Dictionary of British
Social History

The Wordsworth
Dictionary of British Social History

–

L.W. Cowie

Wordsworth Reference

First published as *A Dictionary of British Social History*
by G. Bell & Sons Ltd, London.

This edition published 1996 by Wordsworth Editions Ltd.
Cumberland House, Crib Street, Ware, Hertfordshire SG12 9ET.

ISBN 1-85326-378-8

Printed and bound in Great Britain by Mackays of Chatham PLC.

Preface

This dictionary is intended to be a brief book of reference on the social history of Britain from early times to the present. While it is hoped that it will be of general use, it is written particularly for older children, and this has been borne in mind in determining the nature of its contents.

This, however, could not be the only test. The contents of such a book as this are bound to be determined also by whatever answer is given to the question, 'What is social history?' G. M. Trevelyan once said that it is 'history with politics left out'. Yet this cannot be an entirely satisfactory definition. Political events and movements, such as the Pilgrimage of Grace or Chartism, cannot be disregarded as social portents or influences, and some of these have been included in this book.

Many would think that social history should be concerned with the everyday life of ordinary people throughout the ages; and this principle has been generally followed here (with some extra emphasis on the past life of children), but it raises its own problems. The circumstances of life change, and what is relevant for one period in history may not be so for another. Fighting and warfare, for instance, are not nowadays part of the ordinary life of the people of this country, but this book could hardly omit reference to the castles, armour and weapons of the medieval age. This aspect of warfare has, therefore, been included, but it has not been extended to cover the means of fighting employed in later conflicts with one or two exceptions, such as bombs and stirrup-pumps, which affected ordinary people during the last war. And a similar limitation to relevant periods of history has been followed with other subjects.

Other decisions have been made along equally pragmatical lines. Since this book is about the ordinary people of the past, there are no biographical entries (which can easily be found in other books of reference), though individuals are, of course, frequently mentioned in articles about inventions or movements which affected the everyday life of the people. There are some articles about topics which do not strictly come within the scope of social history, but they have been included to explain references in other articles. There are also a few articles on specific places, such as Salisbury Cathedral, Hampton Court or the New Lanark Mills, or objects such as the Blackfriars Barge or Mons Meg, to show the value of local, particular examples in wider history.

Since the writing of history is so much a matter of selection, anyone who compiles a book of this sort is bound to be guided, when it comes to deciding what should be put in and what should not be put in, by certain considerations which seem relevant to him and might not be so to other people (though none can argue with the overriding consideration of space). Thus, there are here more than a few entries about Christianity and country life (to take two instances), but for many centuries the life of the people of

v

this country has been largely religious, rural and agricultural as opposed to its modern secular, urban and industrial counterpart. For these and other decisions about the contents of the book, the compiler must take full responsibility.

In the arrangement of the book, only one point probably need be mentioned:— whenever a word in an article is printed in small capital letters, it indicates a relevant article in the Dictionary under that (or a closely similar) heading.

At the end there is a list of useful books for finding out more about British social history.

L. W. C.

A

Abbess the head of an ABBEY of NUNS. A medieval abbess was a person of great consequence, addressed as 'My Lady', possessing her own CHAPLAIN, STEWARD and BAILIFF and riding about with a numerous retinue. She was often a woman of some social standing, belonging to an important family and possessing powerful local relatives and influence. Some of the smaller nunneries were almost family perquisites in which the abbess readily benefited her own relations as shown by the frequent occurrence of nuns with the same surname as her.

Abbey a name properly applied to a community of MONKS or NUNS governed by an ABBOT or ABBESS, but it came also to be applied to the MONASTERY in which they lived and particularly to the church in which they held their services. After the DISSOLUTION OF THE MONASTERIES, some churches, though no longer abbeys, still retained the name (e.g. Westminster Abbey or Tewkesbury Abbey), and the name is also kept by some great houses which replaced monasteries (e.g. Woburn Abbey). [F. H. Crossley, *The English Abbey* (1962)]

Abbot the head of an ABBEY, being elected, normally for life, by its MONKS. In the early days of monasticism, the abbot ate with his fellow-monks in the REFECTORY and slept with them in the DORTER, but later the greater abbots became large landowners and important personages. Some (e.g. the Abbots of St Albans, Westminster, Reading and Glastonbury) were MITRED ABBOTS and sat in the House of Lords as TENANTS-IN-CHIEF of the Crown. Such abbots came to have their own separate house in the abbey, apart from the rest of the monastic buildings. They also spent much time travelling about with a train of attendants, visiting estates and staying at country MANORS belonging to the MONASTERY, and they had town houses in provincial cities (e.g. Exeter and Winchester) and in London (e.g. Peterborough Court, off Fleet Street, belonged to the Abbot of Peterborough).

ABC Schools, SEE PETTY SCHOOLS.

Abraham-man a wandering beggar in the time of Elizabeth I. He commonly pretended to be mad in order to gain pity. The term was derived from the Parable of Dives and Lazarus (Luke xvi, 19–31). Another name for such a vagabond was Tom o'BEDLAM, and in Shakespeare's *King Lear* the disinherited Edgar took the guise of one of these.

Additional Curates Society was founded in 1837 by members of the HACKNEY PHALANX to provide CURATES sympathetic with their outlook since the EVANGELICALS in the CHURCH PASTORAL AID SOCIETY laid down doctrinal tests for the curates it assisted and employed lay workers which HIGH CHURCHMEN opposed as being too like the lay preachers of the METHODISTS.

Advowson the right of patronage or appointing a clergyman to a PARISH or other ecclesiastical post. In the CHURCH OF ENGLAND it may be held either by a BISHOP or by some other person or body (e.g. a COLLEGE). Lay patronage goes back to the control exercised by a feudal lord over the churches on his estates. After the Constitutions of Clarendon (1164), advowsons were recognized as a right of property which could be bequeathed or sold. Since the *Benefices Act 1898* (*Amendment*) *Measure* of 1923 advowsons may not be sold after two vacancies have occurred since July 14, 1924, and in 1933 parochial church councils were empowered to purchase advowsons except when the Crown or a bishop is the patron.

In the CHURCH OF SCOTLAND differences over private patronage produced the DISRUPTION of 1843.

Aeroplane was first successfully flown by the Wright brothers in USA in 1903. Louis Blériot flew across the English Channel in 1909. The First World War led to a great increase in engine power, but biplanes remained the most general type because it was easier to brace their wings even though their wind-resistance reduced speed.

The first daily air service in the world for passengers and goods was started between London and Paris in 1919 in

World War I bomber

Early airliner

Flying boat

small bombers. By 1930 the largest airliners were four-engined and could seat 30 passengers. Many were FLYING-BOATS. During the 1930s the wooden biplane gave way to the cantilever monoplane of light-alloy, stressed-skin construction, and landing-flaps, retractable undercarriages and variable-pitch propellers, were introduced. Airliner speeds were about 120 m.p.h. in 1930, 200 in 1939 and were brought up to 450 by the Comet jet airliner in 1952. In 1926 British airlines carried less than 25 000 passengers and flew about 500 000 miles, in 1935 over 200 000 passengers and 4 500 000 miles, in 1961 some 6 500 000 passengers and over 120 000 000 miles. [C. H. Gibbs-Smith, *A History of Flying* (1935).] See also AIRPORT, AIRSHIP, BALLOON.

Agrarian Revolution is the term used to describe the introduction into British farming of the ROTATION OF CROPS and the great increase in ENCLOSURES during

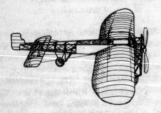

Blériot aeroplane

the 18th century, as well as the invention of the SEED DRILL, improvements in the breeding of CATTLE, PIGS and SHEEP and the replacement of the OX by the HORSE for ploughing. These changes were introduced more gradually than was formerly supposed, but high prices during the Revolutionary and Napoleonic Wars (1793–1815) led farmers to adopt them more speedily. [C. S. Orwin, *A History of English Farming* (1949)]

Airport is an aerodrome which has customs and immigration offices as well as providing refreshment and business facilities to travellers. The first English airport was at Croydon, which by 1926 was handling up to 30 cross-Channel flights a day. After the Second World War, the main international airports became Heathrow (Middlesex), Gatwick (Sussex), Stansted (Essex) and Prestwick (Ayrshire), which were placed in 1965 under the British Airports Authority. Although Heathrow, handling some 450 AEROPLANES a day of about 50 airlines, is the world's largest international airport, it is smaller than a dozen airports in USA. This is because Britain, being a compact and crowded country, has one of the least developed internal systems of air transport in the world.

Airships were planned after the invention of BALLOONS, when men tried to propel and steer them, but not until 1852 did the French engineer, Henry Giffard, build a steam-driven airship, which could fly on a calm day. The first really successful airship was the electrically driven *La France*, built by two French army officers, Charles Renard and Arthur Krebs, in 1884, and petrol-engines were used to power airships in the early 1890s. The first airships were either non-rigid (a gas-inflated envelope with a small car containing crew and engines) or semi-rigid (with a keel suspended immediately

below the envelope to which the car and engines are attached). In 1900 Count Zeppelin in Germany developed the first rigid airship; this had a framework of girders covered with fabric, in which the gas was contained in internal bags and the

Non-rigid airship

Semi-rigid airship

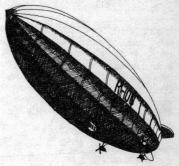

Rigid airship

crew and equipment were housed, but the engines were attached outside. Zeppelins bombed Britain in the First World War.

Britain built a few large rigid airships, including the *R34* which made the first Atlantic crossing in 1919, but the destruction of the *R101* in 1930 led the British

3

government to abandon completely airship development and construction. The German *Graf Zeppelin* inaugurated a regular transatlantic service in 1929, but the wreck of the *Hindenburg* in 1937 brought it to an end, and the great rigid airship was relinquished in favour of the AEROPLANE as a means of long-distance air travel. However, the possibilities of the airship are once again being investigated for loads which are unsuitable for aeroplanes. [E. F. Spanner, *About Airships* (1929); B. Collier, *A History of Airships* (1961)]

Aisle originally an enlargement of the NAVE of a CHURCH made by piercing the side walls with a series of arches and building an extension with a separate and lower roof. In British churches there is usually only one aisle on either side of the nave, but on the Continent there are sometimes as many as three. It is wrong to use the word to describe the passage up the centre of the nave.

Alb a white linen ecclesiastical garment, reaching from the neck to the ankles with tight-fitting sleeves and secured at the waist by a girdle, worn by the clergy at the MASS. It was derived from the under-tunic of the ancient Greek and Roman world and used in Christian worship from an early date. See also VESTMENTS.

Alchemy the pretended art of changing base metals into GOLD, which was brought to Europe by the Moors who conquered Spain. An Englishman, Robert of Chester, in 1144 made the first translation into Latin of many of the Arabic writings which contained ideas derived from ancient Greek and Egyptian alchemists. These were based on Aristotle's view that one substance could be changed into another by changing its primary qualities. The alchemists looked for a 'Philosopher's Stone' or 'Elixir' which could produce GOLD in this way. The Museum of the History of Science, Oxford, has a petition addressed in 1457, by 12 alchemists to Henry VI seeking exemption from the law banning their practice. An English alchemist, George Ripley (d. 1490?), claimed to have the Philosopher's Stone and earned enough to enable him to give £100 000 a year to the HOSPITALLERS. Elizabeth I employed an alchemist to make gold for her in Somerset House and imprisoned him in the TOWER OF LONDON when he did not succeed. Alchemy came to an end with the development of the scientific movement (see ROYAL SOCIETY) of the 17th century. [R. E. Lapp, *Matter* (1969)]

Ale an alcoholic DRINK made from fermented MALT, which consists of BARLEY or other grain steeped in water, allowed to germinate and then dried slowly in a kiln. Tacitus in his *Agricola* (AD 97–8) said that 'wine made from barley' was drunk in Britain. In the Middle Ages ale was mostly brewed by women, ale-wives who kept taverns indicated by an ALE-STAKE outside. CHURCH ALES were a feature of PARISH life. When HOPS were used in the 16th century, ale meant the brew without hops and BEER that with hops, but there is no distinction in the terms today.

Ale-stake a wooden pole with a branch or bush of leaves at the end placed projecting above the door of a TAVERN in the middle Ages as the accepted sign that ALE was sold within. They were sometimes so long and heavy that they damaged the fronts of houses to which they were attached and were dangerous to people riding through the narrow streets of towns. An act of 1375 ordered that ale-stakes must not extend more than seven feet over a public way in London. When a stake was put out, town officials known as ale-conners or ale-tasters would test the ale, and if it were not good, they might confiscate the whole brew or even close the tavern. Ale-stakes were succeeded by INN-SIGNS.

Almack's a famous London gaming-club and suite of ASSEMBLY ROOMS founded in King Street, St James's, in 1764 by William McCall (d. 1781), a Scottish valet of the Duke of Hamilton, who inverted his name to conceal his origin and prevent prejudice against himself. The gaming-club was noted for its high stakes and was patronized by the leading members of fashionable society; the assembly rooms were the scene of weekly subscription balls held during the three months of the London season and organized by a committee of ladies of the highest rank, to be admitted to which was as great a distinction as presentation at Court. The rooms later became known as Willis's, from the name of the next proprietor, being used chiefly for large dinners, and were closed in 1890; but the CLUB transferred to St James's Street in 1778 when it became Brook's Club, which still exists.

Almoner an official in a medieval royal or noble household who had the duty of dispensing alms (see MAUNDY THURSDAY). The almoner of a MONASTERY was in charge of the ALMONRY and had important tasks to fulfil. He cared for poor travellers and collected fragments of food from the REFECTORY to distribute to the poor and also to the boys of the ALMONRY SCHOOL; he supervised the letter-carriers who took round lists of dead MONKS for whom memorial services were to be held in monasteries of the same ORDER; he and his assistant guarded the CLOISTER from intruders, sweeping it and keeping it clean, as well as the chambers of the sick, strewing them with fresh hay and straw.

Almonry the part of a MONASTERY where alms were distributed and where poor travellers were entertained, noblemen being entertained by the ABBOT or PRIOR and ordinary travellers by the HOSTELLER in the guest-house. Both almonry and guest-house were usually situated near the GATE-HOUSE of the monastery. See also ALMONER.

Almonry Schools institutions attached to medieval MONASTERIES, where boys were taught and lived under strict discipline. For their food, they had scraps of meat sent from the REFECTORY, except on HOLIDAYS or when they had done extra work at harvest time. On these occasions they might get extra ALE and BREAD as at Durham in the 15th century. [A. F. Leach, *The Schools of Medieval England* (1915)]

Almshouses institutions, usually for the old and infirm, endowed by charity. The oldest are medieval in origin, being founded by religious communities, corporations or individuals, often for people living in a particular locality or having been employed in some trade. One of the oldest is St John's Hospital, Canterbury (founded 1108), and other examples are St Cross Hospital, Winchester, and Lord Leicester's Hospital, Warwick. Some provide uniforms, as well as maintenance, for their inmates. More recent almshouses are often built as terraces of small houses, one for each person. In 1957 there were about 2500 almshouses in England, mostly in older towns and villages. See also HOSPITALS.

Alpaca a springy, shiny textile, invented in 1838 by Sir Titus Salt, a Bradford woollen manufacturer. Originally it was made of the wool of the alpaca goat (of South America) mixed with SILK, but later with COTTON. It gave the rustling frou-frou of silk much more cheaply and provided an important stiffness to SKIRTS, PETTICOATS and linings of ladies' clothes.

Altar a stone table in churches on which the MASS was celebrated in the Middle Ages, when it was commonly surrounded by curtains on three sides, supported on four posts (riddels), which were often surmounted by carved figures, usually angels, or by candles; the back curtain was sometimes replaced by a carved or painted reredos. Sometimes there were two candles and a cross or crucifix on an altar, but often it had nothing. At the Reformation, stone altars were often replaced by wooden communion tables and sometimes placed in the body of the church. Archbishop Laud (see LAUDIANS) in 1634 ordered them to be restored to the CHANCEL and protected by altar rails at which communicants were to receive the sacrament. A 17th-century altar often consisted of a rectangular table, completely covered by a very full table cloth, falling in heavy folds. Nineteenth-century TRACTARIANS restored stone altars, candles and crucifixes; it also became common to place flowers on altars, which had not been done before. In recent years, an altar has sometimes been placed in the body of the church to enable the priest to celebrate facing the congregation. [Francis Bond, *The Chancel of English Churches* (1916); F. C. Happold, *Everyone's Book About the English Church* (1962).] See also HIGH ALTAR and CHURCH.

Aluminium a very light silvery white metallic element, first isolated by Sir Humphry Davy in 1810 and first commercially produced in France and USA in 1886. Its use for domestic ware became widespread from about 1920. After the Second World War it became the second largest metal industry in Britain, its growth being stimulated by the high cost of other metals. It is cheap, light yet strong, rustless and a good conductor of heat and ELECTRICITY. It is used extensively in the electrical, MOTOR CAR and building industries. It is chiefly used in alloyed form, e.g. Duralumin in which the addition of magnesium increases its hardness and toughness.

Amice an oblong piece of linen cloth tied round the neck by two strings as part of the VESTMENTS worn by the clergy at the MASS. Worn over the CASSOCK and under the ALB, STOLE and CHASUBLE, it originally covered the head like a HOOD and afterwards was worn in the same manner when preparing to go to the ALTAR, but was turned back over the priest's shoulders when the service of preparation was over.

Amphitheatres for public games and spectacles were possessed by many TOWNS in ROMAN BRITAIN, often just outside the walls. Usually they had excavated arenas, the earth from which formed the banks where the spectators sat. Some took advantage of natural slopes. The great Maumbury Rings at Dorchester (Dorset) was a HENGE of the early BRONZE AGE which was adapted by the Romans as an amphitheatre. Most amphitheatres were of simple earthen construction, but others were more magnificent, e.g. at Caerleon (Mon.) which had an arena 200 feet by 150 feet and could seat some 6000 spectators; its banks were faced with stone, and the arena itself was marked by low stone walls. See also THEATRES.

Anabaptists ('re-baptizers'), religious reformers on the Continent from the early 16th century, who objected to the BAPTISM of their children and revived the baptism of adult believers. Many were political radicals, teaching doctrines of non-resistance and the common ownership of property, and, as a consequence, they were bitterly persecuted.

There were some Anabaptists as early as 1534 in England, but throughout the 16th century they were few in number and mainly refugees from the Netherlands. Since they advocated complete religious independence, they probably influenced the ideas of the early INDEPENDENTS. During the 17th and 18th centuries, BAPTISTS were often called Anabaptists, but by then the name had become a term of abuse.

Anaesthetics were first adopted when American surgeons in the early 1840s began to use ether for their operations. Sir James Simpson (1811–70) first used ether in 1847 at Edinburgh in cases of childbirth, but after a few months he introduced chloroform and did much to encourage its use in Britain. This made possible great advances in SURGERY and DENTISTRY.

Anchorites in medieval England were HERMITS who were forbidden by the terms of their vows ever to leave their cells. A BISHOP himself performed the ceremony of enclosing an anchorite, sealing or locking up the door of the cell. In the later Middle Ages, an anchorite's cell was sometimes attached to a parish church. The best-known anchorite was Julian of Norwich (c. 1342–1413), a mystic, who had a cell outside the walls of St Julian's Church, Norwich.

Angel an English gold coin, first minted in 1465 and worth 6s 8d (33p), the original value of the NOBLE, which it helped to displace. It took its name from the obverse showing the Archangel Michael slaying a dragon. Angels and half-angels were minted into the early Stuart period.

Angelus a prayer (beginning *Angelus Domini*, 'the angel of the Lord') commemorating the incarnation, said to the sound of a BELL which was rung from churches in Britain until the REFORMATION. The Angelus bell was rung at night from the early 14th century and also in the early morning from the late 14th century and at midday from the 15th century. The evening Angelus often took the place of the older CURFEW, while the morning Angelus frequently signified the beginning of the day's first MASS, which was frequently said at 4 or 5 a.m.; in some towns it was called the 'Watch Bell' because it acted as a sign for the dispersal of the night WATCHMEN.

Anglo-Saxons first came to England in the 4th century AD when they raided the eastern coast. The most important tribes seem to have been the Saxons from the mouth of the Elbe, the Angles from Schleswig and the Jutes from the lower Rhineland. About 450 their raids gave place to widespread and permanent settlement. By the mid-6th century, the Jutes had occupied Kent, the Isle of Wight and eastern Hampshire; the Saxons settled just above and south of the Thames, establishing the kingdoms of Sussex, Wessex, Middlesex and Essex; and the Angles conquered the rest of the Midlands and the northern and eastern coast, forming the kingdoms of Northumbria, East Anglia and Mercia. The victory of Wessex over the Britons at the Battle of Deorham, Gloucs. (577) brought the Saxons to the Bristol Channel, and the Battle of Chester (616) gave Northumbria access to the Irish Sea. By then the Anglo-Saxon conquest of England was practically complete.

The Anglo-Saxons moved along the river-valleys and Roman ROADS, but established their villages off the main routes for safety. They had no knowledge of urban life. Roman TOWNS and VILLAS were deserted. Many Roman Britons fled to parts of Wales, Cumberland and Cornwall; others remained and intermarried with the invaders. The Anglo-Saxons had a predominant influence on English PLACE NAMES, laws and language. [Beram Saklatvala, *The Origins of the English People* (1969)]

Antimacassar was a covering for chairbacks to protect them, especially from grease, or simply as an ornament. It took its name from Macassar, the proprietary name of hair-oil which was popular in the second half of the 19th century.

Antiseptics were first used in SURGERY by Joseph Lister (1827–1912), who in 1867 began to spray his operating-theatre in Glasgow and to wash the patients' wounds to destroy the infecting organisms. He was immediately successful in reducing the risk of septic infection during his operations, and his practice was quickly adopted in HOSPITALS throughout the country with equally striking results. By 1869 the proportion of patients who died after an operation in British hospitals had fallen from 60 to 15 per cent.

Antler-pick a tool fashioned from the pointed branch of an antler of a red DEER and widely used as a digging implement in mining FLINT and excavating ditches during NEW STONE AGE times and the BRONZE AGE. See also GRIME'S GRAVES.

Apothecaries prepared and traded in drugs made from HERBS and SPICES imported from the East or grown in HERB GARDENS in this country. They joined the Grocers' Company in the 14th century, but early in the 17th century they received from James I a charter for their own Society of Apothecaries. During the PLAGUE of 1665 most PHYSICIANS left London, but the apothecaries remained and treated the sick, which they had already begun to do. Attempts by the Royal College of Physicians to limit their activities failed, and today its member-ship is limited to those who have passed the licensing examination of the Society of Apothecaries which qualifies them to practise medicine, the title of apothecary having now fallen into general disuse.

Apples of several varieties were grown in England during the Middle Ages. During the 14th century grafts of red-skinned 'pippins' were introduced from France, though the two main native kinds, the codlins (tapering towards the apex) and costards (large ribbed), which were both green cooking apples, prevailed until the 17th century. Shakespeare mentioned 'leather-coats' (brown russet apples) as being given by Justice Shallow to Falstaff, who could not endure the 'apple-john', which was so-called from its being at maturity about St John's Day (6 May) and was kept for up to two years because it tasted best when shrivelled.

Apprentices were first bound to a master to learn a trade or art in the 13th century in connection with the GUILDS. The usual term was for seven years, a period which was made universal and compulsory by Parliament in 1563. In 1814 Parliament ordered that trades and handicrafts should be opened to others as well, and in recent years the number of apprentices has declined.

April Fool called in Scotland a *gowk* (cuckoo). Probably from the fact that before the reform of the CALENDAR, March 25 used to be NEW YEAR'S DAY; April 1 was therefore its octave, when the festivities culminated and ended with tricks played upon people. An old April trick played upon children was to send them to a saddler to ask for 'a penny-worth of strap oil' (and get a beating).

Apse a semi-circular eastern end to a CHANCEL, which was adopted in early

CHURCH architecture from the Roman BASILICA. The ALTAR stood in line with the two ends of the apse, with seats for the BISHOP and CLERGY in the curved space behind. It was introduced into England by St Augustine's mission (597), but the Celtic square-ended chancel remained more common. The Normans first adopted the apse for their churches, but later preferred a square end. Only a few old apses are now left (e.g. Norwich Cathedral).

Arcade an arched, covered walk with SHOPS at the sides, first erected in TOWNS during the REGENCY period, at the same time as the first streets designed for shopping were built. The Burlington Arcade from Piccadilly to Burlington Street, the earliest and best-known arcade, was opened in 1819 with 25 double and 22 single shops 'for the gratification of the public and to give employment to industrious females'. It was imitated both in London and other towns.

Archbishops as administrators of PROVINCES, were established on the Continent before St Augustine of Canterbury came to England in 597. Pope Gregory the Great intended that England should be divided into two provinces, with Archbishops of London and York (the two most important towns in ROMAN BRITAIN); but the early conversion of Kent resulted in the permanent appointment of the Archbishop of Canterbury in the CHURCH OF ENGLAND. The ROMAN CATHOLIC Archbishopric of Westminster was founded in 1850. See also CANTERBURY CATHEDRAL.

In the CHURCH OF SCOTLAND, archbishoprics were established at St Andrews (1411) and Glasgow (1494). See also REFORMATION, SCOTTISH.

Within his own DIOCESE, an archbishop performs the functions of a BISHOP.

Archdeacon an ecclesiastical official next to the BISHOP in a DIOCESE, supervizing the RURAL DEANS and holding an ECCLESIASTICAL COURT. They are responsible for the discipline of the CLERGY and also for seeing that CHURCH buildings are kept in repair. In the Middle Ages, archdeacons were very unpopular among the clergy, and it is said that a common topic for discussion set in the UNIVERSITIES was, 'Can an archdeacon be saved?'

Archery was encouraged and protected by laws in the Middle Ages in order to ensure that the country had sufficient trained archers for the royal army, of which they were the most important part after 1330. As late as Henry VIII's reign (1509–47) an Act of Parliament required the inhabitants of all cities and towns to make butts (or targets), keep them in repair, and exercise in shooting at them on HOLIDAYS, under penalty of 20 shillings a month. See also BOW AND ARROW, BOWLS, CRICKET, GAMBLING.

Arminianism the name given to doctrines which originated with a Dutch theologian, Jacob Arminius (1560–1609), who rejected the belief in predestination as held by strict Calvinists and insisted that Christ died for all and not just for the elect. Arminians in England were so called by their opponents because they rejected the tenets of CALVINISM, though it is doubtful whether they had the Arminian doctrines proper. The LAUDIANS were Arminian in theology, and so were the METHODISTS under John Wesley.

Armour probably first consisted of a simple SHIELD with skins to protect the body; later HELMETS were worn. Roman soldiers wore hoops of iron or leather round the body, joined over the shoulders by wide protective braces. After the fall of

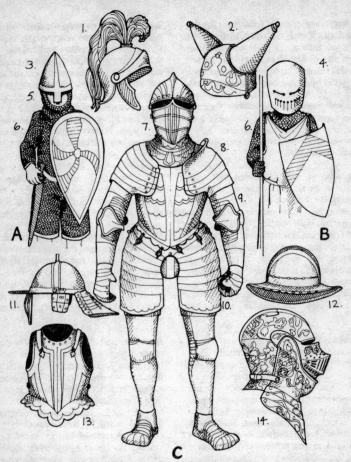

Armour: A 11th cent., Norman soldier; B 13th cent., crusader; C 16th cent., suit of jointed plate armour.

1 Roman helmet; 2 Viking helmet; 3 Nasal pectoral helmet; 4 Pot helm; 5 Coif; 6 Hauberk; 7 Close helmet; 8 Pauldron; 9 Vambrace; 10 Tassets; 11 Lobster tail helmet (17th cent.); 12 Pikeman's helmet (17th cent.); 13 Cuirass; 14 Helmet showing visor and aventail (16th cent.)

the Roman Empire, body armour was little worn for some 800 years. The ANGLO-SAXONS and VIKINGS wore chain-armour (formed of interlocking links), and the main part of Norman armour was the HAUBERK, sometimes worn with mail leggings (greaves). With the development of the long BOW, plate armour was adopted in the late 13th century, and by the end of the 14th century there had been evolved jointed plate-armour for the whole of the body with such pieces as the CUIRASS, AVENTAIL, PAULDRON, PECTORAL, PLACARD, TASSET and VAMBRACE. By the time of the RENAISSANCE, armour had become elaborately ornamented and made useless by the development of GUNS, but it was still used for some time in TOURNAMENTS.

Artillery was preceded by such devices as the CATAPULT, SLING and TRE-BUCHET, and even after the invention of GUNPOWDER these weapons were not rapidly displaced, since gunpowder was at first used as much in BOMBS and MINES as in CANNON, and the efficiency of English ARCHERY delayed the adoption of the arm in England. During the English Civil War (1642-5), Cromwell made great use of artillery in besieging CASTLES. In the early 18th century the Duke of Marlborough had about 99 guns in an army of some 11 000 men. The introduction of

Artillery: 1 Catapult; 2 Trebuchet; 3 Bombard; 4 'Mons Meg'; 5 Cannon; 6 Mortar; 7 Carronade

rifled guns in 1859 made it possible to concentrate gun-power (by accurate aim) without concentrating guns in one spot. Late in the 19th century quick-firing guns could be combined with infantry movement, especially in the 'rolling barrage' of the First World War. In the 20th century anti-aircraft and anti-tank artillery were evolved, but since the 1950s the introduction of rocket missiles has challenged conventional artillery. [H. W. Hime, *The Origin of Artillery* (1915); W. Wilson, *The Story of the Gun* (1944)]

Ash Wednesday the first day of Lent, 6½ weeks before EASTER. The name comes from the pre-REFORMATION practice of the imposition of ashes by the priest upon the heads of the people in church that day as a sign of mourning and penitence.

Some medieval ladies, e.g. Sir Thomas More's wife, put on a FRIAR'S girdle on that day in the belief that they would gain the virtues of its owner by wearing it throughout Lent.

Aspirin is acetylsalicylic acid, a compound of salicylic acid, which was once obtained from plants of the *Spiraea* family (e.g. Astilbe, Meadow Sweet), and so commonly known as spiric acid or spirin. Salicylic acid was shown to quell pain and fever in 1838, but it was found also to cause dizziness and nausea too frequently for practical use. In 1893 the German firm of Bayer devised a method of synthetically producing the forgotten derivative, acetylsalicylic acid, and clinical trials on the new drug proved it to be an effective pain-killer, which was both acceptable and safe. Finally, the firm produced it as a powder in 1898, adding an 'a'—for acetyl—to spirin and selling it under the brand name of *Aspirin*.

Assembly Rooms were built in TOWNS during the 18th century, sometimes being attached to an INN, as places suitable for DANCING, card-playing and other diversions of the county families. Later the MUSIC HALL originated in these rooms. There were similar rooms at SPAS and SEASIDE places where people could listen to the band, attend public tea-drinkings or join in games of BILLIARDS or CARDS. There was a well-known suite of assembly rooms at ALMACK'S in London.

Assizes sessions held periodically in COUNTIES of England and Wales by High Court JUDGES travelling on circuit from town to town to hold their COURTS. This system, which originated in the late 13th century, has been changed by the Courts Act (1970), which has set up new Crown Courts in central towns.

Astrolabe was a simple astronomical device for measuring the height of the stars above the horizon. It originated in antiquity and was used by Arab and

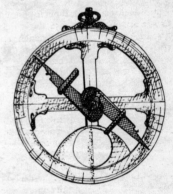

Astrolabe

European astronomers and also astrologers. In the Middle Ages it was a means of telling the TIME and fixing latitude. Geoffrey Chaucer is said to have sent in 1391 to his 10-year old son Lois, a student at Oxford, an astrolabe with a book on its use. It was superseded by the SEXTANT.

Astrology was a pseudo-science which, like ALCHEMY, was much practised in the Middle Ages when men looked for signs and portents in all kinds of things and sincerely believed that the movements of the heavenly bodies forewarned of revolution, war, sudden death and other disasters. The Saxons were dismayed by the appearance of the comet in 1066 which is depicted on the BAYEUX TAPESTRY and now known as Halley's Comet. The heavenly bodies were believed also to determine the inborn desires and abilities of all mortals and govern the success or failure of MEDICINE. As late as Tudor times, a writer said, 'Above all things next to grammar, a physician must have surely his astronomy, to know how, when and at what time every medicine ought to be administered.'

Atomic power was first put to peaceful uses in Britain when, in 1956, the world's first full-scale atomic power station was opened at Calder Hall (Cumberland). By 1970 others had been opened at Berkeley (1962), Bradwell (1962), Hinckley Point (1964), Hunterston (1964), Trawsfynydd (1964), Dungeness (1965), Sizewell (1965), Oldbury (1967), Wylfa, in Anglesey (1968), and Chapel Cross (1969). In these the atomic energy provides heat, which produces steam to operate STEAM TURBINES to produce ELECTRICITY.

Augustinian canons an order of CANONS, founded in the 12th century, who observed a RULE supposed to have been drawn up by St Augustine of Hippo (354-430). They were popular in England, where they were commonly known as the Austin Canons or Black Canons, and at the time of the DISSOLUTION OF THE MONASTERIES had about 170 English houses, including two, Waltham (Essex) and Cirencester (Gloucs.), which were presided over by MITRED ABBOTS. They had a close connection with HOSPITALS, and in London St Bartholomew's and St Thomas's Hospitals were both formerly Augustinian houses.

Augustinian hermits an order of FRIARS founded in 1256 with a constitution modelled on that of the DOMINICANS. In England they had 32 houses at the time of the DISSOLUTION OF THE MONASTERIES. Their most celebrated was the friary at Oxford, a distinguished centre of education, where Erasmus once stayed.

Aumbry a recess or cupboard in the north wall of the CHANCEL of a CHURCH in medieval times for sacred vessels, RELICS, books and sometimes the PYX.

In the Later Middle Ages it was also the food CUPBOARD in a house, consisting of shelves enclosed by a front and fitted at first with a small, pierced central door and considerably later with interlocking double doors. [J. C. Rogers, *English Furniture* (1950)]

Au pair girls have taken the place of SERVANTS in many homes, usually those with young children, since the Second World War. They are usually girls, about 18 years old, who come from abroad to stay for a short period, normally a year. During that time, they live with a family, receiving their upkeep and a small weekly wage in return for helping for a few hours each day in the house.

Aventail was the flap or movable part of a HELMET in front, which could be lifted up so as to enable the wearer to breathe more easily. See also ARMOUR.

B

Bachelor's porch an old name for the north door of a CHURCH. The menservants and other labouring men used to sit on benches down the north AISLE and the maidservants and other poor women down the south aisle, and the arrangement continued even when they married. After the service the men formed one line and the women another, between which the clergy and gentry passed down amid bows and curtseys, and the two lines then filed off. This custom was still observed in some country churches late in the 19th century.

Backboard or deportment board, a wooden board, usually about 3 ft long and sometimes covered with cloth, used in GIRLS' SCHOOLS in the 18th and 19th centuries to improve their posture and prevent them becoming round-shouldered. A girl had to stand for a certain time each day with the board held horizontally behind her back, its handles being looped through her crooked elbows and so holding her shoulders well back. See also DEPORTMENT, STOCKS.

Backgammon a game played by 2 people with 15 men or pieces each, moved according to the throw of dice, on a board of 2 'tables', each marked off into 12 spaces of alternating colours. It was probably played in England as early as the 10th century and was one of the main gambling games of medieval Europe. It was always called 'Tables' until the 17th century. It seems to have remained popular in the 18th century, particularly with the clergy. 'In what esteem are you with the vicar of the parish?' Jonathan Swift (1667–1745) asked a friend. 'Can you play with him at backgammon?' It was played less, however, in the 19th century, especi-

ally late in the century with the invention of ludo, which belongs to the same family. [J. A. R. Pimlott, *Recreations* (1968)]

Badminton a game derived from BATTLEDORE AND SHUTTLECOCK, first played about 1870 at Badminton House (Glos.), the seat of the Duke of Beaufort. It is played with rackets and a shuttlecock over a net in a court like lawn-TENNIS. It is an indoor game, played mostly during the winter, and since the First World War has become very popular.

Bagman a rider who travelled on horseback, with saddlebags, in the late 18th and early 19th century to deliver to the SHOPS in VILLAGES the goods needed by the shopkeepers from manufacturers and wholesalers, and to collect the payments due from them. The bagmen were superseded by cheap POSTAGE in 1840. [E. W. Bovill, *English Country Life 1780–1830* (1962)]

Bagpipes were known in ancient Greece and Rome, but it is not certain when they were introduced into Britain. They seem to have been popular in England in the Middle Ages and were satirised on MISERICORD carvings in which pigs were shown playing them, their noise being compared to a pig's squealing. They do not seem to have come into favour in Scotland until the 15th century, but their popularity survived there when it died out in England. As early as 1633 a London MASQUE described their sound as 'Northern Musick', and Pepys considered them 'mighty barbarous music'.

Bag-ware the name given to much of the POTTERY made by the NEW STONE AGE

14

people because the pots have the same shape as the leather bag which preceded them, sometimes even having two holes at the top to enable a string-handle to be fitted. Sometimes such pots were ornamented with a row of scratched lines made with the finger-nails or with a light wavy pattern made with the finger-tips.

Bail (NORMAN FRENCH *bailler* to deliver) is a legal term for the temporary release of an accused person after one or more people have guaranteed that he will appear in COURT for his trial, often by putting up money which is forfeited if he does not appear. It developed from the medieval practice of mainprize by which mainpernors accepted responsibility for the performance of a contract or other legal undertaking by a person. Under COMMON LAW only murder is not bailable. Formerly, people on lesser charges were arrested (instead of summoned as today) and released through fictitious guarantors, John Doe and Richard Doe, but this ceased in 1832.

Bailey a banked and palisaded area of a CASTLE, sometimes attached to the MOTTE and sometimes enclosing it. The bailey contained domestic buildings for horses and food-storage. Examples built in the 11th and 12th centuries are especially common in Britain, e.g. at Berkhampstead (Herts.), Ongar (Essex) and Windsor (Berks.). In later castles it was common to have two circles of CURTAIN WALLS enclosing an outer and inner bailey or ward.

Bailiff is a legal term for an agent entrusted with responsibility by a superior. The keeper of Dover Castle is called the Queen's Bailiff. On a medieval MANOR the bailiff was responsible, under the STEWARD, for the direction of the estate and to see that the HAYWARD and other servants on the farm did their work properly; he was assisted by the REEVE. The name is now generally applied to officers employed by the SHERIFF to collect fines, summon juries, execute writs and seize the property of a debtor to be sold to provide the money due to a creditor under a court order.

Balconies were adopted for English HOUSES in the 17th century under the influence of the Italian RENAISSANCE; they had stone balustrades, which were often later replaced by iron railings. The development of TOWNS in the late 18th century produced streets of almost completely standardized terrace houses which were given interest by a series of wholly decorative small balconies outside the first-floor WINDOWS, which were taller than the rest and came right down to the floor. These balconies had delicate wrought-iron balustrades, sometimes in elaborate designs; and sometimes there was one balcony for all the first-floor windows, extending across the house-front and having a curving copper or lead roof supported on slender columns. Victorian balconies had iron-work in coarser cast-iron and later were built in various materials. Edwardian balconies were more spacious with white-painted wooden posts and balustrades. Modern FLATS very commonly have balconies. See also VERANDAHS.

Balk a ridge of land left unploughed as a boundary between strips of land in medieval OPEN-FIELD SYSTEM.

Ballads simple narrative poems originally meant for singing, can be traced in Britain back to the 13th and 14th centuries. Many of the earliest describe different adventures in the life of Robin Hood. From the 16th to the 19th century ballads were written, often about contemporary events; sold either in the streets (see STREET CRIES) or by PEDLARS, and printed in CHAPBOOKS. Isaac Walton

(1593–1683) wrote about the room of an INN which had 'twenty ballads stuck about the wall'. [A.T. Quiller-Couch, *The Oxford Book of Ballads* (1910). See also BROADSHEET.]

Ballet a form of DANCING which began with the establishment of the *Académie Nationale de Musique et de la Danse* by Louis XIV in 1661. It was to be seen in England from the 18th century, but it first became an English art when the Russian ballerina, Anna Pavlova (1882–1931), took English dancers into her company from 1910. In 1930 a small ballet company was formed under Ninette de Valois, and this was to become the Sadler's Wells Ballet (later (1957) The Royal Ballet) and gain fame at Covent Garden Opera House. [Mary Clarke, *The Sadler's Wells Ballet* (1955); Mark Edward Perugini, *A Pageant of the Dance and Ballet* (1946)]

Balloons were first constructed in 1783 by two French brothers, Joseph and Etienne Montgolfier. These were open at the bottom and were filled with hot air by means of a fire below the opening. In the same year the French physicist, J. A. C. Charles, perfected his hydrogen balloon, which had all the essential features of later balloons, including a net over the envelope to support the basket, a valve for releasing the hydrogen for descent and ballast to control the height. One of these crossed the English Channel in 1785. In the 19th century balloons were used for sport, military reconnaissance and scientific purposes, but they were later overshadowed by the AIRSHIP and AEROPLANE. During the Second World War barrage balloons, flown from steel cables, protected London and other cities from dive-bombing and low-level air attacks.

Band originally meant a company of singers as well as players of any musical instruments (see ORCHESTRA), but came to designate a body of wind-instrument players, particularly the brass band, which became very popular in northern England from the 1840s and was adopted by the SALVATION ARMY for its open-air meetings.

Banks as institutions concerned with the safe-keeping of money, lending it at interest and providing means of transferring it, really began about the mid-17th century. The legalization of USURY under Elizabeth I enabled GOLDSMITHS particularly to make loans out of their funds, which included COINAGE deposited in their strong-rooms. Until 1640 the Royal Mint was also much used as a repository for valuables, but in that year Charles I requisitioned £20 000 from the deposits there; and though he later returned it, he had undermined the City merchants' confidence in the Mint. The goldsmiths gained accordingly, and numbers became in effect banking firms, which began the practice of lending part of their deposits and issuing bank notes and CHEQUES.

The Bank of England, the first English JOINT-STOCK bank, was founded in 1694 to help finance the war against France; and when its CHARTER was renewed in 1701 a clause was inserted preventing the association of more than 6 persons (other than the Bank itself) to issue notes. Since note-issuing was then held to bring bankers their main profits, the formation of other joint-stock banks in England was prevented. In 1836, however, an Act of Parliament permitted the establishment of joint-stock banks more than 65 miles from London, and when the Bank of England's charter was renewed in 1833 non-issuing joint-stock banks in London were made legal. The first of the new joint-stock banks to be founded were the Westminster and the Midland, both in 1836. In the late 19th and early 20th century amalgamations produced the Big Five—Barclays, Lloyds, Midland, National Provincial and Westminster (the last two being united in 1968).

Meanwhile the Bank of England had become established as the bank of the government and of other banks. Note-issue became its main function, and the Bank Charter Act (1844) was designed to give it an eventual note-issue monopoly by providing that no further banks should issue notes and when a note-issuing bank amalgamated with another, both should lose the right of issue. This object was attained in 1921 when Fox, Fowler & Co., the last of the note-issuing private banks, was absorbed by Lloyds. The Bank of England was nationalized in 1946.

The Bank of Scotland, the first Scottish joint-stock bank, was established by a (Scottish) Act of Parliament in 1695 with a 21-year monopoly. In 1704 it was the first bank to issue £1 notes. As Scotland was not affected by the Bank of England's monopoly, other Scottish joint-stock banks were founded after 1716, the most important being the Royal Bank of Scotland (1727) and the British Linen Company (1727). All Scottish banks still retain the right of note-issue.

The Bank of Ireland was established in 1783. It relied ultimately on the Bank of England, and in 1943 the Central Bank was founded with the sole right to issue legal-tender notes. See also SAVINGS-BANKS.

Baptism was administered in the Middle Ages as soon as possible because it was believed that the souls of unbaptized infants would be consigned to hell, and so the child was usually baptized when a day old. It was believed that if a pregnant woman stood as a godmother, either her own child or her godchild would die prematurely; but to invite the first poor person met with on the way to CHURCH was thought to bring long life to the baby. It was the custom to sprinkle the back of the baby's head, not the forehead, with water, while the heels were dipped in the FONT and the breast anointed with oil. After baptism, a white robe, known as a chrisom, was put on as a sign of innocence, which became the child's shroud if it died within a month.

From Elizabethan times, a baby had to be brought to the parish church to be baptized within a month of birth; infringement of this law by the parents meant a fine, and in the 17th century a Yorkshire RECUSANT was fined £100 for this offence. The PURITANS objected to the use of the sign of the Cross in baptism and also to the appointing of godparents.

During the 17th and 18th centuries the infant was commonly carried to the church covered by a mantle called a bearing-cloth, from which the christening robe later developed. An early Georgian print shows a baptism being held in the mother's bedroom. She is sitting up in an armchair, and a table covered with a cloth has on it a bowl for the baptismal water. See also CHRISTENING PRESENTS, SWADDLING BANDS, BAPTISTS, ANABAPTISTS.

Baptists who believe in BAPTISM by immersion and only for believers, not infants, owe their origin to John Smyth, formerly a clergyman of the CHURCH OF ENGLAND, who had become an INDEPENDENT refugee in Amsterdam. In 1609 he organized the first Baptist congregation among other refugees, and after his death his followers returned to London in 1612. From them a number of other Baptist congregations came into being, particularly during the COMMONWEALTH. Though John Bunyan (1628-88) worked among Baptists, he regarded 'differences of judgement about water baptism' as 'no bar to communion'. [W. T. Whitley, *A History of British Baptists* (1923).] See also ANABAPTISTS.

Barbette a strip of LINEN worn under the chin and pinned on the top or sides of the head by women during the later Middle Ages. It was commonly worn with a white FILLET. See HATS.

Barbican an outward extension of a gateway to a CITY or CASTLE to form an additional defence against attack. Often taking the form of a double tower over a gateway, barbicans usually date from the mid-14th century. Examples are to be seen at Lewes (Sussex) and Carisbrooke (Isle of Wight).

Barley an ancient cereal which probably originated in Asia. Huskless barley was known in the NEW STONE AGE, but by the BRONZE AGE modern types predominated. It was formerly much used in making BREAD, but now is most often converted into malt for the brewing of BEER and distilling of WHISKY.

Barleybrake was a GAME played by 3 couples. One couple remained in a central area known as hell, and had to catch the others who ran together through the area and were allowed to 'break' (i.e. change partners), but when they were caught had to take their turn in hell as catchers.

Barn a farm building in which the corn was stored after it had been cut at HARVEST-TIME. Many dating from the Middle Ages still exist. The big doorway in the centre of a barn was often built high enough to allow a full WAGON of corn to enter. The corn was packed on either side of the doorway, where a space was always kept clear, and here, on a floor of oak or clay, it was threshed with FLAILS. With the introduction of the THRESHING-MACHINE, the corn was stacked in the fields, and later, since the use of the COMBINE-HARVESTER, much of the corn is not even stacked. Consequently barns today are rarely used for the storage of corn. Most have been converted into storage places for farm implements and machinery or sometimes into cowsheds.

Barons were originally all the TENANTS-IN-CHIEF of the King, including both EARLS and KNIGHTS. Gradually, however, a distinction developed between greater and lesser barons, and in the 14th and 15th centuries new titles of nobility (duke, marquis and viscount) were introduced. So the greater barons became the lowest rank in the peerage, while the lesser barons became knights.

Baronet the lowest title that is hereditary, created by James I in 1611. The first baronets had to contribute towards the cost of maintaining troops in Ulster. The recipient was addressed as 'Sir' and his wife as 'Dame' or 'Lady' in the same way as KNIGHTS. He had precedence over knights, but was not a member of the peerage. No new baronets have been created since 1964.

Barrows prehistoric graves, consisting of a stone or wooden chamber covered with earth or stones, of which there are several types. Long barrows of the NEW STONE AGE were communal burial vaults for a tribe or family. Some were 200–300 ft long and 50 ft wide. Among the best-known are Wayland's Smithy (Berks.), Windmill Hill (Wilts.) and Carn Barn (Arran). Round barrows dating from the BRONZE AGE are of several shapes: bowl barrows, resembling an upturned bowl; bell barrows, like a slightly flattened bell in shape and surrounded by a ditch and mound; disc barrows, resembling a shield with a small mound forming the boss of the shield and a flat area with a ditch and mound outside surrounding the whole. The earliest Bronze Age practised BURIAL, but CREMATION, the ashes being then placed in an urn, followed. The burial is always a single one. [L. V. Grinsell, *The Ancient Burial Mounds of England* (1953)]

Bartholomew Fair once the chief cloth FAIR of England, was held at SMITHFIELD in London from 1123 annually, at first on St Bartholomew's Day (August 24) and from 1753, when the CALENDAR was changed, on September 3. The right to hold the fair was part of the grant by Henry I to Rahere for the foundation of a HOSPITAL and PRIORY. By the end of the 16th century there was little trade at the fair, and it had become largely an assembly of shows, exhibitions and popular entertainments, which brought it increasingly into disrepute. It was moved to Islington in 1840 and came to an end in 1855.

Basilica a large oblong building standing on one side of the FORUM in a Roman town and used as an exchange or lawcourt. It was divided lengthwise by two rows of columns and had an APSE at one end, in which were the magistrates' seats, and in front of them was a stone altar on which sacrifice was offered to the emperor before business began. The basilica at Silchester measured 240 ft by nearly 60 ft and is estimated to have stood 60 ft high.

Basinet a light globular HELMET, named from its likeness to a basin. It was worn sometimes with a VISOR or with the great helmet, resting on the shoulders, worn over it.

Baths were part of the VILLA buildings in ROMAN BRITAIN (see ROMAN BATHS), but medieval people were not so clean. In MONASTERIES, the MONKS had a warm bath in the CALEFACTORY two to four times a year. King John took a bath once every three weeks during his reign (1199–1216), but his subjects did so less frequently. Medieval baths were round wooden tubs, but by the late 13th century Westminster Palace seems to have had a fixed, tiled bath, and CASTLES and great HOUSES sometimes had a sort of bath-room, a curtained alcove containing a large tub, to which a visitor was taken as the first act of hospitality. The CRUSADES led to the more frequent taking of more baths.

Elizabeth I took a bath once a month 'whether she need it or not'. A Hurstmonceaux (Sussex) cooper's bill in an account book of the 1640s included 'putting four hoops to the bathing tub'; but though Pepys kept a diary for nine years, he only once mentioned his wife having a bath. In the 18th century tin and copper baths appeared, and the Duke of Wellington took a cold bath daily.

In 1801 a London doctor said, 'Most people neglect washing their bodies from year to year.' In 1832 a bath was fitted in the Mansion House, London, but on her accession (1837) Queen Victoria had to have a portable bath in Buckingham Palace, and Prince Albert did not install one at Windsor Castle until 1847 (though William and Mary had built one at Hampton Court). The first public baths were opened in Liverpool in 1842, and this example was followed by other towns; the baths and washhouses opened in 1845 at the London Docks were used in the first six months by 29 080 people. In 1849, however, at a GIRLS' SCHOOL, Miss Browning's Academy at Blackheath, a weekly hot bath was an extra, and two sisters, whose parents paid for this, were known as 'the bathing Garretts'. From the 1850s bathrooms began to be provided in houses, though they were often no more than a recess in a bedroom, and when in 1859 Philip Webb designed the Red House for William Morris, no bathroom was provided in this revolutionary house. The invention of the cast-iron bath about 1880, however, led to the more rapid installation of baths in houses. [Lawrence Wright, *Clean and Decent* (1960)]

Bathing in public was long thought immoral. In 1571 the Vice-Chancellor of Cambridge University forbade students to bathe in any Cambridgeshire river on pain of public WHIPPING for undergraduates and the STOCKS for Bachelors of Arts; but Shakespeare speaks of 'little wanton boys that swim on bladders', and Thomas Randolph (1605-35) wrote about six girls who one summer's evening 'did gently swim and naked bathe'.

In the 17th and 18th centuries people took to bathing at the SPAS. Sea-bathing began perhaps at Scarborough (which was also a spa); an engraving of 1735 shows men and women bathing and swimming naked in the bay; and another dated 1748, depicts a similar scene on Blackpool beach. Dr Richard Russell's recommendation of bathing did much to develop Brighton and other SEASIDE resorts. [Ruth Manning-Sanders, *Seaside England* (1951)]

Bathing-costumes were unknown when BATHING began in the mid-18th century at the SEASIDE since bathers of both sexes were naked. In the early 19th century women began to wear long, heavy flannel cloaks, tied with string round the neck and left unfastened at the bottom so that they provided concealment by spreading out on the surface of the water, but did not impede the bather's movements. From the mid-19th century women's bathing-dresses were very much like their ordinary COSTUME of the period with skirts, frills and black stockings and commonly of SERGE. From about 1870 men wore close-fitting trunks, but from about 1900 a costume covering the torso. Women's costumes remained quite ample until about 1930 when they adopted at first backless costumes, then two-piece costumes and later the BIKINI, while men reverted to the Victorian trunks.

Bathing-machine is said to have been invented in 1753 by Benjamin Beale, a Quaker, who hired to the public on Margate sands a wooden hut on wheels with a door at each end, which was drawn by a horse into the sea until its floor was level with the water. The bather undressed while the machine was being towed out and dressed again on the return journey.

Bathing machine

It became popular at SEASIDE resorts for over a century, especially for women, and sometimes had a folding hooped canvas awning affixed to it, known as a modesty hood, which was let down to the water's edge to screen the bather when in the water. At Brighton in REGENCY times bathers, on emerging from the machines, were ducked by hired male and female 'dippers' of whom the most famous were Martha Gunn and Old Smoaker.

Battering-ram a device used by besiegers against the walls of CASTLES, consisting of a heavy beam of wood, from 80 to 120 ft in length, with an iron end sometimes shaped like a ram's head. It was suspended in a frame and when swung horizontally by relays of men it dealt heavy blows against the masonry of the wall until the vibration broke up the stonework. Often it was protected from missiles thrown by the defenders by a long wooden shed, sometimes on wheels. See also BORE.

Battle-axe a WEAPON used from very early times, at first with a head of stone, then of bronze and then of iron or steel. The main weapons in the Battle of Hastings were the SWORD and the LANCE, but the English used a formidable two-handed axe, and some Normans had a short axe which could be used with one hand. At the Battle of Bannockburn (1314), Robert Bruce clove an English champion down to the chin at one blow with an axe. The battle-axe was replaced by the more effective PIKE in the 16th century.

Battledore and Shuttlecock a game consisting of batting the shuttlecock, a cork stuck with feathers, with battledores, small rackets consisting of a handle and a flat, expanded board at the top. It is known to have been played in China 2000

Battledore and shuttlecock

years ago. A drawing on an English manuscript of the 14th century shows two boys playing it, and it seems to have been a fashionable pastime among adults in the early 17th century; Prince Henry, the son of James I, often played it. It is the ancestor of BADMINTON.

Bayeux Tapestry an EMBROIDERY in coloured wool on a plain band of linen, 231 feet long and 20 inches wide, worked in two different kinds of woollen thread of eight different colours. It tells the story of the NORMAN CONQUEST from the time of Harold's visit to Normandy (1064) to the Battle of Hastings (1066) in 72 scenes, each separated from the next one by the symbol of a tree or tower, and above them is a commentary in Latin stitched in large letters over an inch high. Made probably for Bishop Odo of Bayeux for the decoration of his new cathedral it is a valuable source of information about CASTLES, COSTUME, WEAPONS and ARMOUR of the 11th century. It is now in the museum at Bayeux, and there is a facsimile in the Victoria and Albert Museum, London. [D. M. Stenton, *The Bayeux Tapestry* (2nd ed., 1965)]

Bayonet was first used about 1640 and gradually replaced the PIKE, but the earliest plug bayonet fitted into the muzzle of the MUSKET, and it was a slow operation to take it off to fire the musket and then replace it. The defeat of William III's army in 1689 at Killiecrankie was supposed to be partly due to the Highlanders charging with their swords before the English troops could fit their bayonets. Soon afterwards the ring-bayonet was invented, which, because it was attached to the musket by a metal band round the barrel, did not interfere with the firing of the gun. [C. Foulkes, *Sword, Lance and Bayonet* (1938)]

Beacon a fire usually lit in a cresset (an iron basket) placed on a tower. Some beacons were to guide travellers through forests or difficult country. For this purpose sometimes special towers were built (e.g. Dunston Pillar, built about 1770 beside the Lincoln–Sleaford road, on which the cresset was replaced by a statue of George III when it was no longer needed), and sometimes the tops of church towers were used (e.g. Monken Hadley, Herts., or All Saints' Pavement, York). Other beacons were lit on high hills to send signals over a long distance, and when the Spanish Armada was sighted in 1588 a system of beacons carried the news all over England. The names of some of these hills are still a reminder of this use (e.g. Dunkery Beacon, Exmoor). See also LIGHTHOUSE.

Beadle an English PARISH or WARD officer, whose duty it was to bid the parishioners to attend the VESTRY meetings. He also kept order among the children with a CANE in church, sometimes acting with the parish DOG-WHIPPER. He commonly wore a BLUE COAT. Under the POOR LAW ACT (1601), he was given duties in connection with the administration of the poor laws, particularly the WHIPPING of vagrants. These duties were transferred by the POOR LAW AMENDMENT ACT (1834) to the Guardians. In Scotland the beadle was a church officer.

Beaker people early BRONZE AGE invaders from the Continent, who were so-called because they made large drinking-mugs or beakers, ornamented with patterns made by pressing shells, lengths of cord or wooden combs into the soft clay. They occupied the greater part of Britain, dispossessing the NEW STONE AGE communities of their best pastures. They were nomadic stock-raisers, who also engaged in trade. They probably usually lived in tents and sometimes in shallow pits sunk into the ground and roofed over. It is likely that the hut-circles on Dartmoor and in Scotland mark the stone foundations of Beaker dwellings. They buried their dead in round BARROWS.

Bear-baiting a popular sport from the Middle Ages to the early 19th century. The bear was tethered by a long chain to

a stake in the middle of a pit or ring, and about half-a-dozen mastiffs were let loose on it. As the dogs were killed or injured, they were replaced until the bear was overpowered or proved the winner. This entertainment was often followed by that of whipping a bear. Five or six men stood in a circle around the bear, each having a whip, with which they struck the bear, and dodging its attacks upon them. Beargardens were full of noise and tumult, confusion and quarrels, and hence the expression 'like a bear-garden'.

Bear-baiting was particularly popular in England during the 16th century. Henry VIII appointed a Royal Bearward, a special officer to look after the King's bears and dogs. The Paris Garden, the most famous bear-garden, was erected at Bankside, Southwark, in 1526, and some of the early THEATRES on the south bank of the Thames, such as the Swan, the Rose and the Hope, were built for bear-baiting as well as plays. Every town had its bearward and pack of dogs, and there was bear-baiting in royal and private parks as well as in special places.

The PURITANS disliked bear-baiting, which was prohibited by Act of Parliament in 1642, but it continued at the Hope until 1656, when the bears were shot by a company of soldiers. It was revived at the RESTORATION and was popular in the 18th century. It was prohibited by Parliament in 1835. See also BULL-BAITING.

Beards and Moustaches were not common among the rulers of ROMAN BRITAIN, it being the fashion to be clean-shaven from the days of Julius Caesar onwards. The ANGLO-SAXONS were proud of their beards, and so also were the VIKINGS, e.g. King Sweyn Forkbeard (d. 1014). The BAYEUX TAPESTRY shows the English invariably with moustaches, but the Normans with both their faces and the backs of their necks shaved. Beards returned in

Henry I's reign (1100-35), and the 13th-century statues of kings on the west front of Wells Cathedral all have short beards. Most of the CLERGY also were bearded in the 13th century, except very young ones, and a young deacon at Wells has a slight moustache only; but by the next century the clergy had become clean-shaven. Beards, however, persisted in the fashionable world until the late 14th century when KNIGHTS began to wear HELMETS

Beards and moustaches: 1 Anglo-Saxon; 2 1580; 3 1640; 4 1850; 5 1940

constructed of steel plates with a movable VISOR; from Henry IV to Henry VII no English king was bearded; but in the 16th century beards became common and general by Elizabeth I's reign. In the 17th century beards began to dwindle and had disappeared by the end of the century, not to re-appear until well into the 1830s, while the return of the bearded soldiers from the Crimean War (1854-56) made them increasingly fashionable; but they became less common again later in the century. Moustaches persisted until the First World War, but gradually dwindled into the 'eleven-a-side', the small, under-the-nose moustache (e.g. Charlie Chaplin and Adolf Hitler), and after the war practically vanished. In the 1920s beards were persecuted out of existence by young

people, who greeted anyone with a beard with the cry of 'Beaver', and by 1930 had almost gone. The Second World War produced RAF 'handlebar' moustaches and submarine and arctic convoy beards; and both beards and moustaches became more common in the later 1960s. See also RAZORS, MAUNDY THURSDAY.

Bedlam originally the Hospital of St Mary of Bethlehem, was founded in Bishopsgate in 1247 by the Sheriff of London for the clergy of St Mary of Bethlehem when visiting England. It was mentioned as a hospital for the sick in 1330, and there is a record of the insane being there in 1402. On the DISSOLUTION OF THE MONASTERIES, it passed to the London civic authorities and in 1547 became a royal foundation for the insane. It moved to Moorfields in 1675 and again to Lambeth Road, Southwark, in 1815. This building became the central part of the Imperial War Museum when the hospital moved in 1930 to Beckenham near Croydon. The word came to mean any lunatic asylum and hence an uproar of any kind.

Beds in prehistoric times were stone box-like structures which presumably had leather and skin mattresses. Roman beds were simple wooden frames on legs with a wooden panel at the head; the more opulent ones were ornamented, the others were plain; and they had mattresses, probably stuffed with fine-combed wool—placed on wooden slats in better beds, on ropes slung between the framework in others.

Anglo-Saxon beds were often sacks of straw laid on a bench with a bolster and pillow, sheets and coverlets and perhaps a goatskin or bearskin on top. Norman beds were low, couchlike frames of massive timbers nailed together or iron-bound and were often combined with a CHEST. By the 14th century beds had

23

become lighter, higher and more elaborate with decorated panels and an embroidered wool wall-hanging behind. Important beds had a tester, a square canopy, hung on a rod or chains from the ceiling, from which hung curtains, often of rich

Roman bed

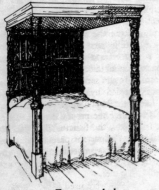

Four-poster bed

Iron bed

material worked with HUNTING scenes or fanciful devices, to be drawn at night around the bed.

Since WINDOW curtains were uncommon until the 18th century, for a long time beds were fitted with hangings to keep out draughts and daylight; but towards the end of the 15th century beds

began to acquire four-poster uprights from which the hangings were suspended, and by the end of the 17th century they had complex hangings and canopies with intricate arrangements of expensive, often embroidered materials, while from the 16th century the woodwork of beds was often carved and gilded. The bases of beds were either loose boards or stretched cords until the mid-19th century when springs were introduced as mattress supports; and about this time Francis Augustus Barnett of Bristol invented iron bedsteads (which did not house bed-bugs). [Lawrence Wright, *Warm and Snug* 1960)]. See also TRUCKLE BED.

Beehive huts were primitive dwellings built of unhewn stones and without mortar by the CELTS of the IRON AGE about the same time as they constructed their LAKE VILLAGES. Windowless and with a single small entrance, they were circular in shape, and the long stones of each course were overlapped by those of the one resting immediately above it and tapered towards a circular roof so that they were like a beehive in shape.

Beer the name given to ALE when HOPS were added in the 16th century. In Elizabeth I's reign there were mainly two grades—single ('small beer') and double; and in the 18th century there was a new dark-brown beer, at first called 'entire' and later 'porter', perhaps because it was popular with London market porters. In the countryside, nearly every cottage brewed its own beer until about 1780. See also BOTTLES.

Beer-drinking increased in the 17th century, when the Navigation Act (1651) and a duty of £4 a tun (1688) made WINE dearer. It declined during the GIN-drinking in the 18th century, but increased again with the heavy taxation on spirits in the 1750s, and did not decline again until the later 19th century when the competition of TEA and other drinks, the spread of temperance and alternative leisure pursuits changed it from an every-day drink to a recreation drink.

Beheading was introduced into England from Normandy (as a less shameful form of execution than HANGING) by William I in 1076 when Waltheof, Earl of Huntingdon, Northampton and Northumberland was the first to be so executed. It became a frequent method of execution, especially in the 16th century, when even noble and royal ladies were beheaded. The rebel lords of 1745 were the last to be beheaded in England. See also TOWER OF LONDON.

Belfry (1) part of the STEEPLE or tower of a CHURCH designed for the hanging of the BELLS. The windows of a belfry are usually large and have placed across them sloping louvre-boards which exclude rain but allow the sound of the bells to be heard outside. See also CAMPANILE.

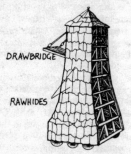

DRAWBRIDGE

RAWHIDES

Belfry siege tower

(2) The belfry was also the name given to a movable wooden tower used in the Middle Ages for attacking a CASTLE. A contemporary chronicle tells how, when the Scots unsuccessfully tried to capture the city of Carlisle in 1315, they 'set up a great belfry, like a tower, which far overtopped the town walls. . . . But the Scot-

tish engine never came against the wall; for when men dragged it on its wheels over the wet and miry ground, there it stuck fast with its own weight, nor could they draw it forward nor harm us.' See also TREBUCHET.

Belgae Celtic-speaking tribes from north-east Gaul that invaded south-east England about 75 BC. Their civilization was that of the IRON AGE, and they were able also to work heavy soils and produce wheel-made POTTERY.

Bells have been used by the Church in Britain from the earliest days of Christianity. The first missionary-preachers used small hand-bells to summon the people, and in the Middle Ages, when the priest took the sacrament to the sick, he was preceded by a bell and a lighted CANDLE, and a bell was rung before the corpse before the procession at a BURIAL. A small bell, the Sanctus Bell, was also sounded at important parts of the MASS, though this was sometimes hung on the ROOD-screen or in a small bell-cot on the CHANCEL gable.

Large bells were used in Scotland and Ireland from the 6th century and in England from the 7th century. They were used to summon people to services and to tell the time in MONASTERIES and CASTLES, where they were struck by a man called a clock-jack, who was guided by a SUN DIAL or HOUR GLASS. The first CLOCKS told the time only by striking a bell; the earliest striking clock with a dial is said to have been made in Italy in 1335.

Benedict, Abbot of Wearmouth, bought a bell from Italy in 680, and Bede mentions one at Whitby Abbey about the same time. Crowland Abbey seems to have had a peal of bells in the 9th century, one of the earliest in the country, and St Dunstan (924–88) is known to have given bells to churches in western England. The size of Saxon church towers suggests that they had rings of bells; and the Return of Church Goods in 1551 rarely mentions less than two bells in a steeple and suggests three were usual even in small churches.

GUILDS of bell-ringers were founded in the early Middle Ages. A patent roll of Henry III confirmed the 'Brethren of the Guild of Westminster, who are appointed to ring the great bells there' in the enjoyment of 'privileges and free customs which they have enjoyed from the time of Edward the Confessor'. Guilds of bell-founders were formed in London and other large cities during the 14th century.

In the past bells were much used for secular as well as religious purposes. There was the CURFEW and the 'pancake bell' on SHROVE TUESDAY, the 'passing bell' to announce a parishioner's death, the 'oven bell' to give notice that the lord of the MANOR'S oven was ready for the baking of the tenants' bread and the 'market bell' to signify that selling might begin.

Medieval church bells were usually heavier than to-day. When change-ringing (which is peculiar to England) developed in the 17th century, the old rings of a few, heavy bells either had new trebles added to them or, more commonly, were recast into a larger number of smaller ones, particularly in towns. Hence there are more old bells in country than in town churches.

Belvedere derived from the Italian *'bel vedere'*—'a fine view', a room or turret raised above the roof of a HOUSE or on an eminence in a park or GARDEN looking upon a view and open to the air on one or more sides to admit the cool evening breeze. Many Italian RENAISSANCE palaces had belvederes, and they were imitated in England in the 17th and 18th centuries. There is one in the grounds of Holland House, Kensington, which is now a public restaurant. See also SUMMER-HOUSE, TEMPLE.

Benedictines the first monastic order founded in western Europe, being organized by St Benedict at Monte Cassino near Naples. Each Benedictine MONAS-TERY was a self-sufficing community under an ABBOT, and the MONKS took vows of poverty, obedience and chastity. The RULE laid down their daily life, and they wore a black HABIT.

Introduced into England by St Augustine of Canterbury in 597, their numbers rapidly increased after the NORMAN CON-QUEST, and they became the most important order in the country. Westminster, Canterbury, Bury St Edmunds, Glastonbury, Peterborough and other important foundations were Benedictine, as was Dunfermline in Scotland. At the DISSOLUTION OF THE MONASTERIES, the Benedictines had 113 ABBEYS and PRIOR-IES and 73 nunneries in England.

In time many Benedictine monasteries neglected their founder's rule, which led to the formation of CLUNIAC, CISTERCIAN and other reformed orders.

Bezique a game of CARDS, usually played by two people, which probably originated in Spain and was introduced into England about 1860.

Bible used in the Medieval Church was the Vulgate, the Latin translation completed by St Jerome in AD 405. The Venerable Bede translated St John's Gospel into English from the Vulgate in the 8th century, but his work has not survived. In the 9th and 10th centuries some translations of the PSALMS and Gospels were made, the most famous being the Lindisfarne Gospels. Little more translating was done until the 14th century when John Wycliffe and his LOLLARDS produced the first complete English Bible (1382-8) in the face of the resistance of the medieval Church to translations as liable to encourage HERESY.

With the advent of PRINTING and the

renewed interest in Hebrew and Greek studies stimulated by the RENAISSANCE, a Hebrew Old Testament (1488) and a Greek New Testament (1516) were published. William Tyndale (who was burnt at the stake for HERESY in 1536) first translated the New Testament directly from Greek and much of the Old Testament from Hebrew. A complete English Bible (based on Tyndale) was produced by Miles Coverdale in 1535; this was revised by Thomas Matthew (the pseudonym of John Rogers) in 1539 as the Great Bible issued with Henry VIII's authority and ordered to be placed in all churches. In 1560 Puritan exiles in Switzerland produced the Geneva Bible, the first to be divided into numbered verses, which became very popular, and the Bishops' Bible, produced by Matthew Parker, Archbishop of Canterbury, in 1568, did not succeed in replacing it. The Authorized Version or King James Bible, authorized at the HAMPTON COURT conference, appeared in 1611; and the Revised Version in 1881-5. The New English Bible was begun in 1947; the old Testament was published in 1961 and the New Testament in 1970.

The Douai Version (1582-1610), the work of ROMAN CATHOLICS abroad, was translated from the Vulgate, and so also was the Knox Bible (1945-55) by Ronald Knox. [Colin Clair, *The Story of the English Bible* (1959)]

Bicycle a term first used in 1868, had as its first real forerunner a machine propelled by cranks attached to the rear wheel and pedals joined to them by connecting rods, which was invented in 1839 by a Scotsman, Kirkpatrick Macmillan (and is now in the Science Museum, South Kensington). The first machine to be sold on a commercial scale had its pedals fixed to cranks attached to a slightly enlarged front wheel and was invented in 1861 by a Frenchman, Ernest Michaux.

These machines were known in England as 'bone-shakers' and in the 1870s, when greater speeds were gained by enlarging the front wheel to as much as 6 ft and decreasing the rear wheel, as 'penny-farthings'. Its days were ended when John

'Bone-shaker' bicycle

Penny farthing bicycle

Early safety bicycle

Kemp Starley invented in 1885 the Rover Safety Bicycle, which went back to a rear-wheel drive by using chain-transmission. This machine differed little from the modern bicycle. Later improvements have been pneumatic TYRES in 1888, the freewheel in 1894 and three- and four-speed

hubs in the early 20th century. See also
MOTOR BICYCLES.

Bikini a scanty two-piece swim-suit
first worn by women in the 1950s and
called after the name of an island in the
Pacific. Professional Roman dancing-girls
performed similarly clad only with small
bands of cloth covering the breasts and

Roman bikini

the groin; and the upper part of such a
bikini, once worn by a Romano-British
girl, was found with its knots still tied,
discarded between AD 60 and 80, near the
Temple of Mithras in the City of London
in 1953 in a well full of water-logged clay
which preserved the cloth.

Bill a kind of concave BATTLE-AXE with a
long wooden handle, which is mentioned
in the Anglo-Saxon poem, *Beowulf*, as part
of a ship-of-war's equipment. It was the
main infantry WEAPON until the PIKE came
into use. A proclamation by Elizabeth I
in 1596 ordered bowmen to change their
bills for pikes. Bills were carried by
WATCHMEN in the 16th and 17th centuries.

The bill-hook, a bill or hatchet with a
hooked or curved point, is used in cutting
thorn-hedges.

Billiards originated either in France
or England in the 16th century. It is mentioned by Shakespeare in *Antony and
Cleopatra*. It was a favourite game for
both men and women in the ASSEMBLY
ROOMS of the 18th century. It was played
with a flat-headed MACE until the cue was
introduced in the early 19th century,
while soon afterwards slate beds were
substituted for those of oak and marble,
and in 1835 indiarubber cushions for
those stuffed with wool and rag.

Bingo a new name for what was formerly known as lotto or housey-housey.
Formerly confined to the nursery and
the army, its wider adoption was made
possible by the Betting and Gaming Act
(1960), and many CINEMAS, through declining attendances, have been given
over to it. The Churches' Council on
Gambling estimated a turnover of £35
million by bingo halls in 1965. It has
become especially popular with housewives. A survey in 1969 showed that some
20 per cent of all housewives and 7·2
million adults played bingo; in the wage-
earning classes more than 50 per cent
played once a week and 70 per cent at
least once a month.

Birch-rod an instrument of punishment consisting of a bundle of birch
twigs, about a dozen in number and two
feet in length, bound together with pack
thread at the thick end to make a handle
and left loose at the other end to form a
spray. 'A good sharp birchen rod and
free from knots, for willow wands are
unsufferable and fitter for a bedlam than
a school' (C. Hoole, 1660); 'or a small red
willow where birch cannot be had' (John
Brinsley, 1612). A birching was commonly administered upon a FLOGGING-
BLOCK with the help of an UNTRUSSER.

Birch-rods were often soaked in brine
(sometimes by putting them in the same
tub as pickled pork) so that the salted
twigs absorbed moisture from the air
which kept them supple; and they were

sometimes placed in LYE to achieve the same effect. A rod was often displayed hanging on the wall of a NURSERY or kept in a ROD CLOSET. Children were made to fetch the rod and kiss it before their punishment as a sign of submission, and afterwards they might be made to wear it tied to their girdle or hanging from their neck to add to their disgrace and as a warning to other children.

In the Middle Ages when masters in grammar received their degree at the universities, they were given (as a sign that they were empowered to teach) a palmer (or FERULA) and a birch-rod with which they displayed their competence by whipping a 'stout boy' in public, giving the BEADLE a GROAT for supplying the rod and another to the boy 'for his labour'.

Birchin Lane a street in London mentioned in Elizabethan times as a locality where ready-made and second-hand clothes were sold. To say to children, 'I'll send you to Birchin Lane', was a threat to whip them, it being a play on the word BIRCH ROD. 'Birchin Lane clothes' came to be a phrase meaning cheap, cast-off clothing.

Bishop the chief administrative officer of a DIOCESE. In the Middle Ages, bishops of the CHURCH OF ENGLAND held considerable lands as TENANTS-IN-CHIEF of the Crown, which may have been why they were summoned to Parliament, and they were often employed by the Crown as ministers and ambassadors, but since the REFORMATION they have ceased to play such a part in the state. Although there are more bishops today, only the two ARCHBISHOPS and 38 bishops sit in Parliament. ARCHDEACONS and RURAL DEANS are their subordinate officers in the administration of their dioceses. Since the 19th century suffragan bishops have been appointed to assist diocesan bishops in particular parts of their dioceses. See also CROZIER, MITRE, WIG. [Cecilia M. Ady, *The English Church and How It Works* (1940)]

Black Death a new and deadly form of bubonic and pneumonic PLAGUE which appeared in Russia and the eastern Mediterranean and spread along the trade routes to the whole of Europe, reaching the western counties of England in the summer of 1348 and in 18 months had swept throughout the country. There were other less severe outbreaks in 1361–62, 1369 and 1379. It was called the Black Death from the black spots appearing on the skin of its victims. It was spread by fleas carried by rats, and the death-rate was increased by unhealthy living conditions, especially in TOWNS and by lack of medical knowledge. The POPULATION fell by a third to a half. Deaths were especially high in some classes, e.g. bakers and weavers, and there was a serious shortage of clergy in the later 14th century. It caused a scarcity of labour and rise in wages and prices. Some landlords ceased to farm the DEMESNE themselves; others took to SHEEP-farming, which required less labour; others tried to prevent the emancipation of their VILLEINS. The Statute of LABOURERS (1351) sought to keep wages down; and the situation contributed towards the outbreak of the PEASANTS' REVOLT (1381). [Philip Ziegler, *The Black Death* (1969)]

Blackfriars barge was discovered during 1962–3 in the mud to the east of Blackfriars Bridge, where the River Fleet once flowed into the Thames. Its shallow lines (it measured only 7 ft from keel to gunwale) and its crude construction show that it sailed only in the river and the estuary. It was flat-bottomed, had no keel fin and only a single mast in the seating of which was a copper coin of Domitian (struck AD 88–9) with the reverse bearing an image of the goddess Fortuna upper-most. Its cargo of Kentish ragstone suggests that it was probably used to bring rough stones from the Medway for building the city wall in AD 193–7. It is typical of the SHIPS employed in ROMAN BRITAIN on the inland waterways. [Alan Sorrell, *Roman London* (1969)]

Black-jack a large, pitch-lined leather drinking vessel, commonly used at one time for small BEER or ALE. It was made in the form of a JACK-BOOT, whence it is supposed that it derived its name. The liquor was poured from a leather pitcher known as a BOMBARD. Both black-jacks and bombards fell into disuse in the 18th century as PEWTER and BRASS came to be used increasingly for drinking vessels, but they continued to be used in some parts of the country well into the 19th century.

Blacksmith was an important figure in both town and country from the time of the adoption of HORSESHOES until the MOTOR CAR and the TRACTOR displaced the HORSE. Town horses needed shoeing every three weeks or month; country horses every three months. A good smith, working a 12-hour day, could shoe nine horses. In addition to shoeing horses, a blacksmith maintained and repaired WAGONS and CARRIAGES and farm implements, forging their own springs, SCYTHES and other simple pieces. [G. E. Evans, *The Horse in the Furrow* (1960)]

Blanketeers a number of spinners and weavers, who set out in 1817 from Manchester, where there was a bad slump and much unemployment, to present a petition to the Prince Regent. As they carried blankets for the night, they became known as Blanketeers. They were quickly dispersed by troops at Derby, and their leader was imprisoned without trial. [R. J. White, *Waterloo to Peterloo* (1963)]

Blazer a name first given to a scarlet flannel jacket worn by members of the Lady Margaret Boat Club, St John's College, Cambridge, in the late 1880s. Other sports clubs soon adopted similar coloured or striped jackets.

Blotting paper was known as early as 1465, and sheets of absorbent unsized paper have been found in several 18th century account books with evidence on their surfaces that they were used for blotting entries. The commercial production of quality blotting paper is said to have been discovered accidentally about 1840 at Hagbourne Mill (Berks.), where John Slade made paper by hand, when some workmen omitted the size from the manufacture of some paper. Someone tried to use a piece of this paper to write a note, and the result was 'Slade's Original Hand Made Blotting', which was soon used regularly by Queen Victoria. Eventually Slade's business passed by marriage to Thomas B. Ford, and now 'Ford's Blotting' is well-known. See also POUNCE.

Blue coat the common costume for APPRENTICES and serving-men in the 16th and 17th centuries and also for boys at Christ's Hospital, London, and CHARITY SCHOOLS, who were often known as 'blue-coat boys'. A blue coat was also the costume of a BEADLE. Blue gowns were worn as a sign of ignominy by women in the BRIDEWELL and other HOUSES OF CORRECTION; and in Scotland the 'blue-gowns' were paupers, who received alms from the kings and wore a cloak or gown of coarse blue cloth with a PEWTER badge which allowed them to beg throughout the whole kingdom.

For these reasons, blue was a colour usually avoided in the past by gentlemen in their clothing.

Bluestockings a term used of women with academic and literary tastes which seems to have originated with London evening parties held about 1750 by Mrs Elizabeth Montagu (1720–1800) and her friends, who included Hannah More, Mrs Thrale and Frances Burney. They met for conversation only instead of the usual card-playing. They were joined by Horace Walpole, Dr Johnson, Edmund Burke and other eminent men of letters, including Benjamin Stillingfleet, who was eccentric in his dress and habitually wore the blue WORSTED stockings of ordinary daytime dress instead of the black silk of evening. It was also said that the ladies themselves wore 'blue stockings as a distinction', so the nickname may be derived from either possible source. Sidney Smith considered that women should conceal their learning—'if the stocking be blue, the petticoat must be long'. [W. S. Scott, *The Bluestocking Ladies* (1947)]

Blunderbuss a short HAND-GUN, unrifled and with a FLINTLOCK and a large bore widening towards the muzzle, which was used especially in the 17th and 18th centuries. It was loaded with many balls and slugs, which scattered when fired, so that some were likely to hit the mark. It was commonly carried by the guards of STAGE-COACHES, but the greater number of vehicles on the new TURNPIKES scared HIGHWAYMEN away, and it was replaced by a long horn for alerting the toll-gates and INNS with fresh horses.

Boars, wild were once common in England, being last seen at Chartley Forest (Staffs.) in 1683 and even later in Scotland and Ireland. They were both dangerous to men and destructive to crops. After the NORMAN CONQUEST, the killing of boars was restricted on pain of death to HUNTING, which was performed on both foot and horse-back and with DOGS and SPEARS. The boar's head was prized as food, and its entrance at the

CHRISTMAS feast was greeted with festivities and CAROLS.

Boater a stiff straw HAT with a flat-topped crown and a narrow brim with a hat-band of coloured ribbon, first worn by men in the late 19th century. See also NECKTIES.

Bodice the upper part of a woman's dress. Sometimes, from the 16th to the 19th centuries, it was stiffened with whalebone strips and laced across the breast and so combined with STAYS. See also BUSK.

Bombard (1) was the earliest form of CANNON, which was introduced by the end of the 14th century and had a large aperture. It threw stone balls or very large shot. See also ARTILLERY.

Bombard

(2) The name was also given to a large leathern vessel used for pouring out liquor. See also BLACK-JACK, BOTTLES.

Bombast the stuffing (of horsehair, flock, wool, rags, flax, bran or cotton) used as padding to distend garments during Elizabethan times by both men and women, especially for TRUNK-HOSE and the sleeves of DOUBLETS.

Bombs originally iron shells filled with GUNPOWDER, were invented in the late 15th century and used by the Turks at the siege of Rhodes in 1522. MORTARS for throwing bombs were cast in England in 1543. Aerial bombs were first dropped on

Venice from Austrian BALLOONS in 1849. The first aerial bomb to be used in England fell on Dover on December 24, 1914. During the Second World War incendiary bombs proved as destructive as high explosive bombs, and fire watchers were organized to assist in FIRE-FIGHTING (see also STIRRUP-PUMP). The first flying-bombs fell on south-east England on the night of August 12–13, 1944; they killed 5475 people in the ensuing months and were followed by rockets which killed 2724. In the First World War British civilian air-raid deaths were 1413 and in the second over 60 000.

Bonfires were commonly lit from early times on occasions like Midsummer's Day (June 24), Hallowe'en (October 31), TWELFTH NIGHT and St Blaise's Day (February 3). In the days before artificial light, festive bonfires in the gloom and darkness of winter were especially popular; and the Guy Fawkes Day bonfires, which started in the 17th century, may be the successor of those lit around All Saints' Day (November 1). The burning of effigies is also old. Around Liverpool Judas Iscariot is still burnt on Good Friday, while in Thanet an image of the most unpopular local citizen is burnt, and formerly a pig's bladder full of blood was tied under the throat of the dummy. The Pope was commonly burnt in effigy on November 5, but at different times it has been Cardinal Wiseman, the Czar, Paul Kruger and the Kaiser. In 17th-century London, Guy Fawkes Day was riotous and noisy with huge bonfires (one having 200 cartloads of fuel) and 30 guys on a single blaze. Most of the great celebrations on that night are a thing of the past with a few local exceptions, e.g. Bridgwater (Somerset) and Lewes (Sussex). See also FIREWORKS.

Bonnet a woman's outdoor HAT without a brim at the back and generally tied by ribbon-strings under the chin, which was first worn in the early 19th century and until the 1880s was adopted by married women as a sign of their status.

Books originated when the papyrus scroll was slowly replaced between the 2nd century BC and the 4th century AD by the codex, made of bound PARCHMENT leaves, which in turn was superseded by the book of double leaves of PAPER in about the 10th century AD. The invention of PRINTING reduced the cost of a book to about one-tenth of that of a manuscript. The early printed books, however, were large and heavy until the Italian printer, Aldo Manuzio, introduced the octavo pocket edition, and this became the usual size; but except for the 18th-century CHAPBOOKS, books did not become really cheap until the 19th century, when the popularity of the novel encouraged book-buying and the establishment of LIBRARIES. The present large sales of 'paperbacks' in Britain began with the publication of Penguin Books in 1935. In the 16th and 17th centuries publishers of books needed a licence from the government, but this system of censorship was abandoned in 1695. See also PILLORY.

Bookcases were not made in England until the later 17th century, it being usual before then to keep the books in CHESTS. The first-known mention of a bookcase, called a press, occurs in the diary of Samuel Pepys, who had two made for him in the summer of 1666, and his set of twelve are now in the Pepys Library at Magdalene College, Cambridge.

Booksellers came into being with the growth of the UNIVERSITIES, being first referred to at Cambridge in 1276. Medieval booksellers were called stationers because they had stalls or SHOPS (Low Latin *statio*), which distinguished them from PEDLARS. Booksellers also sold PARCHMENT and PAPER, the sellers of which are now called stationers. The invention of PRINTING, the RENAISSANCE and the REFORMATION increased the demand for BOOKS and the number of booksellers, who established themselves in London in Amen Lane, Paternoster Row (in which was the hall of the Stationers' Company, incorporated in 1557) and other places around Old ST PAUL'S CATHEDRAL. The earliest bookseller's catalogue is said to be that of Andrew Maunsell, of Lothbury, dedicated to Elizabeth I in 1595. Until the early 19th century, booksellers were publishers as well. The 19th century brought the establishment of railway bookstalls from which multiple book shops developed.

Boots and shoes originated with the SANDALS of ancient times, which were also worn in the Middle Ages. Boots date from early ANGLO-SAXON times and shoes from the Middle Ages; the shape and style of both have varied greatly through the centuries in accordance with purpose and fashion. Thus, the 14th and 15th centuries saw the piked or peaked shoe, which had long spear-like points extending beyond the toes, and the same shape was applied to the PATTENS of the period. Heels were not introduced until the 17th century, when shoes of ankle-height were worn, often decorated with ribbons or rosettes. For 18th-century ladies, high-waisted heels were fashionable; these were replaced in the 19th century by high boots, often buttoned, until late in the century when, as SKIRTS became a little shorter, elegant shoes with high heels were fashionable. Between the wars women wore low-cut shoes with medium heels, and in the later 1950s stiletto heels were fashionable. [E. Bordoli, *Footwear* (1933)] See also JACKBOOT, PATTENS, EMBROIDERY.

Bordar a VILLEIN who held a cottage and a small plot of land at the pleasure of

Boots and Shoes: 1 Sandal of the Middle Ages; 2 12th-cent. boot; 3 15th-cent. piked shoe; 4 15th-cent. patten; 5 18th-cent. shoe with high waisted heel; 6 17th-cent. shoe with lace rosette; 7 19th-cent. buttoned boot; 8 1920s shoe; 9 1950s shoe with stiletto heel

the lord of the MANOR and was bound to menial labour. His status in the FEUDAL SYSTEM does not seem to have clearly differed from that of a COTTAR.

Bore a long pole with a pointed, iron-shod head used in the siege of a CASTLE, after the BATTERING-RAM had broken up the stonework at the base of the wall, to knock the loose stones out and so enable

33

the pick-men to attack the rubble core of the wall. It was called by soldiers the 'mouse'.

Borough or burgh (as it is still called in Scotland) was a fortified TOWN (usually defended by a wall or a bank and ditch) in ANGLO-SAXON times. In the Middle Ages it came to mean a town which had obtained by CHARTER privileges such as the right to hold a MARKET, to have a merchant GUILD, and to govern itself through a MAYOR (PROVOST in Scottish burghs) and corporation. In the 13th century boroughs gained the right to send their representatives to Parliament. See also CRUSADES, CLARENDON CODE, BURGESS, DANES.

Borstal a system established in Britain under the Prevention of Crime Act (1908), by which young persons convicted of criminal offences between the ages of 16 and 23 may be sent, instead of receiving a PRISON sentence, to a Borstal institution for a period of residential, reformative training, usually three years, and subjected, after their release, to further supervision by the Borstal Association. It was named after the village of Borstal, near Rochester (Kent), in the prison of which the first institution of this kind was established. Experiments on similar lines had been conducted there since 1902 and at Bedford Prison since 1900. [L. W. Fox, *The English Prison and Borstal Systems* (1952)]

Bottles at first were made of the whole skins of SHEEP and other animals. Large POTTERY bottles were made some 7000 years ago, and the Egyptians made GLASS bottles as early as 1500 BC. Glass bottles to hold COSMETICS, PERFUME, WINE and other valuable liquids, used in ROMAN BRITAIN, have been found; they were mostly imported from Syria, Italy, Belgium and Germany. As they were expen-sive to make, glass bottles did not come into general use in the late Middle Ages, when quicker ways of making them were developed. The earliest dated English glass bottle (1657) is in Northampton Museum, though a green glass bottle in Canterbury Museum was found in a wall at Whitstable, which was built in 1390. The first practical bottle-blowing machine was designed in 1886.

Bottled BEER was invented by Alexander Nowell (1507?–1602) DEAN of ST PAUL'S CATHEDRAL. But leather-bottles (see BOMBARD) survived until the 19th century, being especially popular in the 16th and 17th century.

Boudoir means literally a room to which a lady retires when she is sulking, the name coming from the French *bouder*, to pout or sulk. The description was first applied to the rooms of the mistresses of Louis XV, King of France (1710–74), at the Palace of Versailles. The name came commonly to be applied in the 18th century to the sitting-room of the lady of the house. Its furniture might include CHAIRS, a DAVENPORT and a CUPBOARD in which was the CADDY containing her TEA. In contrast with the austerity of the NURSERY, it was the fashion for ladies to decorate their boudoirs elegantly. One in the late 18th century was described as having 'white paper with a border of pink silk with white and gold flowers stuck upon it' together with 'window curtains of pink linen with white silk fringes'. See also BOWER, CHILDREN'S HOUR

Bounds small boundary stones marking the limits of parishes and also of a town's meadows and fields in the Middle Ages. From the 9th century 'beating the bounds' was performed each Ascension Day when the children were marched in procession round the bounds, accompanied by the clergy and the parish officers, and beaten with peeled willow switches at each stone.

This was to teach the children to remember the boundary marks of their PARISH when they grew up and so to be able to prevent farmers removing them.

Bow and Arrow is one of the earliest missile WEAPONS. Early bows, which were short, became increasingly important in European warfare from the 10th century. In the NORMAN CONQUEST the invaders had short bows, which had an effective range of 100 yards and an extreme range of 150 yards.

The cross-bow, which was formed of a bow placed crosswise on a stock and winding mechanism for drawing back and releasing the string, was first mentioned by William of Tyre about 1098. The Church forbade its use in the Lateran Council of 1139 because of its deadliness, but its use became widespread. Though it was slower to fire than the simple bow, it was more accurate, and its arrows (called quarrels) had a greater range and penetration.

The long-bow, which was a larger, heavier version of the simple bow, was probably adopted from the Welsh by English troops in the 13th century. Generally made of YEW, it was 6 ft long, and practice in ARCHERY made it a very effective weapon. It was simple and quick to shoot, and a good archer could shoot five or six arrows a minute with a range of between 150 and 250 yards.

Though GUNS were introduced in the 14th century, bows continued to be used as weapons in England until the late 16th century. [Paul Martin, *Armour and Weapons* (1968)]

Bower a chamber in a CASTLE or medieval HOUSE, which was the ladies' sitting-room and which men entered only by invitation. At night the DAMSELS slept in it, their TRUCKLE BEDS being stacked away in a corner by day. A bower-woman was a lady's maid and companion. See also BOUDOIR, SOLAR.

Bowler a hard felt HAT with a narrow, curled brim and dome-shaped crown, usually black in colour. In the early 19th century a hat of much the same shape, known as the bowl hat, because it was like an inverted bowl, was worn, but the bowler hat probably owes its name to William Bowler, a hatter, who popularized it about 1850 as something lighter than the TOP HAT for men.

Bowls an outdoor game played on a level green, the aim being to place the bowls or woods, not perfectly spherical in shape, as near as possible to the jack, a smaller ball. It is one of the oldest British games, having been played as early as the 13th century. The Old Bowling Green at Southampton was in use by 1299. Once it was discouraged because it was alleged that it attracted men away from ARCHERY, and under Henry VIII fines were imposed on all who played bowls in public, but 'every nobleman, or other, having manors, lands or tenements to the yearly value of £100 or above, is free to play bowls without penalty within the precinct of their houses, gardens or orchards', so that bowling greens were laid down in the gardens of great houses in Tudor times. Henry VIII, who was himself a keen player, laid down bowling greens at WHITEHALL; and there is the tradition that Sir Francis Drake was playing bowls at Plymouth when the Armada was sighted in 1588. Charles II settled the laws of bowls, but it became an organized game only after the Bowling Association of Victoria and New South Wales was formed in 1880.

Formerly, women played a game called 'Troll My Dames' in which a wooden or metal ball was rolled along a board to the end where there were eleven holes; and both men and women joined in Carpet

Bowls, which was played with china balls, in the LONG GALLERIES of country houses. The indoor game of ten-pin bowling, played in a bowling alley, which has recently become very popular, is also an old game and more like SKITTLES than lawn bowls. [G. T. Burrows, *All About Bowls* (n.d.)]

Boxing first originated in ANGLO-SAXON times and is the oldest organized SPORT in England. In 1719 James Fig, a wandering showman at FAIRS, opened the Amphitheatre in Tottenham Court Road, London, in which he organized boxing matches. One of his pupils, Jack Broughton, champion of England from 1740 to 1750, drew up the first rules, which excluded biting, kicking and throwing an opponent to the ground, invented boxing-gloves (known as 'mufflers') and taught his pupils to use skill as well as weight and hitting power. There were then, however, only heavyweights, and a fight was won only by a knock-out or retirement.

Boxing in its modern form dates from 1865 when the Marquis of Queensberry drew up rules for matches with boxing-gloves (which had hitherto only been used for exhibitions), which were continued by the National Sporting Club, formed in 1891. See also PRIZE-FIGHTING. [J. W. Kenyon, *Boxing History* (1961)]

Boxing Day the feast of St Stephen, the day after CHRISTMAS. The name is probably derived either from the alms-boxes in churches which were opened on the day after Christmas for the benefit of the poor or from the pottery collecting-boxes taken round by APPRENTICES to householders and later broken open to pay for a feast. This had no association with the presents exchanged by relatives and friends, which were originally given on NEW YEAR'S DAY and transferred to Christmas in the 19th century. Also in the 19th century, the Boxing Day customs were replaced by Christmastide tips to tradesmen, dustmen, newspaper boys, and so on, gifts of game by landowners to estate workmen and tenants, and bonuses from firms to employees.

The PANTOMIME season since the 19th century has begun on Boxing Day.

Boy Bishop a boy elected in many medieval monasteries, schools and parishes on St Nicholas's Day (December 6) to execute until HOLY INNOCENTS' DAY (December 28) the various functions usually performed in church by a BISHOP. The practice was abolished by Henry VIII, revived by Mary and finally abolished by Elizabeth I. The intention of the practice was to express in dramatic form the reverence for childhood shown in the Gospels. The boy bishop wore episcopal robes, including a MITRE, and carried a CROSIER; other choirboys acted as his priests.

Boy Scouts (now known as SCOUTS) were founded in 1908 by Sir Robert (later Lord) Baden-Powell, who expressed his ideas in *Scouting for Boys*. The first great rally of 10 000 boys from all over the country was held in the CRYSTAL PALACE, London, in September, 1909, and a royal CHARTER of incorporation was granted in 1912. By 1910 there were 100 000 scouts; there are now nearly 600 000 in the United Kingdom alone. The sea scouts were formed in 1910; the wolf cubs (8–11 years old) in 1916; the rover scouts (over 18 years) in 1918; the air scouts in 1941; the senior scouts (15–18 years) in 1946. See also GIRL GUIDES.

Bracelet an ornament worn by both men and women from early times. The Romans often gave them as birthday or wedding presents, but they were not usually worn by unmarried girls. ANGLO-SAXON warriors wore large BRONZE bracelets to protect their wrists in battle, and chiefs gave bracelets to brave warriors. Since the Middle Ages, however, bracelets have been worn almost exclusively by women. Nowadays, the only surviving form of bracelet for men is the gold wristband of a WATCH, though recently chain-bracelets have been worn by some young men.

Braces were first used from about 1787. BREECHES were held up by a belt, but this was not strong enough to support TROUSERS, and so braces were invented. At first these consisted of a pair of straps passing over the shoulders and attached to a single button on each side before and behind, but from 1825 came the double-tongued pattern attached to two buttons on each side in front, and by 1850 the two straps were united at the point where they crossed under the shoulder-blades. By this time they were made of indiarubber and by 1860 of plain elastic web with double sliding ends. Victorian young ladies were supposed to embroider braces and slippers for the CURATE of their PARISH. See also POINTS.

Braies in Saxon times, brief, baggy, linen male outer BREECHES, which in the mid-12th century became concealed by the Norman TUNIC and so became an UNDERGARMENT. By the 16th century they had been replaced by DRAWERS.

Branks a bridle formerly used to punish scolding women. It consisted of hoops of metal made to pass over and round the head, opening by means of hinges at the sides and fastened at the back of the neck by a staple with a small padlock. The bridle bit, a flat piece of iron, about two inches long and an inch broad, pressed down upon the tongue to form a gag.

Brandy the spirit distilled from WINE, was originally known in England as brandywine (from the Dutch brande-wijn, burnt wine). It seems to have begun to become known in England at the end of the 17th century, about the same time as PORT (see also CLARET), and much of it came over from France by SMUGGLING. In the 1880s, when the vineyards of the Grande Champagne, the centre of the Cognac district from which the finest brandy comes, were devastated by disease, WHISKY began to rival brandy as a drink in England. [H. Warner Allen, *Through the Wineglass* (1954)]

Branding a penalty often imposed in addition to another (e.g. WHIPPING or the PILLORY). The criminal was branded on his face or hand with the initial letter of his crime (e.g. V for vagrancy; M for malefactor, the most common). The penalty was abolished in 1763.

Brass a metal composed of COPPER and ZINC, has been used since the 5th century BC, being mentioned in the BIBLE, but its use in Europe began about the time of the NORMAN CONQUEST of England, where the earliest traces of its use are to be seen in monumental BRASSES and HORSE-BRASSES. In Henry VIII's reign (1509-47) its export was forbidden, which suggests that it was manufactured extensively in England, and by the 18th century it had largely replaced IRON and BRONZE for many household utensils.

Brasses engraved by masons and set into tombs or on the floors of churches as memorials to the dead, were first introduced to England from the Continent in the 13th century when the desire for spaciousness in CHURCH construction made brass plates preferable to stone tombs and effigies. Throughout the Middle Ages they were made of sheets of brass imported from the Continent and were usually too expensive for any but noble or wealthy families. The oldest surviving brass in England is that to Sir John d'Auberon (d. 1277) in Stoke d'Abernon Parish Church (Surrey), and some 4000 brasses survive, the finest being made in the 14th century, mostly for important families living in the south and east of England.

The figures on brasses in the 13th and 14th centuries are nearly all of noblemen and knights, but in the second half of the 14th century merchants and traders appeared, and brasses became more numerous and smaller as they began to be used by less wealthy classes. In the later 14th century also ladies appeared on the same brass as their husbands, sometimes clasping his hand. Parish priests too were depicted in great numbers on brasses, though most of them belong to the 15th century. After the REFORMATION, the fashion for brasses died out, but they appeared again (though mostly as inscribed plates affixed to the walls of churches and not the floors) in the 19th and 20th centuries. [Jerome Bertram, *Brasses and Brass Rubbing in England* (1971)]

Bread baked from dough made of flour moistened with water and usually caused to ferment by adding LEAVEN or YEAST, has been made from very early times. Cakes of barley have been found in NEW STONE AGE dwellings. The Romans had a fancy bread containing OYSTERS, while to the ANGLO-SAXONS bread was so important that a woman about to be married had to show that she could bake a loaf (see MARRIAGE CUSTOMS).

Bread was an important part of the diet of every medieval household, rich or poor. In 1266 the Assize of Bread fixed the price of a loaf, while allowing its weight to vary according to the price of wheat. Tables were issued showing the weights of various types of loaves as the price of a quarter of wheat rose by stages of 6d from 6d to £5, there being four types of loaves: ½d white, 1d white, 1d wheaten and 1d

household (the roughest and coarsest); in 1329, for instance, when wheat was 6s a quarter, 1d white loaf was 3 lb 13 oz, 1d wheaten 5 lb 12 oz and 1d household 7 lb 11 oz. This law, with some small changes, remained in force until 1815.

The finest medieval bread was made from wheat, but it was also (and more often) made from oats, barley, rye or maslin (a mixture of rye and wheat) as well as peas, beans, vetches or acorns. During the 18th century bread was increasingly eaten at tea-time, when toast became popular, and wheat bread increasingly displaced other sorts until by 1800 it was eaten exclusively almost everywhere in England. Though white bread was prized, most bread was brown or grey in colour until ROLLER MILLS came in. [J. Ashley, *Bread of our Forefathers* (1936); E. Jacob, *Six Thousand Years of Bread* (1944)]

Breeches a garment worn by men from the late 16th century onwards on the lower limbs of the body and coming just below the knee. See also TROUSERS.

Bricks were introduced by the Romans into Britain. They were usually thin and square and red in colour as may be seen from those incorporated into the tower of St Albans Abbey. Roman brickworks, some of which were owned by TOWNS, were often placed near a ROAD for ease in transport. Their use was unknown in the early Middle Ages, but examples of 13th century brickwork exist in East Anglia, e.g. Little Wenham Hall (Suffolk). Many CASTLES were built of brick in the 15th century, e.g. Tattershall (Lincs.) and Hurstmonceaux (Sussex), which encouraged the use of brick in English building. The building of Eton College needed 2½ million bricks (1442–52). Most early bricks were imported from Flanders, but those for Kirby Muxloe Castle (Leics.) (1480–4) were made on the spot, as were those by the builders of later country houses. Brick was only used where suitable building stone was scarce, and for a long time it was used only for large houses. It did not become a common building material for ordinary houses until the end of the 17th century. [W. G. Hoskins, *The Making of the English Landscape* (1955)]

Bride-lace a length of broad blue ribbon, binding sprigs of ROSEMARY, often worn as a 'favour' at MARRIAGES in the 16th and 17th centuries. In the 16th century these sprigs were tied to the arm, but later it became more usual to wear them in the hat. The bride of John Winchcombe ('Jack of Newbury') in Henry VIII's reign 'was led to church between two boys with bride laces and rosemary tied about their sleeves', while Thomas Heywood in *A Woman Killed with Kindness* (1603) spoke of wedding guests 'with nosegay and bride laces in their hats'.

Bridewell originally a medieval royal palace in London, situated near St Bridget's or St Bride's Well, west of the mouth of the Fleet River. Rebuilt by Henry VIII for the entertainment of nobility and foreign princes, it was handed over by Edward VI in 1552 to the city as a house of correction, 'a workhouse where all vagrant and able persons are forced to beat hemp in public view, with due correction of whipping, according to their offence' (Stow). The building was damaged in the GREAT FIRE OF LONDON, but it was reconstructed by 1676. A whipping-room, draped in black, with a balustraded public gallery was built, and in the 17th and 18th centuries it was a fashionable sight to see men and women punished there. The Bridewell was closed in 1855 and the building was demolished in 1863.

The Bridewell in London gave its name to other HOUSES OF CORRECTION and PRISONS elsewhere.

Bridges were probably built from earliest times in Britain, and a few primitive ones still exist in western England (e.g. the East Dart's clapper or plank bridge of four piers supporting three granite slabs some 15 ft long). The Romans built mainly wooden bridges in Britain, but traces of stone or timber laid upon stone piers remain (e.g. at Corbridge, Wroxeter, London and Rochester). The earliest medieval bridges were

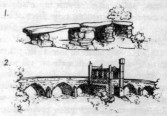

1 Clapper bridge; 2 Chapel bridge

usually of timber, but were gradually replaced by stone structures (e.g. Bideford's 13th-century wooden bridge was rebuilt in stone about 1460). Early medieval stone bridges are at Monmouth (1272) and Huntingdon (about 1300). Many carried houses, the rents of which paid for the upkeep of the bridge (e.g. old LONDON BRIDGE), and chapels (e.g. Rotherham and Wakefield), and some were fortified (e.g. Warkworth and Newcastle upon Tyne).

Modern bridge-building dates from the first wholly IRON arched bridge built over the River Severn near Coalbrookdale in 1779. The first wrought-iron girder bridge was built in Scotland in 1832, and in 1850 Robert Stephenson built the Britannia Tubular Bridge to carry the railway across the Menai Straits. The first major suspension bridge, designed with chains made of wrought-iron links, was the Menai Bridge, completed by Thomas Telford in 1826 to take road traffic over the straits; and the first great steel cantilever bridge was the Forth railway bridge in Scotland, completed in 1890.

Waterloo Bridge (1942) in London is of reinforced CONCRETE construction, while the Forth road bridge (1964) and the Severn road bridge (1966) are STEEL suspension bridges. [Jack Simmons, *Transport* (1962)]

Brigittines a monastic order founded about 1344 by St Bridget of Sweden. There was a single Brigittine house in England—the aristocratic, intellectual and wealthy Sion Convent, near Brentford (Middlesex), founded by Henry V in 1415. It was, like all early Brigittine houses, a double monastery of some 60 NUNS and 25 brethren. They used the same chapel and lived in separate parts of the monastery, the brethren acting as chaplains and directors to the women; and among them were many Cambridge graduates and after 1500 at least six former fellows of colleges in that University. Sion did not share the uninspired and indifferent atmosphere of most English monasteries by the 16th century. It had a reputation for strict observance, a remarkable LIBRARY, a strong interest in the English mystics and important contemporary devotional writers. It was one of the few monasteries restored by Queen Mary, but was suppressed again under Elizabeth I.

British Church, see CELTIC CHURCH.

British Schools were day-schools for poor children provided by the British and Foreign School Society, which was founded by NONCONFORMISTS in 1808. These schools, under the influence of Joseph Lancaster (1778–1838), adopted the monitorial system devised by Andrew Bell (1753–1832) in which elder boys or monitors took charge of the rest and instructed them under the superintendence of the teachers. These schools and the NATIONAL SCHOOLS received from the government in 1833 a grant of £20 000 which was gradually increased in subsequent years. The British Schools gave undenominational religious instruction based on the BIBLE, similar to that provided in the Board Schools set up by the ELEMENTARY EDUCATION ACT (1870). [Mary Sturt, *The Education of the People* (1967)]

Broad Churchmen a popular term in the later 19th century for a group within the CHURCH OF ENGLAND who rejected the position of both HIGH CHURCHMEN and LOW CHURCHMEN and had an outlook similar to that of the earlier LATITUDINARIANS. Some of the Broad Churchmen, such as Charles Kingsley and Thomas Hughes, were among the founders of Christian Socialism, which sympathized with CHARTISM and sought to interest the Church in social reform.

Broadsheet a large sheet of paper printed on one side only in one type and not divided into columns. In the 18th and 19th centuries broadsheets were often sold in the streets and contained short stories, political tracts, dying confessions of executed criminals or BALLADS.

Broadside an older name for BROADSHEET.

Brocade a SILK stuff on which figures are wrought, often with threads of gold and silver. Originally made by the Chinese, it was brought to Europe as a result of the CRUSADES. It was fashionable in Britain for a time after the coronation of King George VI and Queen Elizabeth in 1937.

Brochs a group of CASTLES, peculiar to IRON AGE Scotland and built mostly during the 1st centuries BC and AD. They were round towers about 60 ft high and up to 60 ft in diameter with thick walls of unmortared stone, with no windows and only a low, narrow doorway which could easily be barred. Each had a roof of stone slabs or of timber, little more than 6 ft high, with an opening in the centre and stairs in the thickness of the walls; and many, though not all, had wells. More than 500 sites of brochs have been identified, mainly in the extreme north and the Islands and nearly always near the sea. [J. D. Mackie, *A History of Scotland* (1964)]

Bronze an alloy of COPPER and TIN, the use of which spread from the East to Europe during the BRONZE AGE; and during this time, supplies of tin became exhausted in the Near East, which therefore imported bronze or tin from Cornwall. Many bronze statuettes and toilet articles survive from ROMAN BRITAIN, and the head has been found of a big bronze statue of Hadrian in London. In the Middle Ages bronze tomb effigies became fashionable, fine examples being those of Eleanor of Castile (d. 1290) and Henry III (d. 1272) in WESTMINSTER ABBEY. During the 17th and 18th centuries gilt bronze (ormolu) was favoured for making candlesticks, vases, clock-cases and furniture mounts.

Bronze Age began in Britain about 2000 BC with the coming of the BEAKER PEOPLE, who knew how to use bronze (a mixture of copper and tin) to make more effective weapons and implements than those of the NEW STONE AGE. The Bronze Age saw also the use of the WHEEL for vehicles and the WEAVING of proper garments instead of animal skins; and the HENGES belong to this period. The late Bronze Age (the late 8th century BC) was marked by the arrival of the CELTS, who had CHARIOTS and rode HORSES. The Bronze Age was succeded by the IRON AGE in the 6th century BC. [Stuart Piggott, *British Prehistory* (1949)]

Brooches were worn among the CELTS, being commonly made of BRONZE and in the shape of animals. Enamelled brooches have been found in England belonging to the ROMAN and ANGLO-SAXON periods. Brooches were especially fashionable in the 19th century, the early Victorian period using semi-precious stones for them, while during the years of the Second Empire of Napoleon III in France (1852–70) gold-enamel was favoured.

Brooms until the late 19th century, were besoms, consisting of a bundle of twigs tied round a stick. Originally they were made of the flexible twigs of wild broom (which is not the same as gorse), but later birch twigs were commonly used, and they were made in very much the same way as a BIRCH-ROD. WITCHES were thought to fly through the sky astride a broom; and the ANGLO-SAXONS thought that husbands might give their WIVES 'three blows with a broomstick' if they were disobedient. A broom used to be hung at the mast-head of a SHIP as a sign she was for sale.

Brougham a single-horse, four-wheeled closed CARRIAGE, often with an elevated seat for the driver. Wealthy persons had their own smart, private broughams, but those that plied for public hire (though the most common type of cab) were inferior in speed and comfort to the HANSOM-CABS and were commonly known as 'four-wheelers', 'growlers' or 'crawlers'. The name originally came from the French '*brouette*', but was modified to the name of Lord Brougham (1778–1868), a Whig politician and eminent lawyer.

The name was also given in the early years of the 20th century to a closed electrically-driven private carriage for four or five persons with an open driver's seat (see ELECTRIC CARS).

Building Societies began in the later 18th century when people combined to help each other build and own their HOUSES. The earliest building society was founded in 1775 at the Golden Cross Inn, Birmingham. Each member of these early societies contributed money with which land was bought and houses were built. As the houses were completed, they were allocated to the members by ballot or auction, and when all had been built by a particular society, it was wound up. These societies, therefore, were called 'terminating societies'. In 1836 an Act of Parliament laid down legal regulations for building societies; in 1869 the Building Societies Association was formed; and the Building Societies Act (1874) recognized the societies as corporate bodies.

By the early 1900s the terminating societies had almost disappeared, being replaced by permanent societies which had been formed from the mid-19th century. These new societies benefited both savers, who deposited money with the society and received interest upon it, and house-buyers, who borrowed money from the society (in the form of a mortgage upon their house) for a definite period during which they paid it back with interest. The total funds of all the building societies in Britain amounted to £77 000 000 in 1919, to £773 000 000 in 1939 and to £5 577 000 000 in 1965. At the same time, smaller societies have been amalgamating to form bigger societies; and while in 1900 there were 2250 societies, there were 900 in 1945 and 605 in 1965.

Bull-baiting a SPORT, popular in Elizabethan times, which continued until forbidden by Act of Parliament in 1835. The bull was tied by the horns with a rope about 15 feet long to a ring fixed to a stake driven into the ground. Dogs, trained to seize the bull by the nose, were let loose in turn, and when they did this successfully, it was called 'pinning the bull'. The Bull Ring survives in name at Birmingham, while the iron ring may still be seen in the ground at Brading (Isle of Wight). Bull-baiting was never as popular in England as BEAR-BAITING.

Bullet pudding a Victorian children's Christmas game. The pudding was a mound of flour with a sweet or marble on top. The children cut slices from the pudding, and whoever let the marble fall had to pick it out of the mess with his mouth.

Burgess was originally the FREEMAN of a BOROUGH, being one of the traders, residents and property owners who had the right of voting at borough elections, had a share in the corporate property of the town and paid rates for the upkeep of the town. From 1265 to 1832 each borough was represented in Parliament by two of its burgesses. See also YEOMAN.

Burials in prehistoric times were in BARROWS, but with the coming of Christianity graves in consecrated ground became usual. From ANGLO-SAXON times, the body was taken to a church where MASS was said and then taken to be buried with prayers (see GALILEE). In the Middle Ages bodies were committed to the grave naked or in a LINEN shroud, only the wealthy being 'chested' in a coffin; and in 1666 an Act (not repealed until 1814) said the shroud must be of WOOL. Friends carried CANDLES and ROSEMARY and wore black MOURNING cloaks and hoods (a custom which lasted into the 19th century). The COMMON PRAYER BOOK simplified the burial service, but the PURITANS sometimes had no service at all. See also SIN-EATING, CREMATION, CHARNELHOUSE.

Buses were introduced from Paris into London by George Shillibeer in 1829; his buses carried 22 passengers and were drawn by three horses. From 1833 to 1836 three steam-buses (built by Walter Hancock) ran between Paddington and the City, but they damaged the roads by their weight and were killed by heavy charges imposed by the TURNPIKE trusts.

Buses carrying 12 passengers inside and two outside and drawn by two horses were introduced in 1849, and by 1850 there were some 3000 buses on the London streets. The crowds which came to London for the GREAT EXHIBITION (1851) led to the introduction of double-decker buses which had seats on the roof arranged in 'knifeboard' fashion so that the passengers sat back to back along the length of the bus; these buses each held 26 passengers (12 inside, 14 outside, including one each side of the driver). The London General Omnibus Company was founded in 1855, taking over 580 buses from smaller companies and soon controlling a large proportion of the London services. In 1883 it replaced the knifeboard bus with one having transverse 'garden-seats' on top. Roll-tickets were introduced in 1880 and the bell-punch in 1893.

The largest number of horse-buses ever licensed in London was 3736 in 1901. The first motor-buses ran in London in 1898, and the last horse-buses were withdrawn by October 1911. Change in the provinces was slower. The Birmingham and Midland Omnibus Company introduced motor-buses in 1904, but suspended them from 1907 to 1912. Covered top decks were introduced in 1925, pneumatic TYRES in 1927 and diesel engines in 1932. The London Passenger Transport Board was formed in 1933.

Busk a flat, rigid strip of bone, whalebone, wood or in the 17th century sometimes horn or in the 19th century often steel or brass, which was attached to the front of a BODICE (or STAYS) to keep it a stiff shape and prevent it gathering in folds and wrinkles around the waist. They were particularly worn between 1660 and 1680 and again between 1760 and 1800 when fashion demanded a long bodice, a small waist and a billowing SKIRT. In the 17th and 18th century they sometimes were worn as uncomfortable love tokens by rustic girls, having chip or relief carving on the front and usually girls' names and dates or sentimental messages incised on their backs, and they were worn pushed down a busk sheath in front of the bodice.

Bust-bodice a breast support made of strong white cotton cloth reinforced by wire, laced front and back, and with bones on each side of the lace-holes. It was used by women from 1889 when dress BODICES were very tight, being worn above the STAYS and usually hidden under a CAMISOLE. It was the forerunner of the modern brassière which was introduced about 1916. See also UNDER-GARMENTS.

Bustle a pad or framework for pushing out the top of a woman's SKIRT at the back of the waist. The name was first used about 1830. It was fashionable until 1889, alternating with the CRINOLINE.

Butter was originally made by churning the whole MILK, but by the 16th century butter much more like our own was obtained by using cream rather than milk. Conrad Heresbatch in *The Whole Art of Husbandry* (1577) favoured souring the cream before making butter to give it a nutty taste which is now lost with the disappearance of farmhouse butter. In 1914 there were only two butter factories in England, but now factory butter is general. In 1877 butter-making was revolutionized by the invention of the centrifugal cream-separator which dispensed with the process of skimming and with the large shallow pans in which the cream rose.

As well as being valued as a COSMETIC, butter was originally used as a medicine rather than a food. A 10th-century ANGLO-SAXON treatise advised pounding up butter with YARROW to apply to swellings. In medieval and Tudor times butter was usually made in the spring and summer and much was preserved by salting. 'May butter' was thought to be best for CHILDREN, being especially recommended for growing pains and constipation. In the 17th century, it continued to be despised as a food, Thomas Muffet in 1655 calling it 'the chief food of the poorer sort'; but by the 18th century it was increasingly used for cooking and on BREAD. Cattle-plague in 1865-7 made butter scarcer and expensive and encouraged the eating of MARGARINE. The consumption of butter in Britain was 19 lb per person in 1964 (compared with 43 lb per head in Ireland and New Zealand) of which only 10 per cent was made in Britain.

Butterfly a woman's head-dress worn from about 1450 to 1495, consisting of a wire framework supporting a gauze veil which was spread out over the head on each side like a pair of wings. It was fixed to a small, brimless cap of wool or felt worn closely on the back of the head. The representations of ladies on contemporary BRASSES are often shown wearing it, and their heads are depicted in profile so as to display it fully. See also HATS.

Buttery a storeroom, commonly placed between the KITCHEN and the HALL, in a large HOUSE, CASTLE or COLLEGE in the later Middle Ages, from which the drink was served. The name is derived from the butts or barrels of ALE kept in it. See also PANTRY.

Buttons were used by both the ANGLO-SAXONS and the DANES to fasten their MANTLES, but rows of buttons do not seem to have been adopted until the introduction of tighter-fitting garments in Edward I's reign (1272-1307). They then became more decorative and were worn, especially by women, in larger numbers than necessary. Effigies show that by Edward III's reign (1327-77) it was fashionable to have rows of buttons thickly set on sleeves from the wrist to the elbow. Indeed, buttons had become so popular that servant girls were whipped for ostentatiously wearing sleeves buttoned above the elbow. About this time also COATS and KIRTLES were sometimes worn with closely set buttons down the front, but later were replaced by POINTS.

Buttons reappeared in the 16th century for use and decoration, but were not used much until the end of the 17th century when men began to wear coats and WAISTCOATS instead of DOUBLETS. Throughout the 18th century buttons underwent many changes, being worn mainly by fashionable gentlemen. They were sometimes very costly, set with diamonds and other precious stones, but were very little worn by women until the end of the 18th century. There was no place for them on the flimsy garments of the NAKED FASHION. The early Victorian BODICE frequently buttoned down the front, and in the early 20th century buttons became numerous on women's dresses, while men's buttons ceased to be decorative. Although there have since been other ways of fastening clothes, such as ZIP-FASTENERS, buttons have never ceased to be useful or fashionable.

Byre or cowhouse was probably separated from the dwelling-house in south-east England by the 16th century. The small farmer began to keep his livestock in a separate building for the short part of the year when they could not be kept out-of-doors. The part of the HOUSE formerly used for the cattle now became a KITCHEN, BUTTERY, dairy, brewhouse or store. [M. W. Barley, *The House and Home* (1963)]

C

Cabriolet a light, two-wheeled, hooded, one-horse CHAISE, elegant and easy-running. Its spokes were generally painted red and yellow for decoration, its seat was covered with blue cloth, and its hood was made of shining black leather and (when not needed for protection against weather) was kept open with the aid of a gilded, compass-shaped lever. If it belonged to a wealthy person, a liveried servant stood on the footboard behind. It was very fashionable in the 18th century. See CARRIAGES [L. Tarr, *The History of the Carriage* (1969)].

Caddy a word derived from the Malayan *kati*, a weight of about 1¼ lb which came to give its name to a box containing that weight of TEA. The early caddies had no locks, but were made in sets of two or three, for different varieties of tea, and were kept in an oblong tea-chest provided with a lock, to protect the costly tea; this might be found in the BOUDOIR of the lady of the house, who always served the tea. Not until about 1780 did the single box with a lock (which was really a combination of caddy and tea-chest) become fashionable; but it never superseded the two- or three-compartment chest which, in the late 18th and throughout the 19th century, often contained two caddies for different varieties or grades of tea, and a centrally placed glass bowl in which the tea could be mixed and blended or SUGAR kept. [Edward H. Pinto, *Treen and other Wooden Bygones* (1969)]

Calash (1) a light horse-drawn CARRIAGE used for travelling or pleasure in the 18th and 19th centuries, having low wheels and a folding hood. See also VICTORIA.

(2) This carriage gave its name to a woman's silk hood, supported with hoops of cane or whalebone and projecting considerably over the face, which was worn from about 1770 to 1790 and 1820 to 1840 to protect the high head-dresses that were fashionable during both these periods. See also HATS.

Calefactory or warming-room, the one room in a medieval MONASTERY where there was a fireplace (though the severe CARTHUSIANS had fireplaces in their cells). The calefactory was generally situated beneath the DORMITORY, and a fire was kept burning night and day in it from All Saints to EASTER. This was the only warmth kept for the MONKS, except for those who were ill in the FARMERY. The word comes from the Latin *calefactorium*, a warming-place. See also BATHS.

Calendar of the Romans for a time had 10 months in the year, beginning in March and ending in December; the names of the last 4 months of the year are a reminder of this. Then January and

February were added to give a year of 12 months—4 months of 31 days, 7 of 29 and February with 28, totalling 355 days. By Julius Caesar's time this was clearly inaccurate, so his astronomers added 80 days to the year 46 BC (the 'year of confusion'), making 365 days in the year with an extra day each leap year; the odd months each had 31 days and the others 30, except the last one, February, which had 29 and 30 on a leap year. Julius Caesar also changed the name of the fifth month (Quintilis) into Julius after himself. Augustus similarly changed the sixth month (Sextilis) into Augustus and took a day from February to make it 31 days (equal to July). There were now three consecutive months (July, August, September) with 31 days each, so September and November were reduced to 30, while October and December were increased to 31.

The Julian Calendar had a year of 365 days, 5 hours, 49 minutes (to the nearest minute), but by having an extra day each leap year this produced an error of 11 minutes a year. By 1582 the calendar was 10 days too advanced, and Pope Gregory cancelled 10 days, making October 15 the day after October 4, and providing that the leap year was not to be counted in 'century' years, except when these are divisible by 400. Thus AD 1800 and 1900 were not leap years, but AD 2000 will be.

At the time only Roman Catholic countries adopted the Gregorian Calendar. Britain did not do so until 1752. The British calendar was than 11 days behind those of other countries, and Parliament ordered that September 2 was to be followed by September 14 that year and also that NEW YEAR'S DAY was to be January 1 instead of March 25 as previously. The quarter days, however, were left unchanged as the saints' days which came at intervals of 3 months from March 25 (Lady Day, March 25; St John the Baptist, June 24; St Michael, September 29; Christmas, December 25). The change caused concern and even riots in some parts of the country, the popular cry being, 'Give us back our eleven days!'

Calico a plain white COTTON cloth first brought in the 16th century from the town of Calicut (Calcutta) on the coast of Malabar in India.

Caltrap also called a 'crow's-foot', consisted of four iron spikes, each about three inches long, joined together at their bases, so that when it was thrown down on the ground, one point always stood upwards. It was used in warfare to obstruct the advance of CAVALRY or to increase the difficulty of a ford.

Calvinism the theological system of John Calvin (1509-64) which he put into effect in Geneva. In doctrine its main belief was predestination, the assertion that all men from eternity were predestined by God to eternal salvation or damnation, and in ecclesiastical government it replaced BISHOPS by presbyteries consisting of ministers (clergymen) and elders (laymen). Calvinism was adopted by the CHURCH OF SCOTLAND and by the English PURITANS, though to a different extent by the PRESBYTERIANS and INDEPENDENTS. Later the EVANGELICALS accepted Calvinism, but the METHODISTS were largely ARMINIAN. See also HUGUENOTS.

Camera developed from the camera obscura, which was a device for tracing images invented in the 17th century, consisting of a large box with a lens at one end and a white surface of ground glass at the other on which the image was thrown. In 1814 Joseph Niepce, a French printer, substituted bitumen-coated glass for the ground glass and formed a record of the image which he fixed by washing the glass with solvent, but he could not print positive impressions from his negatives. In 1829 Niepce co-operated with a painter, Louis Daguerre, to produce daguerrotypes in which the image was taken on silver plate sensitized by iodine and developed by exposure to mercury vapour. Finally, W. H. Fox Talbot in England in 1835 used transparent negatives of oiled paper from which, by placing them on chemically treated paper and exposing them to the light, he obtained positive pictures (i.e. in which the shades of light and dark corresponded to the image). Glass was later used, instead of paper, for the negative, but the widespread use of photography only took place with the introduction of the gelatine dry plate in 1880, which reduced the time required for an exposure, and the substitution of the celluloid film for the glass plate in 1889. See also CINEMA. [Helmut Gernsheim, *The History of Photography* (1955)]

Camisole a short-sleeved or sleeveless woman's under-BODICE of white CALICO, often embroidered or trimmed with LACE, worn over STAYS to protect a tight-fitting dress, from the 1820s onwards. See also COSTUME.

Campanile a bell-tower or BELFRY, especially one detached from the main building. Old ST PAUL'S CATHEDRAL had a campanile near the east end, the Jesus Bell Tower, which was a stone square tower crowned with a wooden spire on the summit of which was a gilded statue of St Paul. Other campaniles once stood by WESTMINSTER ABBEY and Norwich, Salisbury and Worcester Cathedrals. Chichester is unique among cathedrals in still possessing its campanile, though spireless.

Canals were first cut in Britain by the Romans. In the Midlands there was the

Fossdyke Canal between Lincoln and the Trent, constructed about 65 AD and scoured in Henry I's reign (1100-35), part of which is still in use today. Though the Exeter Canal was cut as early as 1564-8, the first wholly artificial major navigational canal in Britain was the Bridgewater Canal, from Worsley (Lancs.) to Manchester, opened in 1761, which was the work of James Brindley (1716-72), who designed others, including the Grand Trunk Canal (1766). The

1 LIVERPOOL   4 HULL
2 MANCHESTER   5 BIRMINGHAM
3 LEEDS   6 BRISTOL

——— MAJOR CANAL ROUTES
-------- NARROW MINOR CANALS

Map of Canals

years 1790-4 were a period of 'canal mania' when Parliament authorized the construction of 81 canals. The English network of canals was based on the four great estuaries of the Mersey, Humber, Severn and Thames, linking the important industrial areas with each other and the four great ports of London, Liverpool, Bristol and Hull. The whole canal system of 4000 miles had been practically completed by 1830, but by 1850 the RAILWAY companies had secured control of one third of the canal mileage. Most of the canals were nationalized in 1948. See also NAVVIES. [Charles Hadfield, *The Canal Age* (1968)

Canal lock or pound-lock (with two gates) was first built on the Continent near Bruges (Belgium) in 1396. When Leonardo da Vinci was engineer to the

47

Duke of Milan, he invented the swinging type of lock gate (or mitre gate) to replace the vertically rising or 'guillotine' gates previously used, and in 1487 he built

Canal lock

6 locks with gates of this sort. The first pound-locks in England were fitted by John Trew on the Exeter Canal in Elizabeth I's reign (1558–1603). [L. T. C. Rolt, *Navigable Waterways* (1963)]

Candles were used by the Romans as well as LAMPS. In the Middle Ages wax candles were used in churches and wealthier homes, while poorer people used tallow candles; rushlights, which were simple tallow candles, were used in English country cottages until well into the 19th century. King Alfred used a candle marked with equally-spaced bands to tell the TIME as it burned, the candle being protected inside a lantern of wood and thin horn; and from the 15th to 17th centuries London streets were lit by tallow candles enclosed in lanterns hung from houses. During the 18th century rooms were lit by candles placed first in wall-brackets with reflecting MIRRORS, but later massed in large chandeliers hung from the ceilings. From the early 19th century candles were made of paraffin wax and from about 1820 had woven wicks, which bent over in the flame and were completely consumed, and so did not

need constant clipping or snuffing of the charred wick as had always previously had to be done; but by then candles were being replaced by GAS lighting. See also LACE-LAMP, CANDLEMAS, TORCH.

Candlemas (February 2), the festival commemorating the Purification of the Virgin Mary and the presentation of Christ in the Temple, which took place 40 days after his birth. The name comes from the CANDLES, which were blessed and carried round the CHURCH in PROCESSION before the MASS on that day during the Middle Ages. This was forbidden in England in 1549.

In Scotland it was formerly the custom for children to give presents of money to their teacher on Candlemas Day. The boy and girl who gave most became King and Queen for the day and were carried in procession through the streets on a seat formed of the children's crossed hands. The teacher sometimes made a bowl of PUNCH for the children to drink the health of the King and Queen, but those who had not given anything might get the TAWSE instead. Another Scottish custom was the Candlemas Ba', a FOOTBALL match played on that day by the east end of the town against the west, the unmarried men against the married or one parish against another. The day ended with the Candlemas Blaze, a BONFIRE or setting the furze alight.

Cane the stem of a plant similar to bamboo, was used as a walking-stick by men from the early 16th century onwards, the finer kinds being usually carried under the arm. The fashionable period for canes was the 17th and 18th centuries, and they were of very varying lengths. In the second half of the 18th century they were very long and carried by ladies as well as gentlemen. The most common types of cane were the Malacca or 'clouded cane', made from the mottled stem of a Malacca palm, a long cane carried by gentlemen about 1730; the Rattan, a cane made from an East Indian palm, used in the 17th and 18th centuries —'a little black rattoon painted and gilt' (Pepys, 1660); the Dragon's Blood, made from the frond stem of the Dragon Palm in Malaya, fashionable in the early 18th century; and the Jemmy, a little cane carried under the arm by gentlemen in the 1750s and 1760s and sometimes as part of their fashionable outfit by ladies, who might also have one on their DRESS-ING-TABLE to ensure that their maid-servant did their toilet as they chose.

From the 16th century the cane was also used as an instrument of punishment, especially for children. The accounts of a noble Elizabethan household contain the item: 'For Master John a grammar book and a cane'; and the seal of Blackburn Grammar School depicts the master wielding a slender cane some three feet in length. While the BIRCH-ROD continued to be the usual implement in schools, the cane was sometimes used as a less severe punishment. Edmund Burke said to a schoolmaster who complained of his pupils' indocility, 'You must exert your cane with more vigour, and if that does not do, you must flog—and flog soundly', The cane was used to teach children TABLE MANNERS at home and by the BEADLE to ensure their good behaviour in church. See also NEW LANARK MILLS.

Canning as a means of sterilizing and preserving food owes its origin to a Paris confectioner, Nicholas Appert, who received in 1809 a prize from the French government for discovering a way of preserving food by putting it in bottles, heating to a certain temperature and keeping it airtight. The next year an Englishman, Peter Durand, used tin cans instead of bottles. Australian tinned mutton was shown at the GREAT EX-HIBITION (1851). Today over 5500 million cans of food are eaten each year in Britain, the largest single producer being Heinz.

Cannon the first great pieces of ARTIL-LERY, originated in the early 14th century. The first cannon were 'firepots', crude iron buckets loaded with GUN-POWDER and stones and touched off through a hole at the bottom; but these simple siege engines soon gave way to the familiar tapering tube of IRON or BRONZE. The tube was made of bars running lengthwise, hooped with rings; it was loaded with balls of iron or stone through the breech, and either fixed in place or mounted on a sledge or carriage. The English are said to have used cannon at Crècy in 1346 and at the siege of Calais the next year; and the first CASTLES were bombarded by them in the Wars of the Roses (1455–85). By the 15th century large ones were being made (see MONS MEG), and in 1521 the first cast-iron ones were made in Sussex.

Canon an ecclesiastical title originally given to all the CLERGY in a DIOCESE (excluding MONKS and private CHAP-LAINS), but gradually it was limited to secular CLERGY belonging to a CATHEDRAL or COLLEGIATE CHURCH. From the 11th century there were also regular canons (e.g. AUGUSTINIAN CANONS) who lived under a semi-monastic RULE. There are also Minor Canons (often known in cathedrals of the Old Foundation as Vicars Choral), who sing the priest's part in the daily services; and since 1840 there have been Honorary Canons, who are clergymen who receive the title as a mark of distinction and are not among the regular staff of a cathedral. See also CHAPTER, DEAN, PREBENDARY.

Canon Law comprises the laws of the Church administered by the ECCLESI-ASTICAL COURTS. During the Middle Ages, the Roman canon law was enforced in England, but after the REFORMATION this was modified by the canons of 1603-4. Canon Law was originally binding upon both clergy and laymen, but Lord Hardwicke in 1736 pronounced that it was binding only on the clergy.

Canterbury Cathedral according to Bede, originated when St Augustine (d. 604) consecrated an existing Roman BASILICA as his CATHEDRAL, and beside it grew up a MONASTERY. The present building is in the Perpendicular style (see GOTHIC). The Cathedral became an important centre for PILGRIMAGES, especially to the SHRINE of St Thomas Becket which was dedicated in 1220, but the official receipts for offerings at the shrines and altars in the 15th and 16th centuries show that these had become quite negligible in comparison with the huge amounts given earlier in the Middle Ages. [A. Babington, *Canterbury Cathedral* (1948).] See also HUGUENOTS.

Carbine was a short RIFLE, originally introduced for use by the CAVALRY. See also DRAGOONS and HAND-GUNS.

Cards, Playing probably originated in the East, appearing in Italy in the mid-14th century and then spreading to France and Germany. They probably appeared in England about 1450 since an attempt was made to prevent their importation into the country in 1464. They soon became a popular means of GAMBLING. The court-figures on modern cards are still depicted in late medieval COSTUME. Card-playing was one of the GAMES which the PURITANS tried to stop during the COMMONWEALTH, and it was long thought to be wrong on SUNDAY. In the 18th century it became popular as a game which both men and women could play in ASSEMBLY ROOMS and at SPAS and later the SEASIDE. Whist is mentioned as

'whisk' in 1621 and assumed its present name soon after the RESTORATION. Modern whist evolved in the 18th century and was probably the most widely-played card-game until bridge developed from it about 1894. See also SANDWICH, BEZIQUE.

Carols were originally songs sung with DANCING, particularly at CHRISTMAS, often by MUMMERS, and at WASSAILS. The oldest printed Christmas carol is the *Boar's Head Carol* (see BOAR), which appeared in 1521. Other old carols include 'I Saw Three Ships Come Sailing By' and 'The Holly and the IVY'. The singing of carols from house to house (as described in Thomas Hardy's *Under the Greenwood Tree*) probably goes back at least as far as the NORMAN CONQUEST. During the COMMONWEALTH in England, the PURITANS discouraged the singing of carols, but the practise revived, and many were later sung as HYMNS, while in the 19th century new ones appeared such as 'The First Nowell' and 'Good King Wenceslas'.

Carpets were brought to Europe from the East during the CRUSADES and introduced into England by Eleanor of Castile (d. 1290), but were not used much in England until the 15th and 16th centuries when carpets from Turkish Anatolia were first used for covering walls and TABLES. Floors only gradually ceased to be covered with RUSHES and straw. By the 17th century carpets from Persia and Turkey arrived in larger quantities; some also came from France, and some were made in England, but carpet-making in England died out in the mid-17th century, and was not revived until about 1750 when some weavers, who had left France in disguise, established the English carpet manufacture.

Carpet sweeper in the form of a machine with brushes which revolved when pushed along the floor and swept the dust up into a special compartment, was invented in the middle of the 19th century. See also BROOM, VACUUM CLEANER

Carrel a small alcove in the CLOISTER of a MONASTERY containing a desk and used as a place of study. At both Chester and Gloucester, where carrels can be seen, they were formed by dividing up the outer wall of the church, each occupying the space of half a window.

Carriages started with COACHES, which was followed by the POST-CHAISE; and in the 18th century many types were developed, improvements in the ROADS and in the improvement in the carriage itself, the body being suspended on straps,

attached later to 'C'-shaped springs. Among these were the PHAETON, CURRICLE, CABRIOLET, CALASH, WAGONETTE and CLARENCE. In the 19th century the possession of carriages went with rank— the great house with its large coach-house and all sorts of carriages and a turn-out for important occasions with 4 horses and outriders; then the upper middle-class with a LANDAU and pair and the lower middle-class with a BROUGHAM or a VICTORIA with a single horse; the clergyman's CHAISE and the tradesman's DOG-CART; and the farmer's TRAP or GIG. For public use there were the HACKNEY-COACH, BROUGHAM and HANSOM-CAB as well as the BUS. There is a comprehensive Carriage Museum at Maidstone (Kent). [H. McCausland, *The English Carriage* (1948)]

Carriages: 1 16th-cent. Coach; 2 16th-cent. Hackney Coach; 3 17th-cent. Post Chaise; 4 17th-cent. Chaise; 5 18th-cent. Landau; 6 19th-cent. Cabriolet; 7 19th-cent. Calash; 8 19th-cent. Brougham; 9 18th-cent. Mail Coach; 10 18th-cent. Wagon; 11 18th-cent. Trap; 12 18th-cent. Gig; 13 19th-cent. Victoria; 14 19th-cent. Waggonette; 15 19th-cent. Hackney Carriage; 16 19th-cent. Hansom Cab.

Carriers seem first to have appeared on the roads at the same time as WAGONS late in the 16th century. Stowe's *Annales* state 'about that time (1564) began long wagons to come into use such as now (1598) come to London from Canterbury, Norwich, Ipswich, Gloucester with passengers and commodities'. By the middle of the 17th century there was a regular system of carriers, covering the greater part of the country, running on regular days with fixed prices and fares. From them the stage-wagons developed in the 17th century to carry passengers, and also the faster, dearer STAGE-COACHES. The carrier remained the main means of transport in rural England in the 18th & 19th centuries for conveying small goods, livestock and passengers between villages and nearby towns, being finally driven off the roads by the local motor BUS in the 1920s and 1930s.

Carronade a short, light gun, usually of large calibre, having a chamber for the powder like a MORTAR, first made in 1776 at the Carron Iron Works, Stirlingshire. Having a low muzzle-velocity and being easily handled, it was chiefly used on shipboard, mounted on the upper deck. It made an important contribution to the victories of Nelson's time. See also IRON and ARTILLERY.

Carthusians a monastic order founded by St Bruno at La Grande Chartreuse, near Grenoble, in 1086. It was a very strict order; each MONK had a separate cell and was vowed to silence, solitude and abstinence from meat, while lay brothers prepared his food and brought it to him twice a day. The monks only met each other at daily services and on holy days for meals. They wore a white HABIT with a black cloak over it.

Carthusians came to England in 1180, and their English monasteries were called Charterhouses, but there were only 19 in all, the most famous being just west of Aldersgate in London.

Carucage a tax varying in amount from 3s to 5s on every HIDE or carucate of land, which replaced DANEGELD. It was first levied, on the basis of the DOMESDAY assessment, for Richard I's ransom, and was last levied in 1224.

Cassock a long garment, usually black, worn by the CLERGY and derived from the *vestis talaris* or ankle-length robe retained by the clergy when, under barbarian influence in the 6th century, shorter garments were adopted by other people. The Canons of the CHURCH OF ENGLAND of 1604 forbade beneficed clergy to appear in public 'in their doublet and hose, without coats or cassocks', and the cassock continued to be the normal dress for the clergy until well into the 18th century. See also VESTMENTS.

The Bishops of Durham wore a purple cassock as they were Earls-Palatine in the Middle Ages. The wearing of purple cassocks by all English bishops originated in this century, probably through the encouragement of ecclesiastical tailors.

Castles though the word is sometimes used for the early HILL-FORTS, really began in England after the NORMAN CONQUEST, the first being of the MOTTE and BAILEY type, which was succeeded by the great stone KEEPS with perhaps a HEDGEHOG as an outer defence. New developments were made to meet the dangers of attack by BATTERING-RAMS, BORES, BELFRYS and MINES. Castles were surrounded with CURTAIN-WALLS with WALL-TOWERS and strengthened by CRENELLATION and MACHICOLATION. GATE HOUSES had a PORTCULLIS and a DRAWBRIDGE over the MOAT. The invention of GUNPOWDER and the use of CANNON and MORTARS destroyed the value of medieval castles, though in the 16th century a number of castles, which were really ARTILLERY forts, were built at Walmer, Deal and other coastal points. PEEL TOWERS continued to be used in the

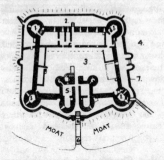

Castle: 1 Towers; 2 Middle bailey; 3 Inner bailey; 4 Outer bailey; 5 Gate house; 6 Drawbridges; 7 Curtain wall

north, and the Napoleonic War brought the MARTELLO TOWERS. [C. Oman, *Castles* (1926)]

Catapult a military engine for throwing projectiles, used in England by the Roman army. The projectile was placed at the end of a movable arm which was propelled by a skein of twisted sinew. The skeletons of men and women hit by catapult bolts have been found in the HILLFORT at Maiden Castle (Dorset), which was captured by the Romans in AD 44. A medieval variant of the catapult was the TREBUCHET. See also ARTILLERY.

Cat o' nine tails a whip, first with three, then with six and lastly with nine lashes once used to punish offenders and in the army and navy. John Lilburne was whipped in 1637 with a whip having three lashes between the FLEET and Old Palace Yard; Titus Oates was whipped in 1685 with one having six lashes between NEWGATE and TYBURN. Probably the punishment was first used on board ship, where ropes are handy and several

ropes were called 'cats'. See also WHIPPING.

Cathedral a CHURCH containing the *cathedra* or throne of the BISHOP of the DIOCESE. In medieval England there were two types of cathedrals—those served by secular CLERGY and those served by MONKS. The secular foundations were Chichester, Exeter, Hereford, Lichfield, Lincoln, London, Salisbury, Wells, York; and the monastic foundations were Canterbury, Carlisle, Durham, Ely, Norwich, Rochester, Winchester, Worcester (all being served by BENEDICTINES, except Carlisle which had AUGUSTINIAN CANONS).

On the DISSOLUTION OF THE MONASTERIES the monastic foundations came to an end, and so these eight cathedrals received new constitutions from the Crown. They became known as the 'New Foundations' in comparison with the 'Old Foundations' which kept their medieval constitutions. There were also other 'New Foundations' founded by Henry VIII—Bristol, Chester, Gloucester, Oxford, Peterborough (and Westminster, which was suppressed in 1550).

During the 19th and 20th centuries a number of fresh Church of England cathedrals have been established. Some were formerly COLLEGIATE CHURCHES (e.g. Ripon, Manchester), some ABBEYS (e.g. Southwell, St Albans), some PARISH churches (e.g. Bradford, Derby) and some new buildings (e.g. Liverpool, Guildford).

The governing body of a cathedral is the CHAPTER composed of the DEAN or PROVOST and the CANONS or PREBENDARIES. [John Harvey, *English Cathedrals* (1950)]

Cats-eyes circular - faceted glass seated in rubber and mounted in metal studs at intervals along the centre of a road so as to reflect the light from the headlamps of approaching traffic. They were invented by Percy Shaw of Halifax

(Yorks). in 1934, but were not widely used until the blackout during the Second World War.

Cattle were first domesticated in the NEW STONE AGE, being used for FOOD and also as beasts of burden (see ox). The small short-horned Celtic or Marsh ox was the only sort domesticated in England before the time of ROMAN BRITAIN, when several other breeds were introduced from the Continent. Systematic breeding for MILK or MEAT began during the AGRARIAN REVOLUTION, being made possible by the incorporation of turnips into the new ROTATION OF CROPS. In the 18th century Robert Bakewell bred the Longhorn, which was a good milker and the first breed with a definite purpose. It was followed by a variety of other milk and beef breeds.

Cavalry became an important part of warfare when the invention of the stirrup made the HORSE more controllable and enabled the LANCE to be used. From the 11th to the 14th century, the heyday of CHIVALRY, the KNIGHT dominated the battlefield and was the central figure of FEUDALISM, but the development of ARCHERY and later of ARTILLERY and the HANDGUN changed the situation. However, cavalry continued to be of use in fighting, being able to charge the MUSKET and PIKE in the English Civil War, and was not finally displaced until the 20th century.

Cellarium the cellar or great storehouse of a MONASTERY, which was in the charge of the cellarer, the most important monastic official not connected with the religious services since he was responsible for the provisioning of the monastery. It was a ground-floor room or basement, usually vaulted from a middle row of columns, as at Chester and Norton Priory (Cheshire), and situated on the western side of the cloister because it had direct access to the outer court (through which provisions reached the monastery) which usually lay on this side.

Celts a people who spoke the Celtic language and first invaded Britain from the Continent about 900 BC in the late BRONZE AGE. They were tall and blue-eyed and had fair or red hair. A later Celtic invasion in the 6th century BC introduced the IRON AGE culture. Celtic replaced all previous languages spoken in Britain and modern Welsh developed directly from it. The most advanced of the Celts were the BELGAE who came to Britain in the 1st century BC. [Nora Chadwick, *The Celts* (1970)]

Celtic Church was established when Christianity reached ROMAN BRITAIN at least as early as the 2nd century, and by the 5th century most of the people belonged to it. It had BISHOPS at London, York and other places The remains of a small CHURCH have been found at Silchester (Hants.), and a VILLA at Lullingstone (Kent) seems to have had its own CHAPEL. After the coming of the pagan ANGLO-SAXONS, it was confined to Wales and other western parts of the island.

Central heating was almost rare in private houses in Britain until after the Second World War, but since the 1960s it has become increasingly common. By 1970 two-fifths of new houses and almost a quarter of existing houses had a full central heating system and many others had a partial heating system, and GAS was the most popular fuel. The highest proportion of centrally heated houses was to be found in London and the south-east.

The first hot-water central heating system in England was introduced from France in 1816.

Ceorl was an ANGLO-SAXON FREEMAN who was not a THEGN. The status of the ceorls gradually declined, and after the

NORMAN CONQUEST most lost their personal freedom and became VILLEINS.

Cereal foods originated in the USA in the 1890s at Battle Creek (Michigan) when two brothers, Dr John Harvey Kellogg and Will Keith Kellogg, steamed wheat and rolled it into flakes as a breakfast food. The annual breakfast cereal consumption in Britain has increased from 1·8 lb a head in 1939 to 5·6 lb in 1967.

Chairs in the Middle Ages were not as common as benches, being often reserved

other new woods, while the 19th century brought machine-turned products. In modern times completely new materials have been used, such as resin bonded glass fibre, which has been moulded into shells for chairs. [J. Gloag, *English Furniture* (4th ed., 1962)]

Chaise a carriage for pleasure or travelling, especially a light, open carriage for one or two persons, drawn by a single horse and provided with a folding hood. A chaise-cart was a light cart with springs used for carrying parcels or light goods

1 Carved oak box chair (settle); 2 Farthingale; 3 Wing; 4 Painted satinwood

for the head of the family in a large household. The typical Tudor chair, sometimes called a 'settle chair', was weighty and had a tall straight back and solid arm supports, while the seat was often made like a CUPBOARD, the seat being hinged to form the lid. In the late 17th century, Dutch influence brought the upholstered wingchair, which has lasted until to-day with its leather or cane seat. Another chair of the 17th century was the FARTHINGALE. Chairs in the 18th century were influenced by the prevailing fashions in FURNITURE and the use of SATINWOOD and

speedily. See also POST-CHAISE, CABRIOLET, CARRIAGES.

Chaldron a somewhat variable measure of coal used in the past. A Newcastle chaldron weighed 53 cwts and a London chaldron 28 cwts. A chaldron waggon contained 217 989 cubic inches or 22·5 bolls. After the Coal Mines Inspection Act (1872), coal has been sold by weight only.

Chalice the cup used to contain the wine consecrated in the MASS or communion service, was at first commonly of glass, wood, tin or pewter, but from the 10th century precious metals gradually became general. The earliest two-handled, vase-shaped chalices continued in use until the end of the 12th century whenever general communion was given. From the 14th century the stem of the chalice was gradually elongated and the bowl made smaller as the people ceased to receive the wine. In England after the REFORMATION, when the people again received the consecrated wine, chalices in the 17th and succeeding centuries were made larger than previously. [James Gilchrist, *Anglican Church Plate* (1967)]

Champagne a sparkling white WINE from the ancient province of Champagne in France, once part of the Kingdom of Burgundy. It became popular in England in the later part of the 18th century. [A. L. Simon, *The History of Champagne* (1962)]

Chancel the part of a CHURCH, east of the NAVE and TRANSEPTS, reserved for the CLERGY and CHOIR, so-called because it was separated from the rest of the church by *cancelli* (screens). In England the upkeep of the chancel fell upon the RECTOR, while the parishioners were responsible for the rest of the church. The chancels of English medieval churches were long, often more than a half of the length of the nave, so that parochial and CHANTRY priests could say their services together. [J. C. Cox & C. B. Ford, *Parish Churches* (1961)]

Chancery was in ANGLO-SAXON times the royal writing-office situated behind a screen (Latin *cancellus*, a screen) and supervised by the chancellor, the head of the clerks. After the NORMAN CONQUEST, the chancellor became an important minister with, since he acted upon petitions for justice to the king, increasing judicial powers. During the 14th and 15th centuries, the Chancery became his COURT and developed its own body of law, known as equity, designed to redress wrongs for which there was no remedy in COMMON LAW. Its increased powers led, however, to its work getting into arrears until it became a byword for delay as pictured by Charles Dickens in *Bleak House*. It was abolished as a separate court in 1873.

Chantry an endowment to maintain a priest to say requiem MASSES and also the small CHAPEL (often part of a parish CHURCH) in which these were said. Some were founded by princes, bishops, noblemen, knights and, later, rich merchants; others were founded by GUILDS. Chantries were first founded in England in the 13th century, but most in the 14th and 15th centuries. Lincoln Cathedral had one in 1290 and 36 in 1530. Most were in the greater churches; Newark Parish Church had 13 by 1530. Among the finest to survive are those of William of Wykeham at Winchester, Abbot Ramryge at St Albans, Henry IV at Canterbury and Henry VII at WESTMINSTER ABBEY.

An Act of 1545 to dissolve the chantries was nullified by Henry VIII's death and replaced by another of 1547. In all, 2374 chantries and guild chapels were suppressed. Much of the proceeds went to the Duke of Somerset, the Lord Protector, and his friends, but the chantry priests were pensioned as the MONKS had been at the DISSOLUTION OF THE MONASTERIES. Many of these priests had kept schools, which were lost, though some were revived as Edwardian GRAMMAR SCHOOLS. [G. H. Cook, *Medieval Chantries and Chantry Chapels* (1947)] See also HAGIOSCOPE.

Chapbooks small, cheap BOOKS sold in the 18th century by PEDLARS, known as chapmen. Usually a chapbook was a slim pamphlet of 16-24 pages, printed on rough paper, illustrated with wood-cuts and sold at prices varying from a farthing to a shilling. They usually contained popular tales or histories, but also BROADSIDES, BALLADS, scandal, accounts of executions and last dying speeches. London was the chief centre for the printing of chapbooks, but Scotland was an especially active area, partly because of the more widespread literacy in the country, and many Scottish chapbooks were pirated south of the border, particularly in Newcastle-upon-Tyne, which, next to London, was the largest centre for their production. The chapbook disappeared in the first half of the 19th century when people were better educated, and improvements in PRINTING and the coming of the RAILWAYS made it possible to supply them with NEWSPAPERS and other literature. [R. K. Webb, *The British Working Class Reader 1790-1848* (1955)]

Chapel a place of worship other than a CATHEDRAL or parish CHURCH, sometimes attached to large HOUSES or institutions such as COLLEGES or the FARMERY of a MONASTERY. Other chapels form part of a larger church or cathedral with a separate ALTAR, such as a LADY CHAPEL, a CHANTRY chapel or a CRYPT chapel. A chapel of ease is one built in a parish for parishioners living far from the parish church, the clergy of which usually have charge of it. Before the 19th century NONCONFORMIST places of worship were usually called 'chapels' and not 'churches', and so 'Church and Chapel' became a common phrase for Anglicanism and Nonconformity.

Chaperon a married or elderly woman accompanying a young unmarried woman when appearing in public, first became customary in Queen Anne's reign (1702-14). Before then it had been thought improper for any unmarried girl or woman to attend any public occasion except in the care of a near relation.

Chaplain was originally a priest in charge of a CHAPEL, especially one belonging to a king, nobleman, bishop or abbot. They have since been appointed to such institutions as colleges, schools, hospitals and prisons and to the armed forces.

Chapter originally meant a section of the monastic RULE which was daily read publicly in MONASTERIES. Hence the name was given also to the assembly of the MONKS or CANONS, belonging to an ABBEY, CATHEDRAL or COLLEGIATE CHURCH, to hear this reading and to transact the business of their community; and now the name is applied to the governing body of such a church. See also PENANCE.

Chapter House a building used for the meetings of the CHAPTER of an ABBEY, CATHEDRAL or COLLEGIATE CHURCH. Separate buildings for this purpose were first built early in the 9th century. It was either oblong, square, apsidal or polygonal, while in CISTERCIAN abbeys it was designed as an aisled hall. The great chapter house at Reading (Berks.), though ruined, is a fine example of the apsidal plan; but the most famous are the polygonal, with vaults either supported on a central pillar or free-standing. There were 25 of these in England and two in Scotland, but more than half have been destroyed. Fine examples, fully preserved, are to be seen at Lincoln and Wells. See also MONASTERY. [F. H. Crossley, *The English Abbey* (1962); John Harvey, *English Cathedrals* (1956)]

Charcoal a form of carbon, is the black residue of partly burnt wood, bones or coal. Charcoal burning took place on a large scale in the woodland and forest areas of England, especially in the Weald of Sussex and Kent where it was used in the manufacture of IRON, but it declined with the change to coke. Charcoal was made by raising the logs of wood into a large domed pile, fired in the centre and covered with earth to ensure slow burning. The process took about five full days and nights, and the charcoal-burner lived in a little hut nearby. Former sites of charcoal-burning hearths or pits may be indicated by such names as 'coalpit' or 'coaldane'.

Chariots were still used in war by the CELTS in Britain at the time of the Roman invasion, though abandoned elsewhere. Their chariots were large, often carrying four men and operating with runners, who might either move independently on the battlefield, discharging arrows and slingstones or else join with the cavalry in charges. The fighting men in the chariot itself traditionally moved out on the shaft between the horses in close combat or dismounted and fought on foot. A few ancient writers describe the chariot as having its axles armed with a SCYTHE to cut to pieces anything which came in its way, but Julius Caesar and the best ancient writers do not mention this, and none of the Celtic chariots found in graves in Britain or Gaul show signs of having been equipped in this way.

Charity Schools were founded in the late 17th and early 18th centuries, many of them under the auspices of the SOCIETY FOR PROMOTING CHRISTIAN KNOWLEDGE, for boys and girls of the labouring poor and were supported by private subscriptions. The children received religious instruction and an elementary education. They wore a SCHOOL UNIFORM and were prepared for APPRENTICESHIP, the girls usually becoming SERVANTS. By 1727 there were nearly 1400 charity schools in England and Wales, a few of them boarding schools; but then the movement lost its impetus. Fewer new schools were founded, and attempts to make the schools self-supporting by setting the children to work at gardening, straw-plaiting, car-

pentry or sewing were not very successful because the children's products were not good enough to sell profitably. In the 19th century many charity schools became NATIONAL SCHOOLS. [M. G. Jones, *The Charity School Movement* (1964)]

Charnel-house a place in which were piled up bones of the dead thrown up in digging because of the medieval custom of making BURIALS of people on top of others in the same churchyard. Sometimes it was a separate building, but often it was part of the CRYPT of a CHURCH.

Charter a written grant of rights and privileges made by a great landowner or (particularly) by the Crown, like the famous MAGNA CARTA (1215). Other charters were those granted to TOWNS to incorporate them as BOROUGHS, and to JOINT-STOCK companies.

Chartism came about largely through working-class disappointment at the failure of the GRAND NATIONAL CONSOLIDATED TRADES UNION. In 1838 the London Working Men's Association drew up the People's Charter, which demanded (1) universal adult male suffrage; (2) annual parliaments; (3) voting by ballot; (4) payment of Members of Parliament; (5) equal electoral districts; (6) no property qualification for Members of Parliament. The struggle of the Charter fell into two periods—1836-9 when the agitation was directed much against the POOR LAW AMENDMENT ACT; and 1840-9 when extremists gained control of the movement. The movement collapsed largely because it never attracted middle-class support and because trade improved in the later 1840s. [M. Hovell, *The Chartist Movement* (1920); N. Steward, *The Fight for the Charter* (1937)]

Chasuble an outer garment worn by a priest in celebrating MASS, which was derived from an outdoor cloak worn by both sexes in late Roman times. Without sleeves, it is made in one piece throughout, and is circular in shape with a hole in the centre for the head to pass through. See also VESTMENTS.

Chatelaine an ornamental metal clasp hooked on to the waist or belt and worn by women from about 1840 to the end of the 19th century. From it hung by short

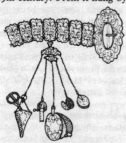

Chatelaine and belt

chains various articles of domestic use (e.g. scissors, penknife, keys, thimble). The word comes from the French *châtelaine*, lady of the castle.

Cheese is made from the curd of MILK, allowed to go sour naturally or artificially soured by the addition of certain vegetable or animal extracts (e.g. rennet or pectin), separated from the WHEY and pressed into a hard mass. In Wiltshire and Somerset early IRON AGE perforated pots have been found, which may have been used for draining off the whey in cheese-making, but there is no positive evidence of cheese-making in Britain before the Roman Conquest, and it was a well-known food in ROMAN BRITAIN.

In Saxon and Norman times ewes' milk was used for cheese-making, but cows' milk was also used as early as the 13th century and replaced ewes' milk by the 17th century. In medieval England there

was only soft cheese, hard cheese, green cheese (which was not fully matured) and spermyse (which was flavoured with HERBS). Local varieties of cheese gradually evolved more or less independently in widely separated regions and were not confined to the areas after which they came to be named (e.g. Cheddar, Lancashire, Wensleydale). Improved transport in the 18th century made local cheese more widely known, e.g. Stilton cheese, though made in Leicestershire, gained its name by being sold at the Bell Inn at Stilton (Hunts.) to coach-travellers on the GREAT NORTH ROAD.

In 1868 the Royal Agricultural Society urged the setting up of cheese-factories to rival American factories set up in the 1850s. The first English cheese-factory was opened at Longford (Derby.) in 1870, and now over 90 per cent of English cheese is factory-made. This has meant the end of the great English local cheeses, and a number have completely disappeared (e.g. Gloucester). [V. Cheke, *The Story of Cheese-Making in Britain* (1959)]

Cheques originated, like BANK-notes, through the custom of entrusting COINAGE to the safekeeping of GOLDSMITHS. Merchants paying debts might give a goldsmith's note (i.e. receipt) to a creditor or send the goldsmith written instructions to make a given sum available to a specified person. The earliest extant example of the latter document (written by hand throughout) is dated 1675. These documents were first known as 'drawn notes' to distinguish them from receipt notes issued, not by the customer, but by the banker. The word 'cheque' originated from the record (or 'check') kept of serial numbers which were placed for identification on drawn notes. Printed cheques are believed to have been introduced in 1672, and cheque books were issued some 20 years later. The use of cheques spread through the convenience of the system and was encouraged by the Bank Charter Act (1844) which restricted the issue of bank-notes. [J. W. Roche & G. R. James, *Getting and Spending* (3rd ed., 1968)]

Chemise an UNDERGARMENT worn by both men and women from the early Middle Ages. Women sometimes wore it next to the skin and sometimes over the SMOCK, but later it became known as a smock when worn by women and a SHIRT when worn by men. From the 14th century the word was not used until the early 19th century, when it returned from France to describe an undergarment with short sleeves which replaced the SHIFT. Later the name was given to a day dress of similar cut.

Cherry was introduced into Europe, according to Pliny, by Lucullus the epicure, who brought it back to Rome from Cerasus, on the southern shore of the Black Sea, in 6 BC; but this probably refers to a particular strain since there is evidence that the Romans possessed the tree much earlier. It was introduced by them into ROMAN BRITAIN and was a common FRUIT by the Middle Ages, being grown chiefly in Kent.

Chess originated in India and was probably brought to Europe through the Moors in Spain in the 8th century it being known in England soon after the NORMAN CONQUEST. In medieval chess the queen and bishop were relatively weak pieces, and the game did not take its modern form until the late 15th century when the value of the queen was increased more than fivefold and the bishop nearly threefold; these changes originated in southern Europe.

Chess was an indoor game which shared with HUNTING and TOURNAMENTS the patronage of kings and noblemen. Among royal chessplayers were John, Edward I and Henry VI of England and James I and James IV of Scotland; John is said to have played chess instead of relieving Rouen. Stories of fatal quarrels over chess are common in medieval romances, and museums have elaborately carved 12th- and 13th-century ivory chessmen, while Edward I is known to have received a present of a jasper and crystal set.

Chest formerly a most common and useful article of FURNITURE, being used for the storage of clothes, books, valuables and other things, as a travelling trunk and also as a seat, TABLE and even a BED. From the middle of the 17th century, it was gradually replaced by WARDROBES, BOOKCASES, CHESTS-OF-DRAWERS and other specialized furniture.

Chest-of-drawers a frame with a set of drawers which began to replace the CHEST for storing linen and clothes from the mid-17th century. The earliest, which were about 4 ft in height, closely resembled a chest placed on stands and fitted with a long drawer. See also FURNITURE.

Children in the past were often welcomed, on the day of their birth, by BON-FIRES, but many of them did not live long, being perhaps carried away by the frequent outbreaks of PLAGUE which were common until the mid-17th century. Their BAPTISM was administered as soon as possible. At the same time they were rigidly brought up. They were expected to reverence their parents, and implicit obedience was demanded from them. Even for minor faults, a WHIPPING, particularly with the BIRCH-ROD, was the usual punishment. A 15th-century Norfolk mother, who used to whip her daughter once or twice a week, instructed her son's schoolmaster in London, 'If he hath not done well, nor will not amend, pray him that he will truly belash him, till he will amend.'

Indeed, the common attitude of medieval parents towards their children was astonishingly cold. Wealthy families sent their babies to be brought up by foster parents until they were 4–5 years old, and boys and girls were sent away at the age of 8 or 9 to be PAGES and DAMSELS in noble households. There they had to act as servants, but were also instructed in ETIQUETTE and TABLE-MANNERS. And it was likely that their parents would arrange for them to be married at an early age (see also CHILD MARRIAGE).

Tudor parents were equally strict, while in the 17th century the PURITANS believed that children must be severely corrected to be saved from the eternal results of their own wickedness. There was, however, more concern for EDUCATION at this time. The first GIRLS' SCHOOLS were opened and also CHARITY SCHOOLS for the poor.

In the 18th century the attitude towards children remained much the same. The children of the 'Proud Duke of Somerset' (who died in 1748) were not allowed to sit in his presence, though later in that century Edward Gibbon said, 'The domestic discipline of our ancestors has been relaxed by the philosophy and softness of the age.' This was also the time when the INDUSTRIAL REVOLUTION by establishing the FACTORY SYSTEM led to a widespread use of child labour the abuses of which were only gradually reformed (see also FACTORY LAWS). In the 19th century, when FAMILIES were large, the attitude of most parents towards their children was still stern. 'Spare the rod and spoil the child' and 'Children should be seen and not heard' were common sayings of the time, which were widely believed and acted upon.

The more sympathetic attitude towards children which gradually gained ground in the later 19th century was helped by Charles Dickens (1812–70), through the way in which he portrayed children in such novels as *David Copperfield* and *Oliver Twist*, and by the Oxford clergyman who wrote, under the name of Lewis Carroll, *Alice's Adventures in Wonderland* and *Through the Looking Glass*. It led to the foundation of the NATIONAL SOCIETY FOR THE PREVENTION OF CRUELTY TO CHILDREN. So also, early in the 20th century, did General Baden-Powell's movement for BOY SCOUTS and GIRL GUIDES. In such ways people came to see that childhood was an important part of everyone's life and that children should be helped to enjoy it in their own way. See also COURTESY BOOKS, FAMILIES. [Ivy Pinchbeck and Margery Hewitt, *Children in English Society* (1970)]

Child marriages occurred in the Middle Ages when parents arranged the marriages of their children. Even the actual ceremony was performed, which became binding at the age of consent (12 years for girls, 14 for boys). In the Berkeley family, for instance, there were between 1288 and 1500 five marriages in which the ten contracting parties averaged less than 11 years.

Children's costume did not exist as such for centuries. After their SWADDLING BANDS, boys and girls wore baby clothes (ankle-length frocks and PETTICOATS) until they were four or five years old, when they were dressed as smaller versions of their parents with at first a few useful additions (e.g. pinafores and reins or leading strings attached to their shoulders).

The change came in the later 18th century, probably through the influence of the revolutionary ideas of the French reformer, Jean Jacques Rousseau (1712–78), who held that childhood was not just a troublesome prelude to adult life, but an important period of life in itself. By 1800 boys wore long NANKEEN trousers, buttoned under their arms on to shirts with frilled collars, short jackets, peaked caps, white stockings and flat, heelless shoes; girls wore long dresses with loose, plain skirts gathered on to a BODICE and confined by a high-waisted sash and with low necks and short sleeves, white socks,

1 Girl wearing pantalettes; 2 Nankeen trousers; 4 Lord Fauntleroy suit; 5 Eton suit

sandals, BONNETS tied under the chin with ribbons, and, for a time, PANTALETTES. By the 1850s boys had belted tunics with wide, knee-length breeches or cut-away coats with long trousers; fashionable girls wore a CRINOLINE and later a BUSTLE. In the 1880s and 1890s boys wore sailor suits or the LITTLE LORD FAUNTLEROY COSTUME, while girls wore the KATE GREENAWAY

DRESS. In the 20th century children's costume has become more informal, light and practical, though it has kept in touch with current trends and fashions. See also SCHOOL UNIFORM.

Children's hour the time, in upper-class families in the 19th century, which was spent by CHILDREN in the evening in the company of their mother in her BOUDOIR. Commonly it was after the children had supper with their GOVERNESS in the NURSERY at about five o'clock until their bed-time, which was also when their parents went to dress for dinner.

Chimneys became usual in the HOUSES of wealthy people in the 14th century and seem to have become common, even in the countryside, by the 16th century. The growing use of BRICK made them easier to build, and COAL fires made them essential. Chimney pots were invented in the 18th century. See also FUMERELL. [Lawrence Wright, *Home Fires Burning* (1964)]

Chivalry was the code of behaviour expected of a KNIGHT during the days of FEUDALISM. An English writer in the 12th century stated he was 'to protect the Church, to fight against treachery, to reverence the priesthood, to defend the poor from injustice, to make peace in his own province, to shed his blood for his brethren and, if necessary, to lay down his life'. These ideals were expressed in the legend of King Arthur and the Knights of the Round Table and in Chaucer's account of the 'very perfect gentle knight'. In fact, it tended to be a code of courtesy towards equals and superiors, consistent with little consideration towards inferiors such as the poor and WOMEN. [L. F. Salzman, *English Life in the Middle Ages* (1926).] See also CRUSADES, TOURNAMENTS.

Chocolate was introduced into Europe, as a drink made from crushed cacao beans and water, by Cortes who found the Aztecs drinking it when he conquered Mexico in 1519; but the drink was not widely known in England until about 1650 (about the same time as COFFEE). The first 'chocolate house' was opened in Bishopsgate, London, in 1657. By Queen Anne's reign it was the aristocracy's favourite drink, costing from 10s to 15s a pound.

In the 19th century the price of chocolate was reduced through the introduction of power-driven machinery and large-scale manufacture to replace hand methods, national distribution by the RAILWAYS and the reduction of import taxes in 1853. In 1824 John Cadbury set up as a tea and chocolate dealer in Birmingham. Not long afterwards he began the sale of solid chocolate as an edible confection. See also COCOA.

Chocolate boxes originated in Britain in 1868 when Richard Cadbury (who got the idea from small boxes coming from France containing sweetmeats) first produced a specially designed small oval cardboard box decorated with an oleograph made from a painting showing his young daughter and her kitten. This was followed by others, and the pictures on these early boxes were usually meant for children to cut out and put in scrapbooks.

Besides these boxes with pictures, the later 19th century brought novelty-boxes, including an S-shaped box for children designed to fit easily into a CHRISTMAS stocking, and other boxes designed for other purposes when the chocolates were eaten, such as a plush-covered glove box with a nickel handle and fittings or a trinket casket with little drawers to hold jewellery.

Until the 1890s, the boxes with pictures mainly depicted children. Then came beautiful young ladies. The Chocolate-Box Girl (the most famous of whom was

Gladys Cooper) had a long sway. There were also pictures of animals and flowers (especially roses), mountains and country scenes; and these continue to be popular. The best sellers were the royalty boxes of the 1930s, which were hand-decorated and had portraits of George V, Queen Mary, the Prince of Wales and Princess Elizabeth.

Recently, the designs of chocolate boxes have been simpler, and there have been fewer novelties, but some have appeared, including, since the early 1950s, big expensive boxes with framed scenes to be hung as pictures afterwards.

Choirs in the Middle Ages existed only in CATHEDRALS and MONASTERIES and were composed of CLERGY or MONKS, being augmented by lay singers about the 15th century. In the 18th century the choir in a CHURCH was often placed in a GALLERY at the west end, and it sometimes consisted of CHARITY SCHOOL children. In the 19th century, under the influence of the TRACTARIANS, choirs were restored to the CHANCEL and wore SURPLICES, which hitherto had been unknown in parish churches. [B. Rainbow, *The Choral Revival in the Anglican Church* (1970).] See also ORGAN.

Cholera an infectious and often fatal disease with violent vomiting and purging, cramps and collapse, first came to Britain from Russia in 1831 and killed thousands of people in successive outbreaks. In England and Wales 53 293 people died of it in 1848–9 and 20 097 in 1854. It is caused by a bacteria carried especially in water, and it spread irresistibly in towns where pumps on which streets and sometimes whole parishes depended for their water, were infected by sewage. Following improvements in SANITATION, which it did much to bring about, there has been no major epidemic in Britain since 1866, though there were minor outbreaks in 1872 and 1894. See also DRINKING FOUNTAINS, WATER-SUPPLY.

Christening presents given to children at their BAPTISM by godparents and others during the Middle Ages and later included cups, cradles, bedclothes and hangings. The favourite gifts for godparents were apostle spoons. A wealthy man might be expected to give his godchild a complete set of the spoons, but others might be content with one, choosing that representing the patron saint of the month in which the child was born. Another common gift was a silver-mounted coral with bells, which was supposed to defend the baby against witchcraft and the evil eye. The PURITANS disliked this superstition, and under their influence a BIBLE became a favourite present. This was still so in the Early Victorian period, and other gifts included a silver mug or a silver knife, fork and spoon in a silver case or a white satin pincushion. A very prevalent fashion was a 'christening glass'—a jug was given to the bridal couple at their wedding and to this was added as each child was born a glass to match inscribed with his or her initials and date of birth. When the couple had their first child, sometimes the mother's friends sent her as a joke a new BIRCH-ROD or CANE with a label tied to it bearing such words as 'For use when required'.

Christian names have remained surprisingly the same in popularity. A sample from medieval records (Feet (list) of Fines, 1196–1307) contains these names in order of use—boys: William, John, Robert, Richard, Thomas, Walter, Henry, James, Peter, Michael; girls: Alice, Matilda, Joan, Margery, Agnes, Margaret, Sarah, Elizabeth, Mary, Susan. A list in the same order from *The Times*, 1967 reads—boys: James, Richard, Andrew, William, Simon, Nicholas, Christopher, David, John, Timothy; girls: Sarah, Emma, Catherine, Victoria, Lucy, Elizabeth, Caroline, Nicola, Joanna, Katherine.

The PURITANS broke with this tradition, some of their names being Comfort (1592), Repent (1599), Faintnot, Obedience (1602), and during the COMMONWEALTH they used texts, e.g. 'If-Christ-hadst-not-died-thou-hadst-been damned'.

The fashion of giving children more than one Christian name began in the 17th century, but did not become general for another 200 years.

Christmas was probably observed on December 25 by the Church to substitute the festival of Christ, the Light of the World, for pagan celebrations at this time of the year when the days grow longer and the nights shorter. In Britain, this was the Yule feast, when the Yule log was burnt to welcome the returning sun. In 601 Pope Gregory told St Augustine to instruct his English converts 'no longer to offer beasts to the devil, but to worship God by feasting' at this Christmas time.

Christmas customs included the appointment of the LORD OF MISRULE and BOY BISHOP, acting by MUMMERS and the singing of CAROLS (a practice brought over from France and Italy). Medieval homes and churches were decorated with holly, mistletoe and other evergreens; pagan shrines were formerly so decorated because their greenness was a sign of life even in winter.

Formerly, the usual FOOD at Christmas was pork, and the boar's head was a special dish; the PIGS were killed in late November, after they had been fattened on acorns and other nuts in the forests. The wealthy also ate roast peacock, but in the 16th century this was replaced by the turkey from the New World. Christmas puddings, still known sometimes as plum puddings, were originally made of dried plums, while mince pies were once called mutton pies, being made of finely chopped or minced mutton.

In the 17th century the PURITANS destroyed many of the observances of Christmas, which were not revived until the 19th century, when four new customs were added—the Christmas tree, from Germany; the PANTOMIME, an essentially English entertainment; the Christmas card, a British invention made possible by cheap POSTAGE; and Father Christmas, from America, where originally the Dutch settlers' Santa Claus (St Nicholas) was believed to bring presents for good children and a BIRCH-ROD for naughty ones. Also in the 19th century, the giving of presents was transferred to Christmas Day from BOXING DAY and NEW YEAR'S DAY, and the eating of a cake from TWELFTH NIGHT. [Margaret Baker, *Christmas Customs and Folklore* (1968).] See also MINSTRELS, WAITS, WASSAIL.

Chronometer an instrument adjusted to measure accurate TIME in all variations of temperature. Since no CLOCKS were accurate enough to calculate longitude at sea, and the absence of such a timekeeper was a serious navigational handicap, the British government in 1713 offered £20,000 for a method of fixing longitude to within 30 miles. John Harrison, a Yorkshire carpenter, set to work and in 1735, after six years, completed his first chronometer. Its sea trials were encouraging, and by 1759 he had built a fourth that allowed longitude to be calculated to within 18 miles. He was not paid the full £20,000 until 1773, three years before his death. His chronometers are at the National Maritime Museum, Greenwich.

Church in the ANGLO-SAXON period usually consisted of a NAVE and CHANCEL, with either a square end or an APSE. After the NORMAN CONQUEST, the chancel was sometimes lengthened to provide

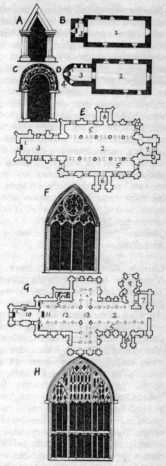

Churches: A Saxon window; B Saxon church plan; C Norman window; D Norman church plan; E Early English Gothic plan; F Early English Gothic window; G Perpendicular church plan; H Perpendicular window.

1 Altar; 2 Nave; 3 Chapel; 4 Apse; 5 Aisle; 6 Porch; 7 Tower; 8 Vestry; 9 Chantry chapel; 10 Lady chapel; 11 High altar; 12 Choir; 13 Transept

space for a CHOIR and the better celebration of the ceremonies of the MASS. Later AISLES became popular, and PORCHES were built, while designs changed with the development of the styles of GOTHIC architecture. With the growing use of BELLS, the 13th century saw the addition of a BELFRY, and STAINED GLASS in the WINDOWS became more common. CHAPELS were also added, especially a LADY CHAPEL and CHANTRY chapels. Large churches were commonly built on the cruciform plan, with nave, transepts, chancel and central tower. The building of churches was checked at the REFORMATION, but the 19th century, under the influence of the EVANGELICAL and TRACTARIAN movements, was a great period of church construction. [N. E. Boyle, *Old Parish Churches* (3rd ed., 1969)] See also MONASTERY.

Church Ales formerly a device to raise money in a PARISH for the CHURCH. The CHURCHWARDENS bought or were given malt which they brewed into strong ALE, often in the church itself, while the girls of the parish stood at the church door, gathering contributions. Church Ales were often held on Whitsunday and were accompanied by merrymaking, DANCING on the green and playing at BOWLS. John Aubrey (1626–96) described Church Ales—'In every parish was a church-house, to which belonged spits, crocks and other utensils for dressing provisions. Here the house-keepers met. The young people were there too and had dancing, bowling, shooting at butts, etc., the ancients sitting gravely by and looking on.' Medieval in origin, Church Ales were disliked by the PURITANS, and few survived the 17th century. [Patrick Cowley, *The Church Houses* (1970)]

Church Army was founded by Wilson Carlile (1847–1942) in 1882 in the slums of Westminster to work within the CHURCH OF ENGLAND on the lines of the SALVATION ARMY. Beginning with evangelistic work, it has since 1889 also undertaken social and moral welfare activities among the poor and in prisons. During the two World Wars it has provided recreation huts, canteens and hostels for the troops and assisted homeless civilians and the relatives of men on active service. [E. Rowan, *Wilson Carlile and the Church Army* (4th ed., 1933)]

Church Missionary Society was founded in 1799 by a number of EVANGELICALS, including members of the CLAPHAM SECT. The first to offer himself to it for service overseas was Henry Martyn (1781–1812), curate of Charles Simeon (1759–1812), Vicar of Holy Trinity, Cambridge, and though he died after a few years in India, his devotion to evangelism among the natives made a great impression in England. The Society sent out five missionaries in its first ten years of existence, but during the 19th century, although later in date than the SOCIETY FOR PROMOTING CHRISTIAN KNOWLEDGE and the SOCIETY FOR THE PROPAGATION OF THE GOSPEL, it became the first effective MISSIONARY SOCIETY of the CHURCH OF ENGLAND and still remains the largest.

Church of England originated with the CELTIC CHURCH in ROMAN BRITAIN, which was driven into the western parts of the island by the pagan ANGLO-SAXONS. England was reconverted to Christianity by the Roman mission headed in 597 by St Augustine (see CANTERBURY CATHEDRAL), and the Celtic and Roman missions were united at the Synod of Whitby (664), which resulted in the triumph of Roman usage. After the Anglo-Saxons, the VIKINGS later became Christians. WESTMINSTER ABBEY and other MONASTERIES were established.

The NORMAN CONQUEST brought the Church into closer contact with European religion. The establishment of the ECCLE-SIASTICAL COURTS led to the development of a system of CANON LAW. New CATHE-DRALS and CHURCHES were built, and new DIOCESES were founded. In the Middle Ages the Church played an important part in the life of the people, controlling EDUCATION, exacting TITHES, establishing HOLIDAYS and organizing PILGRIMAGES to SHRINES, while the MASS was the centre of its worship.

The REFORMATION and the DISSOLUTION OF THE MONASTERIES brought great changes. The Church acquired its COMMON PRAYER BOOK and English BIBLE. PROTESTANT influence, which had began with the LOLLARDS, was strong, and brought about the rise of the PURITANS. It suffered through their rules during the COMMONWEALTH, but was restored at the RESTORATION, which marked a triumph for the policy of the LAUDIANS. This period saw also the rise of the NONCONFORMISTS, who were no more destroyed by the CLARENDON CODE than the ROMAN CATHOLICS had been by the earlier PENAL CODE.

Despite such advances as the SOCIETY FOR THE PROPAGATION OF THE GOSPEL, the SOCIETY FOR THE PROMOTION OF CHRISTIAN KNOWLEDGE and QUEEN ANNE'S BOUNTY, the Church declined in the 18th century and lost the METHODISTS. There followed, however, the movements associated with the EVANGELICALS, TRACTARIANS and BROAD CHURCHMEN. These produced a revival in the 19th century which saw the establishment of the NATIONAL SCHOOLS, MISSIONARY SOCIETIES and the ECCLESIASTICAL COMMISSION. [R. H. Moorman, *A History of the Church of England* (1953)]

Church of Scotland began with missionaries from the CELTIC CHURCH, notably St Ninian (397) and St Columba at IONA. After the SYNOD OF WHITBY (SEE CHURCH OF ENGLAND), it gradually accepted Roman usages, though the CULDEES lingered until the 11th century. After the NORMAN CONQUEST of England, Queen Margaret's influence brought about the establishment of DIOCESES, MONASTERIES and PARISHES. The REFORMATION brought about the triumph of the PRESBYTERIANS and the compilation of the COMMON ORDER BOOK. The early Stuart kings restored BISHOPS in Scotland; these were abolished during the COMMONWEALTH and brought back again at the RESTORATION until 1688. In the 19th century the Church was split by the DISRUPTION, but re-united in this century.

Church Pastoral Aid Society founded by the EVANGELICALS in 1836 to provide more CURATES and lay workers in the PARISHES of the CHURCH OF ENGLAND. See also ADDITIONAL CURATES SOCIETY.

Churchwarden is the oldest and most dignified local official, his position dating from the Middle Ages. His ecclesiastical duties included the care of PARISH finances, the care of the CHURCH building (except the CHANCEL) and the presentation of offenders to the ECCLESIASTICAL COURTS. From the 16th century he was given an increasing number of local government duties, which included the supervision of PEDLARS, the testing of ALE and the keeping down of vermin. He was also associated with the officials responsible for the administration of the POOR LAW and the upkeep of the ROADS. Most of these secular duties were removed in the late nineteenth and early twentieth centuries.

Cigars, Cigarettes are both forms of SMOKING introduced into Britain during the 19th century. Cigars first became popular during the Napoleonic War, being introduced by officers returning from the Duke of Wellington's expeditionary force in Spain during the Peninsular Campaign (1809-14).

The Russian habit of cigarette-smoking was adopted soon after the Crimean War (1854–6), though at first only by the more fashionable young men. Women began to smoke cigarettes about 1900, but not to any extent until after the First World War. Cigarettes were first made of Balkan TOBACCO, 'Virginia' cigarettes not appearing until the 20th century. The first cork-tip cigarettes were sold in 1909. Illustrated cigarette-cards, originally cardboard stiffeners inserted into the flimsy paper packets, were first printed in the United States of America, but by 1895 they were popular in Britain and were issued until 1939.

In 1967 some 120 000 million cigarettes were smoked in Britain (two-thirds being filter-tipped). Filter-tip cigarettes have been smoked in much greater numbers since the Second World War because of recent ideas about the harmful effects of cigarette-smoking upon the health, and for the same reason cigarette-advertising has been forbidden on TELEVISION since 1966.

Cinema films were first made by William Friese-Green in England in 1889, and the first public film show in Britain took place at the Polytechnic, a hall in Regent Street, London, in 1896 by means of a cinematograph machine invented in France the year before by two brothers, Auguste and Louis Lumière. By 1901 films were being shown as novelties in MUSIC-HALLS and FAIRS. The first permanent cinema was the Biograph in Wilton Road, London, built in 1907, and by 1911 there were 94 cinemas in Britain. From about 1905 to 1912 the usual film was a 'one-reeler' on one reel holding 1,000 feet of film and lasting 10 to 15 minutes.

During the First World War people began to go to the cinema to see the newsreels and also Charlie Chaplin's films, and by 1919 many were going twice a week.

In 1927 came 'talkies' and in the early 1930s colour films. This was the golden age of the cinema. The earliest cinemas were plain buildings with wooden benches and a small orchestra or single pianist playing more or less appropriate music while the silent films were shown. Now there were big luxury cinemas in the centre of every town and small ones in the suburbs. The largest had cinema ORGANS, which came up mechanically from a well in front of the screen to play during intervals; and many cinemas had restaurants attached to them. By 1939 there were 19 million weekly attendances at cinema performances.

Since the Second World War, the cinema has been badly affected by the coming of TELEVISION. Many cinemas have been closed or given over to BOWLS or BINGO. Audiences dropped from 1365 million in 1951 to 415 million in 1962, causing a fall in takings from £108 million to £60 million. [E. Lindgren, *A Picture History of the Cinema* (1960)]

Cistercians a reformed BENEDICTINE monastic order founded at Cîteaux in Burgundy in 1098. Their RULE was written by Stephen Harding, an English MONK from Sherborne, who became ABBOT of Cîteaux. While Benedictine ABBEYS were usually in towns, the Cistercians settled in remote places, and their churches were plain and simple without precious ornaments. Benedictines were not supposed to eat meat; Cistercians were not allowed fish or eggs either. They wore HABITS of white, undyed wool.

They first settled at Waverley (Surrey) in 1129. As the Cistercian rule emphasized manual work, they became great SHEEP farmers, especially in the famous Yorkshire abbeys of Fountains, Jervaulx and Rievaulx. In Scotland, Melrose was a Cistercian abbey. At the DISSOLUTION OF THE MONASTERIES there were over a hundred Cistercian houses in England.

City was originally a BOROUGH which had a CATHEDRAL; but in 1889 Birmingham, which then had no cathedral, was made a city. Nowadays there are several cities which have no cathedral (e.g. Leeds and Hull), while Derby, which has a cathedral, is not a city.

Clan (the word should mean 'children') came in the Scottish HIGHLANDS during the 14th century to mean adherents to a definite chief who were bound to him by personal service in return for protection and the possession of land. The Lords of the Isles were head of the great Clan Donald, but it mustered in its ranks many who did not bear the name of MacDonald. The clan, in fact, became somewhat synthetic, though many of its members might adopt the patronymic of their lord. Surnames were not in general use throughout the Highlands until at least the 17th century and in remote areas not for a further 100 years. [J. D. Mackie, *A History of Scotland* (1964)]

Clapham Sect the name given by Sydney Smith to an informal group of EVANGELICALS, who lived near Clapham, a fashionable village just outside London, and worshipped at the Parish Church under John Venn (1759-1813). Among them were William Wilberforce (1759–1833), Henry Thornton (1760-1815), Zachery Macaulay (1768-1838), Lord Teignmouth (1751-1834), Granville Sharp (1735-1813) and Charles Grant (1746-1832). Towards the end of her life, Hannah More (1745-1833) was closely connected with the group. From about 1785 to 1830, largely through the personal position of its members, the group was able to lead public opinion and Parliament in important schemes, such as the abolition of SLAVERY and the formation of the CHURCH MISSIONARY SOCIETY, with a success out of all proportion to its size.

Clarence a four-wheeled closed CARRIAGE with seats for four inside and two outside on the box. It was fashionable in the earlier part of the 19th century and may have been named after the Duke of Clarence, later King William IV (1830-7).

Clarendon Code comprised the laws passed against NONCONFORMISTS after the RESTORATION. These were the Corporation Act (1661), which excluded Nonconformists from the corporations of BOROUGHS; the Act of Uniformity (1662), which reimposed the COMMON PRAYER BOOK and caused the PRESBYTERIANS and INDEPENDENTS to leave the CHURCH OF ENGLAND; the Conventicle Act (1664), which forbade the holding of non-Anglican services; and the Five Mile Act (1665), which prohibited Nonconformist clergy from coming within five miles of any borough. The last two acts were repealed by the Toleration Act (1689) and the Corporation Act in 1828.

Claret the name given in England to the red WINES of Bordeaux for the past 600 years. These were especially popular in the country when the English kings ruled over Bordeaux and Gascony. They were sold for a penny a gallon in the fourteenth century. Dr Johnson considered that claret was the drink for boys, PORT for men, but BRANDY for heroes.

Class meetings a part of the organization of the METHODISTS since 1742 for the purpose of 'fellowship in Christian experience'. Class meetings consist of small sections of a congregation, usually meeting weekly under a class leader appointed by the minister. Its purpose is prayer, Bible study, testimony, inquiry into the moral and spiritual progress of its members and collecting contributions to religious funds.

Clavichord a keyboard instrument, dating from the 13th century, in which the strings were struck. Its shape was that of a small box like a VIRGINAL. Though it was the predecessor of the PIANO, it was largely superseded in England by the more powerful HARPSICHORD, in which the strings were plucked.

Clergy in the Middle Ages were either religious (those who were MONKS) or secular (those who were not). There were also several grades of clergy. In addition to BISHOPS, there were 'Major Orders' of Priest, Deacon and Sub-Deacon and the 'Minor Orders' of Acolyte, Exorcist, Reader and Door-Keeper. In the CHURCH OF ENGLAND, since the REFORMATION, there have only been the three orders of Bishops, Priests and Deacons, while the CHURCH OF SCOTLAND has a single order of Ministers. Medieval clergy had the privilege of 'benefit of clergy', by which they were tried for crimes in the ECCLESIASTICAL COURTS (with less severe penalties) instead of the ordinary courts of the land.

Clicket or snapper, a device used, especially in DAME SCHOOLS, for calling inattentive children to order. They were usually made of box-wood or crab-tree wood and produced a sharp resonant click by pressure and quick release of a trigger. [Edward H. Pinto, *Treen and other Wooden Bygones* (1969)]

Clippers the finest of all sailing-SHIPS, were built in Britain from the 1840s to the 1860s. With the great length and vast area of canvas, they were as fast as the steamships of the time, and they did not have to occupy valuable cargo space with coal, nor had they paddle-wheels which were often broken by rough seas. They were mostly used to bring the new season's crop of TEA back from China to London, and they raced each other to reach England as quickly as possible. One clipper did the voyage in as little as 91

days, but the opening of the Suez Canal in 1869 destroyed their value since they could not use the Red Sea with its unpredictable winds. The most famous of these clippers, the *Cutty Sark*, is now preserved in dry dock at Greenwich; it had ¾-acre of sail. [H. A. Underhill, *Deepwater Sail* (1952)]

Clipping scraping or filing metal from the edge of coins. Though punishable by death, it was a common practice until the Royal Mint prevented it by producing coins with a milled edge from 1663. See also COINAGE, TRADE TOKENS.

Cloak an outer garment, usually long and sleeveless, worn from the ANGLO-SAXON period by both men and women. The length and shape of cloaks varied with fashion from age to age. In the Middle Ages married women and widows wore a draped cloak with a COVERCHIEF. From the reign of Henry I (1100–35) the English nobility wore long, trailing cloaks, but in 1153 Henry II brought over the new French fashion of short cloaks and gained for himself the nickname of 'Curtmantel'. See also DOMINO, MANTLE.

Clocks are known to have existed in several English churches before the end of the 13th century, including ST PAUL'S CATHEDRAL, WESTMINSTER ABBEY and CANTERBURY CATHEDRAL. The oldest surviving clock in the world, dating from at least 1386, is at SALISBURY CATHEDRAL and was restored in 1956. An earlier date, perhaps as far back as about 1335, has been attributed to one made for Glastonbury Abbey and transferred since the DISSOLUTION OF THE MONASTERIES to Wells Cathedral, but only the iron frame is now the original. Exeter Cathedral is said to have had a clock in 1318.

The first clocks were weight-driven, their source of power being the downward force exerted by a weight hung by a cord or chain which was wound round a barrel or drum; the downward pull of the weight caused the barrel to revolve. The introduction of the mainspring to drive the

Astronomical clock

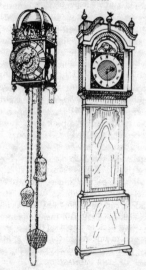

(*left*) Lantern clock; (*right*) Grandfather clock

wheelwork in Germany about 1500 made possible the manufacture of portable clocks (and also WATCHES). The first English domestic clock, introduced about

the end of the 16th century was the lantern clock, which had the movement placed in a brass case surmounted by a BELL, but the driving weights and cords supporting them were outside.

The development of the pendulum in Holland from about 1658 as a regulator and the invention of the anchor or recoil escapement, connecting the pendulum with the wheelwork, brought in the longcase or grandfather clock which was to be found in every tolerably furnished British home for the next 150 years. There was also a portable pendulum or bracket clock in a wooden case, but its shorter pendulum made it less accurate. The development of the balance wheel in place of the pendulum made possible the construction of smaller clocks.

Electric clocks have become common during this century. They are operated from the electric mains, their speed being regulated by the frequency of the AC supply from the generating station, which in Britain was established at a uniform frequency of 50 cycles per second in 1936. [G. F. C. Gordon, *Clockmaking, Past and Present* (2nd revised ed. by A. V. May, 1949)] See also TIME.

Cloister a covered walk or arcade, usually around an open rectangular, grassed space in a MONASTERY with a plain wall on the outer side and on the inner a colonnade, which at first in Britain was open, as in warmer climates, but eventually was enclosed by a series of WINDOWS, which were glazed. It was usually placed south of the church to get as much sunshine and light as possible. It served as a means of communication between the main monastic buildings which were ranged round it and also as a place where the MONKS studied in their CARRELS. The idea of the cloister garth (or open space) was imitated in the quadrangles and courts of the COLLEGES of Oxford and Cambridge.

Clubs originated mostly in the COFFEE-HOUSES of 17th- and 18th-century London, though the first club is supposed to have been the Friday Street or Bread Street Club founded about the end of the 16th century. Many clubs came to retain the name of their original keeper, e.g. White's (1693), Boodle's (1762) and Brook's (1764). See also ALMACK'S.

Cluniacs members of a reformed BENE-DICTINE monastic order founded in 912 at Cluny in Burgundy. They spent more time in prayer and study than in manual labour. Cluniac MONASTERIES were formed into the Congregation of Cluny. Cluny alone had an ABBOT, who governed all the other Cluniac monasteries which only had PRIORS. The first English Cluniac monastery was founded at Lewes (Sussex) in 1077; but their dependence on a foreign abbot led to the suppression of many of them, together with other alien monasteries, in the 15th century.

Coaches large enclosed four-wheeled CARRIAGES for passengers, developed from the WAGONS introduced into England in the 16th century. The first coach in England was made by Walter Rippon in 1555, and he made one for Elizabeth I in 1564, which was a plume-capped, curtained coach. By the end of the 16th century, some of the nobility and gentry owned coaches, and by the early 17th century there were HACKNEY-COACHES for hire in London. The first STAGE-COACH ran between London and Coventry in 1659 and the first MAIL-COACH between Bristol and London in 1784. In 1667 windows were introduced (see also PLATE-GLASS) and springs in 1789. Outside passengers, who sat on the roof behind the driver, travelled more cheaply than those inside, and in 1767 a basket, called the conveniency, was attached to the back of the coach for half-price passengers. [R. Straus, *Carriages and Coaches* (1912);

H. McCausland, *The English Carriage* (1948)]

Coal cinders have been found in ruins of the time of ROMAN BRITAIN, but it was probably not burnt again in houses until the 13th century, when it was thought to be inorganic mineral and was called 'burning stone'. By Henry III's reign (1216–72) it was being shipped from Tyneside to London, where it was known as 'sea coal', but it was not burnt generally until Charles II's reign (1660–85).

Coal at first was quarried from outcrops and from sea cliffs where exposed and gathered from the shore. By the end of the 14th century pits were being dug, chiefly in northern England, but deep-mining did not begin until the mid-17th century, and by the mid-18th century all the present areas were being worked. At first water was drained from pits by subterranean drains, running into some lower river level; pumps were not used until the late 16th century, and later a form of STEAM ENGINE was first devised for this purpose. The Act of 1842 forbade the employment of women and children underground in coal mines. British coal production reached a peak in 1913, when 287 000 000 tons was mined; today it is about 200 000 000 tons a year. In 1945 there were over 800 000 miners, but in 1970 there were less than 300 000. Living in pit villages, the miners came to form closely-knit communities with a strong Trade union tradition, but their declining numbers have reduced their influence on the movement. The coal industry was nationalized in 1946 when the National Coal Board was set up. See also SAFETY-LAMP.

Coat did not begin to have its modern meaning of a sleeved garment until the mid-17th century. In the Middle Ages it was the 'cote', the loose tunic worn by men, the equivalent of the women's

KIRTLE, while in the 16th century it was a short-sleeved or sleeveless jacket worn over the DOUBLET. By the 18th century it had long tails, large sleeves, a low collar and was often profusely ornamented with BUTTONS. This became in the 19th century the frock-coat, which was double-breasted with long square tails or skirts and not cut away in front. Short coats were only worn on holiday or informal occasions, but in the 20th century they began to replace the dress-coat, which was described as 'dead as the Dodo' by 1921. Overcoats began to replace CLOAKS in the 18th century, at first for men and later for women. See also DINNER-JACKET, MACINTOSH.

Cob and thatch a composition of unbaked clay, gravel and straw, faced with plaster, formerly used for building the walls of COTTAGES, especially in south-western England.

Cock-fighting a long-established, popular sport in Britain, having probably been introduced by the Romans. Specially bred and trained cocks, fitted with steel spurs, fought to death in a small round area called a cockpit. A 'main' was a contest between a number of birds on each side, and a 'battle royal' was when victory went to the side represented by a last survivor.

In the Middle Ages, London school-boys on SHROVE TUESDAY brought cocks to school, and the masters arranged matches all the morning. Henry VIII built the Royal Cock-Pit, WHITEHALL, which was used into the 19th century. Cock-fighting was prohibited in Britain in 1849, but is still carried on secretly in some parts of the country.

Cocktail a short mixed drink, usually served as an appetizer, which originated in USA in the 1920s. A great variety can be made by blending various spirits or liqueurs with one or more vermouths, bitters or fruit juices. The cocktail or SHERRY party has largely replaced after-noon TEA as a popular form of enter-taining.

Cocoa a drink manufactured, like CHOCOLATE, from cacao beans. In its modern form cocoa differs from chocolate in having much of the high fat content of the cacao bean removed. It was first made in Holland in 1828 and became a popular drink in Britain during the second half of the 19th century. Much of the excluded fat (known as cocoa butter) is added to solid chocolate as a sweet-meat.

Coffee is said to have been brought into England in 1641 by Nathaniel Canopus, a Cretan, who made it his common beverage at Balliol College, Oxford. Coffee powder at 3s a lb appears for the first time in the Earl of Bedford's accounts in 1685. Unlike TEA, it never became a national beverage and long remained a drink of the upper classes; but since the 1950s there has been a great increase of coffee-drinking in Britain, mainly in instant form. The British consumption of coffee is now over 3 lb per head a year, which is virtually double the level 10 years ago, but must be compared with 18–20 lb in Sweden and 16 lb in USA. See also GROCER.

Coffee-houses were first opened in England during the COMMONWEALTH, the earliest being at Oxford in 1650 by a JEW named Jacobs and the first in London at Cornhill in 1652, by a Greek, Pasqua Rosee, formerly the servant of a merchant, Daniel Edwards, who traded in Turkey. Coffee-houses became very popular, some being patronized by particular professions or politicians. Commercial undertakings, notably LLOYD'S, centred upon them, and they were the forerunners of

CLUBS. In 1700 there were about 2000 coffee-houses in London alone, but thereafter they declined and were replaced by clubs. In the 1870s attempts were made to revive them by reformers to dissuade working-men from drinking BEER. See also NEWS LETTERS.

Coif a close-fitting LINEN cap, covering the top, back and sides of the head and tied under the chin. It was worn by men from the end of the 12th century to the mid-15th century and by women from the 16th to the 18th century when it was often embroidered in coloured silks. See also HATS.

Coif is also the name given to the mail hood, attached to the HAUBERK, worn during the CRUSADES as a HELMET, supplemented by a skull-cap worn over it or under it. It proved inconvenient if the wearers had BEARDS & MOUSTACHES, so they were usually clean-shaven. See also ARMOUR.

Coinage may have existed in Britain before Julius Caesar's expeditions (55 and 54 BC), but it probably came from the Continent. Pieces of COPPER and IRON bars had long been used as currency, while the CELTS used crescent-shaped pieces of GOLD. After Caesar's expeditions, several British kingdoms struck their own coins, which were replaced by imperial coins (minted in London from the 3rd century) in ROMAN BRITAIN. After the departure of the Romans, local rulers struck numerous small, crude SILVER coins, including the silver PENNY from the 7th century.

After the NORMAN CONQUEST, the Roman system of POUNDS and SHILLINGS was adopted for accounting purposes. After Henry III's unsuccessful GOLD PENNY, regular gold coinage began with Edward III's gold FLORIN, soon replaced by the NOBLE. Meanwhile, Edward I had issued the first round HALFPENNY and FARTHING; and the GROAT first appeared under Edward III. The noble was replaced by the ANGEL and ROYAL under Edward IV. The CROWN was first minted in the 16th century. James I minted the UNITE, which was replaced by the GUINEA and this by the SOVEREIGN. First issued in the 16th century. The MARK was never an actual English coin, but used solely for accounting purposes.

Gold coinage ceased to be used during the First World War. The farthing was demonetized in 1960, the halfpenny in 1969 and the half-crown in 1970; and in 1971 a decimal currency was introduced consisting of 100 new pence to the pound. Paper money (in the form of £1 and 10s notes) was first issued in 1914; the 10s note was withdrawn in 1970. [E. V. Morgan, *A History of Money* (1965).] See also CLIPPING, TRADE TOKENS.

Collars were unknown until the 13th century when a narrow strip of material was attached to the neckline of a garment and evolved gradually into the stand-up collar. A collar became part of the SHIRT later, and until recent times a stiff collar was a mark of class distinction. During the last 20 years the wearing of shirts with soft, attached collars has become common. See also RUFF, STOMACHER.

College An organized society of persons joined together for certain common purposes and also the building in which they live, especially at the UNIVERSITIES of Oxford and Cambridge. These first came into being in the 13th century, when BISHOPS and other wealthy men obtained CHARTERS from the Crown to incorporate societies of teachers and students, and these gradually became the dwelling places for students attending the university, when they imitated many of the features of a MONASTERY or a great HOUSE of the time (e.g. the CLOISTER, HALL and CHAPEL). Later every member of the university had to belong to a college and received most of his instruction there. In the 19th century Durham University was founded with a college system and so also was London University. Some of the newest universities (e.g. Nottingham and York) have adopted something like it, but there the colleges are places of residence and not of teaching.

Collegiate church is governed by a COLLEGE (or CHAPTER) of CANONS or PREBENDARIES, but is not a CATHEDRAL. A number were founded in the 14th and 15th centuries, when MONASTERIES were beginning to decline in favour. The purpose was to secure a continual offering of worship in services as in monastic and cathedral foundations. Among such collegiate churches were Fotheringay (Northants.), Crediton and Ottery St Mary (Devon), and Rotherham (Yorks.). Most were dissolved under the CHANTRY Act of 1547 or abolished in the 19th century and became parish churches. The three remaining collegiate churches in England are WESTMINSTER ABBEY, St George's Chapel, Windsor, and the Church of St Endelienta in the parish of St Endellion in Cornwall.

Coloni those who tilled the soil on the estates of the VILLAS in ROMAN BRITAIN. They were not SLAVES, but were attached to the soil like the later medieval VILLEINS, in that they were not free to move from the place where they worked.

Comb has been used from early times for tidying the HAIR, for keeping it in position when arranged and as an ornament for the head. The earliest combs, which were of bone, found in England belong to the NEW STONE AGE. Medieval combs were made of wood, horn, bone and ivory and were often finely carved and fashioned; those used for combing the hair usually had two rows of teeth. Combs are now also made of tortoiseshell, metal and various synthetic materials.

Combinations a male UNDERGARMENT, combining a VEST and DRAWERS in one and of woollen material, was patented in 1862 and commonly worn in the 1880s and 1890s. A similar female garment, a CHEMISE and DRAWERS in one, was introduced in 1877, to be superseded by the briefer, more elegant cami-knickers in about 1918.

Combine harvester which does the work of both the REAPING MACHINE and THRESHING MACHINE, was first devised in America and Australia in the late 1880s; but these were not satisfactory for use in Britain, where the corn is wetter, heavier and longer in the straw. They had, therefore, to be modified for British farms and were not used extensively until after the Second World War.

Comics probably began in Britain with *Ally Sloper's Half-Holiday* (1884–1923); Ally Sloper was a seedy proletarian loafer, who swigged gin and poured scorn on his fellows. There followed (1890–1953) *Comic Cuts* and *Chips* in which Weary Willie and Tired Tim appeared; both were published by Alfred Harmsworth (later Lord Northcliffe), and both originally cost ½d. *Dan Leno's Comic Journal* (1898–1900) featured the actual MUSIC-HALL comedian.

Puck (1908) was the first comic in full colour and for children. It was followed by *Rainbow* (1914) and *Tiger Tim's Weekly* (1920) with the Bruin Boys and *Playbox* (1925) with the Bruin Girls. These lasted until the mid-1950s.

In the 1920s came *Film Fun* featuring Harold Lloyd, Fatty Arbuckle and other CINEMA stars, while from the early 1930s Laurel and Hardy held the front page for over 20 years. The paper lasted until the 1960s.

In the 1930s came *Radio Fun*; and the Dundee firm of D. C. Thomson produced for children *Dandy, Beano* and *Magic*, which were more robust than previous comics, representing school-teachers, policemen and officials as figures of fun. They also dispensed with captions, telling their stories entirely in balloons.

In 1950 the Hulton Press produced its four-colour, gravure publications, *Eagle, Girl, Robin* and *Swift*, which between them covered all ages of children and presaged the space-age comic. In the 1950s TELEVISION also began to influence comics. *TV Fun* appeared in 1953, and then popular programmes had comics devoted to them, e.g. *The Flintstones* and *Thunderbirds*; and in the 1960s came *Smash !*, *Wam !* and *Pow !* containing features from the successful American Marvel Comics, and in 1967 *Fantastic*, which consisted entirely of such reprints. [G. Perry and A. Aldridge, *The Penguin Book of Comics* (1967).] See also NEWSPAPERS.

Common Law a term which came into use in the reign of Edward I (1272–1307), originated in England in the 12th century when the royal JUDGES began work and gave decisions in cases which were accepted as precedents for the future. These decisions produced a body of law which was regarded as common to the whole land and distinct from the law administered by CHANCERY and the ECCLESIASTICAL COURTS. Much common law was evolved in the 12th and 13th centuries in the royal COURTS, checking the power of FEUDALISM and strengthening good government, but with the rise of Parliament, the principle that changes in the law must have Parliament's consent, checked the growth of common law in favour of statute law (i.e. law in the form of Acts of Parliament).

Common Order, Book of a directory of worship compiled by John Knox in 1556 for the English PROTESTANT congregations in Geneva. It was also known as 'The Order of Geneva' and 'Knox's Liturgy'. The General Assembly ordered its use in the CHURCH OF SCOTLAND in 1562, and it was replaced by the DIRECTORY OF PUBLIC WORSHIP in 1645. In 1940 a new Book of Common Order was issued for Scotland.

Common Prayer, Book of the result of the wish of Thomas Cranmer and other PROTESTANT reformers to simplify and condense the medieval Latin services and to produce in English a single, comprehensive volume for the CHURCH OF ENGLAND. The LITANY was first issued in 1544 and the King's Book, containing the Creed, the Lord's Prayer, the Commandments and several canticles and collects in 1545. The First Prayer Book of Edward VI, enforced by the Act of Uniformity of 1549, was a conservative compromise; the Second Prayer Book of Edward VI, which appeared in 1552, was more Protestant.

After Queen Mary's Act of Repeal (1553) had restored the old services, Elizabeth I's Prayer Book of 1559 was largely a reissue of the previous book, and slight changes were made in it in 1604 after the HAMPTON COURT Conference. It was superseded in 1645 by the DIRECTORY FOR PUBLIC WORSHIP, but reissued in 1662, with slight alterations. The Revised Prayer Book of 1928 was rejected by the House of Commons, but the Church is now engaged in experimenting with new services, especially for the Holy Communion.

The Scottish Prayer Book of 1637, though often called 'Laud's Liturgy', was drawn up by BISHOPS of the CHURCH OF SCOTLAND who wanted a revised version of the English Book of Common Prayer. Its use led to riots in Scotland and precipitated the outbreak of the Civil War in England.

Commonwealth the period of PURI-
TAN rule in Britain from Charles I's
execution (1649) to the RESTORATION
(1660). Oliver Cromwell and the army,
after securing the defeat of the LEVELLERS
and DIGGERS, supported the cause of the
INDEPENDENTS and toleration was granted
to all Puritans; but the CHURCH OF ENG-
LAND was suppressed, a censorship of the
press established, heavy taxation imposed
to maintain a standing army and attempts
made to impose by legislation the Puritan
strict moral observances and dislike of the
THEATRE and most GAMES. Resentment at
these measures and a reaction in favour
of the monarchy led to the Restoration.
See also CHRISTMAS, MAYPOLE, SUNDAY.

Compass developed from the knowledge, dating back to antiquity, that a
loadstone will direct itself to point in a
north–south direction, but only in 1190
did Italian pilots begin to use a mag-
netized needle floating on a piece of wood
in a bowl of water. By 1250 this had
developed into the mariner's compass, a
graduated circular card attached to the
needle balanced on a pivot in a glazed box.

Comprehensive schools were defined
by a Ministry of Education circular in
1947 as 'one which is intended to cater for
all the secondary children of *all* the
families in a given area'. They were made
possible by the EDUCATION ACT (1944).
Among the first Local Education Authorities to build large comprehensive schools
in the early 1950s were London and
Coventry, and in the early 1960s other
authorities (e.g. Liverpool, Manchester
and Bradford) grouped existing school
buildings to form comprehensive schools.
In 1965 the Department of Education and
Science issued a circular requiring all
Local Education Authorities to submit
plans for the reorganization of secondary
education in their areas on comprehensive
lines, but not all initiated single schools.

Some areas organized lower and upper
schools with breaks at the age of 13 or
14—an idea first introduced in Leicestershire in 1957.

Concrete dates from the discovery by
Joseph Aspdin in 1824 of the material
which he called Portland cement because
it was like Portland stone in colour.
When mixed with gravel or crushed stone
and sand, it binds these together into a
solid mass. Before this discovery, forms
of concrete had been used since the time
of the Romans, but they lacked strength
and would not set under water. Since
concrete may be moulded into any desired
shape, it is used nowadays in the building
of all sorts of structures.

Conduit a channel or pipe, usually
under ground, for conveying water to be
drawn at a conduit-head, which was often
housed in a building. In London the
Great Conduit in West Cheap (Cheapside) was a stone building housing a lead
cistern fed by a pipe from TYBURN,
3½ miles away, built in 1285. Nearby
householders paid yearly water-rates of
between 5s and 6s 8d. The pipe was
extended to Cornhill in 1378. The palace
of Westminster had a conduit bringing
water from the West Bourne at Paddington which was probably built in 1233. On
occasions like victories or coronations, the
conduits sometime ran with WINE, the
water being turned off and a small pipe
from a wine-barrel inserted in the outlet.
Most of the city conduits were destroyed
in the GREAT FIRE OF LONDON, but some
were rebuilt and several used into the
19th century. See also NEW RIVER, WATER
SUPPLY.

Congregationalists, see INDEPENDENTS.

Constable an official chosen each year
from the inhabitants of a PARISH from the
late 15th century onwards to see that

77

the parishioners kept law and order by serving as WATCHMEN and raising HUE AND CRY. Originally elected by the parishioners, from Tudor times they were increasingly appointed by the JUSTICES OF THE PEACE and acted as agents for them in such ways as apprehending suspicious characters and WHIPPING beggars and other offenders. Constables were unpaid, untrained and often served unwillingly. Parish constables were abolished in the 19th century on the establishment of the POLICE system, and so also were the high constables in the HUNDREDS.

Conservatories ornamental GREEN-HOUSES attached to the house, were popular in the 19th century. Generally flowering plants were grown in other greenhouses under heat, until their blossoms began to develop, when they were taken to the conservatory which was cool enough to extend the flowering period as long as possible. Conservatories often faced south-east, as it then caught the early morning sun in winter and in summer became comparatively cool and shady by the afternoon, which was the time when the family most often sat in it. William Cobbett (1762–1835) wrote, 'There must be amusement in every family. . . . How much better during the long, dreary winter for daughters, and even sons, to assist or attend their mother in the greenhouse [i.e. the conservatory] than to be seated with her at cards or in the blubberings over a stupid novel. . . .' In Victorian romantic novels the secluded, fragrant conservatory was, in fact, often the place for proposals of marriage. Fine conservatories may be seen at Syon House (Middlesex) and Sandon Hall (Staffs.), while there is a Victorian stone 'gothick' conservatory at Foscombe (Glos.).

Convent a word generally applied nowadays to a building occupied by NUNS, but in the Middle Ages it was used to describe the houses of MONKS as well. Thus, Covent Garden in London was originally 'convent garden' because it belonged to WESTMINSTER ABBEY.

Conversi or lay brethren existed in nearly all the religious orders. They were members of the order who were not bound to attend all the services and were occupied in manual work. Being illiterate, they were taught only the Lord's Prayer, the Creed and the necessary parts of the daily services; they were not allowed to wear the full habit. Conversi were first admitted to MONASTERIES in the 11th century through the increasingly usual custom of ordaining MONKS as priests and relieving them of manual work; and at the same time a similar development took place in the orders of women, where lay sisters were employed to leave the NUNS free for worship, prayer and more skilled tasks.

The conversi were especially important and most numerous in the ABBEYS of the CISTERCIANS, where they were needed to cultivate the landed estates. In the early period of the order, they were often more numerous than monks (e.g. there were at Waverley Abbey 70 monks and 120 conversi). The conversi in the houses of the contemplative CARTHUSIANS did much of the more practical work of the household.

The numbers of conversi began to decline, even in the Cistercian abbeys, before the 14th century. The monasteries found it better and more profitable to let out their land or work it with hired labour. The BLACK DEATH and the resulting shortage of labour speeded the process, and the conversi almost wholly disappeared. A few remained, however, and the conversi of the Charterhouse in London were martyred under Henry VIII with the fully professed monks.

Cook-shops (originally cook's shop) were shops where cooked food was sold and often eaten. In London during the 12th century, there was a famous cook-shop on the river-bank where all sorts of ready-cooked food could be bought by those who had to entertain unexpected guests; rich households could have venison, guinea-fowl and sturgeon, while there were humbler dishes for the poor; and all was available 'at whatever hours of night or day'. They were still common in the 17th century. An Act of Parliament of 1678 referred to 'inns and cook-shops'. Pepys frequented them, and early the next century Joseph Addison spoke of them in the *Spectator*. They were the forerunners of the later HOT PIE SHOPS.

Co-operative Societies began with the Rochdale Equitable Pioneers, founded in 1844, which was followed by others all over the country, mainly in the industrial areas and especially in the North. In 1863 the Co-operative Wholesale Society was established to purchase goods on a large scale for co-operative stores, and in 1875 it opened its first factories; the Scottish Co-operative Wholesale Society was founded in 1868. [G. D. H. Cole, *A Century of Co-operation* (1944)]

Cope an ecclesiastical VESTMENT of semicircular shape worn by clergy at services when the CHASUBLE is not used and, like it, derived from the Roman cloak. In the Middle Ages, the cope was widely used as a ceremonial choir habit by MONKS on festivals. The material of copes found in the inventories of Edward VI's commissioners in 1552 varied from cloth of gold to simple SERGE.

Copper has been mined since prehistoric times. There may have been a Copper Age before the BRONZE AGE. Copper was mined in ROMAN BRITAIN in Anglesey and North Wales, but not ex-

tensively. After the NORMAN CONQUEST, copper mines were first opened in England in 1189, but the industry was not very successful until 1568 when the Mines Royal Company, a JOINT-STOCK COMPANY, was incorporated by CHARTER. It opened copper-mines in Cornwall and Cumberland and until the end of the 17th century controlled the mining of copper. In the 19th century there were some 50 copper mines in Cornwall. It is now mainly mined in USA, Chile, Canada, the Congo and Northern Rhodesia. [*Copper Through the Ages* (Copper Development Association, 1934).] See also BRASS, PHOENICIANS.

Copyhold was a form of holding land which, after the BLACK DEATH and the PEASANTS' REVOLT, gradually replaced villeinage on the medieval MANOR. The VILLEIN became a copyholder because he held a copy of the record of his new position. Copyholders paid a money rent to the lord of the manor for their land instead of performing the customary services. Copyhold was abolished by Parliament in 1928.

Copying-sticks consisted of a line of copperplate handwriting, glued on each side of a thin strip of wood, about 8 in. long and 1 in. wide. The wording, in the form of improving texts or proverbs, performed the function of teaching copperplate handwriting. They seem to have been used in all schools until at least the mid-19th century. Those exhibited in the Birmingham City Museum, are inscribed for example: 'Faith dwells with simplicity': 'Silent waters are seldom shallow'. [Edward H. Pinto, *Treen and other Wooden Bygones* (1969)]

Coracle a small oval boat of wickerwork covered over with skins and made watertight by a coating of tar and pitch.

It was about 3 ft by 4 ft in size and propelled by a rower with a paddle. Julius Caesar wrote of coracles being used by the CELTS in England at the time of his invasions of 55 BC and 54 BC. They are still used on rivers in Wales. See also SHIPS.

Coral the hard skeleton of the marine polypus deposited in warm oceans, was very popular as JEWELLERY in Roman and medieval times, the bunches, red, pink or orange in colour, being picked, sorted and polished. Coral NECKLACES were worn as a protection against infectious diseases, and branches of coral were hung round children's necks to preserve them from danger, while babies might be given a piece on which to cut their teeth.

Coriander an annual HERB grown in southern Europe and the Levant, the seeds of which were in general medieval use for flavouring wines, preserves and even meat dishes. Though coriander is now used in pickles and curry powder, it has lost much of its old popularity.

Corn Laws were passed in 1815 to keep the price of corn at a profitable level for farmers and landowners. Until the price of home WHEAT reached 80s a quarter, none was to be imported from abroad, but this was replaced by a sliding scale of duties in 1828. Following the bad harvests of the later 1830s, the Anti-Corn Law League was formed in 1839 at Manchester, which eventually succeeded in getting the Corn Laws repealed in 1846. This had at first little effect on the price of corn. The growing population of the country was still fed by British farmers, but in the 1870s an increasing amount of wheat came from the developing American prairies, and the ruin of British farming began, since it could not compete with the foreign corn grown on a large scale and produced more cheaply. The repeal was part of the free trade movement which by the mid-19th century had abolished all customs duties in Britain.

Coroners were first appointed in 1194 to look after the king's financial interests in place of the SHERIFFS and to keep a check on the sheriffs' powers. With the development of the system of itinerant JUDGES, the powers of their courts, once considerable, slowly declined. Nowadays their main function is to hold inquests on all who die unexpectedly and to investigate cases of treasure trove.

Corrodians persons whom the crown and private patrons were entitled to nominate for board and lodging within a medieval MONASTERY. Such persons were said to possess a corrody. Edward III (1327–77) installed two old servants in Dover Priory and the future Black Prince's nurse in St Augustine's Abbey, Bristol. A monastery might also grant corrodies to craftsmen and others who had served in and sell them to raise ready money. There were usually two kinds of corrodies—one in which the corrodian had the same food as the monks, the other in which he got it from the servants' hall. The prevalence of corrodies caused monasteries serious financial difficulties in the later Middle Ages.

Cosmetics of various sorts were used by Roman women, including white-lead, chalk and rouge for the face and black substances for the eyelids and to lengthen the lines of the eyes (see also BOTTLES). Christian writers condemned make-up for women, Tertullian saying that they should always be 'in mourning and in rags'; and a 12th-century preacher denounced women who powdered their faces with 'blaunchet' (fine wheaten flour) as using the devil's soap; but the CRUSADES led to a greater use of cosmetics.

Queen Elizabeth I favoured a cowslip cream, said to preserve, beautify and whiten the skin, which soon became popular with fashionable ladies; and women and sometimes men, who wished to remove sunburn from their faces, washed in TANSY juice. PATCHES were worn in the 17th century, and both sexes blackened their eyebrows and used rouge. In the 18th century ladies commonly painted their faces, but a CHARITY SCHOOL girl, who powdered herself with flour, was 'instantly stripped, birched and scrubbed before the whole school'.

The cult for simplicity, inspired by the French Revolution, favoured the natural complexion for women, and afterwards the feminine ideal of the ROMANTIC MOVEMENT favoured a pale face, while for a time in the early 19th century some fashionable men (e.g. the Prince Regent) painted their faces, though not women. Throughout the Victorian period a lady who used make-up would be excluded from polite society, and girls were advised just before entering a drawing-room or ball-room to bite their lips and slap their cheeks hard.

Women began to use make-up in the 1920s, but most confined themselves to lipstick and used powder sparingly, only a few painting their nails, cheeks, eyebrows and lashes or bleaching or tinting their hair. All this became more common when cheap cosmetics came into use in the 1930s, and today at least 80 per cent of women in Britain use cosmetics. In 1966 women spent £3 million on nail varnish, £5 million on eye make-up, £8 million on lipstick and £60 million on hair preparations. Men have recently been using cosmetics more, and in 1966 they spent £4 million on after-shave lotions, £1¼ million on deodorants, £750 000 on colognes and £6½ million on hair-dressings. [Brenda Gourgey, *Face to Face* (1969).] See also HAIRDRESSING, PERFUMES.

Costume began with the WEAVING of cloth in the BRONZE AGE, and garments preserved in peat-bogs in Denmark suggest that both sexes wore simple TUNICS of LINEN, CLOAKS of WOOL and SANDALS. Roman men wore the TOGA and beneath it a tunic, which was the only garment of the poor; women wore a long woollen robe, drawn in by a girdle at the waist, and a long linen UNDERGARMENT, pinned at the shoulder. ANGLO-SAXON and Normen men wore a tunic, often with a pattern at the edge, and BRAIES; women wore long dresses, sometimes with girdles, fashionable colours being light blue, red and green. Both sexes wore CLOAKS, fastened with a cord at the neck, those of the wealthy being fur-lined in winter. The CRUSADES brought considerable changes in fashion.

By the 14th century men wore a loose COAT, a low-waisted belt and tight STOCKINGS or HOSE; women wore a sleeveless and often low-necked dress over a tight-fitting KIRTLE. Tudor men wore doublets, square-toed SHOES and flat HATS; women wore full-skirted dresses with PETTICOATS or FARTHINGALES, and the GABLE HOOD or COIF. Figured SILK and VELVET was replaced by SATIN and other plainer materials. The wealthy of both sexes wore RUFFS, which gradually gave way in the 17th century to a wide, turned-down COLLAR, sometimes of LACE. The doublet gave way to a long-sleeved coat, buttoned down in front to hide the BREECHES which replaced TRUNK HOSE. Women's clothes lost their stiffness and padding. During the COMMONWEALTH, the PURITANS favoured sombre fashions, but these lost favour at the RESTORATION.

During the 18th century, the skirts of men's coats slowly diminished, and their WAISTCOATS also grew shorter, while WIGS were generally worn. Women wore dresses over STAYS and linen SHIFTS and had tight half-sleeves trimmed with frills or lace and the neck low in front and

Costume: 1 11th-cent.; 2 16th-cent.; 3 18th-cent.; 4 19th-cent.; 5 19th-cent. ladies undergarments

square at the back. Bold floral designs were fashionable and also an opening to show a plain or quilted petticoat. There was greater simplicity and uniformity after the French Revolution. Women adopted the NAKED FASHION; men abandoned their wigs and wore TROUSERS and plainer, less ornate coats.

In the 19th century men wore the TOP-HAT and dark frock-coat. While women's SKIRTS trailed the ground until the First World War, their attire varied from a number of starched petticoats to the CRINOLINE and BUSTLE and their hats from minute to huge. Nowadays there is a growing tendency for the clothes of both sexes to become less cumbersome and formal and with less emphasis on class-distinction with the spread of ready-made garments. [Alison Settle, *English Fashion* (1948).] See also CHILDREN'S COSTUME, BIRCHIN LANE.

Cottage the dwelling house of country labourers or villagers. From the 12th to

the timbers was filled in with brickwork or WATTLE AND DAUB. See also COB AND THATCH, PARGETTING, WEATHER-BOARD-ING, CRUCKS.

The roofs of cottages were steeply-pitched so that water would run quickly off them and covered with slate, tile, stone or thatch. The WINDOWS, which were small because GLASS was expensive, were placed in any suitable position and often projected into the roof (dormers). The first floor was of boards on wood joists and the ground floor of clay, stone or

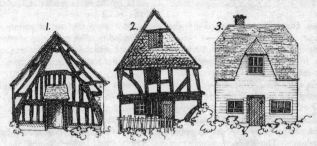

Cottages: 1 Cruck; 2 Timber framework; 3 Weatherboarding

the 18th centuries, its chief character-istics were that it was built by local craftsmen using local materials. Its design was informal, and the simplest construc-tional methods were used because no machinery was available. It was usually a small building, sometimes only one storey in height, but more often two, and its rooms were low, those on the first floor being partially in the roof space.

Constructionally cottages were of two sorts. There were those in which the weight of the roof and the first floor were carried on a solid wall, usually of stone; and there were those in which it was carried by a timber framework, usually of OAK, the rectangles formed by the up-right and horizontal beams being cross-braced to form triangles and make the structure rigid, while the space between

brick. [F. Gibberd, *The Architecture of England* (1938).] See also HOUSE.

Cottar a VILLEIN who occupied a COT-TAGE with a holding of attached land, which was usually between one and five acres, in return for labour service. The word is a translation of *cotarius* to be found in DOMESDAY BOOK and else-where.

Cotton industry was first established in England during Elizabeth I's reign (1558-1603) by FLEMINGS who settled in the WOOL textile districts of East Anglia and Lancashire, importing raw cotton first from the East and then from the West Indies. At first the English industry produced FUSTIAN, and fashionable MUS-LINS and CALICOES were imported from

India until forbidden by Parliament in 1701. This, together with the SPINNING and WEAVING inventions of the 18th century, made Lancashire until 1914 the seat of the world's cotton industry, obtaining most of its raw cotton (after the invention of Eli Whitney's gin in 1793 for cleaning it) from USA. In 1913 Britain exported 7000 million yards of cotton cloth, but in 1967 her total production of cloth was 745 million yards, and she imported 660 million yards. Nowadays 40 per cent of Britain's textile needs are met by imports.

'Cotton famine' was caused by the American Civil War (1861–5) which severely interrupted exports of American cotton to Lancashire and brought the cotton industry practically to a standstill. By 1862 some 500 000 people were being supported by POOR RELIEF or private charity. The government lent money to the Boards of Guardians to enable the unemployed to be put to work on public undertakings. Though new supplies of cotton from Egypt and the East improved the position early in 1863, the famine continued until the end of the war because Lancashire drew four-fifths of her needs from the Southern states. The Lancashire working classes remained firm in supporting the North, which President Lincoln called 'an instance of sublime Christian heroism which has not been surpassed in any age or in any country'.

County the name given after the NORMAN CONQUEST (from the NORMAN FRENCH *comté*) to the SHIRE of the ANGLO-SAXONS. The Welsh counties were organized as they are now in 1536 when England and Wales were united; the first Scottish counties were created by Malcolm III Canmore (1057–93) and his sons, who imitated the English system in the LOWLANDS, while the counties in the HIGHLANDS were organized between the 16th and 18th centuries.

County Court developed from the shire-MOOT of ANGLO-SAXON times which was attended by all FREEMEN of the SHIRE. After the NORMAN CONQUEST it was placed under the presidency of the SHERIFF, and ecclesiastical matters were removed from it to the ECCLESIASTICAL COURTS, but it continued to deal with a great variety of judicial cases. From the later 13th century its jurisdiction was gradually taken over by the royal JUDGES and JUSTICES OF THE PEACE.

In 1846 a new set of county courts, presided over by paid judges, was set up to deal with the recovery of smaller debts and other lesser judicial business.

Courts of law originated in England in the 12th and 13th centuries, largely through the work of Henry II (1154–89), who extended the jurisdiction of the King's Court (see JUDGES) and of Edward I (1272–1307), who divided the King's Court into three divisions—the Court of King's Bench for cases in which the king was interested; the Court of Common Pleas for cases between his subjects; and the Court of Exchequer for cases involving the royal revenue. These developments eliminated the judicial powers of the feudal courts (see MANOR) and of the old COUNTY COURTS, a process assisted by the appointment of JUSTICES OF THE PEACE.

During the same period, CHANCERY developed as a court, which gave its judgements according to equity to supplement the COMMON LAW administered by the King's Courts. There were also the ECCLESIASTICAL COURTS, which administered CANON LAW. In Tudor times there were the Prerogative Courts, the most important of which was the STAR CHAMBER; these were set up by the royal prerogative to deal with matters in which the monarch considered he had special rights or privileges.

In 1873 the Common-law Courts and the Court of Chancery were brought together by the Judicature Act to form a single High Court of Justice in which law and equity are administered equally together, but equity prevails where one conflicts with the other. See also ASSIZES.

Courtesy books were manuals of instruction in ETIQUETTE for CHILDREN which were published in late 18th and early 19th centuries. Their mode of instruction was often indirect, taking the form of a series of letters or anecdotal questions and answers. The older children were addressed as Young People or Young Ladies and Young Gentlemen, the younger Children as Little Masters and Little Misses. It was not thought suitable for the authoress of such a book to reveal her identity, but the authoress of *The Blind Child* (1791) stated in her preface, 'It has always been my opinion that the person of genius who dedicates superior talents to the instruction of young people deserves the highest applause and the most enthusiastic admiration'. She also said, 'My principal aim, it will be seen, is to repress that excessive softness of heart, which too frequently involves its possessor in a train of evils'.

Coverchief a large form of veil or other draped head covering worn by medieval married women of all classes, but largely discarded by the higher ranks in the 15th and generally in the 16th century. See also HATS, COSTUME, HAIRDRESSING.

Crane as a device for lifting heavy objects, has been known from early times. A late 13th century English manuscript shows an illustration of two labourers operating a windlass to draw up hewn stones in a basket, and an illustration in Holinshed's *Chronicles* (1577) depicts a crane with a pulley fixed to an inclined arm or jib and lifting a large block of stone. There was no great development of the crane until STEAM POWER came into use. Steam cranes were first introduced into the London docks in 1801, but as late as 1851, six horse cranes were used in building the CRYSTAL PALACE for the Great Exhibition in London. Derricks, lofty, portable structures, used on land and water for lifting very heavy loads, were invented by A. D. Bishop in 1857, and have been extensively used on building-sites, but are now replaced by tower cranes, in which the moveable arm is mounted horizontally on an extendable tower.

Cravat a neckcloth of LINEN, MUSLIN or SILK with long flowing ends tied with a bow or knot in front outside the SHIRT collar, worn by men from 1660 to the end of the 19th century. During the Regency period, it became very high and stiff, being starched and elaborately arranged; George ('Beau') Brummell (1778–1840) was famous for his skill in tying cravats. During the last 30 years of the 19th century the dangling ends of the bow eventually became the long tie worn by men nowadays. See also COSTUME, STEINKIRK.

Cremation the disposal of the dead by burning, first became general in the late BRONZE AGE and early IRON AGE; the ashes were usually placed in bags or pottery-urns and buried in urn-fields, but were often placed in earlier BARROWS. Both BURIAL and cremation were practised in the Romano–British period. The Emperor Severus was cremated at York in AD 211, and his ashes were taken to Rome.

Cremation lapsed in the Christian period, owing to a belief in the material resurrection of the body, and was reserved for heretics. In 1428, by order of the Council of Constance, the body of

John Wycliffe (c. 1320–84) was taken out of its grave at Lutterworth (Leics.) and burnt, and the ashes were thrown into a river.

In 1873 Sir Henry Thompson, a physician, advocated its introduction into Britain on sanitary grounds, and the next year the Cremation Society was founded, but public opinion only gradually accepted the idea. The oldest crematorium in Britain is at Woking (Surrey) and was built in 1879; the first legal cremation took place there in 1885. Cremation has become increasingly common in the 20th century.

Crenellation the furnishing of the upper part of the parapet of a CASTLE wall with battlements, i.e. openings for shooting through. In the 13th century, the building of lofty, crenellated CURTAIN WALLS and high round WALL-TOWERS made castles almost impregnable and consequently a menace to the peace of the

Crenellation

realm if in wrong hands. Therefore, from at least John's reign onwards, a royal 'Licence to Crenellate' was needed to fortify a castle with crenellated walls and wall-towers. By looking up the date of the licence, it is possible to find almost with certainty the date of erection of a castle.

Crescent as a range of buildings in a curved form, was inaugurated by the Royal Crescent, Bath (1767–74), designed by John Wood II. Its dramatic effect made this one of the most influential innovations in British TOWN-planning, and the idea was widely imitated. The first large crescent outside Bath was at Buxton where John Carr, the architect of Harewood House, built a curved block containing an assembly-room, hotel and newsroom, with an open arcade on the street; it was really a public building. Most crescents are terraces of private houses, and their common feature is their curve rather than any monumentality. They were especially popular with speculative builders at watering-places; the Royal Crescent, Brighton, was one of the first at the SEASIDE. [Geoffrey Martin, *The Town* (1961)]

Cricket which may be derived from STOOL-BALL, first appears in England in a drawing in a 13th-century manuscript *History of England* depicting a batsman holding a bat upright in his right hand with the blade upward and another figure stretching out his hands to catch; and a 14th-century manuscript shows a whole field, all monks. It was, however, discouraged as distracting from ARCHERY. A late 15th-century Act declared that the penalty for allowing the game (which it called 'Hand-in or Hand-out') to be played on one's premises was to be a fine of £20 or 3 years' imprisonment and the burning of all the gear.

The records of court proceedings at Guildford in 1598 show that schoolboys played it there some 50 years previously. Although it was not legalized until the mid-18th century, it was played all over southern England, especially at FAIRS, by the time records became plentiful after 1700. By the end of the century, three stumps had replaced two, straight bats curved ones, and eleven became the normal size of a team, while the men of the famous Hambledon Club (c. 1750–91) introduced a new style of batting.

The first general code of rules was compiled at the London Artillery Club in 1744, and the Marylebone Cricket Club (formed in 1788) through its aristocratic membership gradually assumed responsibility for regulating the game, and in 1835

Early cricket match

it legalized round-arm bowling. The County Cricket Championship started in 1873 and the Test Matches when the first English touring team visited Australia in 1861–2, the 'Ashes' being those of the stumps of the 1882–3 tour sealed in an urn now at Lord's. [H. S. Altham and E. W. Swanton, *A History of Cricket* (4th ed., 1948)]

Crinoline originally a fabric of horsehair or COTTON, invented in 1829 and in the 1840s used to stuff PETTICOATS to set out a lady's SKIRTS. From 1856 to the end of the 1860s the term was applied to a hooped petticoat distended by whalebone, and later by watch-spring hoops. The shape at first was domed, late in the 1850s pyramidical, and by 1862 the fullness began to diminish until in 1866 the front became flat and the back only projected. See also BUSTLE.

Crocodile the name given to the single file, often with the oldest girls in front and the youngest at the end, in which the pupils of girls' boarding schools took their weekly walk outside of school during the 18th and 19th centuries. Often the only exercise such girls got apart from this walk was an occasional saunter along the paths of the school-garden with a lesson-book in their hands. Noisy play, like that indulged in by boys, was a punishable offence lest unladylike habits should be formed.

Crofters are those who rent and cultivate a croft or small agricultural holding, especially in the Highlands and Islands of Scotland, and may also engage in fishing or some other occupation. Between 1790 and 1850 the Highland Clearances resulted in thousands of crofters being driven from their homes by landlords who wished to introduce the hardy Cheviot Sheep into the area. [Calum Maclean, *The Highlands* (1959); John Prebble, *The Highland Clearances* (1963)]

Croquet was probably introduced into England from Ireland in the early 1850s and soon became popular as a country-house and suburban game. The All-England Croquet Club was formed at Wimbledon in 1868. See also LAWN TENNIS.

Crosier or pastoral staff, the symbol of authority carried by BISHOPS and sometimes also by ABBOTS and ABBESSES. Curved at the top, straight in the middle and pointed at the lower end, it was first mentioned in the 7th century. English bishops abandoned the crosier from the REFORMATION to the 19th century. The first bishop to revive the use of the crosier was Walter Kerr Hamilton, Bishop of Salisbury, 1854–69, who was also the first TRACTARIAN to become an English diocesan bishop. See also VESTMENTS.

Crown a coin valued at 5s, first minted in gold in 1526 with a crown on the reverse. From the time of Edward VI to the reign of George III, both gold and silver crowns and half-crowns were issued, but thereafter only in silver. Since 1902 crowns have been struck only on special occasions. See also COINAGE.

Crucks pairs of curving timbers joined to support the roof-ridge of a HOUSE and footed low on the walls, each pair being usually cut from the same curved tree-trunk and then joined blade to blade in reverse. It was a primitive constructional method, common in the Middle Ages and surviving well into the 17th century in some areas, but it is not found in East Anglia or South-East England. It was generally used for BARNS and small dwellings, which were originally one-storeyed and often one-roomed. Often the crucks show in the end wall. [M. W. Barley, *The House and Home* (1963)]. See COTTAGE.

Crusades were undertaken between the 11th and 14th centuries by European rulers to recover the Holy Land from its Moslem conquerors. King Richard I of England joined the Third Crusade in 1190. The TEMPLARS and the HOSPITALLERS helped to maintain the states founded by the Crusaders.

The Crusades brought new luxuries to England and other European countries. These included SPICES, such as GINGER and PEPPER, FRUITS like figs, dates and raisins, and also rice and almonds. SUGAR was probably the most important innovation. Wealthy people began to eat crystallized peaches, cakes covered in almond paste and fine sugar and cheese tarts flavoured with ginger and garnished with SAFFRON.

CARPETS instead of RUSHES on the floor came from the East, and so did CUSHIONS and TAPESTRIES. Changes in COSTUME occurred also. For a time ladies and gentlemen wore turbans, slippers and long, flowing robes of SILK, VELVET and BROCADE; and the knowledge of dyeing came almost entirely from Syria. Ladies adopted new PERFUMES and such COSMETICS as rouge for the face and henna for the hair, and they began to use glass MIRRORS. Some people took BATHS more often. In MUSIC the DRUM and GUITAR were introduced.

The knowledge brought back by the Crusaders led to changes in the design of CASTLES, the adoption of HORSE-BRASSES and the development of HERALDRY in warfare. From the Arabs they learnt the use of anaesthetics in SURGERY and the making of PAPER. The expenses incurred by BARONS when crusading and the increased prosperity of the times enabled VILLEINS to purchase their freedom; and TOWNS gained CHARTERS (especially from Richard I) which increased their privileges as BOROUGHS. [Sir E. Barker, *The Crusades* (1923)]

Crutched Friars an order of FRIARS established in Italy in 1169. They came to England in 1244 and founded half-a-dozen houses in London and elsewhere which survived until the DISSOLUTION OF THE MONASTERIES. The word 'crutched' or 'cross-bearing' refers to the cross of red cloth which they wore upon the back of their blue HABIT. The order was suppressed by Pope Alexander VII in 1656.

Crypt a cellar or vault beneath a CHURCH, often used as a CHAPEL or burying-place. They are rare in parish churches, but more common in CATHEDRALS, where they were often designed, in imitation of the Catacombs in Rome, to contain a SHRINE, but this use was steadily abandoned in England in the later Middle Ages. CANTERBURY CATHEDRAL has a number of crypts of various dates. (See also CHARNEL-HOUSE.)

Crystal Palace the centre-piece of the GREAT EXHIBITION (1851), originally erected on the south bank of the Serpentine, near where the Albert Hall was later built. Three years afterwards it was moved to Sydenham, where it was destroyed by fire in 1936. Made from a metal framework, over 600 yards long, filled with glass, it had the appearance of a huge GLASSHOUSE and was, indeed, designed by Sir Joseph Paxton, head gardener to the Duke of Devonshire. It was very important as a complete breakaway from traditional house-building materials. Since then both glass and metal have been increasingly used, and modern buildings are correspondingly more slender in design and admit more light.

Cuirass a piece of ARMOUR for the body reaching down to the waist and consisting of a breast-plate and a back-plate buckled or otherwise fastened together. Originally it was made of leather and then of metal plates. See also PECTORAL.

Culdees certain MONKS in Wales, Ireland and Scotland (the name being derived from *céli dé*, 'companions of God') whose earliest recorded occurrence is in the first half of the 9th century. By the 11th century they had become indistinguishable from secular CANONS and, as they were hopelessly corrupt, were gradually superseded by canons regular.

Cummin a popular medieval SPICE obtained from the HERB *cyminium*, cultivated in the Levant for its aromatic seeds. Cummin was much used for flavouring poultry. It is still used today, though not in such large quantities as during the Middle Ages. It has an important place in curry powder and also in the liqueur kümmel.

Cup and ball a game in which a ball is attached by a string to a stick surmounted by a shallow cup. The stick is held, cup uppermost, in one hand, and the aim is to move the stick so that the ball is swung and caught in the cup. Originally it seems to have been a children's game in France, called *bilboquet*, which became the craze of the nobility at the French court during the reign of Henry III (1575–89) and thence achieving general popularity throughout the country. It spread to England and became the vogue at the early Stuart court for a time. It was revived as a children's toy in the first part of the 19th century.

Cupboard originally in medieval houses the name given to an open shelf or board on which cups and other plate were set. In the 15th century the cupboard was sometimes provided with an enclosed space beneath the shelf as a receptacle for food, which had doors and was called an AUMBRY, but then became called a cupboard, and so the word acquired its modern meaning. Houses of the 16th century had court cupboards, in which the family kept plate, wine and table-linen, and livery cupboards, in which the servants kept their belongings. In the late 17th century, houses with new panelled rooms had cupboards built into the wall and also corner cupboards to store china. See also FURNITURE, BOOKCASE.

Curate formerly the name given to a clergyman having the 'cure' or charge of a PARISH in the CHURCH OF ENGLAND (i.e. a RECTOR or a VICAR); but nowadays the word is used of the assistant curate who helps the rector or vicar.

From 1662 to 1688 clergymen in charge of parishes in the CHURCH OF SCOTLAND were called curates.

Curfew the ringing of a BELL in towns to give warning that all fires must be put out (*couvre feu*) and lights extinguished as a precaution against conflagrations. It originated in Normandy at an early date and was partially instituted in England by Alfred (871–901), who is said to have ordered its use at the Carfax in Oxford. William I ordered after 1066 that it should be sounded at 8 o'clock every night. The curfew law was abolished by Henry I in 1100, but it continued in many places, probably because Pope John XXII (1316–34) ordered the evening *Hail Mary* to be said at the sound of the ANGELUS bell. The formal sounding of the curfew bell is still continued in some churches today.

Curricle a light, open two-wheeled CARRIAGE, drawn by two horses abreast and used in the 18th century for short journeys by private owners.

Curtain walls were lofty walls built round CASTLES from the mid-12th century for protection against the TREBUCHET, e.g. by Henry II at Dover and Windsor. These high walls blanketed the KEEP, reducing its usefulness and so bringing about its disappearance at this time. The use of MINES led to the provision of HOARDS and the building of WALL-TOWERS to protect the walls.

Cutlery was not used at Roman feasts because the food was cut up previously by slaves, and the guests ate with their fingers; and in the Middle Ages some people used knives and spoons, but only sparingly, and most relied much on their fingers, throwing the bones and scraps on to the RUSHES strewn on the floor for the dogs to eat. Men often carried their own knife in a sheath, but only well-bred people used it entirely for cutting up their meat. Finger-bowls were provided for guests or they washed before and after the meal. Forks were introduced from Italy in the mid-14th century, and Piers Gaveston in Edward II's reign (1307–27) had among his treasures several silver forks 'for eating pears', but they were not generally used until well into the 17th century and were generally two-pronged until the 19th century. See also PLATES, TABLE MANNERS.

D

Dame school a private elementary school for children, usually kept by a single teacher, often a woman, untrained and sometimes unlettered, as a means of getting a scanty living from the few pence paid by the parents. William Shenstone (1714–63) in *The School-Mistress* asserted that every village had such a school kept 'in lowly shed' by a 'matron old' who 'boasts unruly brats with birch to tame'. In the 19th century, for some time after the establishment of NATIONAL SCHOOLS and BRITISH SCHOOLS, many of the children of the labouring classes, who attended any sort of day school, were to be found in dame schools. In the 1830s, of 123 000 children attending elementary schools in Manchester, Salford, Bury, Liverpool and Birmingham, some 50 000 were pupils at dame schools. Most dame schools did, however, at least teach the children to read.

Damsel a girl of gentle birth sent to be brought up in a CASTLE as the companion of the daughter of its noble owner. The duties of these damsels were to make sure that she was never left alone with a man and to join her in DANCING and GAMES. This was to their own social advantage and also provided a means for their education. They slept in the BOWER together with a respectable widow, who also kept an eye on their behaviour all day. Each damsel hoped to marry a household KNIGHT and rule his MANOR, when his father died.

Dancing was a favourite medieval recreation among all classes, although it was forbidden to the CLERGY, NUNS and students at the UNIVERSITIES. MORRIS DANCES, sword dances, and other country dances were performed at CHRISTMAS, MAY DAY and other HOLIDAYS. After a banquet, there was commonly dancing through the night until daybreak, with intervals for refreshment, often WINE and SPICES. SERVANTS also were allowed to dance on special occasions, often to the TIMBREL.

In the 16th century, new dances developed at court and fashionable balls. These included the 'dumps', slow dances with sombre tunes, a stately processional dance known as the pavan, and the galliard, a quick dance with five steps sometimes called the cinquepace. Many foreigners, however, found the English way of dancing strange. A Spaniard at Queen Mary's court, said it was 'not at all graceful', but to 'consist simply of prancing and trotting'.

The PURITANS condemned dancing as 'the science of heathen devilry', but it did not disappear during the COMMONWEALTH. Oliver Cromwell himself danced at his daughter's wedding in 1657 to an orchestra which accompanied 'mixt dancing', and the 'mirth and frolics' lasted until five in the morning. After the RESTORATION, dancing became popular at court

and elsewhere. Pepys in 1666 witnessed 'many French dances, specially one the king called the New Dance, which was very pretty'; this was probably the minuet.

In the 18th century frequent balls were held in ASSEMBLY ROOMS at the SPAS and other places, the minuet being the great dance. There was no frequent change of partners as nowadays. Each lady placed her FAN on the table and had to dance the whole evening with the man who selected it from many.

So far the country dances had been popular at balls, but in the 19th century their popularity at last declined, except for the 'Sir Roger de Coverley' which was often used to close a ball. This was the century of new dances. The waltz first appeared at ALMACKS in 1815; it is said to have been introduced by Princess Lieven, the wife of the Russian Ambassador, and it was considered shocking, especially by the EVANGELICALS, because of its possible 'licentious consequences'. The quadrille also came in about this period (and the later 'Lancers' developed from it); and *Hints on Etiquette* (1836) said, 'Lead the lady through the quadrille; do not *drag* her, nor clasp her hand.' About this time as well there was a rage for the polka, and a writer in *The Times* complained 'the ladies dance polkas in their bathing dresses'. By the 1840s these three dances were fashionable, and later in the century came the Barn Dance.

In the early 20th century there were ballrooms for the wealthy, but the rest had only 'penny-dances' in a room at the back of an INN; but after 1918 dance halls opened in nearly every town. New dances came from USA in the 1920s—the foxtrot and the racy Charleston which combined to produce the quickstep; and the Latin American tango and rumba were also popular, while in 1937 the jitterbug developed to match the complicated rhythms of swing music, to be followed in the

1950s by jive, rock 'n' roll and cha-cha-cha and in the 1960s by the twist. Nowadays, 5 000 000 people go dancing at least once a week in 4000 dance halls and 4000 dancing schools, while 5 000 000 people watch ballroom dancing competitions on TELEVISION. Recently there has been revived interest in 'old time' and country dancing with the encouragement of the Folk Dance and Song Society. [A. L. Haskell, *The Story of Dance* (1960)]. See also BALLET, GUITAR.

Danes were the most numerous of the VIKINGS who settled in England. They made two important contributions to the making of England. First, they restored TOWN life (e.g. London and the Five Boroughs—Derby, Lincoln, Leicester, Stamford and Nottingham—of the DANE-LAW), preferring to live in larger communities than the ANGLO-SAXONS. Second, they opened up overseas trade (e.g. from Chester with Ireland; from Norwich with the Baltic; and from the south-east ports with Normandy and the Rhineland). [Arthur Bryant, *Makers of the Realm* (1953)]

Danegeld was an occasional tax on land originally levied in 991 by Ethelred II to buy off the DANES and several times subsequently. Abolished by Edward the Confessor, it was revived by William the Conqueror and regularly levied until 1163.

Danelaw the name given to the greater part of eastern England which was settled by the DANES in the 9th century. It consisted of about half of England between the Tees and the Thames and east of a line along the eastern borders of Oxfordshire, Warwickshire, Staffordshire and Cheshire. Independent Danish rule over it ended in 954, but details of law and land-holding long remained different in this area from those in the rest of England. See also WATLING STREET.

Darts is a very old game and is known to have been played by young Londoners on HOLIDAYS at least as early as the 12th century. It probably started as a pastime in English INNS where the round ends of beer-barrels provided the first boards, and the earliest darts were primitive spikes with feather flights bound to them.

Davenport a small desk named after Captain Davenport, a customer of the firm of Gillow of Lancaster, for whom the first one seems to have been executed in the late 18th century. It was small, compact and ingenious, being 18–24 inches wide, convenient to use and provided with plenty of space for storage. Its chief

Davenport

characteristics were a sloping top, enclosing a fitted well, supported on a CHEST-OF-DRAWERS, usually with four long drawers, running right through from side to side and pulling out on the right-hand side, and matching dummy drawer-fronts on the other side. The woods most commonly used in its manufacture were WALNUT, MAHOGANY, ROSEWOOD and SATINWOOD. In the 19th century it was often used by ladies in the DRAWING-ROOM or BOUDOIR.

Dean the head of an English CATHE-DRAL or COLLEGIATE CHURCH, who controls its services and, together with the CHAPTER, supervises its fabric and property. In a few cathedrals, the head has the title of PROVOST. See also RURAL DEAN.

Demesne the land in a medieval MANOR retained by the lord and not held by free tenants or VILLEINS.

Dentistry is known to have been practised by early man. The Romans developed considerable skill in dentistry, using gold bindings for teeth in the 5th century BC, but most of their knowledge was lost in the Middle Ages, when tooth-drawing was practised by barbers (see SURGEONS). It became a distinct branch of MEDICINE in the mid-19th century. A dental HOSPITAL was opened in London in 1858. Modern dentistry developed after the introduction of ANAESTHETICS. Vulcanized rubber was used for making dental plates from 1855 and PORCELAIN teeth came into use shortly afterwards.

Deportment was thought very important in the education of girls in the Middle Ages. When seated they were expected to keep their hands crossed on their lap and were told in a book of ETIQUETTE, 'If you are walking out, go with your head turned straight forward, your eyelids low and fixed, and your look straight before you down to the ground at twelve yards, without turning your eyes on man or woman, to the right or to the left, or staring upwards, or moving your eyes about from one place to another, or laughing, or stopping to talk to anyone in the streets.'

Later centuries placed the same emphasis on their bearing, demeanour and manners. The young Lady Jane Grey in the 16th century was punished (she said) if she did not do everything 'in such weight, measure and number, even so perfectly as God made the world'; and a Royalist father in the 1660s whipped his daughter aged 7 several times for her 'rolling, untidy gait', 'wild carriage of the head' and 'wild, unhandsome laughing'; and in the next century a girl of 16 'has as many strokes of the rod merely for curtseying too stiffly'.

Indeed, in the 18th century the fashionable GIRLS' SCHOOLS spent much time in teaching their pupils to perform gracefully such actions as standing, rising, sitting down, walking and curtseying. A school in Queen Square, Bloomsbury, London, had an old COACH taken to pieces and rebuilt in an upper room so that the girls might practise the art of getting in and out of it in a ladylike manner. In some schools girls were made to march up and down a room, each with a book on her head, to make them walk gracefully. The rules of other schools compelled them to walk always with their hands crossed behind their backs and would not allow them to lean against the back of a chair when they sat down or to touch the bannisters when they went up and down stairs. Girls who stooped had their arms strapped to their sides or had to wear the BACKBOARD, while those who did not sit properly were put in the STOCKS; and the future Queen Victoria, as a girl, had a bodkin or a bunch of holly stuck in the BODICE of her dress to make her hold herself upright and was punished if she pricked her chin on it.

The purpose of such severe training in deportment was expressed in a book of instruction for girls in the early 19th century, which said, 'A young lady is known by her manners and carriage. She must be ladylike in all that she does. If she does this, she may not be praised but she will certainly be condemned if she does not.'

Deserted villages of which there are probably several thousand in England, are VILLAGES which were abandoned by their inhabitants for various reasons in the course of history. Detailed study of their sites did not begin until this century, but now aerial surveying is revealing many, though few have yet been marked on maps.

The causes of the desertion of villages are many. The BLACK DEATH, despite what has been commonly supposed, seems only to have caused the evacuation of comparatively few of the sites known. In the Middle Ages, a monastery might compel villagers to move in order to create a sheep pasture, e.g. Balmer (Sussex); and later ENCLOSURES in the later 15th and early 16th centuries had the same effect. Parliament in 1489 passed an Act 'against pulling down of towns', asserting that 'in some towns two hundred persons were occupied and lived by their lawful neighbours [but] now be there occupied two or three herdsmen and the residue fallen in idleness'.

During the 18th century, the new fashion in GARDENS led landowners to destroy villages within their park, e.g. Albury (Surrey), Nuneham Courtenay (Oxon.); a new village was usually built beyond the park wall. In more recent times, the main part of a village might be moved from its original site to border a main highway, e.g. Mountnessing (Essex) or be near a railway station, e.g. Fambridge (Essex). [M. W. Beresford, *The Lost Villages of England* (1954)]

Dewponds round, saucer-like artificial ponds designed for sheep on the dry chalk uplands, especially of Sussex and Wiltshire, where there are no springs. They are filled by dew or rain-water draining into them from a large sloping area around, and they may have originated as early as the NEW STONE AGE.

Diabolo a wooden reel spun on a cord tied to two sticks held one in each hand, the aim of the game being to throw the diabolo into the air as many times as possible, catch it and rotate it skilfully on the cord each time without allowing it to touch the ground. It was a craze in England between 1910 and 1914 and was a revival of *diable*, a French game which was popular from 1790 to 1800.

Diamonds have long been prized as jewellery. Among the presents given by the Earl of Leicester to Elizabeth I were a diamond bracelet, a diamond chain and a gold purse garnished with diamonds. Diamonds formerly came from the East; Brazil became an important diamond-producing country in the mid-18th century, but was overtaken by South Africa in the late 19th century. The diamonds worn in Europe were uncut until 1476, when John de Berghem of Bruges discovered the art of diamond-cutting, though it had been practised from early times in India. In the Middle Ages the CORAL was a fashionable stone and during the RENAISSANCE the PEARL, but ever since the reign of Louis XIV (1638–1715) the diamond has been supreme.

Diggers were a small group of revolutionaries founded by Gerrard Winstanley early in the COMMONWEALTH. They held that the common people should own the land without paying rent, and in 1649 began to assert this right by digging up the common at St George's Hill, Walton-on-Thames (Surrey). They were suppressed by the army. See also LEVELLERS.

Dinner-jacket first appeared at the gaming-tables at Monte Carlo in 1898 and in the early years of the 20th century became accepted for informal evening parties and dinners and in the 1920s for public evening occasions.

Diocese is the area governed by a BISHOP and taking its name from the CATHEDRAL town. By the beginning of the 16th century the English dioceses were Canterbury, York, Bath and Wells, Carlisle, Chichester, Lichfield, Durham, Ely, Exeter, Hereford, Lincoln, London, Norwich, Rochester, Salisbury, Winchester, and Worcester. In 1540 Henry VIII created Bristol, Chester, Gloucester, Oxford, Peterborough, and Westminster (which only lasted 10 years). Since then, these dioceses have been added: Birmingham (1905), Blackburn (1926), Bradford (1919), Chelmsford (1914), Coventry (1918), Derby (1927), Guildford (1927), Leicester (1926), Liverpool (1880), Manchester (1847), Newcastle (1882), Portsmouth (1927), Ripon (1836), St Albans (1877), St Edmundsbury and Ipswich (1914), Sheffield (1914), Southwark (1905), Southwell (1884), Truro (1877), and Wakefield (1888).

Directory of Public Worship was compiled by the Westminster Assembly of PURITAN divines (meeting in WESTMINSTER ABBEY) which was appointed by the Long Parliament in 1643 to reform the CHURCH OF ENGLAND. It was designed on PRESBYTERIAN principles to replace the Book of COMMON PRAYER, though containing general instructions rather than set forms of service. It was ordered by Parliament to be used in churches in 1645.

Disruption the great split which occurred in the CHURCH OF SCOTLAND in 1843 over the question of lay patronage, when over a third of the CLERGY left to form the Free Church of Scotland in which each congregation had the right to choose its own minister. Patronage was abolished in 1874, but complete reunion was not achieved until 1929. See also ADVOWSON

Dissenters, see NONCONFORMISTS.

Dissenting Academies originated in the prohibition against NONCONFORMISTS

teaching in GRAMMAR SCHOOLS or studying at the UNIVERSITIES from 1662. Their educational standards were somewhere between those of grammar schools and universities. They trained candidates for the dissenting ministries, but also taught mathematics, modern languages and other new subjects demanded by the trading classes. Some of the most progressive academies, e.g. Stoke Newington (where Samuel Wesley, senior, was educated and Dr Richard Price later taught) and Warrington (where Joseph Priestley taught) gave instruction in scientific and technical subjects. Such academies contributed a modernizing element to English education, though their importance has been exaggerated. [N. Hans, *New Trends in Education in the Eighteenth Century* (1951)]

Dissolution of the monasteries in England was presaged in 1535 when Thomas Cromwell, newly-appointed Vicar-General for ecclesiastical matters, and his agents made a hurried visitation of a number of MONASTERIES and reported them to be in an evil condition. In 1536 Parliament approved the suppression of all houses with an annual value of less than £200, some 200 in number. This was followed by a rising, the PILGRIMAGE OF GRACE, in Yorkshire and Lincolnshire. Many greater houses were persuaded to surrender themselves to the Crown 1537–40, and Parliament authorized the suppression of the rest in 1539. The last house surrendered in the spring of 1540.

MONKS, but not FRIARS, were pensioned, and many became parochial clergymen; NUNS, who were not allowed to marry until Edward VI's reign, had only meagre pensions. The Crown obtained vast lands from the monasteries, most of which were sold to the nobility and gentry, but six new DIOCESES were founded.

There was no similar dissolution in

Scotland and no systematic destruction of the monastic system at the REFORMATION. Monastic life came to an end, but monks not entering the PRESBYTERIAN ministry were generally allowed to remain in the monasteries until they died, and then the monasteries were suppressed and secularized; but friaries were commonly granted to BURGHS for educational and like purposes, and the friars received pensions. [G. Baskerville, *English Monks and the Suppression of the Monasteries* (1937); M. D. Knowles, *The Religious Orders in England*, III (1959)]

Divorce in the sense of the dissolution of a valid MARRIAGE, was only possible by the passing of a special private Act of Parliament until 1857; but the ECCLESIASTICAL COURTS, which alone administered the matrimonial law, might grant a decree of nullity (a declaration that a marriage was null and void) or a 'divorce *a mensa et thoro*' (i.e. banishment from bed and board, which did not, however, dissolve the marriage, but gave judicial sanction for the couple to live apart from each other). The Matrimonial Causes Act (1857) transferred jurisdiction in matrimonial affairs to a civil court and allowed divorce, in the modern sense, for adultery. The grounds for divorce have been steadily extended in 1923, 1925, 1937, 1950, 1963 and 1969.

Dogs were certainly known in NEW STONE AGE times, the oldest complete skeleton of a dog having been found at WINDMILL HILL; it was a fox-terrier type. ROMAN BRITAIN was renowned for its mastiffs, which were used in the Gallic wars. In medieval England dogs were used mainly for sport—spaniels to pick up birds in FALCONRY, GREYHOUNDS for coursing hares, bull-dogs in BULL-BAITING; and ladies had pet lap-dogs, Maltese spaniels being the favourite. National Kennel Club registrations show

that today the favourite dogs in Britain are (in order) miniature poodles, toy poodles and Welsh corgis; and there are 700 000 dogs in London alone. An ANGLO-SAXON remedy for a mad dog's bite stated, 'Boil and eat the head of the mad dog that bit you.' [C. G. Trew, *The Story of the Dog and his Uses to Mankind* (1940).] See also HUNTING.

Dog-cart a two-wheeled CARRIAGE with two seats back to back, so-called because the rear seat was originally made to shut so as to form a box for carrying sporting dogs.

Dog-whipper a PARISH officer sometimes appointed formerly to help the CHURCHWARDENS and the BEADLE maintain order and quiet in country churches when dogs were brought to services by their masters. If a dog became noisy, the dog-whipper took hold of it around the neck with a pair of wooden tongs and pulled it out of the church. This was especially common in country districts in Wales, and a few Welsh churches still have the dog-tongs hanging on a wall or pillar inside. Some churches also had a dog door, about 30 inches high, through which a dog could be ejected; one such door still survives at Mullion (Cornwall).

Dolls were among the TOYS of CHILDREN in Britain from earliest times and were mostly made of wood, though other materials, such as clay and wax, were also used. All were of men and women, principally women, child and baby dolls not becoming common until the middle of the 19th century. By the 17th century more expensive dolls were being made of rags or leather filled with bran or sawdust. Wax and porcelain dolls became common in the 18th century, and the first talking dolls appeared about 1830. Further realism, such as walking and drinking, has been a feature of modern dolls, and

1 Wooden doll in Puritan style; 2 19th-cent. mechanical doll with built in gramophone turntable and interchangeable discs; 3 Wax doll

they are made in almost indestructible plastic materials. [Gwen White, *Dolls European and American* (1966).] See also FASHION-DOLLS.

Doll's house started with the so-called Nürnberg kitchen imported into England from about 1650 to educate girls in housewifery. It consisted of three sides of a miniature KITCHEN, complete with floor, fireplace and dresser walls and fully fitted with usable scale models of fire-irons, turn-spits, basins, chopping blocks, flour barrels, etc. Other separate miniature rooms were being made by Queen Anne's reign (1702–14), but some seem to be masterpieces of craftsmanship rather than educational TOYS; and miniature shops became common in the 19th century.

Doll's houses may have developed by joining together the miniature rooms, but some were made in the 17th century. A Nürnberg doll's house, dated 1673, is in the collection in the Bethnal Green Museum. In England until about 1850 doll's houses were known as 'baby houses'. In *Gulliver's Travels* the hero had made for him by the Queen in Brobdingnag a minute apartment furnished with silver dishes and plates 'not much bigger than what I have seen of the same kind in a London toy-shop for the furniture of a baby-house'. They were individually designed, often by architects, such as the elegant Blackett house (c. 1740) and Lansdowne house (c. 1860) in the London Museum, and made by skilled craftsmen. Kept in glass cases, usually in the drawing-room, they were intended to be looked at by children, but not normally handled by them.

In the 19th century, doll's houses began to be smaller and less elaborate, intended for ordinary families and as playthings.

Dolly a contrivance, sometimes known as a 'posser', used from the later Middle Ages in LAUNDERING, consisting of a long wooden pole with a handle at the top and a wooden disc with three projecting prongs or arms at the bottom, which was operated in a deep dolly-tub (or poss-tub) for the purpose of stirring the clothes to loosen the dirt. The laundress or house wife pulled on the handle, driving the pole up and down to move the clothes against the side of the tub. In a modern electrical washing-machine the mechanical agitator performs the same service.

Dolmens are small burial chambers belonging to the NEW STONE AGE and generally consisting of a number of large stone slabs set edgewise in the earth to support a flat stone as a roof. They are most common in Scotland and Northern Ireland, but Kit's Coty House near Maidstone (Kent) is a well-known English example.

Domesday Book was compiled as the result of William I's decision (in order that he might know what obligations every landowner owed him) to send officials to survey all the land in England in 1086. Their reports were entered in Domesday Book at Winchester and give a full picture of the manorial system. It records the name of the holder of each MANOR and from whom he held it, the amount of woodland, meadow and pasture, the number of FREEMEN and VILLEINS, the extent of the estate and its value, its mills and fishponds and even its oxen, horses, sheep and pigs. Much of northern England was omitted, the entry 'Hoc est vasta' being a common entry and a reminder of the HARRYING OF THE NORTH. Otherwise Domesday Book includes by name almost every place in England. See also JURY, TOWNS.

Domestic system a common way of organizing industry before the INDUSTRIAL REVOLUTION. In the manufacture of cloth from WOOL, for instance, wealthy merchants (or clothiers) bought the wool from the sheep-farmers and took it to COTTAGES for SPINNING into yarn and WEAVING into cloth. The spinners and weavers usually owned their spinning-wheels and looms, though sometimes a clothier might supply them himself. When the cloth was finished, the clothier collected it from these workpeople, in return for an agreed payment, and then sold it. Other workmen, e.g. blacksmiths or joiners, worked in or close to their own homes; they were on their own and often helped by their own families. This system was largely superseded by the FACTORY SYSTEM.

Dominicans an order of FRIARS founded by a Spanish priest, St Dominic. He gathered followers to preach against HERESY, who became Dominican friars in 1218. The Dominicans built their first PRIORY in England at Oxford in 1221; their second English house was the Blackfriars in London. At the DISSOLUTION OF THE MONASTERIES, there were 58 Dominican houses in England and Wales.

Domino (1) formerly a cape with a HOOD worn by masters or priests, to protect the head and face in winter, of Italian origin and named from the Italian *domino*, master or teacher. In the 17th century it was the name given in England to a mourning-veil for women and in the 18th century to a masquerade-dress worn for disguise by ladies and gentlemen and consisting of a long, ample CLOAK or MANTLE, usually of black silk with wide sleeves and a hood, and commonly worn with a small half-mask over the upper part of the face at masked balls.

(2) The game of dominoes, played with black rectangular pieces of wood or ivory, was probably invented in Italy in the 18th century and played in English INNS from the middle of the 19th century.

Dorter the dormitory of a MONASTERY, usually situated on the eastern side of the CLOISTER and built over the CHAPTER HOUSE or its entrance vestibule. It was frequently linked by night stairs to the adjacent TRANSEPT so that the MONKS had direct access to the CHURCH for their night services; such night stairs are still to be seen at Hexham Abbey (Northumberland). There was also always direct communication between the dorter and the REREDORTER. Good remaining BENEDICTINE dorters exist at WESTMINSTER ABBEY and Durham Cathedral, the latter being 194 ft long.

Doublet a close-fitting, waisted, padded jacket with tight sleeves worn by men next to the SHIRT. It was introduced into England from France in the 14th century and continued to be worn by all classes until about 1670. Its skirts varied from very narrow to covering the hips according to the fashion of the day and in the 17th century consisted of a series of tabs of varying depth. At first the doublet was low-necked, but after about 1540 it had a standing collar, and by this time the front was often partly open so that a STOMACHER had to be worn as well. See also BOMBAST, COAT.

Dovecote a small house elevated considerably above the ground and divided into compartments in which tame pigeons breed. In the Middle Ages only the lord of a MANOR was allowed to have a dovecote so that he might have fresh meat in the shape of squabs or young pigeons which could be lifted from the stone nesting-compartments, since wood pigeons were not easily taken before the invention of HAND-GUNS. His pigeons might not be killed even if they were eating crops.

The oldest known dovecote is one incorporated into the structure of Rochester Castle which was built about 1080. The great dovecote of the HOSPITALLERS, alongside the church at Garway (Herefordshire) has 600 nesting-compartments, while the dovecote, built about 1600, among the monastic buildings of Penmon (Anglesey) has 1000. Sometimes a cheap dovecote was made by walling across a convenient cave or fissure and fitting it with nesting-boxes, such as Culver Hole in a limestone cliff of Gower, near Port Eynon (South Wales).

Dragoons were CAVALRY who were armed with a kind of CARBINE called a 'dragoon'. The first regiment of dragoons was raised in England in 1681, and they were used to assist in putting down SMUGGLING.

Drawbridge came comparatively late in CASTLE construction. The early MOTTE or mound castles had a timber entrance bridge over the ditch often with a removable section of a few planks which could be drawn back into the castle in time of siege. In the 13th century came the 'turning bridge' pivoted, like a seesaw, on an axle and made to swing into a vertical position by heavy weights

attached to the inner edge of the bridge which sank into curved slots at the end of the bridge—and are still to be seen in the GATEHOUSE of Bungay (Suffolk). Later the counterpoise was abolished, and the outer corners of the bridge were attached to chains so that it could be raised by a windlass in a chamber over the entrance passage, e.g. at Manorbier (Pembroke). Later still the chains were attached to the ends of two arms projecting from above the entrance arch, and the slots for these may still be seen in the walls of later castle gatehouses, e.g. at Hurstmonceux (Sussex). These arms were the projecting sides of a sliding door pivoted above the arch and acted as a counterpoise to the bridge, the door being down when the bridge was raised and up close to the roof of the entrance passage when the bridge was down. [Hugh Braun, *The English Castle* (2nd. ed., 1943)]

Drawers an UNDERGARMENT which developed for men in the 16th century from the earlier BRAIES, being usually of LINEN and in the 19th century of WOOL and either knee-length or ankle-length. Later in the 19th century they developed into underpants and then into the more modern shorts and trunks.

Drawers were worn by Frenchwomen as early as the 16th century, but not by Englishwomen until the coming of the NAKED FASHION and not generally until much later. When CRINOLINES were worn, scarlet flannel drawers were fashionable and were often exposed to view (see also PANTALETTES). Later there were two main types—closed knickerbockers (later called 'knickers') and an open-leg type known as 'French drawers'. Towards the end of the 19th century, the latter became almost as wide as PETTICOATS and were frilled and elaborately trimmed. By about 1920 open-leg drawers had disappeared, and knickers remained fashionable, but by 1924 they were often shortened to 'panties' and by 1930 to 'trunks' from which developed the modern 'briefs'.

Drawing room originally withdrawing room, originated in the later 16th century in great HOUSES as the room to which the family withdrew on private occasions. In 18th-century houses it was often placed alongside the SALOON and communicated with it by double doors. See also SOLAR.

Dressing-table dates from about 1630 as an article of FURNITURE in a lady's bedroom or dressing-room. Dressing-tables in the 17th century were small tables with two or three drawers to contain COSMETICS. Later elaborate toilet-sets were made for them, comprising SILVER boxes for COMBS and brushes, powder and PERFUMES. JEWELLERY was kept in caskets. MIRRORS were made with supports to stand on the top; and there might also be a glue-pot with which to stick on PATCHES. In the early 18th century dressing-tables were often draped, while in the mid-century fashion favoured the key-hole style which had a long top drawer fitted with boxes and compartments and a central CUPBOARD flanked by three short, deep drawers on either side. [Ralph Fastnedge, *English Furniture Styles 1500–1830* (1955)]

Drinks before the days of ROMAN BRITAIN are known to include MEAD and ALE, the latter being sold in the Middle Ages at TAVERNS and indicated by an ALE-STAKE; it became BEER when HOPS were added. It was commonly drunk in a BLACK-JACK; and CHURCH ALES were a favourite form of celebration.

Among WINES, CLARET was popular in the Middle Ages, and so was HIPPOCRAS. SACK and MALMSEY were favourites in the 16th century, while CHAMPAGNE, PORT and BRANDY appeared in the next century. MADEIRA and MARSALA came in the 18th century. SHERRY and COCKTAILS are the appetizers of the 20th century.

RUM first appeared in the 17th century, while GROG and GIN were drinks of the 18th century. The 19th century popularized WHISKY and also SODA WATER.

MILK was not at first drunk as much as WHEY. COFFEE came to England in the 17th century and soon afterwards TEA, which was dear and kept in a CADDY. CHOCOLATE was also a drink of the 17th century, but COCOA was not drunk until the 19th century. In order to promote temperance, such drinks were encouraged and DRINKING-FOUNTAINS were erected. In the Middle Ages CONDUITS sometimes ran with wine. See also WASSAIL.

Drinking-fountains in public places mostly were erected in Victorian times, being the gift of prominent people wanting to encourage temperance and reduce the risk of infection from diseases (especially CHOLERA)caused by drinking impure water.

Drove roads were old-established tracks used by drovers to drive livestock from the country to MARKET until the coming of the RAILWAY. Most drove roads had INNS to accommodate the drovers and BLACKSMITHS to shoe the cattle, but other traffic tended to avoid them because of the badness of the surface through the continual passing of animals. As London grew, an increasing number of beasts were sent to SMITHFIELD. Cattle from the HIGHLANDS of Scotland were driven as store beasts down to pastures of Lincolnshire and later on when fat to London. Many Welsh cattle were also sent to England, and the drove road from Tregaron (Card.) to Abergwesyn may still be seen. [John Higgs, *The Land* (1964).] See also GOOSE.

Druids were an order of priests among the CELTS of Britain, Gaul and Germany. They regarded the mistletoe as sacred, especially when growing on OAK trees, and practised sacrifice, animal and human, but little is known of them except from Julius Caesar. They were national leaders of resistance to the establishment of ROMAN BRITAIN, and their centre at Anglesey was destroyed in AD 61. The HENGES were not Druid temples.

Drum is an ancient musical instrument, but the most important type, the kettledrum, was introduced into Europe from the East during the CRUSADES, and from then until the mid-16th century they were known as 'nakers', which was derived from the Turkish word *naqquareh*. French influence made them fashionable, together with the TRUMPET, in England after the RESTORATION. In 1661 Pepys went to WHITEHALL to hear the drums 'which are much cried up, though I think it dull, vulgar musique'. See also TIMBREL.

Dry-cleaning invented in France in 1849 by a tailor in Paris, Jolly-Bellin, who upset turpentine from a lamp on a table-cloth and found that the soaked part was cleaner than the rest. In his dry-cleaning process, he took the garment to pieces and cleaned each section separately in a pan of turpentine. The pieces were then brushed, dipped again and dried to get rid of the smell. Finally, the garment was sewn together again. In 1866 Pullars of Perth, who had been dyers for about 40 years, began a postal dry-cleaning service in Britain and soon afterwards improved the process by using a mixture of petrol, benzine and benzol and discarded the practice of unpicking and remaking the garment.

Dry walls stone walls built without mortar in northern England, usually erected by farmers assisted by expert dry-wallers. Short and often crooked stretches were built near farmhouses in the 17th century when individual farming began, and small portions of land were walled in and agreements made with neighbouring CROFTERS. Larger and higher walls, straddling the moors and surrounding larger fields, were put up at the time of the ENCLOSURES in the late 18th and early 19th centuries. All were made from local stones since as the newly claimed land was tilled, stones were unearthed and used in building the boundary walls.

Ducking-stool a punishment in England for gossipping and quarrelsome women and for dishonest ale-wives. The offender was tied to a chair fixed at the end of a plank and ducked in the water. The Westminster ducking-pond occupied the site of part of Trafalgar Square. A ducking-stool is mentioned in DOMESDAY BOOK as in use in Chester. The punishment became general in the 15th century and prevailed until about 1750. The last recorded ducking of a woman was at Leominster in 1809.

Duels arose from the practice of TRIAL BY BATTLE introduced at the NORMAN CONQUEST. The first formal duel in England was between William, Count of Eu, and Godfrey Baynard (1096); but duelling did not become fashionable until the RESTORATION, though a royal proclamation in 1679 denied pardon to anyone who killed another in a duel. Duels were fought by Wilkes (1763), Byron (1765), Fox (1779), Pitt (1796), Castlereagh and Canning (1809) and Wellington (1829). In the 19th century the Prince Consort was strongly opposed to duelling, and public opinion led to its discontinuance. The weapon used for duelling was usually the small sword until the 19th century, when the PISTOL became more common.

Dulcimer one of the oldest musical instruments, was a primitive form of

PIANO, consisting of wires stretched across a flat box-like frame and played by striking them with hammers held in the hand. It is mentioned in English literature from the late 14th century onwards, but by the 17th century it seems to have become rare, and Pepys (who was interested in musical instruments) first heard one played (at a PUPPET show) when he was nearly 30 in 1662.

Dunce's cap a cone-shaped cap, sometimes with the letter 'D' on it, worn by a dunce at school. The name 'dunce' was introduced by the Thomists (disciples of Thomas Aquinas) in ridicule of the Scotists (disciples of Duns Scotus, d. 1308). When wearing the cap, the dunce was commonly made to stand before the rest of the class and, if whipped, hold the BIRCH-ROD. See also HEADBAND, PLACARD, WHISPERING-STICK.

E

Ealdorman was an ANGLO-SAXON official of the rank of THEGN, who was placed by kings in charge of one or more SHIRES. He kept law and order, commanded the local military forces and sat with the BISHOP in the shire MOOT. From the early 9th century many of his powers were taken over by the SHERIFF and later his title was superseded by that of EARL.

Ear-rings of bone or wood were worn by early peoples. Rich Roman ladies wore PEARL ear-rings that were sometimes so heavy that they distorted the shape of their ears. The early ANGLO-SAXONS wore them, but then they were abandoned for centuries. In the late 14th century Continental ladies wore rings of GOLD, but they were very uncommon in England because of the shape of the HATS of the time. They were introduced into England from Spain in the late 16th century, being worn by both sexes, but abandoned by men (except for some seamen) after the RESTORATION.

Earl was a title introduced into England by the DANES. In the DANELAW the earls performed much the same duties as the EALDORMEN, who were placed by ANGLO-SAXON kings in charge of the SHIRES. In the 11th century the title of earl superseded that of ealdorman. It continued after the NORMAN CONQUEST, and from the 12th century became a hereditary title rather than a position. See also BARONS.

Easter the Feast of the Resurrection of Christ, the greatest and oldest festival of the Christian Church, which superseded an old pagan spring festival. It falls on the first Sunday after the first full moon that occurs on or after the spring equinox (21 March). In the Middle Ages it was sometimes called Egg Sunday because of the custom of taking EGGS, hardened by boiling and coloured, to be blessed by the clergy as symbols of rebirth and so the Resurrection. A record of the 13th century relates that Edward I order 400 painted eggs to be distributed as presents to the royal household. These were known as 'Pask, Paste or Pace Eggs', the derivation being from Pasch, the name for the Jewish Passover, celebrated at the same time as Easter. These eggs were tinged with various colours, but in England the favourite hue was green from a dye distilled from the pasque flower (an anemone blooming about Easter).

In some parts of the country eggs are rolled down a hillside at Easter, but elsewhere this is done on GOOD FRIDAY. See also TANSY.

Ecclesiastical Commission a permanent body, consisting of BISHOPS and certain lay members appointed by the Crown and the Archbishop of Canterbury, created in 1835 by Act of Parliament through the efforts of Sir Robert Peel to hold much of the property of the CHURCH OF ENGLAND and make better use of it. The Commission abolished sinecures, diminished the CHAPTERS of CATHEDRALS, brought the incomes of bishops nearer to equality and increased the endowments of poor PARISHES. In 1948 it was united with QUEEN ANNE'S BOUNTY to form a new body, the Church Commissioners for England.

Ecclesiastical Courts usually presided over by the BISHOP or an ARCH-DEACON in each DIOCESE, existed in the Middle Ages to try laypeople for spiritual offences such as blasphemy or HERESY and the CLERGY for disciplinary offences and any FELONY except treason. The CHURCH OF ENGLAND continued to have its ecclesiastical courts after the REFORMA-TION, but their powers were reduced, and later CANON LAW ceased to apply to lay people. See also PENANCE, COUNTY COURT.

Education in the Middle Ages was largely in the hands of the Church. Boys were taught in the ALMONRY SCHOOLS

attached to the larger MONASTERIES and also by some CHANTRY priests. At the REFORMATION, many of these schools became GRAMMAR SCHOOLS or PETTY SCHOOLS and later PUBLIC SCHOOLS. Medieval teaching was accomplished with the aid of the HORN-BOOK, FESCUE and BIRCHROD.

From the late 17th century poor children were taught in CHARITY SCHOOLS, DAME SCHOOLS and later SUNDAY SCHOOLS. The 19th century brought for them BRITISH SCHOOLS and NATIONAL SCHOOLS and RAGGED SCHOOLS, as well as new schools for the wealthier, including the 'WOODARD SCHOOLS'. Action by the state came with the ELEMENTARY EDUCATION ACT (1870), EDUCATION ACT (1880), EDU-CATION ACT (1902) and EDUCATION ACT (1944). The latest development has been the growth of COMPREHENSIVE SCHOOLS.

The first GIRLS' SCHOOLS were founded in the 17th century, and later there were FINISHING SCHOOLS, but until quite recently many girls were taught at home by a GOVERNESS.

UNIVERSITIES were founded in the Middle Ages, but for a time in the 18th century the wealthier classes preferred the GRAND TOUR. In the 19th century MECHANICS' INSTITUTES provided educa-tion for the working-classes. Nowadays there has been a great extension of the universities and the development of POLYTECHNICS and TECHNOLOGICAL UNI-VERSITIES. [J. W. Adamson, *A Short History of Education* (1930); S. J. Curtis, *History of Education in Great Britain* (4th ed., 1957)]

Education Act (1880) supplemented the ELEMENTARY EDUCATION ACT (1870) by making school attendance up to the age of 10 years compulsory. At 10 a child could obtain an educational certificate entitling him to leave school, but if he had registered too few attendances he had to go on to 13.

Education Act (1902) abolished the School Boards set up by the ELEMENTARY EDUCATION ACT (1870), made the county and county borough councils the local authorities for all secondary and technical education and gave them the same position for elementary education too, except that here the councils of larger non-county boroughs and urban districts were to be the authorities within their areas. It also brought under the new authorities both the board schools and the Church schools, the current expenses of which were now paid out of the local rates.

Education Act (1944) reduced the number of Local Education Authorities from 315 to 146 by making the county and county borough councils the local authorities for education. The Board of Education (founded in 1899) became the Department of Education. It established universal free secondary education (from the age of 12) and abolished all fees in maintained schools. Religious education and a daily act of worship were declared obligatory in every school.

Eggs were eaten in huge quantities in medieval households. The Countess of Leicester's account-book shows 1000 for Easter Day 1265 and nearly 4000 for the following week. Many were used in cooking such dishes as FRUMENTY. In both the Middle Ages and later, because of their cheapness, they were also much eaten by the poorer classes. Egg-consumption per person has risen in Britain from 104 in 1909 to 152 in 1934 and to 240 in 1968. See also EASTER.

Electricity was known as far back as the ancient Greeks, but was not used for power or lighting until the 19th century. In 1821 the English physicist, Michael Faraday, made the first electric motor, but these were not developed on a commercial scale until the 1870s. Electric

LIGHTING began to develop after 1879 when Joseph Wilson Swan produced the first filament lamp. Before then some public buildings had been lit by arc lamps. In 1881 the first private house was fitted with an electric lighting system in Godalming (Surrey), and the first electric street lighting was installed in London near the Bank of England. Small battery-torches were in common use by 1914.

Electric cookers were on show at the CRYSTAL PALACE Exhibition of 1891, and electric toasters, kettles and fires had appeared by 1895, but the first fires looked like radiators, and the common electric bar-fire did not appear until 1908. The VACUUM CLEANER had appeared by then. The electric mixer came in 1920, quickly followed by the washing-machine, hairdryer, domestic immersion heater and domestic REFRIGERATOR. Electric RAZORS came to Britain in the early 1930s. [Percy Dunsheath, *A History of Electrical Engineering* (1953)]

Electric cars were made possible by Gaston Planté's invention of the accumulator or storage battery in 1859. They appeared in USA, France and Britain by 1890 and within 10 years were a commercial proposition. There were electric TAXI-CABS and delivery vans, but especially elegant BROUGHAMS, which were particularly liked by women drivers because they were clean, silent, smooth-running and easy to drive; they were often fitted out luxuriously inside with stuffed seats, silk curtains and flower vases. All electric cars, however, could only make short journeys since the accumulator needed recharging, and much of its power was required just to move its own weight. With the introduction of the self-starter on MOTOR CARS, electric cars gradually ceased to be made from about 1914. They have advantages, however, for use as trollies, delivery vans and milk-floats.

Elementary Education Act (1870) provided that, where there was a shortage of schools, School Boards were to be elected with powers to establish and maintain elementary schools by levying rates, charging fees and receiving government grants. The religious teaching in these Board Schools was not to be 'distinctive of any particular denomination'. The School Boards could, if they wished, make bye-laws compelling children to attend school between the ages of 5 and 12. NATIONAL SCHOOLS, BRITISH SCHOOLS and other voluntary schools were to receive a 50 per cent grant from the government, but building grants were discontinued.

Ell a popular measure of length before the wide adoption of the metric system on the continent especially for cloth, both in Britain and abroad. It was, however, of no definite length. The English ell was officially 45 in., the Scottish 37·2 in., the Flemish 27 in. and the French 54 in. In the 18th century ell wands were in common use, but these were often 27 in. rather than 45 in. because the Flemish ell was adopted by many other Continental countries and was largely used in England for measuring SILK and other imported cloth. Hence the saying, 'Give him an inch and he will take an ell'.

Embroidery has long been an occupation practised especially by WOMEN, who were highly skilled at it in the Middle Ages, as shown by the BAYEUX TAPESTRY and the Syon COPE (now in the Victoria and Albert Museum). NUNS spent much time embroidering VESTMENTS, and in the later Middle Ages embroidery was used for the devices of HERALDRY. In the Elizabethan period the appearance of printed pattern-books encouraged ladies to use it for many domestic purposes, and it was an important subject in the first GIRLS' SCHOOLS of the 17th century. In the 18th century there was much embroidery on women's COSTUME, FANS, GLOVES and SHOES as well as on men's WAISTCOATS, but in the 19th century it was more often confined to PETTICOATS and such objects as cushions, fire-screens and ANTIMACASSARS. In the 19th century also girls had to make samplers to show the various stitches they knew, and on them they embroidered their own names and ages, letters of the alphabet and numbers, patterns and verses or texts. [Therle Hughes, *English Domestic Needlework* (1961)]

Emigrés the name given to the royalist refugees who fled from France during the French Revolution. Some 8000 of these émigrés came to Britain during the 1790s, and funds were raised for their support by parliamentary grants and private subscriptions. Among them were many French noblemen and also a number of bishops and clergymen. French noblewomen opened fashionable GIRLS' SCHOOLS in London and elsewhere. See also SMUGGLING.

Enclosures both of waste and of land used under the OPEN FIELD SYSTEM, occurred in the 16th century in order to increase production of both food to feed the growing POPULATION and WOOL to supply the prosperous cloth industry. The greatest number of enclosures took place in the Midlands, where perhaps 30 per cent of the arable land was enclosed; and for England as a whole some 3 or 4 per cent. Contemporary complaints about the destruction of VILLAGES and the depopulation of the countryside were probably exaggerated, but the enclosures in the Midlands undoubtedly caused unemployment and social unrest (see PILGRIMAGE OF GRACE).

Despite attempts by Parliament to check them, enclosures continued in the 17th century and became much more numerous in the 18th century as part of the AGRARIAN REVOLUTION. These were normally carried out by private bills promoted by land-owners which appointed commissioners to divide out the land. Contrary to common belief, these commissioners seem to have generally acted fairly, and there is no evidence that smallholders suffered because of their awards. The agrarian discontent in the late Hanoverian period was not the result of enclosures, which increased the prosperity of the countryside, but of the high food prices and over-abundance of labour caused by the increase in POPULATION in this period. [G. R. Elton, *England Under the Tudors* (1955); L. W. Cowie, *Hanoverian England* (1967)]

English hood a head-dress worn by women in the first half of the 16th century, consisting of a hood wired up to frame the face and form a pointed arch above the forehead. It fell in thick folds behind to the shoulders and had long embroidered or jewelled flaps, called lappets, crossing the head and falling low on each side. The hair, parted in the middle, was seen under the arch and allowed to fall free at the back beneath the hood. About 1525 the back drapery was replaced by two long, stiffened hanging flaps, sometimes turned up on the crown, and the front lappets were shortened, turned up also and pinned in place. The hair was now bound with ribbons and folded across the forehead or else covered in front by silk sheaths, usually striped, rising to a point and filling up the space under the arch of the headdress. The English hood was succeeded in fashion by the FRENCH HOOD. See also HATS.

English language developed from the Old English of the ANGLO-SAXONS. After the NORMAN CONQUEST, English remained the language of the people, while NORMAN FRENCH was that of the nobility and Latin of the scholars. After the loss of the direct connection with Normandy in King John's reign (1199–1216), English began to gain ground, though enriched by many French words. In 1385 it was said, 'In all the grammar schools of England, children leave French and construe and learn in English'. The earliest surviving English will was made by a London citizen in 1387, and the earliest known English letter was written by a soldier, Sir John Hawkwood, from his home in Florence in 1392.

Epiphany the twelfth day after CHRISTMAS (see also TWELFTH NIGHT), commemorating the showing of Christ to the Gentiles in the persons of the Magi. In the Middle Ages it was the custom for princes, abbots and noblemen to make offerings of gold, frankincense and myrrh on this day, which is still done in England by the sovereign in the Chapel Royal.

Equity, see CHANCERY.

Escalator or moving staircase was developed in USA, and an example was exhibited at the Paris Exhibition of 1900. The first to be installed in Britain was in 1911 at Earl's Court Station, London, between the Piccadilly and District Lines. So many people mistrusted it in the early days that a man with a wooden leg was engaged to travel up and down it all day to give passengers confidence, but he was taken off the job when a woman was overheard telling her small son, 'That's what happens to people who use them fancy inventions.' There are 42 escalators on the Victoria Line (opened 1969).

Escheat the reversion of land to the feudal lord (the Crown or lord of the MANOR) either through the death of a tenant without an heir or through forfeiture if the tenant committed a FELONY.

Esquire see SQUIRE.

Etiquette in medieval books seems to have been largely concerned with TABLE MANNERS for the young and DEPORTMENT especially for girls. It has changed from age to age. In the 17th century, for instance, it was correct for men to wear their hats at meals; and until the beginning of this century, young ladies could not go out alone, but must be accompanied by a maid-servant or parent or some married woman. Again, some rules of etiquette originated in different conditions in the past. Thus, a man walks on the outside of the pavement when he is walking with a woman in the street because once, if she were on the inside, she would not have been splashed by mud from passing vehicles or soaked with water thrown from the overhanging upper windows of houses.

Here are some rules of etiquette from past centuries: *Rules of Civility* (1663)— 'If you meet with a person of quality in the streets, you must run presently towards the channel or post yourself so that he pass by with his left hand towards you and your right hand free, and the same rule is to be observed with coaches'; *The Compleat Gentleman* (1678)—'When he walks, if he meets with any magistrate or other to whom respect is due, let him put off his hat and give them the hand; when he is in conversation, let him not play with his hair, bite his nails, scratch his head, blow his nose without turning aside his head or pick his ears with his fingers or spit often'; *Lord Chesterfield's Letters to his Son* (1774)—'It is extremely rude to answer yes or no to anybody without adding sir, my lord or madam, according to the quality of the person you speak to'; *Hints on Etiquette* (1836)—'Never *nod* to a lady in the street, neither be satisfied with touching your hat, *but take it off*—it is a courtesy her sex demands'; *The Habits of Good Society* (1855)—'One must never smoke, without consent, in the presence of a clergyman, and one must never offer a cigar to any ecclesiastic over the rank of curate.' See also COURTESY BOOKS.

Eton suit worn by young schoolboys from about 1798, consisting of a very short jacket ('bum freezer'), waistcoat and grey TROUSERS and worn with a starched white collar turned down over the jacket collar, a white shirt and black tie. At Eton College the jackets were blue, red or other colours until the school went into mourning for George III in 1820 since when they have been black. The Oppidans (boys living in houses in the town) wore trousers from 1814, but the Collegers (boys living in school) continued to wear BREECHES until about 1820. See also SCHOOL UNIFORM, and CHILDREN'S COSTUME.

Evangelicals owed some inspiration to the METHODISTS, but were largely an independent movement developing from the LOW CHURCHMEN. Their outlook was based on CALVINISM, and they organized themselves on the PARISH system of the CHURCH OF ENGLAND. They were strongest among the upper and middle classes and exercised a strong influence in the 19th century. They founded the RELIGIOUS TRACT SOCIETY and MISSIONARY SOCIETIES, secured the abolition of the SLAVE TRADE and LOTTERIES and promoted the strict observance of SUNDAY. Later they were followed by the TRACTARIANS with whom their ideas conflicted sharply.

Excursions originated with Thomas Cook (1808–92) a wood-turner and BAPTIST lay preacher. He organized in 1841 the first publicly advertised excursion by RAILWAY train (Leicester to Loughborough and back) in connection with the Market Harborough branch of the

South Midland Temperance Association of which he was secretary. Its success led him to make the organizing of excursions at home and abroad a regular occupation and to establish the world-wide travel agency. His arrangements enabled 165 000 people to visit the GREAT EXHIBITION in 1851, and among his other excursions was one to see a public hanging at Bodmin.

The first excursion to the SEASIDE ran from London to Brighton and was organized by the Brighton Railway Company in 1844. The Granville Hotel, Ramsgate, in 1877 chartered a train for the sole use of its clients travelling from London; this 'Granville Express' was the first named train in the country.

Exeter Hall a building in the Strand (London) erected in 1831 by a group of EVANGELICALS as a centre for religious and philanthropic work. Meetings were held here by the MISSIONARY SOCIETIES and by opponents of the SLAVE TRADE. It came to be used allusively as a title for a certain religious outlook. Bishop Wilberforce was told in 1845 that the Berkshire clergy were 'either top-boots or Exeter Hall'. It was bought by the YOUNG MEN'S CHRISTIAN ASSOCIATION in 1880 and demolished in 1909, when the Strand Palace Hotel was built on the site.

F

Factory Laws began with two acts in 1802 and 1819 which applied to CHILDREN in COTTON mills. The first forbade the employment of APPRENTICES (often pauper children bound by the Overseers under the POOR LAW ACT) for more than 12 hours a day; the second, largely due to the efforts of Robert Owen (see NEW LANARK MILLS), forbade the employment of all children under 9 years old and limited the working-day of those between 9 and 16 to 12 hours. Neither of these was effective because they were supposed to be enforced by the JUSTICES OF THE PEACE, many of whom were factory-owners.

Lord Shaftesbury, who was a prominent EVANGELICAL, secured the passing of the Factory Act of 1833, which applied to all textile mills, forbidding the employment of children under 9 and limiting the hours of those between 9 and 13 to 9 hours a day and between 13 and 18 to 12 a day. This was the first effective act because it appointed full-time, paid factory inspectors to enforce its observance. Another act in 1844 fixed a 12-hour day for WOMEN and required the fencing of dangerous machinery.

Meanwhile, the Mines Act (1842) forbade the employment of women and boys under 13 underground. The Factory Act of 1853 established a working-day of 10½ hours for women and boys under 18; this was reduced to 10 by an act of 1874, which also forbade the employment of children under 10, and this was raised to 12 in 1901 and to 14 in 1920.

Factory System replaced the DOMESTIC SYSTEM in many industries as a result of the INDUSTRIAL REVOLUTION, which brought about new machines and forms of power. An early factory was the silk-mill built by John Lombe in 1721 on the River Derwent near Derby in which the machinery was worked by water-power. Richard Arkwright in 1721 established a mill for the SPINNING of COTTON, modelled on Lombe's mill, at Cromford, also on the River Derwent. Other early factories were the Carron Ironworks (1760) and Josiah Wedgwood's Etruria POTTERY (1769), but until well into the 19th century the cotton industry was pre-eminent in the adoption of the factory system.

Fairs gatherings for the sale of goods, held periodically, usually annually and associated with the festival of a saint (e.g. St Giles's Fair, Oxford), and often with amusements and entertainments as well. Fairs met less frequently than MARKETS, but lasted longer (usually for three days) and were larger, being attended by merchants from other parts of the country as well as foreign traders.

Fairs have a very old origin. There was a group of fairs along HADRIAN'S WALL, where the peoples from north and south of the Wall met to trade with each other and with the Roman garrison. One of the oldest fairs in England is at Weyhill, near Andover (Hants.), where the Tin Road from Cornwall and the Gold Road from Wales met six DROVE ROADS. Fairs were important in the Middle Ages as SHOPS were few and travelling was difficult. As trade increased, the legal position of fairs became important and CHARTERS were sought from the Crown. Such charters, recognizing the right to hold a fair, were granted to TOWNS, lords of the MANOR, monasteries or bishops; they were valuable because of the fees charged to traders. By the 12th and 13th centuries nearly all the best-known Eng-

lish fairs had been chartered, and the golden age of fairs began.

The four great fairs of medieval England were Sturbridge (near Cambridge), Winchester, St Ives (Hunts.) and BARTHOLOMEW FAIR (London). An important fair in Scotland was the Lady Mary Fair at Dundee each August. There were also specialized fairs, such as Horse Fairs, Sheep Fairs, Cheese Fairs and the MOP FAIRS. London had its FROST FAIRS and also MAYFAIR. Medieval fairs were controlled by the PIE POWDER COURTS.

Until late in the 19th century, as may be seen from Thomas Hardy's novels, there was still a network of fairs throughout the country, providing the people with holidays and means of making purchases; but changing conditions have brought about their decline, and nowadays fairs are no longer important for trade and are often held mainly for their amusements. [Margaret Baker, *Discovering English Fairs* (1968)]

Falchion a single-edged SWORD with a very wide blade, often with a curved cutting-edge and with the broadest part of the blade near the point. The concentration of weight far up the blade gave it great shearing force, and it was extensively used in the Middle Ages, being shorter than the ordinary military sword and less heavy. Usually it had a hilt like a normal sword, but a few were fitted to a short wooden shaft by means of a socket. [Paul Martin, *Armour and Weapons* (1968)] See also WEAPONS.

Falconry a sport in which falcons or hawks are trained to chase other birds or game. Between flights the falcons are kept on a leash and often hooded to keep them quiet. Falconry probably came to England from France in the 9th century; Harold was a keen falconer. It ranked with HUNTING in the favour of kings and noblemen, and received a new impetus from the CRUSADES, when falcons were imported from the East as well as the Continent. It declined during the 17th century through improvements in sporting firearms, and at the RESTORATION many MEWS closed during the Civil War were not reopened.

Families have become significantly smaller since the mid-19th century. In the 1850s the average married couple had 6 children. The decline began in the 1860s; and between 1911 and 1939 families of 3 or 4 increased from a total of 3·3 million to 5·4, while those of 5 or more fell from 3·7 million to 3·1. Between 1934 and 1943 the average size of a family was 2·1. Since 1945 it has risen to 2·13, but it seems very unlikely that the large families of the past will ever become usual.

Fan commonly used by women from about 1550 and by foppish men in the late 16th and late 18th centuries. Until about 1580, fans were rigid and made of feathers, silk or straw fixed to a decorative handle and variously shaped. Then folding fans came in and became usual in the 18th century. Their size varied greatly from time to time. Some had long enough handles to enable them to be used also as walking-sticks and for beating children. John Aubrey wrote in the 17th century, 'The gentlewomen had prodigious fans . . ., and they had handles at least half a yard long; with these their daughters were oftentimes corrected.'

In the early 19th century fans of ivory were common, and in the mid-century painted fans were introduced. In the 1880s fans decorated with animals (e.g. cats' heads) were fashionable and in the 1890s large folding ostrich-feather fans with frames of ivory, mother-of-pearl or tortoiseshell. See also DANCING, EMBROIDERY.

Farmery the infirmary of a MONASTERY, generally situated east of the CLOISTER, for sick and aged MONKS. It consisted of a pillared hall, where the beds were arranged in the AISLES, with a chapel at one end, and usually its own kitchen, as well as rooms for the IMFIRMARER. The parish church at Ramsey (Hunts.) is thought to have been the farmery of the ABBEY. In later times the aisles were divided into separate chambers, as at Tintern (Monmouthshire), while at Westminster Abbey, when the farmery was rebuilt, the open hall was replaced by a number of small chambers around a small cloister.

The larger CISTERCIAN monasteries also had farmeries for their CONVERSI, generally in the form of an aisled hall, placed, as at Jervaulx (Yorks.) and Roche (Yorks.), near their REREDORTER.

Farthing named from the Anglo-Saxon word 'feorthing', a fourth part and beginning as a quarter of a silver PENNY. Round farthings may have been minted early in Henry III's reign (1216–72), but the first regular minting was in 1272, when they were called 'Londoners' as they were first only minted in London. It became a copper coin in 1672, bronze in 1860 and was discontinued in 1960. See also COINAGE, SPAN-FARTHING.

Farthingale (1) a variously-shaped structure for making the skirt of the PETTICOAT and dress stand out from the body, worn by women from about 1545 to about 1625. It consisted either of a petticoat with hoops of rushes, wood, wire or whalebone or of a stiff horseshoe-shaped cushion (sometimes called a bum-roll) attached to the bottom of the STAYS by tapes. It was revived in the 18th century as the HOOP-PETTICOAT and in the 19th as the CRINOLINE. See also COSTUME.

(2) A farthingale was also a CHAIR with a wide seat, straight back and no arms,

made in the 17th century for wearers of the dress.

Fascine a cylindrical bundle or faggot, usually of brushwood, bound together with twine or withes, for use in warfare to strengthen earthworks or fill in the ditch of a CASTLE under attack. It varied in size from 6 to 18 feet in length and from 6 to 9 inches in diameter. When the limbs were stouter and longer than usual, it was called a saucisse or saucisson. Fascines, dipped in pitch or other combustible matter, were also sometimes used to set fire to the enemy's buildings. See also MINES, MOAT.

Fashion-dolls were dolls dressed in the latest Parisian fashion sent from Paris to the courts of Europe to show the new styles and create a demand for French materials from the 14th century onwards. In 1396, when the seven-year-old Isabella of France came to England to be Richard II's second wife, she was sent fashion-dolls from France, some large enough for her to wear the clothes, others smaller for her to play with. In the 17th century the dolls, usually half size, were shown at the Hotel de Rambouillet before replicas were sent to the various courts; and in the 18th century it became common to despatch abroad a pair of dolls, one dressed *en grande toilette* and the other *en deshabille*, called Grande Pandore and Petite Pandore. These dolls were a recognized way of publicizing fashions. They were replaced in the early 19th century by FASHION-PLATES. [Madge Garland, *The Changing Form of Fashion* (1970)]

Fashion-plates etchings, line-engravings or lithographs, coloured by hand, showing people dressed in the latest fashions, which were invented in the late 18th century and replaced by mechanical reproductions by 1900. Many of them appeared in the ladies' magazines which appeared for the first time in the last years of the 18th century and were taken from London to the provinces by the improved STAGE-COACHES and MAIL-COACHES, spreading a wider knowledge of the latest styles of dressing. About the middle of the 19th century, most English fashion magazines ceased to make their own plates and contented themselves with importing French plates. [James Laver, *Fashions and Fashion Plates 1800–1900* (1943)]

Felony was originally one of the gravest crimes, which included by the 13th century treason, murder, robbery and arson, the penalty for which included death, forfeiture of land and goods to the king and corruption of blood (loss of all rights of rank and title.)

Fennel a fragrant, yellow-flowered HERB of the PARSLEY family, used as flavouring in cooking and sauces. John Parkinson wrote in the 17th century, 'Fennel is of great use to trim up and strew upon fish, as also to boil or put among fish of divers sorts, cowcumbers pickled and other fruits, etc. The roots are used with parsley roots to be boiled in broths. The seed is much used to be put in pippin pies and divers other such baked fruits, as also into bread, to give it the better relish.' It was widely used in the Middle Ages. A conversation in *Piers Plowman* between a priest and a poor woman indicates that it was given to the poor to relieve their pangs of hunger on fast days; and $8\frac{1}{2}$ lb of fennel seed were bought for Edward I's household in 1281 as a month's supply.

Ferula an instrument of punishment in schools, applied to the palm of the outstretched hand. It consisted of a flat piece of wood like a ruler, about ten inches long, of box-wood, crab-tree wood or other hard wood, widened at the inflicting end into a circular shape and sometimes pierced with a hole for raising blisters. Often the ferula was used to punish minor offences and the BIRCH-ROD for more serious ones; and in some grammar schools monitors punished boys with the ferula for talking English instead of Latin in play-time. [J. H. Brown, *Elizabethan Schooldays* (1933)]

Fescue a small quill, straw or pin with which a teacher pointed out the letters to a child learning to read by means of a HORN-BOOK. The name comes from the genus of grass with long stems.

Feudalism was the system in the Middle Ages by which a FIEF was held by a vassal on condition of HOMAGE and services (which included military service) to a superior lord, by whom it was granted and in whom the ownership remained. All land was ultimately held of the king. Those who held it directly of him were his TENANTS-IN-CHIEF, who would have their own tenants beneath them. After the NORMAN CONQUEST, the compilation of DOMESDAY BOOK gave a complete survey of the feudal system in England. [G. W. S. Barrow, *Feudal Britain* (1956)]

Fief land held of an overlord under FEUDALISM by a man and his heirs in return for the performance of HOMAGE and military service.

Field-preaching or preaching in the open air was first adopted in the METHO-DIST movement by George Whitefield (1714–70) and then by John Wesley (1703–91), who made it a regular practice and spoke to huge audiences in places all over the country (e.g. Hanham Mount, Bristol).

The Earl of Egremont gave an account of a field-preaching in 1739 by White-field, who mounted at 6 o'clock on a June evening a stage erected in the open before a crowd of about 200; he began with PSALM 100 in which many joined, then 'made a long pathetic prayer' and finally gave a SERMON on 'the necessity of being born again'.

Fifth Monarchy Men an extremist sect which came into prominence after the English Civil War. It sought to bring in the 'Fifth Monarchy' (Daniel II, 44) which would succeed the four empires of antiquity (Assyria, Persia, Greece, Rome) and when Christ would reign with His saints for 1000 years (Revelation xx, 4). At first its members supported Oliver Cromwell in the belief that the Common-wealth would realize their hopes, but when they were disappointed, they turned against him. Many of them were imprisoned, and their leader, General Thomas Harrison, was deprived of his command. Thomas Venner's unsuccessful rising in London in January 1661 was the last attempt to establish the Fifth Monarchy. The leaders were beheaded, and the sect died out.

Fillet a narrow band of material bound round the head to confine the hair or for ornament by women from the 13th to 19th centuries. In the Middle Ages it was sometimes worn with a WIMPLE (or a BARBETTE) or a COVERCHIEF or both.

Finishing-school was a GIRLS' SCHOOL in the 19th century to which wealthy young ladies were sent to 'finish' their education. Frances Power Cobbe (1822–1904), later to be a prominent SUFFRA-GETTE, was sent in 1836 to a finishing-school at Brighton for two years at a cost of £1000 to her parents. There, she said, 'everything was taught us in the inverse ratio of its true importance. At the bottom of the scale were morals and religion, and at the top were music and dancing.' [*Life of Frances Power Cobbe, as Told by Herself* (1904)]

Firearms, see ARTILLERY, HAND-GUNS.

Fire-dogs also known as andirons, were used to support large logs and prevent them rolling off the hearth. A secondary use, especially in more elaborate KITCHEN varieties, was to carry a roasting SPIT. The top of a tall fire-dog might carry a metal cup, in which was kept warm an inner cup of soup or drink, or a little fire-basket containing CHARCOAL to heat a small dish for which the main

Fire-dog

fire was too fierce. From the 16th century the function of supporting logs and the spit were separated. Smaller and plainer fire-dogs ('brand-dogs', 'dog-irons' or 'creepers') were used to stand between taller, ornamental ones, which, relieved of the dirty work, became more elegant and were often made of BRONZE, bronze-gilt or SILVER. [Lawrence Wright, *Home Fires Burning* (1964)]

Fire-engine was first made in 1672 by the Dutch engineer, Jan van de Heyden (1637–1712), known in England as Jan van der Heide. It was a tank and hand pump on wheels with a flexible leather hose. Between 1721 and 1725 Richard Newsham, a London engineer, added the

airchamber to the pump, which converted the series of water spurts into a continuous stream. STEAM POWER was applied to work the pump of a fire-engine in 1829, but was not widely used until the 1860s,

(*top*) Newsham's fire engine
(*bottom*) Horse drawn steam fire engine

and these were generally not steam-propelled, but pulled by men or horses. The first motor fire-engine was built in 1904. The wheeled fire-escape, as opposed to ladders carried on engines, was invented in 1837 by Abraham Wivell.

Fire-Fighting was primitive in Norman and medieval times, and hence the CURFEW. A PARISH might possess buckets and a THATCH HOOK (often kept in the CHURCH tower). By the time of the GREAT FIRE OF LONDON (1666), there were also primitive hand squirts, which could only throw water a short distance; but FIRE-ENGINES were invented soon afterwards.

At the end of the 17th century, the London fire INSURANCE companies set up their own fire-brigades (see FIREMARKS), which were brought together as the London Fire-Engines Establishment in 1832, which became the Metropolitan Fire Brigade in 1866 and came under the London County Council in 1888. The insurance and the city authorities formed a single professional fire-brigade in

Edinburgh in 1824, and in the 19th century, many towns formed their own brigades, largely manned by volunteers, but the provision of a fire-brigade was not made compulsory throughout Britain until the Fire Brigades Act (1938). During the Second World War, the regular fire brigades and the wartime Auxiliary Fire Service were amalgamated into a National Fire Service in 1941 with a total strength of 213 000 whole and part-time men and women and more than 20 000 appliances (see also STIRRUP PUMP). After the war, the separate fire brigades were restored, but their number was reduced from about 1500 to 150.

Firemarks came into being in the later 17th century with the establishment of fire INSURANCE. The GREAT FIRE OF LONDON (1666) revealed the need for better measures of FIRE-FIGHTING and also for a scheme of compensation for loss from fires through insurance. Dr Nicholas

Firemarks

Barbon, a speculative builder and son of the PURITAN Praise-God Barebones, set up with the help of friends The Phoenix Fire Office (1680), which was the first fire insurance in the world. Other companies were formed and began to form their own fire brigades. They marked the

buildings which they insured with their firemarks (or fire-plates), which at first were of moulded lead and later of stamped metal blazened in colours with their crests or marks (e.g. the 'Sun') and a policy number. Each was fixed on the wall of the insured property in a spot where it could easily be seen by the brigades since the companies only fought fires in buildings bearing such marks. Firemarks were no longer used after 1832 when the companies ceased to have their own brigades, but they may still be seen on old buildings.

Fireplaces first appeared in Britain in the 12th century in HALL of CASTLES and MANORS and were very wide as only wood was burnt, and the stone-walled rooms were draughty and cold. The fire was made on a hearth and the large logs were supported by FIRE-DOGS. The fireplace

15th-cent. Fireplace

at first often had a projecting hood, resting on corbels or columns, which later was replaced by an arch and in the 15th century by a wide slab of stone, frequently carved, or a wooden beam, which became known as chimney breasts. These late medieval fireplaces often had seats on either side and also CUPBOARDS to hold the kindling wood. There was also sometimes an oven beside or behind the CHIMNEY or hearth in which BREAD was baked after it had been heated by being filled with burning faggots and the ashes had been removed.

Elizabethan houses had elaborate fireplaces with carved wooden or stone overmantels built up to the ceiling; there were

16th-cent. Fireplace

18th-cent. Fireplace

sometimes columns on either side of the fire and the panel above it and small figures supporting the chimney breasts. The fire-dogs had become larger with richly decorated uprights, while a metal fireback protected the back of the grate. In the 17th century fireplaces were generally simpler, but in the next century

they were built in refined and elegant styles, and above the overmantel was often a simple panel with a picture or MIRROR let in. [Lawrence Wright, *Home Fires Burning* (1964)]

Fireworks seem first to have been used for celebrations from the late 15th or early 16th century. It is recorded that at the coronation processions of both Elizabeth of York (1487) and Anne Boleyn (1533) there were 'a great red dragon continually moving and casting forth wild-fire' and 'terrible, monstrous and wild men, casting of fire and making a hideous noise'; but true firework displays date only from the reign of Elizabeth I, who seemed to enjoy them. A display given for her diversion at Kenilworth Castle in 1575 included falling fires, rockets, fireballs and coloured lights. In the 17th and 18th centuries coronations, weddings and victories were celebrated with set-pieces which represented the event in fire and light. Handel wrote his *Music for the Royal Fireworks* to be performed at a display commemorating the Treaty of Aix-la-Chapelle (1749). It was also the practice during the 18th century at some BEAR-BAITING rings to release bulls, dogs and bears decked with burning fireworks, and the PLEASURE GARDENS had frequent firework displays. See also BONFIRES.

Fish mainly mullet and carp, were bred in ponds on the estates of VILLAS in ROMAN BRITAIN, and sea-fish was eaten as well. Fish was eaten in great quantities during the Middle Ages in Lent and also on Wednesdays, Fridays and Saturdays (which were usually fish days throughout the year). It was usual for a MONASTERY to have its 'stew pond' in which carp and other fish were bred for food; but wealthy households enjoyed a great variety. Red (smoked) or white (salted) herring was most common, but mackerel, stockfish and cod were also usual. On feast days in such houses, the fish served included pike, lampreys, OYSTERS, porpoise, sturgeon and whale (the last two being regarded as royal fish and highly prized), salmon, dorey, bream, eels and shellfish. The medieval poor had to content themselves with occasionally buying salt fish.

After the REFORMATION, some PROTESTANTS openly refused to eat fish on Fridays and other fast days to show that they were not ROMAN CATHOLICS, but in 1548 and 1563 Parliament ordered these days to be observed in order to encourage the fishing industry, especially the new cod-fisheries off Newfoundland. All sorts of fish continued to be eaten in aristocratic Tudor and Stuart families. In 17th-century Woburn Abbey pike and perch from the ponds in the park were supplemented by salt fish, fresh flounders, herrings and whiting and less often oysters, lobsters and salmon. And Samuel Pepys bought 'a cod and some prawns in Fish Street' and at Hungerford dined on 'very good trouts, eels and crayfish'.

Until the mid-19th century pickled or salted herring was almost the only fish available to the working-classes, but in the 1860s the advent of the steam trawler and other developments changed the situation and particularly popularized FISH AND CHIPS.

Fish and chip shops seem to have risen to popularity during the 1860s when the development of the steam trawler and the use of ice for preservation enabled new supplies of cheap fish (especially cod) to be despatched by railway to inland towns, and also when vegetable fats and oils were becoming more plentiful. Their origin is uncertain, but they probably developed from the Victorian HOT PIE SHOPS, where fish and chips were first sold as a side-line and then became supreme. It had become an important part of working-class diet before 1914.

Fishbourne Palace (Sussex) was built by the Romans about AD 75 probably for Cogidubnus, native ruler of the Regnenses, who had gained favour with the conquerors, and was among the most impressive buildings of ROMAN BRITAIN. It was not merely a VILLA, but a magnificent palace with four wings enclosing an ornamental GARDEN. A road probably led from Chichester directly to the main

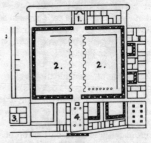

Plan of Fishbourne Palace: 1 Audience house; 2 Formal gardens; 3 Baths; 4 Vestibule

entrance hall in the centre of the east wing; across the garden was the west wing, which was an administrative block with a vaulted audience chamber, flanked on either side by large state and dining rooms; in the north wing the rooms were arranged round 2 small colonnaded gardens to form private suites for visitors; and the south wing is buried under Fishbourne village, but it must have contained the owner's private rooms and is close to the white bath house near the stream.

In about AD 100 alterations were made which suggest a change of ownership. The palace was split into smaller units, and later some parts were rebuilt while others were allowed to fall into decay. In about AD 285 the palace was destroyed by fire. Its walls were dismantled, and the site reverted to farmland, not to be rediscovered until 1960.

Flagellants groups of men and women in the Middle Ages who lashed their bare arms and shoulders with scourges (Latin, *flagella*) as they walked in procession, often singing PSALMS, as a PENANCE for the sins of mankind. They first appeared in Italy in the 13th century, but do not seem to have come to England until about 1350 when, following the BLACK DEATH (1348), there was a revival of their activity all over Europe as part of a belief that the end of the world was near. They marched from town to town, calling upon the people to repent, but were soon condemned by the Papacy.

Flail an implement for threshing corn, sometimes known as a 'stick-and-a-half'. It consisted of a hand-staff usually of ash and a swingle (the 'half') of tough wood like holly or blackthorn. A swivel joint of green ash was fitted on the top of the staff and attached to the swingle by a strip of eel-skin, sometimes reinforced with leather, and thonged with cow-hide. The thresher swung the staff over his shoulder and brought the swingle down across the straw just below the ears so that the grains of corn were shaken out without being bruised. See also BARN, THRESHING-MACHINE. [G. E. Fussell, *The Farmer's Tools* (1952); G. E. Evans, *Ask the Fellows Who Cut the Hay* (1956)]

Flat is defined by the Housing Acts (1936 and 1957) as 'a separate and self-contained set of premises constructed for use for the purposes of a dwelling and forming part of a building from some other part of which it is divided horizontally'. Although flats were built in TOWNS in the 19th century, they have become especially prominent in the second half of the 20th century because of the shortage of building space in modern cities. Examples of big blocks of flats vary from the luxury flats of Dolphin Square, Westminster, to such council flats as those at Roehampton (Surrey). In addition, many large, older HOUSES have been divided into flats.

Fleet Prison a royal PRISON in London, probably established by the Fleet River near to the modern Farringdon Street by the 12th century. It later housed many STAR CHAMBER prisoners and then became almost exclusively a debtors' prison. It was destroyed in the GREAT FIRE (1666) and twice rebuilt. It was closed by Act of Parliament of 1842 and pulled down in 1846.

Fleet MARRIAGES were those performed by clergymen imprisoned in the Fleet without banns or licence. They were abolished by the Marriage Act of 1753.

Flemings were invited over to England as weavers in 1337 by Edward III, who wished to establish a cloth industry. It is not certain how many came over, but some settled at Norwich, York and Cranbrook (Kent) and later at Bristol. Numbers were murdered in London and East Anglia during the PEASANTS' REVOLT (1381). Later Flemings established the COTTON industry in England during Elizabeth I's reign (1558–1603).

Flint a very hard stone found in lumps in the chalk of south-eastern England. Since it breaks with a sharp edge, it was a favourite material for the arrow-heads, knives, scrapers and other implements of OLD STONE AGE men, who found it lying about in the ground or in the beds of streams. The NEW STONE AGE men found that, instead of chipping and flaking the flints, a sharper edge could be obtained by grinding them on sandstone, and in order to get larger flints, they dug mines such as GRIMES' GRAVES.

Flintlock was a HAND-GUN in which flint struck against a hammer produced sparks which ignited the GUNPOWDER. This was invented about the middle of the 17th century and soon replaced the MATCH-LOCK and WHEEL-LOCK in sporting guns, but was not generally used in armies until the 1690s.

Flogging-block a wooden piece of furniture, usually in the shape of a couple of steps, upon which boys were whipped in schools. It was commonly kept, together with the BIRCH-ROD, in the ROD-CLOSET, and when a boy was to be punished he had to bring it out himself. He then had to kneel on the lower step, place his head and shoulders on the flat upper step and his hands on the floor, being prepared for the rod either by himself or by a boy known as the UNTRUSSER. It was also common for the boy to be held down on the flogging-block by one or more boys, 'so as he cannot any way hurt himself or others, be he never so peevish, neither can have any hope by any device or turning or by his apparel or any other means to escape' (John Brinsley, 1612).

Florin a gold coin minted by Edward III when he resumed the English production of gold coins after the unsuccessful experiment of Henry III's GOLD PENNY. By 1337 Edward minted for Aquitaine a gold florin, copied from the *fiorino de oro* of Florence, having on its obverse the lily or *fiore* from which it got its name. The Aquitaine florin, worth 3s, was followed by other gold coins, the *écu* and *léopard*, each worth 3s 4d. In 1344 Edward introduced three new gold coins for England — the florin or two-leopard piece (worth 6s), the leopard or half-florin (3s) and the helm or quarter-florin (1s 6d); but within a year these were replaced by the NOBLE. The florin was re-introduced as a silver coin worth 2s in 1849 as a preparation for decimal coinage. See also COINAGE.

Flute a reedless musical pipe with finger-holes and keys sounded by blowing through a mouth-hole at one side near the end. In 1543 Princess Mary made a gift at the NEW YEAR of 10s to the flute-players and another gift of the same amount to the RECORDER players. Pepys sometimes played 'a little at my flute' at home before he went to bed. The flute in its modern form is largely due to Theobald Boehm (c. 1793–1881).

Flying-boat was an AEROPLANE able to take off or come down on water, having (instead of a land undercarriage) a watertight hull and planing bottom. Between the two World Wars they were used a great deal for carrying passengers, especially on the Pacific routes in the 1920s and on British Empire routes in the 1930s. They were comfortable and popular, but after the Second World War their slower speed (compared with the new jet airliners) led to their abandonment.

Fogou an underground, stone-lined passage associated with IRON AGE settlements in Cornwall. It often has side-chambers or branches and was probably used for food storage, though it could have been intended as a hideout. In Ireland it is known as a souterrain, in Scotland as earth-house.

Folly was the name given to a useless building erected in GARDENS particularly during the period of the ROMANTIC MOVEMENT. With the idea of 'giving a livelier consequence to the landscape', these were of all sorts—castles and towers, cottages and ruins. Among those still to be seen are Ralph Allen's Sham Castle, Bath (Somerset); St David's Ruin, Bingley (Yorks.); Rousham Eye-catcher, Steeple Aston (Oxon.); and

Racton Tower, near Rowlands Castle, Racton (Sussex). [Sir Hugh Casson (ed.), *Follies* (1963).] See also HERMIT.

Font in early times, when adult BAPTISM by immersion was the rule, was a large basin below ground level in which the convert stood while water was poured over him. A modern reproduction of such a sunken font has been constructed in the Church of St Mary in the Castle, Hastings (Sussex).

When infant baptism became usual, fonts as we know them were made and placed at the west end, near the main doorway, to signify entry into the

Medieval font

Church. Very often the font is the oldest thing in a CHURCH. Some Norman fonts are strikingly carved, Early English ones often rest on clustered columns, and Decorated ones are richly ornamented.

Before the REFORMATION, water which had been blessed by the priest was kept in the font, which was covered by a locked lid to prevent people taking the water which was believed to be good for cures and charms. To discourage this superstition, the PURITANS destroyed many of the covers, and water was put in only at the time of baptisms.

During the 18th and early 19th centuries, many old fonts were removed from the churches and replaced by a small marble basin on an iron standard, which could be moved for a baptism up the NAVE and set in front of the congregation; but a number of the old fonts have since been put back in the churches.

Food was eaten raw by early men until they discovered how to make fire and at first consisted of wild animals, which they trapped, and roots, plants, nuts and berries, which they gathered. Later they made flour from the seeds of various grasses, the forerunners of wheat and barley, and made early types of BREAD. Eventually they grew their own crops and VEGETABLES and domesticated CATTLE, SHEEP and PIGS and POULTRY, from which they got MEAT, MILK, CHEESE and EGGS. The development of POTTERY enabled food to be boiled.

In ROMAN BRITAIN all forms of FISH and FRUIT were also eaten, and the OYSTER and the GOOSE were especial luxuries. The Middle Ages prized the SWAN and the BOAR's head at important MEALS and used HONEY for sweetening until SUGAR came in with the CRUSADES. Old English foods which have a medieval origin include FRUMENTY, GINGERBREAD, HOT CROSS BUNS and SILLABUB. Medieval cooking made great use of HERBS and SPICES. The 16th century brought in the POTATO and the 17th ICE CREAM, while the SANDWICH may have been an 18th century invention. CHOCOLATE and MARGARINE were first eaten and the TOMATO was introduced in the 19th century, which also saw the rise of HOT PIE SHOPS, FISH AND CHIP SHOPS and TEA SHOPS. CEREAL FOODS originated late in the century.

In the 20th century CANNING and REFRIGERATION, together with improved land and sea transport, have added greatly to the variety of everyone's diet. After the Second World War two shortlived items of food were WHALEMEAT and SNOEK. [J. C. Drummond and Anne Wilbraham, *The Englishman's Food, A*

History of Five Centuries of English Diet (1939).] See also CHRISTMAS, EASTER, GOOD FRIDAY.

Football in the Middle Ages was a rough mob game played on CANDLEMAS, SHROVE TUESDAY and other HOLIDAYS; it was often forbidden because of its violence and because (like other GAMES) it interfered with ARCHERY. During the later 18th century, the playing of football declined, but was revived in the mid-19th century as an organized game in PUBLIC SCHOOLS, and clergymen encouraged it among the young men in their PARISH. Aston Villa, Bolton Wanderers, Queen's Park Rangers and Everton are among football-clubs which were originally church-teams.

The Football Association was formed in 1863 to give standard rules to the game, but in 1865 some clubs refused to accept a decision to abolish 'hacking' (kicking at the shins). They adopted the game played at Rugby School since 1823 and formed the Rugby Football Union in 1871. At first all the players were unpaid, part-time amateurs, but as the games became more popular, stands had to be built for spectators and expenses met by admission-charges. Clubs soon wanted to pay their players to get good teams and attract large crowds. The Football Association allowed this in 1885, and although CRICKET followed this example, the Rugby Union would not. The result was the northern rugby clubs formed their own Northern Union in 1895 (called the Rugby League since 1922) to have paid players and develop their own rules. Another result was to continue the division between soccer and rugger. In most parts of the country rugger remained the game of the public and grammar schools and of amateur teams, while soccer (especially after the formation of the Football League in 1888) became the chief working-class winter-sport. [Morris Marples, *A History of Football* (1954)]

Football pools a popular modern form of GAMBLING. The first football pool in England was organized in Birmingham in 1922, but they did not become popular all over the country until the 1930s when they expanded steadily. Today the elaborate forms are filled in weekly by nearly 10 million people. The total turnover on the pools in Britain was £8 million in 1934–5, £44 million in 1936–7 and £70 million in 1962–3.

Footman a liveried man-servant, who attended at table, with the carriage or at the door, became a common part of wealthy households in the 18th century. A nobleman might have as many as half a dozen, while a humbler family might have one or two who divided their time between the house and the stables. It was customary to lend one's footmen to friends for special occasions, and a footman might be placed in a box at the THEATRE to keep a seat until his master came. Lord North imposed a tax on man-servants in 1777, which was later increased by Pitt, but this does not seem to have reduced the number kept. Above the footmen was the butler, and below them were the boys who did all sorts of odd jobs and might become footmen themselves when older. See also SERVANTS, RUNNING FOOTMAN.

Forests at one time covered the whole of Britain with the exception of the marshes and high uplands. By the time of the NORMAN CONQUEST, gradual clearing had reduced this to about 32 per cent of the countryside, but in the 13th century there were still forests in 33 counties. William I organized the royal forests under the FOREST LAWS. Medieval forests were a medley of ash, oak, beech, sweet chestnut and other native hardwoods. In the following centuries disafforestation was caused by the need of timber for SHIPS and of wood to produce charcoal for the blastfurnaces of the IRON industry, while the ENCLOSURES of the 18th century brought about considerable clearing.

The Forestry Commission, established in 1919, now owns 1·8 million acres of woodland, planted mainly with regimented alien conifers. [H. J. Fleure and M. Davies, *A Natural History of Man in Britain* (revised ed., 1971)]

Forest Laws originated in England after the NORMAN CONQUEST, being designed to preserve areas for royal HUNTING. Such forests were not always wooded, e.g. New Forest was wooded, but Knaresborough Forest was open country. They were extended in size until by the 13th century they covered about a third of England, hindering farming by restrictive regulations and sometimes even destroying farms and villages. Their area was limited after MAGNA CARTA, and they were increasingly encroached upon for growing crops. The forest laws were finally abolished at the RESTORATION.

Forum the public-place or marketplace in a Roman TOWN. Around it were the BASILICA, TEMPLE, SHOPS, ROMAN BATHS and other public buildings, on the walls of which official notices were displayed. The forum at Silchester (Hants.) covered an oblong about 315 ft by 278 ft.

Fosse Way a Roman road, so-called from its accompanying ditches (Latin, *fossa*). Starting from Seaton or Exeter, it went north-east by way of Ilchester to Bath, Cirencester, Chesterton and Leicester and thence to Lincoln. Most of it was probably built by AD 47 as a fortified frontier road (*limes*) delimiting the civil from the military area. For its length, it was the most direct road in Britain.

Franciscans an order of FRIARS founded by St Francis of Assisi (1182–1226), the son of a rich Italian cloth-

merchant. Renouncing his family and his wealth, he devoted himself to helping the poor and sick and gathered round him a band of helpers, who became the Franciscan friars in 1210. The first Franciscans landed in England in 1224. They founded a great friary at Oxford, taught in the University and gave it a European reputation. At the DISSOLUTION OF THE MONASTERIES there were 66 Franciscan houses in England.

Franciscan Observants a reformed order of FRANCISCANS, founded in the 15th century, who sought to return to the strict rule of St Francis and lead a life of greater poverty. They had only 7 houses in England, but were the only representatives of a recent reform movement, and with the CARTHUSIANS and BRIGITTINES formed the notable exceptions to the decayed condition of English monasticism in the 16th century. Their most important house was the royal foundation at Greenwich, which not only enjoyed Henry VIII's direct patronage, but also supplied confessors to Queen Catherine and her daughter Mary. [A. G. Dickens, *The English Reformation* (1967)]

Freeman in ANGLO-SAXON law was one who was not a SLAVE or a VILLEIN, but there was not equality of status. He might be a THEGN or a CEORL. The word came also to be used for the BURGESSES of a BOROUGH.

Freemasons originated in the medieval GUILDS of working masons, who, since they went from job to job, had signs and gestures to admit them to their lodges (huts on the building-sites). Later the lodges became associations and as early as 1646 a lodge admitted into the craft a member who was not a working mason, and so there developed lodges of 'speculative' masons. Their known history begins in 1717 when four lodges met in

London to form a Grand Lodge, from which the present Grand Lodge of England is directly descended; and Grand Lodges in Scotland and Ireland followed soon afterwards. There are now about 6500 English lodges with 500 000 members. Apart from the performance of masonic rituals, their main purpose is charitable, and they have schools for boys and girls (founded in 1788 and 1789) and a benevolent institution for aged masons, wives and widows (1842). See also FRIENDLY SOCIETIES.

French hood fashionable for women from the 1520s to 1590, but still worn until about 1630. It was a small, rounded bonnet made on a stiff frame and worn far back on the head, exposing the hair, but covering the ears, and was ornamented with two rows of jewels, known as upper and nether billiments. The hood was edged on the front border with stiff-gathered trimming and fell at the back down the neck in formal pleats or, more often, was stiffened, turned up and worn flat on the crown, projecting over the forehead, and was known as a bongrace. See also COSTUME and HATS.

Friars members of religious orders, first founded in the 13th century, who took the same vows as MONKS, but did not live enclosed in a MONASTERY and were mendicants (or beggars). In England the three chief orders were known by the colour of their HABIT—Grey Friars (FRANCISCANS), Black Friars (DOMINICANS) and White Friars (CARMELITES). Other important orders were the AUGUSTINIAN HERMITS and the CRUTCHED FRIARS. The names of these orders are preserved in the streets of the City of London. The friars revolutionized the place of SERMONS in worship and introduced the first stone PULPITS in churches. The parish clergy disliked the friars as intruders, who took away their congregations (hence

medieval MISERICORDS commonly represent a fox, dressed as a friar, preaching in a pulpit to a gaggle of geese); and Chaucer spoke of them with irony. Yet they remained active preachers and frequent legatees in wills until the early 16th century.

Friendly societies began in the 18th century, taking their name from a fire INSURANCE society founded about 1700. Their members paid fixed subscriptions in return for regular payments for themselves in unemployment, sickness or old age and for their families if they died. When TRADE UNIONS were illegal, they were often founded under the disguise of a friendly society.

The first friendly societies were small, local bodies, but in the 19th century they were replaced by 'orders', which were large societies with a central organization and local branches, sometimes known as 'courts' or 'lodges', and admission to these was by secret ceremonies and passwords in imitation of FREEMASONS. They chose names for themselves which were fanciful or romantic (e.g. 'Oddfellows', 'Foresters') or descriptive (e.g. 'Rechabites', a teetotal order—see Jeremiah xxxv, 6, 7).

The friendly societies helped in the administration of NATIONAL INSURANCE in 1911, but have not done since 1946. Their membership has consequently been falling since then.

Frost Fairs unique events on the Thames held, in all, on nine occasions. When the river froze, sometimes to a depth of several feet, normal traffic was halted, and the tradesmen of the city erected booths and shops on the ice, while showmen organized juggling, puppet plays and the other usual entertainments of a fair. There was also sledging, skating, eating and drinking.

In 1554 Elizabeth I patronized a

Frost Fair and led her courtiers around its pleasures. In 1684 Charles II joined in the fun of another Frost Fair, taking part in a fox-hunt on the ice and bringing his queen to an ox-roasting ceremony. At this fair a printing-press was set up on the ice, and people bought sheets of paper with their names printed on it. There were Frost Fairs again in 1715 and in 1739–40. The last fair was in 1814. This ended with a sudden thaw. Masses of ice broke free and floated down the river, carrying with them tents, roundabouts and printing-presses to sink into the Thames.

The freezing of the river was made possible by old LONDON BRIDGE, the piers of which acted as a partial dam across the Thames. Its destruction and the building of the embankment in the 1870s prevented this for the future. [Margaret Baker, *Discovering English Fairs* (1967)]

Fruit eaten in the Middle Ages was mostly grown in orchards. The most common were pears (the most popular of all), APPLES, medlars, quinces, CHERRIES, strawberries, plums and peaches. The CRUSADES brought figs, dates and raisins into the country. In the 16th century fresh fruit was thought to produce colic, and so much dried fruit was eaten, especially raisins, currants and prunes; but ORANGES imported from Portugal were sold in the streets, and Shakespeare speaks of an orange-wife. Fruit remained a luxury in the 17th century, since, when a workman's wage was 6d a day, English cherries cost 8d a lb, a quart of gooseberries 3d and lemons 6d each. In the 18th century imported fruits like oranges and lemons, limes and bananas became more common, but not until about 1870 did working people begin to eat fruit. At first this was in the form of jam, and apples were the only fresh fruit, but this was later supplemented by bananas, which were the first cheap imported fruits.

Frumenty an old English dish, eaten particularly at CHRISTMAS, sometimes as an accompaniment to meat, sometimes on its own and sweetened with SUGAR. A 17th century recipe for frumenty stated, 'Take clean wheat and bray [pound] it in a mortar, that the hulls be all gone off, and seethe [boil] it till it burst, and take it up and let it cool, and take clean fresh broth and sweet milk of almonds or sweet milk of kine, and temper it all, and take the yolk of eggs. Boil it a little and set it down and mess it forth [i.e. serve] with venison or fresh mutton'. In making it, 100 EGGS were needed for each 8 pints of MILK.

Fuchsia was brought from South America to England in the late 18th century by a sailor as a present for his wife. It was seen in the window of their house in Wapping by James Lee, a nurseryman, who persuaded the sailor's wife to let him have it. He raised some 300 cuttings from this plant which he sold for £1 each, and then other nurserymen set out to develop the fuchsia. The first one with a white sepal was raised in 1842 and the first tricolour in 1872. Popular in Victorian GARDENS, there was later a reaction against the fuchsia, but it has now regained favour again.

Fumerell the outlet in the roof of the HALL of a CASTLE or HOUSE above the hearth to allow the smoke to escape from the fire. In the late 13th century it was covered above and given open louvres (horizontal wooden slats tilted to throw off the rain). This was the beginning of the development of CHIMNEYS.

Furniture was scanty in ancient times because most people slept on the floor and spent most of their time out in the open; and in the Middle Ages it was limited and simple in construction. Native woods, mainly OAK, were used to make CHESTS and CUPBOARDS, CHAIRS and TABLES, BEDS and other useful articles. In CASTLES and MANOR houses furniture became increasingly common. It was heavy and plain in style, but decoration such as the LINEN-FOLD pattern was later adopted. RUSHES were strewn on the floors, but CARPETS were introduced during the CRUSADES.

The RENAISSANCE and later the RESTOR-ATION were followed by richer types of furniture. WALNUT became the fashionable wood, to be replaced in turn by SATINWOOD, ROSEWOOD and MAHOGANY. Greater attention was paid to comfort in furniture design, and the wishes of WOMEN had a growing influence on its development and led to the appearance of a wider variety of pieces. These included the DRESSING-TABLE in the 17th century and the WARDROBE and DAVENPORT in the 18th century. During the later 18th century English styles were very influential, particularly the elegant designs of Thomas Chippendale (1718?–79) and the severe lines and simple symmetrical shapes of George Hepplewhite (d. 1788) and Thomas Sheraton (1751–1806).

Victorian times saw the development of mass-production and a liking for heavy, clumsy pieces, and rooms were over-crowded with all sorts of seats, chairs and hanging-cupboards. The 20th century produced functional, cheaper furniture made from steel-tubing or using saw-cut veneer. [R. Fastnedge, *English Furniture Styles 1500–1830* (1955)]

Fustian a kind of coarse twilled cloth, made of COTTON or cotton and LINEN mixed, with a surface resembling VELVET, and hence it was sometimes called 'Mock Velvet'. In 1841, when Feargus O'Connor was seeking to revive CHARTISM, he appealed in his newspaper, the *Northern Star*, to 'the fustian jackets, the unshorn chins and the blistered hands' of true working-men.

The name was also given in the 14th century to a woollen or WORSTED cloth made at Norwich, and in Chaucer's *Canterbury Tales* the Knight wore such a fustian tunic stained with marks left by his armour.

G

Gable hood a women's head-dress during the first half of the 16th century, consisting of a hood wired up to form a pointed arch in front like a little roof with a black cloth at the back. See also HATS.

Galilee a small PORCH or CHAPEL at the entrance to a medieval CHURCH or CATHE-DRAL. The Galilee at Lincoln Cathedral is a porch at the west side of the south TRANSEPT; at Ely Cathedral it is a porch at the west side of the nave.

It was here that the Sunday PROCESSION ended and was so called from the disciples being told that the Master would 'go before them into Galilee'; and corpses were deposited here previous to BURIAL.

Gallery was often built at the end of the great HALL of a CASTLE or MANOR and was sometimes known as the MINSTRELS' gallery, because they performed there during meals. See also LONG GALLERY.

After the REFORMATION, galleries were

built in CHURCHES, usually at the west end, for the CHOIR, it being sometimes the ROOD loft taken down and re-erected at the back of the church. In the 18th century side galleries were also erected to hold part of the congregation, but these were usually taken down in the next century under the influence of the TRACTARIANS.

Gambling was restricted in the Middle Ages because it interfered with ARCHERY, but it nevertheless flourished, especially in TAVERNS and on GAMES such as BACKGAMMON and CARDS. In Tudor times it extended to BOWLS, COCK-FIGHTING, BEAR-BAITING and TENNIS, which was one reason for their suppression by the PURITANS in the COMMONWEALTH. After the RESTORATION, many CLUBS became centres of gambling, and so did the ASSEMBLY ROOMS of the 18th century, one of the most famous being ALMACK'S, and they were followed by the PLEASURE GARDENS. The LOTTERY, conducted by the state, was a favourite form of gambling until suppressed in the early 19th century, though Premium Bonds are a modern version of it. Among the most popular modern ways of gambling are FOOTBALL POOLS and BINGO. Betting on races has also increased since 1960, when Parliament legalized betting-shops, to which people can go for ready-money betting with a licensed bookmaker.

Games popular in the Middle Ages included MARBLES, BOWLS, SKITTLES and DARTS, as well as the semi-military pursuits of ARCHERY, TOURNAMENTS, and QUINTAIN, CHESS, CARDS and BACKGAMMON were common indoor games. BARLEY-BRAKE and HOT COCKLES were liked by both adults and children. The 16th century brought in BILLIARDS and the next century CUP AND BALL, while after the RESTORATION came the pastime of PALL-MALL. Children's games included, then and later, SPAN-FARTHING, SNAPDRAGON and BULLET PUDDING.

In the mid-19th century, when games became compulsory at the PUBLIC SCHOOLS, the old games of FOOTBALL and CRICKET, HOCKEY and TENNIS (see also STOOLBALL and LAWN TENNIS) took their present-day form. Minor games which have been passing crazes include DIABOLO and YO-YO. See also SPORT.

Gardens in ROMAN BRITAIN were probably arranged in orderly fashion, divided by parallel hedges and paths and growing roses, acanthus, rue, rosemary and lilies. The re-created garden of FISHBOURNE PALACE is the only original Roman garden known in Europe outside Italy.

The ANGLO-SAXONS had no gardens. They were revived by the MONASTERIES, which had HERB GARDENS and grew grapes for WINE. Gradually the larger MANOR houses had pleasure grounds with trimmed HEDGES and MAZES as well as orchards. Farmhouses and COTTAGE gardens grew HERBS and VEGETABLES. By the end of the 14th century, as VILLEINS became COPYHOLDERS, cottage gardens and orchards multiplied. Larger gardens had sanded paths, turf mounds, arbours and hedges as well as flowers, though the varieties of these were not yet great, the commonest being roses, single and double dog-roses and sweet-briar.

In the 16th century, flower-beds were surrounded by low trellis-work. Other features were topiary, artificial mounts topped with SUMMER-HOUSES, KNOT GARDENS (as at HAMPTON COURT) and flower-beds forming interlacing geometrical patterns bordered with low hedges. Mazes became popular and so did bowling greens (see BOWLS). In the 17th century the PARTERRE was introduced, and TULIPS became increasingly popular.

The 18th century brought a reaction against formal gardens. Lancelot ('Capability') Brown (1715–83) swept away hedges, walks and enclosed gardens to create parkland scenery (e.g. at Blenheim Palace, Kew Gardens and St James's Park) in which sweeping turf was accentuated by groups of trees, while wooded slopes gave a glimpse of a lake and encircling woodlands (see also HA-HA). GAZEBOS and TEMPLES were built, and the ROMANTIC MOVEMENT brought FOLLIES and HERMITS' caves. ORANGERIES developed into GREENHOUSES and CONSERVATORIES.

In the later 19th century there was, in turn, a reaction against such landscape gardening. Formal flower-beds returned

Garden temple

to favour, while the invention of the LAWNMOWER made LAWNS more popular. At the same time, there was a continuously increasing introduction of foreign trees and shrubs, plants and flowers, such as the SWEET PEA and FUCHSIA.

With the growth of TOWNS in the 20th century into miles and miles of suburbs, there have come into being thousands of small gardens attached to HOUSES. It was estimated in the 1960s that there were over 10 million gardeners in England, but also that to one out of three of them gardening was a disagreeable chore. [Edward Hyams, *The English Garden* (1964)]

Gas originated as a by-product of the manufacture of COKE for the IRON industry. William Murdock (1754–1839), when employed by Boulton and Watt in erecting mining-engines in Cornwall, installed gas-lighting in his own house in Redruth in 1792 and caused a sensation in 1802 by illuminating the Soho foundry at Birmingham with gas burning in fishtail burners to celebrate the Treaty of Amiens. In 1807 the first street in London was lighted by gas, and in 1812 the Gas Light and Coke Company was founded. Gas-cookers were exhibited at the GREAT EXHIBITION (1851). For most of the later 19th century gaslight was unrivalled, and even now gas has maintained its supremacy in cooking over ELECTRICITY.

In 1948 the several British gas companies were nationalized, and since the late 1960s the industry has been turning from coal gas to natural gas obtained from beneath the North Sea. See also LIGHTING.

Gatehouses formed the entrances to medieval MONASTERIES, CASTLES and MANORS and were strongly fortified, having a heavy wooden door in the archway and were protected by BARBICANS and later

Manor gatehouse

MACHICOLATION. They had rooms in the turrets and above the arch, which in monasteries (e.g. St Albans and Ely) sometimes contained PRISONS. When the need for fortification passed, great country houses continued to have gatehouses for decoration and display. Tudor gatehouses were elaborately ornamented with cupolas, oriel WINDOWS and elaborately carved arches, but in the 17th century the gatehouse was commonly replaced by a gateway placed on the axis of a symmetrically planned house or entrance to a park, which had ornamental iron gates framed by stone arches or piers and surmounted

Abbey gatehouse

by urns or heraldic figures; and in the 18th and 19th centuries the park gates of country houses had lodges for the gatekeeper built on either side. Altogether, the purpose was to have a design which afforded an impressive entrance to a house, and the decorative details were often on an imposing scale.

Gazebo a word which first became usual in the 18th century to describe a small two-storied building situated at a

Gazebo

vantage-point in a GARDEN (e.g. in a wall overlooking the carriage-way). The lower part was commonly for storing garden tools or chairs, and the upper storey was built with lavish windows to afford a view. The derivation of the word is uncertain. It is possibly a corruption of some Oriental word or of 'gaze-about' or a mock Latin word comparable with *videbo* ('I shall see'). The East Gazebo at Montacute (Somerset) is in a garden wall, while there is a Georgian one at Walcot Hall (Shropshire) and another overlooking the River Avon at Stoneleigh Abbey (Warwickshire).

General Strike (May 1926) occurred when the mine-owners, forced to lower COAL prices, decided to lower wages also, but the miners went on strike and were supported by the TRADES UNION CONGRESS, which declared a general strike. This was not a complete strike. Workers in all forms of transport and in most industries were called out, but not those in the electrical and gas, sanitary and health and food services. The government, however, had made its plans, and volunteers kept essential services going, while the trade union leaders had made few preparations, and after nine days they called off the strike unconditionally. But the miners remained on strike throughout the summer until they had to accept lower wages and longer hours.

Gig a light two-wheeled CARRIAGE drawn by one horse, often used by tradesmen and farmers in the 19th century. See also DOG-CART, TRAP.

Gilbert's Act (1782) a permissive measure empowering PARISHES to combine to build union WORKHOUSES, allowing the able-bodied poor to be provided with work outside the workhouse and permitting outdoor relief from the rates. These provisions virtually abolished the workhouse test of the POOR LAW ACT (1723) and made the SPEENHAMLAND SYSTEM possible.

Gilbertines the only monastic order founded in England, being established by St Gilbert of Sempringham (1083–1189), incumbent of Sempringham and Torrington, South Lincolnshire. In 1132 he built a house for seven NUNS in a CLOISTER against the north wall of Sempringham Parish Church; a house for CANONS was added later on the south side. At worship the nuns were separated from the canons by a wall down the middle of the NAVE of the Parish Church. By the 14th century a great Priory Church with monastic buildings for 200 nuns and 400 canons had been built close to it. By the time of St Gilbert's death, there were 13 Gilbertine PRIORIES for women in Lincolnshire, nine double MONASTERIES and four for canons only; and at the DISSOLUTION OF THE MONASTERIES there were 26 houses in England. The HABIT of a Gilbertine canon was a black CASSOCK with a white cloak over it and a HOOD lined with lambskin.

Gin a spirit distilled from grain and flavoured mainly with juniper. The low price of corn after 1717 was responsible for the gin-mania in London, which produced among the poor the scenes depicted in Hogarth's cartoon, *Gin Lane*. By the 1730s there were thought to be over 6000 gin-shops, and one could get drunk for 1d. The Gin Act (1736) imposed a duty of 20s a gallon and fixed the cost of a licence to sell spirits at £50, but it caused rioting and was hardly imposed. However, the Gin Act (1751), by forbidding distillers to sell gin retail, was effective. The consumption of gin fell from 8 495 000 gallons in 1751 to 5 946 000 in 1752 and 2 100 000 in 1760.

Ginger a popular SPICE from Roman times and much used in medieval sauces. It was also commonly prescribed by APOTHECARIES since it had a warming and opiate effect. The most expensive sort ('colombine') came from Mecca by way

of Alexandria, while the cheaper sort ('string ginger') came from India and the Malabar coast. Both sorts came into wider use as a result of the CRUSADES.

Gingerbread has long been made from flour, treacle, SUGAR, ground GINGER and other SPICES. It was sold in the form of square, thick cakes or small, button-like cakes known as gingerbread-nuts. The best was made at Grantham (Lincs.), and 'Grantham gingerbread' was famed. Until the middle of the 19th century gingerbread cakes were often profusely decorated with gold-leaf or Dutch-leaf, which looked like gold; this easily peeled off, and hence the saying 'taking the gilt off the gingerbread'. Gingerbread stalls were common at BARTHOLOMEW FAIR, MAYFAIR and other FAIRS. They sold gingerbread figures, known as fairings, baked in moulds, which were an especial favourite with children. These, too, were gilt and were often made in the form of Punch and Judy and other fairy story favourites, while 'gingerbread husbands', made in the form of men, were common.

Girl Guides (now known as Guides) began because many girls paraded as scouts with their brothers at the first great rally of BOY SCOUTS in the CRYSTAL PALACE, London, in 1909. Sir Robert (later Lord) Baden-Powell asked his sister, Agnes Baden-Powell, to devise a similar scheme for girls, whom he called after the Cavalry Guides of the Indian Army. Later brownies (7½–11 years old) and rangers (16–21 years) were formed. There are now more than 560 000 guides in the United Kingdom alone.

Girls' schools in the Middle Ages were confined to a few attached to nunneries in which the daughters of nobility and gentry were boarded and educated. After the DISSOLUTION OF THE MONASTERIES, although girls sometimes when very young attended PETTY SCHOOLS with their brothers, they were usually educated at home by their mothers or tutors.

The earliest girls' schools were founded in James I's reign (1603–25), at first in and around London. They were both day and boarding schools, mostly for the daughters of the nobility and gentry, though they often received the daughters of wealthy merchants. They paid great attention to polite accomplishments (e.g. MUSIC, DANCING and EMBROIDERY) and DEPORTMENT and ETIQUETTE, such accomplishments being thought likely to get a girl an eligible husband. Though many wealthy girls were taught at home by a GOVERNESS, these schools continued little changed throughout the 18th and well into the 19th century, except that some attached more importance to arithmetic (for household accounts) and introduced foreign languages.

After the French Revolution, some girls' schools were established by EMIGRÉ noblewomen; and in the early 19th century schools were established for middle-class girls, who were also prepared for marriage, but in their station of life, being taught reading, writing and arithmetic and (according to a school advertisement) 'lace-making, plain needlework, raising pastry, sauces and cookery'.

Girls in these schools had little freedom or exercise. They did not play GAMES and went only for an occasional walk in a CROCODILE; they had to submit to the BACKBOARD and STOCKS to improve their posture. Discipline was strict, and punishments involved the BIRCH-ROD and CANE, DUNCE'S CAP, and HEADBAND.

Poor girls went to CHARITY SCHOOLS in the 18th century and in the 19th to the NATIONAL SCHOOLS and BRITISH SCHOOLS.

In 1858 Miss Beale was appointed to Cheltenham Ladies' College, and in 1850 Miss Buss founded the North London Collegiate School for day girls; both set out to give girls an education equal to that of boys in PUBLIC SCHOOLS. FINISHING SCHOOLS were also established for wealthy girls. The Girls' Public Day School Trust, founded in 1872, founded high schools, largely modelled on the North London Collegiate School, for middle-class girls, enabling them to go to the UNIVERSITIES. These high schools were in their turn the model for the new secondary schools for girls established under the EDUCATION ACT 1902. [Josephine Kamm, *Hope Deferred* (1965)]

Glaive, Glave a WEAPON consisting of a single-edged blade fixed to the end of a long staff and differing from a BILL in having its edge on the convex curve. Fitted with a circular hand-guard, it was often used by foot-soldiers in the 15th century, being suitable for both cutting and thrusting.

Glass made by fusing silica (sand) with soda or potash was invented in Egypt or Syria about 2500 BC. The blowpipe, invented shortly before the birth of Christ, enabled transparent glass to be made, and glass for WINDOWS was made in ROMAN BRITAIN, but most of the glass vessels used were imported.

In the Weald of Sussex, coarse glass was blown from the 14th century, but most window-glass was imported from France until the 16th century. During the RENAISSANCE, after the art of glass-making had declined for centuries except in the Near East, the Venetians perfected a clear, colourless glass that could be diamond-engraved; and in 1575 Elizabeth I granted Giacomo Verzelini and a group of Venetian workmen a licence 'to make drinking glasses in the manner of Murano, on the undertaking that he bring up in the said art and knowledge our natural subjects'. George Ravenscroft first made flint glass about 1675, in the manufacture of which LEAD was used to make it less fragile, more brilliant and soft enough for deep cutting.

It enabled English craftsmen to make tableware of great beauty, much of which was exported. By the end of the 17th century about 100 glass-houses were making flint glass, London, Bristol, Stourbridge, Birmingham and Newcastle upon Tyne being important centres of the industry. [E. Barrington Haynes, *Glass Through the Ages* (1948)] See also CRYSTAL PALACE, STAINED GLASS, PLATE GLASS.

Gleaning the right allowed to cottagers to gather the ears of corn left by the reapers in the fields after HARVEST-TIME. Often in a VILLAGE the SEXTON rang a BELL from the CHURCH at eight o'clock in the morning and again at seven in the evening to tell the gleaners when they should begin and end work. The gleaned grain was taken to the miller, who returned it ground, after keeping a part of it for himself as payment. Each family depended on this flour as part of its diet during the winter. Gleaning ceased with the introduction of the REAPING-MACHINE and the COMBINE-HARVESTER. [Gordon Winter, *A Country Camera 1844–1914* (1966); Flora Thompson, *Lark Rise to Candleford* (1945)]

Glebe in English and Scottish ecclesiastical law the land devoted to the maintenance of the incumbent of a PARISH. In the Middle Ages, it was often cultivated by the priest himself, who also, in areas of OPEN-FIELD FARMING, shared in the agricultural life of the VILLAGE. By an Act of Parliament of 1925, all glebe in Scotland will ultimately be vested in the General Trustees of the CHURCH OF SCOTLAND.

Glees musical compositions for several male voices (one voice to each part), usually sung unaccompanied. It was a purely English form and most popular from about 1750 to 1830. During this period, Glee Clubs flourished in several

towns, the most famous being the Gentlemen's Catch Club of London, founded in 1761, to which several members of the royal family (including George IV as prince and as king) belonged.

Gloves were worn by Roman ladies to protect their hands both while they worked and at meals, but not often in the early Middle Ages because sleeves were long and often covered the hands. From the 12th century wealthy men and women began to wear gloves, which were often richly ornamented with gold, silver and jewels, and King John, Henry III and Edward I were buried with their gloves on. Later working-people began to wear gloves, but these were more like mittens. Jointed metal gauntlets were a necessary part of ARMOUR, and from them developed in the mid-15th century leather gauntlet gloves with cuffs spreading up the wrists worn by women. In the 17th century both sexes wore elaborately embroidered gloves, white or coloured (see EMBROIDERY), but in the 18th they became tight-fitting, plain and without cuffs. In the 19th century ETIQUETTE required that ladies wore gloves on every possible occasion. See also VALENTINE'S DAY.

Goffering-tongs were used in LAUNDERING from the Middle Ages onwards for IRONING and making wavy the edges of frills and RUFFS.

Gold was mined in ROMAN BRITAIN at Dolaucothy (Carmarthen) and possibly at other places in Wales and in Cornwall and Scotland. It was much valued by the ANGLO-SAXONS (see SUTTON HOO). It was used widely in the Middle Ages for tableware and church ornaments, and a continual object of medieval ALCHEMY was to turn baser metals into gold. By the end of the 15th century there were 52 GOLDSMITHS' shops in Cheapside in London. Most old plate did not survive, however, being melted down in the REFORMATION and the Civil War. See also COINAGE, SILVER.

Gold penny was minted by Offa (757–796), Edward the Elder (901–924), Ethelred II (987–1016) and Edward the Confessor (1016–1066); but gold coins were rarely produced in England until the 14th century. In 1257 Henry III minted a gold penny (or bezant) originally worth 20d, but the value was increased to 2s in 1265. As few needed such a valuable coin, it was withdrawn from circulation in about 1270, and no more gold coins were struck in England until the FLORIN of Edward III. See also COINAGE.

Goldsmiths formed their GUILD in London in the 12th century. The Goldsmiths' Company was founded about 1327 and incorporated by CHARTER in 1392. During the COMMONWEALTH and after the RESTORATION (when GOLD and SILVER plate had been melted down by both sides in the Civil War), the goldsmiths of London increasingly assumed the functions of holding and lending money, and their businesses developed into the first BANKS. See also LIVERY COMPANY.

Golf which may have originated in the Netherlands, was a national game in Scotland by the mid-15th century, being played by all ranks. Its rules were laid down by the Royal and Ancient Club of St Andrews, established by 1754. James VI of Scotland (I of England) founded the existing golf club at Blackheath in 1608, but the first club for English players (as distinct from Scottish exiles) was the Westward Ho! (Devon), founded in 1864. The game did not gain much support until the 1880s, and (unlike Scotland) it began and continued in England as a largely middle-class game. [R. Browning, *A History of Golf* (1955)]

Good Friday the Friday before EASTER on which the anniversary of the Crucifixion is kept. Before the REFORMATION, the ceremony of the Veneration of the Cross (popularly known as 'creeping to the cross') was held. In each CHURCH a cross was set up in front of the ALTAR, and the clergy and people prostrated themselves before it.

In some parts of the country, the custom survives of rolling EGGS down a hillside on Good Friday to symbolize the rolling of the stone away from the tomb of Jesus, but in other places this is done at Easter. HOT CROSS BUNS have long been associated with Good Friday.

Goose is believed to be descended from the Greylag goose and was the first domesticated fowl, being commonly kept in ROMAN BRITAIN. It was a great delicacy in the Middle Ages, especially when MEAT was scarce in the winter, coming into season at Michaelmas and being especially eaten at MARTINMAS. Besides domesticated geese, many wild ones in the fens of eastern England were killed for food. When the fens were drained, it was more profitable to keep tame ones, and there were large flocks in Lincolnshire. See also POULTRY.

Goose-herds drove geese, several thousand at a time, to FAIRS and MARKETS, driving them 8–10 miles a day and often taking weeks on the journey. The geese were driven through first tar and then sand at the beginning of the journey to give them protection for their feet. There were special Goose Fairs, the most famous being at Nottingham, which began on the first Thursday in October, and to which at one time as many as 20 000 geese were driven. See also DROVE ROADS.

Geese were also plucked as often as five times a year to get down for pillows and mattresses, and their quills were used as PENS until the middle of the 19th century.

Goose-riding was a popular rural 18th

century SPORT. A live goose was hung up by its feet, with its head and neck thoroughly greased, and the contestants tried to pull off the bird's head while riding past at speed on horseback.

Gordon Riots (1780) followed a petition presented to Parliament against the Roman Catholic Relief Act (1778) by the Protestant Association under the presidency of the eccentric Lord George Gordon (1751–93). The rioting lasted six days; ROMAN CATHOLIC chapels and dwelling houses, breweries and distilleries were sacked; NEWGATE PRISON and others were attacked and the prisoners freed. Eventually George III insisted on the use of troops. An assault on the Bank of England was repulsed and the rioting suppressed. Perhaps about 500 died in the disturbances, and over 500 private dwellings were destroyed; 25 rioters were later hanged. Though partly due to 'No Popery' feeling, the riots were also a social protest, and mainly wealthier Roman Catholics suffered. Most of the rioters tried were hitherto respectable working-men resentful of the propertied classes. [Christopher Hibbert, *King Mob: the Story of Lord George Gordon and the Riots of 1780* (1958)]

Gothic (originally a term of reproach applied at the time of the RENAISSANCE) was a style of architecture which succeeded NORMAN ARCHITECTURE (or Romanesque) and was prevalent in western Europe from the 12th to the 16th century. In England it developed through three successive types—*Early English* (pointed arch, large windows, deep buttresses, slender, often clustered columns, deeply-recessed doorways); *Decorated* (highly ornamental windows, slender pillars, lavish and naturalistic carving and mouldings); *Perpendicular* (prevalence of vertical lines, flatter arches, lofty windows, frequent panelled surfaces, fantracery vaulting). In the 19th century under the influence of the ROMANTIC MOVEMENT and the TRACTARIANS there was a revival of Gothic styles. [T. W. West, *A History of Architecture in England* (1963); C. W. Budden, *English Gothic Churches* (1933)]

Governess was employed in noble medieval families to teach both daughters

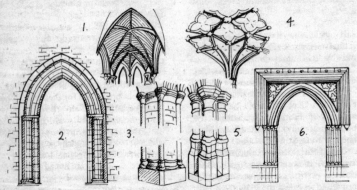

Gothic style: 1 Early English vaulting; 2 Early English doorway; 3 Early English column; 4 Perpendicular vaulting; 5 Perpendicular column; 6 Perpendicular doorway

and DAMSELS, and they continued in wealthy households after the beginning of GIRLS' SCHOOLS in the late 17th century. In the 19th century, often the only employment for a middle-class girl was to become a governess, and she might be badly-paid and expected to undertake housekeeping duties as well as the entire charge of her pupils, besides being humiliated by being treated as a social inferior. Until late in the 19th century the teachers in expensive schools were also called 'governesses' and their pupils 'young ladies'.

Grammar Schools were so-called because originally their main object was to teach Latin grammar. The word 'gramer schole' was first used in English in 1387, but in origin they go back to the Christianization of ANGLO-SAXON England, when the founding of DIOCESES was regularly associated with the establishment of schools to train boys in the use of Latin to fit them to be clergymen, and other schools were associated with MONASTERIES. The rise of the medieval UNIVERSITIES was accompanied by the foundation of a considerable number of grammar schools, and in the later Middle Ages these were often connected with CHANTRIES and GUILDS.

After the REFORMATION, many grammar schools were refounded and new ones were established by private benefactors. Through the influence of the RENAISSANCE, Greek and Latin literature were added to exercises in Latin grammar in the Tudor grammar schools. In the 17th century a number of boarding grammar schools became sharply differentiated and developed into PUBLIC SCHOOLS.

During the 18th century, many grammar schools declined, and their limited classical curriculum led parents to prefer private schools and the DISSENTING ACADEMIES. In the 19th century many grammar schools were reorganized, and new ones

were founded (including GIRLS' SCHOOLS), especially by local education authorities after the EDUCATION ACT (1902). Recently some grammar schools have become merged into larger COMPREHENSIVE SCHOOLS. [A. F. Leach, *The Schools of Medieval England* (1915); J. H. Brown, *Elizabethan Schooldays* (1933); H. C. Barnard, *English Education from 1760* (1947)]

Gramophone began with two inventions made in USA. These were Thomas Edison's phonograph (1877), the first machine to record and reproduce sound, and Emile Berliner's improved machine (1888), which he called a gramophone. Edison traced the sound-waves on tin-foil cylinders, while Berliner used a disk revolving on a turn-table.

The turn-tables of the first gramophones were turned by hand; then clockwork motors were used, and records were made of wax, but cylinders were also made until about 1919. Electrical recording came in 1924, and in the early 1930s the horn, which had been used to amplify the sound, was superseded by an electrical amplifier and loudspeaker, while clockwork was replaced by electrical motors. The first long-playing record was made in USA in 1948, and soon afterwards came 'stereophonic sound' on records.

Tape-recording was developed in Germany during the Second World War and is increasingly replacing the older records.

Grand National Consolidated Trades Union was founded in January 1834 when Robert Owen persuaded a number of TRADE UNIONS, representing both skilled and unskilled workers, to amalgamate themselves into it. He hoped that it would revolutionize society by setting up co-operative workshops and a system of exchanging each other's products instead of selling them for profit; but the working-class were not idealistic and were more interested in strikes for better wages and shorter working-hours. Government alarm led to the prosecution of the 'TOLPUDDLE MARTYRS'. The union reached perhaps about a quarter of a million members, but collapsed by 1835. Most of its funds were exhausted, and its treasurer absconded with the rest. There were a few futile strikes, but they were not supported by the skilled workers, and worsening trade conditions hastened its end. Its failure encouraged the growth of CHARTISM.

Grand Tour a journey through the Continent which became usual for young Englishmen of rank during the 18th century, being made possible by the new wealth of the nobility. The Grand Tour usually lasted for three years, but sometimes more. The young man, accompanied by a tutor, sometimes took his own COACH, but more usually travelled by POST-CHAISE. The object was to enable him to learn French breeding and Italian taste to fit him for his place in society. The Tour usually started in a French provincial town, where he could learn French; then he went on to Paris to acquire fashionable manners; and finally to Italy, which was the most important part of the Tour. Dr Johnson said, 'A man who has not been in Italy is always conscious of an inferiority'; and in Italy the young man saw the famous collections of antique sculpture and Renaissance pictures as examplars of elegant taste and culture. Few young men returned from the Grand Tour without pictures, statuary and bronzes to embellish their great country houses.

From the beginning of the 19th century, as steamships and railways replaced the older forms of travel, the middle classes also began to undertake foreign travel. Entertainment became the aim of foreign travel instead of education and fine manners. The new outlook destroyed the Grand Tour, which was replaced for the wealthy by the PUBLIC SCHOOLS and the UNIVERSITIES.

Great Exhibition (1851) was promoted by the Prince Consort, who saw it as 'an exhibition worthy of the greatness of this country; not merely national in its scope and benefits, but comprehensive of the whole world'. Its centre-piece in Hyde Park was the CRYSTAL PALACE which housed nearly 17 000 exhibitors from Britain and abroad. The articles exhibited in arts, manufactures and the various products of countries were intended to display the technical achievements of the first half of the 19th century. It was visited by over six million people, many brought by special EXCURSIONS, during the 23 weeks it was open. The Exhibition demonstrated Britain's industrial progress and material prosperity and showed the way in which science could increase national prestige. [Asa Briggs, *Victorian People* (1954)]

Great Fire of London (1666) started on September 2 in a baker's shop in Pudding Lane; the spot is now marked by the Monument near LONDON BRIDGE. Fanned by a strong east wind, the fire spread rapidly along the warehouses by the river. The water in the Thames was low, and there were no effective FIRE-FIGHTING measures. Panic spread, and people gave all their attention to seeking to save their possessions. After three days, the wind dropped, and Charles II checked the flames by ordering sailors to blow up with gunpowder houses in the path of the fire. The area devastated covered 436 acres within the walls and 73 without. It destroyed 13 200 houses, 89 churches, ST PAUL'S CATHEDRAL, most of the city gates and bridges and many public buildings, including the Guildhall, Royal Exchange, Customs House, STEELYARD and BRIDE-

WELL. Only six people seem to have died. Popular opinion blamed the ROMAN CATHOLICS for it. It was not the reason, as is commonly supposed, for the disappearance of the PLAGUE, since most of the slum districts, where this had started, survived. [L. W. Cowie, *Plague and Fire* (1970)]

Great North Road between London and Edinburgh, is one of the main ROADS, radiating from London, which emerged in the later Middle Ages, running in part along the route of Roman roads. It follows sections of Ermine Street between London and York and its extension, Dere Street, further northwards. In 1635 a regular postal service was organized along it 'to run night and day between Edinburgh and the City of London', and a MAIL-COACH service was established in 1786. With the constructions of the MOTOR-WAYS, its importance has diminished, but it is being improved to serve as a general purpose road. [Frank Morley, *The Great North Road* (1961)]

Greenhouses were first mentioned by John Evelyn in 1664. These early houses were slate-roofed, brick-walled, small-windowed structures, where plants might 'stand warm and safe from storms, winds, frosts, dews, blastings and other mischiefs'. Late in the 18th century glass roofs were devised, and the repeal of the glass tax in 1845 and the use of ironwork revolutionized their construction. Victorian great houses had massive greenhouses which reached their perfection at the time of Sir Joseph Paxton (1803–65), the Duke of Devonshire's head gardener at Chatsworth (Derbyshire) and designer of the CRYSTAL PALACE. See also ORANGERIES and CONSERVATORIES.

Greyhound which is figured on ancient Egyptian monuments, came to Britain either from the Continent or was brought directly from the north African coast and the Balearic Islands by PHOENICIAN traders. Greyhounds were known in England before the days of ROMAN BRITAIN, and so also was the sport of coursing hares with greyhounds. By Elizabeth I's reign, this was a popular and fashionable sport in England, though public coursing trials only began in Charles I's reign. In 1776 the first coursing club was founded at Swaffham (Norfolk) and was followed by many others; and in 1858 the National Coursing Club was formed and drew up rules for the sport. Coursing now means the pursuit of a hare by a pair of greyhounds in sight (not by scent). See also HUNTING.

Greyhound racing began in USA in 1909. The first English racing tracks were opened at Belle Vue, Manchester (1926), and the White City, London (1927), and by 1928 there were over fifty tracks all over the country, with a total of $13\frac{1}{2}$ million attendances. In 1969 there were about 150 tracks in Britain. See also DOGS.

Grime's Graves a number of NEW STONE AGE mines, six miles north-west of Thetford (Norfolk). The miners, using ANTLER-PICKS, opened up central shafts, some as deep as 40 feet, to reach outcrops

Grime's Graves

135

of FLINT in the sides of an ancient valley and then ran horizontal galleries in all directions from the bottom. Waste material from a new shaft was thrown into an adjacent exhausted mine, and hundreds of filled-in mineshafts exist. Now 16 have been excavated and two kept open for inspection. An altar to a little chalk goddess can still be seen in one of the open pits. Knappers (who broke the flints with hammers) worked at the head of the mines to produce axe, spear and arrow-heads. A small flint knapping industry still survives at nearby Brandon. Other flint mines have been found elsewhere in East Anglia and on the South Downs (e.g. at Cissbury).

Groat the first multiple of the PENNY minted in England, worth 4d in imitation of the French *gros* and the German *groschen*. It was first issued in England in 1279, but not again until it was produced for his Continental dominions about 1339 by Edward III, who also began the regular coining of silver groats (4d) and half-groats (2d) in England in 1351. It was replaced under Elizabeth I by the sixpence and threepence, but revived under Charles II and circulated until the mid-18th century. It was struck again as currency for a short period from 1835. See also COINAGE.

Grocer was originally a 'grosser' or 'en-grosser', one who bought and sold in the gross (i.e. in large quantities). The Company of Grocers (see also LIVERY COMPANIES), said to have been incorporated in 1344, consisted of wholesale dealers in SPICES and other foreign produce. By the 16th century the term had come to mean a trader dealing in spices, dried FRUITS, SUGAR and other foodstuffs which were not sold by specialized shop-keepers. By the end of the 17th century grocers were selling TEA and COFFEE; the Russell family were first able to buy their coffee from the grocer at Woburn (Beds.) in 1685. They extended the range of their sales in the 18th century; and a housewife was able to get from the grocer in the small town of Brackley (Bucks.) currants, raisins, pepper, nutmeg, sugar, oatmeal, soap, treacle and vinegar. From the mid-19th century some grocers began also to sell beer, wines and spirits in bottles. Since the 1950s they have been threatened by the growth of supermarkets (see SHOPS).

Grog the sea term for RUM and water. The name was derived from Admiral Edward Vernon, who wore breeches of grogram (a material of silk and mohair) and so was nicknamed 'Old Grog'. In about 1745 he ordered his sailors to dilute their RUM with water.

Guides, see GIRL GUIDES.

Guilds first became important in medieval England with the merchant guilds, which came into being from the late 11th century. When a TOWN became a BOROUGH, its CHARTER usually gave it the right to have a merchant guild, which controlled trade within the town's boundaries and limited the number of outsiders who wished to become traders there. From the 14th century merchant guilds were increasingly replaced by craft guilds, each of which controlled a particular trade or industry (e.g. the GOLDSMITHS). These developed rules for APPRENTICES, enforced standards of good workmanship and cared for ill and needy members. In the 16th century the guilds steadily declined because industry and trade began to develop on a national instead of a local basis. See also FREEMASONS, LIVERY COMPANIES.

Guinea originally the guinea POUND or SOVEREIGN (20s), which replaced the UNITED in 1663, when it was first minted from gold from Guinea on the West African coast. Its value soon rose to 21s and by 1694 was 30s, but was fixed at 21s in 1717. It was last coined in 1813 and was replaced by the new gold sovereign (20s), which was minted from 1817 to 1925. Some prices and subscriptions, however, continued to be recorded in guineas. See also COINAGE.

Guitar a six-stringed musical instrument, somewhat like the LUTE. In the 12th century the CRUSADES introduced into Europe a stringed instrument much like the modern guitar, which was used by travelling musicians to accompany their songs. The guitar became popular in France and Spain and had a period of popularity in England in the later 17th century; Charles II brought back one from his exile in France, though Pepys thought it was 'but a bawble'. From about 1750 the guitar was very popular in England for about 90 years. In an attempt to prevent ladies selling their HARPSICHORDS and SPINETS, a harpsichord-maker gave away large numbers of cheap guitars to milliners and street-singers to destroy its prestige.

In the 19th century the guitar tended to be the preserve of classical musicians and their followers in Europe, but in America immigrant pioneers in the wagon-trains sang songs of the trail to the guitar around the camp-fires. Then, in the 1930s, from USA came the guitar in the hands of Nick Lucas with 'Tip Toe Through the Tulips', Eddie Lang accompanying Bing Crosby, and the cowboy stars, Gene Autry and Roy Rogers; but the current boom started with the invention in the late 1930s of the electric guitar. In the 1950s came Bill Haley and his Comets with 'Rock Around the Clock', and other groups followed, notably the Beatles. The guitar is the basis for nearly all modern dance music and has replaced the PIANO as the main instrument to the rhythm section.

Guns see ARTILLERY, HAND-GUNS.

Gunpowder seems to have been known to the Chinese in the 11th century, and by the 13th century the Arabs had passed the knowledge of it on to western Europe. Roger Bacon, the FRANCISCAN scholar, writing in the 1260s said that gunpowder was already quite well known as a child's toy in many lands; he later foresaw its destructive force as a BOMB, but not in GUNS. A common recipe for gunpowder in the 14th century was four parts of saltpetre to one of carbon and one of sulphur, ground up fine with a pestle and mortar. It was used in CANNON by the second quarter of the 14th century and also in MINES when besieging fortresses.

H

Ha-Ha a device, invisible from a garden except at close quarters, to divide it from surrounding park-land and consisting of a wide ditch with a shallow slope on the park side and a vertical wall on the inner. It came into general use through Lancelot ('Capability') Brown (1716–83), who enclosed the house and garden of the estates he landscaped with winding ha-has to avoid interrupting the view, as at Blenheim Palace (Oxon.) and Charlecote (Warwicks). Under Humphry Repton (1752–1818) and the early Victorians, when smaller estates were landscaped, the ha-has were often shallower and less imposing. In late Victorian times, the construction of ha-has declined. Iron rails and wire-netting were cheaper and equally effective; and ha-has were also condemned as a 'deception unsatisfactory to good taste'.

Habeas Corpus (literally in Latin 'have the body') is a writ to a jailer or other person detaining someone in PRISON or elsewhere to bring his body before a JUDGE to investigate whether it has been lawful to hold him in custody. At first this was a means by which the crown could withdraw prisoners from trial by private courts (see FEUDALISM, MANOR); but then it became the subject's defence against the crown. The enforcement of this right was improved by the Habeas Corpus Act (1679). To enable the government to imprison persons indefinitely without trial, this act has sometimes been suspended (e.g. in 1715 and 1745, in 1794–1801 and 1817), but not during the two last World Wars when the same result was achieved by the government receiving from Parliament wide powers to intern suspected persons.

Habit the distinctive dress of MONKS, FRIARS and NUNS, consisting usually of a tunic and belt, and hood for men and veil for women. Some religious orders were popularly known by the colour of their habit—BENEDICTINES (Black monks), CISTERCIANS (White monks), FRANCISCANS (Greyfriars), DOMINICANS (Blackfriars).

Hackney-coach a four-wheeled COACH, drawn by two horses and seating six persons, which plied for public hire. It appeared about 1610 in England. By 1625 there were about twenty in London, stationed before the better-class INNS for hire. Their numbers increased, and they made so much noise and caused such congestion in the narrow streets that Charles I for a time restricted their use by passengers to areas at least three miles outside the town's confines. In 1667, when Samuel Pepys had become more prosperous and was considering buying his own CARRIAGE, he wrote, 'I am almost ashamed to be seen in a hackney.' Under William and Mary the number of hackney-coaches in London was fixed at 700, which was raised to 800 in 1710. They faced competition from the SEDAN-CHAIRS and in the 19th century were superseded by BROUGHAMS and HANSOM-CABS.

Hackney Phalanx the nickname of a group of HIGH CHURCHMEN living in the village of Hackney near London. They included Joshua Watson (1771–1855), wine-merchant and first Treasurer of the National Society (see NATIONAL SCHOOLS), William Stevens (1732–1807), London tradesman and Treasurer of QUEEN ANNE'S BOUNTY, and Henry Norris (1771–1850), Rector of Hackney. Rigidly orthodox in doctrine, they disliked NONCONFORMISTS, upheld the rights of the CHURCH OF ENGLAND and the powers of the BISHOPS and CLERGY, and they were politically conservative. Since the EVANGELICALS in the CHURCH PASTORAL AID SOCIETY laid down doctrinal tests for the curates it assisted and employed lay workers, they formed the ADDITIONAL CURATES SOCIETY; they also supported the SOCIETY FOR THE PROPAGATION OF THE GOSPEL instead of the CHURCH MISSIONARY SOCIETY. See also TRACTARIANS.

Hadrian's Wall was begun by the Emperor Hadrian when he visited ROMAN BRITAIN in AD 120; it ran from the Tyne to the Solway. The first fortification consisted of 16 forts in front of the *vallum* (a flat-bottomed ditch 30 ft wide and 7 ft deep with a bank on each side). By about AD 127 these forts were joined by a stone wall about 10 ft thick and 20 ft high, on top of which was a sentry-walk protected by a five-foot parapet. Each fort held 500 men and had barracks and granaries; between them were milecastles, garrisoned

Hadrian's wall

by 100 men, and between each milecastle two turrets, serving as signal stations and shelters for sentries. Behind the Wall was a parallel road for the rapid movement of troops, and every fort and milecastle had gates opening north and south to enable soldiers to be sent out to fight the PICTS and SCOTS if they massed beyond the Wall.

Hagioscope an oblique, slit-like opening (popularly known as a squint) in the wall between an AISLE chapel and the CHANCEL of a CHURCH, through which a CHANTRY priest officiating at a side ALTAR could see the ceremonies at the HIGH ALTAR and avoid reciting his MASS at the same time. [C. M. Durant, *Landscape with Churches* (1965)]

Hairdressing among fashionable Roman WOMEN had become very complicated at the time of the Roman occupation of Britain. Writers speak of the prevailing fashion in which the hair was elaborately curled and dressed high at the back with short curls in front. Martial described it as 'a globe of hair', and Statius called it 'the glory of woman's lofty front, her storied hair'. Wealthy wives employed several female SLAVES merely to dress their hair, and Juvenal told of a slave-girl who was beaten because one of her mistress's innumerable curls was out of place. The slaves are shown in wall-paintings with their own hair long and undressed.

To the ANGLO-SAXONS, however, unbound, flowing hair represented freedom and independence and was permitted only to young maidens. When a girl married her hair was plaited close to her head or even cut short like a slave's to show that she now served her husband. Similarly, medieval WIVES plaited their hair and hid it under a COVERCHIEF, but unmarried girls wore no head covering and either dressed their hair in a plain knot or allowed it to fall loosely to their shoulders.

Hairstyles revived in the 16th century. Ladies curled their hair and dressed it high, drawing it back over a pad of wires (called palisadoes) because a high forehead was fashionable. Rich women adorned their hair with jewels and young girls with garlands of flowers. Later the PURITANS preferred short hair for both men and women; James I in 1620 ordered the Bishop of London to instruct his clergy to preach against 'the insolency of our women and their wearing of broad-brimmed hats, their hair cut short or shorn'.

In the 18th century, though some ladies wore WIGS, hairstyles again became elaborate. Hair was frizzed or closely curled, piled up high over a large pad and whitened with thick powder, but the hair-ornaments fashionable in France were not emulated. 'Parisian ladies', a contemporary wrote, 'wear high towers with an extraordinary number of flowers, pads and ribbons. The English find such boundless display extremely ill-bred, and if any such lady comes to London, people hiss and throw mud at her.' Fashionable GIRLS' SCHOOLS employed maidservants to dress the hair of their pupils, but the

Hairstyles: 1 Roman; 2 1100; 3 1600; 4 1775; 5 1855; 6 1895

girls at CHARITY SCHOOLS had their hair cropped short.

Hairstyles became simpler and shorter with the NAKED FASHION. Later, under the influence of the EVANGELICALS, women's hair was smoothly combed from a centre parting and coiled in plaits or buns at the sides and back of the head, to give an impression of modesty and humility. For most of the 19th century, hairstyles were always small to provide a greater contrast with the voluminous SKIRTS worn, but a more complicated, high-swept style was introduced towards the end of the century.

After the First World War came the radical change when all young women bobbed or shingled their hair. Short hair, with variations, has remained general with women ever since.

Anglo-Saxon men wore their hair long, which was admired by the Normans, who allowed their closely-cropped hair to grow long, though this was denounced by the clergy as effeminate. Long, curled hair was the fashion under the Tudors and Early Stuarts, and the Puritans were called 'Roundheads' because they wore theirs short. From about 1660 to 1760 gentlemen wore wigs and shaved their heads. When wigs were abandoned, short hair was usual, and this has remained so, though some young men adopted long hair in the 1960s.

Halberd a WEAPON consisting of a wooden shaft about 6 ft long, surmounted by an axe-like instrument with a hook or pick on the opposite side. It was introduced in Henry VII's reign and intended to combine the BILL, GLAIVE and PIKE, which were then common weapons in use. Three halberds were stuck into the ground to form a triangle to which soldiers were bound to be flogged.

Halfpenny silver halfpennies or obols (*obolus*, a Greek coin) were first coined in England in the 9th century by King Alfred and the Danish rulers until the reign of King Edgar (d. 975). From then until the 13th century halfpennies were usually made by cutting silver PENNIES in half. Henry I and Henry II may have minted halfpennies. Henry II and Edward, son of Henry III, certainly produced obols for Aquitaine. Edward, when King, started the regular issue of silver halfpennies in England in 1280. The halfpenny minted by Charles II from 1672 was the first English copper coin. See also COINAGE.

Hall was the principal room of the medieval HOUSE. In a CASTLE or MANOR it was used mainly for formal occasions, such as MEALS for a large household and meetings between a feudal lord and his military tenants or between the lord of a manor with his agricultural tenants, while in smaller houses it was a living room in which cooking was done and meals taken. Both were heated by a fire on an open hearth (see FIREPLACES, FUMERELL). In the later Middle Ages a stone wall or wooden screen shut it off from the BUTTERY and PANTRY at the end, and there might be a GALLERY on which MINSTRELS performed. In the 16th century, with the development of the KITCHEN and other separate rooms, the hall assumed its present place in the house as an entrance passage. See also WESTMINSTER PALACE.

Hamlet is usually the term applied to a small VILLAGE which is without a CHURCH.

Hampton Court a palace on the River Thames west of London, was built by Cardinal Wolsey on the site of a MANOR house belonging to the TEMPLARS, which he leased from them in 1514 and later ceded to Henry VIII. The Tudor part of the palace includes the GATEHOUSE, HALL and KITCHEN, while the State Rooms were added by Sir Christopher Wren for William III. There is also a TENNIS court, while the gardens contain an ORANGERY, a KNOT GARDEN and a MAZE. The Hampton Court Conference, between the BISHOPS and the PURITANS, was held here in 1604,

an outcome of which was the production of the Authorized Version of the BIBLE. [P. Lindsay, *Hampton Court, A History* (1948)]

Hand-guns were first used in the late 14th century. These were like miniature CANNON mounted on long wooden stocks, probably held in the left hand and fired with a match held in the right. By 1425 the MATCHLOCK had been invented, and this led to the development of the MUSKET and later the BLUNDERBUSS. In its turn this

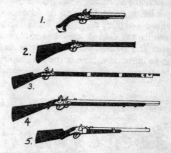

Hand-guns: 1 Pistol; 2 Blunderbuss; 3 Musket; 4 Rifle; 5 Carbine

was superseded by the WHEEL-LOCK and the FLINTLOCK, and the PISTOL was evolved. By 1600 the private possession of light hand-guns was common in England, and the RIFLE came in during this century. Breech-loading (generally) and percussion guns in which the charge was exploded by a cap struck by a hammer released by the trigger were introduced in the 19th century.

Handkerchief first came into fashion for both sexes in Elizabeth I's reign as a small square of LINEN or SILK, often edged with LACE, carried about the person and used for wiping the face or nose. From the early 16th to the early 19th century children had a muckinder, a handkerchief worn at the girdle to which it was sometimes attached by a tape. The taking of SNUFF in the 18th century led to larger handkerchiefs for men since the fashionable article was inadequate for the snuff-taker's sneeze, and such handkerchiefs were also used by the masses for the first time.

Handwriting in its present form originated with Latin writing, which was first used in inscriptions on stone or metal and was similar to modern capital letters; but this was too slow for writing on PARCHMENT, and so cursive writing (done without lifting the pen, so that the letters are joined together) developed. Latin handwriting was used in ROMAN BRITAIN, but after the ANGLO-SAXON conquest, it had to be introduced again in the 7th century by Christian missionaries from Ireland

Handwriting: 1 Italic (cursive); 2 Gothic; 3 Copper plate

(see CHURCH OF ENGLAND), and from it developed the Anglo-Saxon hand in which, for instance, the Lindisfarne Gospels were written (see BIBLE).

After the fall of the Roman Empire, other different kinds of writing developed in various parts of Europe, but from the late 8th century, under the influence of Charlemagne, the Carolingian style, which used large and small letters together according to a definite plan, spread from France to most of western Europe. This was introduced into England after the wars with the DANES and by the 12th

century had developed into a graceful style.

By the 13th century, however, the Gothic or 'black-letter' style, consisting of rather angular shapes, had developed in north-western Europe, and this was used in England until the 16th century. From about 1550 to 1700 the Secretary hand, a particular kind of Gothic writing, was in general use, being replaced by the Italic style, which originated in Florence in the 15th century and was based upon the Carolingian hand. Another style of writing, court-hand, was used in the English law courts from the 16th century until abolished by Parliament in 1731. And from the 17th century with the spread of education through the RENAISSANCE, instruction books in writing were printed carefully engraved on polished copper plates, and hence the name came to be given to a sloping rounded style of writing especially used in legal documents.

Hanging was probably introduced as a form of capital punishment by the ANGLO-SAXONS. The Norman method was BE-HEADING, but by Henry II's reign (1154–89) hanging was established as the punishment for murder, beheading being usually kept as a more honourable death for the nobility. In the early Middle Ages, every TOWN, ABBEY and nearly all important lords of the MANOR had the right of hanging, but from the 12th century only royal courts had the power to hang.

In the following centuries, as the emphasis on the value of property increased, hanging was imposed for more and more offences. In Edward VI's reign (1547–53) an average of 560 persons were executed each year at TYBURN alone and 24 at one hanging in 1571. By 1810, 222 offences carried the death penalty, including shooting a rabbit, forging a birth certificate, stealing a pocket handkerchief, damaging a public building and impersonating a Chelsea pensioner. At Chelmsford in 1814 a man was hanged for cutting down a cherry tree, and at Lynn in 1801 a boy, aged 13, was hanged for breaking into a house and stealing a spoon.

Between 1818 and 1833 hanging was abolished for shoplifting, housebreaking and other offences, for coining and forgery in 1836, for burglary in 1837 and subsequently for other offences until by 1861 it remained only for murder, arson in naval dockyards, piracy on the high seas and treason. The last public hanging in Scotland was in Perth in 1866 and in England in 1868 outside NEWGATE PRISON. Hanging for murder was limited in 1957, suspended in 1964 and abolished in 1969.

Hanging, drawing and quartering was first inflicted upon a nobleman's son for piracy in 1241; the Cato Street conspirators were beheaded after death by hanging in 1820. Hanging in chains, an old penalty for pirates, murderers and others, was abolished in 1834.

Hanse was an association of North German trading towns which in the Middle Ages dominated English trade with northern Europe. From the 12th century it was established in Hull, Lynn, Boston, Ipswich and Great Yarmouth and had its headquarters at the STEELYARD in London. They were granted considerable rights by the Crown, which were increasingly resented by English merchants, and the rise of the MERCHANT ADVENTURERS led finally to the withdrawal of these in 1579.

Hansom-cab a two-wheeled CABRIOLET for two inside, in which the driver's seat was behind the body of the vehicle, and the reins passed over the hooded roof. It was named after its inventor, Joseph A. Hansom (1803–82), and plied for public hire from 1836. Entry was by knee-doors in front, worked from a lever on the driver's seat, and the driver communi-

cated with the passengers through a glass trap in the roof. In very hot weather, a white linen cover kept the cab cool, and in rain, a glass window was lowered in front. It was the fastest and most elegant of public conveyances and, together with the BROUGHAM, replaced the HACKNEY-COACH. In its turn, it was superseded by the TAXI-CAB. See also CARRIAGE.

Harp appeared early in British history and was long associated with the CELTS. Diodorus Siculus in the 1st century BC mentioned a lyre-like instrument used by Celtic bards. The medieval Laws of Wales stated that a man needed only three things —a chaste wife, a cushion for his chair and a harp. The same laws forbade a SLAVE to touch a harp, and a FREEMAN was to be known by his ability to play it. A harp might not be seized for debt, and every house in Wales had its hereditary harp, handed down through generations for the use of the domestic BARD, while until the late 19th century many Welsh villages had their harper or family of harpers.

Chaucer's FRIAR in *The Canterbury Tales* was adept with the harp, and when he played it his eyes twinkled like 'the stars in the frosty night'. Samuel Pepys heard a harp played in a warship and at the Vauxhall Gardens. In early Victorian times, when gentlemen commonly played the FLUTE, a sister or daughter was likely to be able to accompany him on the harp, gracefully displaying her well-rounded arms. See also MINSTRELS.

Harpsichord a keyboard instrument which evolved out of the PSALTERY and the VIRGINAL in the 15th century. It had two or more strings to each note, to permit gradations of sound, and often two keyboards. It was often of considerable size and enclosed in a case like the later grand PIANO. It was much used in the 16th, 17th and 18th centuries. See also PIANO.

Harrow ways early local ROADS, probably made later than the RIDGEWAYS and running on the lower hillside slopes. Gilbert White (1720–93) of Selborne (Hants.) wrote of harrow ways in his locality some 16–18 ft below the field level.

Harrying of the North (1069) was accomplished by William I, when he was faced by a formidable revolt led by Waltheof, Earl of Northumberland, who, with the help of the DANES, captured York and massacred its Norman garrison. William marched northwards, recaptured York and laid waste the whole countryside from the Ouse northwards. Thousands were slaughtered or died from starvation and pestilence. His object was to prevent any further revolts by a general destruction of life, stock, crops and dwellings, and it ensured that the NORMAN CONQUEST of England would endure. See also DOMESDAY BOOK. [David C. Douglas, *William the Conqueror* (1964)]

Hats worn by men in the Middle Ages usually consisted of a crown and a brim in a variety of styles and until the RESTORATION were worn indoors as well as out and also in CHURCH. In the 19th century greater variety and elaboration developed notably in the shape of the TOP HAT and BOWLER and the less formal BOATER and TRILBY. Since the 1930s there has been a growing tendency for men to go bare-headed.

Women hardly ever wore hats until the late 16th century, (an exception being the BUTTERFLY), unless they were travelling. When they did, it was commonly the COIF (which, being insignificant, had been worn by poorer men). Later the MOB-CAP and the BONNET were worn. Since women's hats drew attention to the feminine head, it was not thought proper to wear them on SUNDAYS or in church until about 1875.

Hauberk a long coat of chain mail, with a divided skirt, worn as the main part of the ARMOUR of a Norman KNIGHT. It was formed by sewing interlocking rings or

Hats: 1 Coverchief and Wimple (c. 1200); 2 Barbotte (c. 1170); 3 Coif (16th cent.); 4 Butterfly Headdress (c. 1485); 5 Gable Hood (c. 1520); 6 English Hood (c. 1530); 7 French Hood (c. 1540); 8 Calash (c. 1780); 9 Poke Bonnet (c. 1835)

small overlapping plates of metal on to the leather of the coat. By 1400 it had generally been discarded in favour of plate armour. [Paul Martin, *Armour and Weapons* (1968)]

Hautboys, see OBOE

Hawking, see FALCONRY.

Hayward a servant on a medieval MANOR who was responsible for the proper keeping of the meadows, hedges and woods.

Headband a strip of linen worn as a punishment in GIRLS' SCHOOLS. It was embroidered in coloured thread with the name of the girl's offence and tied or pinned round her head. A number of such headbands, which were used in Christ's Hospital for Girls, Hertford, in the early 19th century, are marked 'Rudeness and Disrespect', 'Gossiping', 'Ill Temper', 'A Dunce', 'Idleness', 'Obstinate', 'Inattention During Prayers'. See also DUNCE'S CAP, PLACARD, WHISPERING STICK.

Hearth Tax or Chimney Tax on every fire-place or hearth was levied in England in the form of PETER'S PENCE during the Middle Ages and was imposed as a national tax by Charles II in 1662 at the rate of 2s a hearth, with exemption for tradesmen and the poor, and it produced about £200,000 a year. It was unpopular and was abolished in 1689, when it was replaced by the WINDOW TAX, and it was last levied in Scotland in 1690.

Hedges were only to be found, in the days of OPEN-FIELD FARMING, round the pastures closest to the VILLAGE and along the PARISH boundary. As a result of ENCLOSURES in the 18th and 19th centuries, the English countryside was gradually divided into numerous fields enclosed by double rows of whitethorn seedlings with a shallow ditch, and protected on one or both sides by a rail. In Northamptonshire blackthorn hedges were even planted in triplicate for cutting down successively for fuel. Nowadays, owing to the use of TRACTORS for ploughing and of COMBINE HARVESTERS, hedges are disappearing in many parts of the country in order to bring into being large, open fields. See also DRY WALLS, KNOT GARDEN.

Hedgehog the outermost defence at the further edge of a CASTLE ditch. It consisted of stakes or specially planted thorn bushes and was called a 'herrison' by Norman soldiers. In some large fourteenth century castles it was replaced by a CURTAIN-WALL.

Helmet of Roman soldiers was round and of iron, while that of the VIKINGS was a close-fitting, round metal cap distinguished by horns and wings. Both sides at the Battle of Hastings (1066) wore a conical iron helmet with a NASAL. The CRUSADES saw the adoption of the COIF. The 13th century brought the POT-HELM, which was replaced late in the next century by the lighter BASINET, sometimes with a VISOR and an AVENTAIL. During the English Civil Wars (1642–8), the CAVALRY wore a triple-barred 'lobster-tail' helmet, and the foot-soldiers, especially those who fought with the PIKE, had a round, brimmed helmet. The British POLICE at first wore TOP-HATS, but later adopted the present type of helmet; the brass helmet adopted in FIRE-FIGHTING during the last century was intended to guard the head and reflect the heat of flames; and the purpose of the round, flat-brimmed 'tin-hat' of both world wars was to give protection against shrapnel, shell-splinters and glancing bullets. See also ARMOUR.

Henge a circle of wooden or stone uprights, enclosed by a bank of earth or stone and usually an internal ditch, forming part of a ceremonial structure for religious purposes, found in Britain and Ireland and dating from the BRONZE AGE. The best known of these monuments is Stonehenge in Wiltshire, and Avebury, the largest stone circle in Europe, is also in the same county. [R. J. C. Atkinson, *Stonehenge* (1956)]

Herald an officer of a royal or noble household, who acted as a messenger between sovereign and noblemen in the Middle Ages. His duties included also the superintendence of TOURNAMENTS, which meant that he had to be able to recognize the devices on the shields and the crests on the helmets of the armour-clad contestants, and so he became expert in HERALDRY and controlled its use. The royal heralds were incorporated in 1484 by Richard III as the College of Arms under three kings of arms (chief heralds), Garter, Clarenceux and Norroy, and they are responsible today for all English grants of arms and state ceremonial. The Scottish heralds, constituted as the 'Court of the Lord Lyon', perform the same functions.

Heraldry arose through the need to tell whether a KNIGHT in full ARMOUR was a friend or foe. Gradually KNIGHTS adopted pictorial signs to distinguish them. These were at first painted on their SHIELDS, but during the CRUSADES they embroidered them on their surcoat or linen garment which they wore over their armour as a protection against the hot eastern sun, so this badge became known as a 'coat of arms'. To further distinguish them in battle, they wore also on their HELMETS a smaller badge or 'crest'.

The granting of arms came under the control of HERALDS, and the heraldic movement developed rapidly during the 13th and 14th centuries, achieving its highest esteem in the reigns of Edward III (1327–77) and Richard II (1377–99). A grant of arms came to infer nobility or gentility. When a man gained a feudal FIEF or other public position, he invariably assumed a coat of arms; and the 14th century saw the rise of the practice of quartering by which, when a family had married successive heiresses, the shield was divided into four or more parts so that the arms of the successive heiresses could all be displayed. Peers, and in Scotland chiefs of CLANS, became entitled to have a pair of supporters, figures standing one on each side of the shield and helmet.

In the later Middle Ages heraldic signs were used in EMBROIDERY and on INN-SIGNS, and corporate bodies, such as CITIES, TOWNS and COLLEGES received grants of arms. [C. Boutell (revised C. Scott-Giles), *Heraldry* (revised ed., 1970)]

Herbs have been used in MEDICINE and for flavouring food since ancient times. Many herbs (e.g. CORIANDER, FENNEL, MUSTARD) were introduced into ROMAN BRITAIN, though some may have died out and been re-introduced later. The ANGLO-SAXONS were not familiar with herbs imported from the East, but they made use of native wild herbs, especially for healing. The use to which they put them is shown by their old English names (e.g. liverwort, lungwort, throatwort and woundwort), 'wort' meaning 'plant'.

From the Middle Ages until the rediscovery of VEGETABLES, herbs, like SPICES, were much used in cooking. A MONASTERY usually had its HERB GARDEN to supply the FARMERY and kitchen, while in large households WOMEN grew the herbs needed for physic and cooking. The most important were SAFFRON and TANSY, but parsley, sage and samphire were among those commonly used. Both RHUBARB and YARROW were used medicinally. In Elizabethan times, herbs were often grown in a KNOT GARDEN.

In the 16th century, ROSEMARY, LAVENDER and other sweet-smelling herbs were often mingled with the RUSHES strewn on the floors. A foreign visitor to England in 1560 wrote, 'Their parlours and chambers strewed with sweet herbs refreshed me'; and the churchwardens' accounts for St Margaret's Church, Westminster, record payment for 'herbs strewn in the church in a day of thanksgiving' in 1650. Herbs also became increasingly used in the manufacture of PERFUMES.

Herb gardens (or Physic Gardens) were first established in MONASTERIES and later by the mistress of the house to provide HERBS for medicinal and culinary use. The earliest garden to be founded for 'physic' purposes primarily was the Oxford Botanic Garden in 1641, and the Chelsea Physic Garden, established in 1673, originally belonged to the Society of APOTHECARIES, who took the herbs down the Thames in their barge to their Hall in the City. The Royal Botanic Garden, Kew, was originally founded in 1760 for the same purpose, but, like the other herb gardens, is now used largely for 'botanic' or scientific purposes. [K. N. Sanecki, *Discovering English Gardens* (1969).] See also KNOT GARDEN.

Heresy the offence of denying the doctrines of the Church. In 1166 some 30 heretics, who came from Germany to London, were branded in the face, whipped and thrust in the depth of winter naked into the streets, where, since none dared to relieve them, they died of cold and hunger. The first record of the burning of heretics in England is in 1210, and in 1222 a deacon was burned as an apostate (he had become a Jew for the love of a Jewess).

There was little heresy in England before the time of John Wycliffe (c. 1320–1384). By an Act of Parliament of 1382 heretics were to be kept in prison until they had satisfied the claims of the Church, and the Act of 1401 (*De Haeretico Comburendo*) stated that heretics were to be tried in an ECCLESIASTICAL COURT and handed over to the King's officers to be publicly burned. It was under this Act most of the executions of LOLLARDS and PROTESTANTS took place in the 15th and 16th centuries. The Act was repealed under Henry VIII, revived under Mary and finally repealed under Elizabeth I. The last person to be executed for heresy in Britain was in Edinburgh in 1696. [K. B. McFarlane, *John Wycliffe and English Nonconformity* (1952)]

Heriot a payment due under FEUDALISM to the lord of a MANOR on the death of a VILLEIN by his kin, usually consisting of his best beast. FREEMEN also owed heriots sometimes in the form of armour or horses to their lord or to the king. In time it came to be accepted that such payments almost always gave the heir the right of possessing the dead man's holding. The heriot was, however, the debt of a dead man to his lord, while the RELIEF was due from his heir.

Hermits (1) in medieval England differed from ANCHORITES since they lived a solitary life, but were not confined to a cell. The earliest, like St Guthlac (c. 673–714) of Crowland (Lincs.) lived in lonely caves, fens or forests; but by the 12th century they mostly lived by high roads or in towns in a hut or hermitage, relying upon the charity of travellers and sometimes keeping a length of ROAD or a BRIDGE in repair. To prevent impostors, Parliament in 1379 ordered all vagabonds to be imprisoned 'except men of religion and hermits having letters testimonial from the bishop'. [J. J. Jusserand, *English Wayfaring Life in the Middle Ages* (1891)]

(2) In the late 18th and early 19th century hermits were occasionally features of country house GARDENS as a result of the

ROMANTIC MOVEMENT. Sometimes a cave was provided with a stuffed figure in a suitable costume, vaguely distinguishable by dim lantern-light, sitting beside an hour-glass and poring over a book in some dark recess, but sometimes a man was paid to be a hermit to live in a thatched wooden house. He was provided with a CAMLET robe and was not to cut his hair, beard or nails. He was also not to talk with the servants nor leave the grounds. The usual contract was for seven years, but few men remained hermits as long. [Edith Sitwell, *English Eccentrics* (1933); Ralph Dutton, *The English Country House* (1962).] See also FOLLY.

Hide an early English measure of land, often taken to mean an area such as could be ploughed by one PLOUGH and a team of OXEN in a season. It therefore varied in different parts of the country, but probably ran from about 40 to 100 acres. See also CARUCAGE.

High altar the main ALTAR of a CHURCH or CATHEDRAL standing in the centre of the east end of the CHANCEL. In English medieval churches, it was commonly the same length as the moulding at the base of the east window, which served as the REREDOS. [N. E. Boyle, *Old Parish Churches* (1951).] See also PYX.

High Churchmen the group in the CHURCH OF ENGLAND in the 18th century which took a 'high' view of the claims of the BISHOPS and the nature of the SACRAMENTS. They were the descendants of the LAUDIANS and like them ARMINIAN in their outlook. See also METHODISTS, TRACTARIANS.

Highwaymen were robbers, usually mounted on horseback, who frequented the highways or main roads in the 17th and 18th centuries and held up passengers, especially those travelling in COACHES. They liked to be known as the 'Gentlemen of the Road' and sometimes dressed and spoke like men of fashion. Their cry, 'Stand and deliver!', became famous, and Pastor Moritz wrote in 1782, 'Even with unloaded pistols they terrify travellers'. The two best-known highwaymen were Jack Sheppard (1702–24) and Dick Turpin (1705–39). They became less frequent with the construction of the TURNPIKES. See also BLUNDERBUSS.

Hill Figures cut into the chalk hills of England (particularly white horses) are unparalleled elsewhere. Despite the fine chalk slopes of Sussex, Dorset and Bedfordshire, Wessex has the greatest number of these figures. Some are really old, notably the Uffington White Horse (Berks.), probably a cult-figure or tribal symbol, cut in the late 1st century BC; the Cerne Giant (Dorset), a revival of a Hercules cult, cut in the 2nd century AD; and the Westbury Horse (Wilts.), which before it was remodelled in 1778 was contemporary with the Uffington Horse. To keep these figures clear of grass, regular 'scourings' were held (often every 7 years —a sacred number) as the centre of a festival of pagan origin.

The 18th century, the time of FOLLIES and pseudo-antiques, produced many hill figures, e.g. Cherhill Horse (Wilts.) in 1780 and Marlborough Horse (Wilts.) in 1804. The largest, at Osmington near Weymouth (Dorset), was cut in 1815 by troops stationed nearby and represents George III on horseback. One at Pewsey (Wilts.) was cut as recently as 1937.

There is only one white horse in Scotland—the White Horse of Strichen (Aberdeenshire). [Maurice Marples, *White Horses and Other Hill Figures* (1949); Kate Bergamar, *Discovering Hill Figures* (1968)]

Hill-forts belong to the IRON AGE period and took many forms. Some were simply promontories or hill-spurs, cut off by a bank and ditch at the narrowest point; but the most characteristic was an enclosed flattish hill-top. At first, a single bank and ditch was reckoned effective as a defence, the bank being strengthened by TIMBER-LACING. Later the weak points were made stronger and the entrances more complex, often being deeply in-turned with gates and guardrooms which might be built over the passageway into the fort. Later still more elaborate forts were built. The number of ramparts was increased with as many as three or even four banks and ditches, wide enough to give protection against enemies armed with SLINGS flinging beach-pebbles.

These improved hill-forts were most numerous in the chalk country and west of England. The finest example is Maiden Castle (Dorset). Such forts provided a commanding view of the countryside and were difficult to storm. The people of the area placed their huts inside the banks and drove their cattle within in times of danger. When the Romans attacked these forts, they used BATTERING-RAMS and large CATAPULTS firing heavy bolts.

An odd variant of the hill-forts are the Scottish VITRIFIED FORTS.

Some hill-forts in England were re-fortified after the Roman withdrawal, e.g. Cadbury (Somerset). [S. Piggott, *British Prehistory* (1949)]

Hippocras a medieval spiced WINE, which is said to have taken its name from Hippocrates' sleeve because the bags, containing the SPICES and hung up for the wine to drip through, were shaped like long, full medieval sleeves. HIPPOCRAS was a favourite warm drink taken before going to bed. [Dorothy Hartley, *Food in England* (1954)]

Hire-purchase began with the invention of the SEWING-MACHINE which the Singer Co. began to sell 'on the new hire system' in the 1850s. PIANO, FURNITURE and COSTUME makers followed. In 1877 some senior civil servants founded the Civil Service Mutual Furnishing Association to help juniors furnish their homes. Meanwhile, 'wagon companies' were formed in northern England to provide hire-purchase for railway trucks (which were not then provided by the railways), and these enlarged their activities to cars and equipment. The North Central Wagon & Finance Co. and the British Wagon Co. became two of the biggest hire-purchase firms; they were followed by other similar finance companies which provide the cash price for the goods sold by the retailer on hire-purchase terms. The mass production of MOTOR CARS led to the growth of hire-purchase and still more after the Second World War for electrical equipment and TELEVISION as well. The total British hire-purchase debt has risen rapidly, and in 1964 it totalled £1,094 million or over £20 per head of the population. The Hire-Purchase Act (1938) was designed to protect the hirer, and there was further legislation for this purpose in 1962.

Hiring fairs. See MOP FAIRS.

Hoards, hourds covered wooden galleries projecting from the top of the external wall of a CASTLE for the defence of the base of the wall. These were supported on wooden brackets, the horizontal holes for which may still be seen just beneath the parapets of some castles. They were made necessary to prevent attack by MINES in the late 12th century when castle-walls were raised as a protection against the TREBUCHET. These galleries often had holes in the floors from which missiles could be dropped on to attackers. See also MACHICOLATION.

Hobby-horse a processional steed used in a MORRIS DANCE or by MUMMERS, consisting of a light wicker cage draped with fabric with a hole in it near the front end large enough to take a man's body. The cage was fastened round the man's waist, and the rear end, fitted with a tail, stuck out behind like a BUSTLE. The man also wore a horse-head mask and his gambolling animated the whole contraption. These hobby-horses were very perishable, and there are few ancient survivors. 'Old Snap', the Norwich hobby-horse dragon is believed to have been made in 1451, while Hob-Nob, a similar figure with snapping jaws, and its companion,

Hobby-horse

the Salisbury Giant, both of which are in the Salisbury Museum, are said to have been made about the same time.

A hobby-horse was also a children's plaything of very ancient origin. In its simplest form it was a stick fitted with a slightly profiled horse-head and a cross-bar grip below which the child grasped while dragging the stick between its legs. The early 19th century brought more realistically carved heads, inserted eyes, rosettes and reins; then the rear end of the stick was fitted with a cross-bar and wooden wheels; and finally came a horse on a stand with four wheels and a horse-headed tricycle. See also ROCKING HORSE.

Hockey may be traced back in England to a game played with sticks and a ball, called the 'London Ball Game' by medieval schoolboys, but this was a rough and tumble. The modern game dates from the mid-19th century. The first organized hockey club, the Blackheath Club, was formed about 1840 and was followed by others in the London area. In 1876 they formed the Hockey Association, which in 1886 adopted the rules of the Wimbledon Club, and these have prevailed ever since.

By this time clubs had been formed all over the country, and divisional associations under the Hockey Associations were formed in the north, the midlands and the west. The first divisional match, North v. South, and the first match between Oxford and Cambridge Universities took place in 1890, to be followed by the first international match, England v. Ireland, in 1895. The International Hockey Board was founded in 1900.

Women soon followed men in playing hockey. It was played by Lady Margaret Hall and Somerville College, Oxford, in 1887 and by Newnham College, Cambridge, in 1890. The Ladies' Hockey Association was formed in 1895 and renamed the All-England Women's Hockey Association the next year.

Hockey is played in some boys' schools, while it is the most regular game in girls' schools. Local varieties include hurling (Ireland) and shinty (Scotland).

Holidays were originally 'holy days' since the saints' days were the holidays of the Middle Ages. In England the Holidays and Fast Days Act (1552) reduced to 25 the number of saints' days to be kept as holidays; in Scotland an act of 1598 set aside each Monday for games and pastimes. In the first half of the 19th century, British public and semi-public offices closed on fewer saints' days each year, e.g. the Bank of England closed on 44 days in 1808, but only on four in 1834. The Bank Holidays Act (1871) gave England six and Scotland five bank holidays. The Holidays with Pay Act (1938) made holidays without loss of pay compulsory in some occupations, and by 1939 about 11 500 000 people were enjoying such holidays, including some 40 per cent of the country's manual workers. This has now become general for all workers. See also CHRISTMAS, BOXING DAY, TWELFTH NIGHT, MOTHERING SUNDAY, SHROVE TUESDAY.

Holiday traffic abroad has grown from 1 500 000 in 1951 to 5 750 000 in 1969, but this still represents no more than 20 per cent of the 30 500 000 holidays taken in Britain in 1969, of which 62 per cent were in July and/or August. In 1968, while 42 per cent of adults had no holiday away from home, 46 per cent took it in Britain only, 2 per cent in Britain and abroad, 8 per cent abroad only and 2 per cent in Ireland. The numbers staying in HOTELS and boarding houses fell from 26 per cent in 1951 to 18 per cent in 1969; the number staying in HOLIDAY CAMPS doubled from 3 to 6 per cent. In Britain 75 per cent of people go to the SEASIDE, and 74 per cent regard shopping as their favourite holiday activity. [*Patterns in British Holidaymaking 1951–69* (British Travel Association, 1969)]

Holiday camps were first established in Britain on the coast after the First World War. The earliest consisted of tents, which were then replaced by huts and sometimes brick bungalows. The growing numbers of MOTOR CARS and CHARABANCS in the 1920s and 1930s brought about a new sort of holiday camp consisting of huts and bungalows in rows and usually a dining-hall and another building for games, competitions and dancing, but none of these camps held more than 300 people. William Edmund Butlin's camp opened at Skegness (Lincs.) in 1935 was the first large camp for 3000 people and more. Others followed after the Second World War, being provided with chalets, lawns, swimming-pools, dining-halls, boating-lakes and amusement-parks as well as organized sports and competitions for the campers. From about 1965, however, their popularity has declined, and some have been changed into self-contained flats and suites.

Hollow way a boundary between two estates, dating from Celtic, Saxon or medieval times, made by each landowner digging out a ditch and throwing up the earth into a continuous bank on his own side, thus forming a double ditch several feet wide and sunk several feet below the level of the fields on either side. [W. G. Hoskins, *The Making of the English Landscape* (1970)]

Holy Innocents' Day (December 28). the commemoration of the massacre of the children in Bethlehem ordered by Herod as recorded in St Matthew's Gospel. It was the custom in some families to whip the children in the morning of that day to remind them of Herod's cruelty. The day itself was considered unlucky for a MARRIAGE or the beginning of any enterprise. Edward IV changed the date of his coronation to avoid being crowned on that day. See also BOY BISHOP.

Homage was the ceremony under FEUDALISM by which a tenant acknowledged himself the man (*homo*) bound to serve the lord from whom he held his FIEF. The usual way of doing this was for the tenant to kneel to his lord, who sat before him, place his clasped hands between those of the lord and declare that 'he did become his man, from that day forth, of life and limb and earthly honour'; and then he received a kiss from his lord.

Honey was used in the Middle Ages instead of SUGAR for nearly all sweetening, and so bees were widely kept. Honey is mentioned in DOMESDAY BOOK. See also MEAD.

Hood from the Middle Ages onwards worn by men and women either as a separate garment or attached to a cloak or other outdoor garment. From about 1530 to the end of the 16th century hoods developed a long extension of the pointed cowl, forming a hanging tail, known as the liripipe or tippet. From the 16th to 18th centuries women wore in the country and when travelling a soft hood, known as the capuchin or riding hood, which had a coloured lining and a deep cape. For special types of women's hoods, see ENGLISH HOOD, FRENCH HOOD, GABLE HOOD.

The English academic hood, an ornament of silk or stuff worn by graduates was derived partly from monastic HABIT and partly from the AMICE. Formerly attached to the COPE and other VESTMENTS, it could be drawn over the head as a protection against cold and rain, and in the universities the hoods of graduates were made to signify their degree by being manufactured in varying colours and materials. In the CHURCH OF ENGLAND the Book of Canons of 1604 ordered all CLERGY when taking services, if they were graduates, to wear upon their SURPLICE, the hood to which they were entitled.

Hoop-petticoat an under-PETTICOAT variously distended with cane, wire or whalebone hoops in the shape of a bell, pyramid or oblong worn by women from about 1710 to 1780 and to 1820 for court wear. It was a revival of the FARTHINGALE and was followed later by the CRINOLINE.

Hops a plant with a long, twining stalk belonging to the nettle family. The use of hops for flavouring BEER probably began in Germany about the 8th century and spread to the rest of the Continent. Hops were brought over to England after the NORMAN CONQUEST, but were at first little cultivated because they were not added to ALE until the mid-16th century. They were originally grown on hedges around farm fields, gathered in the autumn and dried in the old BREAD ovens. Later, when they were grown on a large scale, chiefly in Kent hop-gardens, they were dried in OAST-HOUSES, after families from East London had camped in the fields and gathered the crop; but nowadays they are increasingly picked by machinery and dried by electricity.

Horn-book a cheap and simple primer made from a piece of wood shaped like a BATTLEDORE upon which was pasted a printed page, which contained the alphabet, some numerals and the Lord's Prayer. Over this page was a sheet of transparent horn to keep it clean, and the whole was bound with brass and occasionally backed with leather. Children sometimes called their Horn-Book the Criss-Cross Row because there was a cross at the beginning and end of the alphabet. Its use probably dates from the end of the 15th century and continued until the early 19th century. [Magdalen King-Hall, *The Story of the Nursery* (1958).] See also FESCUE, PETTY SCHOOLS.

Horse was first used by the later CELTS of the IRON AGE for riding and for drawing CHARIOTS and continued to be used in CAVALRY until the 20th century. The SADDLE, HORSESHOE and STIRRUP were introduced into England between the 5th and 7th centuries; but horses were first harnessed to vehicles by a breast-band, which pressed against the animal's windpipe and so reduced its power. The horse-collar may have been invented in China in the 7th century BC, but there is no evidence of its use in Europe until the

11th century AD. It enabled a horse to use its shoulders and increased its pulling power fivefold.

The first example of a horse doing agricultural work appears on the BAYEUX TAPESTRY, but up to the end of the Middle Ages it was not much used on farms and only slowly displaced the OX. In this century the horse has been steadily replaced on the farm by the TRACTOR. In 1939 there were still 750 000 farm horses in England, but now there are less than 10 000.

Similarly, the MOTOR CAR has replaced the horse in transport. In 1844 there were 146 000 horses owned by private persons for riding or drawing CARRIAGES; and in 1901 there were 400 000 horses working in London, but by 1914 the number had fallen to 100 000. Since 1945, however, horse-riding has become more popular, especially for girls, and pony-riding even more so. The countrywide membership of the Pony Club has risen from 17 000 in 1947 to 77 000 in 1963, and summer gymkhanas have grown in number. [A. J. Lamb, *Story of the Horse* (1938); Lynn White, Jr., *Medieval Technology and Social Change* (1967)]

Horse-brasses originated in the East some 2000 years ago as charms to protect the animals from the evil forces of darkness against which light was the safeguard. Made of bronze, their designs usually included representations of the sun, and they were highly polished to reflect the sunlight and so distract the 'evil eye'. They were introduced into England through the trade routes, probably at the time of the CRUSADES. By then their designs were based on Eastern superstitions, e.g. the Lotus Flower, a Buddhist emblem of good fortune, or the Scallop Shell, associated with Venus and credited with the ability to confer beauty of form and so used for brood mares.

In the 18th and 19th centuries their significance changed, and designs became commercial (e.g. the Dolphin by fishmongers), heraldic (e.g. the Knot, the badge of the Stafford family), local (e.g. the Horse Combatant, the emblem of Kent) and commemorative (e.g. the Imperial Crown to mark Queen Victoria's Diamond Jubilee in 1897).

The second half of the 19th century was the heyday of horse-brass manufacturing. The early brasses were hand-cut, but by then they were stamped out by machinery. The Hull Municipal Museum has a collection of horse-brasses.

Horse-racing an ancient SPORT, did not become frequent in England until Henry II's reign (1154–89), being first held at SMITHFIELD; but TOURNAMENTS continued to be more popular. Public races began in James I's reign (1603–25), and races began at Newmarket about 1640. Horse-racing was forbidden during the COMMONWEALTH, but after the RESTORATION it developed with royal support. Charles II regularly visited Newmarket, William III started the custom of offering Royal Plates as prizes, and under Queen Anne the first meeting took place on the royal heath at Ascot in 1711. The earlier Hanoverian kings were not interested in the sport, but Prince George, later George IV, owned race-horses in 1784.

The sport grew rapidly in the 18th century. Many famous races were established at this time: the St Leger (1776), the Oaks (1779), the Derby (1780) and the Ascot Gold Cup (1807). The Jockey Club (1750), founded to control racing at Newmarket, assumed in the 19th century national responsibility for regulating horse-racing; and the General Stud Book (1808) was started as a register kept in London of the pedigrees of all race-horses. Park meetings (i.e. meetings on enclosed courses where gate-money could be charged) became increasingly common after Sandown Park was opened at Esher (Surrey) in 1875. The patronage of Edward VII, who as Prince of Wales won the Derby twice (with Persimmon in 1896 and Diamond Jubilee in 1900) and as King once (with Minoru in 1909), increased the popularity of the sport. [Patrick Chalmers, *Racing England* (1939).] See also STEEPLECHASING.

Horseshoes of iron, nailed on to the hoof of the horse, may have been used by the CELTS, but do not seem to have been in use among the Greeks or Romans and probably were not commonly used in Europe until the end of the 6th century or even later. Before then, horses' hoofs were sometimes protected by 'hippo-sandals', a kind of leather shoe, studded with iron at the base, which could be taken on and off.

Hose in female COSTUME from ANGLO-SAXON times onwards meant STOCKINGS. Chaucer described the Wife of Bath as wearing hose of 'fine scarlet red'.

In male attire hose also meant stockings from Anglo-Saxon times to the 15th century and again after the RESTORATION. During the period from 1400 to 1620 the word came to refer to leg-wear because the long stockings were united at the fork and carried up to the waist, forming a tightly fitting garment known as 'long-stocked hose'. During the last century of this period, the upper part was enlarged and called TRUNK HOSE, round hose or upperstocks, the lower stocking part being called nether stocks.

Hospitals in the Middle Ages were mostly ALMSHOUSES for the aged. Among the few exceptions were lazar-houses (for LEPROSY), BEDLAM, and St Bartholomew's Hospital (founded 1123) and St Thomas's Hospital (early 13th century), both being houses of the AUGUSTINIAN CANONS.

At the REFORMATION the London hospitals survived, and so also did St Bartholomew's, Rochester. In 1697 the Bristol Guardians of the Poor opened St Peter's, financed by both rates and donations. In the 18th century new London hospitals were opened—West-minster Hospital (1719), Guy's (1725), St George's (1728), London Hospital (1740), Middlesex Hospital (1745). By 1789 there were seven general hospitals in London housing about 1600 patients, while some thirty provincial towns had acquired hospitals in the preceding 50 years. In 1800 there was one hospital bed to 5000 persons in England and Wales; in 1961 one to 175. Hospital standards, however, long remained low and the risk of cross-infection was great. 'The very first requirement in a hospital is that it should do the sick no harm', said Florence Nightingale, who greatly improved the training of NURSES. About 1860 specialized hospitals were opened for children, women's diseases, nervous disorders, tuberculosis, etc. By then also Poor Law authorities had established infirmaries for paupers and other poor people, many of which from 1929 were taken over and converted into municipal hospitals; these were rate-aided, but patients paid according to their means. More important still, however, were the independent voluntary hospitals, managed by trustees or governors, supported by endowments, charitable contributions and patients' fees, and caring for both paying and non-paying patients.

The NATIONAL HEALTH SERVICE ACT (1948) placed hospitals under the Ministry of Health and made free hospital treatment available to all.

Hospitallers the Military Order of the Hospital of St John of Jerusalem originated with a HOSPITAL founded about 1070 to care for sick pilgrims in Jerusalem. In about 1120 they adopted a military organization like the TEMPLARS and wore a white cross on a black ground. The international order was ruled by a Grand Master and had various provinces headed by Grand Commanders or Priors. Their head house in England was the Hospital or Priory of St John of Jerusalem in Clerkenwell (London), which was founded about 1144. Among places where they had other houses, which in England were called preceptories or commanderies, were Ossington (Notts.), Clanfield (Notts.) and Mount St John (Yorks.). These gave hospitality to pilgrims, travellers and the poor, but their main purpose was to manage their estates and recruit members. Each one usually housed a Commander, one or two members and a few servants.

In 1338 there were 116 Hospitallers in England. They received about a half of the Templars' properties in 1308 and eventually had about 65 houses in England. The order came to an end in England in 1540 with the DISSOLUTION OF THE MONASTERIES, but it continued on the Continent. In 1827 the English branch was revived in a much altered form with its headquarters at St John's Gate, Clerkenwell (the former English headquarters) and undertook hospital and ambulance work. It obtained a royal CHARTER of incorporation in 1888.

Host a word (derived from the Latin *hostia*, a victim) used to describe the consecrated bread in the MASS, regarded as the Body of Christ offered up in sacrifice. Popular medieval belief held that those who looked on the host would prosper and avoid blindness or sudden death all that day. See also PYX.

Hosteller the MONK in charge of the guest-house of a MONASTERY. He was responsible for the entertainment of ordinary travellers. Noble travellers were entertained by the ABBOT or PRIOR and the poor in the ALMONRY.

Hot cockles a medieval game still played as late as the early 18th century. One player knelt blindfolded, holding his hands behind him, and while the others struck his hands he had to guess the name of the striker. The great idea seems to have been to knock over the 'he' with the force of the blow.

Hot cross buns spiced buns with the figure of a cross impressed upon them, are derived from the ecclesiastical Eulogicae or consecrated bread marked with a cross and given during the Middle Ages in church as alms or to those unable to receive the HOST.

They have long been customarily eaten at breakfast on GOOD FRIDAY and used to be sold early in the morning to the STREET CRY of 'One-a-penny, two-a-penny hot cross buns!' In London during the 18th century the best hot cross buns came from the Chelsea Bun House (closed in 1836).

Hot-pie shops were opened in working-class districts of towns early in the 19th century. They sold hot beef-steak pies and puddings, eel, kidney, meat and fruit pies and, at CHRISTMAS, mince pies. Some also sold sheeps' hearts and tripe and onions. They provided poorer families with a means of obtaining comparatively cheap, hot, ready-made food. See also COOK-SHOPS, FISH AND CHIP SHOPS.

Hotels were first opened in Britain towards the end of the 18th century with the improvements in COACH travel. Among the earliest were Webb's Hotel in King Street, Covent Garden, and Brunet's Hotel in Leicester Square, both in London. They were at first large INNS, at which wealthy people stayed, and were called 'hotels' after the French word for a large house which ÉMIGRÉS introduced into the country.

When the RAILWAYS were built, there

were few inns near the stations, so the railway companies built their own hotels at King's Cross, Paddington, Glasgow, Edinburgh and elsewhere. With the growth of trade and industry, the number of hotels increased. Many were built at SPAS and SEASIDE places for holiday-makers. The coming of the MOTOR CAR added to the number of hotels and also led to the introduction of MOTELS.

Hour glass a simple instrument for measuring intervals of TIME, first introduced in the 15th century. It consisted of two pear-shaped glass bulbs joined by a narrow neck and usually made in one piece. One bulb was nearly filled with dry sand, the hole plugged and the bulbs fixed inside a wooden or metal frame. The size of the neck was such as to allow the sand to run from one bulb to the other in an hour. It was commonly used by preachers to time their SERMON, and a few may still be seen affixed to old PULPITS; and until the 19th century it was used to time the watches kept in ships.

Houses in early times were of such primitive sorts as the PIT-DWELLINGS and BEEHIVE HUTS. ROMAN BRITAIN had its VILLAS with such refinements as HYPO-CAUSTS, but these left no influence behind them, and later houses were built of primitive materials such as WATTLE AND DAUB and THATCH. After the NORMAN CONQUEST, CASTLES and MANOR houses of stone were erected, but humbler people inhabited COTTAGES, which remained much the same for centuries, having such local features as COB AND THATCH, PAR-GETTING and WEATHER-BOARDING.

More peaceful conditions gradually allowed the building of larger, unfortified houses with such additions as a PANTRY and KITCHEN, BOWER and SOLAR, GLASS in the WINDOWS and a FIREPLACE and CHIMNEY in place of the FUMERELL. Tudor

great houses were especially imposing with their GATEHOUSE, PORCH, STAIRCASE, DRAWING ROOM and LONG GALLERY. This was also the time when GARDENS were planned in accordance with the design of the house.

By the 17th century the RENAISSANCE had influenced the design of houses, and the BALCONY and the PARTERRE had been adopted. After the RESTORATION, wall decorations such as TAPESTRY were increasingly replaced by WALL-PAPER. The REGENCY period made VERANDAHS popular. The 18th century brought the CRESCENT and other examples of planned housing, but the INDUSTRIAL REVOLUTION produced large areas of SLUMS.

Manor house plan: 1 Bower; 2 Solar; 3 Fireplace; 4 Hall; 5 Pantry; 6 Buttery; 7 Kitchen

During the 19th century the BATH and the WATER-CLOSET became a common feature of houses. The CRYSTAL PALACE, built for the GREAT EXHIBITION (1851) brought about new ways of construction, as did also the discovery of CONCRETE. The detached and semi-detached suburban houses, built in mock-Tudor style, of the earlier part of the 20th century were a legacy of the earlier ROMANTIC MOVEMENT. Since the end of the Second World War, Georgian styles have become popular, while FLATS have become increasingly built in towns. CENTRAL HEATING has become more common.

In the past, the building of houses has been influenced by the HEARTH TAX and the WINDOW TAX. BUILDING SOCIETIES nowadays play an important part in house ownership. The NATIONAL TRUST has been formed to preserve historic houses and other buildings. [S. O. Addy, *The Evolution of the English House* (1933); A. R. Powys, *The English House* (1929)]

House of Correction was established by an Act of 1576 as a sort of WORKHOUSE under the control of the JUSTICES OF THE PEACE. These institutions had the aim of stopping able-bodied vagrants from receiving outdoor relief by setting them compulsorily to work to earn their keep and also paying them for their labour. By the 18th century, however, they had often become much the same as the common PRISONS, and an Act of 1720 allowed Justices to sentence idlers to a term in either. Therefore, the prison and the house of correction often became virtually the same, or if some distinction was preserved, they were usually in the same or nearby buildings and under the same administration. See also BRIDEWELL, POOR LAW ACT (1601).

Hue and cry a system of arrest set up in England by the 'ordinance of the hundred' issued by King Edgar (d. 975) requiring the men of a HUNDRED to join the hue 'with horn and with voice' and pursue a suspected criminal. If he escaped into another hundred, they had to warn the men of that hundred to continue the chase. They could be punished for failing to take part in the hue and cry and also for raising it without reason. The Statute of Westminster I (1275) re-affirmed the obligation, and it was further regulated by several later Acts, one as late as 1749; and the *Hue and Cry*, a gazette containing the descriptions of wanted criminals, was published in 1710 to aid their pursuit. Though the hue and cry has now disappeared, citizens are still under an obligation to assist the POLICE in arresting suspects.

Huguenots were those who adopted CALVINISM in France in the 16th century. Persecution brought numbers to England as refugees during Tudor times, and the CRYPT of CANTERBURY CATHEDRAL was assigned to them as a place of worship in 1550, but many more came after the revocation of the Edict of Nantes (1685), and they took an important part in the development of the manufacture of SILK, VELVET and LINEN.

Hundred a subdivision of the SHIRE, dating back to ANGLO-SAXON times, which had its own MOOT. By the end of the 12th century, they had ceased to be important, but were not formally abolished as units of local government until 1867. The hundreds were known as wapentakes in the North of England, while in Sussex there were rapes and in Kent lathes, which were groups of hundreds. [W. E. Jackson, *Local Government in England and Wales* (1945)]

Hunting was an economic necessity in the Middle Ages, but was also the favourite sport of the nobility. BOARS and WOLVES were early hunted. Stag-hunting came into England with the NORMAN CONQUEST and remained the most popular until by the 16th century, with the shrinking of the forests, hare-hunting replaced it. Until the 1850s hares were always hunted by mounted huntsmen with harriers; since then hunting on foot with beagles has become a popular winter sport. Foxhunting, which developed in the late 17th century, was first undertaken with packs derived from harriers, and until the 1850s many packs hunted both hares and foxes. During the first half of the 19th century foxhunting became the chief form of hunting in England, and many packs of foxhounds were formed. [Patrick Chalmers, *The History of Hunting* (1936).] See also DOGS, FOREST LAWS.

Hymns were regularly used in monastic services in the Middle Ages, sung to plainchant. At the REFORMATION, since these hymns were really anthems sung by MONKS, they were not suited to the new emphasis on congregational singing. In Germany, the Lutherans introduced hymn-singing, but the CHURCH OF ENGLAND and the CHURCH OF SCOTLAND, under the influence of CALVINISM which held that singing in worship should be restricted to words from the BIBLE, introduced only metrical PSALMS and paraphrases.

The originator of modern English hymn-singing was Isaac Watts (1674–1748), who wrote hymns (including 'When I survey the wondrous Cross') which were first sung in his INDEPENDENT chapel at Southampton. Hymn-singing was a strength of the METHODIST movement, and Charles Wesley (1707–88) wrote about 6500 hymns (including 'Christ, whose glory fills the skies', 'Soldiers of Christ, arise' and 'Love divine, all loves excelling'). The EVANGELICAL movement produced John Newton (1725–1807) and William Cowper (1731–1800), who collaborated in producing the *Olney Hymns,* and Augustus Montague Toplady (1740–78), who wrote 'Rock of Ages'. Among the TRACTARIANS, John Keble (1792–1866) wrote *The*

Christian Year, a collection of poems several of which became used as hymns, but the chief hymn-writer of the movement was John Mason Neale (1818–65), who published translations of the old Latin hymns to be sung to plainsong melodies.

Reginald Heber (1783–1826) published the first hymn-book arranged for use with the services and seasons of the Book of COMMON PRAYER, and *Hymns Ancient and Modern* was first published in 1861.

Hypocaust a heating system from a furnace for ROMAN BATHS or rooms in VILLAS. Hot air was conducted through a

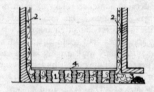

Cross section of Hypocaust: 1 Hypocaust; 2 Flues; 3 Furnace; 4 Floor

hollow space under the floor and by hollow tiles through the walls. A hypocaust used to heat a public bath may be seen at St Albans (Herts.).

I

Ice cream is said to have been invented in England when Charles I's cook added cream to sherbet and stirred it in a vessel surrounded by ice. By the 18th century it had become popular enough for an Eng-

lish household book of 1769 to contain instructions 'to make ice cream' from flavoured or sweetened cream or custard. The general sale of ice cream became common in the later 19th century, being largely popularized by Italian street-vendors; and the ice-cream block was first sold by Lyons in 1923 as an innovation from the USA.

Ice-houses were possessed by large houses for the storage of ice needed for keeping food fresh. They were not common before the late 17th century and were in general use from the mid-18th to the late 19th centuries. An ice-house was often an egg-shaped chamber, usually built underground or covered with a mound of earth, and reached by steps down to it. The ice was cut in slabs from frozen ponds in the winter and laid in layers of straw in the ice-house where it could often be kept all the year round. Ice-houses began to go out of use from the mid-19th century when ice could be made artificially by mechanical REFRIGER-ATION and could be brought at any time by the RAILWAYS.

Icknield Way a prehistoric trackway forming a line of communication between south-west England and the east coast running from the Wash to Salisbury Plain, crossing the River Thames near Goring. Used in the BRONZE AGE, parts of it in East Anglia became a Roman road and in the 6th century was one of the routes by which northern Wessex was settled. It underlies a section of the modern road.

Images of Christ, the Virgin Mary and the saints were venerated in the Middle Ages. PILGRIMAGES were made to them, and miracles were believed to be performed at them. Wonder-working images in England included the ROOD at Bexley Abbey (Kent) and the 'Speaking Crucifix' at Meaux Abbey (Yorks.). In old ST PAUL'S CATHEDRAL, the head of an ANGLO-SAXON king became the fictitious St Uncumber, a bearded virgin able to rid WIVES of unwanted husbands in return for a peck of oats.

At the REFORMATION many PROTES-TANTS were hostile to images. In 1550 an Act ordered their destruction in England, and many were later destroyed or disfigured in the REREDOS and other places in CHURCHES by extreme PURITANS who regarded all images as idolatrous.

Income Tax was first imposed by William Pitt as a wartime tax in 1799 at 2s in the £ on incomes above £60 but with reduced rates up to £200. It was abolished in 1802, but reimposed by Henry Addington at 1s in 1803 and continued until 1816. In 1842 Sir Robert Peel revived it at the rate of 7d, and it has remained ever since. Between 1854 and 1914 it varied between 4d and 1s 2d. In the First World War the rate rose to 6s and in the Second to 10s. The 'Pay As You Earn' scheme (by which the tax is deducted at source) was established in 1944. Earned income relief began in 1907 and child and other allowances in 1909. 'Super-tax' (now sur-tax) on high incomes was first imposed in 1909.

Independents Brownists or Congregationalists originated with the congregation founded in Norwich about 1580 by Robert Browne. They accepted the doctrines of CALVINISM, but not its system of ecclesiastical government; they believed in the complete separation of Church and State and in the independence of each congregation. During the COMMONWEALTH, they had the support of the army and triumphed over the PRESBYTERIANS. [Eric Routley, *The Story of Congregationalism* (1967).] See also ANABAPTISTS.

Industrial Revolution began in Britain in the second half of the 18th century some 50 years earlier than anywhere else in the world. The essential nature of this movement was that it brought about two great changes in the way men did their work. It replaced human muscle power by machines that were driven by new forms of power, especially STEAM POWER; and it replaced the DOMESTIC SYSTEM by the FACTORY SYSTEM, which meant not only a new way of organizing industry, but also a new way of life for many people. [L. W. Cowie, *Industrial Evolution* (1970)]

Infirmarer, Infirmarian the title of the MONK who had charge of the FARMERY of a MONASTERY. The Observances of Barnwell Priory (Northants.) stated that 'he who has the care of the sick ought to be gentle, good-tempered, kind, compassionate to the sick and willing to gratify their needs with affectionate sympathy. He ought to have a servant who is to stay continually in the farmery and wait on the sick with diligence and all gentleness. He should get their food ready at the proper time, and note how they ought to be dieted. He must endure without complaint the foulness of sick persons, and when they die get their bodies ready for burial. The infirmarer ought to say mass daily, and if they cannot go to chapel, visit their bedsides repeating words of consolation, but not disturb them when resting. He should take a kindly interest in each one and should provide a fire if the weather requires it and a lamp to burn all night.'

Ink was made from earliest times of soot, water and gum, but this became easily thick and clogged the PEN. In the 17th century a new sort of black writing ink was made in Europe of a combination of tannic or gallic acid, obtained from the bark of trees, and iron salt. Modern inks are still made in fundamentally the same way, but blue dye may be added to colour it. The ink in ball-point pens is thicker and has an oil base instead of water.

The earliest PRINTING ink was made of lamp black mixed with boiled linseed oil, and this was used until recent times. Today printing ink is usually made by chemical means.

Inns were originally licensed to put up travellers by day and night and not to provide casual drinks and meals to people. At first travellers depended largely on MANORS and MONASTERIES for a night's lodging, and TAVERNS with sleeping accommodation were not known before the 14th century. In the 13th century or earlier, there were ale-houses for drinking and cook-houses for eating, both of which began to erect temporary shelters for travellers, and from these came the first inns. Among the best were those for people on PILGRIMAGES.

By Elizabeth I's reign, English inns were famous for their comfort and good service; a traveller said they were the best in the world. They were usually built round a cobbled courtyard, often entered by an archway from the street; the kitchen and public rooms occupied the main part of the building, while round two sides of the courtyard were other guest rooms, opening out on to a wooden balcony, and along the fourth side were the stables and outbuildings. This courtyard was sometimes used as an early local THEATRE.

The most flourishing period for inns was the age of travel by STAGE-COACH, which began in the 17th century and lasted 200 years. An 18th-century coaching-inn was often the centre of a town's social life with an ASSEMBLY ROOM for balls, etc. It might be owned or leased by a coachmaster, who stabled his horses there and provided board and lodging for passengers. The name of the inn from which a coach was worked was often painted on its doors or its hind boot. The largest and latest of such inns were called HOTELS.

The inns were ruined in the 19th century by the RAILWAYS, and a revival did not come until the development of the MOTOR CAR, which since the 1960s has also been responsible for the growth of MOTELS.

Inn-signs began in the Middle Ages as ALE-STAKES. They were succeeded by inn-signs, often as simple devices to attract various travellers (e.g. a Cross for pilgrims, a Drum for soldiers). Others had religious signs, often derived from the dedication of the church (e.g. the Cross Keys of St Peter or the Lamb and Flag of St John the Baptist). Others had coats of arms, crests or badges (see HERALDRY) belonging to local great families (e.g. The

Inn sign spanning the street

Red Lion or the Green Dragon). Again, other signs indicated that inns were centres of sports (e.g. the Fighting Cocks or the Dog and Bear). In the 18th century and after inns were named after wartime heroes (e.g. Admiral Rodney, Admiral Benbow, Duke of Cumberland, Marquis of Granby, King of Prussia, Iron Duke, Hero of Waterloo). The coming of the RAILWAYS brought new names for inns (e.g. the Great Northern, the Midland or the Railway Inn).

Like SHOP-SIGNS it was usual for inn-signs either to hang out on a pole from the building or on posts between the foot- and carriage-way; but Pastor Moritz noticed in 1782 that many English villages had large inn-signs hanging in the middle of the street from a long beam extending across from one house to another. [Cadbury Lamb and Gordon Wright, *Discovering Inn-Signs* (1968)]

Insurance began with marine insurance, which probably started in Flanders and was brought to England by merchants in the early 16th century, being undertaken by underwriters who later formed LLOYD'S, and at about the same time fire insurance began (see FIRE-FIGHTING, FIREMARKS). Life insurance, usually called 'assurance' in Britain, originated in the Middle Ages when creditors insured, for the duration of a voyage or some other limited period, the life of a merchant debtor handling goods which the creditor had financed. The earliest life insurance on record is dated 1583, and the earliest life insurance company was founded in 1699, but did not long survive; not until the 18th century were a number of successful companies started, and there was a rapid growth in the 19th century; and in the 19th century there was also a great growth of industrial insurance, the name given to life insurance issued in return for small weekly or monthly payments, usually collected from door to door by agents. Personal accident insurance began about 1840; and since the coming of the MOTOR CAR, motor insurance has become an increasingly important form of this insurance, and in Britain the Road Traffic Act of 1930 made third party insurance compulsory for motorists. [H. F. Raynes, *A History of British Insurance* (1950).] See also FRIENDLY SOCIETIES, NATIONAL INSURANCE.

Irish first came to Britain as seasonal workers to help with the hay harvest, and from them the first permanent colonies were largely recruited, one of the earliest in London, established early in the 17th century, being in the parish of St Giles-in-the-Fields. The effects of unequal economic competition, when Irish industry was deprived of protection by the Act of Union (1801), brought an increase of immigrants, among whom was an admixture of Protestants and Ulstermen, and including many tradesmen, artisans, weavers and cotton workers.

From 1810, however, there was an increasingly ROMAN CATHOLIC and peasant migration. Irish poverty was worse than that of the English and Welsh countryside. Successive failures of the POTATO crop (notably in 1821-2) and mass evictions (1820-30) swelled their numbers. Some still came as seasonal harvest workers, but more and more stayed for years or permanently. Probably 400 000 Irish entered England in 1841-51, mostly settling in London and the industrial towns. In 1851 between one fifth and one-third of the population of Liverpool and Manchester had been born in Ireland. The great majority were Roman Catholics and among the poorest paid labourers, including NAVVIES.

Irish immigration reached its peak during the decade of the Great Famine (1847) and thereafter declined, but after the First World War, when mass migration into USA ceased, it revived. In 1961 there were a million persons of Irish birth in Britain. [John Jackson, *The Irish in Britain* (1961)]

Iona a small, rocky island of the Inner Hebrides off the west coast of Scotland. In AD 563, after his missionary activities in Ireland, St Columba came over and built a MONASTERY on it. From there he and his companions started to convert the north of Britain to Christianity. There was a monastery on the island for a thousand years. See also CELTIC CHURCH, LINDISFARNE, MONKS.

Iron came into general use in Britain during the IRON AGE. It was mined in

ROMAN BRITAIN, and this was revived by the ANGLO-SAXONS. DOMESDAY BOOK describes iron-mining in several parts of the country on the eve of the NORMAN CONQUEST. The Forest of Dean became the centre of the industry in the 12th century. There was also some in northern England, but this was on a smaller scale. The industry developed also in the Weald of Kent and Sussex during the 13th century.

Iron was made by the direct process (i.e. in simple ovens to melt the ore) from the Iron Age to the end of the 15th century and even up to 1540 in some places. Blast furnaces (using a forced draught produced by bellows) reached England just after 1490. Between 1709 and 1750 Abraham Darby and his son of Coalbrookdale (Shropshire) found out how to use coke instead of CHARCOAL as the heating agent; and the industry gradually concentrated itself among the coalfields of the North and Midlands, South Wales and the Scottish Lowlands.

The coke-operated blast-furnaces made pig-iron (hardened in shallow ditches called pigs) which was brittle. In 1784 Henry Cort invented a reverberatory furnace which expelled the impurities from the iron and produced stronger wrought-iron. James Neilson's blast-furnace of 1829 economized in fuel by using hot air, and James Nasmyth's STEAM-HAMMER combined power and delicacy in the operation of forging (or shaping).

The first large British ironworks was founded in 1759 at Carron (Stirlingshire), and by 1800 had become the greatest munition works in Europe. [T. S. Ashton, *Iron and Steel in the Industrial Revolution* (2nd ed. 1951).] See also CARRONADE.

Iron Age began in southern England in the 6th century BC, being introduced by a later invasion of CELTS with iron weapons and implements. This enabled them to cultivate and settle in the lowlands, after clearing the forests. Some of them lived in LAKE VILLAGES and BEEHIVE HUTS. Their use of the SLING from the late 2nd century led to the development of HILL-FORTS. The coming of the BELGAE in the 1st century BC brought further advances.

Ironing was first done by means of smooth, water-worn stones, heated in the embers of a fire and wrapped round with cloth to protect the hands. Such primitive smoothing-stones were still being used in the Orkney Islands as late as 1880. Another early implement was a rounded piece of glass, which was used without heating. True flat-irons, heated in the fire, were known in the Middle Ages. From the 17th century heavy box-irons were sometimes used; these stood on three-legged stands and were heated internally by CHARCOAL or a piece of hot metal thrust into one end. Electric irons came into use in the 1920s. See also LAUNDERING, GOFFERING-TONGS.

Irvingites a religious body, called by its members the Catholic Apostolic Church, founded on the basis of the teaching of Edward Irving (1792–1834), a minister of the CHURCH OF SCOTLAND, with a fourfold ministry of apostles, prophets, evangelists and pastors and using in its services incense, lights and traditional Catholic ceremonial. Its numbers have declined, and since 1965 its so-called Cathedral in Gordon Square (London) has become the Church of the Anglican Chaplaincy to the University.

Ivory tablet or *aide-mémoire*, a sheaf of several small, thin rectangular pieces of ivory, fastened together at one end by a metal stud, which was carried by ladies in their RETICULE or handbag to write down notes of engagements, shopping requirements, etc., during the 19th century. The pieces of ivory (which were sometimes seven in number and each headed with the name of a day of the week) were fastened between covers of silver, mother of pearl or ivory, and these might be fitted with a pencil. After use, the ivory pieces could be wiped clean of the pencilled notes and written on again.

J

Jack boot a large BOOT reaching above the knee worn for riding from about the RESTORATION to the end of the 18th century. These boots were made of leather, sometimes hardened by boiling or applications of pitch paint. When worn by CAVALRY, they might be covered with plates of iron to protect the legs.

Jews settled in England after the NORMAN CONQUEST. Their centre was the Great Synagogue, London, but they settled in other towns also. In the 12th and 13th centuries several massacres of Jews took place in London and such places as Norwich, Lincoln and York, but they generally lived in peace. In the 13th century they were placed under the special protection of the King through Justices of the Jews, who formed a court for recovering their debts; but the King could TALLAGE them at will, and their debts fell to him on death. Edward I, who was in constant financial difficulties, expelled them from England in 1290, seizing their property. They were allowed to return under the COMMONWEALTH in 1656, but did not obtain complete equality until the Jewish Relief Act (1858).

The first Jews to come to England in the 17th Century were mainly Spanish and Portuguese, but in the 1890s persecution brought many from Russia who formed a large settlement in east London. The latest to come were those driven from Germany and Austria by the Nazis in the 1930s. In 1970 there were some 450 000 Jews in the United Kingdom.

Jewellery probably came before costume. Early men and women decorated themselves and their garments with ornaments of GOLD and SILVER. NECKLACES, BRACELETS and RINGS were among the earliest forms of jewellery. EARRINGS were introduced in the 16th century, and BROOCHES were popular in the 19th century. WATCHES and CHATELAINES have been designed for ornament as well as use. Among precious stones, CORAL was popular in ancient and medieval times, PEARLS during the RENAISSANCE and DIAMONDS since the 17th century.

Jig-saw puzzles first known as dissected maps or dissected puzzles. Later they became known by the name of the tool by which they were made, and the name remained when the tool was no longer used. They were invented in England by a firm of map-makers, Wallis and Son, between 1760 and 1770. At first they were all of maps as an aid to teaching geography, but soon historical pictures and chronological tables followed. Moralizing puzzles were common in Victorian times, and from about 1850 Biblical stories, Robinson Crusoe and

zoological subjects were all popular, but the dissected map never lost its appeal.

Until about 1840–50 puzzle pictures, apart from maps, usually consisted of numerous small scenes, arranged in sequence, and generally these scenes were divided by wavy vertical and horizontal cuts across the tableaux. Dovetail heads, to hold the whole puzzle together, were used sparingly, if at all, and then only round the perimeter. Also the individual pieces of the early puzzles were usually large, 2–4 in. being common and sometimes larger. Modern jigsaws are only possible through improved means of cutting them.

The first jigsaws cost half a guinea, an expensive TOY in those days. At first the puzzles were usually on $\frac{1}{4}$ in. thick mahogany or cedar and enclosed in mahogany boxes with sliding lids, labelled with the maker's name and sometimes with the title of the puzzle. From about 1850 a varnished-over picture of the completed puzzle was pasted on the lids, and the boxes were of pine or mahogany.

Joint-stock Company came into being in the 16th century. While earlier organizations (see GUILD and LIVERY COMPANY) were associations of individuals, each working separately with his own capital, but licensed by his membership to pursue his trade and subject to its rules, the joint-stock companies each consisted of a number of men who put their capital into it and drew a dividend (a share of the profits earned through its enterprises) proportionate to their investment. Examples of these were the Mines Royal Company (see COPPER) and the Mineral and Battery Works, both incorporated in 1568.

Jube a name for the ROOD-loft dividing the NAVE from the CHANCEL in a CHURCH. The name is believed to have come from the sentence, 'Jube, domine, benedicere'

('Pray, sir, a blessing'), pronounced by the deacon in the MASS before the reading of the Gospel, which was performed on the rood-loft in the Middle Ages.

Judges in early days were BARONS or BISHOPS who dispensed justice in the name of the King, who also did it himself. Gradually officials known as 'justices' were appointed both to preside in the King's COURT and to go through the country with royal authority. These at first not only heard cases, but also engaged in the collection of taxes and other royal business. Henry II (1154–89), however, instituted 'justices of assize' who were empowered to hear cases of every description; and today England and Wales are divided into eight circuits visited annually by ASSIZE judges with much the same powers. See also JURY, JUSTICES OF THE PEACE. [Peter Archer, *The Queen's Courts* (1956)]

Jury originated with the practice, introduced into England at the NORMAN CONQUEST, of authorizing a royal officer to swear in men of a locality to give facts required for some administrative record. DOMESDAY BOOK was compiled in this way. With the abolition of TRIAL BY ORDEAL in 1215, juries began to be used to return verdicts on the facts in judicial cases, and in 1275 jury trial for serious charges was made compulsory. Formerly there were grand juries, which were appointed to enquire into accusations before they were sent for trial by jury, but these were effectively abolished in 1933.

Justices of the Peace received their title when an Act of 1361 provided for the appointment of local knights and gentry by the Crown with the power of arresting offenders and trying felonies, and in 1363 it was enacted they should hold Quarter Sessions four times a year. In the 16th century they were granted summary jurisdiction (Petty Sessions) and also received so many administrative duties that they have been nicknamed the 'Tudor maids-of-all-work'. They were concerned with the POOR LAW, APPRENTICESHIP and RECUSANTS. As unpaid, amateur officials, they became more powerful in local government after the RESTORATION. They were deprived of most of their administrative duties in 1889. See also MARRIAGE, TURNPIKES, TOWNS, FACTORY LAWS.

K

Kaleidoscope a TOY, consisting of a tube through which are seen symmetrical figures, produced by reflections of pieces of coloured glass and varied by rotating the tube, was invented in 1817 by the Edinburgh physicist, Sir David Brewster. [Leslie Gordon, *Peepshow into Paradise* (1953)]

Kate Greenaway dress became popular in the 1880s and 1890s for little girls as a result of the illustrations in children's books by the artist of that name. It comprised a long, high-waisted dress, made of light, flower-patterned material, with puffed shoulder-sleeves and the skirt trimmed with a narrow flounce. It was commonly worn with a wide sash and a MOB CAP. See also LITTLE LORD FAUNTLEROY COSTUME.

Keel an oval-shaped vessel, about 40 ft by 15½ ft, capable of carrying eight Newcastle CHALDRONS (i.e. 21·2 tons of COAL). They were of shallow draught and ferried coal down the River Tyne to ships moored in the open river, but ceased to be needed when the river was dredged in the 1870s, and ships could come up to the quayside. The keelmen, who operated them, were almost extinct by 1886. [S. Middlebrook, *Newcastle upon Tyne* (1950)]

Keep the great tower or donjon of a CASTLE was the successor of the wooden tower of the MOTTE and BAILEY. The keep of Colchester Castle and the White Tower of the TOWER OF LONDON were

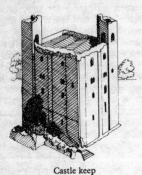

Castle keep

built in the 11th century; all others belong to the 12th century, mostly the second half. The stone keep was tall and square with a single room on each floor, and the entrance, for greater protection, was sometimes on the first floor with an outside stair leading to it, e.g. Castle Rising (Norfolk). Some great keeps (e.g. Rochester Castle) were large enough to contain halls, chapels and many rooms.

The importance of the keep declined with the development of CURTAIN WALLS.

Kilt as an article of highland attire, was probably originally a large PLAID belted round the body. By the early 18th century, the lower part of the garment had become separate as the permanently pleated 'little kilt'. Its wearing was forbidden from 1746 to 1782 by the law against Highland dress, but this was followed by a revival, stimulated by the example of the Highland regiments and the influence of the ROMANTIC MOVEMENT. When George IV visited Edinburgh in 1822 he wore a kilt, though with flesh-coloured STOCKINGS. This revival has also been closely connected with the modern myth of the Scottish TARTAN. [H. F. McClintock, *Old Irish and Highland Dress* (1951).] See also TREWS.

Kirtle was a medieval body garment for women, like a TUNIC, which was worn next to the SMOCK and under the dress or upper garment.

Kitchen of a medieval HOUSE was usually a detached building (because of the danger of fire) before the 15th century and often for the next two centuries, e.g. the kitchen of the ABBOT'S Lodging, Glastonbury (Somerset). In great houses of early Tudor times, e.g. Hengrave Hall (Suffolk), the kitchen was put in the basement, and this continued to be the usual arrangement in both town and country houses until well into the 19th century. [M. W. Barley, *The House and Home* (1963)]

Knight under the system of FEUDALISM developed in England after the NORMAN CONQUEST, was an armed horseman who was bound, in return for his KNIGHT'S FEE, to join the royal army for 40 days a year in wartime. It became customary for a man to be made a knight by a blow on the shoulder from the flat of a SWORD, at first often by the SQUIRE'S father or feudal superior, but later more usually by the sovereign.

During the CRUSADES, knighthood became very important and developed a religious character. A man about to become a knight would keep a solemn vigil in a church beside his arms, and knighthood became the highest order of CHIVALRY. There were, in additions the military orders of the TEMPLARS and HOSPITALLERS.

In the later Middle Ages, the knight's military obligations and cost of his full ARMOUR made the honour increasingly less desirable and the payment of SCUTAGE became more common. As feudalism disappeared, knighthood declined into a lower order of nobility (see BARONET). The title 'Sir' is prefixed to a knight's Christian name, and his wife was first called 'Dame' but nowadays 'Lady'.

Knight's fee   the unit of land under FEUDALISM into which, after the NORMAN CONQUEST, land held of the King by military service was divided. The extent of such an estate bound to provide a fully-armed KNIGHT for the royal army was never definitely fixed, but generally seems to have been worth about £20 a year.

Knot garden   a series of small beds arranged formally, sometimes on a terrace, and edged with dwarf HEDGES and planted with dwarf clipped shrubs and HERBS, like rosemary, box and thrift, in complicated geometric patterns or knots. The background to the pattern might be coloured earth or gravel, and the effect might rely solely on the design of the green plants when seen from above.

Plan of knot garden

Where the pattern was less intricate, the empty spaces in the beds might be filled with topiary-work or flowers. Knot gardens were fashionable in Elizabethan times and very popular throughout the 16th and early 17th centuries, when the more complicated the knots, the better the gardens were liked. Later the knot garden was replaced by the PARTERRE.

L

Labourers, Statute of (1351) was passed by Parliament in an effort to prevent wages rising following the BLACK DEATH. It stated that every able-bodied man, not living of himself or by a trade, must hire himself at the rate of wages paid in 1347 to any master who demanded his services and might not leave his service without his permission. It also forbade masters to offer higher wages. It largely failed because of the continuing labour shortage, but the resentment it produced contributed towards the outbreak of the PEASANTS' REVOLT.

Lace is made in three basic ways: (1) Needlepoint lace evolved from cutwork embroidery, in which a pattern of holes was cut out of the material and edged with buttonhole stitch. By the end of the 16th century, the background material was discarded, and the lace was built up entirely of button-hole stitches. Needlepoint lace developed mainly in Italy, France and Belgium and never became an industry in Britain. (2) Bobbin or pillow lace, made by twisting and plaiting the threads, previously wound on bobbins, also developed in the 16th century. The pattern to be followed is marked upon a parchment, which is laid upon a pillow; pins are stuck at important points in the pattern, and the threads are anchored on these. At first this was mainly a cottage-industry in England, employing women and children, but in the 17th century it was also made in CHARITY SCHOOLS and WORKHOUSES and in the early 19th century in lace-schools in which girls from 5 years old were employed 10 hours a day (see also LACE-LAMP). The two main areas in which lace was made were in and around Honiton and Beer (Devon) and Bucks. and Beds. Lace-making especially prospered in the 18th century, because it could be sold more cheaply than the superior Continental lace. By 1770 some 100 000 people were employed in it. (3) Machine lace developed rapidly in England from the mid-19th century, and nowadays lace-making machines can produce imitations of either type of lace.

Lace-lamp a device for concentrating light for lace-making by means of a glass globe or flash, filled with water, placed in front of a CANDLE. In lace-making schools use was commonly made of a device comprising four tall wooden legs supporting a round board in which were holes for a number of flashes placed around a single candle. The girls sat around this in a circle, so that each would have a flash to illuminate her work.

Lady Chapel an addition to CATHEDRALS and greater CHURCHES from the 13th century onwards as a result of the growing cult of Mariolatry. These special CHAPELS, dedicated to the Virgin Mary (Our Lady), were built as near as possible to the HIGH ALTAR, either at the east end of the CHOIR (e.g. Exeter and Chichester) or by the side of the PRESBYTERY (e.g. Ely) or sometimes forming the two eastern bays of the choir itself (e.g. Worcester and Beverley). [F. H. Crossley, *English Church Design A.D. 1040–1540* (1945)]

Lake villages were built by the CELTS of the IRON AGE in marshes for protection. The remains of several have been found

Lake Village

in Britain, including one at Glastonbury (Somerset), which was built in a marsh probably flooded in winter and spring.

Here a four-acre foundation of logs and brushwood was laid and enclosed by a fence of log piles. On this were built about 60 round huts, 18–20 ft across, with wattled sides, trodden clay floors and roofs thatched with reeds. They had a stone or clay hearth in the middle of the floor, paved doorsteps and sand paths leading between them. Cattle were kept and corn and vegetables grown on nearby higher ground, and food was brought in carts to the village. Dug-out canoes were used for fishing and hunting wildfowl on the water. See also BEEHIVE HUTS.

Lammas Day (August 1), the festival of the WHEAT harvest. People used to go to CHURCH on that day, each taking with him a loaf of BREAD made of new wheat as an offering to God of the first-fruits of the year's harvest. It was one of the oldest of the Church's festivals, probably being derived from the 'loaf-mass' of the ANGLO-SAXONS.

Lamps the oldest form of LIGHTING, consisted in their simplest form of a shallow open dish containing oil on which a wick floated. In GRIME'S GRAVES the roofs of the galleries are still marked by soot from such lamps. In Roman pottery-lamps the wick was led from the oil by a spout, and the oil-container was covered. From the Middle Ages lamps were commonly superseded by CANDLES for interior lighting, but from the end of the 17th century the London streets were lit by oil-lamps enclosed in lanterns, which in the 18th century were fitted with thick convex glass. A great improvement came with the invention in 1784 of the Argand oil-lamp, devised by a Swiss physicist, which gave a brighter light, because the oil was more thoroughly and effectively burned in a tubular glass chimney, and with the introduction from about 1850 of paraffin instead of the vegetable oils previously used which had

given a variable light and were smoky and smelly; but by then oil-lamps were being replaced by GAS.

Lance the chief WEAPON of the mounted KNIGHT. As used by the Normans in the BAYEUX TAPESTRY, it is short and light with a diamond-shape head fitted with a small piece of cloth to prevent the point from imbedding itself at the moment of impact so enabling the weapon to be removed immediately for further use. It is also shown used in the couched position, held under the armpit and supported in the rider's right hand, the head being aimed to the left, a way of using the lance which was then just coming in, being made possible by the adoption of STIRRUPS and high SADDLES. This led to the use from the 13th century of longer and stronger lances, but in TOURNAMENTS special light, readily-breakable lances were used. Despite the introduction of firearms, the lance continued to be used in warfare. In 1816 CAVALRY regiments armed with lances were introduced into the British army, which did not cease to use lances until 1928.

Landau a state CARRIAGE for royalty first made in 1757 at Landau in Germany. It was like a COACH, but the upper part was made in two halves which could be folded back to form an open carriage, and there was also a seat or stand at the back for footmen. A landaulet was a carriage for two with a top opening like a landau.

Latitudinarianism a name given contemptuously in the 17th century to a group of divines in the CHURCH OF ENGLAND who, unlike the HIGH CHURCHMEN and LOW CHURCHMEN, attached greater importance to ethical and moral precepts than to matters of belief, church government and worship. They generally sympathized with the ideas of

ARMINIANISM. Until the coming of the METHODISTS and EVANGELICALS, they exercised an important religious influence in the 18th century. See also BROAD CHURCHMEN.

Laudians the supporters in the CHURCH OF ENGLAND of William Laud (Bishop of London, 1628–33; Archbishop of Canterbury, 1633–45). They held the beliefs of ARMINIANISM, but their distinguishing mark was insistence upon discipline imposed by BISHOPS and obedience to the COMMON PRAYER BOOK in worship. They were opposed by the PURITANS because they sought to revive VESTMENTS and medieval ceremonial. Supported by Charles I, they were influential in the Church before the Civil War and also in Charles II's exiled court. They did much to secure the restoration of the Church in 1660, but declined later through the growth of LATITUDINARIANISM.

The interior aspect of the English parish CHURCH today is largely due to them.

Laundering in its earliest form consisted of washing clothes and household linen in a stream, pounding them with stones to loosen the dirt and spreading them on bushes to dry. By the Middle Ages the washing was done in large households in wooden tubs, and the clothes were beaten on tables with bats or beetles, while a later device was the DOLLY. Most housewives had to wash in their KITCHEN or yard, but by the 16th century substantial houses had their own stone-floored laundry furnished with tables, boilers for heating water, tubs, TALLIES and MANGLES. IRONING was also done, while the introduction of STARCH in the later 16th century was a great advance. SOAP had generally replaced the use of LYE in laundry work by the 17th century. LINEN was finished in a press.

Until the end of the 18th century, it was customary for the laundering in a household to be done only once every two or three months. This meant that so much washing had accumulated that work had to begin as early as 3 or 4 a.m. in order to finish by dusk. Outside washerwomen might be hired to come in to assist the servants.

From the Middle Ages women worked as laundresses, taking the clothes away from households to wash, and Shakespeare refers in the *Merry Wives of Windsor* to the laundresses of that town. In the late 19th century laundries with steam-driven machinery were established in towns, while DRY-CLEANING had already developed. The 1950s saw the establishment of launderettes, in which the housewife can do her own washing; and, in the home, electric WASHING-MACHINES have become common.

Lavender was commonly used in the past as a HERB. Culpeper held that its flowers, when steeped in wine, 'helpeth them that be troubled with the wind or cholic, if the places be bathed therewith'. It is recorded as having been grown for its scent in 1568 at Hitchin (Herts.), and until the 19th century the lavender fields at Mitcham (Surrey) were well-known. Lavender-water was made as a PERFUME by distillation. Like ROSEMARY, lavender was mingled with the RUSHES on the floor, and Izaak Walton in *The Compleat Angler* (1653) spoke of the beds in an inn in which 'the linen looks white and smells of lavender'.

Lawnmower was invented by Edwin Budding, an engineer in a cloth factory at Stroud (Glos.), in 1830 and manufactured the next year. Before then LAWNS were kept short either by stock grazing, mainly SHEEP, or by the use of a SCYTHE and BROOM. The use of the lawnmower was stimulated by the growing popularity of lawn TENNIS in the 1870s, and by then a horse-drawn lawnmower was being used at Kew Gardens, while the motor lawnmower came in the 20th century. The use of the lawnmower has led to a great increase in the area given up to grass in modern GARDENS.

Lawns in the Middle Ages were imitations of a natural meadow with primroses, periwinkles, irises, pinks and other flowers. Later, fashion got rid of the flowers. A monastic CLOISTER had a central lawn planted with flowers and divided into quarters by paths intersecting in the centre. In the 16th century, as GARDENS increased in size, a common arrangement was 'gardens within a garden' (e.g. an orchard, bowling green, physic garden, HERB garden and perhaps a KNOT GARDEN), the whole being enclosed by turf paths and walks. Lawns did not become important, however, until the late 17th and early 18th century when Lancelot ('Capability') Brown brought parks and lawns right up to the house. In the 19th and 20th century lawns became increasingly popular, those in this century being usually smaller and often with flower beds, usually roses. See also BOWLS, LAWNMOWER.

Lawn tennis was invented in England in the early 1870s as an adaptation of TENNIS to the open air. It soon became popular as a game which men and women could play together. In 1875 the Marylebone Cricket Club drew up the first rules for the game, and in 1877 the All-England Croquet Club became the All-England Croquet and Lawn Tennis Club, holding the first lawn tennis championship at Wimbledon in the same year.[Lord Aberdare, *The Story of Tennis* (1959)]

Lead is one of the earliest known metals. It was mined in ROMAN BRITAIN,

many pieces of it with Latin inscriptions having been found, and was important because SILVER could be separated from the ore. Probably it was mined in England even earlier since the remains of primitive furnaces (perhaps belonging to the IRON AGE) have been found in the Mendips and Yorkshire. It was used from the Middle Ages for roofing and plumbing; and lead-mining was important in northern England during the 17th and 18th centuries.

Leading strings in the 17th and 18th centuries were long narrow strips of material attached to the back of the arm-holes of a young child's garment and used to lead him or her when beginning to walk.

Leaven a substance added to dough to produce fermentation in baking. The Egyptians in about 2000 BC discovered the use of leaven using a piece of older, fermenting dough to produce light, aerated BREAD. The Romans made leaven from millet or wheat bran, moistened with water and kneaded with mould from wine tubs, which was then shaped into little cakes and dried in the sun. In making bread these leaven cakes were soaked in water, boiled with fine wheaten flour and mixed into bread dough. Leaven was superseded by the use of YEAST. [R. Sheppard and E. Newton, *The Story of Bread* (1957)]

Lectern a reading-desk in a CHURCH holding the BIBLE from which the lessons are read. Before the REFORMATION, it stood in the CHANCEL to hold the service-book for the conductor of the CHOIR. Later lecterns were often made of brass in the shape of an eagle with dragons at the foot; the eagle symbolizing the carrying of the Gospel to the four corners of the earth with the dragons as evil overcome by the word of God.

Leprosy was known in ANGLO-SAXON times, and occasional cases were recorded under Edward the Confessor, but from the late 11th century it rapidly grew among all classes of society. There seem to have been many cases in the 12th and 13th centuries, but during the 14th century it began to decline steadily and by the 15th century had become rare, though it was still known in south-western England for a century or more.

Special lazar-houses were built and endowed by charitable persons, but lepers could not be compelled to go into them unless they frequented crowded places. The most important lazar-house was at Burton-Lazars (Leicestershire), which was built in Stephen's reign (1135–54), but soon they existed in every considerable town, and in the early 14th century a Bishop of Exeter made bequests to 39 lazar-houses in his diocese.

In the 14th century many towns (e.g. Bristol and London) passed local laws for the expulsion of lepers. A suspected leper, after examination by a parish priest or 'jury of discreet men', was 'secluded' by a special service in church. He was now forbidden to enter churches, markets, inns, mills, bakehouses and other places, and must signal his approach by a bell or clapper. He must not speak with healthy people, walk unshod on a road and bathe or drink in a stream except with a cup. He must have distinctive clothes consisting of a cloak, coat and shoes of fur with plain overshoes or ox-hide boots worn over them. A man had to wear a hood and a woman a thick double veil, black outside and white within. These clothes, together with a girdle were given to them, as well as a clapper, cup, knife and plate. They were also conducted to their own house which was provided with its own well and furnished with such necessities as a couch, coverlets, pillow, chest, table, seat, candlestick and shovel.

Leprosy was also a common disease in Scotland during about the same time, and there were lazar-houses in Edinburgh, Glasgow, Aberdeen, Kingcase (Ayrshire) and Liberton (which is supposed to mean Leper Town). (E. Lanarks.)

Levellers were a party of extreme revolutionaries in the parliamentary army at the beginning of the COMMONWEALTH. They demanded the levelling of all ranks, full individual liberty and religious toleration and a form of republican government with manhood suffrage and annual parliaments. Their activities caused mutinies in 1647 and 1649, which were suppressed by Oliver Cromwell, and after their leader, John Lilburne, had been banished to Jersey in 1652 their influence declined. See also DIGGERS.

Liberties were areas which possessed, usually by royal grant, a varying measure of freedom from royal officials and laws. Their creation began before the NORMAN CONQUEST, and some others came into being afterwards, especially in northern England where the assistance of powerful EARLS was needed to protect the Scottish frontier. The most important was the Palatinate of Durham, where the Bishop of Durham ruled as Prince-Bishop, appointing his own JUSTICES OF THE PEACE and enforcing 'St Cuthbert's Peace' instead of the 'King's Peace'. Other palatinates were Chester and Lancaster. Their most important privileges, such as the right of SANCTUARY, were reduced after 1534, and the rest were gradually diminished and finally disappeared during the 19th century.

Libraries in the Middle Ages were mostly in MONASTERIES since the MONKS wrote or copied manuscripts in the SCRIPTORIUM. The BOOKS were at first kept in CUPBOARDS along the CLOISTER walls, but by the 15th century monasteries, as well as CATHEDRALS and COLLEGES, kept them in a separate room, where they were often chained for safety to LECTERNS. The first public library in the City of London was founded by Dick Whittington (c. 1358–1423) and his friends.

The RENAISSANCE and the invention of PRINTING much increased the number of books and encouraged the establishment of libraries. The royal library of Edward IV was mentioned in 1480, and noblemen began to form libraries; the Duke of Bedford had 152 books at Woburn Abbey and 247 at Bedford House in the Strand in 1700. The first lending library was opened in Edinburgh in 1726, and the term 'circulating library' seems to have been invented in 1742. The first national commercial library was Mudie's Lending Library founded in 1842, followed by W. H. Smith's (1852) and Boot's (1900); all of these are now defunct. The British Museum library was founded in 1753.

Between 1850 and 1892 acts of Parliament authorized towns to provide public libraries out of the rates, and in 1919 county councils were enabled to provide libraries. There are now some 560 public library authorities in England and Wales with over 13 000 000 registered readers.

Life-boats were first stationed on the English coast in the later 18th century. The earliest, stationed at Bamburgh (Northumberland) in 1786, was a converted coble, a local form of fishingboat. The world's first boat designed from the outset as a life-boat was the *Original*, built on Tyneside by Henry Greathead in 1790; it was 30 ft in length and propelled by several pairs of oars. The first self-righting boat was built in 1851, and the first motor-driven life-boat came into use in 1904.

The first life-boats established in

Lifeboats: 1 The 'Original'; 2 Motor vesse equipped with sails

various parts of the country during the late 18th and early 19th century were organized on a local basis and mostly provided by LLOYD'S. The Royal National Life-Boat Institution was formed in 1824 to maintain and operate life-boats around the coasts of the United Kingdom. Apart from the short period from 1854 to 1859, when it received a small annual government grant, it has always relied entirely on voluntary subscriptions, and its life-boat crews are volunteers. Since its foundation it has rescued over 80 000 people. [P. Howarth, *The Lifeboat Story* (1957)]

Lighthouses in Britain were at first BEACONS (towers with braziers), e.g. at

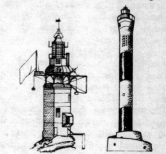

Lighthouses: (*left*) Eddystone 1698; (*right*) Modern design

173

Tynemouth (1608), Eddystone (1698), St Bees (1718) and the Lizard (1751). Coal or wood fires and CANDLES were used for illumination until the early 19th century when Argand's oil LAMP was adopted, to be followed by GAS in 1837. Electricity was first used in 1858. Remote-control lighthouses were introduced in 1934. The chief British authority for lighthouses is TRINITY HOUSE.

Lighting began with oil LAMPS and TORCHES from which CANDLES developed. TINDER-BOXES were long used for kindling a flame before being superseded by MATCHES. The 19th century saw the invention of GAS and later ELECTRICITY for lighting. The LINK and the LACE-LAMP were special forms of lighting; and in the history of transport, the BEACON, LIGHTHOUSE and LIGHTSHIP have been important. [F. W. Robins, *The Story of the Lamp* (1939)]

Lightships were first stationed off the British coasts in the 18th century, the earliest being placed at the Nore in 1732 with a lantern hung at the yard-arm. Later Robert Stevenson (1772–1850) introduced a lantern which surrounded the mast and could be lowered during the day, an arrangement generally adopted until recent times when it was replaced by a fixed lantern mounted at the top of a short, hollow steel mast. TRINITY HOUSE is now engaged in replacing its lightships by light towers.

Lindisfarne a small island off the coast of Northumberland, also called Holy Island from the 11th century. It has been known as the 'Cradle of Christianity' for England because in 635 St Aidan and a party of MONKS of the CELTIC CHURCH came from IONA and established a MONASTERY there from which Northumbria and other English kingdoms were evangelized. St Aidan was eventually followed by St Cuthbert, who carried on the work until 687. In 793 Lindisfarne was sacked by the VIKINGS; in face of another raid in 875 the monks fled with the body of St Cuthbert, and after over a century of wandering the community settled at Durham, where the saint's SHRINE in the CATHEDRAL became an object of PILGRIMAGES. At Lindisfarne there was from 1082 until the DISSOLUTION OF THE MONASTERIES continuous monastic life on the island.

Linen cloth made from the fibres of the stem of flax, was the first textile spun by man. It has been found in early Egyptian tombs and was much used in ancient Greece and Rome. The growing of flax and the making of linen was probably introduced into ROMAN BRITAIN. Though the HUGUENOTS, who were expert at working flax, brought their skill to England, it never became an important industry there, its development being discouraged in favour of WOOL (see also BURIALS). On the other hand, from the early 17th century its manufacture was encouraged in Ireland, where the woollen industry was checked in order to avoid competition with England. During the 18th and 19th centuries, northern Ireland became the largest producer of linen in the world, but it is now declining through the competition of cheaper substitutes such as COTTON and RAYON.

Linenfold a decorative pattern carved on wood, its straight, low relief lines looking like folded LINEN. The design is Flemish in origin and was popular in England in the 15th and 16th centuries, especially as decoration on oak CHESTS. The term itself dates from the 19th century.

Link a TORCH of pitch and tow used in the 17th and 18th centuries to light people along the streets at night and carried by a hired link-man or link-boy who, when he had fulfilled his task, extinguished his link by pushing it up

Link extinguisher

into a cone-shaped extinguisher still to be seen incorporated in the iron front railings of some town-houses built in the 18th century. See also LIGHTING.

Litany a form of prayer consisting of a series of petitions said or sung by the CLERGY and to which the people make fixed responses. Litanies were commonly used during the Middle Ages in PROCESSIONS, during the ROGATION DAYS and on other occasions, especially in time of war, plague or other distress. Thomas Cranmer wrote an English litany for use in processions ordered by Henry VIII when England was at war against France and Scotland in 1544. This was later included in the Book of COMMON PRAYER.

Little Lord Fauntleroy costume was made fashionable for boys by the hero of Mrs Hodgson Burnett's novel of that name (1886). It consisted of a black velvet tunic, knee breeches, a large white lace collar falling over the shoulders and a wide sash round the waist tied in a bow with hanging ends on the hip. It was usually worn with long, curling hair,

the book having described the costume as 'a black velvet suit with a lace collar and with lovelocks waving about . . . the face'. It was slightly reminiscent of the Cavaliers of the 17th century; and since the authoress was an American, she may have been influenced by Oscar Wilde who, while visiting the USA in 1882, asserted the Cavalier costume was the most artistic male style ever known and urged its revival. See also KATE GREENAWAY DRESS and CHILDREN'S COSTUME.

Livery Companies or City Companies are the survivors in the City of London of the medieval GUILDS and take their name from the distinctive costumes or livery which their members wore. The GOLDSMITHS were among the earliest and most important of the 'Great Twelve' companies whose liverymen, as FREEMEN of the City, still elect the Lord Mayor and other officials, a right which they gained in the later Middle Ages. Originally their members genuinely belonged to a particular trade and controlled its affairs, but now they have little to do with any trade except that some of their charitable funds may still be used for the benefit of present-day followers of that trade, and they are the governors of certain schools. [G. Unwin, *The Guilds and Companies of London* (1908).] See also JOINT-STOCK COMPANIES, GROCER.

Lloyd's a London association of underwriters (who accept the risk of INSURANCE). It began in a COFFEE-HOUSE opened by Edward Lloyd in 1688, which was frequented by merchants and ship-owners; and to-day it is still mainly, though not entirely, concerned with marine or shipping insurance. *Lloyd's List* of shipping news first appeared in 1734.

Lollards were the followers of John Wycliffe (c. 1329–84), who in his later years attacked the doctrine of the MASS, questioned papal supremacy, denounced monasticism and upheld the authority of the BIBLE. They drew their numbers from the townsmen, merchants, gentry and even lower clergy, and their name was a nickname meaning 'babblers'. Their earliest groups were in the 1380s in the Midlands and Home Counties, and they circulated English versions of the Bible in manuscript until the middle years of Henry VIII's reign (1509–47).

In the last decade of the 14th century there was a group of Lollard partisans in the House of Commons, but in 1401 the Statute *De Haeretico Comburendo* led to their condemnation for HERESY. After the disastrous revolt led by Sir John Oldcastle in 1414, they lost their chance of becoming a successful political movement and now found most of their members among the poorer classes.

While they were not a united movement and do not seem to have had clear-cut ideas, they contributed towards the anticlericalism of the REFORMATION. Signs of Lollardy continued into Mary's reign (1553–8) and beyond, but by 1530 they were becoming merged into the new PROTESTANTS. [G. M. Trevelyan, *England in the Age of Wycliffe* (1899); H. Maynard Smith, *Pre-Reformation England* (1938).] See also ECCLESIASTICAL COURTS.

London Bridge probably preceded by a Roman bridge and by several wooden structures in Saxon and Norman times, was reconstructed in stone over a period of thirty years from 1176. It had 19 arches and a drawbridge, a two-storied chapel in the middle, a double row of houses and 138 shops built as superstructures on the stone piers. The rush of water between the wooden 'starlings' (platforms built to protect the piers of the arches) made it dangerous to 'shoot the bridge' in a boat. Until the completion of Westminster Bridge in 1750, it was the only bridge across the Thames at London.

In 1754 an Act of Parliament ordered the removal of the houses from the bridge. The old bridge was removed in 1832 after the completion of a new granite bridge of five arches, sixty yards higher up the river, and this is now being replaced by a three-span CONCRETE bridge with a six-lane carriageway and two footways. [J. E. N. Hearsey, *Bridge, Church and Palace* (1961).] See also BRIDGES.

Long Gallery an important room in an Elizabethan great HOUSE (e.g. Haddon Hall, Derbyshire, and Penshurst Place, Kent). On an upper floor, it often ran the whole length of the house and overlooked the GARDENS. It was handsome and comfortable, having the walls panelled or hung with TAPESTRIES and the ceiling decorated with plaster moulding; it was warmed by a fire in a sculptured stone FIREPLACE and might have a CARPET on the floor. Its WINDOWS were tall and filled with small panes of glass. Its furniture included carved oak TABLES, CHAIRS and CHESTS, cabinets displaying silver cups and other treasures, and there were pictures on the walls. Here the ladies sat to read and work and walked for exercise when the weather was bad; here also there was music and DANCING and the playing of a special form of BOWLS.

Lord of Misrule called in Scotland the Abbot of Unreason, was elected in the king's court and the houses of noblemen to superintend the revels from All Hallows' Eve (October 31) to TWELFTH NIGHT (January 5). Sometimes his appointment was made by the company eating a cake; the person finding a ring in his slice assumed the role. The custom of having a Lord of Misrule was prohibited in England in 1555.

Lottery was first promoted in England by Elizabeth I in 1566 for repairing the country's harbours, but it was not successful. Few were held subsequently, and the PURITANS suppressed them completely during the COMMONWEALTH. With the revival of GAMBLING under Charles II, they were held for various purposes; and in 1694 Parliament authorized state lotteries to raise money for the government. These continued until 1826 when opposition by EVANGELICALS, RADICALS and other reformers led to their discontinuance.

Love spoons wooden spoons made and given as a rustic custom for so long in Wales that the term 'spooning' has passed into the English language. The custom also exists in different parts of Europe, notably in Switzerland and Scandinavia, but has never been as widespread as in Wales. The acceptance of a spoon by a girl meant that courting could begin, and it has been said that a coquette might have more than one spoon hanging in her cottage home. The spoons were carved often only with a pocket-knife, the heart motif being most commonly used; but about 1900 the custom of making individual love spoons waned, and commercial examples were manufactured in which the purchaser could insert his sweetheart's name behind a glazed 'window'.

Low Churchmen the group in the CHURCH OF ENGLAND in the 18th century which gave a 'low' place to government by BISHOPS and the administration of the SACRAMENTS. Like the later EVANGELICALS, they accepted the ideas of CALVINISM and sympathized with much in the outlook of the NONCONFORMISTS. See also HIGH CHURCHMEN.

Luddites combinations of workmen formed in 1811 during a period of economic distress with the object of destroying the new SPINNING and WEAVING textile machinery which they regarded as the cause of their troubles. The first outbreak at Nottingham was said to have been led by a young APPRENTICE, Ned Ludd. Later there were serious Luddite riots in various parts of the country, especially in the West Riding of Yorkshire, where many people were killed, mills were destroyed, and numbers of rioters were tried and executed. A Luddite rising is described by Charlotte Brontë in *Shirley*. [E. P. Thompson, *The Making of the English Working Class* (revised ed., 1968)]

Lute a stringed musical instrument, much used from the 14th to 17th centuries, like a GUITAR. It had a pear-shaped body and was plucked with a plectrum (a small spike of ivory, quill or metal, which was sometimes attached to a ring fitting on the finger). See also MUSIC.

Lye an alkaline solution generally used in LAUNDERING until the late 16th century. The source of the alkali was wood or vegetable ashes which the housewife stored from the fireplace in a large barrel. When this was full, she stood it in a second barrel, known as a 'lye-letch', and then poured water over the ashes. The water washed the potash salts from the ashes and drained them through small cracks or holes in the bottom of the first barrel into the outer barrel. The solution was collected and repeatedly poured through the ashes until a strong lye was obtained. An even stronger lye was made by steeping wheat, barley or oat straw in already-prepared lye and burning it and making new lye from the ashes. The earliest home-made SOAP was produced by boiling up the lye with dripping and other fat from the KITCHEN. See also BIRCH-ROD.

M

Macadam a ROAD surface, composed of a tight mixture of broken stones, sand and water, invented by a Scottish engin-

SMALL BROKEN STONES
SAND OR GRAVEL

Macadam surface

eer, John Loudon McAdam (1756–1836), who was Surveyor-General to the London TURNPIKES.

Macaronis the name given to a set of wealthy young men in the 1770s who had travelled in Italy during the GRAND TOUR and on their return introduced contemporary Italian fashions in London. They were so-called because they founded the Macaroni Club in 1764 and introduced Italian macaroni as a dish at ALMACK'S. The dress they adopted made them conspicuous. They wore an immense knot of artificial hair, a very small cocked hat, jacket, waistcoat, small clothes very tight to the body, a large nosegay of flowers pinned on the left shoulder and carried a walking-stick ornamented with long tassels.

Mace was originally just a thick stick with a spiked head or club of Roman times fitted with a BRONZE head. A club made of knotty wood, thicker at one end, is shown on the BAYEUX TAPESTRY, and in this form was a WEAPON used by common soldiers for centuries. It was also adopted by medieval KNIGHTS, who used it as well as the SWORD and kept it in readiness attached to the SADDLE, and as

early as the 14th century its head was reinforced with pointed steel fittings designed to shatter the enemy's HELMET and ARMOUR. In the 14th century also it became the usual weapon of royal guards

Mace

and officers and so became a symbol of authority for JUDGES and others. It was also used in TOURNAMENTS, being then made entirely of ash and bulbous at one end and far less dangerous. It was superseded by the PISTOL in Elizabeth I's reign. See also BILLIARDS.

Machicolation an important feature of CASTLES in the later 14th century, being an opening between the corbels of a parapet or in a floor, through which the garrison could assail besiegers with

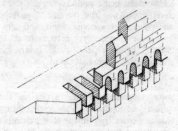

Machicolation

stones and other missiles and sometimes with boiling water or hot pitch, but never with molten LEAD which (then as now) was very expensive. Examples of machicolation are to be seen in the GATE-HOUSES at Bodiam (Sussex), Cooling (Kent) or Raglan (Monmouth).

Macintosh was invented by Charles Macintosh (1766–1843), a Scottish chemist. While experimenting with tar, he evolved a waterproof material consisting of two thicknesses of rubber cemented together by means of naphtha. The macintosh was worn as an overcoat from about 1836 onwards.

Madeira a fortified WINE, resembling SHERRY, produced in the island of Madeira, where the vine was introduced soon after the Portuguese occupation in 1419. From the end of the 17th century, the wine trade was largely monopolized by British merchants, who gained a privileged position through the marriage of Charles II and Catherine of Braganza. During the Revolutionary and Napoleonic Wars the trade was encouraged by the decline in imports of Continental wines by Britain and the temporary occupation of the island by British troops, and during the REGENCY period it was the most popular wine in England. Britain imported 7000 pipes of Madeira in 1774 and 22 000 in 1813; but in the later 19th century the island's vines were badly damaged by disease. They recovered, but much of the British market was lost. Britain now imports about 8000 pipes a year, a pipe being a cask containing 92 gallons. [Rupert Croft-Cooke, *Madeira* (1961)]

Madrigals short part-songs for several voices in elaborate contrapuntal style usually without accompaniment, came to England from Italy in the late 16th century. In 1588 and 1597 Nicholas Yonge, who sang in the CHOIR of ST PAUL'S CATHEDRAL, published a collection of Italian madrigals with the words translated into English and used to gather in his house 'a great number of gentlemen and merchants of good account (as well of this realm as of foreign nations) . . . for the exercise of music daily'. Madrigal-singing then became common, and English composers took it up, but it declined after about 1630.

Magic lantern an optical instrument for projecting magnified and illuminated images of small pictures on glass slides on to a white screen. Its invention has been attributed to Roger Bacon about 1260, but it was first generally made known by Athanasius Kircher, who died in 1680. Harriet Martineau saw one in 1806 when she was four, and it came into common use in the 19th century, being superseded in this century by film and film-strip projectors.

Magna Carta (1215) the 'great charter' of liberties granted by King John, was essentially an expression of the ideas of FEUDALISM and contained concessions made to the CHURCH OF ENGLAND and all FREEMEN. Many of its clauses dealt with the grievances of the BARONS, e.g. no SCUTAGE should be taken without their counsel, and the FOREST LAWS and WARDSHIP should not be abused. The most famous clause is the one reading, 'No freeman shall be taken or imprisoned, deprived of his lands, outlawed or exiled . . . save by the lawful judgment of his peers or the law of the land. To no one will we sell, deny or delay right or justice.' Copies of the charter are in the British Museum and Lincoln and Salisbury cathedrals. [Faith Thompson, *The First Century of Magna Carta* (1925)]

Mahogany was first brought over to England as ballast by ships from the West Indies and (following a WALNUT wood famine in France in 1720) was increasingly used in the making of FURNITURE. After about 1750 it was imported in large quantities, being appreciated for its colour and strength, and was used extensively by the great furniture makers of the time. From about 1820 there was a shortage of West Indian mahogany, but it was also imported from Africa, and its extensive use for furniture continued for the rest of the century.

Mail-coach originated in 1784 when John Palmer persuaded the Post Office to use specially designed STAGE-COACHES to carry mail faster than post-boys on horseback who had done it since the inauguration of the General Post Office in 1635. The first mail-coach travelled from Bristol to London in 15 hours compared with 50 taken by the post-boys. By 1797 there were 42 mail-coach routes in England. Mail-coaches usually charged passengers 10d a mile inside and 5d outside, which was about twice the charge on ordinary stage-coaches, but they were also twice as fast, soon averaging 100–120 miles a day at 10–12 miles an hour. They paid no tolls and TURNPIKE gates had to be opened to them. From 1825 to 1842 was the golden age of the mail-coach, before it was superseded by the RAILWAY. See also CARRIAGES.

Malmsey a strong, sweet, fine-flavoured white WINE, made formerly in Greece, but now also in Spain, Madeira and the Azores. The name comes from Malvasia, a place in the Peloponnese. George, Duke of Clarence, was supposed to have been drowned in a butt of malmsey in 1478. It was a favourite drink in Tudor England, Bardolph in Shakespeare's *Henry IV, Part II* being called a 'malmsey-nose knave'.

Malt is grain, usually BARLEY, steeped in water, allowed to ferment, dried slowly on a kiln and then used in brewing ALE or BEER and in the distillation of WHISKY. In 1697 Parliament imposed a tax on malt, which was replaced by a duty on beer, 1880.

Mangle to press water from clothes after washing in LAUNDERING, was used from the 17th century. The first mangles had a box weighted with stones, which was moved backwards and forwards upon rollers to press the clothes spread flat upon a table beneath. This type was used until the late 19th century when it was superseded by the hand-wringer which had rollers, at first of iron and then of wood, held close together with weighted levers or screws, so that the clothes could be pressed between them; and in the 1920s these rollers were made of rubber. Since the 1950s mangles have been increasingly replaced by electric spin-dryers.

Manor a term used in England after the NORMAN CONQUEST to describe both the manor house and the area of land attached to it. The lord of a manor might be a TENANT-IN-CHIEF or he might hold the manor from one. A manor might contain one or more VILLAGES. There were about 900 manors in England, most of them having a population of between 60 and 100 people each. The lord kept some land, the DEMESNE, for himself, which was worked by the VILLEINS in return for the land they held. Farming was carried out according to the OPEN-FIELD SYSTEM. If a lord had several manors, he would be represented in a particular manor or group of manors by a STEWARD; the work of a manorial estate was directed by a BAILIFF and the workers controlled by a REEVE. The lord had a manorial COURT which dealt with minor offences and breaches of the local farming arrangements. The manorial system began to decline in the early 14th century (see also COPYHOLD), and the last traces of it were finally abolished in 1926.

Mantle originated with the *palla*, a long, wide, sleeveless CLOAK worn by Roman men and women as an outer garment (see also TOGA). In the Middle Ages mantles were rectangular or circular in shape and were fastened either in front or at the shoulders or had a hole for the head. They were everyday garments until the 14th century, when they became generally ceremonial, being fastened for men on the right shoulder with three large BUTTONS to leave the right arm free and tied in front for women.

Manumission the granting of freedom to VILLEINS, who could get it by purchase, through a third person, since theoretically they had no private possessions, or by grant as a reward for services performed. Manumission was a solemn act and, since it might be challenged, was done publicly, often in the COUNTY COURT. The lord declared his villein free of all obligations and gave him arms, the sign of a FREEMAN.

Marbles a miniature form of BOWLS, is one of the oldest of all games and was formerly not just played by children. It was known in Egypt, played by the Roman Emperor Augustus (63 BC–AD 14) and popular in medieval England. It was first played with nuts, fruit-stones and round pebbles, but in the 18th century round balls made from chips of marble were introduced and so the game attained its present name. Alabaster was used for some of the better marbles, which became known as 'alleys', while the cheapest marbles were balls of common clay. Striped glass marbles were not made until the end of the 19th century.

Margarine a mixture of vegetable and animal oils, fats and pasteurized milk, to which are added various flavourings and (since the 1920s) vitamins A and D. In appearance and food value, it is similar to BUTTER. After it was first made in France in the 1860s by a scientist named Mège-Mouriez, it was soon manufactured in large quantities in Holland, but not until the 20th century were there many margarine factories in Britain.

Mark in England a money unit, but never an actual coin. It represented 128 silver PENNIES (10s 8d) in the DANELAW and later over the whole country equalled two gold NOBLES or two-thirds of a pound (13s 4d). The Scottish mark (merk), for which silver coins existed, equalled a twelfth of an English mark. See also COINAGE.

Markets have been held since very early times. Many TOWNS possess markets that date back at least to ANGLO-SAXON days, e.g. Chipping Camden (Glos.) and Chipping Norton (Oxon.) which derive their name from the Anglo-Saxon 'cepinge', a market. After the NORMAN CONQUEST all market rights were granted by the Crown, and the power to levy dues or tolls on goods sold at a market was given to a town or to a private person (e.g. a lord of the MANOR). These brought in such a profitable revenue that the right to hold a market was highly prized, and sometimes it was bought by a town from a private person. Later traders were charged for their stalls instead of having to pay tolls on the goods they sold.

In the Middle Ages markets were usually held weekly, but sometimes more often and sometimes also in separate market-places (e.g. in Leicester for the Wednesday and Saturday markets). A market was often held around a market-cross, which was sometimes called a butter-cross because the farmers' wives stood around it selling their butter, eggs and other produce. In the late 16th century towns began to erect market-halls, often a pillared space where the traders had their stalls and a room above to serve as the town hall or guildhall. The STOCKS and WHIPPING-POST were usually in the market-place, and it was common for offenders to be punished on a market-day when there were crowds present as spectators. See also FAIRS, DROVE ROADS.

Marriage became invariably celebrated by a religious ceremony with the coming of Christianity to Britain. In the Middle Ages the ceremony was performed at the PORCH of the CHURCH, and only after the RING had been placed on the bride's finger did the wedding-party approach the ALTAR for MASS and additional prayers. Medieval marriages were arranged by the parents, and CHILD MARRIAGES were not uncommon.

At the REFORMATION the marriage ceremony remained much the same, though it was in English. In 1563 Archbishop Parker set out the table of prohibited degrees of marriage; and in 1603 the Convocation of Canterbury made several canons regulating marriages, laying down the necessity of banns or license, parents' consent for minors, its performance in a parish church and between the hours of 8 AM and noon (which was extended in 1886 to 3 PM). During the COMMONWEALTH, Barebone's Parliament instituted in 1653 marriage before a JUSTICE OF THE PEACE instead of in church.

By the 18th century scandals had arisen because an irregular marriage performed by any clergyman was still legal, and clandestine marriages were undertaken by impecunious clergymen or those imprisoned in the FLEET PRISON. Lord Hardwicke's Marriage Act (1753) first introduced the principle that marriage was a contract in which both Church and State were concerned and provided that a marriage was invalidated if the requirements about banns, etc., were not observed. In 1837 civil marriage in a District Register Office was instituted, and NONCONFORMISTS and ROMAN CATHOLICS were allowed to marry in their own places of worship. Parliament legalized marriage with a deceased wife's sister in 1907 and with a deceased brother's widow in 1921.

In Scotland, in addition to regular marriages in church or register office, there also exists the long-established irregular (but valid) marriage in which the couple simply make a mutual declaration before witnesses. This led to the Gretna Green marriages by couples from England, but since 1856 it has been required that one of the couple must have lived in Scotland for at least three weeks.

The age of consent for a marriage was 12 years for a girl and 14 for a boy, but the Age of Marriage Act (1929) fixed in Britain the minimum age for marriage at 16 for both. In the 16th century the average age at which men and women married was 27 years, which rose to almost 30 in the late 17th century and did not come down to 25 for men and 23 for women until the mid-18th century. It remained about the same until after the Second World War, when it has fallen further. See also DIVORCE, WIVES.

Marriage customs often date from very early times. The bride's veil was originally worn to protect her from the gaze of anyone possessed of an evil eye. Some old customs were intended to ensure the fertility of the bride. Corn thrown over her was supposed to do this, and the rice and confetti now thrown at weddings is a survival of this. The attendance of a small child on the bride was intended to achieve the same object; and so was the carrying of flowers in bloom: orange blossom has been carried in England since the time of the CRUSADES.

Other customs were meant to indicate the bride's new position. The wedding-cake was originally a loaf made by her to show her proficiency in housekeeping. The slipper was a reminder that at marriage the father's authority over his daughter was transferred to her husband, which was signified by the bride's shoe being delivered to the bridegroom, who touched her on the head with it in token of his supremacy over her. Similarly the custom of carrying the bride over the doorstep of the new house marked the beginning of a new life for her under her husband.

The ceremonial bedding of the bride and bridegroom on the wedding night was usual until the 19th century. At the hour for retiring, the wedding-guests gathered within the nuptial chamber. The bride was undressed by her maids and put to bed, while the men undressed the groom and led him in. There was singing and dancing in the bedchamber and 'throwing the stocking' which was meant to show who would next be married. See also BRIDE-LACE, ROSEMARY.

Martello towers small circular forts with massive walls erected on the south and east coasts of England in 1805–6 to guard against the threat of French invasion. They were named after a stone tower built by the French on Cape Mortella, overlooking the Gulf of San

Martello tower

Fiorenzo in Corsica, which British forces captured with difficulty in 1794.

The Martello towers possessed considerable advantages—they were cheap (they cost only £3000 each to build), they needed only a small garrison, they were impossible to take except after heavy artillery fire, they supported each other and they protected the coast just as effectively as a body of troops. [J. H.

Rose and A. M. Broadley, *Dumouriez and the Defence of England against Napoleon* (1909)]

Marsala a moderately sweet dessert WINE of a SHERRY character, made at Marsala in Sicily. It was brought to England by two English firms in the 18th and early 19th centuries.

Marshalsea prison once a well-known house of detention in Southwark. It stood near to St George's Church and was originally a PRISON for royal servants convicted of offences, but from 1842 until it was abolished in 1849 it was a debtors' prison. It was described by Charles Dickens in *Little Dorrit*.

Martinmas (St Martin's Day— November 11), formerly the time in the country, in the days before the cultivation of TURNIPS made it possible to keep all the CATTLE alive throughout the winter, when most were slaughtered and salted down, leaving only the haulage animals and breeding couples to be maintained until the spring. 'Martinmas Beef' was beef dried in the CHIMNEY in the manner of bacon.

Since geese were common at this time of the year, it was usual for families to eat a GOOSE at Martinmas, and legend has it that when St Martin was elected Bishop of Tours he sought to avoid the post, for which he did not think himself worthy, by hiding, but was betrayed by the cackling of geese.

Masque an entertainment devised in the 14th century and reaching its final development in the last years of Elizabeth I's reign and throughout the reigns of James I and Charles I. Since it was elaborate and costly, it could only be performed in the court and a few noble households. It was part play and part opera, and its plot unfolded in spoken words, but also in songs with solos and choruses. It also included much formal dancing, and the whole performance was set against a beautiful background. The foremost artists, musicians and writers of the time contributed to the staging of masques, but the players were often members of the court, and James I's Danish Queen, Anne, often took part in them herself. See also OPERA.

Mass the name given to the Communion service in the Medieval English Church and the modern Roman Catholic Church. It comes from a phrase at the close of the service, '*Ite, missa est*'—'Go, the congregation is dismissed'. The different kinds of mass are: high mass, sung by three clergy with music, ritual, ceremonies and incense; low mass, said without music by a single priest; requiem mass, for the rest of the souls of the dead. The word 'mass' was retained by Cranmer in the 1549 Book of COMMON PRAYER, but not in the later editions. See also TRENTAL.

Matches were at first sulphur matches for use with TINDER-BOXES. Matches giving instantaneous light were developed in the 18th century. These consisted of a sealed glass tube containing a wax taper tipped with phosphorus which ignited instantaneously when the tube was broken. In 1827 John Walker of Stockton-on-Tees made the first 'friction lights', which were matches tipped with a mixture of antimony, sulphide, potassium chlorate and gum, and could be ignited by being drawn rapidly through a piece of folded sandpaper. These were soon sold widely as 'Lucifers'. The first successful 'strike-anywhere' matches were devised by Dr Charles Sauria of France in 1831 and were tipped with both phosphorus and potassium chlorate. White or yellow phosphorus gave off poisonous fumes which were very dangerous for the workers, and its use was forbidden in match manufacture in 1906. The first true 'safety' match, which used non-poisonous red amorphous phosphorus in a friction surface on the side of the box and potassium chlorate in the match head, was invented in 1855 in Sweden; and in 1898 two French chemists successfully used a non-poisonous compound of white phosphorus, which is now widely used in the manufacture of 'strike-anywhere' matches.

Matchlock was a HAND-GUN in which the match (fuse) was applied by the mechanism of the lock, actuated by the trigger, to the GUNPOWDER. It was invented in the first part of the 15th century and superseded by the WHEEL-LOCK and FLINTLOCK in the 17th century.

Maundy Thursday the day before GOOD FRIDAY and the anniversary of the Last Supper. The name 'Maundy' is said to be a corruption of '*Mandati*' (*Dies Mandati*, the Day of the Commandment), referring to the commandment given that night by Christ to His disciples to wash one another's feet, even as He had washed theirs. Formerly, bishops, monks and noblemen washed the feet of the poor on this day, and English sovereigns washed the feet of 'as many old men as the Sovereign is years of age'. This was done by Elizabeth I in 1572 when she washed the feet of 39 poor people at Greenwich Palace. James II was the last sovereign to do it in person, but in the early part of the 18th century it was performed by the Archbishop of York as the Sovereign's representative.

It was also customary for gifts of money, food and clothing to be given to the poor on this day. English sovereigns did this through their ALMONER, and the Royal Maundy ceremony is still observed, special silver money being coined for the purpose and usually distributed, sometimes by the Sovereign in person, usually in WESTMINSTER ABBEY.

A former popular name for Maundy Thursday was Shere Thursday, the reason for this being explained by the *Liber Festivalis* (1483)—'For in olde faders dayes men wold make hem that day shere hem and pollen her heedes and clippen her berdes, and so make hem honeste [seemly] ageyn ester day'.

May Day (May 1), the ancient pagan celebration of the start of the summer. From medieval times until the end of the 18th century it was a great public HOLIDAY, and its festivities were a regular part of English life. Girls and boys got up with the dawn and went 'a-maying', bringing back branches of trees and flowers to the towns and villages with which they decorated the houses and streets. There followed the crowning of a young girl with a wreath as Queen of the May, the performance of the MORRIS DANCE, in which Robin Hood and Maid Marian figured, and dancing round the MAYPOLE. Samuel Pepys on May Day 1662 saw dancing in the Strand and 'many milkmaids with their garlands on their pails dancing with a fiddler before them'.

Mayfair a district north of Piccadilly, London, which took its name from the annual May Fair held there in the month of May. It received its CHARTER in 1689 and continued to be held (after a temporary suspension in 1708) until George III's reign. A well-known 18th-century character at it was Tiddy-Doll, a GINGERBREAD seller, after whom a London restaurant has now been named.

From about 1800 until 1914 Mayfair was a fashionable residential quarter of London.

Mayor the highest official of an English BOROUGH. He was formerly known, after the NORMAN CONQUEST as the portreeve, but in 1191 the portreeve of London took the title of mayor, and his example was gradually followed in other boroughs. In London, Birmingham, Leeds, Manchester, Liverpool, York and other cities his title is lord mayor. See also PROVOST.

Maypole a pole, gaily painted with spiral stripes and decorated with flowers and ribbons, which was danced round on MAY DAY. In the country maypoles were usually made of birch wood and set up for one day only on the village green. In London and other large towns it was commonly made of harder wood and left standing all the year round. The Church of St Andrew Undershaft in Leadenhall Street (London) received its name because a maypole so high that it overtopped the steeple was erected in front of the church. Another maypole, erected near the Church of St Mary-le-Strand, was taken down by the PURITANS, but in 1661 it was replaced by another one, 134 ft high, which remained there until it was broken by a high wind in 1672.

Mazes cut in the turf in various parts of England, e.g. at Somerton (Oxon.), Hillbury (Surrey) and Appleby (Lincs.), and a maze of pebbles at St Agnes

Maze

(Scilly Isles), probably owe their origin to 'treading the maze', which was an old game in the countryside. Although these existing mazes cannot be shown to be very ancient, they may have been continually renewed for many generations.

The garden maze of dwarf shrubs or

with high hedges first became fashionable, as a development of the KNOT GARDEN, in the 17th century. Charles I had an early one at Wimbledon, and there were many others which were later destroyed as a result of changing fashions; the best-known existing one, at HAMPTON COURT, was laid out in 1689.

Mazer a medieval cup consisting of a shallow bowl of maple wood, usually finished with a SILVER rim, sometimes with a silver foot and cover. Mazers were not as valuable as silver cups, but finer and more permanent than common wooden and earthenware ones. They were prized possessions in middle-class families.

Mead one of the oldest alcoholic DRINKS, being made by the fermentation of HONEY mixed with water and HERBS and SPICES. It was brewed in Britain as early as the 4th century BC. The ANGLO-SAXONS also made it and at their feasts passed the mead round in a great bowl, the wassail bowl, from which each man drank in turn and wished the others '*waes hail*' ('good health'). Until the 16th century much mead was made in England, especially in the west, and in Wales; but when SUGAR replaced honey for sweetening, fewer bees were kept, and by the 17th century hardly any mead was made except in private houses, though it was still served in London PLEASURE GARDENS at the end of the 18th century.

Meals in the Middle Ages were usually two a day, a main, large, formal dinner between 9 and 11 a.m. and a much lighter supper with more emphasis on DRINK than substantial FOOD between 4 and 6 p.m. Breakfast evolved later from a 'morning draught' of ALE and a crust of BREAD. In the 16th century, the gentry dined at 11 a.m. (and the meal might last three hours) and supped about 6 p.m.;

merchants and farmers dined at noon and supped between 7 and 8 p.m.; while the labourer's main meal was BREAD, bacon (see PIG), MILK, WHEY and perhaps BEER. In the 17th century both meals tended to be taken later than formerly, while breakfast developed into a regular meal, consisting commonly of only ale and bread and BUTTER with sometimes, however, MEAT or 'boiled mutton bones' and, more rarely, FRUIT. By the 18th century, OYSTERS were also sometimes eaten at breakfast and TEA drunk at it; and there was a light snack at noon, followed by a heavy dinner between 2 and 3 p.m., while there was tea-drinking (with cake) in the afternoon and supper at 9 p.m. In the 19th century dinner became gradually still later. At the beginning of the century, fashionable people dined between 4 and 5 p.m. and by the mid-century between 6 and 7. This later hour for dinner brought about the introduction of a light luncheon between 1 and 2 p.m. and tea-drinking between 3 and 5 p.m. instead of the old-fashioned supper. See also WORKS CANTEENS.

Meat was not as popular as POULTRY in ROMAN BRITAIN. Roast beef or beef tea was taken as a MEDICINE, but not as food, and nor was mutton. Pork and venison, however, were eaten by the wealthy and bacon by poorer people. While in the Middle Ages the peasants could only have rabbit or hare in the pot and sometimes salt beef or bacon, meat of all kinds was plentiful for richer people, and Tudor England was renowned among foreign visitors for meat-eating. The traveller and historian, Fynes Moryson (1566–1630), said, 'England abounds in cattle of all kinds and particularly hath very great oxen, the flesh whereof is so tender, as no meat is more desired'. In the 17th century, Thomas Tusser, a yeoman, had 'roast beef on Sundays and Thursdays at night', while Oliver Cromwell's favourite dish was roast veal with oranges; and in the 18th century Dr Johnson (according to Mrs Thrale) liked best 'a leg of pork, boiled till it dropped from the bone, a veal pie with plums and sugar or the outside cut of a salt buttock of beef', but a German visitor, Pastor Moritz, said that the ordinary Englishman's midday meal consisted of 'a piece of half-boiled or half-roasted meat and a few cabbage leaves boiled in plain water on which they pour a sauce made of flour and butter'.

The new ROTATION OF CROPS made it possible to have fresh meat all the year, and it has been estimated that by the end of the 18th century some 100 000 head of cattle were sent to the London markets alone. The 19th century working-classes could only afford a small joint once a week, but there were cheap cuts of coarse meat and offal such as cowheels and tripe. The cost of transport made meat dear, but by 1900 REFRIGERATION had made it cheap enough for all but the poorest to eat. Since the Second World War, the consumption of meat has tended to fall, though the sale of cooked and canned meats and meat products has increased. See also GOOSE, PIG, FISH, SPICES, POULTRY.

Mechanics' Institutes conducted evening classes in science and the useful arts, intended for working-men. The London Mechanics' Institute (now Birkbeck College) was founded in 1823 by George Birkbeck, who had already helped to found a similar institute in Glasgow. By 1850 there were 622 mechanics' institutes in England and Wales with 600 000 members; but they were increasingly attended by middle-class clerks and declined during the third quarter of the 19th century, either coming to an end or becoming clubs, libraries or readingrooms giving occasional popular lectures, instead of definite courses of instruction.

Medicine in the Middle Ages was debased by ignorance and superstition (see ASTROLOGY). Many odd beliefs about the prevention and cure of illness were prevalent (see CORAL, DOGS, HOST). However, MONASTERIES had a FARMERY under the charge of an INFIRMARER and also a HERB-GARDEN, while MONKS and NUNS opened HOSPITALS and cared for the sick. HERBS and SPICES were believed to have healing powers, and these were dispensed by APOTHECARIES. PLAGUE occurred frequently from the BLACK DEATH of the 14th century. The BEDLAM in London was a pioneer institution for the care of the insane; and Lazar-houses cared for those who had LEPROSY.

With the revival of learning brought about by the RENAISSANCE, there was renewed interest in medicine. The position of PHYSICIANS was improved, and the foundation of the ROYAL SOCIETY in the 17th century brought about advances in science. In the 18th century SCURVY was conquered and also small-pox by VACCINATION, but far greater advances came in the 19th century. These included better training of NURSES, improvements in SANITATION which removed the menace of CHOLERA and, above all, the development of ANAESTHETICS and ANTISEPTICS which made possible modern SURGERY and DENTISTRY. The advances of the 20th century range from the development of the ASPIRIN to the establishment of the NATIONAL HEALTH SERVICE. [F. N. L. Poynter and K. D. Keele, *A Short History of Medicine* (1961)]

Merchant Adventurers were formed, as the result of the growth of WEAVING in England, to export cloth to the Continent. Formed in 1407 in London, they also had European headquarters at different times in various towns in the Netherlands and Germany. They became serious rivals of the older MERCHANTS OF THE STAPLE and also of the HANSE. They were dissolved in 1808 as a result of Napoleon's conquests.

Merchants of the Staple a body of English merchants who from the 13th century exported and sold WOOL, so-called because they sent their exports through a single town known as the Staple. At first they did this voluntarily since they could organize their ships in convoys for protection against Channel pirates, while it was easier for wool-buyers to come to one place. Edward I and successive kings made the Staple compulsory to facilitate the collection of customs duties on wool. The location of the Staple changed from time to time, being at Antwerp, Bruges or in England, but usually at Calais where it was first fixed in 1363 and finally established in 1423 until the town was taken by the French in 1558. The Merchants of the Staple declined with the growth of the English cloth trade and the rise of the MERCHANT ADVENTURERS. See also SMUGGLING.

Merchet a payment made by a VILLEIN to the lord of the MANOR whenever his daughter was married outside the manor, his son was sent to school or his beast was sold. The villein, his family and his chattels were regarded as belonging to the lord, who received, therefore, this payment to compensate him for the loss of the daughter's children, the son's labour and the beast's value for HERIOT and other payments under FEUDALISM.

Methodists so-called because of the strictness of their discipline, were the followers of John Wesley, an English clergyman who began his preaching tours in 1738. He was an ARMINIAN in theology, but he preached a message of personal conversion to Christ. Soon FIELD PREACHING became a feature of the Methodist campaign, and so also did its HYMNS. The Methodists were carefully organized,

being formed into local societies (under lay preachers) which were divided into CLASS MEETINGS. Wesley intended his followers to remain within the CHURCH OF ENGLAND, but in 1784 he began to ordain his own ministers, and soon after his death in 1791 they made themselves a separate NONCONFORMIST body. They then had over 75 000 members, mostly among the lower classes and particularly in the new industrial districts. [W. B. Brash, *Methodism* (1928)]

Mews originally a small building or cage in which were kept falcons or hawks on the moult (from Old French, *muer*, to moult), which after the RESTORATION were often converted into stables. In London, royal stables were built on the north side of Charing Cross (now the site of the National Gallery) where the king's falcons had been kept since the 14th century (see also FALCONRY). The name later came to be given to a series of private stables built round a yard or on both sides of a lane, especially in towns where there was no space for stables adjoining houses; many of these have now been converted into small houses.

Milestones existed in ROMAN BRITAIN, but the first ones after that were the milemarks set up on the Dover Road in 1663. Other stones were erected on the Great North Road in 1708, but the first true modern milestone is the one still to be seen at Trumpington, just outside Cambridge, which dates from 1727. All milestones were set up by private individuals until official milestones were authorized on the London to Chester road in 1744, but they did not become compulsory until 1773 when an Act required all TURNPIKE trusts to have GUIDE-POSTS and milestones on their roads.

Milk in the Middle Ages was considered only a suitable drink for infants and the old. It was relatively expensive, costing in 1554 3d a gallon or '3 ale pints for $\frac{1}{2}$d' in the summer (compared with CLARET at 8d a gallon and ALE at 4d), and the cream was made into BUTTER and the skimmed milk into CHEESE. By the 17th century, when country milk was often sour and milk from town cows tainted, WHEY was a popular drink in towns. As towns grew, it became more difficult to get fresh, safe milk in towns, and in London in the 18th century the best milk came from cows kept in St James's Park.

The RAILWAYS changed the situation. MILK was first sent by rail to Manchester in 1844 and to London soon afterwards. By 1866 2 000 000 gallons a year were brought into London. It soon became part of middle-class diet, but was not drunk much by the working-classes until this century. The supply of milk was increased by the growing use of root-crops to feed cattle since when most of the cattle were slaughtered in the autumn, the winter milk-yield was less than a quarter of that in the summer.

In 1856 an American, Gail Borden, invented tinned, condensed milk, and milk powder was invented in about 1902, at about the same time that milk bottles began to be used. Milk-bars were opened in the 1930s, the idea coming from Australia. Since the Second World War the National Dairy Council has tried to persuade people to drink a pint of milk a day, but is still far from achieving this target.

Mines as used in land warfare in Roman and medieval times, were tunnels dug through the ground below a besieged fortress by the attacking troops. The wooden props supporting the roof of the tunnel were set alight and the building was undermined (see also FASCINE). Later GUNPOWDER was packed at the end of the tunnel and blown up. This type of mine was last used on a large scale against trenches in the First World War. Smaller land mines, like a kind of BOMB buried in the ground, were used in the Second World War against vehicles and troops. The name was also given to a large bomb dropped by parachute.

Naval mines were first used at the siege of La Rochelle, when in 1573 the French sent small barrels of gunpowder fitted with a burning fuse to drift with the tide against the English ships, but such early mines were not very successful. In the 19th century floating metal containers filled with explosive were used in the Crimean War and the American Civil War, but the first effective use of such mines was in the Russo–Japanese War (1904–5). Naval mines were used extensively in the First World War and again in the Second World War when new types of magnetic, acoustic, limpet and other sorts of mines were developed.

Minster a shortened form of the word 'MONASTERY'; the name came to be applied to churches to which a monastery was formerly attached (e.g. Westminster Abbey or Sherborne Minster) or a CATHEDRAL or parish CHURCH formerly served by secular CANONS (e.g. York Minster or Beverley Minster).

Minstrels were medieval musicians who sang, often to the HARP, verses composed by themselves or others. The most important were those kept in the service of kings and princes for the entertainment of guests. At the Battle of Hastings (1066), William I's minstrel, Taillefer, was killed as he sang in front of the advancing Norman army; and Rahere (d. 1144), who founded St Bartholomew's Hospital, was at one time a minstrel to Henry I.

There were also those who went about in ORCHESTRAS or companies (see also TIMBREL), and these owed their origin to the gleemen of ANGLO-SAXON times. They went round performing in private houses, especially at MARRIAGES and other celebrations. They were organized in London into a GUILD at least as early as 1350, but in Elizabeth I's reign many were treated as rogues and vagabonds. See also WAITS, GALLERY, NIGGER MINSTRELS.

Miracle Plays, Mystery Plays medieval verse plays acted from the late 14th to the 16th century by town GUILDS in a market place, churchyard or other open space. They consisted of a series of dramatized stories from the Bible or Lives of the Saints. Each guild took a suitable scene (e.g. the Shipwrights commonly acted the story of Noah and the Ark), performing in turn on a wheeled stage mounted on a cart until the whole cycle of episodes had been produced. Four great cycles of miracle plays are still extant, being called after the towns where they were probably performed—the York, Coventry, Chester and Wakefield (or Towneley) cycles. These plays are marked by a strong religious sense and also a lively comic spirit (e.g. Noah's wife belaboured her husband and could only be got into the Ark by force).

Mirrors in early times were made of polished metal, and such hand-mirrors have been found in England in BARROWS of IRON AGE times. In the Middle Ages also polished metal discs were used until, through the CRUSADES, glass mirrors came to Europe by way of Constantinople. Such mirrors were first made in Venice about 1300, but not in England until 1637 by Venetian craftsmen at Lambeth. The manufacture of PLATE-GLASS here also made it possible to make large, framed mirrors to stand on ladies' DRESSING-TABLES or hang on the wall of a room.

Misericord a projection on the underside of a hinged seat of a choir STALL to afford support for standing worshippers during long services. Examples exist in British CHURCHES, ABBEYS and CATHEDRALS. The majority extant belong to the 14th, 15th and 16th centuries, ending almost entirely with the DISSOLUTION OF THE MONASTERIES, though there was some revival in the 19th century. They are almost invariably of oak and are often deeply carved with grotesque designs, figures or scenes. [F. Bond, *Wood Carving in English Churches* (1910); M. D. Anderson, *Misericords* (1954)]

Missionary Societies began with the SOCIETY FOR THE PROPAGATION OF THE GOSPEL and the SOCIETY FOR THE PROMOTION OF CHRISTIAN KNOWLEDGE in the late 17th century, but the largest in the CHURCH OF ENGLAND is the CHURCH MISSIONARY SOCIETY founded by the EVANGELICALS and especially the CLAPHAM SECT, the opponents of the SLAVE TRADE. Other societies were established by the BAPTISTS (1792), the CONGREGATIONALISTS (the London Missionary Society, 1795) and the METHODISTS (1813). The British and Foreign Bible Society (1804) provides the societies with the BIBLE translated into native languages. [Stephen Neil, *A History of Christian Missions* (1964)]

Mitre a shield-shaped head-dress worn by BISHOPS since 11th century and also by some ABBOTS. It was rarely, if ever, used

Mitre

by English bishops from the REFORMATION to the 19th century, except at coronations down to that of George III. See also VESTMENTS.

Mitred abbots the ABBOTS of certain great ABBEYS, who were accorded the right to use the MITRE, CROSIER and RING. In England these abbots sat in the House of Lords, but many ceased to do so. In 1305 as many as 75 sat, but on the eve of the DISSOLUTION OF THE MONASTERIES were only 27 and two PRIORS of the AUGUSTINIAN CANONS. Their disappearance brought about, for the first time, a majority of lay peers in the House of Lords.

Moat adopted for CASTLES in the 13th century as a defence against attack by MINES. This meant the abandonment of the mound or high place as a site. Some of the earliest castles were defended by water through damming the end of a valley with earth (e.g. Saltwood, Kent), while others were built on mounds in the middle of marshes (e.g. Knepp, Sussex, and Skipsea, Yorks.); but most were built on low ground enclosed by a broad shallow ditch fed by springs or streams. When a dam was needed to retain the water in a large artificial lake (e.g. Kenilworth, Warwicks. and Caerphilly, Glamorgan.), the dam itself was fortified by walls and towers to prevent it being cut by a besieger and the water drained away. [Hugh Braun, *The English Castle* (2nd ed., 1943)]

Mob-cap a white round indoor cap of fine LINEN or MUSLIN fitting loosely over the whole head, which was worn by women in the 18th and early 19th centuries.

Modesty-piece a narrow strip of LACE or lace-edged LINEN worn by women in the 18th century. It was pinned along the top of the STAYS in front to cover the 'pit of the bosom' in a dress with a low neckline. See also TUCKER.

Mohocks a gang of wealthy young noblemen who terrorized the streets of 18th-century London, so-called from the Indian Mohawks. Among their 'new inventions' were rolling people down Snow Hill in a barrel, overturning coaches on rubbish heaps, pricking gentlemen with swords to make them dance and holding up girls by the legs and beating them with riding-whips. [R. J. Mitchell and M. D. R. Leys, *A History of London Life* (1958)]

Monastery like the word MINSTER, originally applied to any large CHURCH and then later to the house of a religious community. It is only recently that it has come to mean an establishment of MONKS and a CONVENT an establishment of NUNS only.

The organization of the monasteries of the CELTIC CHURCH is uncertain. Their buildings were probably humble and their RULE elementary and informal. Glastonbury was the only one in England to pass intact from British to Saxon hands in the 7th century; it then adopted the BENEDICTINE rule.

The chief buildings of a medieval monastery were arranged around a CLOISTER. The ABBEY church was usually on the north side and the CHAPTER HOUSE on the east side, while the DORTER was often built over the east side. The REFECTORY (with kitchen, cellars and store-room) was likely to be on the south side, and the PARLOUR, SCRIPTORIUM and CELLARIUM might be on the west side. A monastery also probably had a FARMERY, CALEFACTORY, guest-house and ALMONRY, as well as a granary, smithy, brew-house and barns. Around the buildings were the monastery's lands with cornfields, cattle-pastures, woods, quarries, a fishpond and

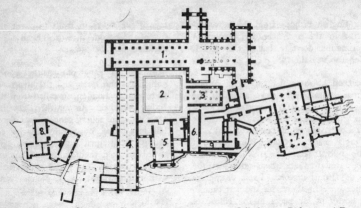

Monastery plan: 1 Church; 2 Cloister; 3 Chapter house; 4 Cellarium; 5 Refectory; 6 Dorter; 7 Farmery; 8 Almonry; 9 Reredorter

perhaps a vineyard. Monasteries were large landowners and aimed at being self-supporting. See also DISSOLUTION OF THE MONASTERIES. [D. H. S. Cranage, *The Home of the Monk* (1926); A. Hamilton Thompson, *English Monasteries* (1913); G. H. Cook, *English Monasteries in the Middle Ages* (1961).] See also CORRODIANS.

Monks existed in the CELTIC CHURCH (see IONA and LINDISFARNE), but the MONASTERIES were simply a cluster of little huts or cells with a CHURCH and perhaps a LIBRARY. After the Synod of Whitby (see CHURCH OF ENGLAND), the Celtic monks gradually adopted the RULE of the BENEDICTINE order. [David Knowles, *Christian Monasticism* (1969)]

Mons Meg a CANNON at Edinburgh Castle probably made in Flanders before 1460. It is 13 ft 2 in. long with a calibre of 19½ in. and fired a stone ball weighing 549 lb. One ball from the gun is said to have been retrieved from a distance of two miles. Guns as large as this were fired lying on the ground and were accompanied on a campaign by a CRANE to lift it on and off its travelling carriage. [J. D.

Mackie, *A History of Scotland* (1964).] See also ARTILLERY.

Moots meeting-places where tribal business was conducted and festivals held in early times, e.g. St Martha's Hill, near Guildford (Surrey), which was probably such a place as far back as the BRONZE AGE. The ANGLO-SAXONS held folk-moots, which later became HUNDRED-moots, meeting of a group of PARISHES every four weeks, from which there could be an appeal to the less frequent SHIRE-moots. The hundred-moots were held at some convenient place—a tree, e.g. Copthorne (Surrey), a post, e.g. Whitstable (Kent), a natural hill, e.g. Swanborough (Sussex), an ancient HILL-FORT, e.g. Badbury Rings and Eggardon (Dorset). The early moots of the citizens of London were held at PAUL'S CROSS to which they were summoned by their 'Common Bell' in the Jesus Bell Tower, a detached CAMPANILE nearby.

Mop fairs were held in the autumn to enable farmers to engage SERVANTS, who were usually hired for a year, from Michaelmas to Michaelmas. The men and women, who sought employment, lined up wearing tokens of their skills—cowmen a tuft of cowhair, carters a piece of whipcord, shepherds a tuft of sheepswool and thatchers a fragment of woven straw, while servant-girls carried a mop or wore a white apron. In some places the regular Mop Fair was followed a week or two later by the Runaway Mop to give a second chance for those who were not already hired or for employers who were dissatisfied. As soon as a man or woman got a job, the token was removed and replaced by a ribbon which was bought with the hiring- or fasten-penny paid by the employer to seal the contract; and the rest of the day was given up to enjoying the amusements at the FAIR. Such a fair is described by Thomas Hardy in *Far from the Madding Crowd*.

Morris dance a form of country dance which may have evolved from the sword dance, which was performed by men and had a religious origin based on nature worship and sacrifice, perhaps involving an actual killing originally. In some places the word 'Morris' is still applied to a sword dance, but usually Morris dancers carried sticks or handkerchiefs instead of swords. The origin of the word may be 'Moorish' since one of the characters originally had his face blacked. Sometimes the dancers represented characters from the Robin Hood legend and performed on MAY DAY.

Mortar a short and very thick GUN with a large bore for throwing BOMBS at a high angle, was first made in England in the 16th century and contributed towards the decline of the CASTLE. See also ARTILLERY.

Mortuary the payment due to the Church on the death of a VILLEIN, usually consisting of his second-best beast, but the Church was forbidden by CANON LAW to claim it unless the dead man had possessed at least three beasts.

Mosaics Greek in origin, were developed by the Romans, who set small cubes of coloured stone in cement to form geometrical or more complex realistic designs. In ROMAN BRITAIN, they were used by Romans and wealthier Britons to cover the floors of their VILLAS. As England is especially rich in varieties of stone, these had a wide range of colours—black and white and countless shades of grey, blue, red, yellow and brown. The earliest mosaic floor so far discovered is at FISHBOURNE PALACE and is in a black and white geometric pattern very similar to contemporary styles in Italy. Such floors came from the pattern-book of the firm which laid the pavement. The richer villa-owners liked themes from classical mythology and especially simple-figured designs of fishes and sea-gods commonly associated with ROMAN BATHS, e.g. the shells and dolphins and head of Oceanus at Verulamium.

Motels are HOTELS designed for those who travel by MOTOR CAR. The motorist drives into a garage adjoining his bedroom and may take his meals in a central restaurant. They originated in the USA, and since the 1960s an increasing number have been built in Britain. They are usually built on the outskirts of TOWNS, especially those which have been by-passed by MOTORWAYS.

Mothering Sunday or Mid-Lent Sunday (the 4th Sunday in Lent) was originally the day when young SERVANTS were allowed to go home to visit their mother, taking gifts with them and feasting on 'mothering cakes'. School-children also sometimes had a holiday when they went home from boarding-school to spend the day with their mother or parents. This Sunday is also known as Refreshment Sunday because the Gospel for the day in the Book of COMMON PRAYER describes our Lord's miraculous feeding of the five thousand.

Motor bicycle was first built in the 1880s in Germany and Britain, but those produced by Werner Frères of Paris between 1899 and 1912 were the real forerunners of the modern machine. Kickstarts and two- or three-speed gears had appeared by 1914, and chain- replaced

Early motor cycle

belt-drive in the 1920s. Motor scooters, mopeds and power-assisted bicycles were developed after the Second World War. See also SPEEDWAY RACING.

Motor-car goes back in history to the first self-propelled road vehicle, which was steam-driven and was built by Joseph Cugnot, a French artillery officer, in 1769 to draw guns. From the end of the 18th century, Richard Trevithick (1771–1833), William Murdock (1754–1839) and others built steam carriages, but the Locomotive Act (1865) enforced a 4 m.p.h. speed limit and required a man to walk in front of a mechanically-propelled vehicle with a red flag. On the Continent and in USA experiments continued, and two German inventors, Carl Benz (1885) and Gottlieb Daimler (1886), made the first petrol-engined cars. The Daimler engine was very successful and was soon made in France and USA as well as Germany.

Soon imported motor-cars and MOTOR-BICYCLES were used in Britain. The Locomotive Act was repealed in 1896, an event commemorated by a London–Brighton rally, still annually repeated. In 1895 F. W. Lanchester formed a company in Birmingham to build motor-cars; in 1897 the Humber Cycle Company of Coventry turned to car-making, and in the same year the English Daimler Com-

pany was founded at Coventry; in 1900 Herbert Austin, who worked for the Wolseley Sheep Shearing Machine Company in Birmingham, began to make cars, and so did William Morris, who owned a BICYCLE repair shop in Oxford; and the first Rolls-Royce car was produced by Henry Royce and the Hon. C. S. Rolls in 1907.

The Motor Car Act (1903) fixed a 20 m.p.h. speed limit, required cars to be registered with local authorities, which

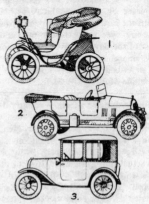

Motor cars: 1 1901 Electric; 2 1915 Morris Cowley; 3 1927 Austin 7

assigned numbers to them, and introduced driving-licences, which anyone over the age of 17 could obtain. A start was made on building new ROADS. Filling-stations with petrol pumps were first opened in 1919. The RAC was founded in 1897, the AA in 1905.

By 1904 there were 25 000 private cars in Britain and 106 000 in 1913, besides many motor commercial vehicles and BUSES. After the First World War, numbers rose to 250 000 in 1921 and 1 475 000 in 1935. British manufacturers began to build cheap, mass-produced cars in imitation of Henry Ford's Model T built in USA since 1908. The Austin 7 sold at £225 in 1922, but at £125 by 1930, and the Morris Minor followed. In 1921 W. O. Bentley produced his first sports car which won a race at 90 m.p.h. In 1928 the British Ford Motor Company opened its factory at Dagenham (Essex) to produce British-designed Fords.

The Second World War brought petrol rationing and a scarcity of new cars until 1950, but then the number of cars on the roads increased faster than ever: 1946—1 750 000; 1961—6 000 000; 1965—8 500 000. Twice as many new cars were bought in Britain in 1958 as in 1938. Casualties on the roads remained constant: 1934—7343 deaths; 1963—6922.

Post-war models included the four-wheel-drive Land Rover, developed in 1948 from the American Jeep made during the War, and the small Mini-Minor, first made in 1959. Driving tests were introduced in 1934 and fitness tests for cars in 1960. The speed-limit was abolished in 1930, but in 1934 imposed at 30 m.p.h. in built-up areas, which were defined as districts with street-lighting, and pedestrian crossings with Belisha beacons were introduced. The first traffic-lights (which were police-operated) were at the junction of St James's Street and Piccadilly in London in 1925; automatic signals (operating on a time-interval) were put up at a junction in Wolverhampton the next year; and the first vehicle-actuated signals were installed at the junction of Gracechurch Street and Cornhill in London in 1932.

The widespread possession of the motor-car among all classes has had important social consequences. It has brought a new freedom of movement unknown before. Fewer people live in the centre of TOWNS since they can reach their work from the country, and the isolation of the countryside has been destroyed. The volume, noise and danger of motor traffic present problems yet to be solved.

[L. T. C. Rolt, *The Horseless Carriage* (1954).] See also ELECTRIC CARS.

Motorways a scheme for wide, straight ROADS, with few intersecting roads, gentle sweeping curves and separate lanes for traffic travelling in opposite directions, were announced in Britain in 1955. The first to be built was the M1 from London to Birmingham and Lancashire. The other four main motorways are Birmingham to South Wales; London to South Wales; London to Yorkshire; and the Medway towns to the Kent coast. There are also shorter motorways interconnecting the three main Birmingham ones and others radiating from London.

Motte a steep-sided, flat-topped artificial mound of earth or turf surrounded by a ditch. The top was ringed by a palisade with a platform on the inner side, to which wooden steps led up. Inside

Motte and Bailey Castle

was a square wooden tower used as a store-house for weapons, a watch-tower and a refuge. Mottes are illustrated in the BAYEUX TAPESTRY, and together with its BAILEY, the motte formed the typical early Norman CASTLE.

Mounting block a wooden or stone step often placed outside a house, church, inn or tavern to enable horseriders to mount or dismount. Outside Merton Parish Church in Surrey there still stands a stone block which was used by Lord

Nelson when he attended services there. See also UPPING STOCKS.

Mourning from the Middle Ages onwards demanded black clothes for all classes, though in the 16th century royal widows wore white. At BURIALS mourners carried ROSEMARY and wore black cloaks. In the 17th and 18th centuries they were given black hat-bands and also scarves, sometimes as long as 3½ yards. Black gloves became common in the 18th century and black arm-bands from about 1820. In the 17th century women adopted veils, and in the 19th century men had 'weepers', broad muslin bands tied round TOP HATS with the two ends hanging down behind to the waist.

Moustaches, SEE BEARDS AND MOUSTACHES.

Muff a tubular covering to keep both hands warm, made of fur, feathers or elegant materials and padded inside, worn by ladies from about 1550 to about 1900. It was also sometimes worn by gentlemen from about 1600 to about 1800.

Among ladies, muffs went temporarily out of fashion in the early years of the 19th century when, owing to the flimsiness of their clothing under the NAKED FASHION, they carried RETICULES instead; but muffs reappeared as soon as SKIRTS grew more ample, and large fur muffs were especially popular during the period of tight skirts at the end of the century. They fell out of fashion during the First World War and have never come back again. See COSTUME.

Mulready an envelope resembling a half-sheet of letter-paper when folded. The space left for the address was enclosed by an ornamental design by William Mulready, the artist. When penny POSTAGE was inaugurated in 1840, these were introduced together with adhesive stamps, but were killed by ridi-

Mulready envelope

cule of their design and remained in circulation only for a year.

Mummers bands of men and women, dressed in fantastic clothes and with blackened faces, who at CHRISTMAS and other HOLIDAYS went from house to house, performing outside or indoors. In Scotland they were called grusards or guisers.

They were most popular in the Middle Ages, but were quite common in some country districts in England until the end of the 19th century. Their performance was once part of ancient religious ceremonies, the words of which lost their original meaning in the course of centuries, and were probably directly connected with pagan rites concerned with the triumph of life over death and with worship and sacrifices to the Corn Spirit. They usually began with a sword dance in which the swords were locked in a star over the head of one of the dancers to represent the death of the year in winter and withdrawn to show the renewal of life in spring. In the 15th century a play was added to the dance, which varied but always had a hero, usually St George, who fought a traditional enemy, sometimes a Saracen from the CRUSADES. See also CAROLS, HOBBY-HORSE.

Music has been performed in many ways from the early MINSTRELS, MUM-

MERS and WAITS to the later MUSIC HALL.
BALLADS, GLEES and MADRIGALS have been
sung, and so also have PSALMS and HYMNS
by CHOIRS in CHURCH and CATHEDRAL.
The MASQUE, BALLET and OPERA have produced their own type of music, as has the
ORCHESTRA, BAND and DANCING.

Wind instruments include the TRUM-
PET, BAGPIPES, SHAWM and OBOE, FLUTE and

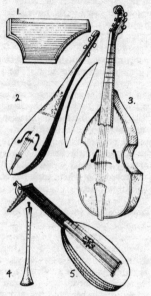

Musical instruments: 1 Psaltery; 2 Rebeck and
bow; 3 Viol; 4 Shawm; 5 Lute

RECORDER; stringed instruments the PSAL-
TERY, REBECK, VIOL, VIOLIN, HARP, LUTE
AND GUITAR; and percussion instruments,
the DRUM and TIMBREL. The DULCIMER,
CLAVICHORD, HARPSICHORD, VIRGINAL and
SPINET lead to the long-lived PIANO and
the short-lived PIANOLA, while the ORGAN
has long dominated Church music. In the
20th century the GRAMOPHONE and the
RADIO have played an important part in
bringing music into the home. [C. Sachs,

The History of Musical Instruments
(1940)]

Music halls originated in the large
ASSEMBLY ROOMS of Georgian COFFEE
houses and INNS which catered for both
the upper and lower classes. 'Catch and
Glee Clubs' and later 'Harmonic Meetings' were organized there. Those 'music-
houses' which were patronized by the
upper classes often developed into
THEATRES (e.g. Sadler's Wells, London),
while others frequented by the lower
classes became tavern concert-rooms. The
first proper music hall, the Canterbury
Hall at the Canterbury Arms, Lambeth,
was established in 1852, and by 1860
publicans all over Britain were building
halls for entertainment adjacent to their
inns. They fitted them with a stage and
tables and chairs, engaged professional
entertainers and charged for admission.
The programmes at first consisted of
MADRIGALS and GLEES sung by choirs,
which later were varied by DANCING and
acrobatics, but comic songs soon became
most popular, and so comedians became
important, one of the earliest being Sam
Cowell (1820–64), who sang 'Villikins
and his Dinah' and other burlesque
BALLADS.

By 1890 the tavern music halls were
being replaced by 'palaces of variety' with
auditoriums complete with circle and
gallery, an orchestra pit before the proscenium arch and a stage equipped for
changeable scenery. The 1890s were the
golden age of the music hall; in the West
End of London there were the Alhambra,
Tivoli and Palace. Among outstanding
performers and their songs were Marie
Lloyd (1870–1922) and 'A Little Bit of
What You Fancy Does You Good';
Albert Chevalier (1861–1923) and 'My
Old Dutch'; and Lottie Collins (1866–
1910) and 'Ta-ra-ra-boom-de-ay'. In
1902 at the London Coliseum Oswald
Stoll introduced variety, consisting of

long song scenes, musical spectacles, short acts and plays.

From about 1912 the music hall began to decline, being challenged by REVUES in West End theatres and then the CINEMA, RADIO and TELEVISION. While in 1900 there had been some 500 music halls in London, by 1960 no working music hall as such was left in the capital. [R. Mander and J. Mitchenson, *British Music Hall* (1965)]

Musket was a HAND-GUN, which was shorter and more effective than previous firearms. Its predecessor was discharged by means of a glowing match (fuse), and was so heavy that it had to be laid across a staff or rest before being fired. The invention of the MATCHLOCK and then the FLINTLOCK made it possible for it to be fired from the shoulder and improved its effectiveness until it was gradually superseded by the RIFLE.

Muslin a fine COTTON fabric with a downy nap on its surface, first imported from India about 1670, when it replaced LINEN and FUSTIAN in feminine fashions. Its large-scale production was made possible in Britain by the SPINNING inventions of the 18th century. This led to the increased use of muslin especially in the NAKED FASHION.

Mustard was known in the Middle Ages as a HERB for flavouring and Culpeper stated that the seed, taken in a drink, 'doth mightily stir up bodily lust and helpeth the spleen and pains in the sides and gnawing in the bowels'. It was not until the 18th century that it was discovered that the seeds can be ground and the powder sifted. Tewkesbury (Glos.) became famous for its mustard, a history of the town saying in 1830, 'The good housewives uniformly pound the mustard in an iron mortar with a large cannon ball and having carefully sifted the flour, mix it with a cold infusion of horseradish and beat it well for at least an hour'. Such mustard powder was popularized in the 19th century by the firm of Colman of Norwich, its founder saying that he made his fortune out of what people left on the side of their plates.

Mystery plays, see MIRACLE PLAYS.

N

Nabobs a nickname given, often in contempt, in the 18th century to those Englishmen who had made their fortune as officials or merchants in India and returned to buy estates and seats in Parliament.

Naked fashion a female fashion introduced into Britain about 1800 from post-revolutionary Paris and inspired by the ideas of the ROMANTIC MOVEMENT. HOOPS, STAYS and even PETTICOATS were replaced by a single one-piece MUSLIN dress with a very low neck, divided into SKIRT and BODICE. The material was too slight for pockets, which had to be replaced by RETICULES, and ladies had to begin also to wear DRAWERS. Hair was worn in its natural colour, cut short into curls or parted in the centre and brushed down smoothly. The fashion lasted into the 1820s. See also COSTUME, HAIR-DRESSING.

Nankeen a plain COTTON cloth of a yellowish-brown colour, named after its original place of manufacture (Nanking in China). In the early 19th century it was a popular material for CHILDREN'S COSTUMES.

Nasal the iron nose-piece attached to the HELMET of soldiers (as shown in the BAYEUX TAPESTRY) which partly protected (and concealed) the face. See also ARMOUR.

National Assistance Board was set up as the Unemployment Assistance Board by an Act of Parliament in 1934 to relieve UNEMPLOYMENT. When an unemployed person had drawn all his NATIONAL INSURANCE benefits, the Board made him payments on a uniform scale according to a 'means test'. In 1940 it was renamed the Assistance Board and in 1948 the National Assistance Board. In 1940 it was given the task of supplementing the Old Age PENSION and in 1947 the whole non-contributory Old Age Pension Scheme was transferred to it.

National Health Service was set up in 1948, providing free medical care for everyone in the country, nationalizing the HOSPITALS and abolishing fees in them. Private medicine was retained for those preferring it and also the patient's free choice of doctors. Since then fees have been imposed for dental treatment and for prescriptions.

National Insurance began with the Insurance Act (1911) which entitled those earning less than £3 a week to free medical attention from a doctor and to sick pay (at 10s a week for 26 weeks and then 5s a week). The Act also set up a scheme of contributory insurance against UNEMPLOYMENT, confined to certain trades and compulsory in them, providing 7s a week for 15 weeks in the year. Originally the employee paid 4d for a weekly insurance stamp (which was deducted from his wages), and in addition the employer paid 3d and the state 2d. Between 1920 and 1937 several acts extended sickness and unemployment insurance to cover most men and women workers, and the amounts paid were also gradually increased, but between the Wars the heavy, long-term unemployment necessitated the 'dole' and 'means test'. In 1946 National Insurance was made compulsory for everyone, and benefits were provided for sickness, unemployment, old age and maternity. See also NATIONAL ASSISTANCE BOARD, PENSIONS, INSURANCE, FRIENDLY SOCIETIES.

National Parks ten in number, have been designated by the National Parks Commission set up under the National Parks Act (1949): Lake District, Peak District, Snowdonia, Dartmoor (1951), Pembrokeshire Coast (1952), North Yorkshire Moors (1953), Yorkshire Dales, Exmoor (1954), Northumberland (1956), Brecon Beacons (1957). The development of these territories is to be controlled so as to preserve their landscape and ensure facilities for people visiting them. The Commission can also designate other 'areas of outstanding natural beauty', and so far these are: Gower, Quantock Hills, Lleyn, Surrey Hills, Dorset, Northumberland Coast, Cannock Chase, Shropshire Hills, Malvern Hills, Cornwall, North Devon, South Devon, East Devon, East Hampshire, Isle of Wight, Forest of Bowland, Chichester Harbour, Solway Coast, Chilterns, Sussex Downs, Cotswolds.

National Schools were day-schools provided by the National Society founded in 1811 as 'The National Society for the Education of the Poor in the Principles of the Established Church'. Like the BRITISH SCHOOLS, they adopted Andrew Bell's monitorial system, but they gave Anglican religious instruction. From 1833 they received grants from the government and after the EDUCATION ACT (1902) financial aid from the local authorities. Under the EDUCATION ACT (1944) they became either 'Aided' or 'Controlled' by the local authorities. [C. F. K. Brown, *The Church's Part in Education 1833–1941* (1942)]

National Society for the Prevention of Cruelty to Children was incorporated under royal CHARTER in 1895 and developed from the London Society for the Prevention of Cruelty to Children founded in 1884 by Benjamin Waugh, a clergyman. Its aim was to find and deal with cases of neglected and ill-treated children, prosecuting offenders where necessary. The Society became a national body in 1889, and largely through its efforts the first Act for the Prevention of Cruelty to Children was passed later that year. Nowadays it concerns itself with about 100 000 children each year, while about another 22 000 come under the care of the Royal Scottish Society for the Prevention of Cruelty to Children.

National Trust was founded in 1894 to hold buildings and land in trust for the people. Its first acquisitions were the Old Clergy House, Alfriston (Sussex), and a few acres of cliffland above Barmouth (Wales). Since 1937 it has accepted houses in which the former owner and his successors reside as tenants, Wallington Hall, Cambo (Northumberland), in 1942 being the first to come under this scheme, and it also possesses farm holdings (e.g. in Great Langdale, Westmorland). [Robin Fedden, *The Continuing Enterprise* (1968)]

Nave the central part of a CHURCH west of the CHANCEL arch or crossing, for the use of the laity. Often it is separated from

the chancel by a ROOD-screen and from the AISLES by columns. Medieval CATHEDRALS had large naves for architectural magnificence and as a pathway for PROCESSIONS; but FRANCISCAN churches had spacious naves to hold congregations listening to their preaching (e.g. St Andrew's Hall, Norwich). The largest nave in Britain is that of St Albans Cathedral (285 feet long).

Navvies the name given to the men working on the construction of the CANALS and later the RAILWAYS. The name 'navvy' is said to have come from the insistence of the self-taught James Brindley (1716–72), one of the greatest canal engineers, on writing 'navigator' as 'navvygator'. They were feared for their drunkenness and rough ways in the parts of the country in which they worked, but their achievements were amazing, especially as all excavations had to be done by hand-tools without the assistance of any machinery. [Terry Coleman, *The Railway Navvies* (1968)]

Necklace is the oldest and most popular form of JEWELLERY. NEW STONE AGE sculptures show women, otherwise naked, wearing long necklaces of shells, beads or teeth covering their necks and breasts. In the 14th and 15th century KNIGHTS, BARONS and members of LIVERY COMPANIES wore necklaces or COLLARS bearing emblems of HERALDRY. The RENAISSANCE favoured PEARL-necklaces. In the 19th century two or three strings of necklaces were worn, while in the 1920s long necklaces, often looped at the end, were fashionable.

Neckties began to displace CRAVATS in male costume about 1830. The practice of wearing distinctive neckties bearing the colours or registered designs of schools, universities, sports clubs, regiments, etc. seems to date from about 1880. It originated at Oxford where BOATER bands were converted into use as 'ribbon ties'. The earliest definitive evidence comes from an order for college ties from Exeter College, Oxford, dated June 25, 1880.

Needlework, see EMBROIDERY

Nef a silver and jewelled model of a ship, containing SPICES for adding flavour to the various dishes, which was placed on the TABLE at a medieval feast.

Negro servants were fashionable in the 18th century, men being commonly employed as footmen or coachmen and boys as PAGES. They were introduced from the West Indies and remained SLAVES until SOMERSETT'S CASE (1772). There were by then between 15 000 and 20 000 of them in London alone, and they continued to be brought to England. They were valued because of their impressive appearance and because they were paid no wages; and they were dressed in splendid liveries (including a silver dog-collar round the neck in the early 18th century) and given pretentious names, Pompey being a favourite.

New Lanark Mills (Scotland) were made into the first model FACTORY by Robert Owen (1771–1858), who married their owner. He started as a shop assistant and became one of Britain's greatest COTTON manufacturers and also a social reformer (see GRAND NATIONAL CONSOLIDATED TRADES UNION). He did not employ CHILDREN under 10 years old and forbade the use of the CANE. He reduced the working-day to 12 hours and later 10. He provided houses for the workmen and their families, cared for the sick and aged and built schools for children from the age of two. See also FACTORY LAWS.

New look the name given by *Life* magazine to dresses introduced by Christian Dior's Spring Collection in 1947. The square-shouldered, short-skirted fashions of the 1940s were replaced by full-skirted, curved-shouldered models. Skirts were 12 in. from the ground, and the high-busted, tiny waist was emphasized by hip-padding. The dresses were often worn with NYLON or stiffened PETTICOATS. At first the fashion was controversial, but it was welcomed by women as feminine and romantic after wartime austerity and was generally adopted. Its tight waists and full skirts remained fashionable until 1957. It was finally killed by the fashion of sack dresses. See also COSTUME.

New River a channel to bring water from springs at Chadwell and Amwell, Herts., to the northern side of the City of London undertaken by Hugh Myddleton and his 'Adventurers' or partners. In 1613 the water was let into the Round Pond at New River Head, Clerkenwell. The site of the Round Pond, abandoned in 1914, is now occupied by the Metropolitan Water Board's head offices. Water from New River Head was distributed to the streets of the City by wooden pipes, mostly of elm, to which were attached small lead pipes leading into houses.

In 1619 the 'Adventurers' became the New River Company. The original length of the New River was about 40 miles, but this was reduced in the mid-19th century by cutting off certain loops, and during the later part of the century the New River below Clissold Park, Stoke Newington, was covered over and the water carried underground in cast iron pipes. From 1618 water was drawn from the River Lee to supplement the springs, and from 1846 wells were sunk along its course to supply the River. The Company introduced STEAM POWER at their works at New River Head in 1768, but since the last century the main pumping station has been at Stoke Newington, where two reservoirs were completed in 1831 and 1833.

As a result of the Metropolis Water Act of 1852, filtration works were established at Stoke Newington, Hornsey and New River Head. The New River Company was merged into the Metropolitan Water Board in 1904. In 1946 the last filter bed at New River Head was abandoned, and the river ceased to flow there. It now ends at Stoke Newington and its length is 24 miles. See also WATER SUPPLY.

New Stone Age people came to Britain about 2500 BC. They were able to polish FLINTS and obtained them from such mines as GRIME'S GRAVES. They also could cultivate the soil and grew crops, living in VILLAGES and huts, commonly PIT-DWELLINGS; and they domesticated animals (see WINDMILL HILL) and made POTTERY, particularly BAG-WARE. See also OLD STONE AGE, BRONZE AGE.

New Towns established under the New Towns Act (1946) are Basildon, Bracknell, Crawley, Dawley, Harlow, Hatfield, Hemel Hempstead, Stevenage, Welwyn Garden City, Corby, Newton Aycliffe, Peterlee, Skelmersdale, Runcorn, Redditch, Washington (in England); Cwmbran (in Wales); East Kilbride, Glenrothes, Cumbernauld, Livingston (in Scotland). Each has its own Green Belt and separate industrial, housing and shopping areas. Other new towns include in the future Milton Keynes (Bucks.) and Thamesmead (London), while Peterborough and Northampton are to be expanded.

New Year's Day was formerly March 25, but was changed in 1752 to January 1 (see CALENDAR). The beginning of the year was formerly the occasion when people gave each other presents, but in the 19th century the custom was transferred to CHRISTMAS. In Scotland, through PRESBYTERIAN influence, the New Year celebrations outstrip Christmas, and the giving of gifts survives in the offerings of bread, money and coal brought by First Footers who visit houses in the early hours of New Year's Day in order to bring luck by being the first person to cross the threshold in the year. See also WASSAIL.

News letters were an early form of NEWSPAPERS, popular in Charles I's reign (1625–49). They consisted of news and gossip, often collected at the London TAVERNS and COFFEE-HOUSES, and sometimes included blank pages on which, when they were sent into the country, readers in turn wrote their own private letters before passing them on to others.

Newspapers first appeared in the form of NEWS LETTERS, but the first English newspaper proper was probably the *Weekely Newes* (1622), and others appeared during the Civil War. The *London Gazette* (1665) still appears twice weekly as the official organ of the government. *Berrow's Worcester Journal* (founded 1690 and appearing weekly since June 1709) is the oldest continuously published newspaper in the world. The first English daily was the *Daily Courant* (1702), which was also the first to publish a special evening edition (after the Battle of Ramillies).

The *Morning Post* (which amalgamated with the *Daily Telegraph* in 1937) was founded in 1772. *The Times* began as the *London Universal Register* in 1785 and took its present title in 1788. It was the first paper to be politically independent through the revenue it obtained from advertising. It also set up the first steam press in 1812, which enabled papers to increase their circulation from hundreds to thousands. The *Manchester Guardian* (renamed the *Guardian* in 1959) began as a weekly in 1821 and became a daily in 1855. The *Daily News*, founded as a liberal paper in 1846 amalgamated with the *Daily Chronicle* to become the *News Chronicle* after the First World War and was absorbed by the *Daily Mail* in 1960. The first Sunday newspaper was the *Sunday Monitor* (1780).

Alfred Harmsworth (later Lord Northcliffe) founded the *Daily Mail* (1896), which began the 'new journalism' with large headlines, short paragraphs and vivid stories; and in 1904 his brother, Harold (later Lord Rothermere) founded the *Daily Mirror* as a woman's journal, and it soon became a cheap popular paper. The *Daily Express* (1900) was the first to adopt the American practice of having news (instead of advertisements) on the front page.

Since the Second World War, the national daily newspapers have gained circulation at the expense of the local papers. They are nearly all now owned by a few large groups as also are many provincial papers. They depend for a large amount of their revenue from advertising, and the coming of commercial TELEVISION has presented them with financial problems because this has taken away some advertising from them.

Newgate Prison was situated near one of the old London city gates. A prison is recorded as being there in the 13th century. Later a new one was built by the executors of Sir Richard Whittington in the 15th century, which was destroyed by the GREAT FIRE OF LONDON (1666). Another one was erected on the site between 1778 and 1780 which was destroyed in the GORDON RIOTS (1780) and re-erected. It was not used as a prison after 1880 and was pulled down and replaced by the Central Criminal Court (opened 1907).

Nigger Minstrels first performed in Britain in 1858 in London and soon became a popular attraction at the SEASIDE. With their faces blacked with burnt cork, they wore TOP HATS, brightly coloured tail coats and striped trousers. They sang both plantation and popular songs and also told jokes, usually calling each other Sambo or Mr Bones. In this century they have developed into the more sophisticated Black and White Minstrel Show of the THEATRE and TELEVISION.

Night-clothes were not worn until the 16th century. Everyone until then slept naked or men in a day-shirt and women in a day-shift. In the 16th century nightshirts and night-chemises were adopted. By the 19th century the night-shirt resembled a day-SHIRT with a loose turned down COLLAR or a loose, ankle-length 'nightgown' was worn by men, while women wore long-sleeved, cotton, longcloth or linen nightdresses. Pyjamas were adopted by men from the 1880s and by women from the 1920s. See also SHIRT, SHIFT, CHEMISE.

Noble a coin called apparently from the metal, gold. Gold nobles (worth 6s 8d), half-nobles and quarter-nobles were issued by Edward III in 1344 to replace the FLORIN. In 1464 it was revalued at 8s 4d and in 1465 replaced by the ROYAL or rose noble and the ANGEL. See also COINAGE.

Nonconformists or Dissenters, those who refused from the 17th century onwards to conform to the CHURCH OF ENGLAND, particularly members of the INDEPENDENTS, BAPTISTS, PRESBYTERIANS, METHODISTS and other Protestant bodies. After the RESTORATION, an attempt was made to suppress them by the CLARENDON CODE, but they were granted toleration at the end of the century. In the 19th century Nonconformity represented a social and political as well as a religious division. Nonconformists mostly belonged to the working and middle classes. Their influence has weakened since the beginning of this century, partly due to the general decline of religion in the country and partly to the tendency for middle-class families, on becoming prosperous, to turn to Anglicanism. [E. A. Payne, *The Free Church Tradition in the Life of England* (1944)]

Norman architecture or English Romanesque architecture is represented in the CASTLES built to subjugate the ANGLO-SAXONS (e.g. Rochester, Dover and the Tower of London) and the CHURCHES and CATHEDRALS built by the incoming BENEDICTINE and CISTERCIAN monks (e.g.

CASTLES. And NORMAN FRENCH was long spoken in England.

Norman French the language spoken by the Normans at the time of the NORMAN CONQUEST. It remained the language of the nobility in England for over two centuries after 1066. Edward III (1312–77) is thought to have been the first post-Conquest King able to speak a little English, with the possible exception of Henry I (1068–1135). Richard II (1367–1400) was the first to use it as his mother-tongue, and Henry V (1387–1422) the first to use it for military despatches. At

Norman style: 1 Doorway; 2 Capital; 3 Base of column; 4 Window

Durham, Peterborough, Norwich and Ely). Its features were thick walls, small windows, semi-circular arches, massive columns and zig-zag ornament. It prevailed from the mid-10th century until the arrival of the GOTHIC style in the 12th.

Norman Conquest (1066) followed the Battle of Hastings (see BAYEUX TAPESTRY) and was enforced by the HARRYING OF THE NORTH. It brought great changes to England. The Normans brought with them strong government (made easier by the compilation of DOMESDAY BOOK) and FEUDALISM. They brought also their own style of GOTHIC architecture and built stone CHURCHES and

the DISSOLUTION OF THE MONASTERIES, the NUNS of Lacock Abbey (Wilts.) were found to be speaking Norman French; they were the less eligible daughters of well-to-do families.

English did not become the official language of the law-courts until Henry VII's reign (1485–1509), and lawyers long afterwards continued to make notes and glosses in a strange mixture of languages (e.g. in 1688 a prisoner, when sentenced by a judge, 'ject un Brickbat a la dit Justice que narrowly mist'). Acts of the English Parliament continued to be transcribed in Norman French until the COMMONWEALTH. The practice was temporarily renewed at the RESTORATION

(1660), but finally abandoned in 1688. See also ENGLISH LANGUAGE.

Nuclear power was made possible when the Italian refugee scientist, Enrico Fermi, built the first nuclear reactor at the University of Chicago in 1942. The first practical nuclear power station began operation at Calder Hall (Cumberland) in 1956, and by 1970 nine others had been opened, which already supplied about a fifth of the ELECTRICITY used in Britain.

Nuns had the same duties in respect of prayers, hospitality and alms as MONKS, but did SPINNING and EMBROIDERY instead of study or manual work. They also educated the daughters of the nobility and gentry. In the Middle Ages nunneries offered the only career open to unmarried women or young widows. At the DISSOLUTION OF THE MONASTERIES about half the nunneries in England were BENEDICTINE, and there were altogether less than 2000 nuns compared with about 5000 monks and 1600 FRIARS. See also CONVENT.

Nurses were members of orders of NUNS in the Middle Ages. St Bartholomew's Hospital in 1544 had 5 'sisters', but they were described as belonging to a very low class of society; and St Thomas's Hospital in 1555 had 200 sick and aged patients in the care of a surgeon, a steward, a porter and two women or sisters 'to attend to the poor and wash their clothes when necessary or convenient,' but a matron is not mentioned until 1557, and there were frequent complaints of drunkenness and brawling by the sisters. The London Hospital in the 18th century employed elderly and decrepit women as nurses, who got £6 a year for a day lasting from 6 a.m. to 10 p.m., while a night nurse or 'watcher' got £4. As late as 1830 many women who were nurses could not read or write.

The great change began when Pastor Fliedner of Kaiserwerth in Germany visited England in 1822 to study the work of Elizabeth Fry among women prisoners in NEWGATE and was so impressed that in Germany he bought a house as a hospital for discharged prisoners and orphans, which became the first training-school for nurses in the world because Lutheran deaconesses were trained there to help him and his wife with the nursing. Florence Nightingale in 1851 spent four months training there and became famous for her work in the Crimea. After the war she spent a public subscription of £50,000 to found the Florence Nightingale School for Nurses at St Thomas's Hospital, which was opened in 1861. The Royal College of Nursing was founded in 1916 and secured the passing of the Nurses' Registration Act (1919) which set up the General Nursing Council empowered to set standards of education and training, recognize School and maintain a Register of qualified nurses. Nurses' Acts (1943 and 1949) have provided for the enrolment and training of nurses. [Cecil Woodham-Smith, *Florence Nightingale* (1951)]

Nursery emerged in wealthy households as a separate room or set of apartments, with its own attendants and its own diet, towards the close of the Middle Ages. Before then CHILDREN were sent away from home, and early MARRIAGE was common.

Until the early 19th century, both the day and night nursery were plain and austere. Both had bare floors and uncurtained windows. The night nursery was furnished with low, curtainless BEDS, and the day nursery with deal TABLES, rush-bottomed CHAIRS, a press for clothes, a cupboard for TOYS and a BIRCH-ROD or CANE, often resting prominently on two hooks over the mantelpiece.

By the mid-19th century parents had begun to decorate and furnish the nursery in a distinctive style of its own, though often there was a tendency to put in it old furniture and pictures that had been rejected for other parts of the house. A ROCKING-HORSE, DOLLS' HOUSE and other TOYS became more common. The windows were hung with muslin, serge or cretonne curtains, and the floor was covered with a carpet.

Children were expected to spend most of their time in the nursery and often only saw their parents once a day during the CHILDREN'S HOUR. They usually had their meals there, though it did become more common, partly in order to ensure that they were taught TABLE MANNERS, for them to come down to the dining-room for the mid-day meal. [Magdalen King-Hall, *The Story of the Nursery* (1958)]

Nylon the first completely synthetic fibre, developed in 1935 by Wallace H. Carothers, an American chemist working for E. I. du Pont Nemours and Company at Wilmington, Delaware, which began to mass-produce it in 1938. Nylon became common for women's STOCKINGS, SHIRTS and UNDERGARMENTS in Britain after 1945. Nylon garments absorb very little moisture and so dry quickly, nor do they need ironing. As nylon is also strong, elastic and durable, it is used to make such things as ropes, bristles and moulds.

Terylene, a material made in much the same way as nylon, was invented in 1939 by an English chemist, J. R. Whinfield, and is commonly used for garments.

O

Oak was much used for FURNITURE from ANGLO-SAXON times. Heavy oak furniture was popular in Tudor times, but was ousted in fashionable houses by WALNUT at the RESTORATION. Nevertheless, it was still used for a great deal of plain furniture, especially in country districts, throughout the 18th century.

Oak was also used for building wooden SHIPS. Some 2000 oak-trees were felled to build HMS *Agamemnon*, a 64-gun ship in Nelson's fleet; and Admiral Lord Collingwood (1750–1810) always had some acorns with him to plant in suitable places in the countryside lest the navy suffered from a shortage of timber in the future.

In the Middle Ages and afterwards PIGS were grazed in forests to feed on acorns.

Oak Apple Day (May 29), the day when Charles II returned to London (1660) and also his birthday (1630). It was declared a day of annual thanksgiving with a special service in the Book of COMMON PRAYER by Act of Parliament in 1660 (which was not discontinued until 1859). To commemorate Charles II's escape by hiding himself in an oak-tree at Boscobel after the Battle of Worcester (1641), people wore oak apples or oak leaves on this day, and boys carried nettles to sting any people not wearing one.

Oast-houses buildings (most commonly found in Kent) containing a kiln for drying HOPS to be used in making BEER. The kiln has an upward draught for the wood-fire lit in the lower half of the round building, the floor above it being perforated and the hops spread out upon hair-cloth to be dried by the heat.

Oats a cereal crop, the origin of which is unknown, but samples of carbonized grains of both cultivated and wild oats mixed with WHEAT and BARLEY have been found in sites in Wiltshire, Somerset and Dorset, dating back to the IRON AGE. It has a higher protein and fat content than most grains. It has long been used as a CATTLE food and in Scotland eaten in the form of oatmeal. Dr Johnson once said 'Pah, Sir! Oats! A food for men in Scotland and horses in England', upon which Sir Walter Scott commented, 'And where do you meet such horses—or such men?'

Oboe a double-reed woodwind musical instrument, which developed in the 17th century from the medieval SHAWM and was at first called the hautboy. The early hautboys were loud and strident, and John Dryden (1631–1701) wrote of a musician announcing his arrival as 'flush'd with a purple grace' he vigorously 'gives the hautboys breath'.

Old Stone Age people were the first who came to Britain about 25 000 years ago. They made their tools and weapons out of FLINT. They lived on berries and nuts, fish and cockles and also hunted animals for food, trapping them in pits, eating the meat raw or cooked and wearing the hides as clothing. They usually lived in caves like WOOKEY HOLE. The Old Stone Age lasted for over 20 000 years and was followed by the NEW STONE AGE [Jacquetta and Christopher Hawkes, *Prehistoric Britain* (1943)]

Open-field System was a medieval method of farming. The land of each MANOR was divided into two or three large open fields which were themselves divided into long, narrow strips, each about ½-acre in area and separated from one another by BALKS. Everyone had strips, the lord about sixty, the poorest COTTAR three or four. Each man's strips were divided among the fields and also scattered about in different parts of the fields to ensure that he had his share of good and bad land alike. Every year one or more of the fields were sown with wheat, rye, oats or barley, but one was always left fallow. Around these fields stretched rough, uncultivated land, which was partly common or waste land (where cattle, sheep and poultry grazed), partly woodland (where fuel was gathered) and partly meadowland (which was divided into strips to grow hay). [H. L. Gray, *English Field Systems* (1915); C. S. Orwin, *The Open Fields* (1938).] See also ENCLOSURES, ROTATION OF CROPS.

Opera in England developed out of the MASQUE largely through Henry Purcell, who wrote *Dido and Aeneas* (1680), *King Arthur* (1691) and other operas. In the 18th century English opera was largely performed in the smaller unlicensed THEATRES in London, but the arrival of George Frederick Handel in England in 1712 led to Italian opera becoming a fashionable pleasure. In the 19th century Britain's main contribution to stage music were Gilbert and Sullivan's comic operas, but in the 20th century a number of British composers from Vaughan Williams to Benjamin Britten have written operas. Since the middle of the 19th century, Covent Garden has been the centre of opera production in England.

Oranges were introduced into southern Europe about the 12th century, but they were the bitter Seville oranges. Sweet oranges arrived in Portugal from India about 1500 and in the 1630s from China. Hitherto the orange had always been a seasoning, but now it quickly became a favourite FRUIT eaten for its own sake. It was imported into England from the groves around Lisbon cheap enough to be sold widely. In London the orange-girls, including Nell Gwynn, became a familiar sight on the streets and at the THEATRES in the 17th century. Pepys drank his first glass of orange-juice in 1669 and wrote 'a very fine drink, but, it being new, I was doubtful whether it might not do me hurt'. Wealthy people grew them in ORANGERIES.

Orangeries were the forerunners of the later GREENHOUSES and CONSERVATORIES. The first ORANGE grown in England from seed was said to have been given by Sir Walter Raleigh to Sir Francis Carew, of Beddington (near Croydon). At any rate, the Carews and Lord Burghley corresponded in 1561 about the purchase of orange trees, and in 1658 John Evelyn said the Beddington orangery was the most famous in England, covered in winter with a 'tabernacle of boards' and warmed by a stove. The great mansions of the late 17th and 18th centuries had dignified, classical stone, orangeries, and sometimes they were an integral part of the house, e.g. Sezincote (Glos.) and Ashridge (Herts.). The oranges were grown in ornamental tubs to form orange groves by garden paths in the summer and taken into the orangery in the winter where their fragrance made it a pleasant place to sit.

Orchestra originally meant any body of players of musical instruments. In the Middle Ages they came into being among the MINSTRELS and WAITS, and there seems to have been a royal orchestra in the household of Edward III (1327–77), but it is difficult to know what their actual instruments were or what music they played. Some evidence is forth-coming, however, in the sculptures of the

Minstrels' Gallery erected in Exeter Cathedral during Edward III's reign. Among the instruments depicted in these carvings are the GUITAR, BAGPIPES, REBECK, PSALTERY and TIMBREL. In 1667, Pepys was serenaded outside his inn at Cambridge by 'the town music'; he 'did give them something', but thought 'what sad music they made'.

From the Middle Ages many parish CHURCHES had a small orchestra to accompany the services with such simple instruments as the VIOL and RECORDER. This was usually placed, together with the CHOIR in a GALLERY at the west end. Such orchestras were replaced by ORGANS in the 19th century (the fate of such an orchestra being told by Thomas Hardy in *Under the Greenwood Tree*).

The modern symphony orchestra (with its four groups of instruments: strings, woodwind, brass and percussion) developed in the 17th century at the French and English courts of Louis XIV and Charles II. After the RESTORATION, an orchestra was introduced into the Chapel Royal at WHITEHALL, but Pepys considered it played 'after the French fantastical light way, better suiting a tavern or playhouse than a church'.

The popularity of the OPERA in the 18th century assisted the development of the orchestra in England. So also did the giving of concerts, often in THEATRES and under royal patronage in the reigns of George III and George IV, the Royal Philharmonic Society being formed in 1813 for the encouragement of orchestral music. In the later 19th century popular concerts were given in EXETER HALL, the CRYSTAL PALACE and the Albert Hall (opened in 1871). [F. W. Galpin, *Old English Instruments of Music* (1907)]

Organs are recorded as being used in CHURCHES at Malmesbury in the early 8th century and at Winchester and Salisbury in the 10th century. They had become common in larger parish churches in the 13th century and almost general before the end of the Middle Ages. At the REFORMATION, the PURITANS strongly objected to them, and most were destroyed during the COMMONWEALTH. At the RESTORATION they were restored in CATHEDRALS and larger churches, but until the 19th century most churches had an ORCHESTRA (or from the 18th century a barrel-organ playing a limited number of tunes). See also RECORDER, VIOL.

In the 1920s and 1930s large CINEMAS had an organ, the great object of which was orchestral imitation and the reproduction of natural and other sounds.

Ox the most common draught animal on medieval farms. The HORSE began to replace it in the 11th century, but the horse was more difficult and expensive to maintain and demanded scarcer foods like OATS, and when it was too old to work, the peasant could not eat it as he could the ox; and it has even been suggested that peasants avoided using horses for farm-work because they were likely to be taken for war. At any rate, less prosperous farmers long continued to use oxen, and they were still employed for farm-work in some parts of the country (e.g. Sussex) into this century. By the time of the First World War, however, only a few teams of oxen remained at work on farms, though on some Scottish islands oxen were still used for ploughing and carting as late as 1946. A team of oxen is still kept for work by Lord Bathurst at Cirencester Park (Glos.). See also YOKE.

Oysters in England were first made famous during the Roman occupation. The Romans discovered the great natural oyster beds on the east coast and exported large quantities of them (in shrouds of frozen snow) from the Essex beds. Interest in English oysters died down when the Romans left. There was a brief revival after the NORMAN CONQUEST, but gradually they sank in status. Pepys often had oysters and wine in TAVERNS, and by the mid-19th century oysters had become part of the staple diet of every poor Londoner, being sold by street-sellers at 8d a bushel. Dickens made Sam Weller say, 'Poverty and oysters always seem to go together.' By 1900, over 40 million oysters were being sold a year, and their price was still low. Their sale slumped during the First World War, revived again, only to slump anew in the Second World War. Then the disastrous winter of 1962–3 almost ruined the beds, but they are now reviving as a delicacy.

P

Page in the Middle Ages was a boy of gentle birth who was sent (as his sister was sent as a DAMSEL) to join the household of the King or some nobleman. While the pages waited on their superiors, they also learnt good TABLE-MANNERS and to sing and play music. They were instructed in horsemanship and other military training as well as in wrestling and fencing. At the age of 14 the page became a SQUIRE. [A. V. B. Norman and D. Pottinger, *Warrior to Soldier* (1966)]

Pall-Mall an old GAME in which a ball was driven with a mallet or club through a high iron hoop suspended from a pole at the end of an alley. The player who knocked the ball through with the fewest strokes was the winner. The game was a fashionable amusement in the reign of Charles II, the King and his courtiers playing it in St James's Park, and the Mall and Pall Mall are a reminder of where their alleys used to be.

Palm Sunday the Sunday before EASTER, so-called because of the pre-REFORMATION practice of placing branches of willow, yew or box on the ALTAR in church to be blessed by the priest after MASS and carried in procession in commemoration of Christ's entry into Jerusalem. Afterwards the branches were burned to provide holy ashes for placing on the people's heads on ASH WEDNESDAY in the following year.

Pantalettes a feminine under-garment in the form of long, straight-legged DRAWERS reaching to below the calf and there trimmed with LACE or tucks, which was worn from about 1812 to the 1840s. Young girls wore pantalettes visible below the SKIRT until about 1850. See also CHILDREN'S COSTUME.

Pantomime now a traditional part of the CHRISTMAS celebrations, the season beginning with BOXING DAY; but it is one of the more recent forms of the English THEATRE. The character of Harlequin, upon which all early pantomimes centred, came from Italian comedy and was made familiar to England by Italian stage players in the latter half of the 17th century. In 1717 the actor-manager, John Rich, developed the character when he presented *Harlequin and Cinderella*, followed by adaptations of other fairy tales and legends with Harlequin as the chief character.

By 1758 the famous family of clowns, the Grimaldis, had become leading pantomime performers. Gradually the emphasis changed. The pantomime became a burlesque and extravaganza and finally a sophisticated revue bound to a plot taken from a few romantic favourites, such as *Dick Whittington, Cinderella, Aladdin* and the *Babes in the Wood*; and the harlequinade gradually faded into the background.

By the last decades of the 19th century, it had become a regular Christmas institution with its conventional principal boy (played by a girl) and dame (played by a man). Dan Leno was then one of the great pantomime actors, and the traditional home of pantomime was the Theatre Royal, Drury Lane, but it ceased to be performed there shortly before the First World War.

Pantomime continued to decline after the First World War. Nowadays there may be only one in central London, instead of four or five at the leading theatres, but it continues to flourish in the suburbs and provinces. The story of a pantomime now has become little more than a link joining a song, dance and comedy show, which is very much like a REVUE. A recent development makes it a parade on ice.

Pantry derived from the Norman-French word for 'bread', a room in a HOUSE or CASTLE from the early 13th century onwards used for serving the food to the KITCHEN and HALL and often situated next to the BUTTERY.

Paper was introduced into Europe through the CRUSADES, the knowledge of its manufacture being acquired from the Arabs who had themselves learnt it from the Chinese, and it gradually replaced PARCHMENT. The first-known English paper-mill, which used LINEN and COTTON as its raw material, was at Sele, near

Stevenage (Herts.), which produced paper for an edition of Chaucer in 1498; and in Scotland mills were erected near Edinburgh in the late 16th century. These mills made coarse brownish paper; white paper was first made by HUGUENOT refugees in 1690; and all paper was made by hand until machinery was devised in France in 1798, which was developed in England by the EMIGRÉ brothers Fourdrinier in 1804, who produced paper in continuous rolls. Since 1864 Esparto grass, imported from Spain, has been largely used in making paper, and since 1866 newsprint has been manufactured from wood pulp.

Pargetting

Parasol a light ornamental UMBRELLA carried by ladies in the 19th century as a protection against the sun. At first a pagoda-shape was usual, but from the mid-century this was replaced by a domed-shape, and parasols became more elegant. In the 1840s they had carved ivory handles, in the 1880s linings in bright colours, in 1886 bows of ribbon near the point and handle, and in 1889 covers of fancy silk in broad coloured stripes.

Parchment a writing material, made from animal skins, which was used by the ancient Greeks and Romans. Until the knowledge of PAPER-making was brought to Europe through the CRUSADES, it was almost the only writing material used. Ordinary parchment was usually made from the skins of sheep and goats, while fine parchment (known as vellum) was made from the skins of lambs, kids and calves. See also BOOKS.

Pargetting consists of ornamental relief work in moulded plaster upon the outside walls and ceilings of old houses, most commonly in East Anglia.

Parish is the area under the care of a clergyman (a RECTOR or VICAR in the CHURCH OF ENGLAND). The earliest reference to parishes is in the 7th century, but a parish is not the same as a settlement. Often there are several distinct HAMLETS in one parish or more than one parish in a VILLAGE; the average is probably about three settlements to two parishes. From Tudor times the parish, acting through the VESTRY, became a unit of local government, and since then the boundaries of ecclesiastical and civil parishes have not necessarily been the same. See also DIOCESE, RURAL DEAN.

Parish Clerk an old-established ecclesiastical official, known from the time of St Augustine of Canterbury, in the CHURCH OF ENGLAND. In the Middle Ages he was often a clergyman in minor orders (a deacon or a sub-deacon); he taught the children singing, read the Epistle at the MASS, assisted the priest when he celebrated and made the responses in the services. After the REFORMATION he was a layman and often acted as VESTRY clerk. In the old three-decker PULPITS, he occupied the lowest stage. The office was an appointment for life until 1921. Few exist nowadays. [P. H. Ditchfield, *The Parish Clerk* (1913).] See also SEXTON, REBECK.

Parlour a room (the word being derived from NORMAN-FRENCH) for speaking in. Originally it was a room in a MONASTERY in which the MONKS were allowed to meet for conversation with laypeople. In the 14th century it appeared in HOUSES as a separate room for sitting and, at first, sleeping. By the 19th century it had become in middle- and lower-class homes the room with the best furniture which was used only on SUNDAY afternoons or to entertain visitors. See also SERVANTS.

A parlour-boarder at a boarding-school was a pupil who, for the payment of extra fees, had meals with the teacher's family.

Parterre a level area in front of a HOUSE below the terrace or WINDOWS. It was introduced into England from France in the 17th century and was part of the movement to introduce the vista into English GARDENS. It replaced the Elizabethan KNOT GARDEN.

Parvise a room over the PORCH of a CHURCH, often built in the Middle Ages for the priest. After the REFORMATION, it was commonly used as a store-room or school-house.

Patches small spots of black velvet or silk, cut into shapes such as crescents, stars, circles, diamonds, hearts or crosses, and applied with glue by ladies as ornaments on their face from the late 16th to the late 18th centuries. Early in the 18th century, the arrangement of the patches on the face sometimes showed the wearer's political party. If she had a patch on the right cheek, she was a Tory; if on the left cheek, a Whig; and if on the forehead between the eyes or on both cheeks, she was of no political bias.

During some periods in the 17th and 18th centuries, patches were also worn by some foppish men. See also DRESSING-TABLE.

Paten the plate used for the bread at the MASS or communion service. Up to modern times it was designed to fit on top of the CHALICE rather than as a separate utensil. In medieval symbolism, the chalice was often said to represent the tomb in which the body of Jesus was laid and the paten to represent the stone placed over it. [James Gilchrist, *Anglican Church Plate* (1967)]

Pattens wooden soles secured by leather loops to BOOTS AND SHOES to raise the wearer out of the dirt when walking. They were worn from the 14th century to the mid-19th century, usually in the country, but in the 15th and 18th centuries were generally fashionable. From about 1630 they were usually secured by an oval iron ring.

Paul's Cross situated in the north-eastern part of the close of Old ST PAUL'S CATHEDRAL. Originally it was a rallying-place for Anglo-Saxon MOOTS of freemen, but from the mid-13th century to 1633 it was the centre for national and religious proclamations, sermons and disputations. When the King came to hear the preaching, he occupied the King's Closet, an erection near the Cathedral itself. Nearby was the Shunamite's House, an INN kept for the entertainment of the preachers at the Cross. The preachers were invited by the Bishop of London and entertained by Corporation of the City from the Thursday before the day of preaching to the following Thursday morning. The Cross was destroyed in 1643. [R. J. Mitchell and M. D. R. Leys, *A History of London Life* (1958)]

Paul's Walk the name given by the end of the 16th century to the central passage of the NAVE of Old ST PAUL'S CATHEDRAL, which since medieval times had been used as a thoroughfare and commercial centre and had by then become the acknowledged place for gossip, newsmongering and business deals and the most popular promenade in the kingdom. It was not unusual for MARKETS and other business to be conducted in CHURCHES.

Pauldron was a separable shoulder-plate in medieval ARMOUR. The left pauldron was larger and reinforced to offer better protection to the chest and upper-arm because mounted KNIGHTS in contest met left side to left side since the LANCE was couched across the horse's neck.

Pearls were highly prized by the Romans, who used them to embroider clothes and shoes as well as for jewellery, but those obtained in ROMAN BRITAIN were disappointingly of little value, being undersized and of very poor colour. Through its study of antiquity, the RENAISSANCE made pearls very fashionable again, especially for necklaces. The art of producing cultured pearls by inserting a mother-of-pearl bead into the body of an oyster was perfected in Japan during the early 1920s.

Peasants' Revolt (1381) was immediately caused by the imposition of a POLL-TAX. It began in Essex and spread to Kent, where the rebels captured Rochester Castle and chose Wat Tyler as their leader. They marched to London, slaughtered many foreigners and lawyers, destroyed the Savoy Palace and seized the Tower, murdering the Archbishop of Canterbury. Richard II met them at SMITHFIELD, where Wat Tyler was killed, but they dispersed on promise of a pardon and the revocation of the Statute of LABOURERS. There were also risings in the eastern counties and other places, which were put down. Probably less than 200 people were put to death afterwards. By alarming landlords, it immediately checked the process towards the abolition of VILLEINAGE, but commutation soon began again. [G. M. Trevelyan, *England in the Age of Wycliffe* (1899)]

Pectoral (1) was a piece of ARMOUR placed over the CUIRASS as an extra protection for the chest and throat and also a piece of JEWELLERY worn by medieval women on the breast. It was applied too in the Middle Ages to the decorative part of the harness of a HORSE.

(2) From the 13th century onwards it was the name given as well to the small cross of gold or silver worn upon the breast by bishops, cardinals, abbots and other dignitaries of the Church. The bishops of the CHURCH OF ENGLAND, who had ceased to wear such pectoral crosses at the REFORMATION, began to wear them again in the later 19th century, and they were called 'abdominal ironmongery' by King Edward VII.

Pedlar one who carried a 'ped' or basket without a lid containing articles to sell in the streets or from house to house. At the Ped Market in Norwich women exposed eggs, butter, cheese and other farm produce in open hampers for sale. A pedlar visited a VILLAGE about twice a year, displaying his wares on the green and going to the servant's quarters of great houses, bringing goods from London and crying, 'What is't ye lack? Fine wrought shirts or smocks. Perfumed waistcoats. Fine bone lace or edgings. Sweet gloves. Silk garters, very fine silk garters. Fine combs or glasses or a poking-stick with a silver handle.' Others sold BALLADS and CHAPBOOKS. And some sold trinkets bought at FAIRS; the household accounts of Grimsthorpe Castle (Lincs.) in 1561 reveal that 2s was given to the children of the house—Master Peregrine and Mistress Susan—'to buy them fairings of a pedlar at the gate'. As ROADS improved in the late 18th century, pedlars came to be replaced by village SHOPS.

Peel towers old square stone buildings in the hill country on the English and Scottish border, mostly in the upper valleys of the rivers Coquet, Rede and North Tyne in Northumberland. They were mainly built from the 14th to 16th centuries as strongholds for farmers to shelter from raiders.

Peel tower

They have thick walls and a single door strengthened with iron. The ground floor room has no windows and was usually for storage; in times of danger horses and cattle were driven into it. The upper rooms, reached by ladders and trapdoors, were living quarters. Each tower was from 15 to 20 feet square.

Pen derives its name from the Latin *penna*, a 'feather', and was originally applied to the quill-pen made from GOOSE feathers, which was used in Europe at least as early as the 7th century AD. The quill was cut with a pen-knife, the tip being pointed and split to hold the INK and enable it to flow straight on to the PARCHMENT or PAPER.

Though the Romans had used pens of BRONZE, quill-pens remained unchallenged until STEEL pens were first made in Birmingham in 1822, and the slip pen, or nib that fitted into a nib-holder, was invented about the same time. At first these metal pens were expensive, hard and stiff, but by 1830 the holes and slits in the nib had been developed, and they began to oust the quill-pen. In 1926 stainless steel was first used for pen-nibs.

The first fountain-pen was made in 1886. They became common in the 1890s, but they had to be filled by taking them apart and squirting in ink with a device like an eye-dropper. Self-filling pens appeared in the 1910s. The first ball-point pen was made in Britain in 1946.

Penal Code comprised the laws passed against ROMAN CATHOLICS in the 16th and 17th centuries. These punished RECUSANTS and also those who celebrated or heard MASS, while those who refused to deny the authority of the Pope were deprived of most of their civil rights and placed almost in the position of outlaws. They were, however, never entirely or continually enforced and by the 18th century were largely inoperative. The greater part of the code was repealed in 1791 and the remainder in 1829. See also CLARENDON CODE.

Penance was a SACRAMENT in the medieval Church, the word coming from *poena* ('punishment') which was imposed on a sinner by a BISHOP, ECCLESIASTICAL COURT or other authority. A penance might take the form of being sent on a PILGRIMAGE or of a WHIPPING or having to stand before the congregation in CHURCH wearing a white sheet or 'shirt of repentance'. In England, penance continued to be imposed after the

REFORMATION. In 1797 Lambeth Parish Church was unusually crowded one Sunday when John Oliver did penance in a white sheet 'for calling Miss Stephenson, the domestic female of a neighbouring baker, by an improper name'.

In Scotland wrong-doers had to sit on a low 'stool of repentance' in front of the PULPIT during service-time and afterwards stand on the stool to receive the minister's rebuke. This occurred into the 19th century.

In medieval MONASTERIES, when the MONKS assembled for their daily meeting in the CHAPTER HOUSE, those who had offended against the RULE had to submit to a penance, which was sometimes correction with a BIRCH-ROD.

Pencil in the Middle Ages was a small fine brush of hair used by painters for laying on their colours. The first wooden pencils filled with graphite or blacklead were made about 1600 following the discovery of a graphite mine in Borrowdale (Cumberland). At first graphite was used in its natural form, but in 1795 N. J. Conté invented a process by which pencils could be made cheaper and harder through combining the graphite with clay and water, pressing it into sticks and firing it in a kiln.

Penny originally 'pending', and probably derived from Penda, King of Mercia (d. 654), who struck such silver coins. Their continuous circulation began in the reign of Offa of Mercia (759–96), 240 being struck from a POUND of silver. Until late in the 13th century, they were the only coins in circulation, all others being money of account. They were cut into two or four parts to produce HALF-PENNIES or FARTHINGS. The penny became a copper coin in 1797 and was later made from a bronze alloy. See also COINAGE.

Pensions were provided for their members by medieval GUILDS, but their funds were seized at the REFORMATION. The first modern pension scheme originated in Charles II's reign through Parliament granting him at the RESTORATION a revenue derived from customs and excise duties. After an unsuccessful attempt to collect the money through tax-farmers, customs-men were employed from 1671, and when they were 'worn out in service', they were granted half the salary of their successor in office, but this proved unworkable in the lower posts, and in the 18th century all customs-men paid 6d in the £ of their wages for a half-pay pension with 10 years' qualifying service and a retiring age of 60. This scheme was ruined by the inflation accompanying the Napoleonic War and in 1810 was taken over by the government and made non-contributory. In 1834 it was extended to the whole of the Civil Service and set a precedent for other occupational schemes.

The first government old-age pensions (varying from 5s to 1s a week) were granted in 1908 to persons over 70 whose income was less than 12s a week. In 1925 widows and orphans were included, and all pensions were made dependent upon weekly contributions by wage-earners, the retirement pension being payable at 65 to men and 60 for women. In 1946 participation in the scheme was made compulsory for everyone, and it became part of NATIONAL INSURANCE.

Pepper was used more in Middle Ages than nowadays since it gave flavour to dried or salted MEAT or FISH. Like other SPICES, it was used more widely after the CRUSADES, when merchants brought it overland from India, but the long journey made it so dear that only the wealthy could afford it. Its price fell at the end of the 15th century after the discovery of the sea-route to India.

Perambulators were first mentioned in Britain in the 18th century, but were not widely used until the first half of the 19th century. At first they were made of wood with solid, iron spoke, cart-type wheels and had only three wheels, being

(*top*) Victorian three-wheel pram
(*bottom*) Early 20th-cent. pram

commonly in later Victorian times called 'mail-carts' because they resembled the hand-carts used in the Post Office. In the 1960s models with fabric collapsible bodies, used earlier on the Continent, became popular in Britain.

Perfumes were first made chiefly from scented resins, leaves, SPICES and HERBS. The perfumes used by ladies in ROMAN BRITAIN came either from the East or from Italy, particularly Capua, where Seplasia, the perfume market, was famous, and Seplasium was the most commonly used toilet water. See also BOTTLES.

Distillation was known to the Arabs, and their perfumes were brought to Europe in the 11th and 12th centuries through the CRUSADES, especially rose-water made by distilling the petals of roses with water. Since an acre of roses yielded about a ton of petals from which about a pound of rose-water was distilled, it remained an expensive perfume.

In the 16th century the new trade routes made perfumes cheaper, and also the production of alcohol, which improved the preparations of perfumes from the petals of flowers and made many more subtle blends possible. *The Queen's Closet*, printed in England in 1663, gave recipes for many perfumes, including one said to have been invented by Elizabeth I—a pomatum made from apples and mixed with the fat of a young dog. In the 18th century perfume was highly fashionable for both sexes, but chiefly through the influence of Beau Brummel (1778–1840) it became used less and less by men.

During the 19th century the first synthetic perfume, nitrobenzine (essence of mirbane), was produced, and by the end of the century most perfumes were produced synthetically with chemicals from such materials as coal tar and petroleum, sometimes blended with flower and plant oils.

From the 13th century onwards perfumes were often carried in little crystal boxes, generally of Arab manufacture. Later POMANDERS and VINAIGRETTES were used.

Peter's Pence a tax formerly paid to the Pope. It was first paid in England by King Offa in 787 and continued by his successors. It lapsed under Edward the Confessor, but was renewed by William I. At one time a HEARTH TAX collected at midsummer from all but the poorest householders (whose property did not exceed 2s 6d—the DOMESDAY price of an ox), it was commuted in the 12th century by the BISHOPS at £200 a year for the country. It was abolished by Act of Parliament in 1534.

'Peterloo Massacre' (1819), the sardonic name (after the Battle of Waterloo) for the dispersal of a reform meeting of about 60 000 people on St Peter's Fields, Manchester (now the site of the Free

Trade Hall) who were charged by the YEOMANRY when ordered by the JUSTICES OF THE PEACE to arrest Henry ('Orator') Hunt as he addressed them. In the ensuing panic, 11 people (including 2 women) were killed and some 400 injured. The incident had the effect of aggravating fear of possible insurrection in official circles and also resentment against the government among RADICALS and the working-class. [E. Read, *Peterloo* (1958)]

Petticoat an UNDERGARMENT worn by women from the 16th century onwards, but commonly called an 'under-petticoat' until the 19th century. In the 16th century it was usually on inferior material and tied to the body of the dress by laces ('points'), in the 17th often of white flannel and in the 18th of cambric or flannel and narrow in shape when worn under the HOOP. In the 19th century it became more elaborate, and in the 1840s the advent of the CRINOLINE made several petticoats indispensable, the undermost usually being of flannel. By the 1890s, when the number had again dropped to one, it was often of silk or satin, lavishly flounced, frilled and bordered with ribbon and lace, producing a 'seductive frou-frou' sound in walking. In the 20th century petticoats again became simple, though they were more elaborate for a short time during the NEW LOOK. See also EMBROIDERY.

Petty Schools or ABC Schools were for little boys, who had to learn to read and write before they could begin Latin at the GRAMMAR SCHOOLS. They learnt the alphabet and numbers up to ten by heart from a HORN-BOOK. See also GIRLS' SCHOOLS.

Pewter a grey alloy of TIN and LEAD or other metal, was known to the ancient Romans, and was revived in Europe in the 11th century for making CHALICES and after the 14th century for PLATES and other domestic articles instead of wood. It went out of use in the 19th century when crockery made from earthenware became cheap. Though unbreakable and fairly cheap, pewter articles were easily bent or dented owing to the softness of the metal. Travelling pewterers toured the country recasting damaged articles, which is why very old pewter is rare today.

Pheasant was a native of central Asia and introduced into ROMAN BRITAIN. It was eaten in the Middle Ages, but was expensive compared with other POULTRY, its local price in 1378 being 13d compared with 7d for a GOOSE.

Phaeton a light, open four-wheeled CARRIAGE, drawn by one, two or four horses, and named after the son of the sun-god, Helios, who drove his father's chariot too near the earth and was killed by Zeus with a thunderbolt to save the earth from destruction by fire. The phaeton was an especially fashionable carriage in George III's reign (1760–1820) and was sometimes built very high. There were several varieties such as the high perch, the low pony, the mail and the spider phaeton. In most the driver was protected by a hood which could be raised or lowered.

Phoenicians were a seafaring people of the sea coast of Syria, who were outstanding navigators and traders. Tyre and Sidon and their other cities were famous for their wealth, and they founded colonies on the shores and islands of the Mediterranean, the greatest of these being Carthage, established in the 9th century BC. They are traditionally said to have reached Cornwall and traded there in TIN and COPPER. See also GREYHOUND.

Photography, see CAMERA

Physic gardens, see HERB GARDENS

Physicians in England during the Middle Ages, since the medical faculties at Oxford and Cambridge were neglected, were usually educated at Continental universities such as Padua, Montpellier or later Leyden, and physicians in royal or noble households were likely to be foreigners. As with Chaucer's doctor of physic, medical training was academic and mostly in books with little bedside teaching or research. The revival of learning during the RENAISSANCE led to a greater interest in the subject. The Royal College of Physicians received its CHARTER in 1518, but it failed to establish a monopoly for its members as against the APOTHECARIES. See also DENTISTRY, MEDICINE.

Piano a keyboard instrument in which the strings are struck, not plucked, invented by Bartolomeo Cristofori of Florence about 1710. The first English piano was made about 1760. Most 18th century pianos were square in shape, 4–5 ft long and formed like the VIRGINAL and CLAVICHORD. The grand piano, based on the HARPSICHORD shape, came into

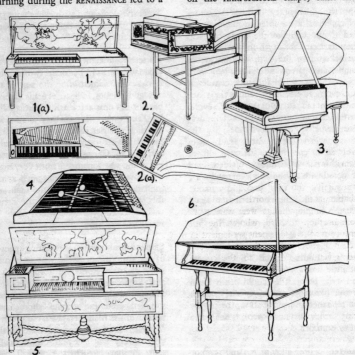

1 Clavichord (1a plan); 2 Harpsichord (2a plan); 3 Grand piano; 4 Dulcimer; 5 Virginal; 6 Spinnet

being in the 1780s; and the upright piano, first made in USA by Isaac Hawkins in 1800, became popular in the 19th century. See also DULCIMER, PIANOLA.

Pianola a form of PIANO played by mechanical means. The hammers were made to strike the strings by means of air pressure, and the passage of air to particular hammers was regulated by the perforations in a revolving paper roll. Skill in pianola-playing consisted entirely in the use of the feet, expression and phrasing being effected by variations of foot pressure on the pedals which operated the blowing. The name was invented by the Aeolian Company (of America), which began to manufacture them at the end of the 19th century. So popular did they become that the London Directory for 1922 showed manufacturers or agents for 52 different makes. Their sale was killed, however, by the economic slump at the end of the 1920s and by the development of the GRAMOPHONE. None have been made since the 1930s. [A. J. W. Ord-Hume, *Player Piano* (1971)]

Picts and Scots were the names given from the late 3rd century to the raiders of ROMAN BRITAIN. Picts, meaning the 'painted [i.e. tattooed] people', were the inhabitants of Britain north of HADRIAN'S WALL, while the Scots were the CELTS from northern Ireland, who in the 6th century made a permanent settlement in Pictish territory and by the 10th century had given their name to the whole country.

Pie Powder Courts special courts controlling medieval FAIRS, the name being derived from a corruption of the old French name for PEDLARS, *pieds poudreux*. GUILD laws did not permit any stranger to trade within a TOWN except for the period of a fair when normal regulations and the regular courts were

suspended in favour of the Pie Powder Courts. As many traders were itinerant, swift justice was necessary, and it was usual to charge, try and punish offenders in a single day, if possible, literally while the dust of the fair was still on their feet. A common penalty for a dishonest trader was to put him in the STOCKS or PILLORY with his bad cloth, cheese or other wares tied around his neck.

The name for these courts came from the Normans, who reconstituted the old English fairs and gave them their first CHARTERS. They were supervised by the STEWARD of the lord of the MANOR, the ABBOT, the MAYOR or a representative of the BISHOP, though usually the merchants attending a fair themselves passed judgement on offenders. The County Courts Act (1888) enabled a lord of the manor or any other fair owner to surrender his rights of pie powder to the Crown, and most of them did so.

Piers became a feature of the British SEASIDE in the 19th century. The first, the Chain Pier at Brighton, built in 1823, was intended primarily as a landing-stage for the Channel crossing to Dieppe, but when the London Bridge to Dover RAILWAY line was opened in 1844, it had to depend increasingly on entertainment. Joined at Brighton by the West Pier in 1866, it was destroyed in a storm in 1896, and the Palace Pier was opened in 1900. Southend Pier, the longest in England, was built in 1846 with a railway having cars drawn by two horses, but in 1889 the old wooden pier was rebuilt, and a single-line electric railway installed, and in the 1920s the pier was extended and improved and a double-line track built. Most British piers were built with a widened platform, commonly at the end, with a concert hall or pavilion for plays, concerts and band performances; and small kiosks and slot-machines have also been a common feature on them.

Pigs appeared in Europe about 1500 BC, but the modern types with short legs and heavy bodies are the result of improved breeding during the AGRARIAN REVOLUTION. The Romans fed pigs on figs to improve their flavour, and this was a favourite recipe for stuffed sucking pig: 'Clean out the interior of pig and fill with the following stuffing. Pound an ounce of honey, pepper and wine, make it hot; break a dry biscuit into bits and mix. Stir with a twig of green laurel and boil until the whole is thickened. Fill the pig with this; skin, stop up with paper, and put it into the oven to bake.'

Since pigs produce three times more meat than other animals in proportion to what they eat, they have during the Middle Ages and later been a common food for poorer people. They were grazed in forests to eat acorns and on the common and waste land before EN-CLOSURES. Until this century bacon and pork were the usual meat of country people.

Pig meat was also liked by wealthier people because it was available fresh all the year, while other MEAT could only be got salted from the autumn to the spring. Fynes Moryson (1566–1630) said that in England 'the flesh of the hogs and swine is more savoury than in any other parts, excepting the bacon of Westphalia'. Pepys ate 'a good hog's harslet [the heart, liver and other edible offal], a piece of meat I love', and also 'some anchovies and ham of bacon'. See also BOAR.

Pike a WEAPON with a shaft about 16 feet long and sharp head, flat like the LANCE, used by foot-soldiers. The head, so that it should not be hacked off, was made with two long tongues of STEEL, nailed down the sides of the shaft. The grip was bound with cloth or leather to stop the hand slipping, and the rear end was bound with steel to prevent it splitting. Pikemen were usually placed in the centre of the line to resist cavalry charges and, if successful, win the day by charging. In the 17th century the pike was considered a more honourable weapon than the MUSKET; if a gentleman volunteered to fight on foot, he trailed 'the puissant pike'. From the end of the 17th century, the pike was replaced by the BAYONET. The pike was used in the English army from the 16th century until George II's reign, when it disappeared except as the half-pike, carried by officers as a mark of rank until the end of the 18th century.

Pilgrimages journeys made in the Middle Ages to shrines containing the relics of saints. The Seventh Council of Nicea (787) forbade the consecration of any church without a relic. The more important relics became objects of special veneration. It was believed that God made His power especially manifest at such SHRINES in the form of the forgiveness of sins and physical healing. The most important English places of pilgrimage were Canterbury (St Thomas Becket), Glastonbury (King Arthur and St Dunstan), Durham (St Cuthbert), Walsingham (the Holy House from the 11th century), Westminster (St Edward the Confessor), St Winefrede of Holywell (healing well and chapel dedicated to a Celtic maiden), St Albans, Bromholm (Holy ROOD). Pilgrimages ceased in Henry VIII's reign, and all the shrines were destroyed except that of Edward the Confessor. [D. J. Hall, *English Medieval Pilgrimage* (1966).] See also PENANCE, PILGRIMS' WAY.

Pilgrimage of Grace (1536) a rising in Lincolnshire and Yorkshire brought about by unrest caused by ENCLOSURES and partly as a protest against the DISSOLUTION OF THE MONASTERIES. The Lincolnshire rising was easily suppressed, but in Yorkshire the rebels, under a banner of the five wounds of Christ, captured York and were only put down after Henry VIII had broken promises he had given them of pardon and reform. The rising hastened the dissolution of the rest of the monasteries. [G. R. Elton, *England Under the Tudors* (1955)]

Pilgrims' Way the name given to a prehistoric (5th century BC) trackway along the southern slope of the North Downs, between Canterbury and Winchester, long thought to have been used by medieval pilgrims going to Becket's shrine in CANTERBURY CATHEDRAL. It was used by the Romans for trade and travel and in many places is still traceable. See also ROADS.

Pillory an instrument for the public punishment of criminals, consisting of a T-shaped wooden framework, with holes in the crosspiece for the head and hands of the offender, mounted on a raised platform in the MARKET-place or other frequented part of a town. Its use was ordered by statute in 1256, and it was commonly used in the Middle Ages to punish forgery, perjury and fraudulent trade practices. After 1637 it was the usual punishment for libellers and printers of unlicensed BOOKS. Persons in the pillory were often pelted by the crowd with rotten vegetables or stones and other missiles and might be injured or even killed It was abolished in Britain except for perjury in 1815 and totally abolished in 1837.

Pins have been used from early times. In the NEW STONE AGE they were used to fasten garments together and to secure and decorate the hair. The earliest known were just thorns or fishbones or made of splinters of bone or horn. Bone pins are frequently found in the BARROWS of the CELTS, and Roman pins of the same material are commonly found in London.

Later pins were made of bronze or iron wire, and they also became an item of jewellery for both sexes. Some ANGLO-SAXON pins were very elaborate. One found in a barrow at Wingham (Kent) has a stem of brass and a head of gold and is ornamented with red and blue stones and filigree work. Silver pins were made in the Middle Ages; in the 16th century there were pins with a pearl in the head, and ladies wore pins in their hair.

Until about 1626 most pins for common use were imported from France and were made of either brass or, if cheaper, iron. In 1636 the London pinmakers formed themselves into a corporation, and later Birmingham became the main centre of the industry. At first the stem and head of a pin had to be made separately, the head being made of fine wire twisted round the stem and soldered or hammered in place; 18 people, each doing a different task, were needed to make a single pin. This was changed through the development about 1830 of a machine that made headed pins from one piece of wire. Most pins today are made from steel with a thin coating of tin to keep them bright. The safety-pin came into use in 1878.

Pinfold (or Pound), an enclosure in a VILLAGE in which the pinder of the MANOR impounded stray oxen, pigs and other animals that were straying. Their owner had to redeem them by payment. Though the pinfold sometimes had access to a spring or stream, it had high walls, which are now usually ruined. Most pinfolds went out of use in the 18th century when stray animals became much less common after ENCLOSURES had shut in the fields with HEDGES.

Piscina a recess including a shallow basin set in a niche south of an ALTAR in a medieval CHURCH for washing the priest's hands and the sacred vessels used in the MASS. The earliest, in a few English parish churches and in the crypt of Gloucester Cathedral, belong to the Norman period. Above the bowl of the piscina was frequently a stone shelf for the cruets, and the bowl was usually pierced by a hole to drain the water and wine down into the consecrated earth of the churchyard. From the 13th century there were sometimes two piscinas side by side, one perhaps for the washing of the priest's hands, the other for the sacred vessels. A piscina was often enriched by a moulded arch. [Francis Bond, *The Chancel of English Churches* (1916)]

Pistol a small HAND-GUN, usually with a curved butt, held and fired in one hand. It appeared with the MATCHLOCK in the 16th century and went over to the FLINTLOCK in the next century and then to percussion detonation in the early 19th century. The use of pistols for DUELS became common in the early 18th century, and small pocket or 'carriage' pistols were carried by STAGE-COACH passengers afraid of highwaymen. The first effective revolver was invented by Samuel Colt in America in the early 19th century, and the first automatic pistol came in the 1890s.

Pit-dwellings were huts made by NEW STONE AGE people, each consisting of a round hole about four feet deep, with the earth piled round the edge and a roof of branches and mud held up by a wooden pole in the middle. These dwellings were commonly grouped together to form small VILLAGES and sometimes defended by a surrounding fence of pointed stakes.

Placard (1) an additional piece of ARMOUR worn as a breast- or back plate over or under the CUIRASS, particularly by mounted soldiers.

(2) An article of dress, often embroidered, bejewelled or trimmed with fur, worn by men and women in the 15th and 16th centuries beneath an open coat or gown. See also STOMACHER.

(3) A square piece of cardboard tied to the shoulders of a child as a punishment and bearing some such words as 'Bite-Finger-Baby', 'Lying Ananias', 'Beware a Thief', 'Idle Boy' or 'Miss Hoyden'. If a child had previously been whipped, the BIRCH-ROD might also be tied to a boy's neck or stuck in the BODICE of a girl's dress. See also DUNCE'S CAP, WHISPERING STICK, HEADBAND.

Place-names in England are mostly ANGLO-SAXON. Examples of these are names with such endings as 'ton' or 'ham' (settlement), 'wick' (farm), 'ley' or 'den' (pasture), 'worth' 'worthy' or 'cot' (village), 'hurst' (wood) and 'fold' (field). In addition, there are Anglo-Saxon versions of earlier names taken over from the CELTS, e.g. Cannock (derived from '*cuno*' 'high'), Penn (from '*pen*' 'hill') and Chatham (from '*ceto*' 'forest').

The VIKINGS introduced names with such endings as 'by' (village), 'thorp' or 'thorpe' (hamlet), 'toft' or 'thwaite' (farm), 'beck' (stream), 'forth' (fiord), 'biggin' (building) and 'fell' (mountain). They also turned the Anglo-Saxon Eoforwic into Jorvik, later York.

After the NORMAN CONQUEST, the new rulers turned Dunholm into Durham and Thornworth into Turnworth. Their own names included Blanchland, Rievaulx and Beaumont. Some of their original names became much anglicized, e.g. Belper ('*Beau Repair*', 'beautiful retreat').

Names derived from other sources include Baldock, which comes from an earlier form of Bagdad and was given by the TEMPLARS who held the MANOR there; Nelson, which was named from the Lord Nelson Inn when it came into being as an industrial town; and Peterlee, one of the NEW TOWNS, which was named after a Durham miners' leader, Peter Lee.

[E. Ekwall (ed.), *The Oxford Dictionary of English Place-Names* (1947)]

Plague occurred at intervals in England from the BLACK DEATH (1348), there being serious outbreaks in 1407, 1564, 1603, 1625 and 1647 in all of which London suffered seriously. The last serious outbreak was the Great Plague (1665), which raged from the early spring for the greater part of the year, being at its worst in September. Some 100 000 people have been estimated to have died in London, and many died in other parts of the country. The court and many people left town, and commerce was badly affected. The reason why there were only small and isolated outbreaks of Plague after this is unknown. It was not because of the GREAT FIRE OF LONDON, nor probably through the gradual replacement of the black rat by the brown rat. Modern parasitologists consider that, after three centuries, people acquired some immunity, and the bacillus itself became less virulent. [L. W. Cowie, *Plague and Fire* (1970)]

Plaid a long piece of twilled woollen cloth of various colours worn by both sexes in Scotland. Until the mid-18th century it was used as an outer garment, made of homespun wool, with the warp and weft of different colours. Thrown loosely over the shoulders or over the head, it was worn by all classes. Then silk or velvet CLOAKS became fashionable and rapidly ousted the plaid. For a while it was retained by matrons and the lower classes, but had been wholly laid aside before the end of the century.

The rural population of the HIGHLANDS wore the 'belted plaid', which was plaited and bound round the waist with a leather belt, the upper part being attached to the left shoulder. By the early 18th century the lower part had developed into the separate KILT.

Plates were largely unknown at table in the Middle Ages. For a long time most food was served on trenchers (thick slices of four-day-old BREAD), which was afterwards given to the poor or flung to the dogs. By the 14th century trenchers or platters (flat plates or dishes) made of wood or metal (often PEWTER) were beginning to come into use, and these developed into earthernware plates (see POTTERY) which became common in the 17th century. Pepys complained that at the Lord Mayor's dinner in 1663 most of the guests had 'no napkins nor change of trenchers and drank out of earthern pitchers' and ate from 'wooden dishes'. See also CUTLERY, TABLE MANNERS.

Plate-glass thick, fine-quality glass rolled out in plates, and used for MIRRORS and the windows of COACHES and SHOPS, was first made in England by Venetian craftsmen at Lambeth under the patronage of the Duke of Buckingham in 1637. In the 18th century, improvements in its manufacture devised in France made it possible to make large plates, and these improvements were adopted by the British Plate Glass Company, established in Lancashire in 1773.

Pleasure gardens or tea gardens were opened on the outskirts of London during the later 17th and the 18th centuries. They were gardens with groves and lawns and buildings in which refreshments were served. The amusements included games such as BOWLS and SKITTLES, HARP and other forms of music and FIREWORK displays. At first social reformers welcomed these gardens as better than the COCK FIGHTING and other amusements of the time, but later they became notorious as centres of gambling and disorderly conduct. Among the gardens were Marylebone (c. 1655–1776), Ranelagh (near Chelsea, 1742–1804) and Vauxhall (c. 1661–1859).

Plough originated in the NEW STONE AGE as a scratch-plough, a vertical stick dragged through the soil by a man. The first important improvement was made in the BRONZE AGE when the plough was hooked to an ox by a wooden YOKE and the ploughman followed, guiding it with a handle. The Roman wooden plough had a horizontal share or cutting edge, which was later strengthened with an IRON tip. Such a plough was drawn first in one direction and then crosswise over a square field of land and was suitable for the light, dry soils of the Mediterranean, but only for the uplands on the heavy, damp soil of northern Europe, and so in Britain ploughing was only possible in restricted areas.

In the 8th century, however, a heavy plough with a blade called a coulter was devised to dig deeper into the soil and a mouldboard, in front of the ploughshare, to turn the soil sideways and form a ridge and furrow. This was probably the first plough to turn the soil as well as loosen it, so both draining and digging the ground. To get it through the stiff soils it was often set on wheels and pulled by a team of oxen, and it ploughed a long strip rather than a square field. It required communal ownership and co-operation in the OPEN FIELD SYSTEM, which was achieved through the organization of the MANOR.

In 1803 Robert Ransome of Norwich patented a cast-iron ploughshare, the under-surface of which was hardened by rapid cooling and remained continually sharp. These were usually drawn by horses, though in the later 19th century some farmers introduced steam ploughing in which two TRACTION ENGINES placed one on either side of a field hauled the plough in turn backwards and forwards between them by means of a long steel cable wound round drums hung under the middle of their boilers. Nowadays direct haulage by TRACTORS has made multi-furrow ploughing possible.

Plough Monday the first Monday after EPIPHANY, the end of the twelve days HOLIDAY of the CHRISTMAS period. The ploughing of the spring corn field usually began on Plough Monday, and on this day boys with blackened faces, decorated with ribbons and wearing masks and cowhides, went from house to house, cracking whips, singing and dancing with swords in their hands and sometimes dragging along a PLOUGH with them. These were pagan survivals of ceremonies originally held to drive away evil spirits from the ground where the new crops were to be sown, the sword dance being a reminder of the sacrifice originally offered.

Sometimes a plough was kept within the tower arch of a parish church for use on Plough Monday, so that it could be blessed for the work it was to do on the land. The ceremony of the blessing of the plough is still performed nowadays in Chichester Cathedral.

Points were laces or strings with a tag or eyelet which were used from the 15th to the mid-17th centuries for attaching HOSE or BREECHES to the DOUBLET. It was also fashionable to use decorative points in bunches or separate bows to adorn the sleeves and other parts of male or female garments in the 16th and early 17th centuries. They were not always strong enough for their purpose—'Their points being broken, down fell their hose', wrote Shakespeare in *Henry IV*, *Part 1*. See also PETTICOAT.

Police forces began with the Metropolitan Police Act (1829) through which Sir Robert Peel founded a regular force in London. Previously law and order had been enforced by the parish CONSTABLE, the practice of HUE AND CRY and WATCH-

MEN in the towns, though about 1750 Henry Fielding, the novelist and JUSTICE OF THE PEACE, founded the Bow Street Runners, who were paid by the rewards they received as thief-takers. BOROUGHS were obliged to have police forces in 1835 and COUNTIES in 1856. The Metropolitan Police force is controlled by the Home Secretary; other forces by local watch committees; New Scotland Yard is the headquarters of the criminal investigation department of the Metropolitan Police, but may be called upon by other forces. Police boxes began in 1888 and took their final form in 1929, but most have now gone as the police are equipped with walkie-talkie radio sets.

Poll-tax a tax by the poll or head and, thus, on each person. First levied in 1222 for the CRUSADES, it became a regular tax in the later 14th century. A poll-tax imposed in 1377 and repeated in 1380 at a higher rate was an important immediate cause of the PEASANTS' REVOLT. The last poll-tax was levied in 1698.

Polonaise a dress which was worn from about 1770 to 1870 and was especially fashionable from 1770 to 1785. It consisted of a BODICE with a SKIRT bunched up behind into about three puffs and open at the front from the waist downwards to show an ornamented PETTICOAT.

Polytechnics were technical colleges for further education founded in the later 19th century mainly in London, the best-known being the Regent Street Polytechnic (1880). In 1967 to supplement the work of the TECHNOLOGICAL UNIVERSITIES, it was proposed that there should be 30 of them in all, formed either from an existing technical college or the merging of two or more colleges. They have not only students reading for degrees on full-time or 'sandwich' courses, but also others

following higher education courses below degree level and many in employment following part-time courses. They have also some students following courses or undertaking research leading to higher degrees generally related to industrial or business interests.

Pomander originally an ORANGE, stuffed with SPICES, the PERFUME of which was thought to be good against infection. Cardinal Wolsey (1471–1530) carried a 'very fair orange, whereof the meat or substance was taken out and filled up again with part of a sponge whereon was vinegar and other confection against the pestilential airs'. This was followed by metal pomanders, balls of gold or silver filled with mixed aromatic substances and carried in the pocket or worn suspended from the neck or waist. Later still this was superseded by the VINAIGRETTE.

Poor Law Act (1601) summed up 16th century legislation for the relief of the poor. The JUSTICES OF THE PEACE were to be responsible for appointing in every PARISH an Overseer of the Poor, who was to collect a poor-rate, relieve the sick and aged, bind poor children as APPRENTICES, set the able-bodied to work and punish 'sturdy beggars' and others who would not work with a WHIPPING 'on the bare back until bloody'. See also HOUSE OF CORRECTION.

Poor Law Act (1723) empowered Overseers of the Poor to establish WORKHOUSES and to deny relief to those refusing to enter them. This workhouse-test was virtually abolished by GILBERT'S ACT (1782).

Poor Law Amendment Act (1834) was passed largely as the result of the consequences of the SPEENHAMLAND SYSTEM. It transferred the administration of the poor law from about 15 000 PARISHES to 643 specially-created unions, each with a WORKHOUSE, administered by elected Boards of Guardians and centrally supervised by three Poor Law Commissioners appointed by the government. It also laid down the principle (which was much resented) that outdoor assistance was to be continued only to sick and aged paupers and no longer to the able-bodied poor, who would have to get relief by entering a workhouse, where conditions were to be such as to make any form of employment seem preferable; but this aim was never fully achieved.

The Local Government Act (1929) abolished the Boards of Guardians in favour of Public Assistance Committees of the COUNTY and county BOROUGH councils; and the introduction of PENSIONS, NATIONAL INSURANCE and the NATIONAL HEALTH SERVICE, together with the National Assistance Act (1948), providing any applicant unable to work with a weekly benefit sufficient for the minimum needs for food and shelter, have replaced the old idea of the Poor Law.

Population can only be estimated until the holding of the ten-yearly British censuses from 1801. The population of England in prehistoric times may have been—OLD STONE AGE, 3000; NEW STONE AGE, 20 000; BRONZE AGE, 100 000. The population of ROMAN BRITAIN was about 1 000 000 and of England at the time of DOMESDAY BOOK about 1 500 000. Estimates of the population of England at various times before 1801 are: 1200, 2 000 000; 1340, 4 000 000; 1400, 2 750 000 (after the BLACK DEATH); 1500, 3 500 000; 1600, 4 500 000; 1700, 5 500 000; 1750, 6 000 000. The population of Scotland was about 1 000 000 in 1700.

According to the censuses, the population of Britain was: 1801, 10 472 048; 1851, 20 185 552; 1891, 35 473 121; 1921,

42 769 196. The estimated figure for 1971 is 55 346 551. The only major country in Europe which is more crowded than England and Wales is the Netherlands.

The population of Britain began to grow markedly in the second half of the 18th century and still more rapidly in the early 19th century. This was not due mainly to a decline in mortality, since the national death rate of about 33 per 1000 only fell to about 20 per 1000 after 1810, when the population growth had passed its peak. It was due rather to an increased birth-rate brought about by younger MARRIAGES.

Porcelain the finest and hardest kind of POTTERY consisting largely of china-clay baked at a high temperature and covered with a coloured or transparent glaze, which was invented in China by the 8th century AD. By the end of the 16th century a few specimens of Chinese porcelain had reached Europe, where they were mounted in SILVER and GOLD as semi-precious stones, but imports increased in the 17th century. Italian potters mixed powdered glass with white clay to make an imitation 'softpaste' porcelain, but the secret of true 'hard-paste' porcelain was discovered in 1708 at Dresden, and near it in 1710 the first European porcelain factory was established at Meissen. China-clay and china-stone were discovered in Cornwall by William Cooksworthy, who opened the first English porcelain factory at Plymouth in 1768; and by the end of the 18th century largescale porcelain manufacture was being undertaken in Staffordshire by Spode, Minton, Davenport and other firms. Bone china (made of china-stone, china-clay and bone-ash) was started in 1805 by Josiah Spode the second.

Porch became fashionable for great country houses in the later 16th century when they were built with a symmetrical front with the storeyed porch making an E-plan, and this plan continued to be followed into the 17th century.

Most medieval CHURCHES had a single porch on the south side, and if there were two (see BACHELOR'S PORCH) that on the south side was usually the more important. Sometimes the porch was built on the north side if the MANOR house or the more populous part of the PARISH lay on that side (e.g. Witney in Oxfordshire). If there was a west porch, it might be a GALILEE. Porches were fitted with stoups, recessed basins which contained holy water into which the congregation dipped their fingers and made the sign of the cross as they entered as a reminder of their BAPTISM. Porches were also fitted with stone benches because the first part of the MARRIAGE service was performed there, and some had an upper chamber or PARVISE. [N. Lloyd, *A History of the English House* (1930); J. C. Cox and C. B. Ford, *Parish Churches* (1961)]

Port a special kind of red Portuguese WINE taking its name from Oporto. It was little known in England until the Methuen Treaty (1703), which permitted it to be imported in return for Portugal allowing the importation of English woollens. The upper classes drank it instead of the lighter French CLARETS, which also suffered from the prohibition of French imports during the wars against France. The well-known 'three-bottle-men' could drink port heavily in the 18th century because it was only after 1820 that it was as much fortified with BRANDY as it is now. [Sarah Bradford, *Port* (1970)]

Portcullis an iron-bound wooden grille, with spikes along the bottom edge, suspended by chains in front of the gate of a CASTLE and let down from an upper floor of the GATEHOUSE to the ground level when necessary, which was invented in the 13th century. It could be wound up by a windlass situated in a chamber over the gatehouse passage (e.g. the Bloody Tower, London) or could be made to act as a counterpoise to a DRAWBRIDGE, so that when the bridge was down, the portcullis was up.

Postage was derived from the organization of king's messengers, who were known as early as Henry III's reign (1207–72). Edward IV in 1482 established relays of horsemen at every 20 miles to carry despatches from London to the Scottish border at 100 miles a day (about thrice the rate of ordinary travel). In the 16th century Henry VIII appointed postmasters to provide these relays, and Elizabeth I laid down regulations for the conduct of the service, after which postmasters began to supplement their income by carrying private correspondence; and in 1635 the public were formally allowed to use the posts.

In 1680 a London merchant, William Dockwra, set up a penny post in London with 400–500 receiving offices, 7 sorting offices and up to 12 deliveries a day in some central areas; but it was opposed by James, Duke of York, to whom Charles II had granted the profits of the royal postal service, and it was taken over by the government. Subsequently local penny posts were extended to many provincial towns, but for long distances the cost was high, being calculated on the distance a letter was taken, and it was paid by the receiver.

By the 19th century, the London rate was 2d, but in 1840 Rowland Hill introduced universal penny post for the first $\frac{1}{2}$ oz. He also introduced postage stamps, which were not perforated until 1854 (see also MULREADY, VALENTINE'S DAY), and post-cards, carried for $\frac{1}{2}$d, came in 1870. Letter-boxes were introduced in 1852 and pillar-boxes in 1874.

Mail was carried by MAIL-COACHES

from 1785 to 1835, when it was transferred to the RAILWAYS; in 1838 came the first railway postal wagon for travelling sorting and the automatic collecting device. The first air mail service (between London and Paris) began in 1919.

The Post Office was made a separate corporation (instead of a government department) in 1969. It employs 97 000 postmen, who deliver mail at 15 million places.

Post-chaise a closed CARRIAGE, hired for travelling from stage to stage or drawn by horses so hired for each trip in relays between the stages, which were usually INNS. The post-chaise is said to have been introduced into England in 1664. Dr Johnson told James Boswell that if he had no duties he would spend his life 'in driving briskly in a post-chaise with an amiable woman'.

Potato was probably brought back to England by Thomas Hariot, on board Sir Francis Drake's ship, from a sojourn of the first Virginia colony on Roanoke Island in 1586. The first mention of it in print by this name occurs in 1596 in John Gerard's *Catalogue* of plants growing in his garden in Holborn. Sir Walter Raleigh probably introduced the growing of potatoes in Ireland.

Since the cultivation of the potato involved less labour and provided more food per acre than any other crop, it became a food especially eaten by the poor. By 1800 it constituted four-fifths of the food of the people of the Scottish HIGHLANDS. It used to be common for a Scottish university student to bring with him from home a bag of potatoes which provided him with much of his food during the session.

The potato did not become a staple national food in England until the 19th century, but by the early part of the century it formed the principal part of the diet of the agricultural labourer, and it remained the most important vegetable diet of the working-class throughout the century. In the 20th century the national consumption of potatoes has only gradually declined, it being 210 lb per head in 1913, 190 lb in 1938 and 180 lb in 1964. See also FISH AND CHIPS. [R. N. Salaman, *The History and Social Influence of the Potato* (1949)]

Pot-helm the typical 13th and 14th century HELMET, which was cylindrical in shape and flat-topped, not unlike a handleless saucepan. It rested on the shoulders and covered the whole head, and its front was perforated with slits to enable the wearer to breathe and see. See also ARMOUR.

Pottery objects made of fired clay, are often divided into earthenware, stoneware and PORCELAIN, according to the degree of heat used in baking. Pottery was made in England from the NEW STONE AGE (see BAG-WARE, BEAKER PEOPLE, BELGAE). Much pottery was imported into ROMAN BRITAIN from Gaul, but most was made in England, especially in the New Forest where it was hard grey stoneware with a purple glaze. For centuries after the fall of the Roman Empire, most European pottery was unglazed earthenware. A lead-glaze had been developed by the 13th century, but until the early 17th century wooden platters (see PLATES), PEWTER tankards and leather jugs (see BLACKJACK) were used more than pottery.

In the 15th century the medieval lead-glaze was replaced by an opaque white tin glaze which made painting on pottery practicable, and in the late 16th century Italian potters settled in England founding potteries in London, Bristol and Liverpool. Josiah Wedgwood (1730–95) revolutionized the making of pottery, which had hitherto been a small-scale craft, most potters employing less than a dozen workmen. In 1763 he developed his 'cream-coloured ware', which was hard white earthernware made of china-clay and china-stone (discovered not long before in Cornwall) which closely approached true porcelain, but was much cheaper; and he made it on a large scale in his new factory which he built in 1769 at a village which he called Etruria (after the ancient Italian state) between Hanley and Newcastle-under-Lyme (Staffs.), the district which has since been known as the Potteries. [Alison Kelly, *The Story of Wedgwood* (1962)]

Poultry was widely eaten during the Middle Ages and, except for PHEASANTS, was cheap, though the local price of a chicken in 1378 was 5d, which represented two days' wages for a farm labourer. By the mid-17th century poultry became something of a delicacy and more expensive. Pepys once had 'a dish of fowl, three pullets and two dozen of larks all in a dish'. The most important change in British diet since the Second World War has been the great increase in the demand for poultry, the eating of which has increased fourfold. This is partly due to the availability of cheaper and smaller birds through broiler production. See also GOOSE, MEAT.

Pounce a fine powder, such as pounded cuttle-fish bones or pumice powder mixed with sanderach resin, originally used to scour or smooth and degrease skins (i.e. PARCHMENT) to form a suitable surface for writing with a quill PEN. When PAPER became generally used, pounce made of pure powdered sanderach was now used to prevent the writing being blurred on the early paper which was virtually unglazed and deficient in size. Then cylindric pounceboxes with a perforated saucer-shaped top were used in place of the earlier one with a single outlet like a salt-pot. The wide, saucer-shaped top allowed the paper to be cupped and the valuable surplus pounce tipped back into the box for re-use after it had been sprinkled on the paper and rubbed in with the fingers. By the end of the 18th century paper had been so improved that this was no longer necessary, but because the INK stayed wet on glazed paper, a new pounce, usually powdered chalk or biotite (powdered magnesium mica) was needed as a drying agent, and pounce-boxes (or dredgers) were still used for a brief period. The adoption of BLOTTING PAPER finally ousted pounce.

Pound (1) originated from the time of the NORMAN CONQUEST when one Tower pound of silver was coined into 240 PENNIES. The sovereign (20s) was a gold coin first minted by Henry VII in 1489 and named from the representation of the enthroned monarch on it. The sovereign became a 30s piece under Edward VI and Mary. Elizabeth I minted gold SOVEREIGNS (30s) and pounds (20s). James I substituted the UNITE in 1604.

The pound Scots equalled one twelfth of an English pound (1s 8d), and it also was divided into 20 SHILLINGS, each worth one English penny. See also COINAGE.

(2) Pound was also the name given to an enclosure for stray cattle. See PINFOLD.

Prebendary a non-resident CANON of a CATHEDRAL of the 'Old Foundation', who originally drew his income from a portion of the cathedral revenues called a prebend because it furnished (*praebere*) a living to its holder. The prebend usually consisted of the revenue from one MANOR of the cathedral estates, and because of this territorial names are still attached to the prebendal stalls in many English cathedrals. In 1840 the incomes attached to all prebends were transferred to the ECCLESIASTICAL COMMISSION, and the Prebendaries have become the equivalent of the Honorary Canons in cathedrals of the 'New Foundation'.

Premonstratensians an order of regular CANONS founded in 1120 at Prémontré in France. They were also known as the Norbertines and in England as White Canons from their HABIT of white wool. They led a life of strict discipline and extreme poverty and often settled in remote places. Their earliest English house was founded at Newhouse (Lincs.) about 1143. Among their later ABBEYS in Britain were Welbeck (Notts.) and Dryburgh (Scotland).

Presbytery the eastern part of the CHANCEL of a large CHURCH or CATHEDRAL, containing the SEDILIA and other seats for the CLERGY.

Presbyterians who accepted the beliefs and system of ecclesiastical government of CALVINISM, gained control of the CHURCH OF SCOTLAND after the REFORMATION and were strong among the English PURITANS. By the early 17th century, they had many supporters among the English clergy and in Parliament, but the triumph during the COMMONWEALTH of the INDEPENDENTS prevented them getting control of the CHURCH OF ENGLAND. After the RESTORATION, they declined in strength, and in the 18th century many of their congregations became UNITARIANS. The present Presbyterian Church in England, revived in 1876, is largely Scottish in origin.

Pressure cooker devised in a simple form by Elizabethan cooks who heated stews in steam-tight bladders, but really invented by the French-born Denis Papin, who demonstrated to the ROYAL SOCIETY his 'new Digester or Engine for softening Bones' (see John Evelyn, *Diary*, April 12, 1682) and gave the members a supper cooked in it. It was a strong, heavy boiler with a steam safety-valve controlled by sliding a weight along a lever, but its high pressure necessitated fast cooking and was dangerous. About 1800 there appeared cast-iron cooking-pots with a flanged lid, secured by twisting under the retaining rim and with a conical weight fitted into a conically sealed hole at the top of the lid so that when the pressure was more than 2–3 lb the weight was raised to allow steam to escape. These, however, were heavy, and pressure cookers only became possible in the home in the 20th century with the advent of lighter ALUMINIUM and the development of resilient packing-rings to effect a steam-tight seal between the lid and the pot. A modern pressure cooker speeds up the rate of cooking to four times that of normal cooking at boiling-point.

Printing was introduced into England by William Caxton in 1476, who set up a printing-press in Westminster. At first Gothic characters were used; these were superseded by Roman letters in 1518. At first wooden presses were used, which were replaced by ones of iron by Earl Stanhope in 1798. Frederick Koenig applied STEAM POWER to printing in the early 19th century, and the first steam press was used to print *The Times* in 1814; it printed 1100 sheets an hour compared with 300 on the best hand-presses. Modern machines can produce 28 000 copies an hour of a 48-page NEWSPAPER. [R. Williams, *Communications* (1966).] See also BOOKS.

Prior normally the second in command (below the ABBOT) of a MONASTERY, but CLUNIAC monasteries (except Cluny) and the houses of AUGUSTINIAN CANONS had a prior at the head and a sub-prior beneath him. Also an offshoot (called a PRIORY) of a monastery had a prior at the head.

As second in command of a monastery, the prior's duty was to watch over its internal discipline and spiritual side. In the early days, the prior, like the abbot, ate and slept with the other MONKS, but gradually he came to have an establishment of his own, where he ate and received guests, and he had considerable interests in the outside world.

Prisons were first used mostly to detain serious offenders before trial and those sentenced to death, minor offenders suffering such summary punishments as the STOCKS, PILLORY or WHIPPING. The crown often used CASTLES, such as the TOWER OF LONDON, as prisons, while other prisons belonged to BISHOPS, BARONS and other private persons. Detention for punishment began in the HOUSES OF CORRECTION, and became a legal punishment in the 18th century, though TRANSPORTATION was a heavier punishment. See also FLEET PRISON, MARSHALSEA PRISON, NEWGATE PRISON.

By the 18th century, conditions were very bad in prisons, and agitation for reform was led by the QUAKERS, especially Elizabeth Fry (1780–1845). The Prisons Act (1791) provided for the establishment of prisons with cells, and the first model prison was built on Millbank (1812–21). Prisons were subjected to state inspection in 1835 and taken over by the state in 1877. Nevertheless, prisons remained harsh places with meagre food, hard beds and the TREADMILL.

The 20th century has brought in many reforms, including the abandonment of hard labour, the reduction of solitary confinement, the provision of libraries and the establishment (after the Second World War) of prisons without bars. [R. S. E. Hinde, *The British Penal System* (1951)]

Prize-fighting (i.e. BOXING for a prize of money) gained popularity with the decline of BEAR-BAITING and was very popular between 1795 and 1825 with all classes of people. It produced such champions as Jim Belcher, Tom Cribb and 'Gentleman Jackson', who was champion from 1795 to 1800. However, the heavy GAMBLING, brutality and crime which accompanied prize-fighting destroyed its popularity. After a few deaths in the 1820s and 1830s, the POLICE took action against it, but it persisted secretly until the great fight in 1860 between Tom Sayers and J. C. Heenan, the American champion, in Lord Palmerston's presence and for a prize of £250. [J. A. R. Pimlott, *Recreations* (1968)]

Processions were a common part of religious services in the Middle Ages, often to the singing of litanies. On Sundays and holy days there was a procession round the CHURCH before MASS to the HIGH ALTAR and ending at the GALILEE, and after Evensong to the ROOD or the FONT or the ALTAR of a saint. There were also outside processions especially on the ROGATION DAYS. In 1545 a royal injunction ordered the procession before Mass to be superseded by the LITANY from the Book of COMMON PRAYER.

Protestants (whose name came from the 'Protest' issued by the reforming princes of the Diet of Speyer in Germany in 1529) a name first given in England to those in Henry VIII's reign (1509–47) who wished to bring about in the CHURCH OF ENGLAND changes such as were taking place on the Continent. They were the successors of the LOLLARDS, and by the end of the 16th century their most extreme group were the PURITANS who had largely adopted the doctrines of CALVINISM. See also HERESY, ECCLESIASTICAL COURTS.

Province a group of DIOCESES administered by an ARCHBISHOP, so-called because such groups were originally coincident with the provinces of the Roman Empire. In England there are two provinces, Canterbury and York, each with its own CONVOCATION. The provinces are independent, but Canterbury secured the primacy in the Middle Ages and has always been larger and dominant. In 1832 the northern province had only 4 dioceses—York, Carlisle, Chester and Durham (and Sodor and Man, which is in the province, but has its own convocation); the southern had 22, including 4 Welsh dioceses, which remained until the disestablishment of the Church in Wales (1920). Today York has 14 dioceses and Canterbury 29.

Provost (1) the equivalent of a MAYOR in a Scottish BOROUGH. Edinburgh, Aberdeen, Dundee, Glasgow and Perth have lord provosts.

(2) It is also the title borne by the head of some of the new CATHEDRALS in England (instead of that of DEAN).

Psalms were said in the Middle Ages in the daily services over a week. The Book of COMMON PRAYER arranged the psalms over a month in the daily services of Mattins and Evensong. The English version of the psalms in the Prayer Book was taken from Miles Coverdale's translation of the BIBLE. When the Prayer Book was revised in 1662, although the text of the Epistles and Gospels was changed to that of the Authorised Version (1611), the psalms were left in the existing version as being 'smoother and more easy to sing'.

In both the CHURCH OF ENGLAND and the CHURCH OF SCOTLAND metrical psalms were sung, following the influence of CALVINISM. At first the 'Old Version' of Thomas Sternhold and John Hopkins (1562), originally drawn up by Marian exiles in Geneva, was used, but this was replaced in Scotland in 1650 by the version of Francis Rouse and in England by the 'New Version' of Nahum Tate and Nicholas Brady (1696), which included two psalms now sung as HYMNS—'Through all the changing scenes of life' (Ps. 34) and 'As pants the heart for cooling streams' (Ps. 42)—and paraphrases of passages from the Scriptures (e.g. 'While shepherds watched their flocks by night'). In England the adoption of HYMNS led to the abandonment of metrical psalms, but they are still sung in Scottish and other PRESBYTERIAN churches. [R. E. Prothero, *The Psalms in Human Life* (1903)]

Psaltery an early medieval triangular stringed instrument which was like a DULCIMER, but played by plucking with the fingers or a small spike of metal or ivory instead of striking with hammers. It was the forerunner of the HARPSICHORD (which had plucked strings), while the dulcimer was the forerunner of the PIANO. It was widely in use in the 14th and 15th centuries and was clearly familiar to the English translators of the BIBLE in the 16th century. See also MUSIC.

Public schools in England developed at first from GRAMMAR SCHOOLS, which succeeded from the 17th century onwards in attracting pupils from a wider area, and today about a third of the public schools are of this sort. Their teaching and discipline declined in the 18th century. Troops had to be called in to suppress a revolt at Winchester College in 1818.

Three headmasters played an especially important part in their revival in the 19th century—Samuel Butler (Shrewsbury, 1798–1836), who introduced modern subjects; Thomas Arnold (Rugby, 1828–42), who introduced the prefect system and organized games, as well as making the chapel the centre of school life and upholding the ideal of the

Christian gentleman; and Edward Thring (Uppingham, 1853–87), who introduced a gymnasium and swimming-bath, workshops and music-rooms. The revival was accompanied by the establishment of many new schools, such as the 'WOODARD SCHOOLS', for the sons of the new wealthy classes, as well as some GIRLS' SCHOOLS; and the typical school today is a mid-19th century Anglican foundation situated in a small country town. There are now about 200, mostly boarding schools, some 120 being for boys and some 80 for girls. Nearly all are in England and most in southern England. [John Rodgers, *Old Public Schools of England* (1938)]

Pulpit first became general in churches in the later Middle Ages through the FRIARS' influence. Previously the ROOD-loft was used for SERMONS. Monastic REFECTORIES also had a pulpit from which a MONK read to the rest from the Scriptures during their meals. Sometimes

Three-decker pulpit

there is a pulpit against the outside wall of a CHURCH (e.g. at Magdalen College, Oxford). After the REFORMATION, when preaching became more important, tall pulpits with large sounding-boards were built. During the 18th century, it was common for churches to have 'three-decker' pulpits—the lowest stage was occupied by the PARISH CLERK, who said the responses, the parson read the prayers in the middle one and preached from the top one. Whitby Parish Church, Yorkshire, still has such a pulpit, but few others now exist.

Pulpitum a double screen in an ABBEY church separating the CHOIR of the MONKS from the NAVE. It had a central doorway with ALTARS on either side on its west face. On great occasions, the Epistle and Gospel at the MASS were read from it, and the ORGANS were housed on it. Generally constructed of stone, it took up a whole bay of the CHURCH and had within it a staircase to reach the platform.

Punch a beverage usually composed of wine or spirits mixed with hot water or milk and flavoured with sugar, lemons and some spice or cordial, was probably brought to England in the 17th century by sailors from India, and as it became popular was generally qualified by the name of a principal ingredient (e.g. BRANDY, CLARET, MILK, RUM, TEA, WHISKY or WINE). John Evelyn had punch in 1662 on an East India Company's vessel when it was docked in London. In the 18th century it was common for a host to mix the punch himself in a bowl with his guests seated around, discussing what and what not should go in, and ladle it into glasses for them. The tenth Earl of Pembroke (1734–94) is reported to have said, 'There, gentlemen, is my champagne, my claret and other wines. I am no great judge. I give you these on the authority of my wine-merchants, but I can answer for my punch for I have made it myself'. This also became a practice in CLUBS and TAVERNS, especially in London, and sometimes to indicate this the word 'Punch-bowl' was added to the existing

INN-SIGN as may still be seen at the 'Magpie and Punch-bowl' in Bishopsgate or the 'Ship and Punch-bowl' at Wapping.

Puppets are a very old form of entertainment, being popular at medieval FAIRS and WAKES and consisting of wooden figures moved about by means of wires attached to them. Puppet-shows were often accompanied by music on the DULCIMER. Puppets were later performed in some THEATRES, Powell's Theatre, Covent Garden, London, being for a time (1710–14) a place where fashionable people went to see them, but they declined with the coming of the PANTOMIME. Punch and Judy first appeared from Italy in English puppet-shows after the RESTORATION, but did not become a glove-puppet street-show until the late 18th century.

Puritans were so-called about 1565 because they were not satisfied with the Elizabethan ecclesiastical settlement and wished to purify the CHURCH OF ENGLAND further than had so far been accomplished by the REFORMATION. Their leaders returned from exile in Geneva during Mary's reign (1553–8) and accepted the beliefs of CALVINISM. They became powerful later in the 16th century, but divided into PRESBYTERIANS and INDEPENDENTS and were opposed by the LAUDIANS. After the RESTORATION, many of them became NONCONFORMISTS.

The Puritans upheld strictness in morals and austerity in COSTUME and opposed many popular amusements. They became disliked during the COM-MONWEALTH when they sought to impose their ideas on the English people.

Purses came into being in the Middle Ages. From the 14th century onwards both men and women wore a purse, to hold money and other small objects, attached to their belt, usually in the shape of a small leather bag with draw strings at the mouth. This was often cut by thieves. In the late 16th century, women began to wear beneath their SKIRT a purse called a little poke or pocket, while men had pockets sewn into their TRUNK HOSE and from about 1570 into their BREECHES. They also had pockets in their sleeves and after about 1610 in the long-skirted COAT and WAISTCOAT which was replacing the DOUBLET. These, therefore, replaced pouches or purses for men with the exception of the Scottish SPORRAN.

From about 1800 the NAKED FASHION made RETICULES necessary for women, though pockets became more common again in Victorian times when skirts were full and stiff, but from 1909 the close-fitting tubular dress with long hobble skirt made pockets impossible. Purses were, therefore, used again and later strong, stiff handbags made necessary by increased number of objects carried by women, such as money, CIGARETTES and COSMETICS. See also COSTUME, SPORRAN.

Pyx a small round box with a conical lid in which the HOST was kept in a medieval CHURCH. It was either kept in the AUMBRY or placed in a ciborium hung above the HIGH ALTAR. The ciborium sometimes took the form of a dove over which was hung a cloth.

Q

Quakers or Society of Friends originated with George Fox (1624–91), a shoemaker, who began to preach in 1647 (exhorting people to 'tremble at the word of the Lord') and formed the first assembly in 1652. Though their interruption of church services got them into trouble, they were sufficiently tolerated under the COMMONWEALTH to be strong enough to survive the CLARENDON CODE after the RESTORATION. From the first they had no CLERGY or SACRAMENTS and no set service or HYMNS in their worship. At first they were derided as rigid PURITANS, but later gained respect for their prominence in humanitarian movements, especially for PRISON reform and the abolition of SLAVERY. [H. Brinton, *Friends for Three Hundred Years* (1953)]

Quadrant an early instrument for measuring angles in astronomy and navigation or for use as a SUNDIAL, which consisted of a wooden frame in the shape of a quarter of the circumference of a circle with a movable wooden arm for sighting the objects to be measured. In astronomy it was superseded by the TELESCOPE and in navigation by the SEXTANT.

Queen Anne's Bounty a fund formed by Queen Anne in 1704 to receive the ANNATES diverted from the Papacy to the Crown during the REFORMATION. They were henceforward to be used to augment the income of poor PARISHES of the CHURCH OF ENGLAND. In 1948 Queen Anne's Bounty was united with the ECCLESIASTICAL COMMISSION to form a new body, the Church Commission for England. [A. Savidge, *The Foundation and Early Years of Queen Anne's Bounty* (1955)]

Quern a hand-mill for grinding corn, consisting of two circular stones, the upper of which was turned by hand. It continued to be used in Britain until well after the NORMAN CONQUEST, although WATER-MILLS had already been in use for some time. In fact, its use was usually forbidden by the lord of the MANOR because it infringed his feudal right to compel his tenants to use his mill, and he might send his servants round the VILLAGE to seek out and break querns.

Quintain a target for a medieval military game of tilting with a LANCE on horseback. It consisted of an upright post with a pivoted cross-bar to one of which was fixed a board (originally a figure of an armed Saracen) and to the other a sandbag. The horseman had to ride fast enough to avoid, when he hit the board, being struck in the back by the sandbag when it swung round. By the rules of CHIVALRY, none under the rank of SQUIRE could take part in TOURNAMENTS, so YEOMEN and BURGESSES resorted to the quintain, which was open to all.

Water-quintain was popular in London during the EASTER holidays in the 14th century. A pole with a shield attached to it was set upright in the Thames, and the players tilted at it with a lance from a boat. Any player failing to hit the shield lost his balance and fell into the water.

R

Radicals a name first used about 1780 and given in the 19th and early 20th centuries to those who wanted wide social reforms. Many supported CHARTISM and became the extreme section of the Liberal party, standing for the disestablishment of the CHURCH OF ENGLAND, reforms in EDUCATION and the provision of NATIONAL INSURANCE and other benefits. By 1914 many of their aims had been achieved, and with the rise of the Labour party, Socialism took the place of Radicalism.

Radio began when Guglielmo Marconi (1874–1937), using an aerial suspended from a kite at St John's, Newfoundland, received the letter S (...) sent by his assistants from the beach at Poldhu (Cornwall) on a crude transmitter. In 1907 a public service for radio messages was opened between England and Canada; and in 1912 the radio was used in the rescue of survivors from the *Titanic*. The first transmission of speech was made across the Atlantic in September 1916. In 1921 the Marconi Co. set up an experimental station at Writtle, near Chelmsford, to broadcast to amateurs and experimenters; and in 1922 the British Broadcasting Co. was set up by six radio manufacturers. Its first broadcasts were from London, but by 1923 it had nine stations (e.g. London 2LO; Liverpool 6LV; Newcastle-upon-Tyne 5NO). King George V made his first broadcast when opening the British Empire Exhibition, Wembley, in 1924. In 1926 the British Broadcasting Corporation was set up with a monopoly to broadcast and was financed by wireless licences; the GENERAL STRIKE that year, during which the corporation broadcast news bulletins, showed the possibilities of radio. There were 80 000 wireless licences held in 1923;

2 300 000 in 1927; 8 900 000 in 1939. During the Second World War the BBC broadcast to Germany and the underground movements in occupied countries. In 1966–7 there were pirate local radio stations, but these were suppressed by Parliament, and from 1967 the BBC began to operate its own local stations.

The earliest radio sets were crystal sets, which needed no batteries or other supply of electricity, but could only be used with headphones. These were replaced by sets with valves and loudspeakers in the late 1920s, and since the 1950s these have been replaced by small transistor sets.

Ragged Schools were founded in large towns during the 19th century for the EDUCATION of destitute children, the instruction being based on the Scriptures and most of the teachers unpaid. The first was probably opened by Thomas Cranfield in South London in 1810, but they did not receive their name until 1844 when the Ragged School Union was founded with Lord Ashley (later Lord Shaftesbury) as its President. By 1884 it had 3211 voluntary workers and over 50 000 children in its classes. Its day schools were superseded soon after the ELEMENTARY EDUCATION ACT (1870), but its SUNDAY SCHOOLS continued into this century. In 1850 the Shoeblack Society was formed to enable boys to earn money by cleaning boots and shoes, part of which was paid to them as wages and part to the Union. In 1898 the Union changed its name to the Shaftesbury Society.

Railways originated in the lines of wooden rails laid down from about 1750 in northern England to enable horse-drawn trucks to take COAL from the mines to the river-quays (see also KEEL); but their growth came with the development of the STEAM LOCOMOTIVE. On the Stockton and Darlington Railway (1825) goods were carried by steam, but passengers at first were horse-drawn; the Canterbury and Whitstable Railway (1830) was mostly cable-worked; but on the Liverpool and Manchester Railway (1830) all the traffic was conveyed by steam power.

Between 1843 and 1849 the 'railway mania' brought a great outburst of investment and construction, notably by George Hudson (1800–71) in north-eastern England. By the time of the GREAT EXHIBITION, all important British towns were linked by rail with London and with each other, and the development of EXCURSIONS promoted rail travel. The Railway Act (1844) required at least one train to run daily each way along every line, carrying passengers at 1d a mile, and between 1850 and 1855 passenger traffic on the railways increased tenfold.

George Stephenson (1781–1848) adopted a gauge of 4 ft 8½ in. for his lines but Isambard Kingdom Brunel (1806–59) built the Great Western Railway with a broad gauge of 7 ft, but in 1846 Parliament fixed the narrower gauge as the standard, though the last broad gauge line was not converted until 1892.

Fixed signals came in 1830 and semaphore signals and audible fog-signals in 1841, followed soon afterwards by signal-cabins. The electric TELEGRAPH was adopted in 1839, and the first express train (between Paddington and Exeter) ran in 1849. An Act of 1868 required the establishment of means of communication between passengers and the guard or driver, and the provision of SMOKING carriages. The Westinghouse automatic brake was invented in 1872; and IRON rails were replaced by STEEL ones from the early 1870s. Sleeping-cars were introduced in 1873 and dining-cars in 1879,

while the first corridor-coaches appeared in 1890.

In 1923 Parliament grouped the 23 separate railway companies into the Big Four—the London, Midland and Scottish Railway, the London and North-Eastern Railway, the Great Western Railway and the Southern Railway. In 1904 the London, Brighton and South Coast had electrified its south London lines, and in 1933 the Southern Railway electrified the London to Brighton and Worthing line, this being the first main line in Britain to be electrified. In 1928 automatic colour signals were introduced.

In 1948 Parliament set up the nationalized British Railways, which ran its last steam train in 1968. Owing to competition from road transport, many lines have been abandoned and stations closed. In 1914 there were 23 700 miles of main track, but by 1961 only 18 000; and in 1960 the Select Committee on Nationalized Industries found that on the average three out of four seats on British Railways were left unoccupied.

Since 1960 a modernization programme has been adopted. Diesel and electric power has made possible fast 'Inter City' trains on main-line routes and new 'Liner Trains' for express freight. By 1963 there were for the first time over 500 trains travelling at more than a mile-a-minute; and the electrification of the London to Glasgow line is proceeding. [O. S. Nock, *The Railways of Britain* (2nd ed., 1962); H. Perkin, *The Age of the Railway* (1970)]

Rattle is a very old TOY. Wealthy CHILDREN in the Middle Ages had ones hung with gold or silver bells, which were called 'baubles'. Other medieval rattles were made of wicker, with bells inside, or of earthenware in the shape of birds or animals or of metal in the form of a knight's head, helmeted. Some 18th-century babies' rattles had gum-sticks of coral or agate, as may be seen in portraits of noblemen's children of the period.

Rayon a semi-synthetic fibre made out of cellulose (obtained from wood-pulp) and COTTON. It was discovered in 1892 by three English chemists; and in 1904 Courtaulds started to make it at Coventry. The greater part of rayon production is still in their hands.

Razors belonging to the late BRONZE AGE, have been found at Syon Reach on the River Thames; they are rough knives made of bronze. In the Middle Ages, the usual type of razor had a wedge-shaped blade with straight sides tapering to a sharp edge and fastened to a handle at the other end. From about 1650 the blade became convex, bulging out in a wide sweep on either side of the handle; and in the early 19th century the sides of the blade began to be ground (or hollowed out), which made it easier to sharpen the blade and improved the fineness of the cutting edge. The safety-razor originated with William S. Henson of London who in 1847 patented a razor 'the cutting blade of which is at right angles with the handle and resembles somewhat the form of a common hoe', and it had 'a comb tooth guard or protector' attached to the blade; but the safety-razor did not become general until a decade after 1901 when King C. Gillette of Boston, Mass., began to manufacture wafer-blades which were so cheap that they could be thrown away after being used several times and so did away with sharpening. This hastened the disappearance of BEARDS and MOUSTACHES. ELECTRIC razors were first manufactured in USA in the 1920s and have since become general; they are a form of dry shaving such as Samuel Pepys practised with a pumice stone in 1662.

Reaping machine originated effectively with a Scottish clergyman, Patrick Bell, in 1826. His machine consisted of two horizontal bars at the front of the reaper each bearing a row of triangular knives, the lower bar being fixed and the upper having a reciprocating motion through being geared to the ground wheels. The corn was held to the clipping knives by revolving sails and laid aside in a swath by a canvas belt on a drum. It

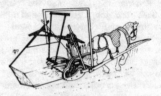

Reaping machine

was pushed from behind by a horse. In 1834 Cyrus H. McCormick, an American, built a machine with the cutting knives on one side of the horse so that it could be drawn without trampling down the corn, and a reaper of this type won a prize at the GREAT EXHIBITION (1851). Later McCormick developed a machine which not only cut and delivered the corn in swathes, but also tied it into sheaves with string.

Rebeck a very early bowed string instrument with three strings and a pear-shaped body, which was a forerunner of the VIOL. Chaucer in the 'Miller's Tale' told of a PARISH CLERK who sang in the INNS of a town and played upon a rebeck and a GUITAR. See also MUSIC.

Recorder a musical pipe played vertically by blowing a mouth-piece at the end, which was very popular during the 16th and 17th centuries. Henry VIII played it and had 76 recorders as well as 78 FLUTES. Milton in *Paradise Lost* writes of 'soft recorders', and Pepys said that the sound of the recorder was so sweet that it almost made him swoon with delight. In the 18th century the recorder began to be displaced by the flute, but in the 20th century there has been a considerable revival of its popularity. It was commonly one of the instruments of the ORCHESTRAS which played in CHURCHES before the widespread adoption of the organ.

Rector a priest in the CHURCH OF ENGLAND in charge of a PARISH, where the TITHES were not partly diverted in the Middle Ages to a monastery, college or private person. A rector was responsible for the upkeep of the CHANCEL of the parish CHURCH and the parishioners for the rest.

A 'lay rector' is a layman receiving the rectorial tithes of a parish. He has by custom the right to seats in the chancel for himself and his family and also the duty of repairing the chancel. Where there is a lay rector, the priest has the title of VICAR.

Recusants a term applied from the reign of Elizabeth I to ROMAN CATHOLICS who refused to attend the services of the CHURCH OF ENGLAND. At first the Acts of Uniformity of 1552 and 1559 imposed a fine of 1s. a Sunday. This was increased to £20 a month in 1581, and an Act of 1587 authorized the seizure of two-thirds of a defaulter's property. These laws, like the PENAL CODE as a whole, were not rigidly enforced and were relaxed in the 17th century. Except in Lancashire, recusants were a very small proportion of the population, probably less than 5 per cent.

Reeve was the local official of a lord, ranging from the king's SHERIFF to the reeve on a MANOR, who was elected by the VILLEINS from among their own number to assist the BAILIFF in organizing the farming of the DEMESNE and to see that the rest did their duties as they should, this being an unpopular post which men tried to avoid.

Refectory the dining-hall of a MONASTERY or nunnery. It had a PULPIT for reading during meals; and at the entrance to the refectory was always a basin where the MONKS could wash their hands and, close by, a recess where towels were kept. The refectory of Beaulieu Abbey, Hampshire, is used today as the parish church.

Reformation, English was political in origin, brought about by Henry VIII's replacement of papal authority by the royal supremacy over the CHURCH OF ENGLAND. The DISSOLUTION OF THE MONASTERIES, which was partly responsible for the PILGRIMAGE OF GRACE (1536), was followed by an attack on the CHANTRIES. Meanwhile, the Reformation was developing as a religious movement which had been foreshadowed by the LOLLARDS. The PROTESTANTS secured an English BIBLE and (in Edward VI's reign) the COMMON PRAYER BOOK. After a reaction in Mary's reign (1553–8), when HERETICS were burnt at SMITHFIELD and elsewhere, the Reformation was consolidated under Elizabeth I, when the PURITANS attempted to continue it further as a religious movement. [M. Powicke, *The Reformation in England* (1941); A. G. Dickens, *The English Reformation* (revised ed., 1967)]

Reformation, Scottish began with a violent popular rising in 1559, which was followed the next year by the adoption of CALVINISM and the abolition of papal authority. The Reformation was threatened by the arrival of Queen Mary, a ROMAN CATHOLIC, in 1561, but she was overthrown in 1567, and the CHURCH OF SCOTLAND became PRESBYTERIAN.

Refrigeration was invented by James Harrison in Australia in 1837, and machines to his design, made by Daniel Siebe, were shown at the International Exhibition of 1862 and were the first to be marketed. In 1882 the steamship *Strathleven* reached London with the first cargo of refrigerated MEAT. Domestic refrigerators were not much used in Britain before the 1920s.

Deep freezing was invented in 1923 in USA by Clarence Birdseye, and the first retail sales of packaged frozen foods were at Springfield (Mass.) in 1930. The sale of these foods has been increasing steadily in Britain since the Second World War, and so also has the number of home-freezers.

Refuse-collection at first did not exist in medieval TOWNS. All householders were required to dispose of their own rubbish, which they commonly did by dumping it outside the walls or into the town ditch and river. When STREET-CLEANING began the authorities hired carters to take away the filth swept up by the scavengers, and they frequently got rid of it in the same way. By 1400, however, increasing population was making such methods unpleasant. Edward III found the stench of the Thames unbearable in 1387 and urged the Mayor and Sheriff to take action, while in 1383 so much rubbish had been thrown into the Walbrook that it was stopped up 'to the great nuisance and damage of the City'. In 1388 Parliament passed an Act prohibiting the pollution of rivers, ditches and water-courses and ordering that refuse should be carried away.

Though this Act was by no means universally obeyed, a number of towns began to take measures for the better disposal of refuse. By the 16th century several had designated special places where it might be dumped, and some, including London, provided laystalls, which were heaps where householders might put their rubbish for collection by the carters. By the 18th century an increasing amount of refuse was sold to farmers and market-gardeners, who sometimes collected it themselves.

The modern system of refuse-collection began with the Public Health Act (1875), which ordered the authorities to provide for the removal of refuse from premises on appointed days and each occupier to place the refuse in a movable receptacle (or dustbin). At present refuse is used for reclaiming land, incinerated or dumped in the sea.

Regency the period in English history from 1811 to 1820 when, because of George III's illness, George, Prince of Wales, acted as Prince-Regent. It was a time of aristocratic extravagance and gaiety, before the country's mood was changed by the EVANGELICALS. The most

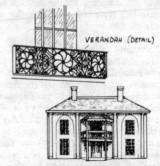

VERANDAH (DETAIL)

Regency House

obvious characteristic of Regency architecture is painted STUCCO and mass-produced ornaments, the buildings being in a simple classical style which still owed much to the RENAISSANCE. It may be seen at its best in the terraces around Regent's Park (London) and in certain streets and squares of Brighton. [R. J. White, *Life in Regency England* (1963)]

Relics the body of a saint or any part of it or objects which were in contact with his body, reverenced by Christians and the object of PILGRIMAGES in medieval England. It was held that, though the saints are in heaven, yet they care for men as much as ever, and where there is a relic of their earthly life, they will agree there to have an earthly habitation and see that God performs miracles there; and much more, Christ performs miracles for those who have relics of his earthly life, not His earthly body which is in heaven, but the Cross, the Crown of Thorns, His garments and the lance.

In western Europe the cult of relics increased particularly during the CRUSADES when numerous relics, often spurious, were brought from the Holy Land. They were kept in magnificent RELIQUARIES, carried in PROCESSIONS and widely venerated. Some were in private possession; Henry VII (1485–1509) treasured a leg of his favourite, St George; but most belonged to the great churches. In the mid-13th century York Minster had nearly 200, which included bones and pieces of clothing of apostles, martyrs, popes and bishops, stones from the Holy Sepulchre, pieces of the Cross, some of the manna which fed the Israelites and a piece of the staff of Moses.

The SHRINE of St Thomas Becket at CANTERBURY CATHEDRAL long remained the most popular in England. Canonization was not essential. The bodies of Edward II (murdered 1327) at Gloucester and Archbishop Scrope (beheaded 1405) at York immediately became popular. In the 15th century offerings at most shrines declined and by the 16th century were very small, the shrine of Our Lady of Walsingham being, however, exceptional. At the REFORMATION all relics were dispersed except the body of St Edward the Confessor (WESTMINSTER ABBEY).

Relief a feudal payment made by the heir to succeed to his predecessor's land, which technically reverted to the king or to the immediate overlord. For a long time the actual sum due was a matter of individual bargaining. William II's demands were so great that Henry I's coronation charter promised that reliefs would be 'just and lawful'. MAGNA CARTA (1215) laid down a scale—£100 for a barony, 100s for a KNIGHT'S FEE and similar sums for other units. See also HERIOT.

Religious Tract Society was founded in 1799 for the publication and dissemination of Christian literature by an equal number of NONCONFORMISTS and members of the CHURCH OF ENGLAND as a result of the EVANGELICAL revival. In 1935 it united with several similar organizations to form the United Society for Christian Literature.

Reliquary a receptacle for RELICS in a CHURCH which often became the object of PILGRIMAGES. The earliest reliquaries were in the shape of boxes, glass vessels, rings and (especially for pieces of the True Cross) crosses; they were often made of precious metals and richly decorated. The body of a saint was placed in a SHRINE or large tomb covered with silver-gilt and ornamentation during the Middle Ages, while smaller relics were kept in reliquaries in the form of arms, legs and heads.

Renaissance the intellectual movement which began in Italy in the 15th century and spread to the rest of western Europe. It was partly a revival of Greek studies (see also GRAMMAR SCHOOLS) and partly a new mood of enquiry and criticism, which influenced literature and philosophy and shaped the development of the REFORMATION. In architecture, the Renaissance had a particular influence on the design of large HOUSES, e.g. Montacute House (Somerset), Wollaton Hall (Notts.); plans became more ordered and balanced, symmetry being sought by balancing bay by bay and tower by tower, while details, such as WINDOWS, also changed.

Reredorter the latrine block of a MONASTERY, which commonly projected at right angles from the DORTER. It was a long, narrow building with a row of seats against the wall, divided by partitions and each having its own window. Beneath, walled in, was either a natural, diverted stream or an artificially cut drain with running water, the origin of many legends about secret passages in monastic ruins.

Reredos the decoration behind or above an ALTAR. The earliest sort were mural pictures painted on the wall against which the altar stood, and those in the form of a separate ornamental screen were not general before the 11th or 12th centuries. The most common type consisted of painted wooden panels fixed in the form of a triptych, i.e. arranged as shutters which could be closed to save the paintings from damage by dust or sun. Larger churches had stone reredoses with rows of statues in niches, and where there was no east window behind the altar these might cover the entire wall (e.g. New College Chapel, Oxford). Many reredoses were damaged or destroyed at the REFORMATION.

Restoration (1660) when Charles II returned to England as King and brought the COMMONWEALTH to an end. The CHURCH OF ENGLAND was restored, and the PURITANS went out of favour (see also CLARENDON CODE). There was a reaction against their strict outlook and a change in the moral and cultural direction of the country as well as a taste for luxury. This

was seen in music (see ORCHESTRA) and in FURNITURE design, together with the replacement of OAK by WALNUT. The THEATRE revived, and so did the observance of CHRISTMAS, dancing round the MAYPOLE and other traditional customs. Henceforward the propertied classes became increasingly powerful in the government of the country. See also OAK APPLE DAY.

Reticule a lady's small handbag, often lozenge-shaped or circular, of VELVET, SATIN, SILK, red morocco or made of coloured beads and drawn in with a running string, to hold HANDKERCHIEF,

Reticule

PURSE, scent-BOTTLE, etc., from about 1800 to the 1820s. It was suspended from the arm or hand by a length of ribbon, and it was made necessary by the NAKED FASHION of the period.

Revolver, see PISTOL.

Revue a theatrical entertainment seeking to give in scenes or episodes a review, often satirical, of current events and fashions. Pioneered in France, it was first introduced to the West End of London with *Rogues and Vagabonds* at the re-opening of the Empire Theatre in 1905. The craze spread and seriously challenged the MUSIC HALLS. By 1912 it was well-established with *Everybody's Doing It* at the Empire Theatre. It declined, together with the living THEATRE, upon the advent of the CINEMA. See also PANTOMIME.

Rhubarb is descended from a wild plant of Central Asia. The roots were imported from the Middle Ages onwards, being used to make tincture of rhubarb for medicinal purposes, being regarded as 'singular good for cramps and convulsions' and for reducing 'the marks remaining after stripes'. Its cultivation in England and Scotland began in the mid-18th century and was at first very profitable; in the late 1770s Edinburgh APOTHECARIES paid a guinea a pound for the root. The use of rhubarb stalks in cookery seems to have not occurred until the early 19th century.

Ridgeways tracks or ROADS used by prehistoric men to travel, generally along the watersheds of high ground (the valleys being undrained marshland), between HILL-FORTS. They may also have a religious significance as they converge from the north, south, east and west on Avebury (Wilts.), the site of the most important of the HENGES. Ridgeways are sometimes known as Green Roads because in the downland country these trackways, where not destroyed by agriculture, may still be traced as broad green roads, their turf from long trampling being finer and darker in colour than on the surrounding land. [R. H. Cox, *The Green Roads of England* (1914).] See also HARROW WAYS.

Rifle a HAND-GUN fired from the shoulder, which succeeded the smooth-bore musket. It was known in the 16th century that by rifling (i.e. making spiral grooves in) the gun barrel, a bullet could be made to spin and so keep a much straighter course, but because rifled fire-arms were harder to load than smooth-bores, though they were used by sportsmen quite early in the 17th century, they were not used generally by the British army until after the Napoleonic War (1803-15). See also CARBINE.

Ring an ancient symbol of fidelity, worn round a finger or other part of the body, e.g. the neck. Wedding-rings originated in the Roman custom of betrothal and were soon adopted by Christians. Episcopal rings are first mentioned in the 7th century and were adopted as the emblem of a BISHOP'S betrothal to the Church.

In England it was customary down to the 18th century for the bride to wear the ring on her right hand, but it has been the left hand ever since. At the beginning of the 20th century most women wore broad gold rings, and in the 1930s platinum rings were the most popular. During the Second World War, when jewellers could only use 9-carat gold, rings grew narrow and remained so even when 22 carats were allowed again, but in 1954 broad rings came back and are still popular.

Roads probably began as suitable animal tracks used by early men, but by 2000 BC trackways had been made connecting BARROWS. The best-established pre-Roman road went from Salisbury Plain to Norfolk, while the outline of one at Brierly Hill, near Broadway (Gloucs.), has been preserved. See also ICKNIELD WAY, PILGRIMS' WAY, RIDGEWAYS, HARROW WAYS, HOLLOW WAYS. The earliest roads kept for the most part to the crests of chalk hills because the low land was largely marshes and forest which could not be cleared with FLINT axes. In southeast England the chalk trackways met on

Salisbury Plain near to Stonehenge. As the country developed, routes between settled places were constructed.

In ROMAN BRITAIN a network of roads was built which traversed in straight lines the settled central and south-east England. Paved and cambered on stone causeways, these were devised at first to provide speedy transport for military needs, but by-roads were also developed for economic reasons (e.g. transporting IRON from the Weald of Kent and Sussex). See also FOSSE WAY, STANE STREET, WATLING STREET.

In the Middle Ages the main Roman highways and their dependent roads remained and were kept in sufficient repair for travellers on horseback, goods on packhorse, and to link TOWNS and VILLAGES, MARKETS and FAIRS. The men of each PARISH were obliged to work for a few days each year on the roads, and BRIDGES were built, often by private benefactors. See also GREAT NORTH ROAD.

When WAGONS and COACHES were introduced in the 16th century, the road surfaces were inadequate for such wheeled traffic and were not improved until the introduction of the TURNPIKES and the MACADAM surface in the 18th century. This made fast STAGE-COACH travel possible, but with the development of the RAILWAYS the roads were deserted and neglected until the coming of the MOTOR CAR. This has led to a growing amount of new road construction, notably the MOTORWAYS begun in the late 1950s. [S. and B. Webb, *The Story of the King's Highway* (1920); R. Devereux, *The Life of Macadam* (1936); L. T. C. Rolt, *Telford* (1957).] See also INNS, HOTELS, ROAD HOUSES, MILESTONES, CATSEYES.

Road houses elaborate INNS built in the suburbs and on arterial ROADS in the 1930s as a result of the coming of the MOTOR CAR. They provided meals and drinks, dancing and a night's lodging, to-gether with TENNIS and swimming in the summer. Every few miles on the Great West Road notices invited motorists to 'Swim, Dine and Dance', but there were also road houses, built in a contemporary concrete idiom, on the outskirts of northern industrial towns. Many had a brief existence and were shut down by 1939. A popular road house of the time was the Ace of Spades at Hook on the London–Guildford road. [J. Burnett, *Plenty and Want* (1966)]

Rocking horse a children's plaything which seems to date from the early 17th century when engravings show it as a flat-topped wooden box supported on a pair of curved rockers with a seat at the rear and a horse-head mounted in front. The 18th century brought both a simpler rocker type with the horse-head attached to a skeleton frame and also an expensive model skilfully carved and painted with a horse-hair tail and mane and perhaps even a covering of real horse-skin. In the 19th century the true rocker type was virtually superseded by the familiar horse on a stand, galloping on two pairs of parallel iron pivots.

Rod-closet a small CUPBOARD in a home or school in which the BIRCH RODS were kept. Children were commonly made to assist in their own punishment by being sent to fetch a rod from the closet and give it to the parent or teacher.

Rogation days from the Latin *rogare*, to ask, were the three days preceding Ascension Day (when the beating of the BOUNDS took place) which were set apart by the Church in the Middle Ages for prayer for the growing crops. This took the form of PROCESSIONS and litanies through the cornfields and was a Christianized version of a pagan observance. It was adopted in England in the 8th century and was suppressed in 1547, but under Elizabeth I royal injunctions of 1559 ordered the 'perambulation of the circuits of parishes' and the use of the LITANY from the Book of COMMON PRAYER.

Roller mills powered by steam, were used for grinding corn from 1835, but their rollers were of chilled iron and rapidly deteriorated. In 1870 porcelain rollers were developed, and roller mills soon spread. The first roller mill of this type in Britain was opened at Glasgow in 1872. The flour ground by roller mills was whiter and more uniform in character than that ground by old methods; between 1880 and 1910 three-quarters of the WINDMILLS and WATERMILLS in Britain became derelict. Nowadays virtually all flour used for making white BREAD is produced by rollers; mill-stones are used only in a few mills making brown and speciality flours.

Roller-skating a sudden craze in the early 1870s when the first roller-skating rinks were opened, which lost favour very quickly, mainly because the current fashion for women ordained steadily tighter SKIRTS. Eventually a fashionable dress made it impossible to skim round the rink, stoop to adjust a skate or struggle up after a fall. A second craze came in the 1910s; skirts were then gored and flared, and so this craze lasted longer. There was another craze in the mid-1920s.

Roman baths were places where people met for both washing and social conversation. Remains of public baths exist at Silchester (Hants.), Verulam (St Albans) and Aquae Sulis (Bath). Many VILLAS had baths, e.g. Folkestone (Kent) and Woodchester (Cotswolds), and so did the hostelry at Silchester. Roman baths were sweating baths, generally having a warm room, a hot-air bathroom, a hot-water bath and a cold-water bath. Heating was by HYPOCAUSTS. Massage after bathing

was normal, and there was often also a swimming-pool and a gymnasium.

Roman Britain lasted from AD 43 to about 410 and left little permanent influence on this country. The Romanized Britons depended on Roman rule and could not manage their own affairs, which made conquest by the ANGLO-SAXONS easier. The TOWNS were largely deserted except as MARKETS and the VILLAS decayed, and these had been the centre of Roman culture.

The main results of the Roman occupation, however, were the survival of the CELTIC CHURCH, the ROADS and the traditional importance of some new townsites, including London. Plants and animals introduced by the Romans include the CHERRY and the VINE, and PHEASANT and hornless SHEEP. [P. H. Blair, *Roman Britain and Early England* (1959); R. G. Collingwood and J. N. L. Myres, *Roman Britain and the English Settlements* (1937); Shepherd Frere, *Britannia* (1968)] See also HADRIAN'S WALL, PICTS and SCOTS, BLACKFRIARS BARGE, FISHBOURNE.

Roman Catholics from Elizabeth I's reign were subject to a PENAL CODE, which especially punished those who were RECUSANTS. Their numbers declined, and by the 18th century they survived largely among some aristocratic and gentry families. Attempts to grant them more toleration resulted in the GORDON RIOTS (1780). During the 19th century, their numbers increased, partly through conversions among the TRACTARIANS and still more as the result of IRISH immigration into Britain. [E. I. Watkin, *Roman Catholicism in England* (1957)]

Romantic Movement was primarily a literary and philosophical movement, which owed much to French and German influence, and also a development in taste taking place during the first 30 or 40 years of the 19th century. It was partly a reaction against the orderly, planned classicism of the RENAISSANCE. Its effect was shown in several aspects of social life. Since the Romantics were interested in solitary man and wild nature, it led to naturalistic, informal designs in GARDENS, the building of FOLLIES and the employment of HERMITS, while in architecture it assisted the GOTHIC revival; and in COSTUME it inspired the naturalness and simplicity of the NAKED FASHION.

Rood the cross of Christ, especially the great crucifix which, in medieval CHURCHES, often stood on the rood-loft, a gallery above the wooden or stone carved screen in the chancel-arch and separating the CHANCEL from the NAVE. This crucifix was sometimes flanked by statues of St John and the Virgin Mary. In greater

Rood

churches, the priest read the Epistle and Gospel of the MASS from the rood-loft.

The roods and most rood-lofts were destroyed during the REFORMATION, but many screens remain, and even when the screen has disappeared, the steps and doorway leading to the loft may often be seen in the wall beside the chancel-arch. See also JUBE, GALLERY.

Rosemary an important HERB, described by Culpeper as used 'not only for physical but civil purposes'. Having a pungent taste, it was taken to cure colds, assist digestion and help weak memories. It was also smoked in a pipe to relieve 'any cough or consumption'. Being a fragrant shrub, it was used with other evergreens to decorate churches at CHRISTMAS and (as an emblem of fidelity) at weddings and (as an emblem of remembrance) at funerals. According to Ben Jonson it was customary also to present the bridegroom with 'a bunch of rosemary, bound with ribands' on his first appearance on his wedding morning; and sprigs of it were distributed to mourners at a funeral before they left the house to carry to the churchyard and throw on the coffin when it was lowered into the grave. See also BRIDE-LACE.

Rosewood the name given to several kinds of valuable close-grained, fragrant wood of dark blackish-brown colour from Brazilian and Indian trees. It was known in England from the 17th century, being used sometimes as inlay and veneer and often in the solid for FURNITURE during the REGENCY period, when it temporarily displaced SATINWOOD in popularity.

Rotation of crops superseded the old OPEN-FIELD SYSTEM of farming during the AGRARIAN REVOLUTION in England and stimulated the carrying out of ENCLOSURES. The rotation of crops, in which corn and roots were sown in alternate years, meant that none of the land needed a fallow year, since the crops used different depths of soil—the corn, being fibrous rooted, drawing its nourishment from the top soil, while the root crops drew theirs from the lower by long tap roots. It also meant that most of the cattle no longer had to be slaughtered each autumn, but could be fed with TURNIPS in the winter. This system was of Dutch origin and was first practised in north-western Norfolk in the closing years of the 17th century.

Roundabouts were at first in the 18th century simply a horizontal wheel or frame furnished with small wooden seats propelled by a man who stood in the centre and turned a capstan. By 1860 STEAM POWER had been introduced and was soon followed by an ingenious arrangement of cams which gave a rising and falling motion as the roundabout rotated, while steam organs blared out popular tunes at the FAIRS. Elaborately decorated horses and cars, ostriches and cockerels replaced the simple seats, and the roundabouts themselves were brightly coloured. From 1885 showmen's TRAC-TION-ENGINES not only hauled the dis-mantled amusement machinery on trucks from fair to fair, but also drove dynamos to produce electricity to provide light and power for it.

Round towers high circular towers of stone with a conical roof and massive walls, built between the 9th and 12th cen-turies as belfries and also probably as lookouts and refuges from the VIKINGS, the door being usually about 12 ft from the ground. They are numerous in Ire-land, and three remain in Scotland, in-cluding that at Brechin which is attached to the church.

Royal a gold coin issued by Edward the Black Prince for Aquitaine in 1364, showing the prince seated under a canopy on the obverse. In 1465 Edward IV issued the first English royal, which replaced the NOBLE and was worth 10s. On the reverse it had a rose in a sun with rays and so was also called a 'rose noble'. The minting of royals ceased by 1470, but was tempor-arily revived by Henry VII. See also COINAGE.

Royal Society was founded in London in 1660 by a group of prominent men in-terested in experimental science. Charles II granted it a royal charter in 1662 defin-ing its purpose as 'the promotion of natural knowledge'. Among its early members were Robert Boyle, the chemist, Samuel Pepys, the diarist, Christopher Wren, the architect, and Robert Hooke, the physicist. Isaac Newton was its 13th President from 1703 to 1727. It has had a longer continuous existence than any other academy of sciences in the world.

Royal Society for the Prevention of Cruelty to Animals was founded in 1824, being the first such society in any country, and was followed by the Scottish society in 1839. Their efforts secured the passing of the first acts for the prevention and punishment of cruelty to animals in the 19th century, which were consolidated by the Protection of Animals Act (1911) and has been followed by further acts in this century.

Ruff a wide white circular collar of fine LINEN or MUSLIN in the form of a frill, stitched, folded and starched and often stiffened with wire, worn fitting close to the neck by men, women and children. It originated in the mid-16th century in Spain and was worn generally in western Europe for about a century. Queen Eliza-beth I's ruffs were masterpieces made by a Flemish woman especially invited to London, while those of the men at her court became so extravagant in size and form that one type was known as 'three steps and a half to the gallows'. See also COSTUME, GOFFERING-TONGS, STARCH.

Rule the way of life laid down for a monastic order. The most numerous order of MONKS in medieval England were the BENEDICTINES, and their rule was the basis of that of other orders except the

CARTHUSIANS. It required complete obedience by the monks to their ABBOT, who was elected by vote, residence in one place and the holding of possessions in common.

The main task of the monks was declared to be the performance of the daily services, work, study and prayer, and the way in which this was to be done was laid down. The monks' day began shortly after midnight, when they went to their church for Matins. Then they returned to their DORTER until they rose again at dawn for Lauds, which was followed immediately by Prime. Breakfast of a little bread and ale in the REFECTORY was followed by MASS and the daily meeting in the CHAPTER HOUSE (see also PENANCE). The next three services were Terce at 9 a.m., Sext at noon and Nones at 3 p.m., after which the monks had their main meal of soup, vegetables, fish and sometimes meat. Between the services they worked for about five or six hours, some in the fields, some studying in their CARRELS and some in the SCRIPTORIUM. They had a short period for recreation before the service of Vespers at 6 p.m. or earlier in winter, which was followed by a light supper. The day ended with the final service of Compline, and the monks went to bed at about 8 or 9 p.m. The events of the day were marked by the ringing of BELLS, either the small bells of the dorter, refectory, chapter house and church or the greater bells of the tower. There were differences in the daily life between individual MONASTERIES, and other orders (e.g. CLUNIACS and CISTERCIANS) had their own variations. [D. Knowles, *The Monastic Order in England* (1930)]

Rum a spirit distilled chiefly in the West Indies from fermented juice of the sugar cane or from molasses. It is said to have been first distilled about 1640 by the planters in Barbados, which was first colonized by the English in 1625. A 17th century writer said, 'Sugar canes distill a hot, hellish and terrible liquor called rum.' It was served to sailors in the British navy from the 17th century. See also GROG.

Running footman employed in the 18th century by noblemen, in the days of bad ROADS to run ahead of his master's COACH to prepare an INN to receive him. Their employers also used running footmen to run messages and arranged running-matches in which each wagered his own man to win. Running footmen sometimes wore the family livery, but more often a velvet cap (sometimes with a tassel), a white jacket and a coloured sash round the neck. As roads were improved, they became fewer, the last one being probably employed by the fourth Duke of Queensberry who died in 1810.

Rural Dean the head of a group of PARISHES in a DIOCESE of the CHURCH OF ENGLAND, appointed by the BISHOP. The office was introduced into England after the NORMAN CONQUEST, when the Rural Dean had his own ECCLESIASTICAL COURT; but in the 13th century his functions were taken over by the ARCHDEACON. The office was revived from 1836, and nowadays the rural dean acts as an important means of communication between the bishop and the parishes in his Rural Deanery. He also presides over the Ruridecanal Chapter, consisting of the clergy in the Deanery.

Rushes were strewn on the floor in HOUSES before CARPETS were used. In some parts of the country, the WAKE or festival of the dedication of a CHURCH was celebrated by rush-bearing, when the parishioners used to strew the church with rushes, ROSEMARY and other sweet-smelling HERBS. See also THATCH.

Rushlights, see CANDLES.

Russet a coarse homespun cloth, reddish-brown or grey in colour, worn by the poorer classes in the 15th–17th centuries. The Elizabethan *Homilies* (for the clergy to read in church) contrasted those who 'wear a russet coat' with the man who 'ruffleth in silk and velvets', and at Newcastle-upon-Tyne 'thick grey russets' were provided as 'the most suitable and warm kind of clothing for the poor'. William Kemp on his dance from London to Norwich in 1600 was accompanied part of the way by a village maiden in 'her russet petticoat'; and Oliver Cromwell in 1643 said he preferred 'a plain russet-coated captain' for the New Model Army.

Rye a relatively recent and very hardy cereal crop, which probably originated in Asia. It will grow on very poor soil and tolerate low winter temperatures. It has never been grown much in England, except on the sandy soils of East Anglia, but was formerly used for making BREAD.

S

Sack an old name for various sorts of dry, SHERRY-type WINES, the best of which came from Jerez (Spain), but there was also Canary sack from Tenerife. Sack was the fashionable drink of the gentry in Tudor England, taking the place of home-brewed ALE among the people. Shakespeare mentioned CLARET only once, but sack more than fifty times in his plays. It was quite common to put SUGAR in it—'Sir John Sack' and 'Sugar' is one of Poins's names for Falstaff. 'Burnt sack', ordered by Ford at the Garter Inn when he called on Falstaff in disguise, was a hot drink of sack with sugar added. [C. Clark, *Shakespeare and Home Life* (1935).]

Sacraments are (in the words of the COMMON PRAYER BOOK) 'an outward and visible sign of an inward and spiritual grace'. In the medieval Church and the ROMAN CATHOLIC Church, these number seven, being in addition to BAPTISM and the MASS, confirmation, penance, extreme unction, holy orders and matrimony. The CHURCH OF ENGLAND after the REFORMA-TION distinguished the first two 'as ordained of Christ in the Gospel' from the other five 'commonly called Sacraments'.

Saddle like the STIRRUP, was unknown to the Romans. It was in use in the 3rd century and mentioned as made of leather in 304. It was known in England about 600, and the BAYEUX TAPESTRY depicts the high war-saddle, with a saddle-cloth, which seems to have been used in Europe from about the mid-9th century. Side-saddles for ladies were introduced into England by Anne, Richard II's queen, in 1388.

Safety-lamp was invented in 1816 by Sir Humphry Davy (1778–1829) for use in COAL mines. He enclosed the flame of the lamp in a cage of fine-meshed wire which allowed the air to enter and promote burning, but also conducted away the heat generated in combustion so that no product of combustion escaped at a temperature high enough to ignite the explosive gases in a mine.

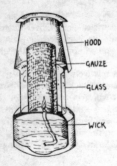

Cut away view of a Safety Lamp

Saffron the most important, although the most costly, of medieval HERBS. It was made from the saffron crocus; only the stigmas of the flowers were used, and about 75 000 flowers were needed to make a pound of saffron. Originally coming from the East, the flower was acclimatized in Spain by the 10th century, and the herb was exported to England by the 13th century. It was used in many medieval sauces; and in the 15th century the main centre of cultivation in England was Saffron Walden (Essex).

St Paul's Cathedral is the third CATHEDRAL on the site, where there was probably, in Roman times, a temple dedicated to the goddess Diana in the FORUM, which became a place of worship of the BRITISH CHURCH. St Melitus, consecrated Bishop of London in 604, is said to have founded the first cathedral, dedicated to St Paul, which was burnt in 1086 and was followed by the second cathedral, commonly known as Old St Paul's. This was ruined in the GREAT FIRE OF LONDON (1666) and replaced by the present cathedral designed by Sir Christopher Wren. Its foundation stone was laid in 1675 and the structure completed in 1710. The central feature is a dome, crowned by a cupola and a lantern with a golden ball and cross. See also PAUL'S CROSS, PAUL'S

WALK. [A. E. Henderson, *St Paul's Cathedral, Then and Now* (1951)]

Salisbury Cathedral is the only English CATHEDRAL to have been built in a single style of GOTHIC architecture. It was built throughout in the Early English style during the 13th century. Since CANTERBURY CATHEDRAL was monastic and followed the BENEDICTINE use in its services, Salisbury Cathedral, which was secular, set the pattern in its Sarum Use for the services in English churches until the coming of the COMMON PRAYER BOOK at the REFORMATION.

Saloon, Salon was the large state room of a great country HOUSE in which important guests were entertained and receptions were held. It was usually a spacious and elegant room, a fine example being the saloon, finished in 1731, at Houghton Hall (Norfolk), which is decorated predominantly in gold and crimson, marble and mahogany. See also DRAWING ROOM.

Salt was used in large quantities in medieval households for preserving MEAT and FISH. It was bought by the quarter or the bushel, sometimes from the famous saltpans of the Bay of Bourgneuf, near the Island of Oléron off the west coast of France ('Bay salt'), but mostly from English salt-mines (e.g. in Worcestershire or Cheshire) or coastal salt-works relying on the principle of evaporation as at Maldon. The price of salt fluctuated with the amount of sunshine each year, a wet year making it expensive.

At medieval feasts the family saltcellar of massive SILVER was placed in the middle of the TABLE. Persons of distinction sat 'above the salt', i.e. between it and the head of the table, while dependents and inferior guests sat below it.

In many parts of England there are ROADS known as 'Salt Ways', along which salt was transported from the coastal and other centres of production.

Salvation Army was founded by William Booth (1829–1912) as the Christian Revival Association in Whitechapel in 1865 and received its present form and title in 1878, being organized on military lines with a 'General' at its head. Booth nominated as his successor in the generalship his son, William Bramwell Booth, but since 1931 the General has been elected by a High Council of leading officers. Booth required 'unquestioning obedience' and self-denial from all its members. He said, 'I like my religion as I like my tea—hot', and insisted upon conversions sought by emotional preaching and public testimony. He also did not see why 'the devil should have all the best tunes', and instituted open-air meetings with BANDS and banners. He rejected the SACRAMENTS and emphasized the moral aspect of Christianity.

The Salvation Army has become increasingly engaged in social activities, which include rescue work, soup kitchens, orphanages, tramps' hostels and night shelters. The weekly *War Cry* is its major publication. The Salvation Army is now an international organization, being particularly strong in the USA. It has training colleges in many countries and its headquarters in London. [R. Sandall, *The History of the Salvation Army* (3 vols., 1947–55).] See also CHURCH ARMY.

Sanctuary was a right recognized as existing in all churches from Anglo-Saxon times. A person taking refuge under this right had within 40 days to take an oath that he would leave the country before a CORONER; the latter named a seaport to which he had to proceed. Sometimes those seeking sanctuary had to touch a particular object in a church (e.g. the sanctuary-stool or 'frith-stool' at Hexham and the sanctuary-knocker at Durham). Special sanctuaries created by royal grant (e.g. the great LIBERTIES of Beverley, Durham, Tynemouth and Ripon) gave permanent sanctuary.

In 1486 the judges decided that sanctuary did not extend to treason and second offences, and the Church never recognized it for sacrilege. Under Henry VIII the privilege of sanctuary was drastically curtailed, and in 1540 eight cities of refuge, on the scriptural model, were appointed (Wells, Westminster, Northampton, Norwich, York, Derby, Manchester, Lancaster), which allowed some sanctuary to debtors. A petition from Manchester against its nomination led to its replacement by Chester. In 1623 sanctuary for criminals was finally abolished and in 1727 for civil offenders. [Christina Hole, *English Shrines and Sanctuaries* (1954)]

Sandals consisting of a sole attached to the foot by thongs, were worn from ancient times until the development of BOOTS AND SHOES. In the Middle Ages they were worn by MONKS, FRIARS and NUNS and by those who went on PILGRIMAGES. In the 18th century ladies, especially if they wore PATTENS outside, changed into 'party-sandals' or 'sandal-shoes' (which had low heels) for indoor and evening wear.

Sandwich may have derived its name from John Montagu, fourth Earl of Sandwich (1718–92), who is said to have had slices of cold beef placed between slices of toast brought to the gaming table to enable him to go on playing CARDS without leaving off for a meal.

Sanitation became a serious problem with the growth of large TOWNS in consequence of the INDUSTRIAL REVOLUTION, when there were outbreaks of CHOLERA especially in the SLUMS. Following the outbreak of 1848, the Public Health Act established a Board of Health, which could set up local sanitary boards where they were wanted, but it was abolished in 1854. The Public Health Act (1875) gave town councils the task of maintaining sewerage and drainage and of REFUSE-COLLECTION. The WATER-SUPPLY was to be controlled by local authorities, who were to ensure its purity. All local councils had to appoint Medical Officers of Health, who were empowered to disinfect premises where those who contracted infectious diseases lived and to examine food. The Public Health Act (1891) required local authorities to provide for STREET-CLEANING.

Satin a cloth of twilled SILK used from the Middle Ages onwards. In such a cloth an appearance of diagonal parallel lines is obtained by passing the weft-threads over one and under two or more (not one as in plain WEAVING) warp-threads. While the back of satin is dull, the surface has been made smooth and glossy by the application of heat.

Satinwood an ornamental wood from the East and West Indies, hard, light-coloured and with a smooth, satiny surface. From the late 18th century, it was used both as veneer and inlay and in the solid for FURNITURE. During the REGENCY period, it was temporarily supplanted in fashion by ROSEWOOD, but later became popular again.

Savings-bank is said to have originated with Joseph Smith, Vicar of Wendover (Bucks.), who in 1799 with two of his parishioners offered to receive from any poor person a sum of 2d upwards to be returned at Christmas with one-third added to the deposit. In 1804 Mrs Priscilla Wakefield of Tottenham with six gentlemen stated they would pay 5 per cent interest on all sums over £1 left

more than a year in their hands; and in 1808 in Bath eight residents, four of whom were ladies, accepted the savings of SERVANTS on which they paid 4 per cent interest. These schemes, however, were anticipatory and were not publicized. The first organized savings-bank was the Parish Bank Friendly Society established in 1810 by Henry Duncan, Minister of Ruthwell (Dumfriesshire); his published account of it led to its imitation elsewhere. By 1817 some 70 savings-banks had been founded. The Post Office Savings Bank was founded in 1861. It is now the National Savings Bank.

Saw-pits were used until the late 19th century for sawing up heavy timber. A long saw was worked by a top-sawyer on a platform at the top and by a bottom-sawyer in the pit. Such pits were not in woods or forests, but outside local joiners' or wheelwrights' shops or in the yards of large houses or estates to which the trees were taken. When the sawing was completed, the timber was stored, with the cut ends protected by a covering of cow-dung, and seasoned in the open for from four to ten years. [George Sturt, *The Wheelwright's Shop* (1923)]

School uniform began when schools for poor children provided their pupils with clothes suitable for their station in life, and such school uniforms were based upon the ordinary dress of poor children at the time. Christ's Hospital in London (founded by Edward VI in 1552) and similar schools dressed their boys in a long BLUE COAT with white bands at the neck and girded at the waist with a leather belt together with yellow stockings and a little black cap. From the late 17th century, CHARITY SCHOOLS put their children into distinctive clothes. The girls wore plain dresses, woollen stockings, white aprons, long mittens and when out-of-doors large round cloaks with tight-fitting hoods and wash-leather gloves, and their hair was cropped short. The boys wore long coats with bands (a pair of white linen strips at the neck), leather breeches, woollen stockings and a small woollen cap. Some of these schools took their name from the colour of the clothes worn by their children, such as the Red Maids of Bristol or the Greycoat Hospital in Westminster.

Late in the 18th century other schools began also to adopt uniform clothes for their pupils. These, too, were based upon contemporary fashions for children. This was true of the ETON SUIT, which was widely imitated; its white COLLAR, for

(*left*) 18th-cent. charity school uniform;
(*right*) Early 20th-cent. school uniform

instance, came from the turn-over collar of REGENCY days. Boys of other schools wore coats with skirts cut back from the waist and brass buttons, peg-top trousers (i.e. wide at the hips and narrow at the ankles) and a cap or mortar-board. In the mid-19th century boys began to wear TOP HATS on Sundays; and about 1860 BOATERS and school caps were introduced and also lounge suits and jackets with knickerbockers. In the 20th century the usual uniform became grey flannel trousers, a coloured BLAZER and a distinctive cap.

At GIRLS' SCHOOLS in the 1860s the pupils wore CRINOLINES and tight STAYS. The two great reformers in the education of girls, Miss Dorothea Beale (in 1864) and Miss Frances Buss (in 1872) also changed their schools' clothes. Pinafores were worn in class and serge tunics over knickerbockers for games, but their school clothes still followed prevailing fashions (e.g. schoolgirls wore BUSTLES in the 1880s). By the end of the 1890s girls usually wore a white blouse, dark, ankle-length skirt and black stockings. In the first part of the 20th century a common uniform was a skirt or gym tunic and blouse in winter and a dress in summer.

The wearing of school uniforms in both boys' and girls' schools is now declining. See also CHILDREN'S COSTUME.

Scouts, see BOY SCOUTS.

Scriptorium the room in a MONASTERY set apart for the writing or copying of manuscripts by the MONKS who acted as scribes. They sat or occasionally stood at sloping desks. The monks of Winchester Cathedral were famous for the illuminated manuscripts they produced.

Scurvy a disease caused by a diet lacking vitamin C, which is found in fresh vegetables and fruit and results in attacks of bleeding from the gums and internally that may cause death. Sailors on long voyages used particularly to suffer from it. The British navy lost more men at sea from it during the wars of 1739–48 than in battle.

A Scottish physician, James Lind (1736–1812), suggested in 1754 the use of green food, fresh fruit and lime juice as preventatives. The plan was adopted by enlightened navigators, especially Captain James Cook (1728–79), who by insisting upon such a diet for his company of 118 men in his voyage of 1772–5 lost only one man from the disease during more than three years. Finally, in 1795 the Admiralty ordered rations of lime juice to be served at sea, and scurvy disappeared. See also SODA WATER.

Scutage was a tax paid to the crown instead of KNIGHT service. It probably developed soon after the NORMAN CONQUEST, and from Henry II's reign (1154–89) any TENANT-IN-CHIEF could arrange with the king to pay 40s for each KNIGHT'S FEE whenever the feudal host was summoned, recouping himself from his own sub-tenants. With the decline of FEUDALISM, it fell into abeyance and was last levied in 1327. See also MAGNA CARTA.

Scythe an agricultural cutting implement used for mowing or reaping, consisting of a long, thin, slightly curved blade with a long, crooked handle set nearly at a right angle to it, and held in use by two projecting handles, called nebs, fixed to the principal handle, so as to be plied with a long, swinging stroke employing both hands. It was used to keep lawns trim before the invention of the LAWN-MOWER. See also SICKLE, REAPING MACHINE.

Seaside had little attraction for people until the mid-18th century. The fashionable resorts were the inland SPAS. Dr Richard Russell's *Dissertation on the Use of Sea-Water* (1752) popularized Brighton (where he lived) which soon had a COFFEE-HOUSE and ASSEMBLY ROOMS. George III made Weymouth known, Londoners went to Margate, at first going down the river by ship. The seaside was patronized mainly by the upper classes until 1830 and by the middle classes up to 1880. The resorts became places, not only for BATHING, but also for such amusements and activities as THEATRES, MUSIC-HALLS, NIGGER MINSTRELS and PIERS. [Ruth Manning-Sanders, *Seaside England* (1951); Osbert Sitwell and Margaret Barton, *Brighton* (1948)]

Sedan-chair a portable, covered-in chair for one person, usually carried on poles by two men, with a hinged door at the front. The first seen in England was a gift from Prince Charles (later Charles I) to the Duke of Buckingham in 1623, and in 1649 Charles was 'hurried away from the Bar into a Common Sedan' after his trial in Westminster Hall. They became popular in all large towns because they eased the congestion on the streets, were cheap and needed no stables or coach-house.

In 1634 Sir Sanders Duncombe was granted a licence to hire out 50 sedan-chairs in London and Westminster. According to John Evelyn in 1645 these early chairs came from Naples. In the 18th century such hackney sedans were

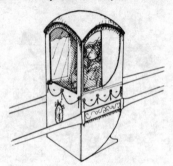

Sedan chair

numerous and plied for hire at public stands usually near COFFEE houses, the best known being in St James's Street and at Covent Garden, Charing Cross and Temple Bar. By 1821, however, only the St James's Street stand survived.

Wealthy people also had private sedans, and one reason why their town houses had imposing entrance halls was because the sedans (with poles up-ended) were stored there. Peers and peeresses had to come to the coronation of William and Mary in 1689 in sedans, horse-drawn coaches and carriages being forbidden to approach WESTMINSTER ABBEY, and as late as the coronation of George IV in 1820, the King was carried from St James's Palace to the Abbey in a sedan-chair. INNS in towns also had sedan-chairs, particularly for customers who had drunk too much.

Sedilia the seats for the three clergy officiating at a high MASS, the priest (celebrant), deacon (gospeller) and sub-deacon (epistler), in a larger CHURCH on the south side of the CHANCEL, westward of the PISCINA. They were introduced into England about the 12th century, being usually stone benches recessed into niches in the wall and often richly carved and surmounted by arches or canopies. Sometimes (e.g. at Maidstone) there was a fourth seat for the PARISH CLERK. [Francis Bond, *The Chancel of English Churches* (1916)]

Seed-drill originated effectively with Jethro Tull in about 1701. He saw that the farmer could weed and also aerate the soil round the growing plants if the seed were sown in rows instead of scattered broadcast by hand. It was not until the 1800s, however, that drilling was practised much in England; and Thomas Hardy mentioned the horse-drill as being a novelty at Casterbridge (Dorchester) as late as about 1846. See also SOWING.

Serf, see VILLEIN.

Sermons since the main duty of the CLERGY was to celebrate the MASS, were not frequent in the Middle Ages until the coming of the FRIARS, whose churches had PULPITS and wide AISLES to accommodate large congregations. Preaching became more important at the REFORMATION, especially among the PURITANS whose influence owed much to the ability as preachers. 'What won them most repute was their ministers' painful preaching in populous places; it being observed in England that those who hold the helm of the pulpit always steer people's hearts as

they please' (Thomas Fuller, 1655). Modern preaching began with John Tillotson, Archbishop of Canterbury 1691–4 and a prominent LATITUDINARIAN, whose sermons were plain, straightforward and moral. John Wesley (see also FIELD PREACHING, METHODISTS) preached fifteen sermons a week to audiences of between 10 000 and 20 000. Sermons used to be much longer than they are nowadays as may be seen from the HOUR-GLASS still to be found in some churches. [Charles Smyth, *The Art of Preaching in the Church of England 747–1939* (1940)]

Servants in Roman VILLAS were often SLAVES and in medieval MANORS often VILLEINS, but as serfdom disappeared, they were paid wages. Medieval WIVES were urged to treat their servants fairly and not allow them to idle; but they were allowed home on MOTHERING SUNDAY, and on HOLIDAYS the maidservants, after evening prayers, might dance in the presence of their master and mistress to the accompaniment of the TIMBREL, and the best dancers were rewarded with garlands. Wealthy medieval families also sent their CHILDREN to be PAGES and DAMSELS in noble households.

Medieval servants were liable to be punished by WHIPPING, and this practice long continued. Adam Eyre, a Yorkshire gentleman, recorded in his diary in 1647 how he punished a maidservant: 'This night I whipped Jane for her foolishness as yesterday I had done for her slothfulness'; and William Cole, Rector of Bletchley (Bucks.), stated in 1766 that his boy, Tom, was 'horse-whipped pretty smartly' for going nutting instead of fetching the letters.

In Stuart times a quarter to a third of the families contained servants, while in the rich London parishes of the 1690s nearly a third of the population were servants. A boy or girl born in a COTTAGE usually left home for service at 10–12 years, though sometimes it might be only 8–9 years. They remained servants until they married, being often as much a part of the FAMILY as the children. Their wages were fixed by the JUSTICES OF THE PEACE, and maidservants were often engaged as APPRENTICES. Servants were commonly engaged at HIRING AND MOP FAIRS.

The growing prosperity of the upper and middle classes in the TOWNS of the 18th century enabled them to have more servants, and some 10–15 per cent of the population was in service. The men slept in the cellar of the town-house, the women in the garret, though servant-girls still sometimes had TRUCKLE BEDS downstairs. NEGRO SERVANTS and FOOTMEN became popular with the rich. Such menservants wore liveries, but maidservants did not wear uniform until the early 19th century. Leigh Hunt described it in 1820: 'Her ordinary dress is black stockings, a stuff gown, a cap and a neck handkerchief primed cornerwise. On Sundays and holidays, and perhaps of afternoons, she changes her black stockings for white, puts on a gown of better texture and fine pattern.'

Victorian prosperity allowed even middle-class families to have an abundance of servants. An upper-middle-class family might have a butler (and probably a footman), a lady's maid, cook, kitchenmaid (and probably a scullery maid) and a laundrymaid. Even the poorest clergyman's wife had a cook and a servant-girl, while her husband employed a man to look after the garden and his horse. A 19th-century nobleman employed 20–100 indoor and outdoor servants in his great house.

In 1851, one in nine of all females over the age of 10 were domestic servants. A young girl started as a kitchen-maid; then she became a still-room maid (making TEA, COFFEE and CHOCOLATE and also biscuits, jams, preserves and cordials) or a PARLOUR maid (looking after the china and serving at table) or a chamber-maid (making the beds and repairing the linen); next she might become a cook; and the best post she could hope for was to be the housekeeper in a large establishment.

In 1901 domestic service was the major occupation of all employed women in the country, there being 1½ million servants among 4 million women at work. By the 1930s this number had halved; and in 1951 the number of women in offices reached exactly the number of domestic servants in 1900. In 1963 there were 22 800 men (including about 600 butlers) and 217 400 women in private domestic service (including daily helps and gardeners). See also AU PAIR GIRLS.

Settlement Act (1662) empowered Overseers of the Poor in the PARISHES to send back to their place of birth or last settlement any new-comers likely to become chargeable on the poor rate. See also POOR LAW ACT (1601).

Sewing-machine was invented in 1830 by Barthélemy Thimmonier, a French tailor, and used to make army uniforms, but through the opposition of Parisian seamstresses and defects in the machine,

Early sewing machine

it was not put into production. In 1846 Elias Howe of Massachusetts devised an improved machine, which was first manufactured in any quantity by another American, Isaac Merritt Singer (1811–

75). The first Singer machine, dating from 1851, was worked by a treadle with the foot, and during the next decade many were exported to Britain by the Singer Co. which increased their sale by adopting a system of HIRE-PURCHASE.

Sextant an instrument used in navigation like a QUADRANT but with an arc of a sixth of a circle, was first constructed practically by John Hadley in 1731. The horizon is viewed through the horizon glass (silvered on its lower half, the upper half being transparent) by means of a TELESCOPE forming part of the instrument, and the index glass (a complete mirror), which is attached to an arm, is moved over the graduated scale of the arc until it brings an image of the sun or star into the silvered half of the horizon glass, which then appears to lie on the horizon.

Sexton an official of a CHURCH employed to take care of the VESTMENTS and communion vessels, assist the clergyman, dig graves and ring the BELLS. Sometimes he held, at the same time, the position of PARISH CLERK.

Shawm was a medieval woodwind musical instrument, having a double reed in a globular mouthpiece, from which the OBOE later developed. See also MUSIC.

Sheep were first domesticated about 6000 BC, and the hornless variety were introduced into Britain by the Romans. The CISTERCIANS pioneered sheep-farming in Yorkshire, and during the Middle Ages nearly all monasteries had flocks of sheep, especially the ABBEYS with estates in the Cotswolds and other great sheep-farming areas; they had great BARNS (e.g. at Milton and Abbotsbury) to store the WOOL, the sale of which was their main asset. In the 16th century ENCLOSURES took place for sheep-farming. During the AGRARIAN REVOLUTION breeds of sheep were developed which would produce wool or meat, e.g. John Ellman (1753–1832) bred southdown sheep and George III introduced a flock of merino sheep on his model farm at Windsor.

Sheffield plate copperware coated with silver by means of a process developed by Thomas Bolsover, who discovered in 1743 that a thin layer of SILVER could be fused over a much thicker ingot of COPPER and that the resultant plate could be rolled into thin sheets and cut, hammered, chased and soldered into wares almost indistinguishable from silver. It was superseded in 1840 by electro-plating, in which silver is deposited by electricity in the form of a thin film coating a cheaper metal.

Sheriff was originally the REEVE of the ANGLO-SAXON kings who administered the royal DEMESNE in a SHIRE. After the NORMAN CONQUEST, as the position of the EARLS changed, he became the king's chief representative in local government and did much judicial and administrative work, but later kings were afraid that they would grow too powerful, and so from the 13th century they lost much power to the CORONERS, JUDGES and JUSTICES OF THE PEACE.

Alexander I (1107–24) introduced the office of sheriff into Scotland, but it became hereditary and remained so until 1748. Today the Scottish sheriff is appointed for life and is the chief judge of his COUNTY, but most of his duties are performed by a deputy, the sheriff-substitute.

Sherry a still WINE named after the Spanish town of Jerez de la Frontera, near Cadiz, varying in colour from pale gold to dark brown and usually fortified with BRANDY. In Victorian times, clear soup had a great deal of sherry in it, but sherry was drunk, with PORT and CLARET, at the end of the MEAL and was often called a 'white-wash'. Nowadays it is usually drunk before a meal as an appetizer. [Rupert Croft-Cooke, *Sherry* (1962).] See also COCKTAIL.

Shields were used in the earliest days of warfare. The Romans during the occupation of Britain used a curved rectangular shield. The VIKINGS had a circular convex shield of wood covered with leather. The BAYEUX TAPESTRY shows the English mostly with pointed shields made of lime-wood measuring about 36 by 15 in., which they locked together on the battlefield into a defensive wall, though some carry round shields; and the Normans with kite-shaped shields, as tall as a man and carried by a strap inside, which were already decorated with devices such as dragons and from which the heraldic escutcheon developed in the 12th century. Shields generally went out of use in fighting in the 14th century, though in Scotland the HIGHLAND 'target', made of wood and studded with nails, remained in use until the 18th century.

Shift the name adopted in the 18th century for the UNDERGARMENT hitherto known as the SMOCK and later known as the CHEMISE.

Shilling the name originally given to a Byzantine coin, the solidus, by the Germans and Franks and introduced for accounting purposes by the Normans into England as equal to 12 PENNIES. Shillings were actually first minted by Henry VII after 1504 and were first known as testoons from the Italian coin of that name. See also COINAGE.

Shire the main division of local government in England under the ANGLO-SAXONS. About a third of the shires represent old kingdoms (e.g. Essex, Kent, Middlesex and Sussex) or tribal divisions (e.g. Norfolk and Suffolk); most of the others take their name from important BOROUGHS (e.g. Derby, Leicester, Lincoln and York). All England south of the Thames, except Cornwall, was divided into shires by King Alfred's reign (871–901); the Midlands were divided as they were conquered from the DANES; but the development was not completed in the North until after the NORMAN CONQUEST. See also COUNTY.

Shirt was from the early Middle Ages an UNDERGARMENT worn next to the skin by men until the appearance of the VEST in the 19th century. A COLLAR was added in the 15th century. Coloured shirts were introduced in the 19th century.

Shoes, see BOOTS AND SHOES.

Ships originated with the CORACLES and other small boats used by early men. The BLACKFRIARS BARGE is an example of the sort of ship which engaged in trade in ROMAN BRITAIN and the ship burial at SUTTON HOO of the ANGLO-SAXON ships which were mostly propelled by oars. The VIKING ships were up to 80 ft long and up to 10 ft across the beam, but surprisingly shallow; they were clinker-built with overlapping OAK planks and had a high prow and stern, a square sail on a single mast and from 30 to 64 oars. This type of ship lasted until the 14th century.

Important developments took place in the Middle Ages. The ships depicted on the BAYEUX TAPESTRY had a single sail, but oars are also shown in use for steering. Oars soon afterwards disappeared, and stern rudders replaced steering paddles in the 13th century. Forward and after castles appeared to give better accommodation for longer voyages, which were also assisted by the invention of the COMPASS. The square stern was introduced in the 15th century, when the full-rigged ship also came into existence with three or four masts. Sail areas became larger in succeeding centuries, a process which reached its culmination with the CLIPPERS.

The first steamship was a TUG-BOAT, and in 1812 the *Comet*, a paddle-steamer, carried passengers on the Clyde. At first steamships had sails as well, the first British ship to steam continuously across the Atlantic being the *Sirius* in 1837. Hulls were first made of IRON in the 1840s and of STEEL in the 1880s, while propellers replaced paddles in the early 1850s. Then came the STEAM-TURBINE and the use of oil fuel. Ships driven by NUCLEAR POWER have already been built. [R. and R. C. Anderson, *The Sailing Ship* (1926); J. P. Spratt, *The Birth of the Steamboat* (1934).] See also KEEL, TRINITY HOUSE, LIFE-BOAT.

Shops in ROMAN BRITAIN were commonly built around the FORUM and often consisted simply of a small front room for customers and a larger adjoining room for displaying merchandise. Medieval town shops were rooms, open to wind and weather, in the lower storeys of houses, which were closed at night by shutters, and APPRENTICES stood outside attracting customers. In the early part of George I's reign (1714–27), shops began to be enclosed by WINDOWS (see also PLATE-GLASS, ARCADE); and in the later 18th century village shops were made possible by improved ROADS (see also BAG-MAN), while the decline of rural industries through the INDUSTRIAL REVOLUTION made them less self-supporting. See also GROCER.

Bainbridge's of Newcastle-upon-Tyne had become by 1845 the first department store in Britain, and by 1900 most large towns had one and London had several which are now famous; most developed from drapery shops. CO-OPERATIVE SOCIETIES opened stores in the second half of the 19th century; and in the 1880s and 1890s Boot's chemists shops spread rapidly. Chain or multiple stores began in the grocery trade. Lipton's had 245 shops by 1898, the Home and Colonial Stores 600 by 1910; the first Woolworth's opened in Liverpool in 1909; and in the 1920s such stores appeared in many other trades (e.g. Victoria Wine Co.,

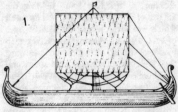

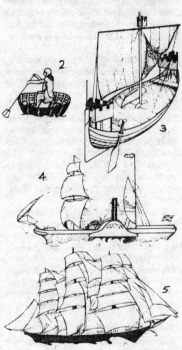

Ships: 1 Viking; 2 Coracle; 3 Castle ship; 4 Paddle steamer; 5 Clipper

MacFisheries, Sainsbury's, Montague Burton). At the same time branded goods replaced those made or packed by the staff of shops. The 1950s saw the establishment of self-service stores and supermarkets, some selling as many as 5000 separate items. By 1961 there were nearly 1400 supermarkets in England. [Alison Adburgham, *Shops and Shopping* (1964)]

Shop-signs from the Middle Ages onwards either hung from the house above the SHOP or posts between the foot- and carriage-way in the same way as INN-SIGNS. With increasing traffic these became inconvenient and even dangerous for vehicles. In 1762 an Act of Parliament ordered them to be placed flat against the front of the house. The numbering of houses in a street began with New Burlington Street, London, in June 1764, and the practice soon became common in towns.

Shorthand a system to enable speech to be recorded at great speed. The first real inventor in England of such a system was Timothy Bright, a clergyman, who produced an arrangement of arbitrary marks in 1588. John Willis in 1602 produced an alphabetical system, and there were other advances in the 17th century. A means of shorthand was wanted by the government for recording state-trials and by the PURITANS for taking down SERMONS, but probably no greater speed of writing than 50–70 words a minute was achieved; and the average speaker pronounces 120 words a minute and a fast one 180–200. Sir Isaac Pitman's system, devised in 1837, came into general use because of its outstanding legibility. Most modern systems of shorthand enable a writer to keep up with the average speaker by accepting the principle that a word can be recognized by its consonants only and vowels can be omitted except to avoid ambiguity; but Gregg's system of

1888 and others have exchanged geometrical forms in favour of something approaching ordinary script. [Sir Isaac Pitman, *A History of Shorthand* (4th ed., 1918)]

Shrine a casket or tomb holding the RELICS of a saint (see also RELIQUARY), which was the object in the Middle Ages of PILGRIMAGES. Among famous English medieval shrines were those of St Edward the Confessor at WESTMINSTER ABBEY and St Thomas Becket at CANTERBURY CATHEDRAL. Originally it was common for a shrine in a CATHEDRAL or other large CHURCH to be in the CRYPT, but in the later Middle Ages it was usually moved to a place of greater prominence and honour immediately behind the HIGH ALTAR.

Shrove Tuesday the day immediately before ASH WEDNESDAY, so-named from the shriving (confession and absolution) of the people in the churches on that day. It was also a holiday in preparation for the Lenten fast days ahead and the day when housewives used their butter and eggs to make pancakes to conserve the perishable food in their larders before the fast. The 'pancake bell' was rung in the morning to show that the holiday had begun and again towards sunset to show that it was over.

The day was marked by COCK-FIGHTING and other sports. The pancake race at Olney (Bucks.), probably 500 years old, is a survival of these sports, and so also is the FOOTBALL played in the streets of Ashbourne (Derbyshire) and Alnwick (Northumberland) and the hurling of the silver ball (made of wood covered with silver leaf) at St Columb (Cornwall).

Sickle an agricultural implement used for lopping and trimming HEDGES and for cutting growing grain, having a short handle and a hooked blade, flattened in the plane of its curve and sharpened on its inner edge, one side of the blade being notched so as always to sharpen with a serrated edge. FLINT sickles belonging to the early NEOLITHIC AGE have been found, and a MISERICORD in Worcester Cathedral, dating from 1379, shows three men reaping wheat with sickles. The sickle was still sometimes used to cut corn until the early 20th century. [G. E. Fussell, *The Farmer's Tools* (1952).] See also SCYTHE, REAPING MACHINE.

Signposts of some sort are considerably older than MILESTONES. Several medieval roads, such as the track across Dartmoor, had stone crosses to mark the way. Private individuals set up signposts in the late 17th century, and an Act of 1698 required JUSTICES OF THE PEACE to erect standing-posts at cross-roads, but this does not seem to have been effective, and sign-posts did not become compulsory until the Act of 1773.

Silhouette the portrait of a person in profile showing the outline only, this being filled in with black and cut out in paper. The art originally came from the East (China, Persia and Turkey) and was named in Europe after Etienne de Silhouette, who was Controller-General of Finance in France in 1759, on account of his reputation of being a shadow-figure. The first portraits in this technique were made in England, the country of portrait-painting, and from there they spread to the Continent. They were very fashionable in the second half of the 18th century, being favoured because they were quickly accomplished and inexpensive, and they were executed by both professionals and private persons. Though usually in black, sometimes the dress and hair were painted in colours.

Silk was probably first reeled and made into cloth in the 26th century BC in China. It was first manufactured in Italy in the 12th century AD, later spreading to Spain and southern France, where the mulberry tree, on which the silkworm feeds, flourishes. Silk was introduced into England through the CRUSADES at the end of the 13th century, the wives of some noblemen first appearing in silk dresses at a ball in Kenilworth Castle (Warwicks.) in 1286. The weaving of silk in England was introduced by Flemish refugees in the 16th century and greatly developed after 1685 when HUGUENOTS from France established themselves in London at Spitalfields. Its use has declined since the development of man-made fibres, especially RAYON and NYLON. See also SATIN, SMUGGLING.

Sillabub an old dish, a favourite during the reign of Queen Elizabeth I, made by mixing wine or cider with cream or milk into a soft curd, flavoured with sugar, and whipped into a froth or made solid by adding gelatine and water, and boiling.

Silver objects and COINAGE have been found in the graves of the BELGAE, and silver was probably obtained in ROMAN BRITAIN in connection with the production of LEAD. Few examples of ANGLO-SAXON silverware survive, but it is known that both kings and churches had considerable quantities. By 1300 so much was being made that an Act of Parliament ordered the London GOLDSMITHS to check the standard of silver used in every piece of plate and to stamp it with a leopard's head, which led to the present system of hall-marking. The Tudor and early Stuart period was a prosperous time for silversmiths; silver tableware became fashionable, but most of it was melted down and made into coin by both sides during the Civil War (1642–6). After the RESTORATION, much of the silver, for a century and more, was gilt (covered with GOLD) to protect it from tarnishing caused by the use of COAL.

Sin-eating a custom common in Wales, Shropshire and Herefordshire until the late 18th century at FUNERALS. The village sin-eater, usually an old man, attended the funeral and for a small fee consumed a loaf of bread and a bowl of beer over the coffin, so taking upon himself the sins of the dead person.

Skirt the lower part of a woman's dress hanging from the waist over the hips, though until the 19th century the term PETTICOAT was usually used. The original medieval skirt was a draped garment reaching from the neck to the knees in one piece and generally girded, which was worn by both sexes until about the 13th century, when women began to wear a separate bodice. The length, width and shape of skirts have continually changed with contemporary fashions.

In the late 1870s skirts grew steadily tighter, became wider and a little shorter at the end of the century and about 1910 became so tight again that fashionable women could only hobble. Shorter skirts came first from USA where they were worn on rainy days in muddy streets and were known as 'rainy daisies'. The Women's Page in the *Observer* spoke in December 1914 of 'short full skirts' with 'more than a suspicion of ankle visible' and in February 1915 of 'skirts six inches off the ground'. By the end of 1915 skirts came down to just below the calf, and in 1925 the knees were exposed for the first time, but in the 1930s they usually came to just below the knees. For a time after the Second World War the NEW LOOK brought fuller, longer skirts, but in 1967 came the shorter-than-ever-before mini-skirt.

Skittles an indoor form of BOWLS, sometimes called ninepins, which came to England from Germany in the 13th century and was sometimes played in INNS, though it was at one time forbidden lest it should lead men to neglect ARCHERY. Since the Second World War new elaborate bowling alleys, at which this game is played, have been opened in many British towns.

Slaves are those who belong absolutely to another and have no freedom or personal rights. Slaves were employed in ROMAN BRITAIN in many industries and on the estates of landowners, while there were domestic slaves in the VILLAS. The institution of slavery was part of the earliest ANGLO-SAXON law, and the early English CEORL was usually a slave-owner. DOMESDAY BOOK recorded 100 000 VILLEINS and 25 000 slaves, who comprised 9 per cent of the counted population, the figures being as high as 20 per cent or more in the western counties. There was less slavery in the DANELAW than in most parts of the country. Slavery was rare in contemporary Normandy, and it seems that in some parts of England many slaves were emancipated by their new Norman masters and became COTTARS on the MANOR. Within a century of the NORMAN CONQUEST slavery had practically disappeared. In the 18th century many NEGRO SERVANTS in England were slaves until SOMERSETT'S CASE.

Slave-trade was carried on with the Continent by the tribes of Sussex, Kent and Essex in Celtic times and continued after the Roman occupation. In ANGLO-SAXON times Bristol was the centre of a thriving slave-trade with Ireland. After the NORMAN CONQUEST attempts were made by the Church to check the traffic. Archbishop Anselm at the Council of London (1102) issued a canon against the selling of Englishmen 'like brute beasts', and Wulfstan by his preaching checked the Irish trade.

John Hawkins in 1562–7 led English participation in shipping negro slaves from West Africa to the Spanish plantations in the New World, and this trade developed steadily in the 17th century through the demands for negro labour in the West Indies and the southern English colonies in North America. In the 18th century Bristol and Liverpool merchants acquired most of the trade, and British ships carried more slaves than those of any other nation.

The QUAKERS from 1727 opposed the slave-trade, and in 1787 the Anti-Slavery Committee was established in London largely under the influence of the EVAN-GELICALS led by William Wilberforce, but it was not until 1807 that Parliament passed an Act forbidding British participation in the slave-trade, and slavery was not abolished in the British Empire until 1833.

Sling a military weapon, consisting of a strap or a pocket with a cord attached to each end, for hurling stones or other missiles. A store of 20 000 sling-stones has been found in the HILL-FORT at Maiden Castle (Dorset). Foot-soldiers in medieval armies were sometimes armed with slings. See also CATAPULT, TREBUCHET. See also ARTILLERY.

Slums came about through the rapid growth of TOWNS during the INDUSTRIAL REVOLUTION. The word, first used in the 1820s, derives from the old word 'slump' meaning a 'marshy place'. The first industries had to be on low ground beside CANALS, and the working-class HOUSES built there endured terrible problems of SANITATION. Moreover, houses were run up as cheaply and as close together as possible; and in Birmingham, for example, by the 1830s there were over 2000 built round small, dark courtyards and many of them also back to back. Many such houses had no WATER SUPPLY, and CHOLERA and other diseases were prevalent.

Early acts to deal with the problem were the Common Lodging-Houses Act (1851), requiring the registration and inspection of all lodging houses, and the Artizans' Dwellings Act (1875), fixing standards for future house-building and empowering local authorities to pull down slums and build working-class houses. In the 1860s Octavia Hill founded a trust which bought slums and reconditioned them, and her example led to the passing of further measures by Parliament.

At present about 60 000 old houses are pulled down every year, and another 80 000 wear out. Nearly 500 000 houses are still officially classified as slums, and the real figure may be much more. Three million homes have no baths, and two million are without a lavatory.

Smallpox was known to have existed in Arabia about AD 900 and is supposed to have been introduced into Europe from the East by the Saracens. By the 17th century it was a common disease in England, Queen Mary dying of it in 1694, and in London in 1713 one out of fourteen deaths was due to it. Inoculation (using the contents of the actual 'pocks' or spots on the skin) was brought to England from Turkey by Lady Mary Wortley Montagu in 1718, but it often led to serious disease and was made illegal in 1840. Meanwhile, Dr Edward Jenner discovered vaccination (inoculation with the virus of cow-pox) in 1796, and it was made compulsory from 1853 to 1948. Despite this, there were severe epidemics of smallpox throughout the 19th century.

Smithfield or 'smooth field' was an ancient open space outside the walls of the City of London. At one time it was the chief horse-market in England and consequently a place for HORSE-RACING. From early times it has been also a meat market (see DROVE ROADS), and for many years the annual BARTHOLOMEW FAIR was held there. Later it became the scene of TOURNAMENTS. It was a place of execution from the 12th century, and 43 PROTES-TANTS were burnt at the stake there as HERETICS during Queen Mary's reign (1553–8). [R. J. Mitchell and M. D. R. Leys, *A History of London Life* (1958)]

Smock (1) was the term from ANGLO-SAXON times for a woman's UNDER-GARMENT worn next to the skin. In the 18th century it became known as the SHIFT and in the 19th century the CHEMISE. (2) In the 18th and 19th centuries it was also the name for an outer garment of coarse white LINEN or COTTON, about knee-length, worn by agricultural labourers.

Smoking began in Elizabethan times, when it was thought to be medically beneficial as well as pleasurable. The Pied Bull Inn, Islington, is said to have been the first house in England where TOBACCO was smoked. Sir Walter Raleigh (1552–1618) patronized the cult and popularized the habit, which survived a royal proclamation of 1584 against it. In the 16th century tobacco was smoked in short clay pipes, and long-stemmed pipes were introduced from Holland after the Glorious Revolution (1688). They became known as 'churchwardens' in the 18th century because the CHURCHWARDENS used to smoke them when they met together in the INN after they had made up their PARISH accounts in the VESTRY or been elected to office at the EASTER meeting. They were replaced by briar-root pipes in the middle of the 19th century.

Until about 1900 smoking was almost entirely a masculine habit, practised in special smoking-rooms and smoking-compartments. Many people, including Queen Victoria, disapproved of smoking. It was not generally allowed in RAILWAY trains until 1868, when the Regulation of Railways Act required the provision of smoking-carriages, though smoking-saloons had been started on the Eastern Counties Railway as early as 1846; Brad-

shaw's first *Guide*, printed in 1840, noted that it was forbidden also on railway stations. *Hints on Etiquette* (1834) insisted, 'If you are so unfortunate as to have contracted the low habit of smoking, be careful to practise it under certain restrictions'; and in 1859 Oxford undergraduates 'in the habit of smoking at public entertainments' were cautioned by the university 'against the repetition of such ungentlemanlike conduct'. Recently there has been a reintroduction of restrictions on smoking in trains, shops and public places. See also CIGARS, CIGARETTES, ETIQUETTE.

Smuggling In Edward I's reign (1272–1307) was of English WOOL by night across the Channel from Romney Marsh (Kent) to Flanders and France (see MERCHANTS OF THE STAPLE); and in the 14th century smugglers brought in woven cloth, the importation of which was forbidden to protect English clothiers (see DOMESTIC SYSTEM). After the RESTORATION, when the first duty was imposed on TOBACCO, it was smuggled into Cornish creeks in English, French and Flemish ships. To check smuggling, a corps of 'Riding Officers' was formed in 1698, who could call in the help of DRAGOONS; they were later replaced by coastguards under the control of the Customs Board.

Sir Robert Walpole's Excise Bill (1733) was an unsuccessful attempt to defeat smuggling, which reached its height in the 18th and early 19th century, especially in Kent and Sussex, the chief cargoes brought in being TEA, SILK and BRANDY. During the Napoleonic War (1803–15), the French government bribed smugglers with such cargoes in order to get them to bring out British cloth and boots for the French army. The smugglers also helped EMIGRÉS to escape to England. Smuggling was cut down in the 19th century and made profitless by the advent of free trade (see CORN LAWS).

Snapdragon a traditional pastime on CHRISTMAS EVE, probably associated with Scandinavian fire-rites and initiation rituals. It consisted of plucking raisins with the fingers out of a bowl of flaming brandy.

Snoek a large, edible tropical fish, allied to the horse-mackerel. In 1948 the Ministry of Food, while still trying to persuade the British people to eat WHALE-MEAT, imported large quantities of tinned snoek from South Africa. It was advertised by a snoek-tasting party at the Ministry, which also issued a leaflet containing recipes which included 'Snoek Piquante', but it could not be popularized and disappeared from the shops the next year. [Michael Sissons and Philip French (eds.), *Age of Austerity 1945–51* (1963)]

Snuff powdered TOBACCO, often left to ferment and flavoured, for inhaling as a stimulant or sedative. The Spaniards introduced it into Europe from Central and South America where it was widely used. It became popular in Europe in the late 16th century, but was not used much in England until Charles II's reign when it was introduced from France, and it became very widespread and fashionable in the 18th century. Queen Anne took snuff, and her ladies copied her. In 1702, when a large Spanish convoy was captured in Vigo Bay by Admiral Sir George Rooke, among the loot was a large consignment of snuff, which was distributed throughout the country by sailors who received it in part payment of their wages and prize-money, thereby increasing the popularity of snuff-taking. Indeed, in the 18th century this was held to be the most polite form of tobacco-taking, and the wealthy carried it in finely-made snuff-boxes. It largely superseded pipe-SMOKING, and probably reached the apex of its popularity during the Regency period. There were snuff-mills in London, Bristol, Sheffield, Kendal and other places. In the 19th century, however, snuff was eclipsed first by the CIGAR and then by the CIGARETTE.

Soap was known in a crude form in ROMAN BRITAIN and again in the Middle Ages. The Romans used a mixture of oil and sand, while medieval soap was at first home-made by boiling fats with the LYE (which was used for LAUNDERING) and sometimes perfuming it by adding oil of almonds, musk, rose leaves or lavender flowers. It was a 'soft soap', and early pictures of bathing show it being handed to the bather in large wooden bowls. Wealthy people imported soap from abroad, mostly Venice and Spain (particularly the fine white soap from Castile). This was sold in tablets, on each of which was the maker's 'soap mark' (e.g. a half-moon, sun or chain).

Soap was made commercially in England from the 14th century, at first at Bristol and then at Coventry and London. It was first manufactured in balls, though large households bought it by the barrel at FAIRS. The Soapers' or Soapmakers' Company was incorporated in 1638. Until the 19th century soapmakers usually had to prepare their own caustic soda or potash (for treating animal or vegetable fats and oils), but the development of the chemical industry made plentiful supplies of these available. In 1789 Andrew Pears began making his transparent soap by dissolving ordinary soap in alcohol, distilling off the alcohol to produce a transparent jelly and drying this slowly in moulds. From 1785 to 1800 the consumption of soap in Britain increased by 41·7 per cent. [Lawrence Wright, *Clean and Decent* (1960)]

Societies for the reformation of manners were founded towards the end of the 17th century by religious people to check vice and intemperance. They did this mainly by enforcing the laws against such offences as drunkenness, swearing and immorality among the poor and by distributing religious literature. From 1691 to 1738 these societies made 101 638 prosecutions and distributed more than 444 000 books and pamphlets. Their activities gained them much unpopularity, especially because they seemed to spare rich and influential offenders. Much of their work was taken over by the SOCIETY FOR PROMOTING CHRISTIAN KNOWLEDGE, and they became extinct by the middle of the 18th century. [J. H. Overton, *Life in the English Church, 1660–1714* (1885)]

Society for Promoting Christian Knowledge was founded in 1698 to promote the establishment of CHARITY SCHOOLS and the dispersion of BIBLES and religious tracts. Like the SOCIETIES FOR THE REFORMATION OF MANNERS and the SOCIETY FOR THE PROPAGATION OF THE GOSPEL, it was one of the religious societies formed in the late 17th century with spiritual and moral aims, which were mainly controlled by laymen. It is still an important educational and publishing society of the CHURCH OF ENGLAND. [W. K. Lowther Clarke, *A History of the S.P.C.K.* (1959)]

Society for the Propagation of the Gospel founded in 1701, was the first of the MISSIONARY SOCIETIES of the CHURCH OF ENGLAND. At first it worked mainly in the American colonies, but in the 19th century extended its activities all over the world. After the formation of the CHURCH MISSIONARY SOCIETY, it became increasingly representative of the TRACTARIAN outlook. [H. P. Thompson, *Into All Lands* (1951)]

Soda water or aerated water was first produced in the 18th century by Joseph Priestley, who produced carbonic acid gas by adding crude hydrochloric acid to marble, capturing the escaping gas and adding this to water in a sealed barrel, which was frequently shaken. It was drunk medicinally, as an imitation of the waters taken at SPAS and was added by the Admiralty to the lime-juice given to sailors to prevent SCURVY. It was first made on a commercial scale at Geneva in 1790 by Nicholas Paul, whose partner, Jean Schweppe, set up business in England. It is now used to produce various sparkling fruit drinks, 8 gallons of which are drunk per head in Britain. Charles Plinth in 1825 patented a 'Regency portable fountain', and in 1837 Antoine Perpigna substituted for its stopcock a valve closed by a spring, which could be opened to allow the pressure of the gas to force the soda water up a tube to a curved spout. This was the beginning of the modern soda siphon.

Solar was the upper room, designed especially for the private use of the family, and sometimes known also as the great chamber, which was added to later medieval HOUSES. It might be used both as a bedchamber and a sitting room and might be above the BOWER and was reached either by a STAIRCASE from the HALL or on the outside. The name means the sunny room, being derived from the Latin *sol*. [Ralph Dutton, *The English Country House* (1962).] See also DRAWING ROOM, HOUSE.

Somersett's Case (1772) concerned James Somersett, a slave brought by his master as a NEGRO SERVANT from Jamaica to England. He escaped, but was recaptured, whereupon a writ of HABEAS CORPUS was sued for his freedom. Lord Mansfield, who heard the case, said in his judgement, 'The state of slavery is of such a nature that it is incapable of being introduced on any reasons, moral or political, but only by positive law. . . . I cannot say this case is allowed or approved by the law of England; and therefore the black must be discharged.' See also SLAVERY.

Sovereign an English GOLD coin, eventually worth a POUND, which is still minted as gold bullion, but ceased to be minted for general circulation in 1925 and had been replaced for ordinary use by paper money in 1914. There was also a gold half-sovereign. See also COINAGE, GUINEA.

Sowing seed in the past was usually done broadcast. The sower scattered it by throwing it from the hand as he advanced over a field taking it from a seed-tray held in the other hand or a sack hung from his shoulder. A MISERICORD in Worcester Cathedral dating from 1379 shows a man sowing grain by broadcasting it. In the early stages or on small holdings the holes for the seeds were made by dibbles, a pair being used by a man walking backwards and followed by women or children who dropped four seeds in each hole, the saying being, 'One for the rook, one for the crow, one to rot and one to grow'. See also SEED-DRILL.

Span-farthing a 17th-century children's game in which one player tried to throw FARTHINGS so close to those of his opponent that the distance between them could be spanned with one hand.

Spas places with mineral springs, were first frequented for medicinal reasons in the late 16th century. In the 17th century the most important were Harrogate, Buxton, Epsom (where London merchants took their families for the day), Tunbridge Wells (made fashionable by Charles I's queen, Henrietta Maria), Bath (where Pepys stayed 'above two hours in the water') and Scarborough. The 18th century was the great age of the spas, and under Richard Nash (1674–

1761) Bath became the model for the others. There the leisured classes not only took the waters, but also indulged in the pleasures of BATHING and frequenting the ASSEMBLY ROOMS and the THEATRE. In the 19th century spas were superseded largely by the SEASIDE. After the Second World War, 8 spas were operational and were incorporated in the NATIONAL HEALTH SERVICE, but only Bath, Royal Leamington and Woodhall Spa (Lincs.) are now flourishing. See also SODA WATER.

Spear a very ancient WEAPON used in both war and HUNTING. The Roman soldier had the *pilum*, a heavy javelin meant to be hurled. The BAYEUX TAPESTRY shows both Norman and English soldiers armed with spears. Later it developed into the PIKE and LANCE. The spear was especially used in hunting WOLVES and wild BOARS in Britain until these animals became extinct.

Spectacles were invented in Italy in the late 13th century, and by the middle of the 14th century appeared on representations of saints and heroes. At first these had convex lenses (held together by a joint or hinge stiff enough to keep them on the nose), and were used to assist the elderly seeing at close range; they were long used only by scholars as most people could not read. By the 16th century spectacles were in common use among learned men in England and became more common with the spread of literacy. Scales of lens-strengths proportionate to the number of years past middle age had been worked out by the 17th century; women were held to require double the strength of lens of a man of the same age owing to an 'inherent feminine weakness'.

By 1500 a curved nose-piece had been introduced, and side-pieces came about a century later. The early rims of metal gave way in the 16th century to leather which did not slip down the nose so much; horn came in at the time of William and Mary, silver with Queen Anne, and tortoiseshell with George III. The pince-nez appeared in the 1840s, but disappeared almost completely in the early 1920s. Until the early 20th century lenses were usually small and oval and surrounded by gold rims. Now they are usually rimless or horn-rimmed. Fashion has constantly changed the shape of lenses and frames (as well as the colour and material used), especially for women.

In the 18th and 19th centuries spectacles were not fashionable except for the elderly and scholarly. In the 18th century the 'quizzing glass', a single lens with a handle, was fashionable for both ladies and gentlemen, to be replaced at the end of the century by the lorgnette, a pair of lenses similarly mounted. In the second half of the 19th century, a monocle was fashionable for gentlemen.

Concave spectacle-lenses did not become freely available until the end of the 19th century, but many oculists still believed that they were harmful to the eyes, even provoking the short-sightedness which they would, in fact, have relieved. Such spectacles were largely sold from itinerant vendors' trays until this was made illegal by an Act of Parliament in 1952.

Women spectacle-wearers now outnumber men by about 7 per cent. Bifocal lenses were invented in France towards the end of the 18th century. Contact lenses were made from the middle of the 19th century, but until the Second World War their fitting was laborious, and they could rarely be worn for more than a few hours with any comfort. Sun-glasses came into fashion in the 1920s, and tinted glasses have come into greater demand in recent years.

Speedway racing or Dirt Track Racing by MOTOR BICYCLES was introduced into England by Australian riders at a meeting at High Beech (Essex) and soon became a popular SPORT. In 1963 there were 24 tracks in Britain.

Speenhamland system a scheme of poor relief, devised by the Berkshire JUSTICES OF THE PEACE meeting in the Pelican Inn, Speenhamland (now part of Newbury) in 1795, which supplemented wages from the poor-rates according to a scale which depended on the price of corn and the size of a labourer's family. It systematized a practice already allowed by GILBERT'S ACT (1782), and by 1834 it had been adopted in every county except Durham and Northumberland. Though designed to meet the distress among agricultural labourers caused by high prices and low wages, it kept down wages, often demoralized the labourers and increased the rates. It came to an end with the POOR LAW AMENDMENT ACT (1834).

Spices as well as HERBS, were used in ROMAN BRITAIN to disguise unwelcome flavours and vary monotonous MEALS before the rediscovery of VEGETABLES and when fresh MEAT and FISH were not common. Among the common spices were CUMMIN, GINGER and PEPPER. Such spices were used both in cooking and at the table (see also NEF). They also went to the making of spiced foodstuffs (e.g. GINGERBREAD) and drinks (e.g. MEAD and HIPPOCRAS).

Spices became more commonly used as a result of the CRUSADES. They were brought from the Mediterranean region and the Far East mainly by Venetian merchants, being sent thence overland to Bruges or direct by sea to England. The discovery of the sea route to India made spices cheaper. The trade then passed into the hands of the Portuguese and afterwards the Dutch; and in 1600 the East India Company was founded by English merchants to participate in it. See also GROCER.

Spinet a keyboard instrument, in which, like the VIRGINAL and the HARPSICHORD, the strings are plucked, not struck. It was like the virginal in having only one string to a note, but, instead of having its rectangular form, was of 'trapezoid, pentagonal or wing-shape'. Though known earlier on the Continent, it was not introduced into England until about the mid-17th century, when it displaced the virginal and remained popular until replaced in its turn by the PIANO late in the 18th century. See also PIANO.

Spinning of WOOL, COTTON or FLAX into threads was at first done by the spindle and distaff. The distaff, a cleft stick about 3 ft long, was held under the left arm, and the fibres of wool drawn from it were twisted spirally by the forefinger and thumb of the right hand. As the thread was spun, it was wound on the spindle, which was suspended from and revolved with the thread during spinning.

The spinning-wheel was invented in Nuremberg about 1530 and introduced into England soon afterwards. It consisted of a revolving wheel operated by a treadle and a driving spindle. In 1764 James Hargreaves invented the spinning-jenny, a spinning-frame with a number of revolving spindles worked by one spinner, and Richard Arkwright in 1769 the water-frame, worked by water-power; then followed in 1779 Samuel Crompton's spinning-mule, which could be worked by water or steam power and spun MUSLIN and other fine materials.

Spinning was long carried on in private houses by the WOMEN of a family, and hence the name for a maiden was a 'spinster'. In ANGLO-SAXON times, a young woman before MARRIAGE had to make from her own thread a set of body, table and bed linen. A HOUSE OF CORRECTION was sometimes called a spinning-house because the women there were obliged to spin or beat hemp as a punishment. During the FAIR at Sturbridge, offenders were sent to the Spinning House at Cambridge, and, a 17th-century writer recorded, 'thither doth the Town Crier oft-times resort, to discipline the Ladies of Pleasure with his whip'. See also WEAVING, DOMESTIC SYSTEM.

Spit a slender bar on which MEAT to be roasted was made to rotate before a fire. Turning the spit was rated the most menial of domestic duties. Sometimes it was done by the 'dogwheel', a contraption in which a DOG ran endlessly inside a cylindrical cage. A special breed of 'turnspits', rather like dachshunds, came from Pembrokeshire, but any low-built, muscular dog would do. There was also the 'chimney-wheel' (or 'draft-mill' or

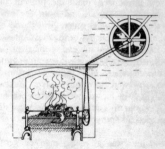

Spit turned by a dog

'smoke-jack'). This is to be found in Leonardo da Vinci's note-books and was used in England by the 17th century. It consisted of a horizontal, multi-bladed fan, hung in a narrowed neck in the flue and turned by the rising current of hot air from which power was transmitted through gears to the spit. Such chimney-wheels are still in place in some of the halls of the LIVERY COMPANIES in London. [Lawrence Wright, *Home Fires Burning* (1964)]

Sporran the pouch or large PURSE worn as part of HIGHLAND costume and usually made of the skin of some animal with the hair left on, being slung round the waist and hanging down in front of the KILT.

Sport as well as GAMES, was at first discouraged in all its forms in favour of ARCHERY. Popular sports in the past have been BEAR-BAITING, BULL-BAITING and GOOSE-riding. BOXING (from which developed PRIZE-FIGHTING) is the oldest English organized sport. HORSE-RACING is also of ancient origin, and to this form of racing have since been added MOTOR CAR racing, SPEEDWAY RACING and GREY-HOUND racing.

Spurs with a short single spike were used by the Romans. Spurs with a number of points of considerable size were introduced about the time of the NORMAN CONQUEST, and from the early 13th century were generally replaced by the rowel, usually bearing six points, rotating freely at the end of the shank. A KNIGHT wore gold or gilt spurs, a SQUIRE silvered ones, and those of ordinary soldiers were in iron or steel. A man might 'win his spurs' (gain knighthood) by valour in battle, and if he were degraded his spurs were hacked off.

Squire was a young man of gentle birth in the days of CHIVALRY who attended a KNIGHT often bearing his ARMOUR or SHIELD. In rank the squire (or esquire) was next to the knight. See also PAGE.

Stage-coach with scheduled stops appeared about 1640, supplementing the slow stage-WAGONS carrying goods and passengers between the big towns. By the mid-1650s there were stage-coaches operating on all the great highways radiating from London, taking two days to Oxford and six to Edinburgh. In the later part of the 18th century the use of the stage-coach for the mail service produced the MAIL-COACH. Stage-coaches usually required one horse for each mile of route (e.g. 150 horses were kept for the coaches travelling the 158 miles between London and Shrewsbury) and changed horses about every 10 miles, the stages being sometimes farms and more often INNS. At Hounslow, the first stage out of London on the Bath and Southampton roads, some 800 horses were maintained for the 500 coaches passing through daily by the end of the 18th century. See also BLUNDER-BUSS, PISTOL.

Staircases in medieval CASTLES and MANORS, where the HALL was usually on the first floor, were of stone and outside most commonly. Where stairs were built inside the building, they often wound in a spiral round a central pillar (a 'newel') and were in a turret, like those in many CHURCH towers. These too were usually of stone, but as carpenters grew more skilful, wooden stairs became more common. In the 16th century they were designed more spaciously. Elizabethan staircases had short flights of steps, divided by square landings around an open well and often had elaborately carved newel-posts, handrails and balusters; but 18th century staircases were more slender and elegant, being fairly narrow (especially in town HOUSES) and ascending round three sides of a staircase-hall with a square quarter-landing between flights or in two flights of opposite direction joined by rectangular half-landing and separated by a narrow well, while they often had turned wooden or delicately scrolled iron balusters and moulded handrails. In the 19th century winding-staircases with winders (winding steps) were sometimes built. In modern times open, ladder-like staircases have become popular.

Stane Street the name of two Roman roads, so-called from the Old English *stan*, stone. One ran from London to Chichester, the other from Braughing (Herts.) to Colchester.

Staple see MERCHANTS OF THE STAPLE.

Starch made by steeping in water the ground-up seeds or roots of vegetables, was introduced for stiffening garments after washing in about 1565. This made possible the wearing of RUFFS, which became widespread, and every young lady of fashion took lessons in the art of starching. The earliest form of starch used in England was yellow in tone, imparting a somewhat rich creamy shade to the material, but this colour was only fashionable for a few years, and after the hanging of a notorious woman who wore a 'yellow ruff', starch was changed to the blue tint it has retained ever since. [Iris Brooke *A History of English Costume* (1968)]

Stained glass in the early Middle Ages was mostly imported from France. The earliest example of stained glass in England is probably in York Minster, being part of the panel of the Jesse Tree window dated between 1142 and 1151. The increasing size of WINDOWS in GOTHIC architecture encouraged the use of stained glass, which was probably at its best in England in the 14th century. Much was destroyed at the REFORMATION.

Figures of kings and bishops, small in the 12th century, later increased in size. The 14th century introduced naturalistic foliage, the 15th century five-petalled roses and the 16th century heraldic devices. Until the 15th century each colour was a separate piece of glass held together by grooved lead strips, like a MOSAIC, the details being depicted in a brown enamel. Painted glass came into use through the influence of the RENAISSANCE, and by the middle of the 16th century the older method was little used until the Gothic

revival of the 19th century. [N. E. Boyle, *Old Parish Churches* (1951)]

Star chamber originated as a COURT in the 14th century when the royal council, sitting in the 'star chamber' (the ceiling of which was decorated with stars) of the Palace of Westminster, heard cases, especially those concerning the 'over-mighty subjects', the nobility who defied the ordinary law courts. It became very efficient under the Tudors, but under the early Stuarts it became disliked, particularly by the PURITANS whom it punished for religious offences. It was abolished in 1641.

Stays an UNDERGARMENT with whalebone ribs embracing the chest and confining and supporting the waist and body, which was first worn in England by Norman ladies. From the 18th century steel ribs were introduced, and 'tight-lacing', to restrict the waist to the 18 in. decreed by fashion for ladies, became common. A lady said in the mid-19th century that 'tight-lacing produces delicious sensations, half pleasure, half pain'. From the 17th to the 19th century stays were sometimes worn by gentlemen as well. The French word 'corset' was first used as a refinement for 'stays' in the late 18th century and in the 19th century gradually replaced it. See also BUSK.

Steam engine was first made by Thomas Savery (1650?–1715), who patented in 1698 a machine used for pumping water out of mines by the use of steam. The water was sucked up by creating a vacuum through condensing steam in an enclosed vessel, but it was not very successful.

More reliable was the 'atmospheric engine' of Thomas Newcomen (1663–1729) in which steam, injected into a cylinder, was condensed to make a vacuum so that atmospheric pressure forced a piston down, and then a fresh injection of steam forced it up again. The upright piston was attached to a pivoted beam, the other end of which was attached to a pump. By 1765 there were over 100 Newcomen engines at work in mines in north-eastern England alone.

This engine was improved by James Watt (1736–1819), who added a separate condenser in 1765, fitted a crank-shaft and cogwheel to the piston, which gave it a rotary movement, in 1781, and made it a double-acting steam engine, in which steam was admitted alternately on each side of the piston, in 1782. He entered into partnership with Matthew Boulton (1728–1809) at the Soho Ironworks, near Birmingham, in 1774. By 1800 some 500 of their engines were operating in mines, ironworks and cotton-mills.

Later 18th-century inventions included the slide-valve and 'compounding' (the addition of a double cylinder). Richard Trevithick (1771–1838) invented high-pressure engines and internal-flue boilers in 1802. The reciprocating steam engine began to be replaced by the STEAM TURBINE at the end of the century.

Steam hammer was invented by a Scottish engineer, James Nasmyth (1808–90), in 1839 and was of great value in the development of the IRON industry. The hammer, fixed to the end of a piston-rod passing through the bottom of an inverted cylinder, weighed up to 80 or 100 tons and was so perfectly controlled by STEAM POWER that its action could be gauged with sufficient accuracy to enable it to crack the glass of a watch without actually breaking it or to be brought down on a mass of red hot iron with a force representing many hundreds of tons. [Leslie Halward, *Famous British Engineers* (1954)]

Steam locomotive was first built expressly for rails and operated in Cornwall in 1804 by Richard Trevithick (1771–

1833), who also operated one on a circular track in London near the present site of Euston Road in 1809. George Stephenson (1781–1848) built a locomotive in 1815 which hauled trucks of coal from Killingworth Colliery to the River Tyne on existing RAILWAYS in 1815. In 1825 he persuaded the Stockton and Darlington Railway to use his locomotives, and in 1830 his *Rocket*, the most important early locomotive, won the competition at the Rainhill trials of the Liverpool and Manchester Railway. The Newcastle and Carlisle Railway in 1834 was the last to begin by using HORSES instead of steam locomotives; and the last steam locomotive completed in Britain was in March 1960. [O. S. Nock, *The Railways of Britain* (1962)]

Steam power made the INDUSTRIAL REVOLUTION possible. The STEAM ENGINE, for the first time in history, gave man a source of power which on a large scale replaced his own muscles. By 1800 it was used in Britain for SPINNING and WEAVING and to work CRANES, STEAM HAMMERS and many other machines. From the 1870s ELECTRICITY became an increasingly serious rival to steam power, and in the 20th century NUCLEAR POWER is becoming steadily more important.

Steam turbine in which the steam turns the blades of a wheel instead of moving a piston up and down, was invented by Sir Charles Parsons in 1884. He fitted it into a small boat, the *Turbinia*, which he sailed at the Spithead naval review in 1897, where it moved between the warships at the incredible speed of 34½ knots. In 1905 the first Atlantic turbine-liner was launched, and the steam-turbine also became important in power-stations for generating ELECTRICITY.

Steel which is IRON combined with carbon to increase its hardness, was made in England from the Middle Ages, especially at Sheffield, but the process of heating the iron with charcoal was costly, and the steel was mostly used for the manufacture of cutting implements, such as SWORDS. In 1856 Henry Bessemer devised a converter which turned iron into steel with a small consumption of fuel; in 1866 William Siemens invented the alternative open-hearth furnaces; and in 1879 the Gilchrist–Thomas process, invented by two English chemists, eliminated the phosphorus found in most iron ores. From then onwards steel was increasingly used instead of iron, because of its greater strength and elasticity, in making ships, railway engines, wagons and all sorts of machines and machine-tools.

Steelyard a property in the city of London, owned by the HANSE, between Upper Thames Street and the river. The German merchants, who had rights of self-government there, possessed it from 1320 and were given more premises by Edward IV about 1475. It was closed in 1598 and until 1611 was used as a naval storehouse. The buildings were destroyed in the GREAT FIRE OF LONDON (1666), but were rebuilt, sold in 1853 and demolished in 1863 when Cannon Street railway station was built on the site.

Steeple (1) the pointed spire above the BELFRY of the tower of a CHURCH, most commonly those of the perpendicular period.

(2) The name given to the high, pointed HAT worn by women in the early 15th century. It came from France (where it was known as a Hennin) and was never very fashionable in England.

Steeplechasing originated in the 18th century when riders or hunters used to match their mounts in HORSE-RACING from a given starting-point to a neigh-bouring STEEPLE, which was a mark easily seen from a distance. These impromptu races originated jumping-races as opposed to flat-races and led to 'point-to-point' fixtures at the end of the HUNTING season. The best-known steeplechase, the Grand National, has been run at Aintree, near Liverpool, since 1839.

Steinkirk a long CRAVAT, loosely knotted under the chin with lace ends hanging down or twisted and passed through a ring or a button-hole of the coat. It was fashionable for gentlemen after the Battle of Steinkirk (1692) until the mid-18th century. It was also worn, often highly coloured, by ladies on horseback.

Stereoscope a binocular instrument constructed to obtain a single image giving the impression of solidity or relief from two paired photographs, invented by Sir Charles Wheatstone in 1838. As the MAGIC LANTERN took time and trouble to set up, the craze for viewing with a stereoscope quickly spread through Europe and USA in the middle years of the 19th century.

Steward was the representative of the lord of a MANOR in the Middle Ages and usually had to deal with several manors. He was responsible for their management and had to see that the lord's interests were upheld. He also held the manorial court. Under him was the BAILIFF. In the 17th and 18th centuries the steward was the head of the household of a noble family.

Stirrup a leather strap suspended from the side of a SADDLE and having at its lower end an iron loop with a flattened base to receive the foot of the rider, assisting him in mounting the HORSE and sitting steadily in the saddle while riding. Stirrups were not known to the Romans, who placed stone blocks along their ROADS to enable horsemen to mount. Stirrups were introduced in about the 6th–7th century, but were not generally used until the 12th century. They made possible the use of the LANCE by CAVALRY in warfare.

Stirrup-pump a small pump, worked by hand, with a stirrup-shaped foot-rest and a nozzle for producing a jet or spray of water, used for extinguishing small fires. It was issued to air-raid wardens and fire-watchers in Britain during the Second World War to put out incendiary BOMBS.

Stocks an instrument of punishment used for the public disgrace of minor offenders, especially drunkards, until the 19th century. The offender sat for several hours upon a bench with his feet confined in holes cut in movable planks fitted into wooden posts, one of which was often also used as a WHIPPING-POST. They were usually placed on village greens, MARKET squares and other frequented places. It is uncertain when they were introduced, but the second Statute of Labourers (1350) prescribed stocks as the punishment for unruly workmen, and in 1376 the House of Commons prayed Edward III that stocks should be established in every village. The last stocks in London were removed from outside St Clement Dane's Church in the Strand in 1826, but they are known to have been used later in other places, e.g. Colchester (1858), Tavistock (1863) and Rugby (1865).

Stocks were also used, together with the BACKBOARD, in GIRLS' SCHOOLS during the 18th and 19th centuries to make the pupils sit upright and with their legs stretched straight out.

Stockings of cloth, generally reaching to the knee and held up by garters, were worn by both sexes from ANGLO-SAXON times, but until they began to be knitted in the later 16th century, they were known as HOSE. At first, in the early 16th century, stocking meant the leg-portion of the TRUNK-HOSE and not a separate garment. When BREECHES were replaced by TROUSERS, men took to wearing socks. In this century, when women's SKIRTS became shorter, SILK, RAYON and later NYLON stockings in flesh colour became general. In the early 1960s thicker stockings in bright colours became fashionable, and the middle 1960s the advent of the mini-skirt made nylon tights universally popular. See also BLUE STOCKINGS.

Stole a narrow strip of coloured silk worn by a priest round the neck and hanging down in front. One of the oldest Christian VESTMENTS worn by the CLERGY, it was probably originally a scarf in Roman times and later came to be regarded as representing the yoke of Christ. It is worn by a deacon like a sash across the breast and tied under the right arm.

Stomacher an ornamental covering for the breast and pit of the stomach, generally forming the lower part of the BODICE, worn as part of a lady's dress from the 15th to 17th centuries. It was often embroidered or set with gems. Henry VII (1485–1509) bought 'an ostrich skin for a stomacher' for £1 4s.

Stool-ball a game at least 600 years old, played especially in the north of England, in which originally one player stood before a stool set upon the ground and another player threw a ball at the stool. The first player had to beat the ball away with his hand; if the ball touched the stool or if the player who threw the ball caught it when the other beat it back, then the players changed places. The game was usually, though not always, played by young women, and CRICKET may have been derived from it.

Street-cleaning in medieval TOWNS was at first confined to requiring every householder to keep the pavement outside his house clear. Soon well-to-do people began to employ street-sweepers, and then the authorities in some towns began to employ scavengers or rakers to remove refuse from the middle of streets, from the fronts of unoccupied houses and in the MARKET place. In London they were placed in 1345 under the supervision of the BEADLE and CONSTABLE of each WARD and were empowered to levy a charge on householders who did not keep the pavements clean in front of their houses. They also sometimes made arrangements for REFUSE-COLLECTION.

These arrangements, though they lasted for centuries, did not, however, keep the streets very clean nor prevent people dumping their rubbish out on them. In 1551 William Shakespeare's father was fined for depositing refuse in the street at Stratford-on-Avon; and in 1741 the streets of London were described as 'abounding with such heaps of filth as a savage would look on with amazement'. One great heap at the bottom of Gray's Inn Lane was not moved for a century until 1815 when the dust was extracted and sold to Russia to make bricks for the rebuilding of Moscow after Napoleon I's invasion.

The Public Health Act (1891) required local authorities to ensure a sufficient number of scavengers to sweep and clean the streets and dispose of the refuse. This gradually led to the disappearance of crossing-sweepers, who depended upon tips from passers-by for a livelihood. Since the disappearance of the HORSE, streets have been much cleaner, and though children are killed by the MOTOR-CAR fewer now die of disease in the towns.

Street cries were commonly heard in towns in the past. At different times, people with all sorts of goods to sell advertised them by calling through the streets. The muffin man, carrying on his head a wooden tray of hot muffins, covered with a green baize cloth to keep them warm, rang a bell and sang, 'My bell I keep ringing and walk about merrily singing my muffins'. The flower man, with his plants and flowers on a small cart drawn by a donkey, cried, 'All a-growing and a-blooming'. BAKERS invited people to take their own dough to be baked in the ovens when they were hot by blowing horns, ringing bells and shouting, 'Come to the bakehouse!' And on GOOD FRIDAY they sold HOT CROSS BUNS in the streets. The TOWN CRIER and the WATCHMAN were also to be heard, and so too the BALLAD-singers.

Craftsmen had their street cries. The scissors-grinder took his grindstone around, crying, 'Scissors to grind! Umbrellas to mend!'; and the chair-mender called out, 'Old chairs to mend, rush and cane bottom'. Among street cries sung to simple tunes was the lavender-seller's, 'Will you buy my sweet blooming lavender, three bunches a penny?', and that of the sandman, who sold fine sand for dusting on letters to dry the ink, 'White sand and grey sand! Who'll buy my white sand? Who'll buy my grey sand?' Other street cries included, 'Quick periwinkles, quick, quick, quick'; 'Fine Seville oranges, fine lemons'; 'Sweet juniper, juniper, will you buy my bunch of juniper?'; 'I ha'ripe cowcumbers, ripe, ripe, ripe'; 'Buy my fine Jemmies, my little Tartars, but a half-penny each' (these being CANES and BIRCH-RODS for use in home or school).

The *Illustrated London News* in 1848 stated that 'many of the London cries, which once resounded through our crowded thoroughfares, and which the old inhabitants still remember, are no longer heard', having been drowned in 'the rattle and roll and thunder of our modern vehicles'. In the London suburbs and the larger towns, street cries were still to be heard until about 1890 and into the turn of this century in smaller places. Today the scrap-metal merchants, carol-singers at CHRISTMAS and loudspeaker-vans at election-times are still to be heard.

Strip lynchets usually to be found on the scarp faces of chalk downland, repre-sent the contour ploughing of the ANGLO-SAXONS, though some belong to the early Middle Ages. After ploughing, the top-soil on the hillslope tended to slide down-hill and pile up in terraces wherever it met some such obstruction as a fence, wall or other field boundary. [James Dyer, *Discovering Archaeology in England and Wales* (1969)]

Stucco a plaster of lime and sand used as a coating in buildings. A fine stucco is used in internal decoration to cover walls and ceilings and for making cor-nices and mouldings. A coarser stucco is a sort of cement for covering exterior sur-faces of walls in imitation of stone. In REGENCY architecture, the whole of the exteriors of buildings were finished with painted stucco.

Suffragettes the name given by the *Daily Mail* in 1906 to members of the Women's Social and Political Union formed in 1903 in Manchester by Mrs Emmeline Pankhurst (1858–1928), who believed in direct action, including what she called the 'argument of the stone'. It organized a campaign of violence to secure the parliamentary vote for WOMEN in which election meetings were dis-turbed, shop windows broken and churches burned. Their militancy may have delayed the granting of the vote; the work of women in jobs such as munitions workers and bus conductors in the First World War probably did more to bring it about. See also TEA-SHOPS, TYPEWRITER. [Roger Fulford, *Votes for Women* (1957)]

Sugar was first introduced into Europe in small quantities from Asia in about AD 625, but in the Middle Ages HONEY was mostly used for sweetening. As a result of the CRUSADES, it came into Europe in sufficient quantities to be used in wealthy households by the mid-13th century. It was grown in Syria and processed in the factories of Acre and Tyre. In about 1148 the sugar-cane was transported to Cyprus, and thenceforwards the sugar industry flourished in the Venetian and Genoese colonies of the eastern Mediterranean. It was also introduced into Madeira about 1420 and into the West Indies about 1506.

Sugar was first imported through Bristol in Henry VI's reign (1422–71), and cookery books of the 15th century show that it was a frequent ingredient in the food of rich families. In the 17th cen-tury imports by the East India Company made sugar much cheaper and led to the custom of serving sweets or puddings at MEALS. After the RESTORATION, the Eng-lish planters in the West Indies grew less TOBACCO and more sugar and hence-forward supplied Britain and Europe with most of its sugar.

Sugar was first obtained from beet in Germany in 1747, but little use was made of the discovery until Napoleon I encour-aged its development in order to attack the British monopoly of cane-sugar. The growing of sugar-beet was subsidized in Britain in 1914–18 and again from 1924 onwards. In 1928 there were 18 sugar-beet factories in Britain, and by 1934 Britain produced nearly a quarter of her total consumption of sugar. In 1936 an Act of Parliament joined all the factories into a single British Sugar Corpora-tion on the management of which the government is represented. Since the Second World War the government has fixed the price paid for sugar-beet to farmers and also each year the maximum acreage of beet which the Corporation may contract with farmers to grow.

The consumption of sugar in Britain has been growing since the early 19th century, partly owing to increased drinking of TEA. It has quadrupled over the last 100 years to reach an average consumption per person of 110 lb a year, though it has recently shown signs of declining, probably through medical insistence upon the dangers of over-weight to health.

Sugar-loaf a conical mass of refined sugar, usually about 14 lb. in weight and resembling in shape a DUNCE'S CAP. This was how sugar reached the grocer in the 19th century. It was broken by him into chunks to be sold and further cut into small pieces in the home by means of sugar-nippers.

Summer-house a feature of GARDENS since the 16th century. Elizabethan gardens were designed as a series of more or less enclosed spaces, and one or more might have a summer-house as a focal point; Montacute House, Somerset, has two square towers at the corners of the

Summer house

wall enclosing the PARTERRE in front of the house. The 18th-century garden and surrounding park were laid out as a single whole with little summer houses, often like classical temples, to give interest to a view; it also had GAZEBOS, BELVEDERES and HERMITS' caves. The ROMANTIC MOVEMENT in the late 18th and early 19th cen-

turies led to a fashion for fantastic summer-houses in GOTHIC and eastern styles, some with walls lined with shells and lit by coloured glass. Victorian summer-houses were commonly of wood and had thatched roofs.

Summer time originated with the idea of William Willett, a London builder, who first urged in 1907 that clocks in Britain should be advanced one hour beyond Greenwich Mean Time for a period during the summer months so as to have longer summer evenings. Adopted in 1916 as a wartime measure to economize in artificial lighting, it was continued after the war and became permanent in 1925. Double Summer Time (two hours in advance of Greenwich Mean Time) was adopted during the later summers of the Second World War with Summer Time throughout the rest of the year. From 1947 to 1968 the period of Summer Time was fixed each year by an Order-in-Council. In 1968 British time was fixed permanently one hour in advance of Greenwich Mean Time, but this arrangement was abandoned in 1971.

Sunday was enforced as a day of religious observance by ANGLO-SAXON kings with increasing strictness, and medieval GUILDS and BOROUGHS regulated Sunday trading. The Sunday Fairs Act (1448), the oldest Sunday observance law still in force, was passed because 'for great earthly covetise' some towns refused to close their Sunday MARKETS. John Wycliffe (1329?–84) said that Sunday was for thinking about God, speaking to God and worshipping God, while William Lyndwood (1375–1446), the leading contemporary English canonist, said that Sunday should be kept only in hymns and psalms and spiritual songs; but by the later Middle Ages it was marked by games and dancing, and preachers lamented that there was more crime and drunkenness on

Sundays than during the rest of the week.

After the REFORMATION, the PURITANS identified the Jewish Sabbath with the Christian Lord's Day. James I's *Book of Sports* (1618) enjoined 'lawful and harmless' recreation after divine service, but it was burned by Parliament in 1643. Under the COMMONWEALTH all recreation, even going for a walk, was prohibited on Sunday. After the RESTORATION, observance was slightly relaxed; the Act for the Better Observance of the Lord's Day (1677) forbade all work and travel by horse or boat on Sunday, but did not mention recreations. The early 18th century was marked by greater liberty, but the Lord's Day Observance Act (1781), passed through EVANGELICAL influence, required that any place of entertainment or debate where there was payment for admission should be closed on Sunday.

In Scotland Sabbatarianism was strong. From the beginning of the 17th century all recreation, including even books and music not strictly religious, was forbidden. When Shelley visited Edinburgh he was threatened with imprisonment for laughing in the street on a Sunday.

In the 19th century Sunday in Britain was still largely given to religious observances, but in this century relaxation has been progressive. Parliament agreed to the opening of museums and art galleries on Sundays in 1896, and in 1932 the Sunday opening of cinemas was permitted under a system of local option. The Lord's Day Observance Society (founded 1831), however, succeeded in preventing the opening on Sundays of theatres during the First World War and of the Wembley Exhibition (1924 and 1925) and the Fun Fair at Battersea in the Festival of Britain (1951). The Crathorne Committee (1961) recommended the removal of restrictions on Sunday entertainments.

Sunday schools were first founded in the later 18th century, some of the earliest being by Hannah and Martha More in the Mendip district and Hannah Ball in High Wycombe (Bucks.), and in 1780 Robert Raikes (1735–1811) organized the schools in Gloucester into a successful movement and publicized them in his *Journal*. In 1803 the interdenominational Sunday School Union was founded and was supported particularly by EVANGELICALS and NONCONFORMISTS. The schools usually met on a Sunday morning and taught both religion and reading and writing. In 1833 it was stated that, while six out of ten children attended some sort of school, three of these were at a Sunday school. With the development of BRITISH SCHOOLS and NATIONAL SCHOOLS, Sunday schools devoted themselves to religious education and became more denominational. [Catharine R. Newby, *The Story of Sunday Schools* (1930).] See also RAGGED SCHOOLS.

Sundials are known to have been used in ROMAN BRITAIN since they are depicted on the MOSAICS of VILLAS, e.g. Brading (Isle of Wight). The ANGLO-SAXONS had mass or scratch dials, roughly carved on the south walls of CHURCHES or on churchyard crosses; many may still be seen, though the gnomon, which cast the shadow, has usually disappeared. They were divided into four periods (called 'tides'), probably to give guidance for the tolling of the BELL for MASS. The earliest such dials are on Bewcastle Cross (Cumberland) and Escomb Church (Co. Durham), both dating from about AD 670.

After the NORMAN CONQUEST, sundials appeared with 12-hour lines. At Bishopstone (Sussex) a dial inscribed with four mass lines and the Anglo-Saxon name 'Eadric' has eight shorter lines added by the Normans to conform to the duodecimal system of measurement. After 1350, through the investigations of the

Arab mathematician, Abdul Hassan, into the positioning of the gnomon in relation to the earth's axis, greater accuracy was obtained by the more careful construction and siting of the dials. One result was the use of multiple dials, each face giving the time at a different season of the year; Hitchin Church (Herts.) has two dials, while some in the Cotswolds have six or

Anglo Saxon sundial

Portable sundial

seven. In the 15th century the sundial set like a table-top on a stone pillar was first introduced; and at the same time day and night were divided into 24 *equal* hours, a change necessitated by the introduction of mechanically-driven CLOCKS. Even after the introduction of clocks, village churches still used sundials, which were cheaper and often more reliable. Before WATCHES became common, small portable sundials were used, which often incorporated a small COMPASS so that they could be set in the right direction. See also TIME.

Surgery is known to have been practised by early men as skulls have been found with little round holes cut out of them, presumably with FLINT knives and in order to relieve severe headaches or let out evil spirits from the head. The army surgeons in ROMAN BRITAIN ranked as non-combatants, enjoying many privileges, and memorial inscriptions to those who died on service have been found. The practice of surgery was at a low ebb during the Middle Ages, but the revival of learning during the RENAISSANCE revived interest in it. Surgeons and PHYSICIANS were exempted from bearing arms and JURY service in 1513, but there were only 13 in London. In 1540 the Company of Barber-Surgeons was founded as a craft GUILD, but the barbers were not allowed to perform any operations except the drawing of teeth. In 1745 the surgeons left it, and the Royal College of Surgeons was established. Modern surgery owes its development to the introduction of ANAESTHETICS and ANTISEPTICS. [W. J. Bishop, *The Early History of Surgery* (1960).] See also DENTISTRY, MEDICINE.

Surplice an ecclesiastical VESTMENT of white linen with wide sleeves. Originally it was a loose, knee-length garment worn by the clergy in church (except at the ALTAR) in place of the short, narrow-sleeved ALB because it was better-suited to be worn over the fur coats customary in northern countries (hence its name derived from the Latin, *superpellicum*, 'over a fur garment'). From the 12th century it was the distinctive dress of the lower CLERGY and was used by priests for services other than the MASS. It was also worn by members of CHOIRS in church.

In the CHURCH OF ENGLAND, the Book of COMMON PRAYER of 1552 made it the only prescribed vestment for the clergy, but the Ornaments Rubric ordering this was removed in later editions. The

PURITANS objected to the wearing of the surplice, but Archbishop Parker in Elizabeth I's reign and Archbishop Laud in Charles I's reign ordered all clergy to use it during services. In the 18th century it became usual for the clergy to exchange it for a black gown when they went into the PULPIT to preach. The EVANGELICALS continued this practice, but it was abandoned by the TRACTARIANS, an action which gave rise to great controversy in the middle of the 19th century.

Sutton Hoo site of an ANGLO-SAXON ship burial (about AD 650), near Woodbridge (Suffolk), probably in commemoration of an East Anglian king or warrior. The 80-ft-long ship was laden with rich grave goods, including a silver bowl from Byzantium, two silver spoons marked Saul and Paul (indicating Christian influence), another bowl from Egypt, a helmet, shield and sword from Sweden, and money in bejewelled gold purse from Merovingian Gaul (i.e. France). This exceptional treasure is now in the British Museum.

To Anglo-Saxon warriors, GOLD, SILVER and other treasure were symbols of wealth and grandeur, and so, as shown in this hoard, they were gathered from afar by loot, tribute, gifts and trade. Though no corpse was found in the BARROW, this burial was an example of the custom of setting a warrior adrift after death in his own boat and with his own possessions into the after life. It is thought that the owner of this boat was perhaps drowned. [R. L. S. Bruce-Mitford, *The Sutton Hoo Ship Burial, a Provisional Guide* (British Museum, 1956)]

Swaddling bands or sheath bands, long bandages used for wrapping round the body and limbs of a baby, giving it the appearance of a mummy. The baby usually remained thus swaddled until it was weaned. This was the usual practice

from the Middle Ages to the end of the 18th century, but among the upper classes swaddling was replaced by long clothes from the late 17th century in the form of a long gown, some 3 ft or even

Swaddling clothes

more in length, fastening at the back, with short sleeves, and the whole was often richly ornamented with lace and embroidery. This garment appears to have been adapted from the 'Christening Robe' formerly only used on that occasion.

Swans were kept from the 13th century by the wealthy for both ornament and food, being eaten at banquets and at CHRISTMAS. The bird was plucked, impaled on a spit and, after it was cooked, was dressed in its feathers and brought ceremoniously to the table with a piece of blazing camphor on a wick in its beak. Among the provisions ordered for Henry III's Christmas in 1247 at Winchester were 40 swans. King's College and Trinity College, Cambridge, each had a swan-house, and the Hospital of St Giles, Norwich, had until the Second World War a swan-pit in which swans were kept. The swan was largely replaced for eating by the turkey in the 17th century. The Crown has a monopoly of the swans on the River Thames.

Sweet pea originally came from Sicily in 1699, but it was an insignificant flower and proved difficult to hybridize or 'cross' until Henry Eckford, a gardener employed by a Gloucestershire doctor in the 19th century, resolved to seek to develop it. His laborious work in producing new varieties resulted in the first 'modern' sweet pea, which was exhibited in 1882. The first variety with wavy edges appeared in 1902 and was immediately popular in GARDENS.

Sweet pig a sweetmeat model of a PIG commonly sold by street-hawkers in the 18th century. A vendor of such pigs was described in a CHAPBOOK in these words— 'This man makes pigs of paste and fills their bellies with currants and places two little currants in their heads for eyes.' It was not a live pig, but this sort of pig which was stolen and straightway eaten by Tom, the piper's son, in the nursery rhyme. [I. and P. Opie, *The Oxford Dictionary of Nursery Rhymes* (1951)]

Sword has developed from the FLINT cutting WEAPONS of the Stone Ages. The Romans used a short thrusting sword about 20 to 30 in. long and the Normans a cutting broadsword. The 14th century brought the 'saddle-sword' with a long, thin blade used by mounted soldiers. The sword became an emblem of CHIVALRY, used to make a man a KNIGHT and as a crucifix to comfort the dying on the battlefield. Swords were long worn by well-dressed gentlemen in everyday life, but to prevent DUELS in the SPA Nash prohibited their wearing at Bath, and they became replaced by CANES.

T

Tables used by the Romans were made of wood or marble and were low because the diners reclined on couches. In the HALL of a medieval HOUSE, the tables were of trestle-construction, being long boards of oak or elm resting on two or more supports, which could easily be dismantled after a meal and propped against

17th-cent. gateleg table

the wall. The joined table, in which the main underframe was fixed into the tops of legs, was first used in England early in the 16th century and was often fitted

Roman table

281

with leaves that could be drawn out from underneath. See also CHEST, CARPET.

The 18th century saw a multiplication of special sorts of tables, which may be divided into eating, console and gaming types, and eating tables were further divided into breakfast, dining and tea tables. A large house had a small separate breakfast room, and the table was small

18th-cent. console table

with end flaps to make it less obtrusive during the day; for dining tables the gate-leg style was popular early in the century, to be replaced from about 1735 by oval or circular table with carved legs; tea tables were usually small, just large enough to take the tea-tray, and often delicately carved. Console tables were decorative rather than functional, often having one

19th-cent. oval table

side supported against a wall by a bracket, and commonly had marble tops. Gaming tables often had hinged side flaps which could be folded away when not in use; the playing surface was covered with green baize or needlework; the corners were dished for candlesticks and provided with wells for money.

Table manners do not seem to have been considered so important in early medieval society as the proper seating of people at the TABLE. It was particularly necessary at a feast to decide who was to sit above and below the SALT.

Some of the earliest directions about table manners seem to be those issued for MONKS in their REFECTORY—'The bretheren ought to eat what is set before them temperately, cleanly and cheerfully; they ought to speak sparingly and not let their eyes wander. None should sit chin in hand or spread his hands across his face; each brother should sit straight and keep his arms off the table. He must not wipe his teeth on the table-cloth or cut or wipe the table-cloth with his knife'. To prevent them speaking unnecessarily, an elaborate sign-language was evolved for use at meals, e.g. 'Fish—Wag thy hand displayed sideways in the manner of a fish tail'; 'Mustard—Hold thy nose in the upper part of thy right fist and rub it'; 'Ale—Bow thy right finger and put it on thy nether lip'.

Later medieval books of ETIQUETTE for the young were more concerned with table manners, especially for boys entering a great household as PAGES. One written in the 15th century urged, 'Set never on fish, flesh or fowl more than two fingers and a thumb'; 'Look thy nails be clean, lest thy fellows loathe thee'; 'If thou spit over the table, thou shalt be considered discourteous'. The refectory of the MONASTERY and the hall of the CASTLE had, indeed, a strong effect in spreading good table manners among the young noblemen who were educated there.

The English were not, however, thought to be particularly well-mannered at the table in the 16th century. A French visitor complained in 1558 that they 'belch at table without reserve or shame'. It was still then customary to gnaw bones, but not good manners to throw them on to the RUSHES on the floor or give them to cats or dogs.

The *Rules of Civility* in the 17th century warned, 'You must not blow your nose publicly at the table, or without holding your hat or napkin before your face, wipe off the sweat from your face with your handkerchief'. CUTLERY was then slowly coming into use; and in 1774 Lord Chesterfield warned his son against eating with his knife, picking his teeth with his fork and putting his spoon, 'which has been into his throat twenty times, into the dishes again'.

In the 19th century increasing emphasis was placed upon the need for good table manners among well-to-do children. In some families a CANE was kept in the dining-room, perhaps stuck behind the great ornamental mirror over the mantelpiece, and when the maids laid the table for dinner it was placed at the father's right hand to enforce good behaviour among the children with a sharp cut or two across their shoulders. However, a doubt was expressed by *Hints on Etiquette* (1834)—'Fashions are continually changing, even at the best tables; and what is considered the height of good taste in one year, is declared vulgar the next'.

Tally a length of wood scored right across with notches or cuts representing the amount or quantity of goods delivered or the amount of debt or payment due between two persons. After being notched the tally stick was split in two lengthwise across the notches, the buyer and seller or payer and payee each keeping a half as a record. This way of keeping accounts was introduced into England at the NORMAN CONQUEST, and it was long used by the Exchequer, which used small notches to represent pence; larger, shillings; still larger, pounds; and proportionately larger and wider, £10, £100 and £1000. When an account was paid, the two halves of the tally were tied up together and stored in the Tally Office of the Exchequer. The use of tallies by the Exchequer was abolished in 1782, and the accumulated tallies were ordered to be destroyed in 1834. These were burnt in a stove in the House of Lords, but the stove, becoming overheated, set fire to the panelling of the room, and the Houses of Parliament were destroyed.

In LAUNDERING a tally was also sometimes used, especially if the maid-servants could not read. It was an oblong block of wood, bound with brass and faced with transparent horn, which was inscribed with the names of various articles of clothing, etc. Under each word was a small disc to be turned to show the numbers of articles of each kind to be washed on any particular day.

Tansy a strongly aromatic, bitter-tasting HERB with small yellow flowers and erect feathery leaves growing in abundance on marshy ground. The leaves formed an ingredient of a kind of cake or fritter called Tansies and eaten especially at EASTER in remembrance of the bitter herbs eaten by the Jews at the Passover. John Parkinson (1567–1650) said tansy should be 'eaten young, shred small with other herbs, fit for the purpose, beaten with eggs and fried into cakes'; and John Selden wrote in his *Table Talk* (1689), 'Our Tansies at Easter have reference to the bitter herbs, though at the same time 'twas always the fashion for a man to have a gammon of bacon to show himself to be no Jew'.

The juice of tansy was also used for COSMETIC purposes.

Tapestry a thick, hand-woven fabric, usually of wool, in which the picture or pattern is woven (see also WEAVING). In the later Middle Ages the craft was especially developed in France, notably in Arras, which was so famous that from the 14th to 16th centuries the name of the town was often given to any tapestry. The only important English factory was at Mortlake (1619–1703). Tapestries were hung on the walls of houses from about the 14th century until replaced by WALLPAPER. Leather wall hangings, which were popular in Spain and other Continental countries in the 17th century, never seem to have found much favour in England. See also BAYEUX TAPESTRY.

Tartan the term used today for the pattern of colouring characteristic of the cloth or PLAID made in the Scottish Highlands and used for KILTS; but this type of pattern is not peculiarly Scottish. It is one of the simplest types to invent and is found in many parts of the world as a native production.

Not until the early 19th century was it identified with particular CLANS. In the later 18th century, as Highland regiments were raised for the British army, regimental tartans were systematized. Persistent interest in tartans began in 1822 when George IV visited Edinburgh wearing an exuberant form of Highland dress. They were made popular by Sir Walter Scott's novels and the efforts of the two Sobieski Stuart brothers, who claimed descent from the Young Pretender and possession of an ancient manuscript laying down systematically all the correct clan tartans.

There is no suggestion of this identification in contemporary portraits before the 19th century. In the range of Grant portraits at Castle Grant no tartan is repeated, and none is like the modern Grant tartan. All pictorial evidence suggests that there was no agreed system of design for tartans throughout the Highlands in the 18th century or earlier, but rather that Scottish gentlemen and ladies chose the patterns in their clothing to suit their taste. The present-day myth is due to a combination of manufacturing enterprise, patriotism and tourism. [H. F. McClintock, *Old Irish and Highland Dress* (1951)]

Tasset overlapping plates hanging from the CUIRASS in medieval body ARMOUR and protecting the thighs.

Taverns as distinct from INNS, originally could only provide casual refreshment and were not licensed to entertain and put up guests. They existed in England at least as early as the 13th century and were often kept by women or ale-wives. An act of 1284 ordered them to be shut at the CURFEW. In the mid-14th century there were only three taverns (or alehouses) in London: one in Cheapside, one in Walbrook and one in Lombard Street. An act of 1552 permitted forty in London, eight in York, six in Bristol, four each in Norwich, Hull, Exeter, Gloucester, Chester, Canterbury, Cambridge and Newcastle-on-Tyne and three each in Westminster, Lincoln, Shrewsbury, Salisbury, Hereford, Worcester, Southampton, Ipswich, Oxford, Winchester and Colchester. Taverns were first licensed in 1752, and in 1830 there were nearly 4000 in London. In the 19th century they became commonly known as public houses, and the late Victorian town ones were extravagant, exuberant and highly ornamented with ironwork, wood carving, engraved glass, polished mirrors and tiled pictures. In the 1930s the MOTOR CAR brought ROAD HOUSES and large, new public houses on the arterial roads and by-passes with bright mock-Tudor lounges.

Tawse a leather strap, usually with its end slit into several narrow strips, used in Scotland for chastising children in schools and families.

Taxi-cab came to be so-called after the taximeter, a German-invented automatic device fitted on to a cab to indicate to passengers the distance travelled and the fare due. It was first fitted to London motor-cabs in about 1907, and they soon became known as taxi-cabs or taxis.

Tea reached Europe in 1610 and was introduced into England about 50 years later from Holland. Pepys wrote on October 25, 1660, 'I did send for a cup of tea (a China drink) of which I had never drank before'. When first introduced it cost £6–£10 per lb and remained at 16s–60s per lb until 1689 when the EAST INDIA COMPANY first imported it directly from China and carried it in its own ships; in 1721 the Company was granted the sole right to import China tea and enjoyed this monopoly until 1833. The price remained more than 10s per lb in the 18th century. See also SMUGGLING.

At first tea was drunk by the well-to-do in TAVERNS and COFFEE-HOUSES, but in the early 18th century tea-drinking developed in private houses, though it was still mainly a luxury of the urban rich. It was carefully kept in a CADDY, and in larger houses the company withdrew to a 'tea-room' where the cups and saucers were kept and tea was drunk. Taken by both sexes, it contributed to the softening of manners, and by the end of the century was replacing the conventional drunkenness after dinner. See also TABLE.

By the early 19th century, other classes were drinking tea, and the estimated annual consumption per head of the population was 2–3 lb. The abolition of the East India Company's monopoly brought the price down, but a heavy duty kept it at over 3s. a lb. until the 1850s. It was made cheaper and became the drink of all classes through lower tariffs and the introduction from 1839 of Indian tea which gradually superseded China tea.

Tea was first retailed in sealed packets under a proprietary name in 1826 by John Horniman, whose sealed, lead-lined packets soon became popular. Packeting was first put on a mass-production basis when the Mazawattee Tea Company offered a high-priced, extensively advertised pure Ceylon tea. Lipton's stores in 1889 sold tea at 1s 7d per lb; until then no tea had sold under 2s 6d per lb. Such cheap tea was made possible by selling it in multiple stores together with provisions and by centralized buying and control. By 1914 there were over 500 Lipton stores, and these and rival multiple stores dominated the trade. By 1967, 86 per cent of tea was sold by five manufacturers. (See also GROCER).

The British are still the biggest tea-drinkers, consuming 500 million lb a year or 9 lb each, compared with 1 lb a year in India and 0·8 lb in USA. Most Britons drink 5–6 cups a day. Most of the tea now comes from India, next Ceylon and then the African countries (Kenya, Uganda, Tanzania and Malawi); little now comes from China.

Tea-shops began in London in the later 19th century. The first ABC shops were opened in 1880 and the first Lyons tea-shop in Piccadilly in 1894. These were the first places where WOMEN could have a meal on their own and so meet friends outside their own homes. Previously they had to go to restaurants escorted by a husband or brother. This was of considerable importance for the SUFFRAGETTES.

Technological universities (Aston, Bath, Bradford, Brunel, City University, Heriot-Watt, Loughborough, Salford, Strathclyde, Surrey) are former Colleges of Advanced Technology which were made UNIVERSITIES in 1966. Although best known for their conventional engineering and technology courses with an emphasis on integrated industrial training 'sandwiched' with teaching they are individually increasing the subjects they teach, (e.g. in the social sciences, modern languages and regional studies). See also POLYTECHNICS.

Teddy boys youths in the early 1950s who adopted an Edwardian style of dress consisting of drainpipe trousers, drape jackets, slim-jim ties, shoes with thick crepe soles and greasy hair styles. The garb was first propagated in the late 1940s by the *Tailor and Cutter* magazine, but was abandoned in fashionable circles when it was taken up by young gangs, the first of these being the Elephant Mob at the Elephant and Castle in South London, as a uniform which signified rebellion. The gangs met on bomb-sites, fought with flick-knives, knuckle-dusters and bicycle-chains and 'bowled' along the pavements in line abreast pushing everyone else into the gutter. [Vernon Bogandow and Robert Skidelsky (eds.), *The Age of Affluence 1951–1964* (1970)]

Telegraph began with several forms of mechanical telegraphs or semaphores used in Britain by the end of the 18th century. These had to be placed in conspicuous positions, such as the numerous 'Telegraph Hills' in different parts of the country. During the Napoleonic War, the naval authorities used a series of semaphores, displaying frames with various signal devices, to send messages from London to the south-coast ports. The early RAILWAYS had similar devices to communicate with signalmen.

Electric telegraphy began with the invention of Samuel Morse, who demonstrated it in 1844 by sending a message from Washington to Baltimore. In 1839 the Great Western Railway installed an electric telegraph service between Paddington and Slough, and in 1842 the arrest of a murderer at Paddington after the police had been alerted by telegraph popularized the invention.

Submarine telegraph cables were laid between England and France in 1850–1, between England and Belgium in 1853 and between England and USA (after a failure in 1858) in 1866.

From 1846 private companies in Britain were offering telegraph services; but in 1869 the Post Office was granted a monopoly of British inland telegrams.

Telephone was invented by an American, Alexander Graham Bell, in 1875, was exhibited in 1876 at the Centennial Exposition, Philadelphia, as the 'lover's telegraph' and was launched commercially in 1877. A telephone exchange with seven or eight subscribers was opened in London in 1879, and soon afterwards the Post Office also opened its exchanges. A number of private and municipal telephone companies operated under licence from the Post Office; the largest, the National Telephone Company, had 700 000 telephones in 1912, the year when the Post Office took over all telephone services, except in the city of Hull and the Channel Islands where they are still operated municipally. Subscriber dialling was invented in 1896, but the first British automatic exchange, at Epsom, was not opened until 1912 and the first large automatic exchange in London in 1927. Subscriber trunk dialling was initiated in the Bristol area in 1958. In 1921 Britain had nearly one million telephones and 47 people per telephone; in 1968 there were over 11 million telephones and 6·2 people per telephone. The USA had 8 people per telephone in 1921 and 2·5 people in 1968.

Telescope was invented about 1608 by the Dutch optician, Hans Lippershey, who discovered that a double-convex lens, as object-glass, and a double-concave lens, as eye-piece, placed together some distance apart magnified distant objects. This refracting telescope, however, was subject to chromatic aberration, which produced coloured edges round the image, blurring the outline. In the 17th century, however, Italian GLASS-makers, who had come to England, solved this problem by making lenses of different kinds of glass which dispersed the spectrum.

Television was first demonstrated in October 1925 when John Logie Baird (1888–1946), transmitted an image in his laboratory in Soho (London). His system was demonstrated by Selfridge's store and used by the BBC for its first television transmission in 1929, but it adopted the Marconi system for its first regular television service from Alexandra Palace in 1936. This service was closed down on the outbreak of the Second World War and resumed in 1946. The BBC opened its Manchester transmitter in 1949; Independent Television began in 1955; and Channel 2 (BBC) in 1964. Colour television began in 1967 on BBC 2 and on the other channels in 1969. By 1958 there were more homes with television than with a RADIO alone, and by 1961 there were 12 million television sets in use (i.e. 9 homes out of 10 had one).

Templars the military order of the Temple of Solomon, founded in 1118 by Hugh de Payens, a knight of Champagne, to protect pilgrims on the road from the coast to Jerusalem, but they soon took to fighting Moslems. They wore a red cross on a white ground and in 1128 adopted a form of CISTERCIAN rule. In the 12th century they grew greatly in numbers and wealth, being organized under a Grand Master and a General Chapter and arranged in provinces, each under a Commander. Within each province they had churches and 'preceptories' or houses. Their churches, e.g. the Temple Church, London, and the Round Church, Cambridge, were circular in imitation of the Holy Sepulchre, Jerusalem. The Old Temple in London was their headquarters in England from about 1128 until replaced by the New Temple in 1184. English PLACE NAMES, e.g. Temple Cressing (Essex), Temple Newsam (Yorks.) and Templecombe (Somerset), record that they had preceptories there, a few of which were HOSPITALS, but most were for managing their estates and recruiting members.

The numbers were usually small, being only 165 in England in 1308 when the English revenues of the order totalled £4720 a year. When driven out of Palestine, their members returned to Europe, where they became powerful and independent. They were expelled from England in 1308, and some of their property was given to the HOSPITALLERS, who leased their headquarters in London to a body of lawyers, from which developed the Inner and Middle Temple.

Temples were built in large GARDENS in the 18th and 19th centuries to adorn the landscape. They were usually constructed of stone and round, rectangular or octagonal with pedimented porticos, Corinthian pillars and domes. They do not seem ever to have served any purpose other than to draw the eye along a vista, enhance the pastoral scene or add a point of interest to the view. Fine examples of such temples can be seen at Stowe (Bucks.), Stourhead (Wilts.), Castle Howard (Yorks.) and Studley Royal (Yorks.).

Tenant-in-Chief was, under FEUDALISM, a man who held a FIEF directly of the king (see also BARONS). After the NORMAN CONQUEST, they were very numerous in England, including not only those who held large estates, but also a large number who held only a single KNIGHT'S FEE and a single MANOR. See also WARDSHIP.

Tennis was introduced into England from France in the 13th century, being a game for two or four players, at first probably played with the palm of the hand, but later with rackets. The walled oblong court (measuring about 96½ × 30 ft) is divided by a net, about 3 ft high. The ball is driven against the wall to make it rebound beyond the net, and it then has to be kept in motion, points being lost by players who let it fall to the ground. The tennis court at HAMPTON COURT was completed in 1530. By 1615 there were 15 courts in London, and the game remained popular until some years after the RESTORATION. It has now been almost completely superseded by LAWN TENNIS.

Thatch has been used for the roofing of HOUSES from early times when people sought something more substantial and more permanent than foliage or herbage, being usually of RUSHES (and later straw as well) laid on a foundation of brushwood. Its replacement by tiles began in the 12th century, and in 1212, because of the danger of fire, its use was forbidden in London. It gradually ceased to be used generally in the 19th century.

Thatch hook a medieval FIRE-FIGHTING implement used for pulling THATCH from burning houses. A law of Edward II (1307–27) required every London PARISH to have a fire crook or thatch hook of iron, with a wooden handle, together with two chains and two strong cords. It also enacted that stone party walls of houses in London should be continued above the roofs to form fire barriers and that roofs should in future be of lead, tiles or straw and not stubble; but, despite the law, party walls were not always of stone or brick before 1666, even in London, and in many country places the walls rarely continued above the roof until recent times. The only way, therefore, of

creating a firebreak was to tear down the thatch and isolate the burning building or buildings from others which were not yet alight. The chain hung hooks were mounted on 16–20 ft long poles and were wielded by several men or harnessed to horses.

Theatres may have been quite numerous in ROMAN BRITAIN, but the sites of only four are known—St Albans (Herts.) Colchester (Essex), Canterbury (Kent) and Brough (Yorks.). The one at St Albans was built about 150 AD. It is open to the sky with tiered seats embracing a circular arena for three-quarters of its circumference. The arena, 80 ft in diameter, was probably not used for

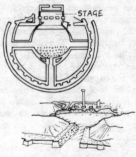

Roman theatre

classical plays, but singers and dancers may have performed on the small stage at one end, and as no AMPHITHEATRE has been found, it was probably used also for COCK-FIGHTING and wild beast hunts.

In the Middle Ages MIRACLE PLAYS were performed, and actors played in the galleried courtyards of INNS and the HALLS of CASTLES and MANORS. In 1576 James Burbage built the first theatre at Shoreditch, which was modelled on the inn-yards and BULL-BAITING and BEAR-BAITING rings south of the River Thames. Others followed in Elizabeth I's reign, including the Globe (1599) and the Blackfriars (1596). These had a platform stage projecting into the auditorium, so that the audience surrounded it on three sides. Only the galleries and stage were protected by a roof, and the stage had neither front-curtain nor artificial light. There were also smaller, rectangular, roofed-in, candle-lit private theatres, and one belonging to Burbage was the winter home of Shakespeare's company during his last years. Early in the 17th century Inigo Jones, influenced by Italian developments, introduced the picture-frame stage with a proscenium

16th-cent. theatre

arch. Set in this was a painted curtain on rollers which lifted to reveal a painted scene which was changed during the play. This made the playhouse much like a modern theatre.

During the COMMONWEALTH the theatres were closed, but at the RESTORATION Charles II licensed two companies of players, which had theatres, one being in Drury Lane. This was lit by candelabra and had a fixed proscenium arch and a large apron stage stretching as far in front of the arch as the stage for scenery stretched behind. On each side of the apron stage were two doors with boxes or balconies above; these doors were the usual means of entering or leaving the stage. Most seats were now in the pit, the dearest in the boxes and the cheapest in the upper galleries.

For over 200 years after 1737, only two theatres in London, Drury Lane and Covent Garden, were permitted to show plays, but many smaller theatres evaded the law by mixing plays with concerts and other entertainments, and in them evolved the OPERA and PANTOMIME. Their productions were expensive, and so the apron stage was shortened to make room for more seats. There were, however, a number of provincial theatres in the 18th century, some of which have survived, e.g. at Bristol and Richmond (Yorks.)

In 1843 the monopoly of the two London patent theatres was ended, and the smaller London theatres could legally produce plays. There are now about 250 professional theatres in Britain, 40 of them being in London. [R. Mander and J. Mitchenson, *A Picture History of the British Theatre* (1957)]

Thegn or thane was originally in ANGLO-SAXON England a member of a royal bodyguard, who gradually held land in return for their service and acquired a hereditary status. The NORMAN CONQUEST reduced their powers and position, and the title ceased to be used soon afterwards.

In Scotland, the title of thane was given to the ruler of a county or province or the chief of a CLAN.

Threshing-machine was invented in 1784 by Andrew Meikle, a Scottish millwright. It was first driven by horses, but later by steam. Its introduction into England was one of the reasons for the rural riots in 1830 because it deprived men of the constant winter-work provided by threshing with the FLAIL in the BARN, and many were destroyed during the disturbances. By the second half of the 19th century, however, it had been adopted on most farms.

Timber-lacing a method of strengthening the ramparts of HILLFORTS of the IRON AGE period by securing horizontal cross-timbers through the body of the

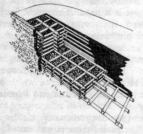

Timber lacing

rampart to connect with vertical posts at the front and rear. They were often also connected with stone revetting or facing. See also VITRIFIED FORTS.

Timbrel a small DRUM, played with the hand, of ancient origin, like the modern tambourine. It was commonly used in the Middle Ages to accompany DANCING. Timbrel-girls (or timbesteres or balance-mistresses) were women who danced and played upon the timbrel, occasionally tossing it into the air and catching it again on one finger. Like MINSTRELS, they often went about in bands or companies.

Time has been measured in various ways in the past. Among the earliest devices were the SUN DIAL, HOUR-GLASS, CANDLE and ASTROLABE. These were followed by the CLOCK (see also BELL) and later the WATCH. See also CALENDAR, CHRONOMETER.

Tin was mined in Cornwall both before and during the time of ROMAN BRITAIN.

Under the ANGLO-SAXONS the mines seem to have been neglected, but were revived after the NORMAN CONQUEST. Until the discovery of tin in Germany in 1240, these Cornish mines were the only ones in Europe. Nowadays tin comes mainly from Malaya, Bolivia, Indonesia and the Congo. See also BRONZE, PHOENICIANS.

Tinder-boxes for kindling fire are very old in origin. Excavations on the OLD STONE AGE site of Starr Carr (Yorks.) c. 7000 BC. have revealed a lump of iron pyrites used for striking with FLINT to produce a spark and also bracket fungi used for making tinder by boiling, drying and heating the fungi and impregnating them with saltpetre. Some of the bracket fungi had been sliced, perhaps for making tinder. Flint with iron pyrites has also been found among the grave goods in BARROWS of the BRONZE AGE in Britain. Later steel was used more effectively than iron. Until the 18th century most people had a tinder-box, containing a flint, steel and charred rag tinder. In the 17th and 18th centuries sulphur MATCHES became common, these being slivers of wood with their end dipped in melted sulphur, which would ignite easily from the smouldering tinder. From the 17th century also wealthier people had tinder pistols, based upon the 17th century flintlock PISTOL, but most still used tinder-boxes.

Tithes a tenth part of the produce of the land paid from quite early years of the Church to maintain the CLERGY. In England, when the lord of a MANOR built a CHURCH on his estate, he often enforced payment of tithes to its priest as its endowment, and in time such allocation of tithes became general law. A SYNOD in 786 strongly enjoined the payment of tithes, which was enforced by law in 900. Tithes were of three sorts—'praedial', of the fruits of the earth; 'personal', of the profits of labour; and 'mixed', partly of the ground and partly of the industry of man. They were further divided into 'great' (tithes of wheat, oats and other major crops) and 'small' (tithes of lambs, chicken and other minor produce). A RECTOR had all the tithes, but a VICAR only the small tithes. Gradually many landowners substituted annual cash payments instead of tithes. The Tithes Commutation Act (1836) converted tithes into rent charges dependent on the varying price of corn, but in 1918 the value was fixed, and in 1925 and 1936 further acts were passed to extinguish tithes. There are now no such things as tithes in England. See also TITHE-BARN.

In Scotland the question of tithes or teinds was settled by the Church of Scotland Properties and Endowments Act (1925).

Tithe-barn the building in which the RECTOR of a PARISH stored his TITHES. At HARVEST-TIME, before the corn was taken into the farmers' BARNS, he took every tenth sheaf and often had his own WAGON to cart it; and he stored it in his own tithe-barn. In some parts of Suffolk the turnips also had to be set in heaps for the rector to tithe. Tithe-barns still exist in the country, though many of the oldest were built by a MONASTERY which took the greater share of the tithes by gaining possession of the rectory.

Tobacco was first brought to England in 1565 by Sir John Hawkins and attempts were made to grow it. Francis Bacon in his *Sylva Sylvarum* (upon which he was engaged at the time of his death in 1626) wrote, 'English tobacco hath small credit, as being too dull and earthy.' Its cultivation was forbidden in England in 1684 to assist the American colonies.

Despite James I's *A Counter-Blast to Tobacco* (1604), SMOKING increased, and by 1614 there were no fewer than 7000 tobacconists in London. Grinning for tobacco was a popular competition for women at rural FAIRS in the 18th century. From about 1700 to 1900 the consumption of tobacco in Britain remained at about 2 lb a head, but since 1900 it has gone up to 4 lb a head. The bright Virginia tobacco is most popular in Britain. Until the Second World War it was grown mainly in the United States of America, but its cultivation has since been developed in other countries, notably Rhodesia.

In 1614 the STAR CHAMBER imposed a duty of 6s 10d a lb on tobacco, and today it is the most important source of government revenue from indirect taxes. In the 1960s British expenditure on tobacco products averaged £1500 million a year of which nearly £1000 million went in taxation. See also CIGARS, CIGARETTES, SNUFF, SMUGGLING.

Toga was the outer garment worn by Roman freemen. It was a flowing cloak or robe of a single piece of material covering

Toga

the whole body except the right arm. It was put on by boys at the age of 14 as a sign that they had reached manhood. See also TUNIC.

'Tolpuddle Martyrs' six farm labourers who formed a branch of the GRAND NATIONAL CONSOLIDATED TRADES UNION in 1834 at Tolpuddle (Dorset) and were sentenced at Dorchester to TRANSPORTATION for 7 years because they had administered oaths contrary to an Act of 1797 (passed during the naval mutiny at the NORE). Lord Melbourne, the Prime Minister, rejected a petition of protest with a quarter of a million signatures presented by a long procession of TRADE UNION members marching behind banners. The men were sent to Australia until public opinion obtained a pardon for them in 1836.

Tomato a plant of the POTATO family, a native of Central and South America, introduced into Europe in the early 16th century. Tomatoes first came to England in 1596, but were not cultivated until the late 19th century. The tomato was known as the Love Apple in Britain until the late 1850s. It was regarded as medicinal in the 18th century, but later was thought to cause gout or cancer and only slowly became popular.

Top is a very old TOY. Examples have been found of tops, made of boxwood and terra-cotta, belonging to the period of ROMAN BRITAIN. An illustration in a 12th-century manuscript shows children whipping peg-tops, which are pear-shaped with a metal peg, and Shakespeare in *Twelfth Night* speaks of 'a schoolboy's top'. A book called *Trifles for Children* (1801) said of topspinning, 'This is good exercise, and we know no reason why girls should not use it, in moderation, as well as boys; for, when they have been working with a needle for some time in cold weather, the exercise will tend much to promote their health.'

Top hat a tall HAT worn by men from about 1805 or earlier and throughout the 19th century remained the general wear in the upper classes. It was usually made of black silk, though in the early years brown beaver was used, and white was a fashionable colour in the 1830s and 1840s. Sportsmen wore top hats of grey or white from about 1820. The wearing of the top hat by gentlemen led to their use of the UMBRELLA. Ladies wore top hats when riding from the 1830s.

The top hat was invented by John Hetherington, a London haberdasher, and first worn by him on January 15, 1797, and causing a riot for which he was charged 'with a breach of the peace for having appeared on the Public Highway wearing upon his head a tall structure having a shining lustre and calculated to frighten timid people' (*St James's Gazette*, January 16, 1797).

Torches were, together with oil LAMPS, the oldest form of LIGHTING. In the OLD STONE AGE they were made of resinous wood or from twigs or rushes soaked in fat or wax. From torches were developed CANDLES, though the LINK long remained as a special form of torch.

Tournaments came to England in the 12th century, probably from France, and were at first very rough affairs, consisting mainly of a mock battle fought between groups of horsemen over open country with the object of disabling as many opponents as possible in order to obtain their horses, arms and ransoms. In one vast mock battle, fully 3000 KNIGHTS are said to have taken part; they tore up acres of vines in the French countryside.

By the end of the 14th century, however, the main feature had become the joust in which one competitor tilted or rode against another in order to dismount him or break his LANCE. Other forms of single combat were included (see MACE), ceremonial was introduced; HERALDS acted as masters of ceremonies; prizes were given by the presiding lady or 'queen of beauty'; and the proceedings ended with feasting, minstrelsy and dancing. Special tilt-yards were built, the main London ground being at SMITHFIELD. Tournaments were humanized by the use of blunted weapons and the observance of sets of rules, of which that drawn up by John Tiptoft, Earl of Worcester (1427?–70), in Edward IV's name, is the best-known.

By then, nevertheless, tournaments were declining. The decay of CHIVALRY and the introduction of heavier plate ARMOUR made them less attractive in the 15th century. Tilting continued to be popular, but by the 16th century tournaments were little more than pageants.

Tower of London was one of the first stone CASTLES erected after the NORMAN CONQUEST. The central KEEP or White Tower was begun by William the Conqueror in 1078 to protect and overawe the City. An inner CURTAIN-WALL with 13 WALL-TOWERS was added by William Rufus (1087–1100), a MOAT by Richard I (1189–99) and an outer wall by Henry III (1216–72). It was commonly used as a PRISON, and Tower Green was the scene of many BEHEADINGS. See also ZOOS.

Towns were the main means by which civilization was introduced into ROMAN BRITAIN. There were three chief types— military settlements for veteran soldiers (Colchester, Lincoln, Gloucester and York); towns on sites naturally fitted for particular purposes, e.g. London (trade), Cirencester (market), Bath (spa); centres of government for each British tribal district, e.g. St Albans, Canterbury, Winchester, Leicester. Roman towns were built with two main streets crossing in the middle, where were situated such public buildings as the FORUM and BASILICA, and other streets branching off

from the main ones, forming a grid pattern.

Since the ANGLO-SAXONS were not town-dwellers, they allowed the Roman towns to become deserted and ruined, but in the 7th century some of their walls were again used, and the early BISHOPS also settled in them (see CITY). Town life was further renewed with the growth of trade and the development of MARKETS. The coming of the DANES also stimulated the expansion of the towns, and they too founded BOROUGHS or strongholds. By 1086 DOMESDAY BOOK

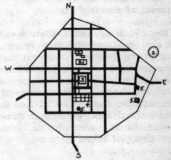

Plan of Roman town: 1 Baths; 2 Amphitheatre; 3 Forum; 4 Shops; 5 Temples

recorded over 100 boroughs in England besides less important market towns.

The NORMAN CONQUEST in its turn encouraged the growth of towns. From the 12th and 13th centuries towns got CHARTERS which gave them rights of self-government, a development much influenced by the CRUSADES; and in the 13th century each borough was invited to send two BURGESSES to Parliament. In the 15th century, as towns grew larger, their government tended to become oligarchic, and in the 15th century the mayor, aldermen and council of a borough commonly formed a close corporation which filled its vacancies by co-option; and in the 16th century certain of the officials of most boroughs acquired the powers of JUSTICES OF THE PEACE without appointment by the crown and had the privilege of holding courts. The Municipal Corporations Acts (1835 & 1882) gave all boroughs a uniform constitution, transferring the powers of the old corporations to town councils elected by the ratepayers. [Clive Rouse, *The Old Towns of England* (1936); Guy Parsloe, *The English Country Town* (1932); Geoffrey Martin, *The Town* (1961); Sir William Savage, *The Making of our Towns* (1952).] See also NEW TOWNS.

Town and Country Planning began in Britain with the Public Health Act (1875), which regulated street widths and spaces round buildings. The Housing and Town Planning Act (1909) empowered local authorities to plan areas likely to be developed. These powers were extended by the Town and Country Planning Act (1932), and all land in England and Wales was brought under public planning control by the Town and Country Planning Act (1947).

Toys of early times included RATTLES, TOPS, DOLLS and models of animals, furniture and crockery, including the ancient HOBBY-HORSE. The ROCKING-HORSE and the DOLL'S HOUSE both originated in the 17th century, the JIG-SAW PUZZLE in the 18th century and the KALEIDOSCOPE and the MAGIC LANTERN in the 19th century. The 20th century has brought in all sorts of new mechanical and scientific toys, as well as revivals of old ones such as the YO-YO. [Lesley Gordon, *Peepshow into Paradise* (1953).] See also GAMES.

Tractarians (also known as the Oxford Movement) sought to revive the LAUDIAN ideals of the 17th century in the CHURCH OF ENGLAND. The movement began with John Keble's sermon on 'National Apos-

tasy' at Oxford in 1833, which was followed by the publication of a series of *Tracts for the Times*, many of them written by John Henry Newman, who became a ROMAN CATHOLIC in 1845. Later in the century there was an emphasis on ritual, which led to the revival of ceremonial and VESTMENTS in worship. Their activities resulted in opposition from the EVANGELICALS. [S. L. Ollard, *A Short History of the Oxford Movement* 1963)].

Traction-engines first appeared on British roads as load-pulling steam-engines in 1869, some of them hauling loads which would have needed sixteen horses. From these developed the general purpose traction-engine, which was usually used in agriculture for driving THRESHING-MACHINES, and engines for drawing heavy loads by road, such as boilers, girders and factory machinery. Most picturesque of these heavy engines

Traction engine

were the showmen's engines, which became a familiar sight on fair-grounds between about 1885 and 1939, pulling up to five trucks, working ROUNDABOUTS and generating electric light. At the beginning of the 20th century more traction-engines were sold than petrol lorries, which could then only carry smaller divisible loads (e.g. bricks and fuel); but after 1920 their use declined rapidly. [W. J. Hughes, *A Century of Traction Engines* (1968)]

Tractors as a means of pulling a PLOUGH instead of HORSES or OXEN, first took the form of the steam plough engines, manufactured from 1861 to 1926. Two of these engines, placed one on either side of a field, pulled the plough in turn backwards and forwards between them by means of long wire ropes. Though this method of ploughing is still used on some farms, it has been declining since 1918. In the second half of the 19th century, light steam tractors were made; they proved too unwieldy and costly for the direct traction of ploughs, but were used for pulling WAGONS and tree trunks. In 1902 Daniel Allborne of Biggleswade (Beds.) built a motor tractor, but they were first used extensively on British farms in 1917 when several thousand Ford tractors were imported from USA to speed up ploughing to meet wartime needs. Since then tractors have increasingly become supreme on the farm for ploughing and other purposes.

Trade tokens brass and copper tokens made and issued by individual traders from the 17th century onwards to meet the need for COINAGE in small denominations, which was often in short supply because coins were damaged by CLIPPING and because in George III's reign the Royal Mint issued no copper coins for twenty-three years, and there were similar lapses earlier and later. These tokens were made without authority and often against the law; in 1643 a royal proclamation prohibited their use, but their circulation greatly increased during the Civil War. They were commonly stamped on the face with the name of the issuing trader and occasionally his trade and on the reverse with the name of the town or village. In the later 18th century, when there was not enough cash to pay workmen and labourers, they were issued by large manufacturing concerns and could only be spent at shops under their control, which was a form of TRUCK. Trade tokens were finally declared illegal by Act of Parliament in 1818 and a new copper coinage was minted in their place. [J. R. S. Whiting, *Trade Tokens* (1971)]

Trade unions began with the INDUSTRIAL REVOLUTION, but were forbidden by the Combination Acts (1799 & 1800), which were not repealed until 1824. Ten years later came the GRAND NATIONAL CONSOLIDATED TRADES UNION and the 'TOLPUDDLE MARTYRS'. The Amalgamated Society of Engineers (1850) was the first of the 'new model unions', which were of skilled, better-paid workers, provided sickness and unemployment benefits and sought agreements with employers rather than strikes. These established the TRADES UNION CONGRESS.

The London dockers' strike (1889) was followed by the 'new unions' of low-paid, unskilled workers. The Conspiracy and Protection of Property Act (1875) had allowed 'peaceful picketing' and permitted trade unions to do whatever would be legal if done by an individual; but in the Taff Vale Case (1901) a railway company was awarded compensation for loss of earnings during a strike, a decision which was reversed by the Trade Disputes Act (1906); and the Trade Union Act (1913) reversed the Osborne Judgment (1909) to allow a trade union to spend its funds on political objectives.

Trade union membership rose from 2 500 000 in 1910 to 4 100 000 in 1914, and there were many strikes between 1911 and 1914. Between the wars the trade unions were weakened by the GENERAL STRIKE; they did not recover their 1926 membership (5 200 000) for ten years. Since then they have recovered their importance and now have a membership of nearly 10 000 000. See also FRIENDLY SOCIETIES.

Trades Union Congress was founded in Manchester in 1868 as the official representative body of TRADE UNIONS in Britain, mainly for the purpose of exerting influence on Parliament. It now also co-ordinates the activities of the unions, though each keeps it independence of action. [Lionel Birch (ed.), *The History of the T.U.C. 1868–1968* (1968).] See also GENERAL STRIKE.

Trams were first introduced into England from the USA in 1861 when a line was laid for horse trams from Marble Arch to Bayswater, but the rails projected above the road, and the attempt soon came to an end. The Tramways Act of 1870 required grooved rails flush with the road surface, and thereafter tramway construction became common.

Trams: (*top*) Horsedrawn; (*bottom*) Electric

The Metropolitan Street Tramways Company ran London's first regular trams between Brixton Station and Kennington Gate, using double-deck horse cars. It was immediately followed by the North Metropolitian Company between Whitechapel and Bow. By 1880 there were in London nearly 500 trams and about 4000 horses carrying more than 64 000 000 passengers a year on ten routes. Other large towns also had their horse trams.

In 1878 the Vale of Clyde Tramways at Govan provided a regular service of steam trams. In 1880 Parliament required that steam trams were not to exceed a speed of 10 m.p.h., their working parts were to be concealed and they were not to discharge smoke, steam or water. These restrictions limited the use of steam trams, but they were run in some towns and had the advantage of carrying more passengers than horses could manage. Some cars carried as many as a hundred persons.

Short stretches of electric tramway were first laid down in 1884 in Brighton, Blackpool and Ryde. By 1887 there were six electric tramways in operation in Britain, including one at Leeds and another in London (from Stratford to Manor Park). In 1901 Glasgow, Liverpool and Cardiff changed their entire system over to it, and other towns followed.

The last horse tram in London was withdrawn in 1915, and by then the electric tramway system was at its height in Britain. It could not, however, compete in flexibility with the motor BUS, and from 1926 it was steadily displaced. London finally abandoned its trams in 1952. [Jack Simmons, *Transport* (Vista Books, 1962)]

Transportation grew out of the medieval punishment of banishment. In the 17th century Royalist prisoners were sent to the West Indies and North America and so were Monmouth's followers. By Act of Parliament in 1666 the King obtained permission to sentence criminals to be 'transported to any of His Majesty's dominions in North America', and another Act in 1717 empowered the courts to order men or women convicted of burglary, robbery, perjury, forgery or other offences punishable by death to be transported for at least 7 years. These were handed over to private contractors, who shipped them across the Atlantic and sold them to employers as virtual slaves. In the mid-18th century about 1000 convicts were transported each year, and by 1775 (when the outbreak of the American War of Independence brought the system to an end) a total of 50 000 had been sent to North America.

It was then decided to transport convicts to serve their sentences in penal settlements in Australia. In 1787 Captain Arthur Philip took more than 700 convicts to Botany Bay, and by 1820 there were some 28 000 convicts in New South Wales. Convicts were also sent to other parts of Australia. When their sentences expired, they were not taken back to England, but were granted land in the colony if they wanted it. The practice of transportation was finally abandoned in 1868.

Trap a light, two-wheeled CARRIAGE on springs, like a GIG, which had under the seat a box extending a few inches beyond the back of the seat in which originally dogs and later all sorts of things were carried. See also DOG-CART.

Treadmill a cylindrical wheel driven by the weight of persons treading upon steps on its exterior. It was advocated by PRISON reformers in the 19th century as a means of making imprisonment more of a deterrent. St Albans had one about 1790, but the first to be erected in London was in Brixton prison in 1817, and then other large prisons followed. In some prisons, treadmills performed a useful purpose, such as grinding grain or pumping water, but in most the labour was quite useless, the necessary resistance being provided by large vanes turning in the air. Treadmills were abolished in British prisons late in the 19th century.

Trebuchet a siege engine introduced into England at the beginning of the 13th century. It depended for its power on a counterpoise, the impetus of a descending weight on a pivoted beam. At one end of the slender arm was a scoop which, when held down and secured, could be loaded with a missile. By releasing this arm, the box full of earth and stones at the other end would swing downwards, causing the scoop to hurl its contents, often weighing many hundredweights, for distances up to a quarter of a mile. Some trebuchets had an additional weight, which could be moved along the arm partially to balance the main weight in a fashion similar to a butcher's beam balance. In this way the machine's range could be roughly adjusted. These machines were generally built near a besieged CASTLE or anywhere else where they were needed, and a quite normal size for one was 18 ft long and 12 ft high. The timber was cut near the site, and it was built by a carpenter in the besieging forces. Its size was determined by the needs of the circumstances and the size of timber available. Stone balls hurled by trebuchets are sometimes discovered among castle ruins, but they also threw horses, masses of manure and even live prisoners. See also ARTILLERY.

Trental a set of thirty requiem MASSES for the repose of the soul of a dead person, said on a single or on successive days, which was regarded as especially effective in the Middle Ages. King Henry VII (died 1509) ordered a total of 10 000 such masses for his own soul at the rate of sixpence each, at least half as much again as the usual fee.

Trews close-fitting TROUSERS or BREECHES combined with STOCKINGS, were an ancient garment said to have been worn by the CELTS in Roman times. Until the late 18th century they were worn by Scottish highlanders and the Irish. The trews were a mark of distinction and worn by gentlemen; the KILT was the dress of the common people.

Trial by battle a form of judicial DUEL, was introduced as an alternative to TRIAL BY ORDEAL at the NORMAN CONQUEST. Battle was fought before a JUDGE between the defendant and the man who accused him in the belief that God would defend the right. The practice declined with the development of the JURY system, but battle was waged as late as 1817, which led Parliament to abolish it in 1819.

Trial by ordeal was an ANGLO-SAXON means of trying an accused person by an appeal for divine justice. There were three main ordeals: for a FREEMAN, to carry a hot iron for nine steps or plunge his hand into boiling water, and if his scars healed in three days he was innocent; for a VILLEIN, to be thrown bound into cold water, sinking proving his innocence; and for the CLERGY to eat a morsel of bread or cheese, choking proving guilt. All these required the supervision of the clergy, but in 1215 the Lateran Council forbade this, which brought the practice to an end and assisted the development of the JURY system. See also TRIAL BY BATTLE.

Trilby a soft felt HAT with a narrow brim and a dint in the crown, which first became fashionable for men about 1895. Its name originated from George du Maurier's novel, *Trilby* (1894), describing life in the Latin quarter of Paris in the mid-19th century. The heroine, Trilby O'Ferrall, an artist's model, wore a black hat of that description.

Trinity House so-called since 1547, originated when Henry VIII granted a charter in 1514 to a body of mariners at Deptford, which was originally a religious foundation, the Guild, Fraternity or Brotherhood of the Most Glorious Trinity and of St Clement. Since the 19th century the Corporation has been the general LIGHTHOUSE, LIGHTSHIP and buoy authority for England, Wales and the Channel Islands and the chief pilotage authority for England and Wales.

Trolleybuses electrically propelled, passenger-carrying road vehicles, which obtained their current from two overhead wires. Being trackless, they were more flexible than TRAMS, and they were more reliable than the early motor BUSES. They were introduced in 1909 in Hendon and

Early trolleybus

in 1911 in Leeds, Bradford and Aberdare and then in other towns up to the beginning of the Second World War. Between 1931 and 1941 they replaced trams on 250 miles of route in London; but in the 1950s they themselves were replaced by buses.

Trousers were worn from about 1730 by men of the lower orders in town and country and by soldiers and sailors. They were also occasionally worn by country squires, but BREECHES were general wear for all classes. From 1807 trousers began to be fashionable for day wear and from about 1817 for evening wear, though not entirely replacing evening-dress breeches until 1850. They were often worn with instep straps from the 1820s until the mid-19th century. Turn-ups began about 1910 and became usual in the 1920s until the mid-1960s; creases began in the early 1900s. See also COSTUME.

Truckle bed a simple, low bedstead, running on castors, used by servants and children during medieval times and later, which could be pushed conveniently under the great BED and brought out at night.

Trumpet is an ancient musical instrument, which had become very popular by the 16th century. Of Henry VIII's 42 musicians, 14 were trumpet-players. The earlier instruments could play only in a single key, but in the 17th century detachable crooks allowed changes of key on the same instrument, and in the early 19th century valves were added.

Trunk-hose a kind of short, full, often padded BREECHES, gathered in about half-way down the thighs, worn by men from about 1550 to 1610. They were at first joined to the stockings, but later worn with thigh-fitting extensions, called canions, to the knees or just below, which were often of a different colour and material from the trunk-hose and over which STOCKINGS were drawn up. See also COSTUME, HOSE, BOMBAST.

Tucker or neck-piece, an ornamental frilling of LACE, LINEN or MUSLIN worn by women in the 17th and 18th centuries round the top of the STAYS or BODICE and descending to cover a great part of the shoulders and bosom. See also MODESTY-PIECE.

Tug-boat was devised by Jonathan Hull in 1736, when he was granted a patent for an engine-driven boat 'capable of taking vessels or ships out of any harbour, port or river against wind or tide or in a calm', but his experiments on the River Avon were unsuccessful. In 1803, however, William Symington's *Charlotte Dundas* towed two 70-ton barges on the Forth and Clyde Canal, and by the 1830s tug-boats were in common use in the major British ports, though near Bristol the watermen of the Avon, who towed becalmed SHIPS with their rowing-boats, tried to sink the *Fury*, the first tug on that river. J. M. W. Turner's painting, *The Fighting Téméraire*, shows the old battleship being towed up the Thames to Rotherhithe by the paddle-tug *Monarch* in 1838. Nowadays steam tugs are being replaced by diesel or diesel-electric tugs, which are more powerful and have their engines controlled directly from the bridge.

Tulips were developed from wild tulips which are native to eastern Europe and the Levant. They were brought in seed from Turkey to Augsburg in 1559, and both seeds and bulbs came to England from Vienna about 1578. By the late 1630s they had become popular in GARDENS, especially the striped or 'broken' varieties.

Tunic in Roman times was a sort of SHIRT worn under the TOGA with short sleeves, buckled round the waist with a girdle and reaching just below the knees. The Norman and medieval tunic was of varying length; it was worn by men and was similar to the KIRTLE worn by women. From the 17th century it came to mean a COAT, at first loose-fitting and from the 19th century tight-fitting. See also BRAIES.

Turnips formed an important part of the new ROTATION OF CROPS brought in during the AGRARIAN REVOLUTION, but their introduction was not due to Viscount Charles Townshend (1674–1738), whose estates were at Raynham Hall, Norfolk.

They had been grown on the Walpole estates at Houghton Hall some years before 1700 and continued to be cultivated throughout Sir Robert Walpole's lifetime (1676–1745). Indeed, J. H. Plumb has suggested that had Walpole lost his political struggle in 1730 with Townshend and retired to *his* Norfolk estates, he would have become known to posterity as 'Turnip Walpole'.

Turnpikes began when an Act of 1663 empowered JUSTICES OF THE PEACE of several counties to erect turnpikes (gates) and charge tolls for maintaining ROADS. From the early 18th century local companies secured similar powers as turnpike trusts, and they increased rapidly in 1750–70 when about 1000 trusts controlled over 21 000 miles of roads. They only maintained a minority of the highways, and many were inefficient and in debt, but by the end of the 18th century they had linked the larger towns with usable roads and made fast COACHES possible. Most of them had come to an end by 1895. See also MACADAM.

Twelfth Night the evening preceding Twelfth Day (the EPIPHANY), twelve days after CHRISTMAS, was formerly a time of merry-making presided over by the LORD OF MISRULE. The 'Twelfth Cake' was an ornamented cake, containing a bean or coin, the drawer of which became the 'King' or 'Queen' of the festivities. At midnight the Christmas decorations were taken down. See also WASSAIL.

Tyburn a former small tributary of the Thames which gave its name to the district where now stands the Marble Arch, Hyde Park. A gallows stood there permanently and from the Middle Ages it was the place of HANGING for criminals convicted in the county of Middlesex until 1783 when it was transferred to outside NEWGATE PRISON. The yearly average of executions at Tyburn in Henry VIII's reign has been put at 140. By the 18th century a 'hanging day' at Tyburn was a public spectacle, and crowds lined the three-mile route of the condemned prisoners from Newgate to Tyburn.

By an Act of Parliament in 1698 prosecutors who secured a capital conviction against a criminal were exempted from all offices within the PARISH in which the FELONY had been committed. The certificate granting this exemption was known as a 'Tyburn Ticket' and might be sold. The Act was repealed in 1818.

Typewriter was first made successfully in Milwaukee (Wisconsin) by Christopher Sholes and Carlos Glidden in 1873 and was manufactured by the Remington Small Arms Co. of Ilion (N.Y.). It had no shift-key and printed only in capitals. It was exhibited at the Centennial Exposition of 1876 in Philadelphia, but was overshadowed by the TELEPHONE. Remington then promoted it by lending the machines to some 300 firms, and after that its use spread. The Underwood typewriter of 1898 was the prototype of most modern machines, but the apparently haphazard arrangement of the alphabet was due to Sholes who placed the letters commonly occurring together as far apart as possible to prevent jamming. The typewriter did much to assist the SUFFRAGETTES in securing the emancipation of WOMEN by providing extensive employment for them.

Tyres at first were iron rings fitted to the wooden WHEELS of WAGONS. They were fixed in place when hot and soused with water to prevent the wood being scorched and hasten the cooling and subsequent shrinking which ensured a close fit.

Solid rubber tyres began to replace iron for BICYCLES and other road vehicles in the 1860s, and pneumatic tyres were invented in 1888 by John Dunlop, a Scottish veterinary surgeon living in Belfast. When his son asked him to think of some way to protect his tricycle from damage on the cobbled streets on the way to school, he constructed a tube inflated with air through a valve and protected by a rubber-impregnated outer casing.

U

Umbrella in the 17th century was used chiefly as a sunshade by women, but it was heavy and clumsy, covered with leather or sticky oiled SILK, and nearly flat in shape. A lady often had it held up over her by a servant. In the 18th century the use of whalebone or cane ribs made it lighter, and the shape of the cover became domed.

The use of an umbrella by men was considered effeminate. In about 1750 Jonas Hanway used one in the London streets and caused a disturbance among sedan-porters and public coachmen; but gradually men began to use it and more commonly from about 1805 with the adoption of the TOP HAT. Umbrellas had metal ribs from about 1800 and COTTON or ALPACA covers in the 1840s. Samuel Fox in 1852 patented a grooved steel frame combining strength with lightness. In the second half of the 19th century it was fashionable for gentlemen to carry an umbrella provided it was always rolled up and for ladies to carry little umbrellas in their CARRIAGE. Until about 1912 all umbrellas were black; more recently the invention of RAYON and NYLON has made it possible for women's umbrellas to be manufactured in bright colours. [T. S. Crawford, *A History of the Umbrella* (1970).] See also PARASOL.

Undergarments began for both men and women with the garment known variously as the SMOCK, SHIFT, CHEMISE and VEST. For the lower limbs of men, BRAIES developed into DRAWERS, which were not worn until much later by women. Women at one time wore PANTALETTES and men and women COMBINATIONS. The PETTICOAT became a usual garment for women, and men and women have at different times worn STAYS. [C. Willett and Phillis Cunnington, *The History of Underclothes* (1950).] See also COSTUME.

Underground railways began in London with the opening of the Metropolitan line from Paddington to Farringdon Street in 1863. It was steam-operated with ventilating shafts, and so also was the District Railway which was opened from South Kensington to Westminster in 1868. Both these systems made extensions east and west until by 1884 they joined to form the Inner Circle, which was steam-operated until 1901. The first 'tube' (i.e. deep tunnel) railway, electrically operated, was the City and South London Railway opened in 1890, which was followed in 1900 by the Central London Railway nicknamed the 'Tuppenny Tube' because the fare was 2d to any station. The latest line, the Victoria

Line, was opened in 1968. The Fleet Line is under construction.

Unitarians a religious body rejecting the doctrines of the Trinity and the Divinity of Christ, first appeared in England after the REFORMATION. John Biddle (1615–62) is generally reckoned as being the father of English Unitarianism. Their numbers grew during the COMMONWEALTH and still more in the 18th century, when many chapels of other NONCONFORMISTS, especially those of the PRESBYTERIANS, passed into their hands. Joseph Priestley (1733–1804), the scientist, was a notable Unitarian. [H. Gow, *The Unitarians* (1928)]

Unite a gold coin (value 20s), also called a broad from its size, minted by James I in 1604 (instead of the POUND) to commemorate the union of England and Scotland. It was replaced by the GUINEA in 1663. See also COINAGE.

Universities began in Britain with the establishment of Oxford about 1167, its oldest COLLEGE being said to be University College (1249), though its foundation is less well documented than that of Merton College (1264). The earliest college at Cambridge was Peterhouse (1284). The oldest Scottish university is that of St Andrews (Fife), founded in 1410.

Medieval universities generally had four faculties or departments of learning —theology, law, medicine and the arts (grammar, logic and rhetoric, forming the first part, the *trivium*; arithmetic, geometry, astronomy and music, forming the second part, the *quadrivium*). The first three faculties gave students a professional training, while the fourth was either a qualification for teaching or a preliminary to the other faculties.

The RENAISSANCE resulted in the replacement of the *trivium* and *quadrivium* by dialectic, rhetoric, mathematics, philosophy, civil law, theology, medicine,

Greek and Hebrew. By the later 17th century academic conservatism was prevalent in the universities, and in the 18th century they were challenged by the DISSENTING ACADEMIES.

The 19th century saw the development of new subjects (e.g. history, modern languages, science) and also the foundation of new universities. Durham was founded in 1832 and associated with the college at Newcastle in 1852. London was formed in 1836 from University and King's College there, but was only an examining body until 1900.

Other universities (the 'Redbrick Universities') were founded in the 19th and early 20th centuries in important industrial towns—Manchester (1884), Birmingham (1900), Liverpool (1903), Leeds (1904), Sheffield (1905) and Bristol (1909). A number of university colleges, which gave London degrees, were founded mainly between the two World Wars, and these have since become universities, among them being Southampton, Exeter, Leicester, Nottingham and Reading. The first university to be founded after the Second World War was Keele (1949), which has been followed by others (the 'Plateglass Universities'), including Sussex, Warwick, East Anglia, York, Lancaster and Kent. See also MECHANICS' INSTITUTES, POLYTECHNICS, TECHNOLOGICAL UNIVERSITIES. [V. H. H. Green, *The Universities* (1969)]

Untrusser the name given in the 16th and 17th centuries to a boy appointed in a SCHOOL to prepare other boys for WHIPPING by letting down their BREECHES or HOSE by untrussing or untying the POINTS which held them to the DOUBLET. It was also sometimes his task to hold a boy down on the FLOGGING-BLOCK while he was being punished.

Upping stocks stone steps commonly placed outside farmhouses and useful for mounting horse, especially since women usually rode pillion behind a man. Upping stocks were usually placed so that they could be reached from the house without having to cross a muddy or dirty yard. See also MOUNTING BLOCK.

Utilitarianism was an attitude of thought and practice expounded especially by Jeremy Bentham (1748–1832), whose sayings included, 'The greatest happiness of the greatest number is the foundation of morals and legislation'; 'The game of push-pin is of equal value with the arts and sciences of music and poetry. If the game of push-pin furnishes more pleasure, it is more valuable than either'; 'Every man is to count for one, and no man for more than one'. Utilitarianism had a strong influence on political and social reform in the 19th century.

V

Vaccination against small-pox was preceded by inoculation, which was popularized in England by Lady Mary Wortley Montagu (1689–1762), on her return from Turkey in 1718. It was increasingly practised during the 18th century, mainly by quacks, to inflict the disease in a mild form. In 1769 Edward Jenner (1749–1823), a country PHYSICIAN, first vaccinated from cow-pox to confer immunity from small-pox, having heard that milk-maids who had the cow-pox never took the small-pox.

Vacuum cleaner began when H. C. Booth, an Englishman, invented in 1901 a large, piston-operated vacuum pump, worked by a petrol engine. This was mounted in a horse-drawn van which was drawn up at the kerbside outside the premises to be cleaned, and hose-pipes from the vacuum chamber were run across the pavement and in through doors and windows to suck up the dust from carpets and curtains. Household vacuum cleaners originated in USA with David Kenny's stationary 'apparatus for removing dust' in 1903, and in 1908 James M. Splenger invented an electrically-driven suction carpet-sweeper, such a machine being manufactured by the Hoover Company soon afterwards, using the rotary suction fan and bag for receiving the dust, both of which are still fundamental in vacuum cleaners. See also BROOM, CARPET SWEEPER.

Valentine's Day the name given to February 14 after two Roman saints martyred on the same day. It was an old-established custom, probably a relic of mock betrothals marking the pagan spring festival, for girls to draw lots for lovers or husbands, who were known as 'valentines', and each gave the girl a present, often a pair of GLOVES. The giving of presents continued into the 18th century, but was slowly superseded by the practice of girls sending hand-written cards to their valentines, which were not signed so that the man to whom it was addressed must guess who sent it. The first printed valentines appeared in stationers' shops in 1761, and were folded sheets of flimsy paper with bright hand-coloured engravings and verses. From 1800 they became more substantial with embossing and paper-lace. The advent of penny POSTAGE led to a great increase of valentines as the sender could more easily remain anonymous. The 19th century produced comic valentines and also romantic, sentimental cards made of swansdown or silk ribbon, silver lace-paper or dried flowers, cards made in the shape of fans, circular or three-dimensional cards and cards containing mirrors or sachets of PERFUME. It also became the practice for men to send them as well as women. A Victorian manufacturer urged men to buy a valentine and add 'a delicate sentiment of your own, seal and direct the same to the dear object of your affections, thereby laying the foundation of the most true of all earthly happiness, viz. matrimony'. [Frank Staff, *The Valentine and its Origins* (1969)]

Vambrace was a piece of plate ARMOUR, approximately shaped like a half-cylinder, to protect the forearm. The equivalent piece protecting the leg was the greave.

Vegetables were cultivated from the BRONZE AGE to the end of ROMAN BRITAIN, the oldest being peas, beans, onions, leeks, globe artichokes, cabbages and carrots. Their cultivation was neglected until the 14th century, when they were mainly grown in the GARDENS of MONASTERIES, though in Britain even by the end of the 16th century many banquets consisted of courses of meat, poultry and game, but no vegetables; and even Victorian and Edwardian dinners had much meat and few vegetables. Meanwhile, the range of vegetables was slowly widened, e.g. by the POTATO and TOMATO. From the early 20th century cookery books devoted more space to vegetables, but they were eaten more by the upper than the lower classes.

Vellum, SEE PARCHMENT.

Velvet a cloth made from SILK with a close, dense pile, the manufacture of which was brought in the 13th century from the East through the CRUSADES to Italy and France. King Richard II of England directed in his will that his body should be clothed '*in velveto*' in 1399. It was first made in England by HUGUENOT refugees at Spitalfields about 1685. COTTON-velvet was first made in England in 1756.

Verandahs were common features of late Georgian and REGENCY town HOUSES. They had lead or copper roofs supported by slender iron columns. The ROMANTIC MOVEMENT of the Victorian period led to a fashion for rustic verandahs. See also BALCONIES.

Vest originally the name for the WAISTCOAT, which was an UNDERGARMENT. It appeared as a woollen or flannel undergarment, first known as an under-vest about 1840. The modern singlet was derived in the 1930s from the vest and partly replaced it.

Vestments were originally the everyday garments worn by the early Christians, which were adapted for use by the clergy when taking the services of the Church. By the 10th century the principal vestments used in the Medieval Church had been established and were not afterwards altered much. In the CHURCH OF ENGLAND after the REFORMATION the COMMON PRAYER BOOK of 1549 enjoined the use of the medieval vestments with little change and so again did the Book of 1559, but thereafter they fell into disuse except for the SURPLICE. They were reintroduced from about 1851 under the influence of the TRACTARIANS. [F. C. Happold, *Everyone's Book about the English Church* (1962).] See also ALB,

Vestments: 1 Priest wearing cope; 2 Cope; 3 Priest wearing surplice and cassock; 4 Priest wearing amice, chasuble, alb, stole and cassock; 5 Chasuble; 6 Bishop wearing mitre, amice, chasuble, alb, stole and holding the crosier

AMICE, CASSOCK, CHASUBLE, COPE, DOMINO, HOOD, MITRE, PECTORAL, STOLE.

Vestry the part of a CHURCH where the clergy put on their VESTMENTS, which was used by the parishioners in the Middle Ages when they met to decide local affairs, and so the name came also to be used for their meeting. The vestry elected each year the CHURCHWARDENS to care for the furniture of the church and agreed and levied a rate of contribution towards the maintenance of the church. This was the beginning of local government, and the vestry concerned itself increasingly with the life of the PARISH. By the 16th century there were 'open vestries' (meetings of all the parishioners) and 'closed vestries' (meetings of only a selected few, probably originating as a committee of an open vestry). The Local Government Act (1894) transferred the civil functions of the vestries to elected parish councils.

Vicar from the Latin *vicarius*, a 'substitute'. It is the title in the CHURCH OF ENGLAND for a priest in charge of a PARISH in place of the RECTOR and drawing originally only part of the TITHES. Priests in charge of more-recently created parishes, though legally styled perpetual CURATES, are usually called vicars.

Victoria a light, four-wheeled CARRIAGE with low seats for two people, a CALASH top and a raised driver's seat in front.

Vikings or Northmen, the Scandinavian adventurers who began to attack the British Isles from the late 8th century, settling in the Western Isles of Scotland about 810 and in England about 874. The DANES were the most numerous of those who came to England. Viking SHIPS, about 80 ft long and masted, with a square sail, carried about 50 warriors who rowed in turn the 32 oars and hung their SHIELDS round the bulwarks for extra protection. They were armed with long BATTLE-AXES with which a horse and rider could be cut down at a blow. They especially plundered churches, and by the middle of the 9th century it was said that, from the Humber to the Solent, hardly one remained intact within a day's ride of the coast. The ANGLO-SAXONS prayed, 'From the fury of the Northmen, Good Lord deliver us!'

Villa a country house in ROMAN BRITAIN, belonging to a Roman official or trader or a Celtic landowner, who had adopted Roman manners and Latin speech. It usually consisted of a dozen or more single-storied rooms joined by a corridor, but the end rooms were often enlarged to form projecting wings, and these might be joined again in front to make an enclosed

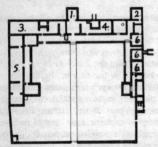

Plan of Roman villa: 1 Lodge; 2 Furnace; 3 Dining room; 4 Baths; 5 Sitting room; 6 Bedrooms

courtyard with a long verandah and a GARDEN. The wealthier houses had MOSAIC floors, glazed WINDOWS, ROMAN BATHS and heating from a HYPOCAUST. There were also farm buildings, granaries and quarters for dependents and the COLONI. The remains of about 500 villas have been found in south-eastern England alone. See also FISHBOURNE PALACE.

Village life began when the people of the NEW STONE AGE grew crops and so lived in settlements. Early village remains are those of the LAKE VILLAGES. In ROMAN BRITAIN the VILLA was introduced in the southern and central part of the country, but the native people continued to live in their own settlements. The ANGLO-SAXONS established their villages often some distance from the Roman ROADS for safety, which is why in some parts of the country (e.g. south Lincolnshire) many villages are not on the main roads. Anglo-Saxon village names commonly end in 'ham', 'ton' or 'cot'. Medieval villages were commonly dominated by the MANOR and the OPEN-FIELD SYSTEM of farming. See also DESERTED VILLAGES, HAMLET, PARISH, PLACE NAMES.

Villein an unfree man who in the Middle Ages held about an average of a VIRGATE of arable land and pasturage from the lord of the MANOR for which he had to till the DEMESNE with his own implements two or three days a week, perform cartage or carrying duties, give additional 'boon' services at the spring and autumn sowings, harvest-time, haymaking and sheep-shearing, and render on special days a seasonal tribute of farm produce (e.g. eggs at EASTER). He had to grind his corn in the lord's mill and bake his bread in the lord's oven, for which he had to make payment; and he also had to make MERCHET, HERIOT, MORTUARY and other payments.

The villein was personally bound to his lord and could obtain his freedom only by escape, admission to holy orders or MANUMISSION. In the 13th and 14th centuries, partly through the CRUSADES and the BLACK DEATH, commutation of services for money rents everywhere became general in England, and by the end of the 15th century villeinage was everywhere replaced by COPYHOLD. It also disappeared about the same time in Scotland, being replaced by various forms of tenancies or leaseholds. See also BORDAR, COTTAR.

Vinaigrette a small bottle or box of gold, silver or glass, having perforations in the top, for holding aromatic vinegar contained in a sponge or smelling salts, used in the 18th and 19th centuries, usually by women. See also PERFUME, POMANDER.

Viol a late medieval stringed instrument, the successor of the REBECK and forerunner of the VIOLIN. It was shaped like a double bass and had a flat back. It usually had six strings and was played with the hand under the bow, being held downwards on or between the knees like a cello. It was popular from the 15th to 17th century and was commonly one of the instruments of the ORCHESTRAS which played in CHURCHES before the wide-spread adoption of the ORGAN. See also MUSIC.

Viola a four-stringed musical instrument, slightly larger than the VIOLIN, having a lower pitch and less bright quality of tone.

Violin was first produced in Italy in the early part of the 16th century and had ousted the VIOL by the end of the 17th century. With the development of the symphony ORCHESTRA, it became the chief of the group of stringed instruments played with a bow which forms its largest section. Pepys enjoyed 'the music of all sorts, but above all the 24 violins' at the state banquet after the coronation of Charles II in 1661.

Virgate or yardland, an early English measure of land, the rough equivalent of a quarter of a HIDE or carucate.

Virginal the earliest and simplest form of HARPSICHORD. Oblong in shape, it was usually only a small box that could be placed on a table, though sometimes it stood on a four-legged frame. It may have been so-called because it was meant as an instrument for young ladies, a 'clavicordium virginale'. It was popular in the 16th and 17th centuries, but in the later 17th century was gradually superseded by the SPINET and the HARPSICHORD. Pepys noticed, during the GREAT FIRE OF LONDON, that a large number of the boats on the Thames, in which people were taking away their household goods, contained virginals. See also PIANO.

Visor was the front part of a HELMET, which defended the face. It could be lifted up at will and was perforated with holes for seeing and breathing. See also ARMOUR.

Vitrified forts remains of fortified places found in Scotland. The stone walls in places show evidence of molten rock, and it is thought that the forts were originally of TIMBER-LACING and when set on fire the heat of the burning timbers caused the stone to take on a glass-like consistency. These forts are apparently post-Roman in date.

W

Wagon a four-wheeled, horse-drawn vehicle for carrying heavy loads, probably introduced from the Netherlands in the 16th century. By 1600 it was used by CARRIERS for the transport of merchandise and also as stage-wagons, carrying 20–30 people. The English wagon was a strong, heavy vehicle, drawn by from two to eight horses yoked abreast in pairs. The fore-wheels were smaller than the hind-wheels, and their axle was swivelled to the body of the vehicle to make turning easier. It was often provided with wooden bows over which could be stretched a tilt or cover of canvas to protect goods and passengers from the weather. Since a wagon had only one team of horses, however long the journey (unlike a STAGE-COACH), it only covered 10–15 miles a day, and the waggoner commonly walked beside his horses. Until the coming of MACADAM surfaces government regulations restricted the number of horses and the narrowness of WHEELS in an attempt to prevent heavy wagons damaging the ROADS. Stage-wagons were the means of travel for poor people and were displaced by the RAILWAYS, but carriers' wagons were still used in the country until finally made obsolete by the MOTOR CAR soon after the end of the First World War.

The farm-wagon (or harvest-wagon) was derived from the stage-wagon and remained basically similar in its structure, though it was more lightly built and had no form of cover. There were also great variations in design and detail from county to county. They were hauled at first by OXEN and then by HORSES and remained in use until replaced by TRACTORS and their trailers. See also CARRIAGES.

Wagonette a four-wheeled, horse-drawn CARRIAGE of light construction, open or with removable cover, used for pleasure in the 18th and 19th centuries. It was built to carry six or eight people and had one or two seats crosswise in front and two back seats arranged lengthwise and facing inwards.

Waistcoat from the 16th century an undergarment, commonly known as a VEST or under-waistcoat, worn by both men and women. From 1668 it became an under-coat for men, cut on similar lines to a coat. See also EMBROIDERY.

Waits were originally town WATCHMEN, who accompanied their hourly proclamations by sounding a musical instrument, usually a horn, and so became good enough musicians to form a uniformed ORCHESTRA which performed on ceremonial occasions and at CHRISTMAS. The surnames Waite and Wakeman come from this occupation. Orlando Gibbons (1583–1625) was the son of a Cambridge wait. From 16th century the waits often attended at INNS on the arrival of any guest likely to recompense them, and at some seaports they welcomed sailors back from voyages. They were not suppressed during the COMMONWEALTH, and in many towns they survived until the late 18th century.

Scottish waits were usually termed 'tounis minstrels'. In the 17th century they were employed by the Edinburgh city authorities to play in the streets every morning and evening and give a special concert at noon. See also MINSTRELS.

Wake was originally an all-night vigil kept from ANGLO-SAXON times onwards on the eve of some festival, especially the feast of the dedication of a parish CHURCH, but it soon came to refer to the feasting and merry-making which marked such a festival, when tents were often erected in the churchyard to feed the people. The name survives for the annual local HOLIDAYS observed by a whole town or village in the North and Midlands of England. In Scotland and Ireland it referred to the watching of a dead body by friends and neighbours before the funeral. See also RUSHES.

Wall-paper originated with medieval book-printers and wood-engravers, who occasionally produced decorated sheets for CHEST and CUPBOARD lining-papers. The earliest form of cheap wall decoration, however, was painted cloths (consisting of canvas stretched on wooden frames and fixed to the walls), and by the 16th century this was used even in farmhouses and COTTAGES. Wall-paper first came into use soon after 1660, when the decorated sheets were pasted on to the canvas on these wooden frames. By the end of the century it was pasted on the wall and began to replace TAPESTRY, wall-painting and other types of hanging; but in 1712 Parliament taxed it, and at the end of the 18th century it was used only by the gentry, a few wealthy clergymen and farmers and professional people in towns. Even the middle-classes had only one or two rooms hung with it (usually the PARLOUR and the best chamber over the parlour); most people had only whitewashed walls.

For the wealthy, however, there was in the 18th century a great variety of wall-papers. Some were in imitation of more costly forms of hangings—silk, leather, velvet, wood and even marble. Chinese wall-paper was much admired, especially with a design of birds and plants, entirely hand-painted in imitation of the painted silk hangings in wealthy Chinese homes.

By 1800 printing with wood blocks and distemper colours began to oust flock, stencilled and hand-coloured papers, but the great change came in the early 19th century with the introduction of cylinder printing machines. The technical difficulties had been mastered by 1850, and the tax was repealed in 1861. Prices fell considerably, and the widespread use of wall-paper began. [M. W. Bailey, *The House and Home* (1963)]

Wall-towers were built at intervals projecting outwards from the CURTAIN WALLS of CASTLES to enable archers to protect the whole external face of the wall from attack. Framlingham Castle (Suffolk), built 1190–1200, has thirteen rectangular towers projecting from its wall, but soon afterwards circular towers became more common, as they were less easily destroyed by MINES, e.g. Conisborough Castle (Yorks.), and in the latter part of the 13th century they were often D-shaped to give more space in the rooms of the tower while preserving its solidity, e.g. Pevensey Castle (Sussex).

Walnut was used for some fine pieces of FURNITURE, especially court CUPBOARDS, at the end of the 16th century, but became really fashionable when it replaced OAK after the RESTORATION. In its turn, it was replaced by MAHOGVNY from 1730 and was almost abandoned by 1745.

Wardrobe meant originally the department in a royal or noble household which was charged with the care of wearing apparel, and for some centuries after Henry III's reign (1216–72) the King's Wardrobe organized the finance of the royal household.

From about the middle of the 17th century onwards the name was given to a large piece of furniture for storing clothes which developed from the CUPBOARDS and CHESTS where they were at first stored. The first wardrobes were not generally made with doors the full height, but had a hanging section above a number of drawers.

Ward was originally a district of a BOROUGH or a CITY under the charge of an alderman, who might also be the chief official in a GUILD. The wards of London are mentioned by name as early as the 12th century, being sometimes called by the name of an alderman and sometimes by their locality.

Wardship was the power conferred under FEUDALISM upon the King if a TENANT-IN-CHIEF died leaving heirs who were minors. Until they came of age (a boy at 21, a girl at 14), he had custody of their persons and managed their lands, and he could generally control the marriage of a ward, while a tenant-in-chief's widow was in his gift. Often the wardship was sold to the highest bidder, which led to grave abuses, and MAGNA CARTA attempted to regulate the practice. Wardship was abolished in Charles II's reign (1660–85).

Warming-pan a long-handled, covered metal pan for holding hot CHARCOAL, formerly used for airing and warming a BED, which had become common by the 15th century. Samuel Pepys was presented with 'a noble silver warming-pan' by a ship's captain. The earliest brass pans used in England were imported from Holland, English-made ones dating from about 1585; and at first handles were of metal, not wood. From about 1770 copper replaced brass in their manufacture. Warming-pans gave way in the 19th century to mass-produced stone and tin hot-water bottles, which were followed by rubber ones in the 1930s and then electric blankets. [Lawrence Wright, *Warm and Snug* (1962)]

Washing-machines originated in the middle of the 19th century, these early models usually having an agitator, which was a central shaft with blades that were swung backwards and forwards by hand.

An electrically-operated model produced in 1930 was simply a tub on wheels with a MANGLE. Water heating was introduced

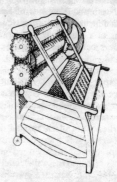

An early washing machine

in 1948, and in the later 1950s the introduction of the spin-drier led to fully automatic machines with a choice of water temperatures and washing and rinsing times.

Wassail was a festive occasion at which healths were drunk such as at CHRISTMAS, TWELFTH NIGHT and NEW YEAR'S DAY. The DRINK on such an occasion consisted of ALE (sometimes WINE), sweetened with SUGAR and flavoured with SPICES and was sometimes called Lamb's Wool. It was mixed and placed on the table in a large bowl, the wassail-bowl, and it was the custom to go about with such a bowl, singing CAROLS, drinking the health of householders and collecting money to replenish the bowl.

Watches rely upon a coiled spring as a source of power, and it is believed that this was first used by Peter Henlein (1480–1542) of Nuremberg about 1500. These early 'pocket clocks', often called 'Nuremberg eggs', were first introduced into England during Henry VIII's reign and became popular with the wealthy under Elizabeth I. Thomas Tompion (?1639–1713) has been called the 'father of English watchmaking'; he became famous for his finely constructed and beautiful watches. Indeed, watches of the 16th and 17th centuries, often in gold or jewelled cases, were made for ornament rather than for use since they were inaccurate and had only an hour-hand.

The invention of the balance spring by Robert Hooke (1635–1703) ensured sufficient accuracy in watches to make worthwhile the addition of a minute-hand and

(*left*) Thomas Mudge watch;
(*right*) James I puritan watch

later a second-hand; and Thomas Mudge (1717–94) invented the detached-lever escapement which is still a usual feature of modern watches. Cheap watches began with the introduction in the USA by Robert H. Ingersoll (1859–1928) in 1892 of a 'dollar watch' which sold in Britain for 5s.

Wrist watches originated about 1890 and were first known as 'bracelet watches', being worn only by women and considered too effeminate for men; but men found them useful in the First World War, and since then they have become more usual than pocket watches. [T. P. Camerer Cuss, *The Story of Watches* (1952).] See also CLOCKS, CHRONOMETER.

Watchmen originated with the Statute of Winchester (1285), which required each TOWN and VILLAGE from Ascension Day to Michaelmas to have two or more able-bodied householders to serve in rotation under the CONSTABLE to watch from dusk to dawn and stop strangers. If they seemed suspicious, the watchmen had to detain them, and the next morning the constable would take them to a JUSTICE OF THE PEACE. Should the travellers refuse to stop, the watchmen might raise HUE AND CRY to capture them, beat them and put them in the STOCKS until the morning. It became common in many places for householders to make money payments instead of service and hiring watchmen to take their place. In London and other large towns the Watchmen proclaimed each hour with some such shout as, 'Past twelve o'clock and a cold, frosty night!' The Statute was not repealed until 1827. See also ANGELUS, BILL, WAITS.

Water closet was known as early as 1597 when Elizabeth I's godson, Sir John Harington, described one he had erected at Kelston, near Bath. The Queen had it tried in her palace at Richmond, but it did not come into general use until it was re-invented by Alexander Cummings in 1775 and Joseph Bramah in 1778. [Lawrence Wright, *Clean and Decent* (1960)]

Watermills are an older invention than the WINDMILL, dating from antiquity and were introduced into Britain in about the 9th century AD. DOMESDAY BOOK enumerated over 5000 of them in England.

Until the 13th century most watermills were still of the undershot type (driven by the impact of the stream of water on the lower paddles of the wheel). The overshot water-wheel (driven by the impact of falling water on the top of the wheel) came into use in the early Middle Ages. A further advance in the construction of the overshot wheel was the enclosure of the paddles on three sides to hold water, the weight of which added to the force of the impact of the overhead stream of water. See also ROLLER MILLS.

Water-supply was brought to TOWNS in ROMAN BRITAIN by a covered channel cut in the ground from a nearby stream, but this often supplied only the ROMAN BATHS and houses had their own wells, as did the VILLAS. In the Middle Ages water was largely drawn by hand from rivers and springs, wells and CONDUITS, though some large towns had small systems of wooden or lead pipes; and MONASTERIES were often built by a stream to ensure their water-supply. Piped water schemes were further developed in the 17th century, and London had the NEW RIVER. Many towns also built public pumps in the 18th and 19th centuries, but these were found to be a source of CHOLERA as the population increased. Waterworks were built throughout Britain from the early 19th century as the STEAM-ENGINE

and cast-iron pipes enabled water to be pumped up slopes and for long distances. The Public Health Act (1875) compelled water companies to provide a constant supply of water to houses in towns. See also DRINKING-FOUNTAINS, SANITATION.

Watling Street a Roman ROAD, so-called from the Old English, *Waeclingastroet*, the road to Waeclingaceaster (St Albans). It went from Dover through Canterbury to London and then north-westwards through St Albans, Dunstable, Stony Stratford, Towcester and High Cross, across the FOSSEWAY, through Mancetter and Penkridge, a little south to Wroxeter, where it joined the East Wales road coming up from the south at Kenchester, and so proceeded to Chester.

For about ten years in the late 9th century, the boundary of the DANELAW ran along Watling Street.

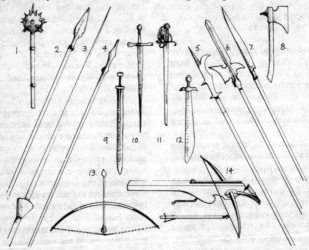

Weapons: 1 Mace; 2 Spear; 3 Lance; 4 Pike; 5 Bill; 6 Halberd; 7 Glaive; 8 Battle axe; 9 Sword (10th cent.); 10 Sword (13th cent.); 11 Sword (16th cent.); 12 Falchion; 13 Bow and arrow; 14 Crossbow

Wattle and daub a rough method of constructing the walls of COTTAGES, consisting of twigs interwoven and covered with a mixture of mud or clay and chopped straw, sometimes re-inforced with horsehair as a binding agent.

Weapons of many sorts have been used in the past, both in war and in DUELS and TOURNAMENTS, among the earliest being the SWORD, SPEAR, MACE and BATTLE-AXE. Variants have been the FALCHION, BILL, GLAIVE and PIKE, to which was later added the HALBERD. The LANCE was the main weapon of the medieval KNIGHT. The CALTRAP was devised to be used against CAVALRY, but eventually the BOW AND ARROW proved the most effective.

Siege weapons used against fortifications from HILL-FORTS to CASTLES, were the CATAPULT, SLING and TREBUCHET, the BATTERING RAM and BORE, the MINE and FASCINE.

The invention of GUNPOWDER, used first in BOMBS and then in ARTILLERY and HAND-GUNS, gradually changed the main weapons used in war.

Weather-boarding a series of overlapping horizontal boards, fastened to wooden uprights and covering the outside of the walls of COTTAGES, especially in the Weald of Kent.

Weaving a process consisting of crossing or interlacing one set of threads of WOOL or other textile with another, i.e. the warp threads are crossed at right angles with the weft threads so that the warp threads lie parallel with each other, while the weft thread is continuous and carried under and over alternately by the shuttle of the loom. The simple loom was invented before 10 000 BC, and the more complicated multishaft loom was probably devised by the Chinese over 2000 years ago, so that by the Middle Ages weaving in England had reached a high degree of perfection.

During the INDUSTRIAL REVOLUTION, several inventions accelerated weaving and made possible the rapid progress of the COTTON industry. In 1733 John Kay devised the fly-shuttle, which enabled a weaver to jerk the shuttle across the loom and back again using one hand only. The speed of weaving was doubled; and a single weaver could make cloths of any width, whereas previously two men had sat together at a loom to make broad cloths.

Since this was followed by inventions in SPINNING which enabled thread to be

Hand-loom

produced more rapidly than it could be used, a period of prosperity began for the hand-loom weavers. The first power-loom was invented in 1785 by a Leicestershire clergyman, Edmund Cartwright, but it remained a clumsy machine until improved early in the 19th century by William Radcliffe and John Horrocks. It then had ten times the capacity of a hand-loom, but it was not introduced rapidly until after the Napoleonic War. In 1813 there were only about 2400 power-looms in Britain and nearly a hundred times as many hand-looms; but there were about 14 000 by 1820 and 100 000 by 1833. The hand-loom weavers suffered severely from unemployment and distress and provided many of the LUDDITES during this period. See also DOMESTIC SYSTEM.

Westminster Abbey is said to have been built on the site of an old CHURCH of the 7th century and to have become a MONASTERY of the BENEDICTINE order in St Dunstan's time (960). Edward the Confessor rebuilt it, with a palace nearby, shortly before the NORMAN CONQUEST, and his RELICS were placed in a SHRINE there in 1161. William the Conqueror chose it for his coronation, since when all English monarchs have been crowned there. The building of the present ABBEY in the French style began under Henry III in 1245, the latest addition being the fine eastern CHAPEL completed in 1519 by Henry VII and bearing his name. The western towers and front were rebuilt by Christopher Wren and Nicholas Hawksmoor in the 18th century. It became known as the MINSTER in the west in contrast to ST PAUL'S CATHEDRAL in the east. Since the DISSOLUTION OF THE MONASTERIES it has been a COLLEGIATE CHURCH.

Westminster, Palace of was probably founded by Edward the Confessor before the NORMAN CONQUEST. The kings of England, who had previously held court at Winchester, moved there in the 11th century. They added to and partly rebuilt it until, after a fire in 1512, it was abandoned as a royal residence in favour of WHITEHALL, and became the meeting-place of Parliament. After the fire of 1834, nothing remains of the old palace except the CRYPT (the Chapel of St Mary Undercroft) and Westminster Hall, begun by William Rufus in 1097 and rebuilt by Richard II in 1397, which is a fine example of the HALL of a great medieval HOUSE, a small pinnacle on the roof marking the original position of the FUMERELL.

Whalemeat was imported by the Ministry of Food in 1947, when food RATIONING was still in force in Britain, to supplement the meat ration. It was powdery-textured, rather resembling a meaty biscuit, with overtones of oil. It was not, however, popular, though it was officially described as 'rich and tasty—just like beef steak'. Whalemeat lay unwanted for months in warehouses on Tyneside, and by 1950 the Ministry, having now diverted its attention to SNOEK, ceased to attempt to popularize it. [Michael Sissons and Philip French (eds.), *Age of Austerity 1945–51* (1963)]

Wheat the oldest and most important of the cereal crops, probably developed from a wild grass in the Near East. It was brought to Britain in the NEW STONE AGE, being grown on bare downlands, where there were no FORESTS to clear, and harvested with SICKLES of FLINT. After threshing, it was often stored in underground pits. The same soil was cultivated and cropped each year until it was exhausted, when the cultivators moved on to a new settlement. Wheat flour has always been regarded as the best for BREAD. During the AGRARIAN REVOLUTION, ENCLOSURES enabled more to be grown in England, but from the 1870s an increasing amount came from abroad (see CORN LAWS).

Wheel has been described as the most important invention ever made. Wheeled vehicles of some sort were used in Britain in the BRONZE AGE about 1000 BC. They were probably two-wheeled, pulled by OXEN and used for carrying Cornish TIN to ports in Essex and Kent for shipment to the Continent. Later, in the IRON AGE, carts having wooden wheels with spokes were used, the number of spokes varying from four to as many as fourteen, and the wheels had well-turned wooden hubs and also iron TYRES. The CELTS had CHARIOTS with a metal band round the hub to prevent it splitting when the chariot went over rough ground; the ruts in the entrances of HILL-FORTS show that the distance between the wheels of these chariots was 4 ft 5 in.; the wheel-tracks of Roman vehicles are about 2 in. wider.

In the Middle Ages carts and wagons continued to be used, and the wheels were sometimes studded with iron nails to grip the muddy ROADS; but there were few developments until the four-wheeled WAGON was introduced in the 16th century. From the 17th century, when tolls were levied on TURNPIKES, regulations prohibited heavy wagons with narrow wheels which it was thought would cut up the highway surface; and in 1751 an Act of Parliament required them to have wheels at least 9 in. wide and excused them from tolls if their wheels were 16 in. wide. It was believed that wide wheels would roll the roads flat, but heavy, clumsy vehicles appeared and did much damage. The situation was changed with the coming of MACADAM roads late in the 18th century.

The flanged wheel, used by RAILWAYS, was invented by William Jessop in 1800. Rubber TYRES for road vehicles were invented in the 19th century and used by BICYCLES and MOTOR CARS.

Wheel-lock was a HAND-GUN with a form of lock consisting of a small wheel of steel (wound up with a spring), the friction of which against a piece of flint produced sparks which fired the GUNPOWDER. It was invented in the 17th century, when it superseded the MATCHLOCK, but it was itself soon superseded by the FLINTLOCK.

Whey the watery part of MILK remaining after the separation of the curd in making CHEESE. It was a popular drink in the 17th century. Pepys had his 'morning draft of whey' and visited 'whey houses'. Nowadays it is used for animal food or to enrich the flour for bread-making.

Whipping was a punishment inflicted in medieval times upon men and women of low rank convicted of small thefts and other minor offences. It was also the punishment for MONKS and NUNS when offences were corrected in the daily assembly in the CHAPTER-HOUSE, and it was commonly imposed upon SERVANTS and APPRENTICES, while undergraduates at the UNIVERSITIES were birched for misbehaviour. The POOR LAW ACT (1601) ordered vagrants to be whipped. See also CAT O' NINE TAILS, WHIPPING-POST.

The public whipping of women was abolished in 1817 and their whipping in private in 1830. The Criminal Justice Act (1948) abolished sentences of whipping. Flogging was abolished in the army in peace-time in 1868 and on active service in 1880.

Whipping was also the accepted punishment for children at both home and school. The BIRCH-ROD, CANE and TAWSE were at different times frequently used. The ANGLO-SAXONS spoke of their childhood as 'when I was under the rod'; and in the 18th century, Susannah Wesley, the mother of John, the founder of METHODISM, taught her children 'to fear the rod and cry softly'. For long the prevalent attitude was that expressed by Robert Mulcaster, who was a schoolmaster and said in 1581, 'The rod may no more be spared in schools than the sword may in the Prince's hand', and, 'My Lady Birchly will be a guest at home or else parents shall not have their wills'.

Whipping-boy a boy kept to be whipped when a prince deserved chastisement. Barnaby Fitzpatrick stood for the future Edward VI and Mungo Murray for the future Charles I.

The child King Henry VI (who came to the throne in 1422 at the age of 9 months) was made to give, by way of an official record, permission for his own WHIPPING by his tutor, Richard Beauchamp, Earl of Warwick, who is said to have used this permission with such severity that his charge was soon brought 'for awe thereof . . . (to) forbear the more to do amiss and attend the more busily to virtue and learning'.

Whipping-post an upright post, furnished near the top with iron clasps to fasten around the offender's wrists and hold him securely during the infliction of punishment. Often one of the supporting posts of the STOCKS was fitted as a whipping-post. Whipping at the cart's tail was ordered for vagrants by a statute of Henry VIII, but another statute of Elizabeth I, which also ordered them to be whipped, did not specify this. It was at this time, about 1596, that whipping-posts were probably set up in village greens and MARKET places.

Whisky a spirit distilled from cereal grains and MALT. It was distilled in Ireland by at least the 12th century, and the art was perhaps brought from there to Scotland sometime in the early Middle Ages. In the great whisky-producing area of Scotland, a large rectangle immediately south of the Moray Firth in the north-east of the country, barley has long been grown in the coastal plain and valleys, while the bogs provide peat to smoke and dry the barley into malt, and the highland springs and streams provide clear water to turn the malt into a fermented liquid before distilling it into spirit. It became popular in England and began to rival BRANDY in the 1890s, especially when drunk with SODA WATER. [David Daiches, *Scotch Whisky* (1969)]

Whispering stick a device formerly used to punish school-children who spoke in the classroom. It consisted of a short piece of flat wood inserted as a gag into the mouth of the child; it had strings tied to each end which were fastened at the back of the child's neck. The child might also have to wear a PLACARD with some such words as 'He Whispers' or 'Miss Prattler'. See also DUNCE'S CAP.

Whitehall was originally York House, the London palace of the Archbishops of York. Cardinal Wolsey, when Archbishop of York (1515–29), rebuilt it and renamed it Whitehall. When he fell from favour in 1529, Henry VIII seized it and made it his chief residence. It remained a royal palace until 1698 when most of it was destroyed by fire. The Banqueting Hall, completed to the design of Inigo Jones in 1622 and with a painted ceiling by Rubens completed in 1635, still stands. [J. E. N. Hearsey, *Bridge, Church and Palace* 1961).] See also BOWLS, COCK-FIGHTING.

Wigs were fashionable for men during a short period in Elizabeth I's reign (1558–1603), but not again until after 1660 they copied the French fashion of shaving the head and wearing an elaborate

Wigs: 1 Full bottomed periwig; 2 Tie wig; 3 Bag wig; 4 Ramillies

wig of curls descending to the shoulders and even below. This attained its largest proportions in the early 18th century, and the wigs of BISHOPS and JUDGES were derived from that period. By the 1740s the long, curled wigs had been replaced by bob-wigs, which merely covered the back of the neck, for everyday use, and thereafter wigs continued to become gradually smaller. Soon after George III's accession (1760) men began to wear their own hair again, and by the end of the 18th century wigs had been generally abandoned. See also MACARONIS.

The wig today is still part of the official dress of English lawyers and judges. Charles James Blomfield, Bishop of London (1828–56), tried unsuccessfully to induce George IV to sanction the disuse of the episcopal wig, but it was not until the accession of William IV (1830) that bishops ceased to wear wigs.

Throughout the 18th century some fine ladies wore wigs, but women generally wore their own hair elaborately dressed and powdered. Since 1962, however, there has been a growing demand for female wigs (usually made of NYLON), a trend which originated in USA. See also HAIRDRESSING.

Wimple a long piece of linen or silk, draped over the front of the neck and swathed round the chin with its ends pinned to the hair above the ears. It was worn by women from the late 12th to the mid-14th centuries, either alone or with a COVERCHIEF or a FILLET or both. Originally it was white, but later was also coloured. See also HATS.

Windmills were introduced into England for grinding corn into flour about a century after the NORMAN CONQUEST and from the 16th century were also used for draining the Fens. The earliest known windmill in England was the post-mill at Bury St Edmunds (Suffolk) recorded in 1191, but the oldest one still complete is the Born Mill (Cambs.) dated 1636.

The post-mill, the earliest, simplest type, had a wooden-framed body supported by a massive upright post, which was held in position by quarter bars resting on horizontal cross-trees. The entire mill body was turned to face the wind,

either by the miller by means of a long tiller beam or later by a fantail, a device to adjust the mill to any change in the direction of the wind, which was developed about 1650.

About the same time came the smock-mill, which had its sails and windshaft attached to a revolving cap. The oldest is at Lacey Green (Bucks.) and was originally built about 1650.

The culmination of mill design was the tower-mill. While the smock-mill had a

Windmills: 1 Tower-mill; 2 Post-mill; 3 Smock-mill

wooden frame, the tower-mill was constructed of stone or brick. The finest tower-mills were built in the late 18th and early 19th centuries.

The sails of early mills were covered with cloth or canvas; but in 1772 a Scottish millwright, Andrew Meikle, invented a new type of sail composed of a series of shutters arranged like a Venetian blind, which opened or closed according to the strength of the wind, and in 1807 William Cubitt, the engineer, invented a method of setting the shutters from inside the mill.

The decline of the windmill began when STEAM POWER was applied to flour-milling (and to pumping in the Fens) in the middle of the 19th century. Later ROLLER MILLS began to dominate the flour trade. Millers were reduced to grist milling, and many were forced out of business after 1918. [J. N. T. Vince, *Discovering Windmills* (1968); R. Warles, *The English Windmill* (1954).] See also WATERMILLS.

Windmill Hill   near Avebury (Wilts.), has on it the remains of a circular enclosure made of earth banks with openings at intervals. The ditches, dug in making these banks, contain the bones of OX, SHEEP, PIGS and other animals. Every autumn the local NEW STONE AGE people drove their animals into the enclosure and killed them all except a few they could keep alive on corn during the winter. Bones found on the hearths of the campfires, which they lit in the ditches, show that they ate some of the meat immediately. They may have salted some of the rest and certainly used the hides for clothing.

Windows   had glass in the VILLAS of ROMAN BRITAIN, but in the Middle Ages windows existed only for ventilation and had only wooden shutters to close them at night. Window-glass was not used for private HOUSES until the late 12th century and throughout the Middle Ages remained a rare extravagance, and a nobleman who possessed a set of windows carried them with him from house to house.

In Tudor times (under the influence of the RENAISSANCE), windows became larger, and the bay-window (projecting from the wall) and the oriel-window (a recess built out from the wall on an upper storey) became common. In the early 18th century sash windows were invented in England with wooden frames divided into equal rectangular panes, and later in the century bow-windows (curved bays) became fashionable, as did French windows, often opening on to BALCONIES. In

modern houses methods of construction and heating make large windows possible.

CHURCH windows varied according to the periods of GOTHIC architecture—*Norman* (1050–1200): small and narrow with

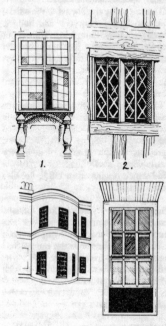

Windows: Casement; Mullion; Bow; Sash

rounded heads; *Early English* (1150–1300): larger and with pointed heads, often in groups; *Decorated* (1250–1400): mullioned (divided by vertical shafts) and pointed heads often traceried; *Perpendicular* (1350–1500): larger with flattened heads. See also STAINED GLASS, NORMAN ARCHITECTURE.

Window Tax   first imposed in 1695 to defray the cost of replacing COINAGE damaged by CLIPPING, replaced the HEARTH TAX. It was increased in 1747,

1778, 1784, 1797, 1802 and 1808. Houses with fewer than seven WINDOWS were exempted in 1782 and with fewer than eight in 1825. It was reduced in 1823 and abolished in 1851 when it was replaced by a duty upon inhabited houses. Scotland was exempted under the terms of the Act of Union (1707). Houses were often designed with few windows to avoid the tax, and owners of houses, to achieve the same end, commonly had windows bricked up, and they may sometimes still be seen in this condition today.

Wine was made in ROMAN BRITAIN, and Bede (c. 673–735) mentioned the vine as one of the country's plants. DOMESDAY BOOK recorded about 40 vineyards, mostly in Gloucestershire, Kent, Suffolk and Norfolk, many belonging to MONASTERIES and CATHEDRALS (e.g. Rochester), but they virtually disappeared in the later Middle Ages when a considerable international trade in wine developed, and England became a large importer, especially from Burgundy and Bordeaux, as much as three million gallons a year being imported in the 15th century. White wine was the last to be produced locally, though some vineyards have recently been established in Hampshire. In the Middle Ages, wines of all kinds were drunk by the better-off and by all classes on festive occasions (see also CONDUIT), the minimum siege ration at Dover Castle being a quart per person per day. By the 14th century English MEAD cost 1s 6d a gallon, but imported CLARET only 1d. See also HIPPOCRAS.

In the 16th century, SACK and MALMSEY were favourite wines. In the accounts of the Earl of Bedford at Woburn, CHAMPAGNE appeared for the first time in 1665 and PORT and BRANDY in 1684. Generally in the 17th century, however, wine-drinking declined in favour of BEER. In the 18th century only white wines were served at MEALS; red wines were considered indelicate (like PORT) and so also

was CHEESE; and therefore the custom arose of serving the pudding, before the ladies left the table to drink TEA, and then the gentlemen had the cheese and red wine.

In the last hundred years, three of the great fortified wines—PORT, MADEIRA and MARSALA—have fallen from favour, but SHERRY is more popular than ever. Sales of table wines are now double those of the 1930s, British wine imports in 1967 being from France 6 067 000 galls, Spain 1 770 000, Italy 1 642 000, Germany 1 074 000, Portugal 677 000, Australia 600 000, South Africa 198 000, other countries 801 000.

Witches in England were punished as early as the NORMAN CONQUEST in the ECCLESIASTICAL COURTS by fines, PENANCE or burning at the stake. After the REFORMATION in England, an Act made witchcraft a felony in 1543. Another Act made causing death by witchcraft a capital offence in 1563, and in that year an Act in Scotland imposed the death penalty for witchcraft and sorcery.

Trials for witchcraft were most numerous in England in the 17th century, but were never as frequent or harsh as in Scotland or on the Continent. This was because of the declining powers of the ecclesiastical courts and because TORTURE was not employed to extort 'confessions'. James I encouraged witch-hunting, and in 1603 an Act inflicted the death penalty for invoking evil spirits. In 1612 twelve witches were condemned at Lancaster and in 1634 seventeen at Pendle Forest (Lancs.) on the evidence of a boy who was found to be an impostor. There was a great increase in persecution especially in the eastern counties during the COMMONWEALTH. The 'Witch-Finder General' Matthew Hopkins from 1644 to 1647 pricked, waked and swam hundreds of women in East Anglia with an assistant and a female searcher and charged 20s expenses in every town he visited. He hanged 60 women in Essex in 1644, 40 in Bury and more elsewhere. Eventually he was himself swum and hanged as a wizard.

The last execution in England for witchcraft was in 1706 when a woman and her daughter, aged 11, were hanged at Huntingdon for having sold their souls to the devil and causing their neighbours to spit pins. The last conviction in England was that of Jane Wenham at Hereford in 1712, but she was pardoned since she had been accused of flying, and the judges held that there was no law against flying. In Scotland, however, a woman was burned alive as a witch at Dornoch as late as 1722. The laws against witchcraft were repealed in Britain in 1736, but superstitions about it lingered, especially in Northamptonshire and Huntingdon. As late as the 1760s in the country women were still being thrown into ponds, with their thumbs and toes tied together to undergo the ancient test to see whether they were witches or not. If they floated, they were pulled out to be punished as witches; if they sank, they often drowned.

Wives in ANGLO-SAXON times, were regarded as serving their husbands, and so wore their long flowing hair plaited close to their head or even cut it short like slaves. Medieval wives were expected to be meek and obedient to their husbands. An early 14th century theologian wrote, 'Moreover, a man may chastise his wife and beat her by way of correction, for she forms part of his household; so that he, the master, may chastise that which is his'. This right became obsolescent in the 17th century, though Blackstone, writing in 1765, said that 'the lower rank of people, who are always fond of the old common law, still claim and exert their antient privilege'. Many MISERICORDS show wives being chastised by husbands, but sometimes a scold beating her husband with a wooden ladle or washing bat (see also BROOMS).

In the Middle Ages and later, WOMEN were married for social and economic reasons, their MARRIAGE being arranged by their parents. A wealthy heiress was considered a good property and a good investment. In law, while an unmarried woman or a widow, had the same position as a man, a married woman during marriage was treated very differently. As Coke put it in the 17th century, husband and wife were one person in law, and that person was the husband. She had no separate existence for judicial purposes; her property was controlled by her husband. There was no DIVORCE, but medieval wives prayed to the IMAGE of St Uncumber.

The Married Women's Property Act (1882) gave married women the same right of acquiring and disposing of property as unmarried women; they could sue and be sued for contracts and dispose of their own property by will, but a husband remained responsible for his wife's debts unless this liability were explicitly disavowed.

Wolves were once common in England. In 961 King Edgar demanded 300 wolves' heads yearly as a tribute from Wales; and in 1289 Edward I ordered their destruction in several counties in England. They became extinct in England at the end of the 15th century; the last wolf is said to have been killed in Scotland in 1680 and in Ireland in 1710. The ANGLO-SAXONS called January the 'wolf-month' because so many people were killed by them then, and one of their remedies stated, 'Lay a wolf's head under the pillow, and the unhealthy shall sleep.'

Women were regarded by medieval law-givers and moralists as essentially inferior. Their view was based upon Biblical texts: if God had meant women to have a position of superiority or equality, He would have taken her from Adam's head rather than from his side. Inferiority in such an age of violence meant subjection to corporal punishment—hence the frequent beating of daughters, sisters and WIVES. The community also had its special punishments for women: the BRANKS and the DUCKING-STOOL.

Nevertheless, the medieval woman had her own authority within the FAMILY. Even a wealthy lady had to supervise the HERB garden, the preparation of MEALS and the affairs of the household. She also had the care of the SERVANTS and of her CHILDREN. One of the earliest books of household conduct, *How the Good Wife Taught her Daughter*, said simply that if her children were disobedient or badly behaved, she should not curse nor cuff them, but take 'a smart rod' and beat them till they cried for mercy and acknowledged their fault.

The chief task of medieval women was SPINNING and EMBROIDERY, but by the 15th century some women were acting as merchants and as members of the craft GUILDS; others were MINSTRELS and ale-wives in charge of TAVERNS. Women could also inherit estates and titles in England and act as CHURCHWARDENS. In Tudor times, indeed, foreigners envied the liberty enjoyed by Englishwomen. A traveller wrote, 'England in general is said to be the Hell of Horses, the Purgatory of Servants and the Paradise of Women.'

In 1620, however, James I ordered the Bishop of London to instruct his clergy to preach against 'the insolency of our women and their wearing of broad-rimmed hats, their hair cut short or shorn'; and during the COMMONWEALTH the PURITANS denounced the pride of women. The 18th century continued to regard women as inferior. Lord Chesterfield said, 'Women, especially, are to be talked to as below men and above children.'

GIRLS' SCHOOLS began in the 17th century, and the next century had its BLUE-STOCKINGS, but for long MARRIAGE was regarded as the only future for women, and great emphasis was placed in their education upon training in DEPORTMENT and ETIQUETTE. Their entry into the professions and UNIVERSITIES did not come until the 19th century and their political emancipation through the efforts of the SUFFRAGETTES in this century. The proportion of women at work in 1956 in Britain was the same as 50 years earlier (i.e. about one-third of all women and girls of working-age), but the number of married women with children at work had more than doubled; and of seven million women at work, over three million were married.

Women's fashions in COSTUME, HAIR-DRESSING, COSMETICS and PERFUME have changed over history. The ideal medieval woman had to have a slim, gently-curving S-shaped figure, head inclined slightly forward, breasts seemingly drawn inwards and hips pushed outwards. In the 1920s the ideal was that of the film-star, Greta Garbo; flat chest, square shoulders, narrow hips and long calves. Since then the average woman's waist has decreased by an inch, while her hips have increased by four inches and her bust by six. See also CHAPERON.

'Woodard Schools' founded by Nathaniel Woodard (1811–91), a clergyman, who sought to establish PUBLIC SCHOOLS which would provide a sound middle-class education on a definite Anglican basis. Among the schools he founded are St Nicolas's College, Lancing (1848), and St John's College, Hurstpierpoint (1850), in Sussex; St Nicolas's College, Denstone, Staffs. (1873); King Alfred's School, Taunton, Somersetshire (1887); and St Winifred's School, Bangor, North Wales (1887), for girls. [Brian Heeney, *Mission to the Middle Classes* (1969)]

Wookey Hole the name of a series of huge caverns in the Mendip Hills (Somerset), formed by the shallow river Axe which has its source in the limestone of these hills. One is known as the Hyena Den because in it have been found bones of wild horses, bison, reindeer, cave bears and woolly rhinoceroses, nearly all having teeth marks as if they had been gnawed. At one time, in the OLD STONE AGE, hyenas lived there and dragged the bodies of their prey into the cave to eat. Later, Old Stone Age men lived there and left behind the ashes of the fires they lit near the cave-mouth and burnt bones and FLINT tools. Such caves were the usual dwellings of these men.

Wool was the greatest source of wealth of Medieval England. Some of it was used in England, but much was sold overseas. The MERCHANTS OF THE STAPLE bought the raw wool and sold it in France and Flanders, where it was woven into cloth; over 35 000 sacks of wool a year were shipped to Flanders during the 12th century, much of it coming from the SHEEP flocks of monasteries. The wool that remained in England was spun into knitting yarns and woven into strong cloth, but neither was as fine as that of Flanders. It came to be called 'Home-spun'.

Edward III (1327–77) invited FLEMINGS over to England to weave the finer woollen cloths. Many settled at Worstead (Norfolk), which gave its name to WORSTED cloth. The industry spread to other parts of the country, especially the West Riding of Yorkshire, and the cloth was exported by the MERCHANT ADVENTURERS. Both SPINNING and WEAVING were organized on the DOMESTIC SYSTEM, and the success of the industry was partly responsible for ENCLOSURES in the 16th century. See also BURIALS.

During the INDUSTRIAL REVOLUTION, wool was slower than COTTON to adopt the FACTORY SYSTEM, and as late as 1856 only about half those employed in the Yorkshire woollen industry worked in factories. However, Yorkshire (especially around Leeds) remained the centre of the woollen industry. The first mill, for instance, was built in Bradford in 1798, and by the end of the 19th century there were over 300. Nowadays, wool is meeting increasing competition from RAYON, NYLON and other synthetic fibres.

Workhouses were established, sometimes in connection with CHARITY SCHOOLS, in the later 17th century as shelters for the poor in which the able-bodied were made to work. The POOR LAW ACT (1723) led to the establishment of workhouses in PARISHES, but GILBERT'S ACT (1782) and the SPEENHAMLAND SYSTEM led to such abuses that the POOR LAW AMENDMENT ACT (1834) brought about a new way of organizing the workhouses. See also BRIDEWELL, HOUSE OF CORRECTION.

Works canteens originated early in the 19th century. Robert Owen (1771–1858) provided eating facilities for his workers at the New Lanark cotton-mills as part of his social experiment there. By the close of the 19th century Rowntree's (York) offered a canteen dinner (which featured a pint of soup at 1d; a choice of Irish stew, fish or meat pasty at 2d; and stewed fruit at 1d), and Cadbury's (Bourneville, Birmingham), a Nottingham lace-works and a few other firms did the same. The Factory Order of 1940 advised firms with 250 or more employees to provide dining-areas for their workers, and by 1941 some 1600 companies had installed canteens. In the same year, the BBC began the *Workers' Playtime* programme broadcast from different canteens around the country. There are now more than 30 000 works canteens in Britain.

Worple a rough bridle path left by ploughmen in medieval times so that people could cross newly ploughed land. Sometimes the name of a road today indicates that it follows the line of an old worple (e.g. Worple Road, Wimbledon; Worple Way, Richmond—both in Surrey).

Worsted fine, smooth-surfaced thread spun from long-fibred WOOL, which has been combed straight and in the spinning is twisted harder than ordinary. It is knitted or woven into cloth, stockings, carpets, etc. It originated in the 13th century as 'Cloth of Worthstede', being first made at Worstead (Norfolk). See also FUSTIAN.

Y

Yarrow a HERB, remarkable for the divisions of its leaves, which was believed to have strong healing properties. It was made into an ointment to apply to wounds and chewed to ease the toothache. See also BUTTER.

Yeast in the form of brewer's yeast or barm, was used in the 1st century AD by bakers in Gaul and Spain, instead of LEAVEN, for their BREAD. They got it from the thick scum strained from the surface of fermenting wine. In Britain bakers used brewer's barm from fermenting malt liquors until comparatively recent times, though others used barm made by themselves from a mash of BARLEY, MALT and HOPS. Modern bakers use compressed yeast made by specialist manufacturers from grain or molasses. [R. Sheppard and E. Newton, *The Story of Bread* (1957).] See also ALE.

Yeoman was the name given at first to a SERVANT, but after the 15th century to a small farmer who owned his land. It is a mistake to suppose that the ENCLOSURES of the AGRARIAN REVOLUTION led to the disappearance of this class in the countryside. From 1430 to 1832 yeomen who owned free land of 40s annual value alone had the right to elect two knights of the shire to represent each county in Parliament. See also BURGESS.

Yew trees often planted in the past in country churchyards and also alongside cottages and farmhouses. It is not certain why they were planted in either situation. It was not to provide wood for BOWS (which were made from the trunk timber of yew trees and not from the branches). The foliage was cut as 'palm' on PALM SUNDAY, and the trees certainly gave protection from the prevailing south-westerly rain and gales; but possibly the practice goes back to ancient, heathen veneration of the yew as a strong evergreen enduring tree to be worshipped as a protector of men.

Yoke a curved or hollowed piece of wood placed over animals' necks and fastened at the centre to a chain extending backwards by which a PLOUGH or vehicle is drawn. The yoke was most commonly used to couple two OXEN together. Since the neck of an ox projects forward from the body horizontally, unlike the rising crest of a horse, and since its vertebral column forms a bony contour in front of which a yoke can easily be placed, the ox could be harnessed more easily than the HORSE until the adoption of the horse-collar.

Milkmaids and others also used a yoke fitted to their neck and shoulders for carrying a pair of buckets or baskets suspended from each end of the yoke.

Young Men's Christian Association was formed in London in 1844 by George Williams (1821–1905) from his meetings for prayer and Bible study with the aim of gaining young men and boys for the Christian life. It now possesses club buildings for religious, social and educational activities and also has hostels in some large towns. Its wider work lies among members of the armed forces, apprentices and trainees, and it organizes camps and holiday centres. Like the YOUNG WOMEN'S CHRISTIAN ASSOCIATION, it is now an international organization with its headquarters in Geneva. [L. L. Doggett, *History of the Young Men's Christian Association* (1922).] See also EXETER HALL.

Young Women's Christian Association a similar organization to the YOUNG MEN'S CHRISTIAN ASSOCIATION, came into being through the union in 1877 of two organizations, both founded in 1855—a Prayer Union begun in southern England by Miss Robarts and homes and institutes for young business women opened in London by Lady Kinnaird. [Ann V. Rice, *A History of the World's Young Women's Christian Association* (1948)]

Yo-yo a grooved wooden wheel made by a flick of the wrist to run up and down a piece of string. A TOY in the Far East in ancient times, it became a craze in England and France in the 1790s, being then known in France as *emigrette* and in England as the bandalore, and again in England from 1820 to 1830. There have been yo-yo crazes in this century in England and America in 1910 and 1933.

Yule, see CHRISTMAS.

Z

Zinc a hard, bluish-white metal, found in abundance in many parts of Britain and known since prehistoric times. It is used with COPPER to make BRASS.

Zip-fastener in its modern form was produced in 1913 by a Swedish engineer, Gideon Sundback, who was employed by a firm in Chicago, but little notice was taken of it until the First World War, when it was used by the US army on belts and pockets and by the navy on flying-

suits. In 1919 it was made by an English firm in Birmingham, but sales were slow, though one shown at the British Empire Exhibition, Wembley (1924 and 1925), was opened and shut by visitors over three million times. It began to be used on clothing from the late 1920s.

Zograscope also known as an optical machine or an optical diagonal machine and probably invented about 1750. It was used mainly by short-sighted people, who according to the conventions of 18th-century society could not be seen wearing SPECTACLES in public, for viewing prints, etc., in a magnified form. It consisted of a framed mirror, mounted above a telescopic stem on a rectangular base. It usually measured about 27 in. in height when closed, rising a further 8 in. by means of the telescopic stem and a set-screw. It had a suspended magnifying glass in front of the pivotally adjusted mirror. When stood on a table, with the mirror correctly adjusted and the print placed on the table under the mirror, it enabled the viewer standing in front of the magnifying glass to see the print magnified in the mirror.

Zoos in England originated with the 'lions at the Tower', the wild beasts kept in the TOWER OF LONDON soon after it was built. Henry I had a number of lions, camels, wild deer and ostriches there, and Henry III received a gift of three leopards in compliment to the royal arms. In the 13th century the Tower had an elephant and a bear, which may have been a polar bear and was kept on a long chain so that it could swim and catch fish in the Thames. By the mid-18th century there was a large collection of animals at the Tower, but then the numbers began to decline and were not increased again until the early 19th century.

Meanwhile, James I had established a collection of birds in St James's Park, which included cormorants and ospreys; Charles II added pelicans, storks, a gannet and a famous crane with a wooden leg; and some of these birds were kept in Bird-cage Walk. Later private zoos were founded. The Duke of Bedford had a menagerie at Woburn Abbey, and the sixth Duke of Devonshire had a collection at Chiswick which included emus, kangeroos, Indian cattle, elks, goats, a giraffe and an elephant which escaped and tried to swim away across the lake when the Czar Nicholas paid a visit there in 1844.

In 1834 the animals of the Tower of London were given to the Zoological Society of London, which had been founded at Regent's Park in 1826 by Sir Stamford Raffles and already had some animals there. The Society founded another zoo at Whipsnade (Beds.) in 1931. Before and since then other zoos have been founded in a number of places in Britain; and in 1964 the Marquess of Bath established at Longleat House (Wilts.) a game park in which exotic animals roam free to be viewed by visitors from their motor cars, setting an example to be followed by other landowners.

Useful Books

Apart from the particular books mentioned at the end of some of the articles, there are a number of general books which are of great use in finding out more about British social history. There are articles in books of reference, some of which are written especially for children. These are the *Encyclopaedia Britannica* (and the *Children's Britannica*), *Chambers's Encyclopaedia*, the *World Book Encyclopaedia*, *Black's Children's Encyclopaedia*, the *Oxford Junior Encyclopaedia* and the four volumes, edited by G. Grigson and C. H. Gibbs-Smith, on *People, Places, Things, Ideas*. Three valuable specialized books of reference are *A New Dictionary of British History*, edited by S. H. Steinberg, *The Oxford Dictionary of the Christian Church*, edited by F. L. Goss, and *The Oxford Companion to Music*, edited by P. A. Scholes.

The best one-volume introduction is G. M. Trevelyan, *English Social History* (3rd ed., 1946), which has also been published by both Longman and Penguin as an excellent illustrated version, *Illustrated English Social History* (4 vols). It deals with English and Scottish social history from the fourteenth to the nineteenth centuries. R. J. Mitchell and M. D. R. Leys, *A History of the English People* (Pan, 1967) is about everyday life from roughly the Stone Age to the First World War. P. Lasett, *The World We Have Lost* (Methuen, 2nd ed., 1971) describes life in England before the Industrial Revolution.

Among multi-volume histories, there are the twelve volumes of the English life series, each written by a specialist (e.g. A. Birley, *Life in Roman Britain*) and the five volumes of M. and C. H. B. Quennell, *Everyday Things in England;* both these series are published by Batsford. There are also the small, paperback 'Discovering' books of Shire Publications, which are ideally suited for carrying when looking for social history in town or countryside. The *Shell Country Book* and the *Shell Book of Country Crafts* are similarly to be recommended for this.